The McMahon Line
and After

Library of
Davidson College

The McMahon Line and After

A Study of the Triangular Contest on India's North-eastern Frontier Between Britain, China and Tibet, 1904–47

PARSHOTAM MEHRA

© *Parshotam Mehra*, 1974

All rights reserved. No part of this publication
may be reproduced or transmitted, in any form
or by any means, without permission.

First published in India by
THE MACMILLAN COMPANY OF INDIA LIMITED
Delhi   Bombay   Calcutta   Madras

First published in the U.S.A. 1976 by
SOUTH ASIA BOOKS
P.O. Box 502, Columbia, Missouri 65201

ISBN 0–88386–616–1

Printed in India at the Macmillan India Press, Madras 600 002

For Kamla
and
Divya

Contents

Acknowledgments	ix
Introduction	xi

PART I THE FORGOTTEN FRONTIER

1. The Forgotten Frontier	1
2. The Aftermath of Younghusband: Negotiating the Adhesion Agreement	16
3. A Chinese Come-back into Tibet	30
4. Tibet and the Convention with Russia (1907)	41
5. The Trade Regulations of 1908 and Tibet's 'Autonomy'	52

PART II CHINESE PENETRATION AND BRITISH REACTION

6. Chao Erh-feng and Chinese Administration in the March Country	67
7. Chinese Penetration into the Assam Himalayas	80
8. British India's Policy Towards the North-East Frontier: Before and After Williamson's Murder	86

PART III TOWARDS A TRIPARTITE CONFERENCE IN INDIA

9. The October (1911) Revolution and the 'Outer Dependencies'	103
10. Chinese Withdrawal and Tibet's Independence	123
11. China and the British Memorandum of August 1912	137
12. A Tripartite Conference in India	147
13. 'Negotiations' in East Tibet, 1912–13	154
14. China and Tripartite Negotiations (June–August 1913)	162

PART IV THE SIMLA CONFERENCE 1913–14

15. The Simla Conference: Some Preliminaries	171
16. The China–Tibet Boundary and the Birth of Inner-Outer Tibet	181
17. The Conference Gets Underway: October 1913–January 1914	198
18. A Territorial Settlement in East Tibet	208
19. Negotiating the India–Tibet Boundary	221
20. The First Simla Convention, 27 April 1914	233

Part V Failure at Simla: Negotiations with Russia and China

21. Negotiations with Russia: Mongolia and Tibet ... 247
22. Negotiations with China: Peking and London ... 261
23. Towards a Second Simla Convention, April–June 1914 ... 273
24. The Second Simla Convention, 3 July 1914 ... 283

Part VI 1919: China Revives the Simla Proposals

25. Shatra, Tibet and Teichman's Memorandum of May 1917 ... 295
26. China and Fighting in Eastern Tibet, 1915–18 ... 307
27. Teichman, Tibet and China: The Boundary and Truce Agreements of 1918 ... 317
28. May 1919: China Revives the Simla Proposals—and Then Backs Out ... 330

Part VII Bell's Policy Towards Tibet

29. The Kansu Mission and the Question of Arming Tibet ... 347
30. A New Tibetan Policy: Bell's Mission to Lhasa, 1920–21 ... 356
31. Tibet: Modernism versus Conservatism ... 370

Part VIII The Tripartite Basis Vanishes 1931–33

32. The Tripartite Basis Vanishes, 1931–32 ... 383
33. Bilateral Talks: Chinese Initiatives, 1920–33 ... 393
34. Bilateral Talks: Their Limitations, 1932–33 ... 401

Part IX India Rediscovers the McMahon Line: End of British Rule 1935–39

35. India Rediscovers the McMahon Line, 1934–36 ... 413
36. Tibetan Encroachments South of the McMahon Line ... 425
37. China's Cartographic Aggression: New Delhi and London ... 437
38. Tibet and China, 1940–47 ... 442
39. End of British Rule: Tibetan and Chinese Encroachments on the Eastern Frontier ... 452

Epilogue ... 462
Bibliography ... 489
Index ... 493

Acknowledgments

THE BACKGROUND story of the *McMahon Line* is briefly told. While my interest in the subject is not easy to date, it was the summer break of April 1966 at Chandigarh that enbaled me to repair to Delhi to get a first-hand acquaintance with that vast bulk of material housed in the National Archives. What was initially viewed as a three-month assignment spilled over into eighteen and, since it had to be combined with teaching and administrative chores at the University, it was neither easy nor perhaps that satisfactory. By October 1967, a large, if seemingly confused, pile of index cards dutifully recorded the 'notes' that had been gleaned. A rough preliminary draft was knocked into shape over the winter months but was, at best, half-done when, in July 1968, I obtained leave to visit London. The objective was to get acquainted with the Whitehall end of the picture—an extremely rich, fascinating and revealing, one—without which an understanding of the whole is, at best, incomplete. Predictably, this one-year sojourn helped both to widen and deepen the scope of the work which comprehends a much larger canvass than it was initially designed to.

By mid-1969, the first hand-written draft was ready, part of it even typed out. Between then and early 1972, when the manuscript was finally handed over to the publishers, a lot of rewriting and rearranging was done. What the end result of all this has been, only the reader can tell.

Inevitably over the years a large number of obligations, at once personal and institutional, were incurred and it is pleasant indeed to be able to acknowledge them here. The pride of place in all this is to my parent University which has nurtured and sustained me all these years—first as an alumnus and now a member of its faculty. The authorities were both good and gracious in meeting my all-too-frequent requests: for funds, adjustment of teaching schedules, leave of absence. In particular, I should record my deep debt of gratitude to my Vice Chancellor Padam Bhushan Shri Suraj Bhan who, in more ways than one, was understanding and extremely helpful.

It would be no exaggeration to say that this work owes a lot to the University Grants Commission and its then Secretary, P J Philip. The Commission underwrote my frequent visits to Delhi for almost two years, a trip (February-March 1967) to NEFA and the one-year sojourn in London. Refreshingly different from most governmental organisations, it encouraged my writing by often overruling pettifogging procedural delays so as not to hamper the work.

The National Archives and, more especially, the two young men who then managed its research room, were generous in meeting my seemingly insatiable quest for records which often strained them physically and, I believe, mentally.

Acknowledgments

Among those who were particularly helpful, I should mention Sourin Roy, D V Desikachar, T R Sareen and R K Perti.

At the India Office Library in London my principal and indeed unfailing guide was Martin Moir. The staff in the Reading Room was forbearing and met my many demands with unfailing courtesy. So did their counterparts at the Public Record Office in Chancery Lane.

I had the privilege of long and detailed discussions with well-known authorities in the field, both at home and abroad. Among them were S Gopal, K R Narayanan, T S Murthy and S L Poplai. The late P C Chakarvarti, whose own contribution to the subject is second to none, gave me some insight into its many facets. In England I was lucky to meet two distinguished visiting Americans—Leo Rose and Bob Huttenback. I had the opportunity too of discussions with the late Dorothy Woodman whose own study is a competent piece of sustained research. That I have benefited from Alastair Lamb's two excellent volumes and G N Rao's slender yet useful book goes without saying.

The work owes a lot to Sir Olaf Caroe who was good enough to look through a preliminary draft and make several useful suggestions.

I should record a word of special appreciation for my New Delhi and London hosts—the India International Centre in one case and No. 8, Chalcot Square in the other. Both were homes—havens of goodwill, comfort and retreat—away from home.

It is pleasant to record my debt to Mrs Shirley Knight who (in 1968-69), despite her own full-time load, undertook, for a pittance, to give shape and form to my first hand-written and shamelessly criss-crossed draft. Nearer home the task fell to the lot of another fine young man, Ved Parkash. He was at once professionally competent and unusually indulgent. For the maps I owe a word of thanks to O P Sarna who did his job with patience and skill.

From the first, through more than half a dozen years of its uneasy gestation, my wife bore with me and with this study, patiently, persistently; so did Pradip—there was a lot they sacrificed.

Chandigarh   PARSHOTAM MEHRA
March 1974

Introduction

RECENT STUDIES of India's landward periphery have barely even scraped the surface of the real problem—namely, to provide a framework of reference in which developments on the frontier could be viewed in their proper historical perspective. Instead, attention has been riveted principally on the armed encounter of 1962 in all its varied ramifications: there has been talk of the critical years that followed; of the motives and motivations of the so-called 'forward policy' which, allegedly, led to India's war on China; of betrayal by a trusted neighbour; of men guilty; of stories untold; of Himalayan blunders. *The McMahon Line and After*, in sharp contrast, delves into the evolution of India's north-eastern frontier from about the opening years of the century to almost the present day. In so doing the objective is not to apportion blame, much less to vindicate individuals, policies or points of view; it is to lay bare allt he known, rich, but varied, facets of men and events leaving it to the reader to formulate his judgments and reach his own conclusions.

Touching briefly on the principal strands in this vast panoramic, yet strangely fascinating, story of the birth and growth of a definitive boundary line, it may be noted that the beginnings go back to the first decade of the present century—to all that followed the return, from Lhasa, of the victorious British Commissioner, Colonel Francis Younghusband. An interesting, if seemingly paradoxical, result of this resounding military, and diplomatic, triumph for the Raj was the almost unchallenged domination, and control, of Peking's unbridled authority in the land of the lama. This was the easier for in 1907, through a self-denying ordinance, both Whitehall as well as St. Petersburg bowed out of the great game on Tibet's windswept, barren and treeless wastes. Albeit well-intentioned, in actual fact Chinese control came to be synonymous with the high-handedness and strong-arm methods of Chang Yin-tang, Lien Yu and Chung Ying who rode roughshod over the known susceptibilities of the Tibetan 'barbarians' and all that their god-king, their land, and faith meant to them. What was more, there was a well-planned, even systematic, extension of authority beyond Lhasa and the well-worn provinces of U and Tsang to the sensitive areas of Nepal, Bhutan and Sikkim and the hitherto sleepy, if woefully neglected, border districts on India's north-eastern frontier. Again, not far from Lhasa, there was the redoubtable Chao Erh-feng whose great dream of sketching out the contours of the new province of Hsi-kang spilled over into Pome, Pemako and Dzayul.

Sustained Chinese activity roused British ire and they set about mending their fences, probing, in the bargain, into areas which had hitherto remained a no man's land outside their administrative pale. Here were all the makings of a cold war with rival predatory imperialisms, in battle array, heading for a direct confrontation. An important development which brought things almost to a boil was the flight, early in 1910, from the Potala of the 13th Dalai Lama —Tibet's supreme spiritual as well as lay ruler. He sought refuge from his tormentors in the land of Buddha's birth, fondly hoping the British could be persuaded to intercede on his behalf; failing them, perhaps the Great White Tsar, whom he had assiduously cultivated over the years. Unfortunately for the Lama, he drew a blank on both counts. Presently however, the October Revolution (1911) in China came to his rescue and proved to be a powerful catalyst in this complex yet explosive situation. On its morrow, the superstructure of Chinese rule in Tibet came tumbling down for ' the web of policy', to borrow Lytton's picturesque phrase from a different context, ' so carefully and patiently woven ' stood rudely shattered. As a result, the Dalai Lama repaired home to resume his twice-interrupted rule over a long-suffering, if patient, people.

Among the factors responsible for convening the tripartite conference were: (i) Tibet's desire for recognition of her new-gained status and eviction of a ruthless, if now powerless, Chinese soldiery; (ii) India's desire to stabilise an unsettled frontier; (iii) and China's desire to regain what seemed to have been irretrievably lost. The conference was to be convened at Simla where, *inter alia*, the 1914 Convention came to be concluded and the McMahon Line drawn.

The going was tough. Parts IV and V of this study bring out the problems, the intricacies and the frustrations of negotiating with the Chinese; of the drama attending the initialling, the signing and sealing of the Simla Convention; and of how, above all, everything appeared to have been settled except the tangled skein of the territorial question. Essentially it was the inclusion, or exclusion, of Batang or Litang, of Chamdo or Draya in Inner/Outer Tibet—and *not* of Tawang or Walong north/south of the McMahon Line—which bedevilled all progress and led to interminable wrangling for nine long and weary months. The Chinese, and sometimes the Tibetans as well, continually indulged in the familiar game of procrastination, of a chronic, mulish, refusal to compromise, or reach final conclusions. An interesting revelation is the enormously important role played by Sir John Jordan, the all-powerful British Minister in Peking, who literally led Whitehall by the nose and, in private if not in public, lambasted the Indian authorities for their intransigence and temerity in not falling in line. Another figure that emerges is of the little-known, yet immensely important, Lu Hsing-chi, the self-styled Amban-designate at Lhasa, who, enjoying the confidence of the highest authorities in Peking and operating from distant Calcutta, masterminded the Simla conference and played a part that was far more pivotal than the better-known, and much-maligned, Ivan Chen.

Thanks to Chinese repudiation, the developments after the Line was laid and the Conference adjourned are extremely relevant and revealing. Based on archival material never fully used before and supplemented by personal, on-the-spot knowledge of the frontier itself, the author for the first time documents, with great care and thoroughness, the aftermath of the 1914 parleys. Among some of the more important, if lesser known events, in the decades that follow may be listed the well-nigh endemic in-fighting in East Tibet resulting, through British mediation, in a one-year (1918–19) truce that lasted almost twenty; serious Chinese overtures, down to 1919, to revive the earlier (1914) basis for a settlement with Tibet; and the varied problems that beset the Dalai Lama and, what Hardinge called, his 'tin-pot' diplomacy.

Later in the thirties, the developments which crowd in become inextricably mixed up and are less easy to disentangle. For one the Chinese knocked out, nay repudiated, the earlier tripartite basis for a settlement with Tibet; the British, in a spasm of semi-absent-mindedness, 'rediscovred' the McMahon Line which had been almost forgotten for nearly a score of years; Kuomintang China's cartographic aggression on the eastern frontier was played down, if not condoned, by Whitehall; and, on the eve of World War II, the occupation of Tawang ruled out by the Raj on the plea that an annual expenditure of a hundred thousand rupees would seriously jeopardise the equilibrium of the central budget.

In its essence, this study draws to a close here. What follows is an epilogue somewhat sketchy and, to an extent, even unsatisfactory. Its main objective is to bring the story to-date; based on evidence that is far from conclusive, it scrupulously refrains from offering any definitive judgments.

In the evolution of boundaries, as of the men who make them and of the people who live on either side, there is a remarkable flux and a variety of developments impinge. In the case of India's north-eastern frontier, this variety is the greater, if more complex, for, in the period under review, not only India and Tibet but China, too, is directly, at times even intimately, involved. This would largely explain why it is necessary at every stage to bring the three together, to ensure that each falls into its proper place in the larger context of the whole. While doing so, an attempt has also been made to pinpoint some tentative conclusions, partly by juxtaposing the past with the present with a view not so much to delineate what it may unfold, as to view it in sharper focus, widen the horizon and thereby place the frontier in its true historical perspective; important, yet by no means preponderant.

PART I   THE FORGOTTEN
        FRONTIER

Chapter 1

The Forgotten Frontier

AN APT study of a frontier wherein elements both of political as well as human geography have played significant roles is that of India's long, and sprawling, land frontier divided, for convenience, into the north-west and the north-east. In sharp contrast to the western half, long-embattled and a trouble-spot down the ages, the eastern, remarkably quiescent for most part, has been called a 'neglected', and a 'forgotten', frontier. To go no farther back than the middle of the nineteenth century, the youthful Lord Dalhousie, then British India's Governor-General, pronounced it to be 'a bore', while nearly fifty years later, his more pushful, if equally controversial successor, Lord Curzon categorically disclaimed any desire to develop 'a North-east Frontier Province, policy or charge'. Later, in the early nineteen thirties, Sir Charles Bell, a well-known authority on Tibet and this part of the frontier, publicly confessed that the latter 'does not receive the attention it deserves'. More recently, a noted Indian scholar bemoaned the fact that 'serious students of frontier history' continued to confine their attention to the routes taken by Alexander, and were 'altogether indifferent' to the eastern part of the frontier which, he felt, was of the greatest significance from the political no less than the military standpoint.[1]

An initial, and by no means unimportant, step in the direction of dealings with tribes on the north-east frontier of British India was the induction, towards the end of 1882, of Jack Francis Needham as Assistant Political Officer at Sadiya, not far from the bend of the Brahmaputra, known here as Dihang. His appointment had followed in the wake of the British occupation, in 1881, of Bomjur and Nizamghat. The APO's principal task was to be political. Placed in a subordinate capacity to the Deputy Commissioner of Dibrugarh, the latter was directed to issue, through Needham, orders on 'all matters relating to... the Abor, Mishmi and Singhpho frontiers'. Besides,

> arrangements regarding the location of all frontier posts, their supplies, the patrolling between them... as well as the political relations with the Abors and Mishmis was to be carried on through him....[1a]

---

[1]Charles Alfred Bell, 'The North-east Frontier of India', *Journal of the Royal Central Asian Society*, London, 17 (1930), pp. 221–26, and Anil Chander Banerji, *The Eastern Frontier of India*, 1st Edition, (Calcutta 1943), Preface. The journal, et seq, has been abbreviated as *JRCAS*.

[1a]Cited in Sir Robert Reid, *History of the Frontier Areas Bordering on Assam* 1883–1941 (Shillong, 1942), p. 183. In subsequent pages this work has been referred to as *Reid*.

The creation of the post of Assistant Political Officer at Sadiya was recommended by Mr Elliott, then Chief Commissioner, Assam, on 25 September 1882. It followed the occupation by the British, in 1881, of Bomjur and Nizamghat.

A little over a decade after his appointment, Needham faced, in November-December 1893, the incipient rebellion of the Bor Abors, the Passi Abors and the Mishmis.[2] His view that severe punishment, and a blockade, be imposed on the erring tribes was overruled because of the Assam Chief Commissioner's rigorous limitations both in terms of the men and money he could spare.[3] With the latter view the Supreme Government broadly agreed for above all it was keen that operations be conducted, ' so far as possible ', by the Military Police.[4]

The long and short of it was that an ' expeditionary force ', under Captain Maxwell, conducted ' operations ' in January-March 1894, resulting in their occupying the offending villages and, as was their wont, burning them. It is not without significance that the objectives in view were severely limited. *Inter alia*, Needham was told to confine himself to

> punishing villages you have good reason to believe concerned in outrage, insisting on delivery of murderers' and sepoys' rifles. Don't go further inland than is absolutely necessary for the purpose, and give villagers clearly to understand that we have no desire to annex their territory, but only to punish offending villages....[5]

The most important, as no doubt the most effective, punishment in these cases always turned out to be the blockade of tribal territory which would deny the tribes access to British marts. Other measures, adopted in such cases, were the withholding of *posa* and the refusal to allow new villages to be built on the site of those already burnt down.

Summing up the results of the expedition, the Chief Commissioner wrote to Calcutta on 1 June 1894 that these had

> now proved to the Abors for the first time that we can march through their country from one end to the other with the greatest ease and destroy every village they have, their cattle, their household goods and their crops. They are not likely to forget this however much they may boast that they succeeded by treachery in preventing the force from reaching Damroh....[6]

Though the Commissioner expressed himself as being ' satisfied ', the conduct of the expedition drew adverse comment from the Government of India who felt that its instructions had been violated and its authority subverted. More specifically, the advance to Damroh was

> not altogether beyond what the Chief Commissioner admits he had originally contemplated, but it was evidently unprovided for by the orders of the

---

[2]Assam to India, telegram, 4 December 1893, *Foreign*, External A, April 1894, Procs. 72–86.
[3]Assam to India, 10 December 1893, Ibid.
[4]India to Assam, 7 December 1893, Ibid.
[5]These were among the instructions drawn up for Needham, cited in *Reid*, p. 193.
[6]Assam to India, 1 June 1894, Ibid., p. 197.

Government of India and it seriously enlarged the field of operations of a force organised for action within much more restricted limits....[7]

Not only had the Chief Commissioner incurred 'a grave responsibility' in authorizing the advance but, what was much worse, compounded it further by failing to consult the General Officer Commanding, Assam. No wonder that after a

> careful consideration of all the circumstances the Governor General in Council is constrained to record the opinion that Mr Ward (Assam's Chief Commissioner) in sanctioning the advance to Damroh without the knowledge or approval of the Government of India, altogether exceeded his authority and committed a grave error of judgement.[8]

Nor was that all, for Needham who had been in charge was accused too— of 'want of judgment and political foresight'.[9] All this, however, was for the short run. Later, thanks to the effectiveness of the blockade, the Abors of Membu, Dadu, Sillak and Bomjur soon grew anxious for peace and, by the end of 1895, the lesson seems to have been driven home to some of the other tribes. Consequently, the blockade against the Passi Minyong Abors was lifted by the end of the year, and against the Bebejiya Mishmis in 1896. The Bor Abors, however, had to face this ordeal for a good five years before they realised their weakness for it was only in 1901 that they showed any willingness to resume normal relations with the Assistant Political Officer at Sadiya.[10]

Needham's appointment as Assistant Political Officer, as has been briefly noted, was made in 1882 and his role was defined as that of 'special advisor' on all political questions relating to the frontier and its tribes. Before long Authority noted that his views were entitled to 'considerable weight' because of his intimate knowledge, and complete familiarity, with his charge at a fairly early stage.[11] Between December 1885 and January 1886 he had journeyed to a point very close to Rima,[12] and was among the first Europeans who

---

[7]India to Assam, 31 August 1894, cited in Ibid., p. 200.

[8]Loc. cit.

[9]Loc. cit.

[10]Assam to India and India to Assam, 18 December 1900 and 5 January 1901, in *Foreign*, External A, February 1901, Procs. 4–5.

Also see Assam to Deputy Commissioner, Lakhimpur, 27 February 1896, and India to Assam, 24 March 1896 in *Foreign*, External A, May 1896, Procs. 65–66 and India to Assam, 11 March 1897, in *Foreign*, External A, April, 1897, Procs. 3–5.

[11]These comments were contained in a report made in 1894 by W E Ward, then Chief Commissioner, Assam, cited in *Reid*, p. 184.

[12]Needham who took no armed escort was accompanied by Captain Molesworth, Commandant of the Lakhimpur Frontier Police. Starting on 12 December (1885) he marched a distance of 189 miles up the course of the river from Sadiya and, on 4 January 1886, reached within a mile of Rima where he was turned back. *Assam Administration Report*, 1885–86, cited in *Reid* p. 185.

had travelled by this route without a mishap—his forebears on this journey, Krick and Boury, back in 1854, had been killed by the Mishmis in the Zayul valley.[12a] The main geographical interest of his journey lay in the confirmation it afforded to the narrative of A K Pandit of the Trigonometrical Survey of India who had made his way from the Tibetan side to Rima in 1882 and lived in the Zayul valley for some weeks. On the great mystery of the Tsangpo, Needham affirmed

> that no river in any degree comparable to the Sanpo in size joins it between Sadiya and Rima, and consequently the Sanpo must pass into the Brahmaputra west of Sadiya, and my opinion is that it can be no other than the Dihong.[13]

Needham's zeal and enthusiasm about Rima notwithstanding, the Government of India's response was far from encouraging. It was clear that for official expeditions beyond the frontier Government's prior sanction was necessary, nor was there any ambiguity about Calcutta's considered view that without ' clear evidence of their necessity and utility', no such expeditions were called for.[14]

Despite this 'douche of cold water' Needham, in 1888, visited the Hukong valley on the borders of Burma. This survey established the possibility of reaching Hukong by either of the two routes—one by the Nongyond Lake and the other by way of Yogli, Phoong, Morang and Shangye.[15] Three years later, in 1891, Needham, at the instance of the Government of Burma, visited the Hukong valley again. The aim now was to join hands, from the Assam side, with a column from Burma which was being sent to Mungkhom to subdue the tribes living north of Mogaung, between the Irrawaddy and the Hukong valley. In a long and detailed report on his journey, Needham was far from complimentary to the Burmese column or the arrangements made for their advance.[16]

In December, 1898—a few weeks before Lord Curzon took over the Viceroyalty—the Chief Commissioner of Assam suggested that the blockade against the Bor Abors should be maintained, albeit other tribes in the north of Assam had been absolved from its rigours. The main reason, of course, was the continually hostile attitude of the Abors who it was feared might, in the event of the blockade being lifted, descend upon the Miris.[17] Assam's recommendation was agreed to by the Supreme Government.[18]

[12a]For details see Colonel R H Phillimore, *Historical Records of the Survey of India* (Dehra Dun, 1945–58), 4 vols., Vol. III.
[13]Loc. cit.
[14]*Reid*, p. 186.
[15]Loc. cit.
[16]*Reid*, p. 192.
[17]Assam to India, 16 December 1896, in *Foreign*, External A, January 1899, Procs. 65–66.
[18]Loc. cit.

Later that year, an outrage was committed by the Bebejiya Mishmis on a hamlet at Mithagaon, nearly 16 miles to the north-east of Sadiya, necessitating the despatch of an armed expedition. Its objective was to arrest and punish the perpetrators of the massacre and recover the guns and the children abducted. Apart from acquiring information about 'this unknown country', the gams of Aiyu Mimi village who, allegedly, were guilty of perpetrating the 1893 outrage, were to be arrested.[19] Plainly the principal aim was punitive and the Commissioner noted that there was

> no question of annexation or of the permanent occupation of new territory for this hilly and inhospitable country is not only worthless to us from every point of view, but it is bounded in the far distance by the inaccessible mountain ranges which are the frontier of Tibet. We do not desire to have any closer relations with the savage Mishmi tribes than we have at present.[20]

Needham who acted as Political Officer of the expedition found it difficult to define accurately the physical limits of the country occupied by the Bebejiya Mishmis in contradistinction to their more pushful, if aggressive neighbours, the Chulikattas.[21] The expedition also brought to the fore the question of defining more accurately the precise connotations of Inner and Outer Lines as indicated on maps, or observed in practice. Some of these pronouncements throw an interesting sidelight on controversies which were to rage, and violently, later. Thus the following comments regarding the Inner Line make interesting reading:

> the Inner Line is really our administrative border....[22]

Or again,

> what was subsequently called the Inner Line is a line fixed for purposes of jurisdiction. Our Officers need not actively govern upto it, but they must not attempt to govern beyond....[23]

These somewhat restrictive definitions were not accepted by the Chief Commissioner of Assam who held that the local authorities

> have jurisdiction and in practice exercise authority anywhere beyond the inside boundary as far as they can get their orders obeyed, and their juris-

---
[19]*Reid*, p. 204.
[20]Assam to India, 11 July 1899, *Foreign*, External A, January 1900, Procs. 70–96.
[21]Needham (Political Officer, Mishmi Expedition) to Assam, 1 March 1900, in *Foreign*, External A, October 1900, Procs. 43–70.
[22]Office Note, 25 July 1899, by H S Barnes, Secretary, Foreign Department, *Foreign*, External A, January 1900, Procs. 70–96.
[23]Loc. cit.

diction is not limited by the Inner Line which was laid down for a very different purpose....[24]

The Commissioner amplified these remarks by two further pronouncements. Firstly, that it was 'not necessary... to raise the question as to what is the precise boundary of British territory in the direction of the various independent or semi-independent tribes....' Secondly, that 'for all practical purposes British territory extends wherever the Deputy Commissioner can enforce obedience', without calling in the aid of a military expedition.[25]

That the Inner Line in terms of jurisdiction over the tribes was not restricted in scope, is further made clear in a communication which the Commissioner addressed to his political superiors in Calcutta:

> The tribes far beyond the Inner Line are required to work on local roads. Elephant 'Mahals' beyond the Inner Line are let on lease to Khamti and Sinappho gams, and a poll tax is levied from Bor immigrants who settle in the plains below the foot of the hills. Practically speaking jurisdiction is exercised up to the foot of the hills, and all claims put forward by Abor and other tribes to plains-land as a portion of their own territory have always been repudiated. In the several agreements executed between the Deputy Commissioner of Lakhimpur and the Abors in 1862, 1863 and 1866 it was recited that British territory extended to the foot of the hills. It is for this reason that the Chief Commissioner has insisted on the payment of poll by all settlers ... and has allowed of no misconception on their part in regard to their status when allowed to settle in the plains. The degree of protection [he] is bound to afford to trans-Inner Line settlers is a matter which calls for determination when the question arises....[26]

How clearly defined the 'Inner Line' was, should be evident from the above. But what of the Outer Line? In 1899 the then Secretary to the Foreign Department of the Government of India made it clear that 'the Outer Line on the map of Assam is only an imaginary boundary'.[27]

A week later his deputy confessed that 'if the Outer Line ... has ever to be precisely defined' it may not be easy, for the information possessed by Authority on these areas was 'admittedly very vague'.[28] That the whole thing

[24]Assam to India, 14 August 1899, in Ibid.
Earlier, on 4 August, the Government of India had told the Chief Commissioner that, as it understood the matter, 'the Inner Line is the administrative frontier in this direction of British India' and that 'no authority or jurisdiction is exercised by our Officers beyond it'.
[25]Assam to Deputy Commissioner, Lakhimpur, 27 July 1886, cited in Assam to India, 14 August 1899, Ibid.
[26]Assam to India, 14 August 1899, Ibid.
[27]Office Note by H S Barnes, *supra*, n. 22.
[28]Office Note by H Daly, Deputy Secretary, Foreign Department, 2 August 1899, *supra*, n. 22, p. 204.

needed clearer definition is evident from Lord Curzon's somewhat terse noting:

> we seem to do things in a rather unscientific and haphazard manner (so far as boundary, authority and jurisdiction are concerned) upon the North-East Frontier.[29]

In the light of the heated debate that was to envelop these terms later it may be useful at this stage to spell out the manner in which Authority viewed the symbols used on Survey of India maps. Thus in a communication to Assam on 11 March 1904, Calcutta noted that the

> symbol to be ordinarily adopted in the case of provincial frontiers should be dash-dot-dash (_____ . _____ . _____) line and this should be employed wherever the boundary has been settled by inter-provincial arrangement or by demarcation.
>
> Where a territorial boundary though undemarcated is settled in practice, it should be indicated as an approximate boundary by a plain broken line.
>
> Where the territorial boundary of the province has not been determined either by inter-provincial agreement, by demarcation, by recognised practice, no attempt should be made to show any territorial frontier on the map either by engraved symbol or by any coloured band. The outermost borders delineated on the map in such parts should be jurisdictional boundaries indicated in the same manner as ordinary district borders that is to say in the present case by an engraved dotted line (. . .) coloured by a thin ribbon.[30]

His dissatisfaction about the 'haphazard manner' of boundary, authority and jurisdiction apart, Lord Curzon had also been unhappy about the local government's conduct of the expedition against the Bebejiya Mishmis which he had earlier sanctioned. Thus on 14 May 1900, he noted that far from viewing it as 'satisfactory', either in its inception or in its results, he held

> it to have been marked by serious miscalculation from the start, by a sacrifice of life which ought, with reasonable precautions, to have been avoided, by an expenditure of money for which there has been no . . . return and by political and scientific results that are all but worthless.

The worst, as Curzon saw it, and in his own inimitable prose:

> Finally, to cap the whole story, the Bebejiyas, who were the objects of the expedition, and had hitherto been described ' as a fierce race of cannibals,

[29] Office Note, 27 August 1899, by Curzon, *supra*, n. 22.
[30] India to Assam, 11 March 1904, in *Foreign*, External A, April 1904, Proc. 31.

a very savage, bloodthirsty and dangerous race', were discovered by the Political Officer to be a petty community of only 3000 to 4000 souls (including not more than 1500 adult men) who are described by him as ' on the whole well-behaved and inoffensive tribe, very desirous of being on friendly terms with us'.[31]

This was contrary to what the Chief Commissioner of Assam thought. The latter had put forth the view that, as a result of the expedition, ' peace and obedience along the frontier for many a long day to come', would be ensured and further recommended that the blockade against the Bor Abors, which had been maintained for a period of five years, be withdrawn. If his proposal were accepted, as it actually was, there would be no blockade in force against any of the frontier tribes north of Sadiya.[32]

A couple of years later, the Assam Chief Commissioner recommended the establishment of a military police post at Lungchang, beyond the then Inner Line, to the north-west of Lakhimpur district.[33] And even though Lord Curzon was fully alive to the fact that this proposal would accelerate the ultimate projection of the Inner Line to the Tirap.[34] he accorded it his approval.[35]

Meanwhile as ground was being prepared for the despatch of the Younghusband expedition to Lhasa, British exploration on the North-east Frontier continued with unabated zeal. Thus in a memorandum of 13 April 1903, collating all available information on trade routes between India and Tibet. O'Connor noted that

> Tawang is a mart of some importance as the distributing centre of goods from Lhasa and Eastern Tibet, from Bhutan, India and Assam and from the fertile though savage districts of south-eastern Tibet and no doubt the commerce of this place will someday assume fairly large proportions.[36]

But the physical contours of the country remained for most part an unknown quantity:

---

[31] Cited in *Reid*, p. 204.

[32] Assam to India, 18 December 1900, *Foreign*, External A, February 1901, Procs. 4-5.

[33] Assam to India, 17 December 1902, in *Foreign*, External A, February 1903, Procs. 7-9.

[34] Thus Dane, then Foreign Secretary, recorded that ' it was expected that on account of the rise of the Tirap river in flood ' the proposed outpost ' would result in the extension of the Inner Line to that river '. Note, 17 January 1903, by L W Dane, Secretary, Foreign Department, in Ibid.

Also see note by Curzon, 18 January 1903, in Ibid.

[35] India to Assam, telegram, 19 January 1903, in Ibid.

[36] ' Note on Trade between India and Tibet ', by WFT O'Connor, 13 April 1903, enclosed with letter dated 13 April (1903), to L W Dane, Secretary, Foreign Department, in *Foreign*, Secret, June 1903, Procs. 303-4.

As regards the lower course of the Dihong, we know very little except that it flows through a thickly wooded mountainous country inhabited by savage tribes....[37]

That knowledge at this stage was patchy, is further borne out by the hazy outlines and the unmarked boundaries of the map O'Connor attached to his report.[38]

Again, by the time Younghusband was preparing to leave for Gyantse, the question of securing, at an early date, a definition of the physical boundaries of Tibet became a subject of considerable interest and was indeed driven to the fore. Thus in an annotation of 8 July 1904 the then Foreign Secretary of the Government of India urged that the matter be brought to the notice of HMG:

Colonel Younghusband will probably be able to supplement our inadequate existing information on this point and all that would be required would be a written recognition by China and Tibet as to what these boundaries are....[39]

Efforts were also made, though these proved still-born thanks to Tibetan obstruction, to explore the Assam-Batang trade route from the Assam side. Thus on 21 April 1904 Curzon recorded his keen disappointment:

Could anything be more unfortunate than that the party, even though they got through the Mishmi country, should be turned back as soon as they reached the Tibetan frontier.[40]

The same lack of precision was evident from a comprehensive report which the Chief Commissioner of Assam submitted to the Government of India regarding the 'undefined' territory of the Bhuteas of Tawang, of other independent Bhuteas, of the Akas and the Daflas on the north-east frontier. Among the principal points made by him, the following may be listed:

1. That the agreements which the British Government had with the Bhuteas of Tawang, who are dependent on Tibet, and with the independent

---

[37]Loc. cit.

[38]Loc. cit. The map in question bears the following markings: I.B. Top. Dy. No. 4.468, Exd. C. 5A., April 1903, No. 2033–I, 1903. The sheet is signed by W F O'Connor and bears the date 13 April 1903.

[39]Note by Dane, Secretary, Foreign Department, 8 July 1904, in *Foreign*, July 1904, Procs. 443–464.

The definition of Tibet was required in terms of Clause 2 of the proposed draft convention with Tibet, which excluded foreign influence and made the British supreme arbiters. Later this clause became Clause IX of the Lhasa Convention of September, 1904.

[40]Note 21 April 1904 in *Foreign*, External A, October 1904, Procs. 311–17.

Bhuteas and the Akas to the east do not provide for any delimitation of territory nor did the British have any agreements with the Dafla tribes farther east.

2. That between the Dihong and the Subansiri rivers the boundary had, by a notification of 12 March 1897, been pushed northwards to the foot of the hills and from the Subansiri to the Sisri it followed a demarcated line along the foot of the hills. From the Sisri the line leaving the hills approaches the Brahmaputra, following the right bank of that river for some distance and finally crossing it at the confluence of the Noa Dihong.

3. That in some of the published maps a second line was shown as an 'outer line' along the northern border of Lakhimpur district. This line followed the foot of the hills more or less closely. For part of this strip of the country, no provincial boundary had been laid by treaty, although treaties existed with some of the Abor tribes which specifically mentioned that British territory extended to the foot of the hills. The frontage of the Abor territory covered by these agreements extended from a point near Masaki on the east to Nizamghat on the west.

4. That in the map (which he had attached) the outer line was shown in broken colour and was carried south-east from Nizamghat at a considerable distance beyond the Inner Line. After crossing the Brahmaputra, it followed approximately the Dephakrun range to the south and then, turning south-westward, followed the crest of the Pakoi range as far as the north-east corner of Manipur territory.

5. That the Khamtis, the Singhphos and the Nagas accepted the British Government as the sovereign power up to the water-parting dividing the tributaries of the Brahmaputra from those of the Irrawaddy.

6. That although the tract of country enclosed between the Inner and the Outer Lines was uninhabited and had no present value, indeed it was regarded as unsuitable for tea cultivation, yet the maps issued by the Surveyor-General of India should no doubt throw light upon the rights of the British Government to this territory.

7. That 'at present' there appeared to be no advantage in exhibiting, on the map, as British territory extending eastwards and southwards to the crest of the Daphudeh and Patkoi ranges including extensive tracts of mountain and jungle. With this the British just then had nothing much to do nor was the area likely to be taken up by the settlers. Later, however, if it were found desirable to extend British jurisdiction over their country, ' we shall not be prejudiced by the fact that it lies across a line which is professedly only an Inner Line and is not marked on the map as a final boundary'.[41]

Actually, as a result of the Chief Commissioner's self-assurance, the Foreign Department felt confident that the proposed expedition to Eastern Tibet

---

[41] Assam to India, 9 December 1903, in *Foreign*, External A, April 1904, Procs. 30-31.

would have 'no difficulty' in securing from the Mishmis a 'safe conduct' through their territory or 'even an agreement' for a road to be constructed to the borders of Tibet.[42]

Whatever the over-all impact of activity on the eastern frontier in the wake of Younghusband's march to Lhasa may have been, one thing is fairly obvious. And it is that neither Lord Curzon nor his government were yet prepared to have anything to do with a north-east frontier. Indeed the categorical tone of the Viceroy's views is starkly revealing. Thus on 12 March 1905 he minuted:

> We do not want Mr (J C) White or anybody else to present us with a North-east frontier problem or policy. There being no problem beyond that of remaining on peaceful and friendly terms with our neighbours and quietly developing our relations . . . there is no occasion for a policy.[43]

A few days later, Lord Curzon wrote,

> I have no desire to develop a North-east Frontier Province, policy or charge.[44]

Despite the Indian potentate's unambiguously authoritative assertion in regard to a north-east frontier policy or province, the expedition to Lhasa gave a powerful impetus to activity on this part of the frontier. This is noticeable in a number of developments which, though individually of little moment, did collectively lend themselves to a considerable impact.

Towards the end of 1905, Jack Needham, who had for nearly a quarter of a century held the post of Assistant Political Officer incharge Sadiya, retired from service. Years later, in its preface to the Sadiya Frontier Tract Gazetteer of 1928, the Assam Government paid him a handsome and indeed a well-deserved encomium:

> By his explorations and discoveries, Mr Needham acquired an international reputation and his work . . . laid the foundations of the modern North East Frontier of Assam.[45]

Verrier Elwin, than whom no one in recent times knew the frontier and its people better, has remarked that Needham's appointment was 'the first important step' towards some elementary administration in the area and the establishment of more friendly relations with the tribes. He (Needham) had achieved these objectives both by his 'long tours in hitherto unknown

---

[42] Note by Dane, 25 August 1904, in *Foreign*, External A, February 1905, Procs. 507–37.
[43] Note by Curzon, 12 March 1905, in *Foreign*, External A, April 1905, Proc. 44.
[44] Note by Curzon, 17 March 1905, in *Foreign*, External A, July 1905, Procs. 21–45.
[45] Cited in *Reid*, p. 181.

country' and by the singular fact of his 'remaining at his post' for such a length of time.[46]

What comes out clearly from Needham's explorations in the Lohit valley—and his manner and methods left a lot to be desired—is the fact that there was no known sanctity then attached to the crossing of the Inner Line or of going beyond the Outer. True these concepts had themselves been defined, in the 'Bengal Eastern Frontier Regulation—I' of 1873, but it is evident that they were often violated and some of the trespasses condoned at the highest levels of government. Not as a matter of deliberate policy, but fairly markedly, British control continued to grow and its dominion expand into what later came to be christened the North East Frontier Agency.

Just before Needham laid down the reins of his office, a murderous outrage was committed in British territory on two Chulikattas by some of the Bebejiya Mishmis, allegedly as a measure of revenge for the punishment meted out to them in the earlier expedition of 1899–1900. As a result a blockade was imposed both on the Chulikattas (whom Needham tried, though in vain, to exempt) and the Bebejiyas.[47]

Needham's sucessor as Assistant Political Officer, was Noel Williamson. Not long after he took over, the whole gamut of policy towards the tribes in this area came under severe criticism. In a note penned in September 1907, the Lieutenant-Governor of East Bengal and Assam[48] (the new name acquired by this easternmost province after the partition of Bengal, towards the close of 1905) pronounced the earlier policy of 'aloofness' towards the tribes as one 'foredoomed to failure.' What was worse,

> apart from the urgent need of preventing interference with the development of trade, the fact that over half a century of proximity to civilization has failed in any way to redeem the tribes on our border from their native savagery is in itself a condemnation of the policy of non-interference.[49]

Redemption apart, there was a more vital issue involved,

> the economic value of the strip of country between the Brahmaputra and the foot-hills, on the north bank, in the Lakhimpur district appears to lie at present wholly in its forest produce. It is the main source of tea-box timber to the Lakhimpur and Sibsagar districts and therefore of great importance to the stable industry of those districts.[50]

---

[46]Verrier Elwin, *A Philosophy for NEFA*. (Shillong, 1959) pp. 2–3.
[47]*Reid*, p. 210.
[48]The then Lieutenant-Governor was Sir Lancelot Hare.
[49]East Bengal and Assam to India, 9 September 1907, in *Foreign*, External A, June 1908, Procs. 33–38.
[50]Note, 28 October 1907, by Price, Under Secretary, Department of Revenue and Agriculture, in Ibid.

Humanitarian considerations in terms of redeeming the barbarians, and the economic by way of exploiting the rich natural resources of the land, important as these undoubtedly were, had a powerful impact on policy. Yet something more vital and urgent had in the meantime raised its ugly head. Authority noted that

> in view of the activity of China in Tibet, it is also desirable to ascertain the northern limits of the Abor and Mishmi country where this can be done peacefully.[51]

Before long, two things were quite apparent. At the outset, and in order to afford proper protection to the people in the plains, the foot-hills and indeed the mountains beyond ('which form the northern boundary of Hindustan'), had to be adequately secured. This supervision was a part of the duty of government which it had long 'neglected', for from the

> point of view of the dwellers in the plains next in importance to the mountains which we have in so many instances ignored, is the strip of land which lies at their foot—it is essential at least that this area should be protected if the industries below it are to be secured.... [52]

Nor was the inevitability of such an advance a matter of any doubt. Sooner or later the country's government must administer to its natural boundaries for it was

> clear that the extension of our boundaries must come some day and that the line will not remain at the foot of the hills.... [53]

A development that was to focus considerable attention on the frontier was a tour which Noel Williamson undertook between December 1907 and January 1908. His principal objective, apart from the general one of gathering more information about the country and its people, was to explore 'the practicability' of a trade-route with south-eastern Tibet. Unaccompanied by an escort and with but few companions,[54] the farthest point Williamson reached was Sati, 35 miles south of Rima.[55] His report of the tour makes interesting

---

[51]Note, 18 October 1907, by Dane, Secretary, Foreign Department, in Ibid.

[52]Note, 31 October 1907, by S Earchly-Wilmot, Inspector General of Forests, in Ibid.

[53]Note, 13 November 1907, by G O Miller, Member, Revenue & Agriculture Department in Ibid. Miller noted that ' Mr Williamson indeed already looks forward to the establishment of police posts in the hills and doubtless that will come in time '.

[54]Williamson's party consisted of, besides himself, Chowna Khamti Gohain, two other Khamtis and one servant.

[55]' I did not,' he noted, ' go further and enter Tibet.' Actually he had orders not to. Letter, 27 February 1908 to Deputy Commissioner, Lakhimpur, in *Foreign*, External A, October 1908, Procs. 37–40.

reading. *Inter alia*, he

> found the inhabitants respectful and obliging. In fact, I might have been travelling in an administered tract.

The Lohit, of course, was the natural highway into Tibet and large flat tiers running parallel to it provided the main artery of intercourse. The real obstacle to the development of trade, however, had been the absence of any incentive for to the

> north she (Tibet) has no market; to the south the country is mountainous and inhabited by savages; to the east her nearest market is Batang . . . and to the west . . . a wild and tedious route inhabited by a people of whom the Tibetans stand in some dread. . . .

No wonder, south-east Tibet was 'absolutely' isolated—it had no industries and no exports. If, however, communications were developed along the Lohit valley, and facilities for exports made available, while a good bridle path developed from the borders of Tibet to Sadiya, the shape of things would change. For

> once the Tibetan learns that every hide and every pound of wool has a marketable value in Assam, which can be reached quickly, comfortably and safely, and where in return he can purchase tea, clothing, etc., commercial interchanges are assured and expenditure on the route justified.

Later in his report, Williamson let his imagination run riot visualising a railway running from Eastern Tibet to Szechuan and on to the plains of Assam:

> With such improved communications, the resources of Szechuan, one of the wealthiest provinces of China, would develop enormously, with an easy and expeditious route there is no reason why the Chinese coolie should not seek for employment on the tea-gardens of Assam. . . .[56]

No wonder the Assistant Political Officer was singularly impressed by the 'comparative ease' with which it should be possible 'to forge a link in a chain' connecting India with China.[57]

Williamson's tour of 1907–8 marks what may be termed the powerful im-

---

[56]This and the preceding citations are from Williamson's report, dated 27 February 1908, in Ibid. Also see *Reid*, pp. 211–12.

[57]Not that he was not conscious of some of his harebrained schemes: 'I trust I may be pardoned for writing at such length on a route which at present is politically impossible, and the cost of which may be considered prohibitive.'

pact, direct as well as indirect, on this part of the frontier, of Younghusband's expedition to Lhasa. The emphasis on trade and the opening up of Eastern Tibet, which may be regarded as characteristic features of this period, gradually give way to a growing interest in the exploration of tribal areas and of extending the governmental sphere of influence. The latter itself was a direct result of mounting, yet inexorable, pressures from the north. For China, in the last decade of Manchu rule, had suddenly awakened to the power vacuum that was Tibet, and Mongolia.

Chapter 2

The Aftermath of Younghusband: Negotiating the Adhesion Agreement with China

'EXPLORATION', a term then considered synonymous with political probing followed by territorial expansion, was gradually—albeit imperceptibly—taking the British administration from the plains of Assam to its foothills and beyond. In this process, 'the punitive expeditions' of Needham and his successor Noel Williamson played an important role. And, as may be evident from the preceding pages, a good deal of the stimulus in this direction came from the Lhasa expedition of 1903-4. While taking account of its impact on the 'forgotten' frontier, it would help a better, more rounded, perspective if the aftermath of Younghusband's march to Lhasa on the politics of India's immediate northern neighbour are kept constantly under review.

According to a Tibetan proverb, the British are the road-makers of Tibet (i.e. they have shown to others the path leading to Lhasa). This role was dramatised by Younghusband's march to the Tibetan capital at the head of a victorious army and, having dictated terms of peace to a stop-gap, residuary regime in the absence of the Dalai Lama,[1] his complete withdrawal from the scene. In doing so, the British demonstrated conclusively that they had the power to intervene in Tibet whenever they chose to do so and that neither the Chinese, with their proud boast of 'supervising' the Tibetan administration, nor yet the Dalai Lama with his much-vaunted 'spiritual and temporal authority', could stop them from doing so. Additionally, the bubble of Russian intrigue, of the great White Tsar rushing to the help of the Lama, was pricked.[2]

---

[1]Chinese authorities have never tired of maintaining that, in the absence of the Dalai Lama, 'neither the Chinese Resident nor the Tibetan representative' had full power to enter into a treaty with Younghusband; that the new status of Tibet was 'without legal foundation' and that the only validity that the Convention had 'was derived from the continued exercise of force'. Tieh-tseng Li, *Historical Status of Tibet* (New York, 1956), pp. 107-8.

The Tibetan viewpoint, however, runs counter. It maintains that the British were dealing with Tibet as a 'separate and independent' state and that the provisions of the 1904 Convention 'completely negate' any Chinese claims of sovereignty or suzerainty over Tibet. Shakabapa, *Political History of Tibet* (Princeton, 1967), pp. 217-18.

There is an interesting revelation (by Rockhill) to the effect that the seal left by the Dalai Lama with the Ganden Ti Rimpoche was the Tibetan seal—'not the seal conferred on him by the Chinese Emperor'. W W Rockhill, *The Dalai Lamas of Lhasa and their Relations with the Manchu Emperors of China* (Leiden, 1910), p. 75, n. 1.

[2]There is no evidence, according to Tibetan records, of any political relationship with Russia, except for Dorjieff's later visits. Kawaguchi, the well-known Japanese traveller, however, reported that there were Russian firearms in Tibet: 'But if that had been the case, the Tibetans

And yet, despite his undoubted success, the limitations of Younghusband's performance soon became apparent. For while the Commissioner had no doubt exceeded his instructions in certain respects, there were others in which he failed to carry them out.[3] Of the latter category, two bear a mention here. The first related to new trade regulations designed to replace those negotiated in 1893; the second, to make the Amban ratify the terms of the Lhasa Convention in the name of his Government.[4] Both were of considerable importance.

A provision for separate trade regulations had been made in Article III of the Lhasa Convention which laid down that the

> question of the amendment of the Regulations of 1893 is reserved for separate consideration, and the Tibetan Government undertakes to appoint fully authorised delegates to negotiate with representatives of the British Government as to the details of the amendments required.[5]

To put the record straight, a copy of the proposed regulations had even been despatched to Younghusband at Lhasa but largely owing to his preoccupations with negotiating the main Convention, and Macdonald's insistence on an almost immediate withdrawal thereafter, these were left over to a later date.

As for the Amban's ratification, Younghusband had done his best to carry that Chinese functionary along in all that he did at Lhasa; and for reasons that were fairly obvious Yu T'ai had cooperated fully with the Commissioner.[6] Since he had been a party to negotiating the Convention in all its details, it would stand to reason that, left to himself, he may possibly have appended his signatures too, had not Peking at the very last moment specifically barred him from so doing.[7] Thus China's pose of injured innocence on the morrow of the Convention's conclusion had little if any justification except in terms of an exercise in 'saving face'.

Peking was conscious of the fact, as no doubt were the British Government, that the Anglo-Chinese Convention of 1890 had implicitly recognised China's

---

would have used such weapons against the British'. *Shakabapa*, p. 219, n. 1. Also see P L Mehra, 'Tibet and Russian Intrigue', *JRCAS*, XLV, January 1958, pp. 28–42, and its sequel in Ibid., XLVI, 1959.

[3] For a detailed study of Younghusband's performance at Lhasa see Parshotam Mehra, *The Younghusband Expedition, an Interpretation*, (Bombay & London, 1968).

[4] On 17 August, Younghusband had called on the Resident and given him a draft of the proposed Adhesion Agreement to which evidently Yu T'ai 'raised no objection'. A fortnight later Younghusband told the Tibetans that Chinese suzerainty was 'fully recognised' in the proposed (Adhesion) Agreement.

[5] 'Political Diary of the Mission' in *Tibet Papers*, Cd. 2370 (1905), Part II, Encl. in No. 320 and No. 339, pp. 250 and 259.

[6] *Supra*, n. 3, pp. 304–15. Also see *Li*, n. 1, pp. 104–6.

[7] *Supra*, n. 5, Encl. in 334, p. 258.

unquestioned right to speak for, and on behalf of, Tibet.[8] The unratified Lhasa Convention had, therefore, in the eyes of international law and practice, no validity. Britain's anxiety, born of this predicament, was to become China's opportunity. Later, owing to its refusal to accept the separate article of the Lhasa deal which provided for visits to the Tibetan capital of the Trade Agent at Gyantse,[9] Britain would appear to have thrown away its only effective weapon of intervening purposively in Tibet.

Having negotiated the Lhasa convention after a great deal of time and effort, Younghusband was, understandably, reluctant to be a party to modifying it in any important particulars. This was all the more evident inasmuch as he was known to be considerably out of step with the policy of the Government of India, and even more so of HMG.[10] Thus even though he had received clear instructions that Whitehall had 'authorised' the reduction of the indemnity, and consequentially an early termination of the occupation of the Chumbi valley, and that it was 'most desirable' that before leaving Lhasa he should endeavour to secure Tibet's consent to this change, the Commissioner had refused to oblige.[11] Convinced from the outset that his settlement had incurred ' the minimum of responsibility with the maximum of reparation ',[12] he had 'deprecated any alteration' of terms 'at present'. It is clear that he had received the telegram containing these instructions before he left Lhasa, and yet wired back to say that it had been communicated to him too late, and that the present arrangement was 'distinctly preferred' by the Tibetans. Briefly, that if he had attempted to alter, 'at this stage', a settlement made with 'much solemnity', it would have defeated the main objectives in view.[13]

Other things apart, Younghusband clearly saw that further protracted negotiations with the Tibetans might prove, as those earlier had threatened to, well-nigh interminable. The additional mart desired, as also the securing of customs revenue as payment for the indemnity, may have turned out to be a long drawn-out agony. The fact that the Chinese were ready to jump into the foray just about this time would have made Younghusband's stay at Lhasa far more prolonged than his masters may have initially anticipated. For, on 27 September, Peking, confident that the Commissioner was still at the Tibetan capital, announced that Tang Shao-yi, then a Taotai at Tientsin,

---

[8]The preamble to the Lhasa Convention had made a specific reference to the ' meaning and validity of the Anglo-Chinese Convention of 1890 and the Trade Regulations of 1893 and as to the liabilities of the Tibetan government under these agreements '. For the text, *supra*, n. 3, pp. 385–88.

[9]This article was allowed to drop out at the time Lord Ampthill ratified the Convention in November 1904. For the text see *supra*, n. 3, p. 389.

[10]For details *The Younghusband Expedition*, *supra* n. 3, pp. 257–66.

[11]*Tibet Papers*, *supra*, n. 5, No. 169, p. 68.

[12]Ibid., No. 164, pp. 67–68.

[13]*The Younghusband Expedition*, *supra*, n. 3, pp. 331–32.

had been ordered to Tibet to talk things over with the British.[14]

The Chinese who were not even mentioned in the Lhasa Convention knew of the special position they held in Tibet and were acutely conscious of the lacunae in Younghusband's treaty. India under Curzon which had inaugurated its Tibetan policy by ignoring China, whose control the Viceroy had characterised as 'a constitutional fiction and a political affectation', would have, left to itself, continued to deal direct with Tibet. Whitehall, however, was more sensitive and hated to think that the precedent of Tibet conducting its own foreign relations, to the exclusion of its suzerain, might be made use of, to Britain's own grave disadvantage, by the Amir of Afghanistan taking a leaf out of the Lama's book.[15] And London could scarce view with equanimity the Amir's right of direct relations with the Russians.

Difficulties of another nature had also cropped up. France, Germany, Italy and the United States had protested strongly to the Chinese Foreign Office about Article IX of the Lhasa Convention.[16] It may be recalled that with all that it contained, and implied, this article was tantamount to an unmistakable British protectorate over Tibet. *Inter alia* it had stipulated that, without British consent

(a) no portion of Tibetan territory shall be ceded, sold, leased or mortgaged or otherwise given for occupation, to any Foreign Power;
(b) no such power shall be permitted to intervene in Tibetan affairs;
(c) no Representatives or Agents of any Foreign Powers shall be admitted to Tibet;
(d) no concessions for railways, roads, telegraphs, mining or other rights, shall be granted to any Foreign Power, or the subject of any Foreign Power. In the event of consent to such concessions being granted, similar or equivalent concessions shall be granted to the British Government;
(e) no Tibetan revenues, whether in kind, or in cash shall be pledged or assigned to any Foreign Power, or the subject of any Foreign Power.[17]

What Peking feared most was that as a counter to a British protectorate over Tibet, and Article IX could be explained in no other light, Germany in Shantung, Japan over Fukien and France in Yunnan would press their respective claims—claims that it may find itself powerless to resist. Unless Britain was working for the dismemberment of China, she must, Peking argued, either forswear Article IX or explain it away to the satisfaction of these hungry wolves at China's doorstep.[18]

---

[14]Tang was actually appointed to 'proceed to Tibet to investigate and conduct affairs', *Tibet Papers, supra,* n. 5, No. 167, p. 67.
[15]*F O* 535/5, No. 15, Lansdowne to Satow, 6 October 1904.
[16]*F O* 17/1752, Satow to Lansdowne, 5 October 1904.
[17]For the full text see *The Younghusband Expedition, supra,* n. 3, pp. 385-88.
[18]*Supra,* n. 16.

This line of reasoning appeared to carry conviction and Satow in Peking, duly impressed, proposed that he negotiate with the Chinese their acceptance of the Lhasa Convention in return for a British recognition of Peking's claims as a suzerain of Tibet.[19]

Curzon, already ruffled by the idea of re-negotiating, with its inevitability of a further watering down of what he had always viewed as a weak Convention, was now additionally alarmed at the prospect of Peking being chosen as the venue for these talks.[20] Hence the change to Calcutta whither Tang Shao-yi, initially appointed for talks with Younghusband at Lhasa, was now directed to repair.[21] His western education and background, coupled with some unhappy experiences at the hands of the British, had turned Tang into a bitter, even rabid, nationalist.[22] And where China's integrity was concerned, he was not the man to compromise. In negotiating with him, therefore, Curzon's government had met more than its match.

Tang's basic premise was that the Lhasa Convention, concluded without Chinese participation, was invalid *ab initio*. A new Anglo-Chinese treaty, without Tibetan participation, must, therefore, take its place. Citing as his evidence the investiture of the Dalai and Panchen Lamas, the appointment of members of the Kashag and local Tibetan functionaries by the Chinese Emperor, as well as the supervision of Tibetan troops by the Amban, Tang maintained that Chinese sovereignty in Tibet was a fact that had to be recognised. If the British were averse to the term sovereignty he proposed, as an alternative,

> the insertion in Clause I of the recognition by the British of the original and existing rights enjoyed by the Chinese Government in Tibet and the amendment of Clause IX to the effect that the Chinese Government should be the sole intermediary in all communications between India and Tibet.[23]

When it was clear that it would be impossible for the British to accept this, Tang changed his stance, bringing forth a Supplementary Convention to take the place of the Lhasa deal. *Inter alia*, he now proposed that China undertake all the obligations which the 1904 Convention had imposed upon Tibet. Thus, while the new trade marts specified in the Convention would be accepted, any change in the 1893 Regulations governing them would be left to future Anglo-Chinese, *not* Anglo-Tibetan, parleys. Similarly British functionaries in Tibet would deal with Tibetan authorities, but through Chinese officials. Again, while the indemnity would be paid, it would be China doing

---

[19] Loc. cit.

[20] *F O* 17/1753, Satow to Lansdowne, 1 November 1904.

[21] *I O* to *F O*, 5 November 1904, in Ibid.

[22] Note on a conversation between Sir G Clarke and G E Morrison, 15 November 1905, in *F O* 17/1756.

[23] *Li*, n. 1, pp. 109–10.

so, through a Tibetan official. The crux of the matter was Article IX and Tang proposed a clarification through an unequivocal British denial of any intention either to annex Tibetan territory or to interfere in Tibet's internal affairs. At the same time it was to be made plain that all prohibitions in Article IX applied to Britain as well as to other foreign powers, but *not* to China.[24]

The Indian position was summed up by Fraser, then Foreign Secretary, who along with Wilton was the principal negotiator. At the outset, the British were prepared to recognise Chinese suzerainty, but *not* sovereignty, to which term Tang had persistently referred. As a corollary, and owing to India's physical proximity to Tibet, Britain's special position in its (Tibet's) affairs was to be recognised by China. As for Article IX, which had proved to be a hard nut to crack, so long as no other power violated its terms, the British too would be prepared to accept it. There would be exceptions, however, arising for instance out of the presence of British Trade Agents in the country, or the building and maintenance of telegraph lines between the Indian border and Gyantse.

In reply to Chinese claims of controlling Tibet, Fraser is said to have pointed out to the actual situation which the British had found to be so entirely at variance, for here was

> an autonomous country (which) managed its own administration, collected its own taxes and made its own treaties with its neighbours.[25]

Another problem, to which the Indian government now addressed itself, was the somewhat paradoxical situation created by the presence, in Tibet, of British incumbents of the Chinese Imperial Maritime Customs Service. To the uninitiated Tibetans, it may not have been easy to draw a line between a British Officer of the Government of India, supporting and buttressing the policies of the Viceroy and a British Officer in the pay of the Chinese Imperial Customs trying, as a loyal functionary of his masters, by every possible means to subvert those very policies. Men like James Hart, who headed the Chinese Customs organization and whom Mortimer Durand disliked intensely, were not directly involved. But Parr, the Chinese Customs official at Yatung during the period of Younghusband's expedition to Lhasa, and Henderson who, as Parr's successor, had not only been defying the British Trade Agent in Chumbi but was acting as Tang's official adviser during the period of negotiations in Calcutta, had, each of them, at times created embarrassing situations.[26] Fraser, therefore, proposed that in any modifications of Article IX of the Lhasa Con-

---

[24] Lamb, *McMahon Line*, I, pp. 31-38.

[25] Cited in Ibid., p. 38.

[26] O'Connor, then Trade Agent at Gyantse, and White, then Political Officer in Sikkim, had been particularly unhappy about Henderson's activities. The latter had, among other things, declared that the Lhasa Convention was invalid—a viewpoint that was galling to British Indian officials who swore by its validity and sought to enforce it. Henderson's personal relations with White had been none too happy either.

vention, Peking should agree to forego the right to employ any Europeans, including personnel of the Chinese Maritime Customs, in Tibet.[27]

Although the implications of the British demand may not be viewed as far-reaching, Tang was unwilling to accept any limitations whatsoever on his country's right to station its public servants wherever it chose to do so. This apart, there was a fundamental difference in his approach, as contrasted to Fraser's. Basically, what Calcutta wanted was that the Lhasa Convention should be accepted by China with as little change as possible and, to make this palatable, it was prepared to make such minor concessions as a recognition of China's suzerainty over Tibet. Such claims may not have been seriously in conflict with the actual authority which Peking allegedly wielded at Lhasa. On the other hand, as the Chinese viewed it, the British government was prepared to agree only to a recognition of Chinese suzerainty in Tibet and would

> abate nothing to their (Chinese) right to enforce the fulfilment of the terms of the Lhasa Convention by such means as may be found convenient although by seeking Chinese adherence, they intended to secure help in the execution of the Convention and wanted to be relieved of the pain of enforcing it alone.[28]

The two sides thus operated on what may be called different wave-lengths and there was little, if any, meeting of the minds.

By July 1905, after the Calcutta parleys had been in progress for over three months, heated arguments about China's right to *sovereignty* over Tibet, as claimed by Tang, as against *suzerainty*, as conceded by the Indian Government, became interminable. Precise legalistic interpretations apart, what the Chinese claimed was much more than what the British were prepared to concede. Unfortunately for the British, and luckily for the Chinese, none of the earlier treaties, namely those of 1890 or 1893, had defined either the precise status of Tibet or the supervisory rights which China was entitled to exercise in that country.[29] Here, apart from Chinese semantics about *Chu Kuo* and *Shang Kuo* there was the difficulty, as Dr Eekelen has pointed out, of a basic 'deficiency' in the concept of suzerainty in defining or comprehending accurately Tibet's relationship with China. At best, it was inadequate; at worst, it led to considerable misunderstanding.[30]

[27] Lamb, *McMahon Line*, I, p. 39.

[28] *Li*, n. 1, p. 110.

[29] Thus the convention of 1890 while it defined the Sikkim–Tibet boundary, admitted Britain's protectorate over the tiny Himalayan kingdom and provided for increased facilities for trade across the frontier, had failed to spell out with any precision either the political status of Tibet or the relationship which China bore to that country.

[30] W F Van Eekelen, *Indian Frontier Policy and the Border Dispute with China*, 2nd Edition (The Hague, 1968), p. 211.

The long and short of it was that in September (1905), on a plea of illness,[31] which was widely regarded as an excuse, Tang interrupted the negotiations and, on earnest requests, was duly recalled by his government.[32] As his *locum tenens* he left behind in Calcutta his secretary, Chang Yin-tang, who despite his willingness to carry on the negotiations had little or nothing to offer beyond a readiness to discuss the ' alteration ' of the Lhasa Convention. Not that the Indian side was in any better position. For, with his resignation having been accepted, Curzon was preparing to hand over to Minto while Fraser, the Foreign Secretary, was on the way out, to be replaced by Dane. Thus a breakdown in communication, which seemed inevitable, came to a head in November when, on declining to accept the Indian draft, Chang was informed that negotiations were at an end.[33]

On his own, Curzon had never set much store by China's ' adhesion ' and with his experience of dealings with Tang, and later Chang, he was disillusioned further. No wonder that on the eve of laying down the reins of office, he advised his political superiors in London

> to intimate officially at Peking that they (the British) dispense with China's adhesion to the Lhasa Convention which they nevertheless have always regarded and still regard as in itself complete and of full validity and that they will themselves without reference to the Chinese Government take such measures as they may find necessary for the execution of its terms.[34]

Nor was the attitude of Curzon's successor materially different. Negotiations with Chang had broken down before Minto was sworn in but he placed himself firmly on record as being none too keen to re-open the parleys. To him, as to Curzon, China's ' adherence ' was really superfluous

> so far as the actual working of the convention on the spot is concerned; and we regard as a question of greater moment the settlement of the future position of the Dalai Lama. Matters are working smoothly at present in Tibet,

---

[31] 'Tang's illness was regarded with much distrust by Curzon and his advisers. It was said that all that had happened was that the Chinese Representative had knocked his foot against a croquet hoop, and that he then took to his bed for purely diplomatic reasons '. Lamb, *McMahon Line*, I, p. 46.

[32] 'Being unable to break the ensuing deadlock, Tang asked leave to return home. In September, his request was granted ....' *Li.*, n. 1, p. 110.

According to Shao Hsung-cheng's review of ' Tibet in Modern World Politics ' by W K Lee, in *Chinese Social and Political Science Review*, XVI, 1932–33, p. 540, Tang requested his recall in the hope of avoiding the deadlock that had ensued and to make room for a possible success in the future. He was conscious too that his government did not want to compromise its ' sovereign rights ' and that negotiations devoid of substance were ' nothing but solicitation'.

[33] *Li.*, n. 1, p. 111.

[34] Curzon to Secretary of State, 14 November 1905, cited in Lamb, *McMahon Line*, I, p. 47.

and this result will be further assisted by the return of the Tashi Lama after his visit to India, which has been most successful.[35]

If at all, Minto argued, China's 'adhesion' had relevance only if the Dalai Lama were kept out of Tibet. For the Tibetan ruler's previous record had been one of active hostility to the British, nor may he be well-disposed towards a Convention to which he had not been a party. Things, however, did not seem to work that way, for when Satow sounded the Wai-wu-pu on the question, its reaction was a firm negative.[36] The fact was that Peking had already pressed the Lama twice over to return home, a course which, it was well known, the Russians would strongly support.[37]

Minto's counsels, however, did not carry much weight in Whitehall where a new (Liberal) Government was now actively engaged in the task of sorting out, settling and getting out of the way some of the principal areas of conflict and discord with the Russians. It was an operation essentially similar in nature to the one conducted with the French a few years earlier. More relevant, the Lhasa Convention had invited sharp criticisms from other European powers, including the Russians, and Whitehall smarted under the hostile comments of friends and foes alike.[38]

As time came around for the payment of the first instalment of the indemnity, and Peking notified that it would step in on behalf of Tibet, its ward, things began to move again. Suspicious of the Chinese move, Calcutta viewed it as an attempt ' to force ' its hands, making it accept an arrangement that could later be cited as a precedent. Besides, in this way, Peking would be able to establish ' its theoretical right ' to supremacy over Lhasa and thereby ensure that the British hold over Chumbi would not be maintained, in default of payment. HMG's rejoinder, therefore, was to the effect that ' unless China adheres to the Convention in the form in which it is now presented', the arrangement regarding payment would not be acceptable.[39] Later, in January 1906, Tang, now Minister in the Chinese Foreign Office, presented some fresh proposals to the British envoy in Peking which became the basis for the Adhesion Agreement eventually signed on 27 April 1906.[40]

[35]Minto to Morley, 23 January 1906, cited in Ibid., p. 49.

[36]Satow to Grey, 24 February 1906, cited in Ibid., p. 50.

[37]Hardinge, then back from St Petersburg, had expressed the view that the Russians considered the Tashi Lama as ' our creature ' and would strongly resist any British pressure at Peking to exclude the Dalai Lama from Tibet. Hardinge's minute in *I O* to *F O*, 30 January 1906, *F O* 371/176.

[38]As Mr Richardson points out, Britain's anxiety to obtain Peking's ' adhesion ' was ' due partly ' to allay ' foreign criticism ' of the Anglo-Tibetan Convention of 1904. Richardson, *History*, p. 94.

[39]*Li*, n. 1, pp. 110–11.

[40]*The* (London) *Times*, 27 April 1906, noted that the negotiations were conducted in a friendly spirit, a fact that did credit to Tang Shao-yi, ' that accomplished Yale graduate whose appoint-

Officially, as the British government in London viewed it, the new agreement

> secures the adhesion of China to the (Lhasa) Convention....It does not alter the arrangements arrived at....It contains an engagement on our part not to encroach on Tibetan territory nor to interfere in the Government of Tibet, the Government of China undertaking on their part not to allow any foreign state to interfere in the government or internal administration of Tibet. It also states that we do not seek for ourselves any of the concessions mentioned in Article IX of the Convention of Tibet which were denied by that Article to any other states or to the subjects of any other state. It does not alter the amount of Tibetan indemnity in any way.[41]

As usual in such pronouncements, a lot more remained unsaid. Thus while both the expressions, 'sovereignty' as well as 'suzerainty', were scrupulously avoided, the privileged position which had accrued to Britain from the terms of the Lhasa Convention appears to have been completely surrendered. For China was not only not a foreign power in terms of Article IX of the Lhasa Convention, but the responsibility for maintaining the integrity of Tibet now devolved fully upon her (China).[42] As a Chinese scholar has maintained,

> China's payment of the indemnity for the Tibetans not only established her right to supremacy over the Tibetan Government ... with Russia definitely excluded and the British tied to a self-denying clause, the way was paved for her to consolidate her power in Tibet....In fact ... for a time she resumed full sovereignty and ruled Tibet through the Lhasa Government which was brought under her control during the absence of the Dalai Lama.[43]

To be candid, any re-reading of the Peking Agreement strongly reinforces the conviction that from the Indian, and Tibetan, point of view the sell-away was complete. Thus Article I made it clear that China was 'to take at all times such steps as may be necessary to secure the due fulfilment' of the terms of the Lhasa Convention. In other words, Tibet was to be recognised, for all practical purposes, as a part of China. Article II which specifically barred Britain from

---

ment as one of the Ministers of the (Chinese) Foreign Office is the most satisfactory appointment made by China for a long time'.

[41] *Parliamentary Debates*, Vol. 156, pp. 372, 553.

[42] 'Chinese rights in Tibet were thus recognised to an extent to which the Chinese had recently been wholly unable to exercise them'. Richardson, *History*, p. 94.

[43] *Li*, n. 1, p. 114. According to another Chinese scholar, by agreeing to attach the confirmation of the Lhasa Convention as an annexe to the Peking Convention, the Chinese Government 'tacitly recognised' that Tibet had the right to enter into commitments with foreign powers. Yao-ting Sung, *Chinese-Tibetan Relations, 1890–1947* (unpublished thesis, University of Minnesota, 1949), p. 48; cited, *et seq*, as Yao-ting Sung.

interfering in Tibet's administration thereby equated its position to that of any other foreign state. Again, apart from laying down the telegraph lines connecting India with the trade marts in Tibet, Britain, like all other foreign states, was barred from any concessions or privileges spelt out in Article IX (*d*) of the Lhasa Convention. It was obvious that fresh trade regulations, provided for in Article III of the 1904 Convention, were now to be negotiated with the government of China while, additionally, the indemnity due from Tibet was to be Peking's responsibility. It is patent all through that the Tibetan Government was neither a party to the Agreement of 1906, nor was it at any time consulted with regard to its terms.[44] As a matter of fact, the Dalai Lama had been away from Lhasa since he took flight before Younghusband's arrival and, in his absence, the structure of Tibetan administration was far from steady. Before discussing developments relating to the Trade Regulations of 1908, it may thus be worthwhile investigating the Lama's movements in the intervening years.

It may be recalled that in August 1904, as Younghusband neared Lhasa, he was keenly desirous of making the Dalai Lama a little less uneasy, confiding in his father that he (Younghusband) was 'angling delicately for him'.[45] When, on reaching the Tibetan capital, he found that the Lama had bolted

> (As to the Dalai Lama) I said I was quite prepared to give him the most positive assurance that he would be safe from us if he returned here. I did not wish to discuss personally with him the details of the settlement, but wished him to affix his seal in my presence; and it would certainly be more convenient if he were nearer Lhasa for reference during the negotiations. The Regent said he would send two messengers to him tomorrow, advising him to return.[46]

As is well known the Lama, after sending word to the Commissioner that he had 'gone into religious retreat', had left his seal with the Ganden Ti Rimpoche, Lobsang-Gyaltsen and, 'following a precedent set him four years before by his suzerain', fled from Lhasa accompanied by his personal attendants and a small bodyguard.[47] He took the road to Nagchuka and made with all haste for Urga, the seat of the third great Huthukhtu in the Lama hierarchy. We

---

[44]*Shakabapa*, p. 205 contents himself with the bald statement that the 1906 agreement was signed 'without the knowledge of the Tibetan Government' while Richardson, *History*, p. 94, maintains that if the Tibetans had been consulted they might 'reasonably' have pressed for the 'specific restriction' of Chinese overlordship to what it had been in 1904.

[45]*Supra*, n. 3, p. 292.

[46]Younghusband, *India and Tibet* (London, 1910), p. 275.

[47]Shakabapa's construction of events is slightly different. According to him, before Younghusband arrived in Lhasa, the Dalai Lama had gone to Reting and Taklung monasteries accompanied by a small escort. While at Reting he decided to go to Mongolia and sent a message to the Ganden Ti Rimpoche to this effect. *Shakabapa*, p. 220.

are told that the Jetsung Dampa Lama, more popularly the Bagdo Gegen, initially at any rate welcomed him with open arms. Later, however, things were different for the

> reverence he (Dalai Lama) received from the Mongolians made Jetsung Dampa somewhat envious, and for sometime the relations between the two lamas cooled. Finally, the Mongolian Ministers brought about a reconciliation between them.[48]

The Dalai Lama appears to have remained in the vicinity of Urga till the late spring of 1907, changing his residence from one to the other of the three monasteries in its neighbourhood. Nor were his preoccupations altogether spiritual for he is said to have been in touch with affairs in Lhasa and in Peking.[49]

Well-informed as he was about men and affairs, it may be safely presumed that the Lama must have known about the Anglo-Chinese Agreement of April 1906. Equally that the news of its conclusion persuaded him to start afresh on his travels and, crossing Mongolia and the Kokonor, he took up his residence, towards the end of 1907, in the Kumbum monastery. It is said that while out there he received two invitations, one from the Tibetan Government urging him to return home, and another from the Manchu court asking him to visit Peking.[50] The latter, it seems, wanted him to return immediately to Lhasa for just then Chinese administrators were having a hard time suppressing large-scale tribal revolts in Kham, or Eastern Tibet. Tibetan officials in this region are also said to have complained to him that the Chinese were constantly encroaching upon their rights, a fact that may have further reinforced the Lama's determination to go to Peking in the hope that ' a short visit to China ' might prove ' beneficial '.[51]

Towards the middle of 1908, on his way to Peking, the Lama arrived at Sian-fu, the ancient capital of Tang China. Here he is said to have received another letter from Lhasa urging him to return.[52] Meantime, the Manchu court announced the impending visit to Peking of the Panchen Lama and the

It would thus seem that the decision to flee was taken *after* the Lama had been at Reting and not at the time of his departure from Lhasa.

Rockhill maintains that in this, as in the earlier arrest of his councillors, the Lama had followed ' well-established Chinese precedents in such emergencies '. *Rockhill*, n. 1, p. 74.

[48]*Shakabapa*, p. 221. Also see *Rockhill*, n. 1, p. 75.

[49]*Rockhill*, n. 1, p. 76.

Shakabapa would have us believe that ' in 1906, Dalai Lama returned to the Kokonor region and visited the Kumbum monastery '. *Shakabapa*, p. 221.

[50]*Rockhill*, n. 1, p. 76, believes that only after the Adhesion Agreement had been signed did the Lama come to believe that he might ' with safety ' come a little nearer to Peking, ' as a first step on a return journey to Lhasa '. See also *Shakabapa*, p. 221.

[51]*Rockhill*, n. 1, pp. 76–77. The Chinese evidently believed that the Lama's ' presence and influence ' might allay their fears and anxieties in East Tibet.

[52]*Shakabapa*, p. 221.

reported arrival of the latter's chief of ceremonies may have lent further credence to this report.[53]

In the autumn of 1908, the Dalai Lama and his followers, then on their way to Peking, stopped over in the well-known Buddhist monastery of Wu-tai-shan, in the province of Shansi. Urgent messages from Peking were now sent to him to hasten his arrival thither for

> hostilities had broken out in Chinese Tibet, and the small Chinese force available on the spot was hard-pressed; the Lama's influence with his people was now necessary to the Imperial Government.[54]

The Tibetan ruler arrived in Peking towards the end of September 1908 and stayed there for almost three months. He took up his residence in the Huang Ssu, a palace specially built by the Emperor Kang-hsi for the Fifth Dalai Lama. He was received in separate audiences by the Emperor Kuang Hsu and the Dowager Empress Tzu Hsi and, in deference to his wishes, the ceremonial kowtow was waived to be substituted by genuflexions.[55] Later, however, on the birthday of the Empress, he is said to have kowtowed and received his new title. As an Imperial Edict explained:

> In past times the Dalai Lama received the title of 'Most Excellent, Self-Existent Buddha of the West'. His title shall henceforth be, 'The Sincerely obedient, Reincarnation helping, Most Excellent, Self-Existent Buddha of the West'....Furthermore an annual stipend of ten thousand taels is accorded the Dalai Lama to be paid quarterly out of the Szechuan (special) Treasury for the Fan-tzu....After being invested with his title the Dalai Lama will at once return to Tibet. All officials along the route will furnish him escorts and insure him protection. After his return to Tibet he must be reverently submissive to the laws of the Sovereign state and make known everywhere the sincere purposes of the Chinese Government.

As if this were not clear enough,

> he (Dalai Lama) must enjoin the Fan (i.e. the Tibetans) to obey the laws and to practise virtue. Anything which he may have to communicate must be reported, as the Regulations require, to the Minister Resident in Tibet, who will then memorialise for him, and he must await the decision.
>
> We trust that the border lands may enjoy perpetual peace, that the differences between the priests and laity may be entirely removed, and that due appreciation will be shown for the firm intention of the Court to support the Yellow Church and bring peace to the frontier.

[53] *Rockhill*, n. 1, p. 77.
[54] *Rockhill*, n. 1, pp. 91 and 77, and *Shakabapa*, p. 221.
[55] 'On hearing that he would be required to kowtow in disregard of all precedents, the Lama refused to go to the audience. It had to be countermanded'. *Rockhill*, n. 1, pp. 78–79.

The Board of Dependencies is ordered to notify the Dalai Lama to reverently receive the above and respectfully obey it.[56]

The Lama, though heartened by a reaffirmation of the Manchu court's continued support to him and his faith, was deeply upset by the specific denial to memorialise direct to the throne. The latter appeared necessary in order that he may be able to bring direct to the authorities in Peking his own complaints, and those of his people. The denial of this right had placed him, and his predecessors, in a somewhat humiliating position and at the mercy of Chinese officials in Tibet.

Deeply agitated, and in spite of the distinctly categoric terms of the Edict of November 3, the Lama asked the Board of Dependencies to make the Chinese Government reconsider the Edict of the Empress and grant him the right ' to address direct communication to the Throne in his own name or jointly with the Amban at Lhasa, as the case might require'. He wrote to the Board that the right be granted to him ' in conformity with the old rules ' and that all the officials, civil and military, be notified accordingly.[57]

Unfortunately for him, before his request could be considered, both the Emperor and the Empress died. Their sudden passing away, and the period of strict mourning that followed, severely curtailed his stay in Peking, although there were some outstanding questions that he had hoped to take up. Since he would have fewer opportunities to make his stay useful, the Lama left the Chinese capital on 21 December (1908).[58]

At Kumbum, where he arrived in February (1909), the Imperial Commissioner of Hsining presented him, at an elaborate ceremony, with the Letters Patent for the new title that had been bestowed upon him by the Empress. Here the Lama is also said to have instituted a number of reforms in the administration and rituals of the monastery. Towards the close of the year, he reached Nagchuka and later arrived at Lhasa. It is said that his people now presented him with a new seal, with the inscription ' By the Prophecy of the Lord Buddha, Gyatso (Dalai) Lama is the holder of the Buddhist faith on the face of the Earth', which was ' a symbol of Tibetan independence ' and ' a mark of defiance ' against Chinese interference. This was the more remarkable in that the seal was presented at a time when, as would be noticed presently, a strong Chinese army was advancing on Lhasa.[59]

---

[56] Ibid., pp. 83-85.
The title conferred on the Fifth Dalai Lama was ' Most Excellent, Self-existing Buddha, Universal ruler of the Buddhist Faith, Vajradhara, Dalai Lama '. Ibid., pp. 17–18.
[57] Ibid., p. 86.
[58] Ibid., p. 87.
[59] Ibid., p. 89. Also see *Shakabapa*, p. 223.

Chapter 3

A Chinese Come-back into Tibet (1904–7)

FROM PEKING, by the end of 1908, the Dalai Lama had started again on his travels which were to take him another twelve months on the road. The years since he fled from Lhasa in 1904 had been momentous, and not only in terms of his own political education and awareness of the complicated skein of international rivalries in which Tibet was deeply entangled. They had been memorable too in the near-metamorphosis that had come about in the political landscape of his own country. Here, long before he reached his capital, the transformation which increasing Chinese activity had brought about in Eastern Tibet was deeply imprinted on his mind. Lhasa too he found to be a very different place from the one he had left, for the lingering shadow of Lord Curzon's India across the Potala had gradually given way to the unremitting grip of Peking's new representative who, for a time, seemed to supersede the time-worn institution of the Amban itself.

It was generally expected that Lord Curzon's departure from India would be a curtain-raiser for a complete break with the past, and not only in regard to Tibet. And yet, as has been briefly noticed above, in one major particular at any rate, viz. negotiations concerning the Adhesion Agreement with China, Minto's thinking was in no way materially different from Curzon's. Like the latter, he too had been opposed to a resumption of negotiations, for the price that had to be paid seemed prohibitive. Soon other issues came up for decision and, unwittingly perhaps, the new Viceroy seemed to be toeing his predecessor's line.

A major by-product of the Younghusband expedition was the spate of activity that it unleashed in exploring parts of what had hitherto been a forbidden land. And, in view of the hurdles which such exploration had to contend with in the past,[1] this seemed natural enough. One of the first probes in this case, and for which permission had been obtained before Younghusband left Lhasa, was the Gartok expedition which set out in October 1904. Led by C G Rawling and accompanied among others by Captain O'Connor, the newly-designated Trade Agent at Gyantse, the principal aim of the expedition was to explore the upper valley of the Tsangpo.[2]

[1] Parshotam Mehra, *The Younghusband Expedition* (Bombay and London, 1968), pp. 58–68. Also see Graham Sandberg, *The Exploration of Tibet* (London, 1904), Sir T. H. Holditch, *Tibet, The Mysterious* (London, 1908), and perhaps the best hitherto, John MacGregor, *Tibet, a Chronicle of Exploration* (London, 1970).

[2] For the results of the expedition see C G Rawling, *The Great Plateau* (London, 1905).

In the wake of Rawling's success, other expeditions suggested themselves. Among these, one was that of Captain Ryder, an ex-member of the Younghusband mission, who proposed a journey east, down the Tsangpo. The aim was to help resolve the conundrum posed since the eighteen eighties by the Survey of India explorer, the intrepid Kinthup, more popularly known as A K Pandit. Another was a suggestion of E C Wilton, a member of the British Chinese Consular Service, who had been Younghusband's principal adviser on Chinese affairs, to return to his post (in China), overland through Tibet. Still another great, and ambitious, project was that of the well-known Swedish doctor, Sven Hedin, who in the early summer of 1905 had conceived the idea of crossing into Tibet from the south, across the Indian frontier. Curzon, while by no means in favour of a blanket permission being accorded to all exploration, yet supported each of the projects enumerated above. To Seven Hedin, for whom he had considerable respect, he wrote

> I shall be proud to render you what assistance lies in my power while I still remain in India, and only regret that before your great expedition is over I shall have left these shores....[3]

It is not without significance that Minto too, while he agreed that government control over all exploration into Tibet should be strictly enforced, lent his countenance and gave support to most of the proposals listed above, including Sven Hedin's. For the latter he waged a battle royal with Whitehall nor was it due to his want of trying that some of the other projects proved still-born.

Morley at the India Office, though he swore by the policy of Brodrick in terms of isolating, if also perhaps insulating, Tibet had an entirely different approach to the question. He was 'horrified' at the idea of Minto allowing or even supporting any proposals for exploration and, in his characteristic way, told the Governor-General:

> What may be our ultimate relations with Tibet, I do not venture to predict. Is it not certain that our policy is to satisfy Tibet, China and Russia —that we mean to keep our word—deliberately given to all three—that we mean no intervention or anything leading to intervention? Why else did we take such trouble, after I came to this office, to procure the adhesion of China?[4] Yet, here before the ink on the Chinese settlement is dry... here is a policy from Simla, of expeditions, explorations, and all the other provocative things—that in the case of Tibetan resistance would mean either

---

[3]Sven Hedin, *Trans Himalaya: Discoveries and Adventures in Tibet* (London, 1910), 3 Vols, I, pp. 3–4.

[4]As has been noted, *supra*, Chapter II, the Peking negotiations between Sir Ernest Satow and Tang Shao-yi had been authorised by the Liberal Government which succeeded Balfour in December 1905. It may also be recalled that Minto and his advisors in India were opposed to the concessions which HMG finally made.

another senseless mission, or else humiliating acquiescence. What may be done in the way of exploration by and by... I do not presume to say. But today! Consider the language held by Spring-Rice to Lamsdorff only a few weeks ago—each of them solemnly and emphatically declaring that he would have nothing to do with intervention.[5] Consider the row we made (very rightly) about the Buriat escort for the Dalai Lama.[6] And now here we are, sending a whole squad of explorers in every direction, a force of Gurkhas, and a British Officer in charge. I cannot but think of this as Curzonism pure and simple.[7]

Understandably, the smaller explorations Morley did not find it difficult to countermand; his greatest battle was against the Swedish doctor who had set his heart on entering Tibet from British India. What was worse was that considerable pressure was brought to bear on him, among others from Prime Minister Campbell-Bannerman and the Swedish King himself, through the British Ambassador in Stockholm.[8] Morley, however, stuck to his original stand and in so doing underlined the fact that HMG ' considers it advisable to continue the isolation of Tibet ' which the late Government ' so carefully maintained '.[9]

Paradoxically, it was not that Morley under-rated the Russian bogey which had so completely preoccupied the Curzon-Younghusband thinking; only that, as he claimed it, his manner of tackling it was different. His approach, as that of the Liberal Government of which he was a member, was one of building a bridge of confidence with St. Petersburg. If the Russians disclaimed any interest in Tibet, why not take them at their word and, by underpinning Britain's own anxiety to isolate Lhasa, bring about a *modus vivendi*. This would not only scotch the flames of controversy, but develop a modicum of trust and confidence in which the mutual professions of lack of interest in Tibet of both the Powers could be given a more concrete, a more tangible, form. It was this approach which eventually resulted in the conclusion of the Anglo-Russian *entente* embodying a mutual hands-off policy of strict neutrality and non-interference, *vis-a-vis* Tibet, by both the powers. It is discussed, at some length, in the latter part of this chapter. Two corollaries of

[5]Reference was to Russian dealings with, and alleged support to, the Dalai Lama, more specifically in the context of Dorjieff's activities and the attentions showered on the Lama at Urga by the Russian Ambassador in Peking.

Spring-Rice was the then British Charge d'Affaires in St. Petersburg.

For Russian and British assurances see Spring-Rice to Grey, 2 and 7 May 1906 in Nos. 90 and 100 in *F O* 535/7.

[6]Grey to Spring-Rice, 1 May 1906, No. 87 in Ibid.

[7]Morley to Minto, 7 June 1906, cited in Lamb, *McMahon Line*, I, p. 63.

[8]Renell Rodd to Grey, 23 July 1906, Ibid., p. 64.

[9]*Sven Hedin*, I, n. 3, pp. 8–11.

For some intimate letters of Sven Hedin to Dunlop Smith (Minto's Private Secretary), bearing on Morley's denial of permission to the Swedish explorer, see Martin Gilbert, *Servant of India* (London , 1966), pp. 99–118.

this policy may, however, be noted here. One, that it involved, on the part of Whitehall, a periodic dressing-down of the Indian authorities who repeatedly raised the issue of Russian activity, often based on the flimsiest of evidence. Two, making re-doubled efforts towards fostering that power vacuum in Tibet which had resulted from British withdrawal on the morrow of Younghusband's resounding march into Lhasa. It was this power vacuum which the Chinese were to fill and which, in turn, created its own hiatus. To this hiatus Morley's policy, as would be noticed presently, offered no solution.

To large-scale Western domination of China in the closing decades of the 19th century—a domination which to many percipient minds appeared to be a prelude to the whole country being carved up[10]—Peking's reaction took varied forms. An interesting manifestation was strengthening the hold of the central government over the outer dependencies, viz. Korea, Sinkiang, Mongolia, Manchuria and Tibet. While the dread hand of the maritime powers over a major part of the country's sea-frontage appeared to be irresistible, the Chinese argued that the securing of their land frontiers would no doubt arrest the processes of further disintegration. The early beginnings of this policy may be seen in the struggle over Chinese Turkestan, freshly reconquered and newly christened Sinkiang, the 'New Dominion'. This was towards the latter part of the nineteenth century and recalls to mind the campaigns of Tso Tsung-tang, the intrepid warrior-statesman who both defeated, and nipped in the bud, Yakub Beg's nascent dreams of an independent Kashgaria.

Traditionally, Chinese control in the outlying dependencies had been maintained indirectly through such cleverly wrought contrivances as the Lama Church, or the hierarchy of Muslim tribal chiefs. For fairly obvious reasons, direct Chinese governmental authority, as in the case of the eighteen provinces on the mainland, could neither have been extended to these areas nor perhaps worked in practice. In Tibet, the fount of Chinese power and prestige were the Manchu Ambans who, since the middle of the 18th century, had been agents of Imperial control and channels of communication for the Dalai Lama and his functionaries.[11] In much the same way, the Imperial Resident at Urga and the Military Governors at Uliassutai in Mongolia and at Kuldja

[10]John King Fairbank, Edwin Reischauer and Albert Craig, *East Asia, the Modern Transformation* (Boston, 1964), pp. 365–84.
Also see Vinacke, *A History of the Far East in Modern Times* (New York, 1960), pp. 146–63, Owen and Eleanor Lattimore, *The Making of Modern China* (Washington, 1944), p. 123, and Hu Sheng, *Imperialism and Chinese Politics* (Peking, 1955), pp. 109–76.
[11]W W Rockhill, *The Dalai Lamas*, p. 90, maintains that the Manchu Amban Yu Tai's proclamation of 10 September 1904 in which he stated that the Dalai Lama ' will hereafter be responsible for religious matters and shall only be concerned slightly in the official matters ' while the Amban will conduct all Tibetan affairs with Tibetan officials and all important matters will be referred to the Emperor, was ' absolutely in accordance with the Regulations of 1793 ' and that it neither added to nor subtracted from the authority of China.

in Chinese Turkestan, were the custodians of Peking's authority in these far-flung dominions of the Empire. As pressures on Mongolia from the direction of Russia, and on Tibet from that of British India, increased Chinese policy of indirect rule gradually yielded place to one of direct control.

Symptomatic of the change was the creation, in 1901, of two new (Chinese) government departments, the Boards of Territorial Development and of Frontier Defence, both primarily concerned with Mongolia and Tibet. Partly, the aim was to colonize these areas with Chinese settlers[12] and, in the process, through intermarriages and cultural assimilation, integrate them into the larger body-politic of the mainland. Elaborate schemes were drawn up for opening Chinese schools, imparting language instruction, setting up institutes for elementary military training, and even establishment of banks. So also were plans for railroad construction from Kalgan to Urga and for prospecting of minerals. The major objective in all these cases, as may be apparent, was to integrate Mongolia, and its economy, into the larger family of the Motherland. It should have been clear nonetheless that there was a basic incompatibility between China's 'old intensive-type' economy and the distortions it underwent as it moved into an area of nomad mobility with its own extensive tribal organisation. No wonder it was clear that, after the Manchus,

> Mongolia and China would have tended to cleave apart along the Great Wall frontier . . . as the old underlying values of mobility and immobility, extensive economy and intensive economy re-asserted themselves and gravitated toward their natural geographical environments and social forms.[13]

Long-term economic incompatibilities apart, in the short run the rapid induction of these measures into the hitherto staid life of the Mongols led to violent reactions. Two principal vested interests, the Lama hierarchy with its strong and powerful backing in the Dalai Lama's church, and the landed nobility in the shape of the Mongol princes who sustained and supported that church, felt visibly threatened. Additionally, there was the powerful impact of Tsarist Russia whose land frontiers were now contiguous with that of Mongolia and which had, over the years, cast covetous glances across the frontier. An upsurge of Chinese activity was thus far from welcome to the Russians who had, over the years, built powerful interests and acquired important rights and privileges in Mongolia.[14]

---

[12] ' The Peiping-Suiyuan railway reached up to the southern edge of Inner Mongolia.... From the east and south the railway despatched into Inner Mongolia even more Chinese colonists than Chinese traders because rail transport reversed the direction of grain export, making the Chinese market more profitable than the steppe market '. Lattimore, *Inner Asian Frontiers of China* (New York, 1951), p. 99.

[13] Ibid., p. 100.

[14] In 1861, the Russians had opened a Consulate at Urga while in April 1899, the British had, through an exchange of notes, recognised Mongolia as lying within the Russian sphere of

Not to go farther, Russian interest in Mongolia went as far back as the Treaty of Kiakhta in 1727. More recently, in 1861, St. Petersburg had opened a Consulate at Urga where it had not only set up a commercial firm but otherwise enjoyed a privileged position in the internal trade. By what Peking now calls the 'unequal' treaty of 1881, Russia acquired, *inter alia*, the right to set up more consulates in Mongolia. By 1900, a Russian gold mining enterprise, the 'Mongolor', had begun to operate while a year previously the British had recognised, through an exchange of notes, Russia's special, and indeed exclusive, position in the building up of rail roads in the country. Thus by the time Peking embarked upon its new policy of integrating Mongolia into the body politic of the mainland, Russian interests in the country were no longer of a purely academic nature.

To these interests, commercial no less than political, China's new policy posed a powerful, if sinister, threat. No wonder that in every plan that the Mongols evolved for resisting Chinese pressures and in every scheme they contemplated to defy them, the hand of Russia, direct or indirect, was not only suspect but often crudely overt enough to be noticed.

China's policy in Mongolia was only another facet of its policy towards Tibet. The watershed here was the Younghusband expedition which had lost Peking not only a great deal of its authority but what was more valuable, if less tangible, its 'face'. It was with a view to regaining its lost prestige that the negotiations over the 'Adhesion' Agreement had been, from the British point of view, such a long drawn-out agony. Thanks to 'the sell-out' which the Liberal Government of Campbell-Bannerman and the political philosophy of Morley and Grey made possible, Peking's success in these parleys was significant.[15] This lent it a new determination to exercise to the hilt its newly acquired privileges; what was more, a conspiracy of circumstances was to prove propitious.

To recount events briefly, Curzon's Tibetan policy had virtually met its Waterloo long before he returned from England towards the close of 1904, to commence his ill-starred second term as Governor-General. On the eve of his arrival, Ampthill had ratified the Lhasa Convention and, in the process, thrown away its two principal gains which would have given the British the major instruments through which they could exercise power and wield influence. Whatever Curzon could salvage of the residue was surrendered at the time of the Adhesion Agreement, in April 1906, although it was clear that by then his responsibility for the conduct of affairs had ceased. The final blow was struck not so much by the terms of the Peking agreement, compromising as it was in more ways than one, as by Morley's determination subsequent thereto, to desist from doing anything that would smack of creat-

---

influence. A year later, in 1900, 'Mongolor' a Russian goldmining enterprise was founded. By then nearly ten Russian trading firms had established themselves in Urga and over 200 Russians were carrying on some kind of peddling trade throughout Mongolia.

[15]*Supra*, Chapter II.

ing even the semblance of a quarrel or a dispute that may invite any overt intervention. One result of this approach was that the Tibetans, and later the Chinese, reverted to a position with which the British had long been familiar and which ante-dated Younghusband's arrival in Lhasa. Another, not unexpectedly, was the helplessness which the British Trade Agents felt in the new situation that had now been created for them.

All that remained of the Lhasa Convention, therefore, was the occupation of the Chumbi Valley and to this British officials now stuck tenaciously. Charles Bell was the first administrator of Chumbi, to be succeeded briefly by W L Campbell. As an administrator, Bell had carried out some far-reaching reforms designed not only to simplify the processes of government but to leave on the people a deep imprint. *Inter alia*, Tibetan and Chinese officials were to be excluded from all organs of administration, and what Bell called ' a simple organization ', based on the principle of ' freedom from oppressiveness', was evolved. Government was left mainly in the hands of village headmen; the practice of forced labour, without payment, was abolished while an annual sum—' substantial but reasonable '—was fixed as taxation for each of the five divisions into which the valley was split. The village headmen, who were responsible for collection of revenue, were also vested with powers in ' petty matters ' of justice and police.[16]

Chumbi apart, Tibetan reluctance to implement the terms of the Lhasa Convention, after it had been plain that there could be no second military expedition to enforce its authority, was patent. Nothing, however, did more to undermine British prestige in Tibet than the personality of Chang Ying-tang who repaired to Lhasa, via India, as Chinese Imperial Commissioner after the failure, early in 1906, of the Calcutta negotiations over the Adhesion Agreement.

Chang stopped over briefly in Chumbi but while out there behaved in a manner that completely ignored British occupation of the valley. Thus he lived at the Chinese yamen in Pipitang, suggesting there had been no interruption in the continuity of their (Chinese) rule; demanded, and received, free transport as an entitlement; issued orders to the headmen of the Tromowas; and, on leaving after a few weeks, presented them with small sums of money as gifts from the sovereign.[17]

There was another string to Chang's bow, namely to bring the pro-British Panchen Lama to heel. On his way to Lhasa, the Chinese Commissioner had worked out tentative plans for a possible visit to the Lama at Shigatse. An inkling of this was enough to upset Bell, then acting, during White's leave of absence, as Political Officer in Sikkim. The latter feared lest Chang's visit, or even that of Henderson, should be interpreted by the Lama as an

---

[16]Bell, *Tibet*, pp. 73–81, comprising a whole chapter entitled 'Administering the Chumbi Valley'.

[17]Minto to Morley, 2 October 1906, No. 64 in *F O* 535/8 and Bell to India, 9 October 1906, No. 76 in Ibid.

attempt to punish him for his unauthorised sojourn to Calcutta to meet the (British) Prince of Wales, in the winter of 1905. There was the additional argument that while the British Trade Agent in Gyantse, and indeed the Political Officer himself, was barred from visiting the Lama, Chinese officials were being allowed uninhibited access. In the final analysis, Bell was given permission to visit Shigatse, although it is not clear whether this helped to re-establish confidence in the Lama about British bona fides or assure him the support that he sought but which Bell had no authority to pledge. The latter's description of the visit is fairly detailed and, one would imagine, frank. The Lama's interest, apart from animals and novelties was

> centred chiefly on the political situation. He had accepted the Indian Government's invitation to visit India, depending on their support if his acceptance should subsequently lead him into trouble. The Chinese were regaining power in Tibet, and he feared their reprisals.[18]

Besides Chumbi and the Panchen, Chang's main effort to reassert Chinese position in Tibet was designed to be achieved through an embargo on direct communication between the British and the Tibetans in commercial transactions at the trade marts. He even went a step further and by appointing Chinese, instead of Tibetans, as diplomatic and commercial representatives, made the position of the British Trade Agents increasingly difficult, if not impossible. Chang's own views on the subject were quite categorical and admitted of no compromise. He held *inter alia* that

> virtual recognition of Chinese sovereignty over Tibet was involved in the signature of the Adhesion Agreement, and that ' Chinese authorities in Tibet ' should ' consequently ' be the interpretation placed on the phrase ' Tibetan Government ' wherever the latter occurs in the Lhasa convention.[19]

In pursuance of this policy, Chang argued somewhat speciously, that British Trade Agents, then posted at the marts, were strictly *persona non grata* insofar as they had occupied their positions before their Chinese counterparts had been inducted into office. In other words, the trade marts, although already in existence, could not have been functioning *officially* before Chang, or his appointees, had arrived on the scene. Apart from the embarrassments which this seemingly difficult situation created, Chang's whole concept of the new relationship made the day-to-day functioning of British Trade Agents virtually impossible.[20] Bell, who went through all this, recaptures the situation vividly:

> It soon became apparent that our position in Tibet was precarious. Our Treaty rights were infringed in various ways....The Tibetan officers at

---

[18] Bell, *Tibet*, p. 84.

[19] *Tibet Papers*, Cd. 5240, No. 141, p. 86.

[20] Chang, ' a vigorous High Commissioner ', let it be seen that he interpreted the 1906 Convention ' as a recognition of Chinese sovereignty in Tibet ', Richardson, *History*, pp. 95–96.

Gyantse were unable even to accept invitations to lunch from British Officers there, without first obtaining permission from their Chinese masters.[21]

Nor were Chinese activities confined only to Tibet. For the

> power of China was recognised in Sikkim, where people said openly that the Chinaman was the equal of the Englishman. I was told by more than one good authority, that the Maharaja and Maharani of Sikkim would prefer to be under China rather than under Great Britain, if this were possible. And Mr Chang was already stretching out his hand towards Nepal....[22]

Embarrassing the British was only one part of Chang's overall strategy. Another was to eliminate every single individual who had directly, or indirectly, been associated with the humiliations of the British expedition. Thus Amban Yu T'ai for the dubious crime of not being able to prevent Younghusband from coming to Lhasa was not only arrested but, allegedly, put in chains and sent back home. The Ganden Ti Rimpoche and a host of Tibetan officials, who had been associated with the negotiations at Lhasa, were openly humiliated.[23] The Panchen Lama was left in no doubt that his hobnobbing with the British had been viewed with severe disfavour and that it was foolhardy of him to depend upon them. The Tibetan administrative structure was recast on the pattern with which Chang had been familiar in China— Boards of Revenue, of War, of Communications taking the place of the hitherto loosely organised Tibetan government. A Tibetan army too was on the cards. For those who saw a great deal that was wrong about China and all that it did, a fair corrective may be the thought that its new officials lessened the bribes taken by Tibetan functionaries from the poorer classes and in ordinary, non-political, cases dispensed better and more equitable justice. Thus Bell testifies to the fact that there

> was no doubt some foundation for the Amban's claim that the poorer classes in Tibet were in favour of China.[24]

Where Peking's new agents faltered was that, unlike the British, they were a lot more impatient and a lot more meddlesome in the time-worn habits

---

[21] Bell, *Tibet*, p. 92.

[22] According to Bell, Ibid., pp. 92–93, Chang wrote to the Nepalese agent at Lhasa that Tibet and Nepal ' being united like brothers and under the auspices of China ' should work in harmony ' for the mutual good '. Here was, Bell concludes, ' a tentative assumption of Chinese suzerainty over Nepal to be pressed or disavowed later by Mr Chang's government ' as circumstances might suggest.

[23] Richardson, *History*, p. 96, maintains that all the Tibetan Ministers ' who had taken part in the negotiations of 1904 ' were dismissed.

[24] Bell, *Tibet*, p. 93.

and customs of 'this most conservative of peoples'. Hence the seething cauldron of an incipient revolt that gripped the land and that was brought to a head by events on the mainland. In the short run, however, before this ground-swell of discontent could take form, Chang's plans appeared very close to success. O'Connor, the British Agent at Gyantse, had even concluded that Chang's tenure would see Tibet transformed into a Chinese province in which trade marts would be indistinct from treaty ports and where the British would not be entitled to any special privileges or rights.[25]

A sizeable part of Chang's later activity developed into an unseemly wrangle between him on the one hand and O'Connor on the other. Shorn of overtones, it was largely a clash of personalities. Thus we know that Bell had developed a wholesome respect for the Chinese Commissioner for his

> personal relations with Mr Chang, official and social were uniformly excellent. Though some of his methods were not such as to commend themselves to the British mind, one had to recognise that our presence in the country was distasteful to him. He worked, as he believed in the best interests of his country, and the policy of our Government, right or wrong, gave him the means of promoting those interests.[26]

Unfortunately, with O'Connor it was just the reverse. From the first, the two of them never hit it off as it were. As for Gow, Chang's under-study at Gyantse with whom O'Connor came into daily contact, there was an unending battle which, starting with such minor inanities as Gow preventing O'Connor from obtaining willow cuttings for the Agency garden to O'Connor ignoring Gow in a judicial proceedings which he conducted in his official capacity, grew into a perpetual running sore.[27] It is not germane to this narrative to go into the sickening details of this conflict except perhaps to record that one of the major 'victories' which the Chinese scored related to Sven Hedin. Despite O'Connor's best efforts he was unable to obtain permission for the celebrated Swedish explorer to travel from Shigatse to Gyantse and then, across the Himalayas, into India. For Chang, to O'Connor's great chagrin,

---

[25] O'Connor's Diary, 6 April 1907, No. 174 in *F O* 535/9; Minto to Morley, 3 February 1907, No. 47 in Ibid.

According to a Chinese scholar, on 13 January 1907 Chang submitted 24 articles to the Tsungli Yamen ' with a view to consolidating and strengthening Chinese rule in Tibet '. He recommended, *inter alia*, that the Dalai and the Panchen should be ' mere religious heads '; that Tibet have a Viceroy of ' royal rank and power '; that at least 6,000 Chinese troops should be stationed in Tibet, apart from 10,000 natives ' trained and commanded ' by Chinese officers; that telegraph lines be laid all the way from Batang to Lhasa; that the road from Tachienlu to Gyantse and Yatung be improved; that mines be opened; that 1/10 of revenue be collected as tax; that an arsenal be set up for manufacturing small arms and last, but not the least, relations with Bhutan and Nepal be improved. *Yao-ting Sung*, p. 65.

[26] Bell, *Tibet*, p. 89.

[27] O'Connor's Diary, 5 January 1907, No. 92, in *F O* 535/9.

successfully insisted on the Swede's retracing his steps across Western Tibet and Chinese Turkestan.[28]

At the height of the conflict, O'Connor made two proposals for which Minto lent him full support. The first was to arm the Panchen Lama with 400 Martini-Henry rifles and, at the same time, encourage him to proclaim his political independence from Lhasa! The second was to transfer the headquarters of the Trade Agent from Gyantse to Shigatse—a move which, apart from its political overtones in terms of buttressing the authority of the Panchen Lama, O'Connor justified on purely commercial considerations.[29]

Morley at the India Office resisted the pressures to which he was thus exposed, countermanded O'Connor's proposed visit to Shigatse and refused ' any despatch of rifles'. He was emphatic that, as he saw it, the British aim was *not* ' to oust China so long as it does not violate the Convention'.[30] To get over O'Connor's difficulties, however, Jordan was able to secure Gow's removal from Gyantse and later O'Connor himself was quietly eased out of his post at the trade mart. He did not like it and though

> sorry to leave Tibet, it was clear that in the circumstances I could no longer be of much use there....Our representative at Lhasa would, for the future, have only a passive role to fulfil.[31]

---

[28]Sven Hedin, I, n. 3, pp. 388–401.
[29]O'Connor to India, 3 February 1907, No. 1226 in *IOR*, Political/External File 1908/22.
[30]O'Connor, *Things Mortal* (London, 1940), p. 94.
[31]Ibid., p. 96.

Chapter 4

Tibet and the Convention with Russia (1907)

LONG BEFORE the Liberals took the reins of office, the Conservative administration of Arthur Balfour had initiated far-reaching moves towards easing tensions, and to that extent cutting its losses, with Tsarist Russia. As a close, and careful, student of the end of Britain's ('splendid'?) isolation has put it, in the opening years of the century 'the two countries were not however negotiating an *entente*; rather they stood on the brink of negotiations'.[1] Even as early as March 1903, Lansdowne, then Foreign Secretary, expressed himself as 'extremely anxious' to convince the Russian Government that

> we cannot deal with these occurrences as if they were isolated incidents. If we are to come to an understanding it should have reference to Tibet, Afghanistan, Seistan and Persia generally.[2]

And not only did he not despair of finding a 'reasonable solution' to the Russo-Afghan difficulty, and perhaps of other 'tiresome questions', but was in 'great hopes' of a settlement with Russia on questions connected with India.[3] By early in December (1903), his efforts to find a workable understanding with Russia had reached an advanced stage for at

> about this time Lansdowne was circulating to the Cabinet drafts of an *entente*, and it was in the course of the discussion of these that Balfour, on the 21st, entered his caveat. He was, however, prepared to accept Lansdowne's policy as a temporary palliative, and on New Year's day Lansdowne circulated to all his colleagues a final draft approved by the Prime Minister.[4]

What bedevilled Conservative efforts was the outbreak of the Russo-Japanese War (December 1903–March 1905) which, owing to Great Britain's commitments to Japan, now an ally, made a rapprochement with Russia impossible—at any rate, during its pendency. No sooner was it over, the Germans challenged the as yet embryonic Anglo-French *entente* in Morocco. The crisis

---

[1] G W Monger, *The End of Isolation* (London, 1963), p. 118.
[2] Lansdowne to Scott, 23 March 1903, cited in Ibid., n. 1, p. 118.
[3] Lansdowne to Balfour, 12 April 1903, and Lansdowne to Curzon, 24 April 1903, ns. 2 and 3, p. 118 in Ibid.
[4] Ibid., p. 143.

that ensued lasted until December (1905) when the increasingly rickety administration of Balfour gave way to the Liberals under Campbell-Bannerman.

It was thus left to Grey, the new Foreign Secretary, to pick up the threads where Lansdowne had left them. Within less than three months, he had reached an accord with Benckendorff to work for a definite understanding. Before long, Nicolson was especially despatched to St. Petersburg with instructions to hammer out an agreement.[5] Among the subjects which had aroused considerable bad blood, and created a miasma of mutual suspicion and distrust, Tibet and Afghanistan—and latterly Persia—figured most prominently. In fact, at an early stage in the negotiations, the bases for British proposals had been well sorted out: Britain's special interest in Tibet, owing to the fact of its physical proximity, was to be recognised; for the rest, neither government was to send its representatives to Lhasa, nor seek any concessions for themselves nor their subjects on railways, roads, mining or other rights, nor were they to have any Tibetan revenues assigned or pledged to them. Russia, of course, even as Britian had earlier, was to recognise China's suzerainty over the country and respect the latter's territorial integrity.

Thanks to their previous background, each question was to become a subject of considerable debate and even long drawn-out disputation. Thus the relationship of the Tsar's government to the Dalai Lama evoked a lot of controversy, as did St. Petersburg's insistence on the right of the Buryats, and other Buddhist subjects of the Tsar, to have free and uninhibited access to both the Lamas. Dorjieff and much more so his master, now in exile, were subjects of lively discussion. As it turned out, the British could offer no concrete evidence to establish their thesis that the Buryat was a Russian Agent and discovered to their surprise that the Dalai Lama was not always amenable to Russian discipline. Indeed Isvolsky, it seemed, was quite as keen as they were themselves to keep the pontiff temporarily away from his seat of authority. As Nicolson noticed at a fairly early stage in the negotiations, the Russians conceded that

> it would be undesirable, in the interest of both our countries, that this personage should return to Tibet.[6]

A week later, the Russian Foreign Minister proposed that both parties should come to a mutual understanding ' not to facilitate ' his return to Tibet.[7]

What had worried the British was not only the threat of the Lama's own

---

[5] The understanding with Grey was arrived at on 19 March while Nicolson reached St. Petersburg on 28 May. Meanwhile Lamsdorff had been replaced by Isvolsky and it was with the latter that Nicolson opened official talks on 29 May, the day after he arrived. Ibid., pp. 281–83.

[6] Nicolson to Grey, 13 July 1906, No. 35 in *F O* 535/8. On his part, Nicolson had expressed the view that in Tibet the Lama might prove to be an element of ' danger and trouble'.

[7] Nicolson to Grey, 20 July 1906, No. 33 in Ibid.

return but that he should be escorted on his journey by an armed band of (Russian) Buryats. Since the Lama himself, as also his entourage, the Russians argued, felt that his life was threatened and as a large number of Russian subjects were Buddhists (for whom the Lama was both a high-priest and a Divinity) it was 'understandable that some of their number might accompany their master to his home in order to defend him from attacks on his sacred person'.[8] Later, when Lamsdorff was succeeded by Isvolsky and negotiations proceeded apace, the latter changed his earlier stance and even held out categorical assurances on this count. Nicolson noted that the Russian Government

> had given the Dalai Lama, who was staying at Gumbum, to understand that it was not desirable that he should return at present to Tibet and he (Isvolsky) firmly assured me that no Russian official nor any person subject to Russian control would accompany him if he were to return there.[9]

The Russian Foreign Minister was also to state, quite frankly, his own view of the Lama's place in the scheme of things. The Dalai, he told Nicolson,

> exercised great influence over all the Buddhists, both Russian and Mongolian, and it was, therefore, of interest to the Russian Government to keep in touch with him, presumably through M. Dorjieff, not as the Grand Lama of Tibet, but as the spiritual chief of so many Russian subjects.[10]

About Dorjieff's goings-on too, the Russian Foreign Minister became increasingly communicative. Thus in November (1906) he informed Nicolson, 'privately and confidentially', that the Buryat was in St. Petersburg consulting with his Foreign Office officials in regard to Mongolian affairs, that on his own he (Isvolsky) had no plans to see him (Dorjieff) lest it should unduly inflate his importance. It was clear, Nicolson concluded, that Dorjieff was the instrument through which the Russians would like 'to use' the Lama in regard to the influence which he wielded over the Mongols.[11]

The Dalai Lama apart, another subject that presented difficulties related to what the British claimed to be their special rights derived from the Lhasa Convention, the most tangible of which was the stationing of Trade Agents at Yatung, Gyantse and Gartok. The British were, not unnaturally, keen that their special, and privileged, position should be recognised. Isvolsky, understandably, appeared equally concerned that it be watered down. Nicolson pointed out in December (1906), after negotiations had continued for six months, that it was clear to him

---

[8]Spring-Rice to Grey, 2 May 1906, No. 100 in *F O* 535/7.
[9]Nicolson to Grey, 19 November 1906, No. 79 in *F O* 535/8.
[10]Loc. cit.
[11]Nicolson to Grey, 19 November 1906, No. 82 in Ibid.

that the Russian Government desire to place themselves on an equal footing with us in regard to Tibet and to ignore as far as possible our recent expedition and the consequences flowing therefrom.[12]

India Office was shocked, as well it might, for the Russian stance

> practically reduces Great Britain's special interest to an obligation to see that the existing state of the foreign relations of Tibet with ourselves, as with other foreign powers, is maintained in its integrity. This does not appear to correspond with the special position we hold as compared with Russia....[13]

Grey told Nicolson that the British had ' a special interest ' in the external relations of Tibet generally owing to ' our geographical position ' and that the Convention must reflect it fully. It did finally, even though this required a great deal of horse-trading. As concluded, the preamble stated that

> Great Britain, by reason of her geographical position has a special interest in the maintenance of the status quo in the external relations of Tibet.

Another subject that created difficulties was the British occupation of the Chumbi valley. The occupation was, for reasons easily intelligible, not very palatable to the Russians and even though it had been made clear that there was no intention to stay beyond the stipulated three years, Isvolsky was sceptical. To start with, both Morley and Grey held that nothing more was called for than to repeat the words used at the time of the ratification of the Lhasa Convention by Amphill: that ' the British occupation of the Chumbi valley shall cease after the due payment of three annual instalments of the said indemnity....' The two riders attached being that the trade marts had been ' effectively opened ' for three years and that the terms of the Convention were ' faithfully complied with'.

At an early stage in the negotiations, Isvolsky had made it plain that if occupation was prolonged, the British would be in a privileged position and the Convention would require ' re-negotiation'. Nicolson spelt out the position, as Isvolsky saw it, clearly enough:

> In short, the two Governments proposed ... to draw up a kind of self-denying Convention with regard to Tibet, but if we remained in possession of a portion of Tibet, the self-denying clause would not be applied by us. Russia should therefore have the right to reconsider the provisions of the Anglo-Russian Convention if the situation had not returned to a normal condition after a specified period.[14]

---

[12]Nicolson to Grey, 26 December 1906, No. 7 in *F O* 535/9.
[13]*I O* to *F O*, 6 February 1907, No. 50 in Ibid.
[14]*Supra*, n. 12.

In other words, if the British occupation was prolonged—'and he (Isvolsky) appeared sceptical that it would terminate at the date fixed'—the Russian Government would be entitled to ' some concessions'.[15]

It was not easy for Nicolson to persuade his Russian counterpart to modify this position. Besides, the evacuation of Chumbi was ' entirely dependent ' on the fulfilment by the Tibetan Government of the terms of the Lhasa Convention and

> it is clear that His Brittanic Majesty's Government could not agree to discuss with another Power whether the stipulations of the Convention of 1904 had been complied with.[16]

Finally, the separate annexe to the Convention while it did not provide for negotiations *de novo*, stipulated nonetheless that

> if the occupation of the Chumbi valley by the British forces has, for any reason not been terminated at the time anticipated in the above Declaration, the British and Russian Governments will enter upon a friendly exchange of views on this subject.

Still another bone of contention related to travel by officials of the two countries. While Morley was keen that a blanket moratorium on Russian explorers, who sometimes appeared in the guise of leaders of scientific expeditions, would prevent any possibility of intrigue and therefore of avoidable misunderstanding between the two Powers, Isvolsky was opposed to any such plan. More than once he had confessed to Nicolson his embarrassing position in regard to a public interdict on all scientific missions. Although, on his own, he would be prepared to prevent these, yet to proclaim this policy in a solemn agreement was something he could not easily stomach. As Nicolson told Grey, ' he (Isvolsky) did not object so much to the substance of our proposal as to the form in which we desired to clothe it'.[17] Here was a tune that struck a sympathetic chord in the hearts both of Grey as well as Nicolson. The latter argued that the suspicion that the Russians would exploit these explorations for political intrigue and thereby raise ' complicated questions ' was misplaced. For, if the Russians did want to manipulate the Lhasa authorities, or Tibetan nationals, to subserve their ulterior political purposes, they would have plenty of such opportunities, even outside the sphere of scientific exploration. Grey was even more outspoken and, after Sven Hedin's success in reaching Shigatse, pin-pointed the ' ineffectiveness ' of such a prohibition, implied that its opera-

---

[15]Loc. cit.
[16]Aide Memoire to Russian government, dated 22 April 1907, Encl. in No. 146, *F O* 535/9.
[17]Nicolson to Grey, 23 February 1907, No. 84 in *F O* 535/9; also Nicolson to Grey, 23 February 1907, No. 74 in Ibid. Earlier, on 6 January 1907, Nicolson told Grey that Isvolsky ' still felt great difficulty ' in agreeing to the interdict, No. 29 in Ibid.

tion would only place the two countries in a ' disadvantageous ' position (' for prohibition would not apply to others '), hinted that Morley may like to withdraw it and made it plain that British insistence on this question accounted for Russian ' reluctance or unwillingness ' to accept the Convention's terms.[18] Morley, however, refused to be persuaded, indicated that he ' cannot modify ' the views he had expressed earlier although ' not to a point where breakdown of present negotiations becomes inevitable'.[19] In the end, Grey, who in the Cabinet leaned heavily on Morley, gave way and persuaded Nicolson to tell the Russians that British

> anxiety to avoid complications which might compromise evacuation of Chumbi valley is the reason why we desire to maintain the prohibition ... (that it would be) difficult to carry out engagement regarding Chumbi valley if a British scientific mission were attacked or destroyed in Tibet.[20]

Despite this, he cautioned Nicolson against referring to the subject ' unless reopened ' by Isvolsky.[21] The long and short of it was that in an exchange of notes between Nicolson and Isvolsky, the interdict on scientific expeditions was accepted.

Not unrelated to the question of scientific expeditions was that of Buddhist pilgrims visiting Lhasa, their holy of holies, and establishing some contact with the Dalai (or the Panchen) Lama. At an early stage in the negotiations, Isvolsky had told Nicolson that ' it would be impossible ' to cut off ' all communications ' between the Tsar's Buddhist subjects and the Lama.[22] India was rather touchy on these questions and conceded only grudgingly the principle of visits by Russian subjects to holy places in Tibet. An early formulation of its thinking on the subject may be gauged from the following:

> Deputation to Tibet of Russian representatives should not in any circumstances be permitted. Distinction between political and religious matters in Tibet cannot be drawn and if representatives (were) admitted all previous troubles (would ensue).... Mere fact of visits by Russian subjects to holy places (is) no argument for establishment of relations between Russia and Tibet.[23]

---

[18] *F O* to *I O*, 28 February 1907, No. 82 in Ibid. A fortnight later Nicolson wrote to say that Isvolsky faced ' opposition from his colleagues ', that there was an element of ' general inacceptability ' about the prohibition, that he (Isvolsky) feared ' public odium ' and above all was unable to justify the interdict to himself. Nicolson to Grey, 13 March 1907, No. 104 in Ibid.

[19] *I O* to *F O*, 7 March 1907, No. 94 in *F O* 535/9.

[20] Grey to Nicolson, 9 March 1907, No. 99 in Ibid.

[21] Grey to Nicolson, 19 March 1907, No. 106 in Ibid.

[22] Nicolson to Grey, 17 June 1906, No. 128 in *F O* 535/7.

[23] India to Morley, 13 July 1906, Encl. in No. 14, *F O* 535/8.

It was the fear that Russia might use its Buryat subjects for political intrigue, under the thinly veiled guise of religious intercourse, that caused concern to Whitehall and against which it wanted to safeguard.[24] It was soon apparent nonetheless that, however desirable the objective, it was not perhaps easy of realisation in actual practice.[25] Here not only the government in Calcutta but Nicolson himself was quite candid on the implications:

> If Russia contemplates entering at any time into secret relations with the Tibetan authorities, it would, I imagine, be rather through agents of the standing of Dorjieff than through Russian officials....I fear it would not be possible to devise formulae which would prevent and forestall any future desire to get behind the Convention....[26]

These twin props: that, as framed, the Convention had enough safeguards to prevent pilgrims from being used as political agents or go-betweens and that, in practice, no fool-proof system could be devised that may prevent its abuse, were ultimately to sustain both the Viceroy and the India Office against their fears. As signed, the Convention stipulated that

> The two High contracting Parties agree to respect the territorial integrity of Tibet, and to abstain from all interference in its internal administration.

and as for Buddhists,

> It is clearly understood that Buddhists, subjects of Great Britain or of Russia, may enter into direct relations with the Dalai Lama and the other representatives of Buddhism. In Tibet, the Governments of Great Britain and Russia engage, so far as they are concerned, not to allow those relations to infringe the stipulations of the present agreement.[27]

A subject of considerable interest in the context of the new agreement on Tibet was a clearer and more precise definition of what constituted the physical limits of the country. The question was relevant and was raised by Isvolsky at an early stage in the negotiations. He asked Nicolson if the British considered the Kham and Tsaidam regions as falling ' within Tibetan jurisdiction ' and as to ' what was forbidden ground and what was not.'[28] In

---

[24] *I O* to *F O,* 17 October 1906, No. 70, and *F O* to *I O*, 26 October 1906, No. 72 in Ibid.
[25] India to Morley, 5 November 1906, Encl. in No. 75, Ibid.
[26] Nicolson to Grey, 30 January 1907, *F O* 371/382, cited in Lamb, *McMahon Line*, I, p. 96.
[27] It was difficult, Bell explained, to distinguish between Russian Buryats or Buddhists in general in their dealings with the Panchen Lama. At Tashilhunpo out of 2,500 monks, roughly 300 were Buryats: ' how many of the latter came from Russia, was not known; if they do they kept this fact to themselves.' Bell to India, 6 November 1906, Encl. 2 in No. 35, *F O* 535/8.
[28] Nicolson to Grey, 6 January 1907, No. 29, in *F O* 535/9.

reply, Calcutta indicated that it regarded the Kuenlun as the northern boundary of Tibet while in the east the country touched the Tsaidam basin: the Chinese Minister in Tsaidam was said to have conceded that Western Thaiji and Upper Tsaidam lay in Tibetan territory.[29] Furthermore India was not prepared to accept the proposition that Tibet was an administrative province of China for it held it to be a

> feudatory state under the suzerainty of China, possessing wide autonomous powers, together with power to make treaties in respect of frontiers, mutual trade and similar matters with conterminous states.[30]

Nicolson, while intimating the above to the Russians, suggested that 'instead of trying to define the boundaries ourselves', it might be as well to accept a definition put forth by the Chinese Government.[31] The real snag herein, of course, was—as Isvolsky was not slow in pinpointing at once—that the Chinese themselves had 'no very clear and positive ideas' on the subject.[32] This was borne out fully after Jordan made his soundings in Peking, for while the Vice-President of the Foreign Affairs Board feigned ignorance, its President conceded that 'there was no map of Tibet later than the 18th century in the possession of the Chinese Government'. No wonder Jordan concluded that it was

> impossible to ascertain boundaries by inquiring privately in Peking and if we ask the Wai-wu Pu officially, some time must elapse before the local authorities can furnish the necessary information.[33]

Nicolson therefore proposed, and Isvolsky 'seemed to concur' in the view, that 'we could describe that country (Tibet) in the Convention under its simple designation' without necessarily defining its precise limits.[34] In retrospect, the attempt to define those limits was not to be taken up until about seven years later at the Simla Conference itself and with results that were far from satisfactory.

In the course of these negotiations over Tibet, early in 1907, Isvolsky had brought up the Mongolian question, underlining the

---

[29] *Supra*, n. 23.

[30] Loc cit.

[31] Nicolson to Grey, 29 November 1906, No. 84 in *F O* 535/8.

[32] Nicolson to Grey, 6 January 1907, No. 29 in *F O* 535/9.

[33] Jordan to Grey, 16 February 1907, No. 65 in Ibid. Also see Jordan to Grey, 21 January 1907, No. 34 in Ibid.

[34] Aide Memoire to Russian Government, in Nicolson to Grey, 2 June 1907, No. 182 in Ibid. *Inter alia*, it was proposed that China be asked to state Tibet's boundaries, and when these had been ascertained the two governments 'would then sign a declaration recording their adherence to the limits laid down by the Chinese Government'.

very great importance which the situation in Mongolia had for Russia and how any alteration in those provinces would affect Russia's interests. Russia had no aggressive designs in regard to Mongolia, all that she desired was the maintenance of the status quo and he wondered if it would be possible to mention in our convention regarding Tibet the desire of the two Governments that no alteration should be introduced in the existing administrative system of Mongolia. The Chinese Government were seeking to replace the ancient feudal system by a centralised Chinese administration and this was causing much discontent among all the inhabitants of Mongolia.[35]

Chinese infringements were bad enough. What was worse was that the Japanese were active too for, as Isvolsky told Nicolson, they had 'many emissaries in Mongolia actively assisting' the new policy of the Chinese Government. Since Mongolia bordered Tibet, the Russian Minister felt that the British 'may have some interest' in the matter.

Whitehall, from the first, had been far from receptive. The fact that the Russians had consistently opposed recognition of a consular status for Britain's own representative in Kashgar, that Peking would not relish British guarantees to Russia in regard to Mongolia at the expense of its territorial integrity and that, as Whitehall viewed it, it would have been a one-sided deal, made the British hesitate. Grey argued that even if the Russians offered him a free hand in Tibet—and as matters stood they had resisted it—little would be gained. For, by the Anglo-Chinese Convention of 1906, the British had burnt their bridges and severely restricted such options as they may have had in Tibet. Hence meeting Russian claims vis-a-vis Mongolia offered Britain no *quid pro quo* and was, therefore, not attractive. It followed that what the British offered the Russians was a vague, colourless declaration regarding the integrity of China's frontiers, and a pledge not to violate them—something which St. Petersburg thought meaningless. Luckily for them, Russian anxiety was soon over, for, by a secret treaty with Japan, the latter recognised their 'special interest' in Outer Mongolia and pledged 'to refrain from all interference' that might prejudice such interests. Once this assurance had been secured, Russia had no stake in, nor much use for, a vague and fatuous British guarantee. Thus it was that Outer Mongolia dropped out of the gambit of Anglo-Russian parleys.

It now remains to sum up the results of these long drawn out, if tortuous, negotiations which took the form of the Anglo-Russian Convention signed in St. Petersburg on 31 August (1907). As applied to Tibet, it consisted of a preamble, five articles, an annexe and an exchange of notes. The preamble recognised both the 'suzerain rights' of China in Tibet as well as Britain's 'special interest', owing to its geographical position, in the maintenance of the status quo in the external relations of that country. The articles that follow

[35]Nicolson to Grey, 6 (21) January 1907, No. 30 in *F O* 535/9.

were largely an effort at defining how the two powers would keep away from interfering in Tibet and thus ensure both its territorial integrity as well as the maintenance of Chinese suzerainty. Thus both Russia and Great Britain engaged 'not to enter into negotiations with Tibet except through the intermediary' of the Chinese Government—the two exceptions being the direct relations between British commercial agents and Tibetan authorities and of the Buddhist subjects of both the empires with the Dalai Lama or his understudies (Article II). Further, the two Governments were not to send representatives to Lhasa (Article III), and neither seek for themselves, nor yet obtain for their subjects, any concessions for railways, roads, telegraphs and mines or other rights in Tibet (Article IV). And finally, no part of the revenues of that country, either in cash or kind, were to be pledged or assigned to Great Britain or Russia or to any of their subjects (Article V).

The annexe re-affirmed Britain's earlier pledge, appended by Lord Ampthill to the Lhasa Convention at the time of its ratification, that the occupation of the Chumbi valley was to cease at the end of three years—provided, of course, that the trade marts had been opened effectively and the indemnity paid fully. If, however, the occupation was not terminated at the end of the stipulated three years, the two Governments were to 'enter upon a friendly exchange of views' on the subject.

The notes exchanged on the occasion and appended at the end related to the embargo to be imposed by the two countries on scientific missions to Tibet for a period of three years. Additionally, they were to approach China for a similar prohibition from undertaking such ventures. The whole question was to be examined *de novo* at the end of three years when it was to be decided 'if any further measures' were necessary.

It is interesting to note that while the Afghan clauses of the Anglo-Russian Convention required the consent of the Amir before they could be regarded as operative (Article II)—and, in fact, owing to the Amir's categorical refusal they remained defunct—the Tibetan clauses made no such reference to the Dalai Lama. To be sure, Tibet had no official knowledge of the Anglo-Russian deal either then or later. The fact that the British themselves had been privy to the opening up of the country and of concluding a treaty direct with her, made this extremely objectionable. This callous, and high-handed, disregard of Tibet apart, the fact that a great deal of what had been gained previously was now thrown away, invited severe criticism. Curzon and Younghusband underlined this latter aspect, of 'a wholesale abandon', with growing bitterness.[36] As for disregard of Tibetan interests, a keen student of that country's history has expressed the view that while 'a British Government' has

of course, the right to upset or whittle away the actions of its predecessor;

---

[36] Curzon cited in Ronaldshay, *The Life of Lord Curzon*, 3 vols, (London, 1927), III, p. 38.
According to Dr Sung the results of the Anglo-Russian Convention (in conjunction with the

(but) it seems extraordinarily high-handed or negligent that, after a treaty had been signed directly with the Tibetans, the British Government should have made no attempt to keep them informed of other acts affecting and modifying that treaty.[37]

A later Tibetan writer barely contents himself with the remark that his government 'knew nothing' of this Agreement,[38] even though it may be conceded that by 1908 the Dalai Lama 'at least was well aware' of its contents.[39]

---

earlier Peking Convention) were 'far reaching'. Since 'no essential concessions' concerning Tibet could be made without the previous consent of the British government, Tibet, he concludes, was made a 'de facto if not a de jure' British protectorate. Additionally, the new agreement 'impaired' Tibetan confidence in Russian power. *Yao-ting Sung*, p. 48.

[37]Richardson, *History*, pp. 94–95.

[38]*Shakabapa*, p. 220.

[39]In November 1908 an envoy of the Dalai Lama in Peking asked Jordan about the Anglo-Russian Convention and the Trade Regulations of 1908 of which the Lama 'had heard but not told anything by the Chinese Government'. Jordan, curious why the Lama did not apply directly to the Chinese, nevertheless condescended to assist him in obtaining copies of the English text. Jordan to Grey, 25 November 1908, No. 5 in *F O* 535/12.

Chapter 5

The Trade Regulations of 1908 and Tibet's 'Autonomy'

THE ANGLO-RUSSIAN Convention had shown scant regard for Tibet's rights nor, while it was being negotiated, had the Lama been consulted at any stage. Whatever the moral justification for ignoring her, from Tibet's point of view this was tragic enough. What was worse was that during the years immediately following the British expedition of 1904, such rights as were still left to her were being systematically nibbled away. And in this respect nothing had been more eloquent than the abortive Calcutta negotiation in 1904–5 and of the role therein of Tang Shao-yi and later Chang Yin-tang. These had indeed been a revealing curtain-raiser.

After Chang Yin-tang's arrival in Lhasa—and, as it happened, his progress through Chumbi and Gyantse had been marred by incidents that foreshadowed increasing trouble with the British Trade Agents and all that they stood for—he had made his own, and China's, authority felt in a manner that was unmistakable. Chang's attack had been two-pronged. In the first place, he asserted his full measure of control over Tibetan officials who, for a variety of reasons, not the least important of which was the absence of the Dalai Lama, were soon cowed down. Briefly, he dismissed, or at any rate disowned, most of those who had in any way been associated with Younghusband or the members of his expedition. Those that Chang thought to be 'collaborators' were gradually weeded out and although the Ganden Ti Rimpoche, who had signed the Lhasa Convention and was the recognised Regent, stayed on in his place, his wings were severely clipped. In place of these officials, Chang appointed his own protégés, men known to have opposed the British and whom he could trust to do his bidding. His actions were sufficiently obvious as not to escape notice and, although ulterior motives were loudly denied, few could have been deceived either as to the purport or the impact of such measures. Actually it was only when these instances assumed the form of a pattern that Grey told Jordan of the basic 'incompatibility' in recognising the Lhasa Convention on the one hand and the 'punishment' of officials who were concerned with negotiating it with Younghusband and his men, on the other. For, as he argued, the British had concluded the Adhesion Agreement principally to ensure that China was 'not prejudiced' by the maintenance of the Lhasa Convention.[1]

[1] Grey to Jordan, 9 February 1907, No. 67 in *F O* 535/9. Also Bailey to White, 4 February 1907, Encl. 2, No. 107; and Bailey's Diary for the week ending 2 February 1907, entry for 29 January, Encl. 4, in No. 109, both in *F O* 535/12.

What was more, Chang went the logical step in degrading and even humiliating the Amban Yu T'ai and his men who, in his eyes, had helped Younghusband's cause. Reports held that the old Amban was put in chains and that his secretary was pursued with an unforgiving, if relentless, vendetta through Chang Thang's barren wastes to Nagchuka.[2] Peking later maintained that there had been charges of corruption against Yu T'ai and his officials, that one of the tasks with which Chang was charged, as Imperial Commissioner, was to investigate the old Amban's administration, that a decree had been issued to detain Yu T'ai in Tibet itself where alone witnesses who knew about his actions at first-hand were available. Understandably, the fact of his being put into chains was stoutly denied and Peking maintained that Yu T'ai had still remained ' unpunished '.[3]

O'Connor, though prone to exaggeration owing to his own strained personal relations with Chang, appears to have visualised the over-all picture clearly enough. His diary entries all through 1906–7 scrupulously catalogued the names of Tibetan officials who had been demoted and replaced by those whose views were known to be pronouncedly anti-British. He noted too that since the advent of Chang there had been an upsurge of unrest in the minds of Tibetan officials and that the latter refused to accept the premise that, as between them and the British, issues had been settled. What was more, the power of the Lhasa monasteries which had been far from broken by Younghusband's expedition was now again in the ascendant and they were said to cherish ' a resentment (against Great Britain) not sufficiently tempered by fear '.[4]

Another difficulty that presented itself was that of conducting day-to-day business in the Trade Agencies, more particularly at Gyantse. An earlier reference to the conflict made it plain that, by 1907, the situation had, from the British point of view, become intolerable.

A major snag in all these instances was that, when pressed to answer charges of violation of treaty rights, Chang, thanks to his extremely sympathetic principals at Peking,[5] denied them categorically. All that he had done, he claimed, was to prohibit malpractices. For ' no obstacles ' had been placed in the way of direct dealings ' between the British authorities and the people of Tibet '; the boot, he insisted, was on the other foot. Thus Chang complained that at

[2] In O'Connor's Diary for the week ending 26 January 1907, the entry for January 23 reads:
On the 12th Yu T'ai sent off his baggage to China and handed over his seals of office and was preparing to start, he was arrested by the other two (Chang Yin-tang and Amban Lien Yu), chains were fastened to his wrist and neck and he was placed in close custody incharge of the Chinese magistrate in a house near the yamen. Amban Yu T'ai's baggage was recalled to Lhasa, sealed up and taken charge by Chang and the new Amban.
Yu T'ai's secretary, O'Connor reported, who had made good his escape was ' overtaken and caught and dragged back in sorry plight to Lhasa '. Encl. 2 in No. 109, Ibid.
[3] Jordan to Grey, 4 March 1907, No. 144 in Ibid.
[4] Encls 2 and 4 in No. 109, *supra*, ns. 1–2.
[5] It was well known that Tang Shao-yi, who was then Vice-President of the Wai-wu-pu, had in Chang a personal protégé. The latter's rear and flanks were thus well-protected.

Gyantse, on his way to Lhasa, he had received complaints from the Tibetans that 'Indian sowars (troopers) there and at Chumbi' were paying short for supplies. Chang's version, that he had 'a pile of petitions' regarding such exactions and that he was determined to punish such people 'over whom he had power', may be exaggerated, and yet there may well have been an element of truth in these complaints. Thus we know that Bell wrote to Government on 28 November (1906) that he

> used to hear such cases occurring and immediately on arrival warned Bailey to investigate.[6]

Exercised as Calcutta undoubtedly was, and worried as Whitehall did become, they were on the horns of a veritable dilemma. Morley, whom Churchill called 'a martinet in the India Office', had early made up his mind not to be stampeded, much less nose-led, by the Indian Governor-General.[7] Besides, he argued convincingly, HMG were precluded by the terms of its Convention with Russia from interfering—'even if they had the desire to do so'—with Chinese action in Tibet or for that matter in the relations of the Lhasa Government with the Tashi Lama at Shigatse. That position, it was now argued, would become 'exceedingly difficult', indeed untenable, if 'it should be found necessary' to call in the Tibetan government to fulfil the obligations of the Convention 'in opposition to the Chinese Government', and their Amban at Lhasa. Hence the by now pretty useless recourse of an appeal to Peking to direct its local officers in Tibet to give effect to the provisions of the Lhasa and Peking Conventions 'in a friendly spirit' and 'to avoid occasions of friction' with British officers! Pro forma, however, the British continued to reiterate that while they had no desire to interfere in Tibetan affairs, they were 'bound to take such action as may be necessary' to ensure fulfilment of the conditions of the Convention.[8] The Chinese, of course, knew, even as the British did, that there was no question of another Younghusband marching into Tibet.

Thanks to Chang the situation continued to worsen for the British, while, in sharp contrast, Chinese prestige remained on the upswing. There was talk too of an increase in the Tibetan army—for there had been complaints of 'too many monks' and 'too few soldiers'—maintained and financed by Peking and of Chang's own appointment as a Junior Amban.[9] Symptomatic of the

---

[6]Bell to India, 28 November 1906, Encl. 14 in No. 37, *F O* 535/9. Also Gow to Bailey, 4 December 1906, Encls. 27 and 30 in No. 37 in Ibid.

[7]Morley, *Recollections*, II, pp. 177–78, told Minto (in the context of negotiations with Russia regarding Afghanistan) that H M G having determined their course it was 'for their agents and officers all over the world to accept it'.

Also see Churchill, *Great Contemporaries*, p. 98.

[8]*I O* to *F O*, 6 February 1907, No. 56 in *F O* 535/9.

[9]O'Connor to India, 10 and 26 December 1906, Encls. 10 and 12 in No. 62 in Ibid.

Also see 'Extract from translation of a letter from Nepalese representative at Lhasa', Encl. in No. 93 in Ibid.

change was the Viceroy's acknowledgement, despite advice to the contrary by the Political Officer, of the intimation that Lien Yu, the new Assistant Amban at Lhasa, had assumed office.[10] All the while, Chang continued to throw to the winds both the letter and spirit of the Convention's terms by notifying the appointment, at the trade marts, of Chinese commercial and diplomatic representatives, some of them Tibetan officials others Chinese nationals.[11] Chang's reported statement that he had been vested with ' plenary powers ' to reorganise the government of Tibet and that he was determined to throw out the British ' bag and baggage '[12] had an unsettling effect and created a fear psychosis. At the receiving end were the Tibetans, buffeted between the dread of another British invasion and the much more active role, with all that it implied, of their Chinese suzerains.

It was thus clear that, as Calcutta viewed it, the situation had become impossible for until the Lhasa Government

> formally appoints Tibetan Agents at trade marts and our representatives are allowed unfettered communication with them, little improvement in local situation can be expected.[13]

The Foreign Office in London took up the question and Grey told Jordan, in no uncertain terms, that ' we cannot accept ' Chinese appointees of Chang as 'Agents at the Trade marts ' in terms of Article V of the Lhasa Convention. He

> should, therefore press the Wai-wu Pu to take immediate steps to compel the local authorities of Tibet to carry out this engagement by the appointment of Tibetan Agents.[14]

When pressed, the Chinese Foreign Office took the view that the appointment of Tibetan Trade Agents could only follow the negotiation of fresh Trade Regulations. To effect this, Chang was designated Imperial Commissioner

---

[10]India to Lien Yu, 13 December 1906, Encl. 8 in No. 62 in Ibid. Actually Bell had suggested that Lien Yu's letter of 14 September (1906) announcing his appointment may be acknowledged by himself as Political Officer, but Jordan counselled that the Foreign Secretary should do so on the Viceroy's behalf. The latter course was eventually adopted.

[11]India to Morley, 14 February 1907, Encl. in No. 63 in Ibid.

[12]Bell informed Government that it was given out at Lhasa that Chang 'will settle all outstanding questions '; at Gyantse, Bailey noted that there were rumours that ' the whole of British Agency and escort was to be removed ', that Campbell (Bell's Assistant) had been ' dismissed ' by Chang and that the government of Chumbi was to be ' immediately taken over ' by the Lhasa authorities. Bell to India, 10 December 1906, Encl. 10 in No. 62 in *F O* 535/9. Also see Bailey's ' Diary ' for the week ending 1 December 1906, Encl. 1 in No. 37 in Ibid.

[13]India to Morley, 23 March 1907, Encl. in No. 119 in Ibid.

[14]Grey to Jordan, 29 March 1907, No. 124 in *F O* 535/9.

and directed to proceed to Calcutta where, for the next round in the battle, the scene shifted.[15]

With its earlier, far from happy, experience of the Adhesion Agreement of 1906, the Government of India had understandably been none too keen in regard to negotiating the new Trade Regulations. Additionally, for want of the new, the old Regulations of 1893 were operative and, from the strictly Indian point of view, worked far more satisfactorily than anything that could take their place. Here again it was the over-bearing Secretary of State who forced the pace. ' In view of strained relations at Gyantse ', Morley wrote to the Indian Government, the ' balance of advantage ' lay in embarking on the proposed negotiations.[16] It would have been difficult for Calcutta at any time to resist such a peremptory command but in 1907, with the situation at the trade marts being what it was, refusal would have been impossible. All that remained, therefore, was to ensure that negotiations were conducted as best they might and all necessary precautions taken well in time.

One of the major British desiderata in the impending parleys was to associate a duly authorised Tibetan representative who would sign on behalf of his country. To be sure, Article III of the Lhasa Convention had stipulated that the Tibetan Government was to appoint ' fully authorised delegates ' who were to negotiate the new regulations, so that later on Tibet would find it hard either to evade or disclaim responsibility as it had so often done in the past.

It is significant that in his directive to Jordan, Grey underlined the fact that while HMG would not insist on ' their right ' to negotiate the regulations ' exclusively ' with Tibetan delegates, Chang in Lhasa should ensure that

> Tibetan Government must appoint their delegates *before the commencement of the negotiations with full powers to negotiate and sign on their behalf*, and in such a manner that they cannot disclaim responsibility for any settlement which may be arrived at between the delegates. . . .[17]

India too now asked the Secretary of State if he would

> object to arrangements being made with China being communicated to Lhasa Government and latter being required to furnish credentials to their Representative authenticated as suggested. . . .[18]

Peking's reaction to any such communication being made was, predictably, far from friendly and Jordan wired back that the Foreign Board ' demurred to moving the latter Government (i.e. Tibet) to make any such notification.'[19]

---

[15] Jordan to Grey, 8 April 1907, No. 134 in Ibid.
[16] Morley to India, 16 April 1907, Encl. in 142 in Ibid.
[17] Jordan to Grey, 8 May 1907, No. 155 in Ibid.
[18] India to Morley, 1 July 1907, Encl. 2, No. 5 in *F O* 535/10.
[19] Jordan to Grey, 16 July 1907, No. 17 in Ibid.

This was taken note of in London and Morley directed the Viceroy to write 'a friendly and uncontroversial letter' to Lhasa notifying about the 'friendly' negotiations scheduled to be held at Simla and trusting that it would despatch its delegate 'with proper credentials.'[20]

Chinese assurances on the question, albeit often repeated, were far from being specific or categorical. At one stage they suggested that the Indian and Tibetan delegates could sort out their differences at Gyantse and present a joint draft to their superiors—the British and the Chinese—to negotiate and agree to.[21] This was a clever ruse through which the British could clearly see and which they summarily rejected. Later Jordan was told that 'full powers to negotiate and sign' had been conferred upon the Tibetan representative, although there was no assurance that he had 'written credentials'.[22] Subsequently he was informed that the (Tibetan) delegate had been given 'written authority to sign'.[23] A few days later, Jordan was told that Chang had given Dane 'a telegraphic assurance' in regard to the Tibetan delegate and that the respective credentials of the three representatives could be 'mutually examined' when negotiations got under way.[24] The long and short of it was that, despite India's strong fears—which, for the record, proved genuine enough—that the Tibetan delegates would be 'mere puppets', there was little that could be done. Morley ruled that

> unless on examination credentials of the Tibetan representative are found to be unsatisfactory, no further action is considered necessary.[25]

The difficulty of course was, and this was confirmed by actual experience, that by then it would be too late, and perhaps impossible, to retract.

Later, when negotiations did commence, Chang strained every nerve to ensure that the Tibetan representative, who was under his complete control and surveillance, would be treated as a *sub*-delegate. Thus within a few days of his arrival in Simla, Wilton, who was assisting Dane in the negotiations, noted that

> Chang desired Dane to ignore the Tibetan delegate firstly because negotiations might then have been carried on entirely between the two commissioners and secondly because Tsarong Shape and his Tibetan assistants, hurt

---

[20] Morley to India, 18 July 1907, Encl. 1 in No. 20 in Ibid

[21] The Wai-wu-pu's memorandum, dated 21 May 1907, is referred to in Jordan's own memorandum to the Foreign Affairs Board on 13 June (1907). Encl. 1 in No. 28 in Ibid.

[22] *Supra*, n. 19.

[23] Jordan to Grey, 23 July 1907, No. 19 in *F O* 535/10. The written authority was given by 'acting Dalai Lama Galdan Chipa'.

[24] Wai-wu-pu to Jordan, 30 July 1907, Encl. 1 in No. 82 in Ibid.

[25] Morley to India, 7 August 1907, Encl. in No. 33 in Ibid. Also India to Morley, 20 July 1907, Encl. 2 in No. 20 in Ibid.

by the slight, would have been prejudiced against Sir Louis Dane right at the outset.²⁶

The same story was repeated at Chang's formal interview with the Viceroy on 6 September (1907) for he desired that the latter receive the Shape along with himself (Chang), and *not* separately. Later Liu, Chang's secretary, was to ask Wilton in pained surprise why the British should take 'such notice' of the Tibetan delegate considering that, according to Liu, in 1890 Shape Shatra, who accompanied the then Amban to Darjeeling, had been ' ignored ' and even ' grossly insulted '.²⁷ Subsequently, in the course of negotiations, when Dane demanded a Tibetan rendering of Chang's draft regulations duly signed by Tsarong Shape, the latter at first evaded the issue by pointing out that as this was

> only a draft, I do not wish to sign it. The Chinese and Tibetans are of one opinion, and there is no difference between them. As some disparity might occur in translating the Chinese into Tibetan and delay and confusion might follow.²⁸

When Dane persisted, the Shape was more blunt. 'I fail to see', he told the British delegate,

> the reason for your idea that much time must be wasted in discussion if I have not a Tibetan version of the document under examination and that a Tibetan translation of Tibet Trade Regulations is enclosed, for, so far as I can see, the cause has not the least connection whatever with the effect.²⁹

As will be noticed presently, the refusal to provide a Tibetan version of the Regulations finally agreed to was later to prove a major stumbling block in bringing the negotiations to a successful conclusion.

Symptomatic of the Chinese attitude in the case of the Shape was Chang's determination to claim for his country both suzerainty as well as sovereignty over Tibet.³⁰ This was evident in many ways, not least in the matter of ' credentials' issued to Tsarong Shape. These enjoined, earlier assurances to the contrary notwithstanding, upon the Shape not only to accompany Chang to Simla but further that he ' must carry out Chang, the Great Minister's instructions '. As if this were not enough, Wilton noted that

---

[26] 'Note on Conversations between Liu (Chang's Secretary) and Wilton (then Secretary to Dane) on 10 and 13 October 1907 ', Encl. 2 in No. 118 in *F O* 535/10.

[27] *I O* to *F O*, ' Note on the conversations between Mr Wilton and Mr Liu in September and October 1907 ', Encl. 1 in No. 104 in Ibid.

[28] Shape to Dane, 4 October 1907, Encl. 4 in No. 104 in *F O* 535/10. Also *supra*, n. 26.

[29] Shape to Dane, 10 October 1907, Encl. 10 in No. 104 in Ibid.

[30] *I O* to *F O*, 1 November 1907, No. 103 in Ibid.

Mr Liu declared that Tibet had belonged to China for centuries and was as much a part of the Chinese Empire as India (was) of the British empire. A Tibetan was a Chinese subject in the sense that a native of India was a British subject. There was no word in the Tibetan language for Tibetan Government.[31]

Before long, the Chinese attitude crystallised into a persistent, backstage, rear-guard action that would prevent the Shape from signing the Trade Regulations along with the two Commissioners. Thus as early as 11 November 1907 Jordan informed Grey that Peking while

> willing to accept Sir Louis Dane's proposed description of Shape and to agree to latter's taking part in the negotiations ... (wanted) me to support the view which they held that it would be derogatory to China that Shape should sign the Regulations.[32]

Whitehall, however, 'insisted' that the Regulations 'must be signed' by the Shape and 'a definite assurance' on this point must be forthcoming, before it would agree to Peking's compromise formula on the Preamble.[33] Chang at Simla, in his talks with Dane, had made no secret of his refusal to consider the Tibetan delegate as his co-equal in the negotiations;[34] at Peking, he had urged that the Shape being an appointee of the Chinese Emperor had no independent existence. Since, in Chinese view, the Lhasa Convention had been 'rectified' by the Adhesion Agreement (1906), all matters had to be sorted out as between the two 'High Contracting Parties'—the British and the Chinese. It followed that Tibet had no *locus standi* and its delegate no legal status to sign the Regulations.[35]

Opposition to providing a Tibetan text flowed from the same line of reasoning. In January (1908), Jordan had telegraphed to the effect that Chang

> urges that owing to the difficulties attendant on accurate translation there should be no Tibetan text.... He suggested that instead of this a separate Tibetan version should be officially communicated to the Indian Government after signature of the Treaty.

---

[31] 'Translation of the Tibetan copy of the credentials handed by the Tsarong Shape to Sir Louis Dane on 12 September 1907', Encl. 18 in No. 104 in Ibid. For Liu's remarks, *supra*, n. 27.

[32] Jordan to Grey, 11 November 1907, No. 108 in *F O* 535/10.

[33] Jordan to Grey, 25 November 1907, No. 115 in Ibid.

[34] 'Notes by E C Wilton on Negotiations in connection with Tibetan representative', Encl. 5 in No. 118 in Ibid.

[35] Jordan to Grey, 13 November 1907, No. 126 in Ibid. For the Memorandum communicated by the Wai-wu-pu to Jordan, 10 November 1907, see Encl. 2 in No. 126 in Ibid.

And then, in an addendum marked 'Confidential',

> Chang considers signatures of the Tibetan text will involve infringement of sovereign rights and his real object is to prevent this. Wai-wu Pu have admitted this in conversation.[36]

Nor were Chang's obstructionist tactics confined to the status of the (Tibetan) delegate or the provision of a (Tibetan) text. He was determined too that, at the trade marts, the British Agents should not deal 'direct' with the Tibetans but only through the intermediary of the Chinese. Such intercourse as was to be vouchsafed, would be on 'petty matters'. The British traders, as also the Agent, were to be confined to especially demarcated areas 'beyond which they could not carry trade, nor reside' while within (these areas) it would be easy 'to prevent all intercourse' between them and the Tibetans.[37]

By January 1908, so stultifying had the position become, with Chang refusing to yield ground on what Dane and the Indian Government regarded as basic principles, that Grey asked Jordan if there was a 'better chance' of negotiations at Peking

> since it seems hopeless to expect satisfactory results by continuing discussions with Chang....[38]

Jordan was far from enthusiastic. The Chinese, he felt, were 'really anxious' to settle and for his part he would straighten out such points as were 'not settled' in Calcutta. But breach of negotiations at the latter place would involve revoking Chang's commission and this, Jordan feared, would present 'great difficulty'. As for the broader question, Chinese

> policy in Tibet, as elsewhere, is imbued with ideas of 'recovery of sovereign rights' and Chang is, I fear, only reflecting their views.[39]

It was not only the issue of 'direct' relations between the British Agent and the Tibetan officials—and, as was soon apparent, the Foreign Board in Peking confessed to having 'failed to find' in the Lhasa Convention 'any specific mention' thereof[40]—that came in the way. Additionally, Chang was keen that British trade officials be replaced by native agents, that their escorts be withdrawn, such protection as they afforded being taken over by the Chinese

---

[36] Jordan to Grey, 11 January 1908, No. 13 in *F O* 535/11.
[37] India to Morley, 11 January 1908, Encl. in No. 15 in Ibid.
[38] Grey to Jordan, 23 January 1908, No. 22 in Ibid.
[39] Jordan to Grey, 25 January 1908, No. 26 in Ibid.
[40] Jordan to Grey, 26 January 1908, No. 27 in Ibid.

police. Interestingly enough on all these questions Morley was very responsive[41] much to the annoyance, tacit if not overt, of the Indian Government.

These issues apart, in the final count, two questions stood out on which a stalemate threatened to wreck the talks—others such as the import of tea or the fixation of a tariff were shoved off to later discussions. The first related to a direct reference being made by the Government of India to higher Tibetan authorities at Lhasa and the second to a Tibetan text of the Regulations being prepared and signed by the three representatives.

From the middle of February when Dane left,[42] his place being taken by Wilton, until about the third week in April, when the Regulations were at long last concluded, Chang proved tenaciously unyielding. The Indian Government were equally clear that if the right of direct communication guaranteed to it by the Lhasa Convention were denied, the Amban

> may be unable, as in the past, to induce Tibetan Government to take any action, even if he put the matter before them at all—a state of things (that may result) in (a) most regrettable friction.[43]

The Tibetan text presented much the same problems, for in its absence Tibetan officials could always take shelter behind the plea that they could not enforce the Regulations because they did not understand them. This had been part of the frustrating, stultifying Indian experience in the case of the Regulations of 1893. Here too Chang, unwilling to yield on the basic principles, was prepared nonetheless to modify the peripherals. Thus he assured his Indian counterpart that he 'shall have furnished' to Lhasa 'a copy of the Tibetan translation' and would ensure that they 'quite understand' the whole agreement.[44]

Tenacious and unyielding the Chinese proved, if also tough, 'hard' bargainers. A compromise, however, was finally wrought in regard to a reference to 'higher Tibetan authorities', the formula laying down *inter alia* that

> questions which cannot be decided by agreement between the Trade Agents and the Local Authorities shall be referred for settlement to the Government of India and the Tibetan High Authorities at Lhasa. The purport of a reference by the Government of India will be communicated to the Chinese Imperial Resident at Lhasa. Questions which cannot be decided by

---

[41] Morley to India, 13 February 1908, Encl. in No. 45 in Ibid. *Inter alia*, Morley had told the Governor-General that 'to remove' Chinese suspicions, HMG proposed to replace British Trade Agents by 'native' agents.

[42] Dane was appointed Lt. Governor of the Punjab and for a time it was debated whether negotiations with Chang may not be transferred to Lahore. Later, however, this was ruled out as being impractical.

[43] India to Morley, 18 February 1908, Encl. in No. 51 in *F O* 535/11.

[44] India to Morley, 3 March 1908, Encl. in No. 63 in Ibid.

Agreement between the Government of India and the Tibetan High Authorities at Lhasa shall, in accordance with the terms of Article I of the Peking Convention of 1906, be referred for settlement to the Governments of Great Britain and China.[45]

It is significant that on the question of the Trade Agents' escorts, an important concession was made to the Chinese position. In a letter addressed to Chang and the Tsarong Shape on the day the Regulations were signed, Wilton undertook that the strength of the escorts at Gyantse and Yatung would not exceed 50 and 25 respectively, that even before 'their absolute withdrawal' under Article XII, the desirability of reducing their number was to be 'carefully' considered—'as occasion may offer and the conditions of the marts may admit'. Additionally, the British

> will take special measures to ensure that the armed guards are kept under close control and that discipline is maintained at the fullest pitch and that they are not allowed to interfere with the people of the country unnecessarily.[46]

Despite the long drawn-out agony of nearly eight months of interminable wrangles—Chang arrived in Simla on 26 August (1907) and the Regulations were signed in Calcutta on 20 April (1908)—no agreement was reached on such questions as extradition, levy of customs duty, export of tea from India, and appointment of Chinese Trade Agents with consular privileges. Of these, the question of the levy of customs duty and of the export of Indian tea soon came to the fore; for, early in 1909, the Chinese Customs Officer at Yatung seized some cases of Indian tea and sent them back—there had been complaints of a similar nature from the Punjab government and the British Trade Agent at Gartok.[47] Nor was that all. For despite persistent denials, the Chinese Amban at Lhasa, and his understudies at Gyantse and Yatung, obstructed intercourse between the British Trade Agents and Tibetan officials at the marts. A typical, though by no means exceptional, instance was the fate that befell the Panchen Lama's letter to the British Agent at Gyantse condoling with him on the death of King Edward VII. The Lama's epistle was received by Bailey through Ma Chi-fu, the Chinese Trade Agent at Gyantse, who enclosed it with a forwarding note. And this despite a most categorical assurance by the Foreign Board in Peking that 'all intercourse' was being conducted 'in accordance with the provisions of the treaties'.[48] The subterfuge of divergent versions of the Amban's orders, in Chinese and in Tibetan respectively, was also

---

[45]For the text, see Encl. 3 in No. 86 in *F O* 535/11.
[46]Loc. cit.
[47]India to Morley, 10 February 1909, Encl. in No. 13 in *F O* 535/12. For complaints from Punjab and the Trade Agent, Gartok see Encls. 1 and 2 in No. 25 in Ibid.
[48]*I O* to *F O*, 3 April 1911, No. 26 in *F O* 535/14.

The Trade Regulations of 1908

resorted to.⁴⁹ Fortunately for the British it was not long before matters came to a head with the revolt of Chinese troops in Tibet, in November 1911. The chain of events that followed helped to resolve many a contentious dispute in regard to questions not exclusively relating to trade or commerce.

---

⁴⁹Jordan to India, 19 June 1911, and India to Jordan, 18 July 1911, Encls. 1 and 2 in No. 64 in Ibid.

Jordan's protest to the Wai-wu-pu concerning this tricky behaviour of the Amban was contained in Jordan to Prince Ching, 14 August 1911, Encl. in No. 67 in Ibid.

PART II CHINESE PENETRATION AND BRITISH REACTION

Chapter 6

Chao Erh-feng and Chinese Administration in the March Country

CHANG'S ASSERTION, in full measure, of the authority of his Chinese masters with its resultant pin-pricks to the British and almost complete bull-dozing of Tibetan resistance was but a part of the larger picture. Broad details in the latter included the dressing down of the Dalai Lama during his stay (1908) in the Chinese capital and the concerted effort by the Imperial Commissioner, Chao Erh-feng, to reduce Western Szechuan and the March country to a semblance of orderly government so that the assertion of the Emperor's authority in the uplands of Tibet and the provinces bordering it on the south should be the easier and more effective. It is to Chao Erh-feng, therefore, one has to turn in order to have a clearer appreciation of the situation which the Dalai Lama faced (and the Indian government had to contend with) on the morrow of his arrival in Lhasa, in December 1909, seemingly at the end of his long travels.[1]

Chao Erh-feng was the Chinese Taotai who, until then relatively unknown, was able in the course of a little less than half a dozen years (1905–11) to transform completely the political landscape in eastern Tibet and on India's north-eastern frontier. He, it may be recalled, was the successor of the ill-fated Fung Chuan who had in 1905, in the wake of the Younghusband expedition to Lhasa, been appointed Assistant Amban at Chamdo in a newly-created post. Taking over the task hardly yet begun by his trail-bearer, Chao's was an important assignment, the essence of which was to punish and pacify the turbulent, lama-ridden tribes who controlled the twilight country between China and Tibet comprising the western districts of Szechuan, the northern areas of Yunnan and what the Tibetans vaguely referred to as the province of Kham! It was necessary too, other things apart, to open the road to Lhasa, both as symbolic of a rejuvenated China as well as providing a physical link with the great motherland. These bonds, visible or otherwise, had broken down under the 13th Dalai Lama and even resulted in his complete defiance of Peking's writ and, what was more, getting away with it with impunity. With Younghusband's withdrawal, and the Dalai Lama a fugitive from his native land, the task appeared both urgent and, more important still, capable of early realisation.

A line or two on the political spectrum in Tibet and the March country,

---

[1] Eric Teichman, *Travels of a Consular Officer in Eastern Tibet* (Cambridge, 1922), offers an excellent background knowledge of the entire area. It was gained at first-hand during his travels in 1918–19.

on the eve of Chao's appearance on the scene may help to explain his campaigns with greater clarity. The Dalai Lama's Tibet in the opening years of the century, it may be recalled, extended all the way to the Thang La range in the north which separated it from the Kokonor. In the east it touched Bum La, the frontier pass near Batang, where a pillar erected in 1727, in the reign of Emperor Yung Chung, marked the boundary. Besides its hard core of U, Tsang and Ngari, Tibet included the frontier provinces of Markham and Gonjo, the lama-ruled dependencies of Draya, Chamdo and Riwoche and the somewhat remote, if half-forgotten, province of Nyarong.

What was strictly called the March country comprised the 'native' states on the Szechuan border east of the old Sino-Tibetan frontier on the Bum La. It embraced the kingdom of Derge, and the five Hor states, besides Chala or Tachienlu, Batang and Litang—the first two closely aligned to Lhasa, the latter three powerfully oriented towards Chengtu and Peking. All were under China's nominal protection and from time to time sent, or were supposed to send to that country, tribute missions. Notwithstanding Peking's political hegemony, its military officials and commissariat officers stationed at Tachienlu, Litang, Batang and other places on the main south road had, over the years, become an almost extinct species while the soldiers detailed in the Imperial Institutes existed only on paper, for purposes of pay-roll.

Chao's analysis of the situation that he was up against was fairly simple. The key to controlling the tribal areas, he argued, was to break the power and influence of the vastly rich and prosperous lamaseries which filled the entire area. Not only did the monks hold the land and, as it was, the richest estates belonged to them—what was worse, they held complete sway over the minds of their lay flock. Be it birth or death, disease or man-made calamity, the intercession of the lama with the powers-that-be, was a *sine qua non* of all existence, worldly or even other-worldly. No wonder the lamaseries while on the one hand they fattened on the vast income of their rich lands and the fees of this vast concourse, on the other tightened their dread hold over their minds and hearts. Ignorance and superstitious belief was the bed-rock of the system for while the lamas prospered on ignorance, their laity were hide-bound by a blind faith, nurtured on omens, sorcery and supernatural divination, to which they clung tenaciously.

Towards the end of 1904, on the eve of his appointment, Feng Chuan, Chao's short-lived predecessor, had witnessed the conversion of Tachienlu, hitherto capital of the semi-independent Tibetan state of Chala, into a district headquarters, with a Chinese magistrate. From here, along the southern road to Tibet, he had repaired to Batang, the seat of a large, and powerful, Buddhist monastery. With means so meagre, in proportion to his ambitious ends, he set himself to interfering with the lamas on a sensitive point, viz. reducing the size of their monastery. Here was a frontal assault, the more galling in that China's prestige in the wake of Amban Yu T'ai's powerlessness in Tibet—a British expedition had marched to Lhasa with impunity—stood shamelessly exposed.

The lamas' disaffection and unrest took the form of a rebellion and although by the clever, and ingenious, stratagem of scattering money among those who had besieged him, Feng Chuan escaped from Batang, he was ambushed not far outside the town and done to death in cold blood.[2]

Not long after, General Ma Wei-chi, a commander of the Szechuan army, avenged Feng Chuan's death in a manner that was to leave a deep and abiding imprint. He razed the Batang monastery to the ground, severely chastised the rebels and visited rack and ruin on the countryside through which his armies had marched.[3] In the sequel, Feng Chuan's barely begun task now fell on the shoulders of Chao Erh-feng, who was appointed by Hsi Liang, the then Viceroy of Szechuan, to undertake both punitive measures and a pacification of the country.

The first phase of Chao Erh-feng's campaigns, 1905–6, was at once short-lived and singularly successful. He suppressed the incipient revolt among the tribesmen with a stern hand, destroyed the monasteries without exception and cut the monks to size. An echo of this ruthlessness was to be heard many years later when the charge of 'excessive severity' in these campaigns was pressed against Chao and he was impeached before the Imperial Censors by his Tibetan detractors.[4]

A highlight of Chao's campaigns was the siege of Changtreng—Hsiang-cheng to the Chinese—an impregnable fortress housing a large and powerful monastery and lying athwart the southern road, through Batang, to Lhasa. The siege lasted nearly seven months, from the end of 1905 to the summer of 1906, when the monastery finally fell not indeed to the valour of Chao's soldiery but the treachery of a renegade lama who had betrayed his men.[5]

The fall of Changtreng, soon converted into the headquarters of a Chinese official placed incharge of a newly-carved military district, was a singularly prestigious feat and redounded to Chao's credit. Not long after, in November 1906, he was publicly honoured at Chengtu with the title of 'Bataru', an approximate Manchu equivalent of the British 'Order of Merit'.[6] A new office was now given to him, that of Frontier Commissioner, equated in rank and status to that of the Imperial Residents at Lhasa and Sining. What was more, he was placed in charge of a vast domain that extended all the way from the Kokonor and Kansu in the north to the borders of Yunnan, Burma and Assam in the south, from Tachienlu in the east to the very confines of central Tibet in the west.

[2]For details, Satow to Lansdowne, 30 May and 6 July, 1905 in *F O* 17/1754. Also *Teichman*, n. 1, p. 20.

[3]*Teichman*, n. 1, p. 21.

[4]'China in 1908', General Report by the British Legation in Peking in *F O* 371/637/18298,

[5]For a detailed account, see 'Siege of Hsiang-Cheng', from the Diary of Revd. J Muir. Encl. 2 in No. 55, Jordan to Grey, 7 January 1908 in *F O* 535/11.

[6]Jordan renders it as 'Ba Tu Lu'. Jordan to Grey, *supra*, n. 5. Also see *Teichman*, n. 1, p. 23.

Chao's campaigns for the pacification of the Marches, temporarily interrupted for a little over a year in 1907–8 by his taking over as Acting Viceroy of Szechuan, did not cease. For he now set himself the task of converting the areas he had conquered into Chinese administered districts. Nor must one view as purely negative in content his work concerned primarily with suppressing revolts, razing monasteries and exterminating the lamas. For, as he conceived it, Chao was desirous of filling these regions with Chinese colonists, whom he sought to attract by generous, if seemingly wild, promises of what the new land could offer. Another measure that he planned was the opening of schools (one such, for both Chinese and Tibetans, was set up at Tachienlu), for the spread of education would, by itself, sound the death-knell of the lamas' power. He hoped thereby to isolate them, while attracting their lay flocks towards their new Chinese masters—their liberators from the monastic yoke. The indigenous populace, Chao argued, released from the lamas' dread hold, along with the colonists newly implanted, would together constitute the twin pillars of Chinese rule and set at nought the insidious attempts of the gompas to subvert it.

A word here about Chao's attempt to attract Chinese colonists from Szechuan to these tribal territories may not be out of place. In one of his earlier proclamations calling for settlers to the new districts of Batang, Chao declared:

> Cultivators here (use) wooden ploughs, no manure (is necessary).... The climate too is very similar to that of China.... Living beyond the frontier is very cheap and it is easy to keep pigs, cattle, sheep and chickens. While the hill-sides are covered with fuel which simply needs to be cut.... A native girl taken as wife will prove of great assistance in the work.... The over-populated state of Szechuan renders the struggle for existence very difficult. Why then do you not hasten to this promising land?[7]

Strange as it may have seemed to him, and despite repeated affirmations of the 'integrity' of his intentions and firm assurances that he had taken this step 'entirely out of consideration for your sorry plight',[8] there were not many who volunteered to be the denizens of this 'promising land'. It is on record that Chao endeavoured to grow rice and mulberry trees in the area, yet, even though he could overpower the lamas, the climate and the soil were too much for him—Batang is over 13,000 ft above sea-level.[9] What defeated him even more was the cultivators' traditionally conservative instinct. Understandably, for the more prosperous and assured farmer of Szechuan to exchange his fertile soil and temperate climate for the barren mountains and rigorous winters of East Tibet, would have been completely out of the question.

[7]'Proclamation issued by H E Chao Erh-feng', Encl. 2, Proc. 165 in *F O* 535/9.
[8]Loc. cit.
[9]Report by Captain F M Bailey, September 1911, *I O R*, L/P & S/10/183, p. 7.

Besides, talk of pacification from the house-tops would not convince many that the operation was anything but a temporary palliative; nor, in the context of the often-repeated erosions of Chinese authority, was it likely to be permanent. Again, unless the settlers moved *en masse*, there was the grim prospect of their being swept away, and absorbed, by the more virile, and sturdy, albeit ' uncivilised barbarians '—the border tribes.[10]

Another aspect of the problem was that those who did move to the promised land had to face the stark reality of having to do without their staple food—rice and pork. Nor would they be easily grafted on to barley and mutton or, more commonly, yak meat. No wonder that most of those who did come returned home in disgust. Disgruntled at best, they would have been poor advertisement for Chao's great dream!

Thus, unfortunate as it was, Chao's constructive efforts, and well-meaning plans, miscarried. Nor was it true only in the case of transplanting Szechuanese farmers. In the fertile uplands around Batang and Litang, in the summer of 1911, on the eve of the October Revolution in China Captain Bailey found 13 colonies deserted and could scarce set his eyes on more than 30 of those miserable looking left-overs of Chao's great colonisation effort! Much the same may be said of the industries he endeavoured to set up—the leather tannery was a financial fiasco.[11] Inevitably, the great Chao's name came to be synonymous not with his constructive endeavours, however well-meaning, but with his strong-arm methods. The epithet that stuck was of ' butcher ' (Chao).

The second phase of the Frontier Commissioner's work belongs to the years 1908-11 and there was a lot that he compressed into this period. Apart from his own ability, which could scarce be gainsaid, he had started on an excellent wicket. For early in 1908, two Imperial edicts had appeared: one appointing him as (Imperial) Commissioner for Tibet, a second Amban; and another designating his brother, Chao Erh-hsun, as Governor-General of Szechuan.[12] Nothing could be more propitious, nothing better designed to ensure the success of Chao's effort, and of Chinese policies, aiming at the complete subjugation of Lhasa. As a Peking edict, not long after the appointments, spelt out, the two brothers were to cooperate with each other in a common endeavour—that of reducing Tibet to subjection.[13] The uninhibited flow of resources, in men and money, Szechuanese dovetailed to the military skill and prowess of Chao Erh-feng, did indeed achieve the impossible—if only for a time. In a letter to Grey, years later, Jordan praised the two brothers as successful administrators. Chao Erh-hsun, he noted,

---

[10]For Chao's failure see Encl. 3 in *supra*, n. 7. Also ' General Report on China 1907 ', in *F O* 371/231/25162.

[11]Chao had invested 15,000 taels, nearly £2,000, in establishing a tanning industry which succeeded only in making bad, and expensive, boots. In the summer of 1911, when Bailey visited the area, the factory could account for only 13 Tibetans and 6 Chinese employees. Bailey's Report, *supra*, n. 9, p. 7.

[12]*Teichman*, n. 1, p. 24.

[13]Loc. cit.

has the reputation of being the most upright and efficient official in the Empire... is a wizen-faced little man of 68 years who prides himself on being a life-long tee-totaller and non-smoker and justly claims considerable credit for having totally suppressed poppy cultivation during his three years as Viceroy of Szechuan. The forward policy which China recently assumed in Tibet and the Western frontier generally was largely due to Chao Erh-hsun who found a most active ally in his brother, Chao Erh-feng, the Warden of the Szechuan Marches....[14]

From the Marches to Tibet. Here it may be recalled that on the morrow of Younghusband's withdrawal from Lhasa, the Chinese had started mending their fences in a truly herculean fashion, a feat the more remarkable in that the fortunes of the ruling dynasty on the mainland had begun to ebb precipitately. For a regime so shaky at home as the C'hing, to be able to project itself with an outward appearance of such firmness and determination in the peripheral regions, demanded two basic desiderata. One, the policies to be pursued were not a subject of serious debate at home; two, the instruments employed to execute them would have both an unflinching devotion to the major objective in view as also the necessary wherewithal to carry it out. In both respects, the choice of Chao was, for Chinese imperialism, a happy coincidence.

By the autumn of 1906, thanks to Chao's early campaigns, the new Amban Lien Yu, who had replaced Yu T'ai, had reached Lhasa—taking the Tachienlu-Batang road via Chamdo, after the fall of Hsiang Cheng had made it secure. Meanwhile, as has been noticed, Chang, the Special Commissioner, had already arrived overland through India, and between the two of them they set about to undo the embarrassments which Peking had suffered during the preceeding years.

Prior to taking over as an additional Amban at Lhasa,[14a] to which post he had been nominated early in 1908, Chao was determined to complete his work in the border districts. With this end in view, in the autumn, he set out from Chengtu along the North road, via Sining and Jyekundo, his heart set on Derge or Dege—the largest, the wealthiest and the most important of the autonomous Tibetan principalities, with a proud ruling house that could trace its ancestry back a thousand years. His task here was rendered easier by a fratricidal conflict for the throne within the ruling house. Cleverly playing the two brothers against each other, he eventually installed his own nominee to the rival brothers' total exclusion. After Dege, Chao struck at Chamdo, doubly important because of its strategic location at the junction of the main

---

[14]Jordan to Grey, 1 May 1911, in *F O* 371/1078/289.

[14a]According to a Chinese scholar, Chao's appointment as Amban 'frightened' the Dalai Lama who petitioned the Throne for its withdrawal and ordered the Tibetans to create disturbances so as to frustrate Chao's designs. Lien Yu, in Lhasa, too urged the three monasteries to 'oppose' Chao's entry and warned the Chinese government that if he did set out, the Tibetans would 'stop' him. 'Finally', we are told, his appointment was cancelled. *Yao-ting Sung*, pp. 61–62.

roads from Yunnan, Szechuan and Kham to Central Tibet. Chamdo's fall was achieved without much ado largely because of the confusion in Tibetan ranks (albeit there were sizeable levies not far outside the town), as to whether a fight was to be joined. The confusion, to which a fuller reference has been made in the following paragraphs, was largely a reflection of the state of affairs in Lhasa itself. From Chamdo, Chao's armies helped to reduce the neighbouring states of Draya and Markham-Gartok.[15]

The fall of Chamdo, the age-old, time-worn nerve-centre of political activity in Kham, signified that the road to Lhasa was now open. Towards the late autumn of 1909, convinced that Chinese mastery over Tibet could best be demonstrated, and indeed sustained, not so much by loud wordy protests of Lien Yu as by the physical presence of Chinese soldiery, Chao determined to despatch 2,000 of his well-equipped and well-drilled troops to the Tibetan capital. The news, and exaggerated rumours had for long preceded the actual march of the troops, frightened the Tibetan government, or whatever was left of it. So indeed it did the Dalai Lama who, as we noticed, had, towards the end of 1909 after nearly five years of political wilderness, arrived at Nag-chuka, a few stages to the north of his capital. Tibetan resistance to the Chinese advance was on the cards but was stultified both by the temporizing tactics adopted by Lien Yu as no doubt by the element of surprise inherent in a relatively rapid advance of the troops themselves, in the cold wintry months, along an almost impassable highway. The result was that those who had prepared themselves for offering resistance were completely confused and virtually without a sense of direction. And, in the bargain, Chao succeeded in planting at Lhasa, and in Tibet, a sizeable Chinese army that could set at nought all the dark webs of intrigue that the Dalai Lama could conceivably weave and all the resistance that he could possibly muster. So difficult, in fact, was the position, that the appearance of the Chinese advance-guard in Lhasa, under the command of the young, and ambitious General Chung Ying—and he had the clearest directive to seize the Dalai Lama—found the latter a refugee again, even though he now headed south, instead of towards the north.

On the face of it, Chung Ying's troops were no innovation. For since the days of Emperor Chien Lung, the Imperial Institutes had provided for 150 officers and troopers to man the China-Tibet borderlands. Drawn from the provincial forces of Szechuan and in no way indistinct from the irregular constabulary, these men were scattered in small detachments on the roads from Tachienlu to the Tibetan capital. A number were also spread out, somewhat thinly, over the entire expanse of Tibet, with a major concentration of around 500 at Lhasa.[16] May not Chung Ying's well-trained troops then be viewed as

---

[15] *Teichman*, n. 1, pp. 7, 24–25.
Also see Louis King to Alston, 5 November 1913, Encl. in No. 219, *Foreign*, March 1914, Procs. 1-251.

[16] William Fredrick Mayers, *The Chinese Government*, 2nd edition, (London, 1886), p. 102.

a substitute for the irregular levies sanctified by the Imperial Institutes which, through the intervening century and more, though intact on paper, had all but disappeared in fact?

It is possible, however, to view the situation differently. In more ways than one, Chung Ying's troops constituted an invasion of Tibet and, to that extent, a complete break with China's past. As Mr Richardson, a keen student of Tibet's history, has underlined, here

> was the first Chinese army to reach Lhasa against the will of the Tibetans. The expeditions of 1720, 1728, 1750 and 1792 all came to restore order and were not opposed by Tibetans. After each expedition there had been some reorganisation of Chinese relations with Tibetan Government but, except for a brief period in 1720, there had been no question of taking over the administration. In all that had been done before the Tibetans had acquiesced.... The Emperors on their side had been careful... to do nothing to upset the ostensibly amicable basis of that relationship.[17]

Whatever else it may have implied, the occupation of the Tibetan capital was a major victory for Chao's campaigns in the Marches; it could, with justifiaction, be termed their coping stone. To an extent, it may well be argued that here was proof positive of the fact that the Marches were now securely within Peking's grip, even though the latter's 'specific authorisation' for Chao's actions has been openly questioned.[18] Conversely, British prestige received a crushing blow. With much fanfare, and even more acriminious debate, the British had marched an army to Lhasa, not so much in the face of Chinese protests as in the teeth of futile Tibetan resistance. Not directly perhaps, for Amban Yu T'ai had repeatedly exhorted the Tibetan 'barbarians' to behave and was always found on the right-hand side of the British Commissioner, but indirectly every success of Younghusband drove the nail deep into the coffin of Chinese authority, and prestige, in Tibet. Partly that prestige had returned with the resounding success attendant upon Chao's campaigns in the eastern regions. With the fall of Lhasa to his men, China was restored to the position that she had always claimed to enjoy in theory, though but rarely in practice.

An important result of the induction of Chinese troops into Lhasa was that it relieved Chao of an anxiety, however remote, about the Dalai Lama's regime subverting or endangering his efforts, behind his back as it were, towards stabilising his work in the border areas. It is thus significant that no sooner did Chung Ying, the young commander who led the army, reach Lhasa, than Chao felt it was time to push his troops into the district of Zayul to the north of Assam and even Rima, at the door-step of the Indian frontier to the east. Thereby he made live and sensitive the Abor and the Mishmi areas

[17]Richardson, *History*, p. 100.
[18]Ibid., p. 101.

which had hitherto been relatively quiescent and peaceful. The full impact of his policies which had, at one time, seemed to the British Foreign Office a matter of little concern,[19] now began to be felt in a powerful way, for the chickens had come home to roost.

Nor was that all. Chao was determined that whatever was left of Tibet would be within its smallest physical confines. In the summer of 1910, he memorialised the throne that Tibet's frontier in the east should be fixed at Giamda, beyond the Salween-Brahmaputra divide, and not more than 100 miles, and a few days' march, to the east of Lhasa! However problematic the success of the Dalai Lama in defying Peking may have been, in reducing his domain Chao was severely clipping his wings and cutting him to size as it were.

Apart from Lien Yu, whose jurisdiction had progressively shrunk since Chao's emergence on the scene and who was, therefore, if secretly, opposed to the revised physical limits to which Tibet was to be confined, expert opinion was sharply split on Chao's new boundary marks for Tibet. Thus Teichman had expressed the view that the

> Giamda boundary appears to have been an arbitrary line, probably drawn for strategic purposes, and unsupported by historical claims of any kind.[20]

And yet during the negotiations at Simla, in 1913–14, the Chinese were to invest the (Giamda) boundary with a sanctity that was clearly alien to it!

Besides managing his own affairs, and the task of holding the March country was no child's play,[21] Chao was able to come to the rescue of Lien Yu as well. It may be recalled in this context that with Chinese forces in Lhasa, the Amban had felt encouraged to undertake a major campaign against Pomed, a difficult country of heavy rains, dense forests and precipitous snowy ranges lying to the north of Assam and west of the Tibetan district of Zayul. Pomed subserved an important strategic purpose too in that a road planned to run from Batang to Lhasa traversed through it. Initially an expedition had been sent there from Lhasa under Lo Ching-chi but it had met with serious reverses. Con-

---

[19] Answering India's argument that Chao's, and China's, doings in Tibet in 1909–10 necessitated the lodging of a strong protest in Peking, Max Muller wrote that no 'protest' was warranted either 'against a possible change of the status quo' or 'infringements' of the Agreement of 1906. Max Muller to Grey, 15 February 1910, in *F O* 371/853/498.

In the Foreign Office, Campbell minuted that 'we have not much of a *locus standi* for making representations'. Loc. cit.

[20] *Teichman*, n. 1, p. 30 recalls that initially the Lhasa Amban's jurisdiction extended to Tachienlu, that when the Frontier Commissionership was created in 1906, the Amban's sphere of authority was cut down to correspond with the old limits of Tibet proper as laid down in the reign of the Emperor Yung Ching (1723–36) 'including...the states of Chamdo, Draya and Markham'.

[21] Thus, to cite one instance, towards the end of 1910, the Chinese garrison at Hsiang Cheng mutinied, and local Tibetans rose again in revolt against Chinese rule. The rising was suppressed with an unusual measure of severity.

sequently, early in 1911, Lien Yu appealed to Chao to help pull him out of the morass. In response, the latter rushed troops from Batang and Shoupando and ere long resistance was smothered and Pomed reduced to submission. Chao went the logical step forward and even drew up blueprints for converting both Pomed and Zayul into regular Chinese districts.

A climax to his tireless work, as also a well-deserved reward for his labours, was Chao's appointment, in the spring of 1911, to the Viceroyalty of Szechuan, a post of trust and responsibility that was additionally rated as the most lucrative in the Empire. In a sense, his work as Warden of the Marches had now drawn to a close. As he surveyed the scene, the sight of Chinese administration with its hierarchy of Fu, Chou, Hsien and Ting, stretching all the way from Tachienlu to Markham, must have filled his heart with joy. West of the Mekong and the Salween too, he had carved out and planned administrative units, though the incumbents were not as yet firmly installed in the saddle. Additionally, he could see Amban Lien Yu and General Chung Ying established squarely in Lhasa and, with the Dalai Lama a fugitive, Tibetan administration shrunk almost into a nothingness. While from the Chinese point of view it (Lhasa) may have retained a nuisance value, its capacity for harm had come to nought. Perhaps in a way, its pro forma existence was essential if only to satisfy the British, and to an extent the Russian, penchant for an 'independent' Tibetan administration!

A fitting epitaph to Chao's work in the Marches was the Memorial which his successor, General Fu Sung-mu, drew up for the Emperor on the morrow of his appointment. *Inter alia*, Fu supplicated that the whole of East Tibet be constituted into a separate province and christened 'Hsi-kang'—Western Kham.[21a] The memorial was on its way to Peking, via Chengtu, when the October (1911) revolution intervened and consigned to the melting-pot, and the flames, not only Chao's handiwork but much else besides.

There was an uncanny paradox in all that the Warden had done. On the one hand, his reforms took the Tibetans of the in-between regions towards Chinese education, civilization and moral codes which, outwardly at any rate, were harbingers of considerable improvement in life as they knew it. And yet on the other, as an astute contemporary observer of the scene put it, there was the realisation

> that the reforms which are influencing the moral, mental and physical life of the people are emanating from Peking—conservative, utilitarian and unsympathetic—the puzzle becomes decidedly Chinese.[22]

[21a] According to a Chinese scholar, Fu Sung-mu's principal argument for the creation of the new province was that it would safeguard the territory 'against possible foreign encroachment' as well as 'remedy' the difficulties of the Szechuan provincial authorities in their attempts to exercise 'effective control' over this 'vast and turbulent' region. *Yao-ting Sung*, p. 65.

[22] 'Extract from a private letter from Batang dated 18 July 1910', Encl. 1 in Max Muller to Grey, 30 September 1910, in *I O R*, L/P & S/10/183.

What was more, Chao's efforts, as has been observed, to implant a large number of Chinese husbandmen from Szechuan who, married to women of Tibetan stock, would help make the land a part of China, or at any rate better oriented towards that country, proved miserable, if also costly, failures. They would be amusing to contemplate if they were also not so pathetic. There was still another aspect. Behind an impressive facade of military victory— Chao had achieved his conquest and ' pacification ' with a woefully inadequate force of less than 4,000 men—lurked the inconvenient shadow of a diplomatic debacle. As one who lived through these years and saw it happen at close quarters observed:

> There is no doubt, before very long, a great part of Tibet will be recognising the authority of China. But two questions arise. Can China do anything with the conquered country? And is the alleged subjugation a policy on the part of the Tibetans to avert the vengeance of the one invulnerable Chinaman? ' Wait ', they say, ' Chao will go some day and then our turn will come.' And there is probably something in such rumours, for has not China's conquest and reconquest in this land been the wearying tale of the ages? Conquer a turbulent country at great expense, hold it at great inconvenience, and at the same time get nothing from it, and what happens?[23]

It was this ' wearying tale ' that made Chao's otherwise remarkable achievement look so shallow in retrospect. The harsh fact is that if his achievement was phenomenal, his failure was even more so. And the key to this seeming paradox may be found largely in the tribal organisation and the monastic discipline of this entire area. Broadly, what Chao did was to depose the tribal chieftains while at the same time promising the tribesmen, through his (Chinese) officials, that not only would their taxes be reduced but that their independence will not be interfered with. He pursued his policy of conciliating the tribesmen even to the extent of abolishing the hated ' Ula ', the much-abused right of free transport for all officials, which imposed such a heavy burden on the countryside.

To his revolutionary innovations, the chieftains who exercised a sort of remote control over the tribesmen, through their landlords, offered but scant resistance. In turn, the landlords accepted the new dispensation because their rights and privileges had been left untouched. And finally, the newly-inducted Chinese officials found themselves to be instruments of a policy that was unexceptional. They were accepted without much friction.

All this displayed a great insight into political conditions obtaining in the Marches. The Warden also kept a stern hold over his own officials and maintained the strictest discipline among his troops, ensuring at the same time that

[23] Loc. cit.

if and when military action was necessary, it came quickly and with a strong, powerful impact.

What undid Chao and his work was primarily the October 1911 Revolution and the fall of the C'hing which unleashed forces of disorder, loosened discipline and snapped what was left of the slender threads that held the ramshackle empire together under the weak regency (1908–11) of Prince Ch'un. If partly, there was the hostility of the large monasteries with their armies of well-fed, but ignorant, lamas. The monks' power over their laity was at once spiritual as well as temporal. For the gompas were, in their own right, feudal landlords. Thanks to the ignorance and superstition in which the tribes were encompassed, the hold of the lamas was the greater and they were dreaded all the more. The fear and vengeance of the gods which took the form of natural calamities could only be averted through the intercession of the lamas which meant, in turn, the growing enrichment of the gompas and the consequent impoverishment of the tribesmen.

Unlike the landlords, the vast hordes of ignorant lamas served as private armies for the monasteries and their feudal estates. Besides, as has been noticed, the dread hold of the lamas over the minds and hearts of their lay flocks was unquestioned. It was this elemental force, this stranglehold of the monasteries, which Chao dared to antagonise; in turn, their stern, yet well-organised, resistance blighted his path and stood in the way of his cherished goal.

His assault was frontal. Chao limited the number of monks in each lamasery; tried to force into these strongholds men who favoured Chinese rule; posted proclamations in every district that natural calamities could not be averted by prayer; much less priestly intervention; and prohibited tribesmen from paying for such services to the lamas.

The ire of the gompas was easily aroused. Against Chao's determined assaults, they held Hsien Cheng for upwards of six months. When he did finally capture their fortress, they fled across the border into Tibet—only to re-organise and bide their time for another opportunity. Nor were the tribesmen easily weaned away, for the spiritual hold of their faith remained firmly entrenched.

What then was the element of durability in Chao's work? Uncharitable critics were not averse to pointing out that his ' much-vaunted ' reforms and innovations—implanting colonists, cultivating rice and vegetables at high altitudes, giving widespread encouragement to matrimony with Tibetan women—were but desperate endeavours to save ' face ', put a veneer on his otherwise ruthless suppression of a way of life different from his own; that, in fact, the whole exercise was an 'impudent farce'.[24] For the stark reality was that Chao's rule was based on armed conquest over a populace that failed to be reconciled, that the greater the measure of his repression, the more unpopular he and his regime became. In the final analysis, his system had

[24]Jordan to Grey, 2 September 1909, Encl. Letter from J H Edgar, Batang, 4 July 1909, in *F O* 371/620/974.

rested on the uneven pillars of small garrisons maintained at strategic, but isolated, places throughout the March country. And when the men revolted, or their loyalty tended to waver—and instances were not unknown when, in his own lifetime, his soldiers had risen in rebellion and were put down with the greatest severity—the system collapsed.

Chapter 7

Chinese Penetration into the Assam Himalayas (1906-11)

BESIDES THE sweep of his arms and administration over Kham, re-christened Hsi-kang, an important adjunct to Chao Erh-feng's activity was, as has been briefly noticed, the planting of Chinese troops into the provinces that bordered Assam and Burma. British surveyors who were at the time conducting a fairly systematic probe into what constituted the southernmost limits of Tibetan administration, as distinct from areas in which tribal influences prevailed and persisted, came into contact with these (Chinese) officials, and troops. For India, strategically of the greatest import in this context were the south Tibetan districts of Zayul, Pome, Pemako and Takpo. A word about how much penetration was achieved, and its impact, may be of some interest if only as a measure of the threat posed to the frontier areas by these incursions.

The district of Pome includes the valley of the Nyang-chu, also called Po-Tsangpo or Po Chu in its lower reaches. The inhabitants, referred to as Po-bas, are spread all the way down to the Abor frontier. The capital is Showa. Three estates, then directly under Lhasa's authority and independent of Showa, were Samdzong, Chudzong and Dashing.

The valley of the Tsangpo, below the gorge, constitutes Pemako. The term is vaguely used, for the district has no definitive boundaries. At an earlier stage, the inhabitants are said to have been Abors but later a large number of people from eastern Bhutan and the neighbourhood of Tawang came to this country in search of a land of promise alluded to in ancient lore. It was held that when religion came to be persecuted in Tibet, people would repair to Pemako, a land of plenty where reportedly rivers flowed with milk and honey and crops grew without labour. From here then, it was prophesied, would true religion spread to the whole world.

Bacot, a French traveller with an intimate knowledge of the Marches, has maintained that owing to the ravages of Chinese soldiery in East Tibet, there was, in the first decade of the 20th century, a fresh migration in search of this land. Victims of Chinese fury particularly sought it out. It was this migration which accounted for large numbers of Tibetans who entered the Dibang valley about the same time.[1]

With the new migrants, the Abors, who were the former inhabitants of this area, were gradually pushed south, even though some remained behind to be absorbed by the Monbas or the Drukpa, said to be among the earlier

[1] J. Bacot, *Le Thibet Revolte* (Paris, 1910), cited in Bailey and Morshead, ' Report on the Exploration of the N E F, 1913 ', in *Foreign*, October 1916, Procs. 76–83.

settlers. As a consequence, the valley claims many Abor villages besides those where the Lopas and the Monbas live together. The Abors in Pemako have adopted Tibetan dress and language; many have even taken to Tibetan religion. In a Lopa village, Bailey noticed a line of water-turned prayer-wheels, while the people professed to be Buddhists. 'Before the Monba immigration', the British traveller recorded, 'the whole of Pemako belonged to the Lopas and was independent of Pome'.

Po-bas, the people of Pome, lay claim to the levying of taxes on the people of Pemako. That these claims were far from substantiated is borne out by the fact that the Po-bas were not sure of the names of Pemako villages which allegedly paid them tribute. Besides, the taxes were said to vary from village to village. The administration of the valley itself was in the hands of three petty officials under the Po-ba authorities.

In Pemako, according to Tibetan tradition, there was, somewhere in the Lohit-Dibang watershed, a holy mountain of glass which, thanks to the determined hostility of the Mishmis, was not easily accessible to them.

Pemako grows the usual sub-Himalayan crops of rice, maize and murwa. There is an abundance of the mader dye plant too, a little cotton and some indigo. In the Po-Tsangpo valley and other parts of Pome, the main crops are barley and wheat albeit a little maize and murwa is also grown. There are peach and walnut trees too. The cattle in the hills are yak and dzo; in the valleys, the dzo with a mithan strain. Pome is said to be famous for breeding ponies.[2]

The Chinese occupation of these districts was a phased development. The first visitors, who preceded the arrival of Chao Erh-feng in the Marches, were the surveyors who strode about 'counting their paces and writing down notes' as they went. One wonders if this alleged activity was not an amplified version of the story of the Chinese lama who, a trainee of the Trigonometrical Survey of India, had accompanied Kinthup. It may be recalled that he not only sold the latter into captivity but got rid of his own surveying instruments and a pistol. In any case, neither he nor his compatriots could have been very welcome among a people who perhaps suspected them for the worst.

Not long after the surveyors came the troops, their numbers inflated particularly after the Tibetan capital itself had been occupied. It would appear that the Chinese at first told the Po-bas that besides laying down a telegraph line, they would cut a road through the country. This activity, however, was stoutly resisted and led to severe fighting. According to Po-ba accounts, four principal engagements were fought besides which numerous ambuscades were laid along the road. The number of Chinese killed is said to be 500, a figure sometimes inflated to 1700, while Po-ba losses are rated at 300-500 men. Whatever the truth, it was clear that the first phase of the fighting ended in favour of the Po-bas.[3]

[2]Bailey and Morshead, Report, Ibid.
[3]J L R Weir, then Trade Agent, Gyantse, noted in his diary for June 1911 that the 'Po-bas

After their initial discomfiture, the Chinese returned with fresh reinforcements; as many as 1,000 troops are now said to have entered the country via Poto. Some of the inhabitants who resisted were killed, others aided and assisted the invaders—the worst offenders in this respect being the gompas or the monasteries. A gruesome business was the murder of the ruler, his eight ministers and four chiefs, all on a single day. Followed an orgy of destruction—the palace and the gompa in Showa were burnt down, besides many a village and gompa all over the valley.[4]

In this fashion, the Chinese are said to have overrun the whole country and established their garrisons at Yortong on the right bank of the Tsangpo and at Chundro. From these two main centres, small parties were despatched to the outlying villages.

In contrast to Pome, in Pemako, with its mixed population of Monbas and Lopas, the damage appears to have been less because resistance was not too well-organised. There was, however, considerable hardship, an acute shortage of the bare necessities of life, and an almost complete breakdown of all communications. This was mainly due to the fact that a large number of troops, and their accoutrement, were continuously on the move. No wonder people deserted their villages *en masse*. In Pome, all the villages on the road from Showa to Tangkyuk ' had been devastated ' and Bailey reported having passed all along the road, ' ruined houses and uncultivated fields'. At one place, he noticed, ' this year's barley crop when it was green and before it had ripened' was being eaten up, for there was nothing better people could do.[5]

Besides Pome and Pemako, the neighbouring district of Zayul was of considerable interest to the Chinese, for by this route Lhasa was much nearer to Yunnan than via the longer, and often-disturbed, Szechuan-Lhasa detour.

In 1911, a small Chinese force, part of the large army of Chung Ying, found its way to Rima whence it is said to have expelled all Tibetan officials. In the course of their occupation of this territory, they erected on the Menilkrai flat, three miles south of Walong, a post and claimed it to be the southern boundary of the Ching empire. This post was noticed by the then Assistant Political Officer, Dundas, in December 1911. Three years later, in his tour diary for February-March 1914, O'Callaghan, another APO, found a short distance from Menilkrai, ' on the hill-side carefully placed between two pine-trees ', a thatch ' covering another boundary post '. In his own words,

> the new post, a pine plank 7' × 16' on which was inscribed neatly in English, Tibetan and Chinese: The southern boundary of Chuan Tien Tsa Yu of Chinese Republic established by special Commissioner Chiong

(Po-Pas) are giving the Chinese troops who were sent to conquer them a lot of trouble' as a result of which reinforcements of Chinese from Shigatse and Gyantse ' will probably be sent '. Extract from the Diary of J L R Weir, No. 292 in *Foreign*, August 1911, Procs. 225–301.
[4]Loc. cit.
[5]Bailey and Morshead, Report, *supra*, n. 1.

Fong Chi and magistrate of Tsa-Yu, Kes Win Chin-Tsa-Yu, June 9th 1912.[6]

O'Callaghan, conscious that allowing the pine planks to stand would be tantamount to ' a tacit admission of Chinese or Tibetan claims ' to a new boundary line, had both of these removed and left them in the jungle, opposite the village of Kabas. Thereby, he hoped, no fresh Chinese claims would be made, much less acknowledged.

The headman of Walong, who at first denied any knowledge of Chinese activities, later confirmed that he had been sent for and warned that, if the British put in an appearance again, he should ' show (them) the post'.

As a result of his enquiries, O'Callaghan endorsed what Dundas had found out in 1911 namely, that the village of Walong, north of Menilkrai, had been established by the Miju Mishmis many years earlier. Its ostensible purpose was to look after their cattle as also to give refuge to the Tibetans who came down, or ran away, from the north. In addition to Walong, there were other villages of which some remains were extant and which at one time had been settled but were now deserted, their people having died or returned to Tibet. There was clear evidence too that at one time the Miju-Mishmi influence dominated Walong and the area beyond it.

O'Callaghan was of the view that before erecting their boundary pillar at Menilkrai, the Chinese had conducted a survey. For at the place where the pine plank had been put up, one enters an area of large arable flats on both sides of the river which continues northwards and terminates at the broad valley of the Zayul, at Rima. These flats of arable land are conspicuous by their absence between Menilkrai and the foothills adjoining the plains of Assam, thereby making it difficult for the latter to man or support a frontier post in this area. It followed that being shut to the south of Menilkrai and Walong, the Lohit valley garrisons could only be maintained from Sadiya. This would largely explain why O'Callaghan was

> more than ever convinced of the necessity of finishing of the road to our frontier and the opening of the post as near our frontier as is practical as soon as possible.[7]

From Walong to Rima, however, there was no difficulty in road-making for all that was necessary was to extend the Lohit valley road to the Manglor flat, a distance of less than 30 miles. This would make the opening, and the rationing, of the post at Walong a practical proposition. After local enquiries, O'Callaghan was convinced that, within a few years, the majority of rice and

[6] T P M O'Callaghan was Assistant to the Political Officer, Central and Eastern Section, N E Frontier and was placed in charge of the Walong promenade. His tour diaries for the period may be seen in *Foreign*, December 1914, Procs. 156–84.

[7] Loc. cit.

other items required could be purchased on the spot. Since at, or near, Rima large quantities of grain were raised, O'Callaghan argued, all that needed to be done was to divert this trade southwards.

The populace in these districts had been the plaything of fortune in the disturbances during the last few years (1910–13), being harassed by a rapacious Chinese and Tibetan soldiery alike. No wonder O'Callaghan found the inhabitants in favour of British occupation! Again, the unsteady nature of an administration which, with all its followers, including even cattle and ponies, moved to the Rima plain during the cold weather because of its rich grazing and crops, made things doubly unsatisfactory.

To recapitulate the broad detail of events. By August 1910, Chinese control over Zayul had been firmly established and apart from the fact that recalcitrant Tibetan officials were removed from office, there was a Chinese garrison of some 300 men stationed at Chikong, north of Rima. Chao Erh-feng had plans too for large-scale Chinese colonisation of this area; for here, as at Pome, the land and climate were rated peculiarly suitable for intensive rice cultivation. This was a prospect which as long as it lasted—and Chinese rule was short-lived, from about the middle of 1910 to the summer of 1912— was enough to frighten the British. There was, however, considerable evidence that the Tibetans were well-disposed towards the ' Sahibs ' if only because Chinese rule was oppressive. Understandably, the two Tibetan officials who met O'Callaghan and his party at Rima wrote thus to the stalwart young man, ' of wise address, great Lord, great Sahib ' and his companions:

> You came to and we are sorry you stayed so short a time. If you come again, we will come and meet you below Walong. We will come to the boundary of the Mishmi country. We will welcome you to Zayul. The Chinese continue to oppress us. We and the English mix like milk and water.[8]

Although the Tibetans were friendly and well-disposed, there was fear of an adverse reaction should the British penetrate into what was admittedly Tibetan territory. Thus, after the Mishmi Mission (1911–12) had reported on the friendly attitude of the Tibetans in Zayul, the Foreign Department in Calcutta noted that any talk of pushing to or cutting a road to Rima

> may alarm the Tibetans ... our object in establishing posts and making the road is merely the defence of our own frontier, that we hope it will be the means of maintaining and extending our intercourse and friendly relations with the Tibetans.[9]

The Army General Staff, conscious of the importance of Zayul and of Chinese encroachments on the border with Assam, underlined the need for a

---
[8]Loc. cit.
[9]Office note by L W Reynolds, in *Foreign*, February 1914, Procs. 261–337.

'promenade' to Walong. Meanwhile on 8 July 1913, General Lake, then Chief of the (Indian) General Staff, noted that

> having regard to the forthcoming negotiations with China, and the latter's known designs on the fertile province of Zayul which is the portion of Tibet bordering on Assam. It seems highly desirable that Government should persevere in its policy of establishing British influence up to the frontier which it claims, so as to prevent Chinese encroachments and avoid boundary disputes in future.[10]

A week earlier, on 1 July 1913, the Secretary of State had refused to sanction expenditure for the 22-mile monorail from Sanpura to Paya river, a project on which the Assam Government had set its heart. Equally, Whitehall's decision made Calcutta visibly unhappy. The latter still thought it necessary, 'in view of the eventualities', to establish ' our position ' on the Assam frontier and determine the boundary. It was accepted, however, that the urgency would disappear 'if the Chinese agree', as a result of the forthcoming tripartite (British–Chinese–Tibetan) Conference, 'to relinquish their claims' to Zayul.[11]

---

[10] Office note by Chief of the General Staff, General P. Lake, 8 July 1913, in Ibid.
[11] Office note, referring to Secretary of State to Viceroy, 1 July 1913, No. 285 in Ibid.

Chapter 8

British India's Policy Towards The North-East Frontier: Before and After Williamson's Murder

APART FROM moving into the south Tibetan districts of Pome, Pemako and Zayul, the closing years of Chao's stewardship of the Marches had also witnessed Chinese incursions, through Yunnan, into northern Burma including Hpimaw or Pienma, the Ahkyang valley and Khampti Long. Burma being then a part of the larger whole of the Indian Empire, Chinese movements in these areas understandably upset the British a great deal more for here above all they posed the problem of a direct confrontation.

It may be recalled that as early as the spring of 1904, the British had informed the Chinese regarding the Shweli-Salween-Irrawaddy watershed as the accepted boundary with Yunnan. A year later, by mutual arrangement, British and Chinese representatives were to meet when the actual position and features of the frontier were to be marked. This meeting, however, never took place as the Chinese showed a pronounced tendency to procrastinate and delay.

Until early in 1910, no further advance towards a settlement was registered; in April that year, however, when the British Consul stationed at Tengyueh visited Hpimaw, he found it occupied by 20 Chinese soldiers.[1]

In the meantime, with the Chinese occupation of Tibet and advance into Zayul, the British administration in Burma had felt alarmed. To start with, an expedition to counter Chinese moves was despatched under W F Hertz, then Deputy Commissioner of Myitkyina. This took about four months, December 1910-April 1911, and achieved some permanent results. One was the consolidation of British jurisdiction throughout all the territory as far north as latitude 26°/18'; another was the establishment of a military police post at Lankhang near the Nmaikha river. And finally, the Myitkyina-Seniku mule track was further extended.

Hertz's expedition pointed to some important conclusions. Firstly, that the Chinese were unable to establish any claim to jurisdiction over any part of the tract in question, barring a small area comprising the Hpimaw, Gawlum and Kangfeng group of villages. For the rest, there had been no attempt, on their part, to control, much less administer, any territory. Again, relations between village officials and Chinese authorities across the watershed had been

---

[1] For a summary of the major developments during the years 1910-13, see Encl. 5 entitled ' NEF of India (with map)' to No. 36, *Foreign*, May 1915, Procs. 36-50.

confined to an occasional exchange of presents which indicated nothing more than a desire on each side ' to preserve amicable relations ', necessary to the fostering and continuance of ' trans-frontier ' trade.

All this notwithstanding, the fact that the Chinese were pushing into these areas could not be gainsaid. Thus it was noticed that efforts were afoot

> to distribute appointment orders, hats and other official tokens to headmen and others holding positions throughout this territory. The object... could only be with a view to assert at a later period that the villages... were shown thereby to be subject to Chinese jurisdiction.[2]

Another significant development was the visit to Hkampti of a Chinese official accompanied by a military escort. This not only violated the northern extremity of the boundary claimed by the British, but demonstrated Peking's growing interest in the Shan states. So far as India was aware, the Chinese had not asserted any formal claims to Hkampti which had been regarded as subordinate to the British, while the principal Sawhwa in the Shan states had sent tributary offerings to Rangoon and thereby acknowledged his allegiance to the Raj.

To forestall Chinese designs, which were now far too pronounced to be ignored, Rangoon proposed that a civil officer, with an escort of military police, be despatched from Myitkyina to Hkampti to assert British supremacy ' in a formal manner '. Additionally, he was to deliver to the recently-installed Sawhwa, a *sanad* indicating that his authority was recognised by, and derived from, the British government. Since the precise nature of the Chinese move was not clear, it was felt that a protest at Peking may not precede the projected visit of the British officer.

With this proposal broadly approved in Calcutta, J T O Barnard was deputed to undertake the work. Unfortunately for the British, his visit was not a success: no detailed description of the territory adjoining Hkampti was made for want of a surveyor, nor could the *sanad* be presented to the Sawhwa. While Barnard found no Chinese personnel, nor any evidence of their occupation of the (Hkampti) valley, it was evident that some of the tribes paid tribute to both Tibet and China. Such information as he gleaned came from tribal sources and was found to be incomplete, if also perhaps partly unreliable.

A fresh expedition, being deemed necessary, was undertaken in October 1911. In addition to his earlier tasks of presenting a *sanad* to the Sawhwa and of surveying the country, Barnard was to ascertain traces of Tibetan or Chinese influence, open communications with the Mishmi mission, then in the Lohit valley, and concert his own findings with that mission.

Barnard's expedition, as well as Clerk's tour farther to the east, were carried

---

[2]From an office note, initialled ' GMG ', dated 3 June 1914 and entitled ' Summary of Correspondence attached to Sir Henry McMahon's Report on the NEF ', in Ibid.

out in 1911–12. The latter showed that between Ngawchang and Mekh streams, the Chinese possessed no rights in the Nmaikha valley, while Barnard's enquiries farther north in the Hkampti region revealed that Peking had no rights over any part of Hkampti Long as far north as the Sein Ku Wang. The latter river was said to mark the northern limits of the Shan sphere of control, the people farther north being under Tibetan influence.

Another interesting finding was that tribes living in the valleys of the Tazewang, and Taron, north of the Tsangpo's big bend, paid tribute to and were under a measure of Chinese control. This further supplemented the information furnished by Captain Bailey who, in his journey from Peking to Sadiya, had crossed the headwaters of both these rivers and found a portion of the country to be definitely Tibetan.

During the open season of 1912–13, further exploration became necessary to clarify a number of doubtful points before a definitive boundary could be laid in this region. In the course of these explorations, a number of Chinese were found in the Ahkyang valley, it being further ascertained that other (Chinese) parties had entered by the Yurgan pass and, after crossing the Taron and Nam Tamai rivers, had reached Putao itself. This fact seemed to demonstrate that the major objective of the Chinese was to seize and occupy the country on this side of the main watershed. To counter this move, the British felt that the whole of this region, including the Ahkyang valley, ought to be occupied by them.

Another conclusion seemed equally inescapable, namely that there must be occupation in strength followed by the actual administration of the area, for that alone would prevent 'future incursion' by Peking.

On the diplomatic front, in December 1910, the Chinese had protested against British activity and demanded a joint delimitation of the frontier. In reply, Jordan was directed to point out that no such delimitation could be agreed to, unless the Chinese accepted his predecessor, Sir Ernest Satow's note of 1 May 1906, stipulating their acceptance of the watershed principle as a basis for determining the frontier.[3]

Peking, in turn, rejected the British note, refused to accept the watershed frontier, and pointed out that it had never agreed to it. In any case, it argued, its acceptance of the British position would take away an area most of which was under the rule of native Chinese chieftains. Further notes of protest from the Wai-wu-pu charged that the British had violated the frontier, demanded their immediate withdrawal and maintained that Hpimaw was in Chinese territory.

It was Britain's turn now. Whitehall stoutly contested the Chinese claim and pointed out that as early as 1905 'the country between the Nmaikha watershed and the Ngawchang' had been jointly surveyed by the two sides

---

[3]The Chinese note was presented on 10 December 1910 and Jordan's reply was dated 17 December 1910. For a summary see Ibid.

when the earlier position had been re-affirmed.[4] The Wai-wu-pu resisted this stance, declared that the question of the undelimited frontier 'had been in a state of confusion' for many years, that the watershed principle enunciated in 1906 was 'merely an ex-parte pronouncement' and had never received China's consent.[5] That, however, was not the way Whitehall viewed matters for it declared that the watershed

> not only offered the most suitable frontier on geographical and administrative grounds but was, in fact, the only line offering any hope of a final settlement, and that in the circumstances, HMG must continue to press for its acceptance as the general basis of the frontier, subject to the understanding that any claim China might be able to substantiate west of this line would be dealt with in an equitable spirit.[6]

Later, to repeated Chinese protests, the British reply was that all measures which had been taken on the British side of the frontier were of a purely administrative character.

The eastern frontier with Tibet spans the whole area from Bhutan up to and including the Mishmi country. Until Burma was separated from India, in April 1937, it extended southwards too, down to the Myitkyina district of Upper Burma. Purely for administrative convenience, the British had laid down what used to be called the Inner and the Outer Lines. This was largely a matter of dealing with the tribes who, for most part, were settled in the vast expanse of hill and dale between the plains and the high mountain peaks that formed the natural boundary with Tibet. Starting with Bhutan and moving east, the principal tribes were the Tawang, Charduar and the Thengla Bhutias, the Akas, the Daflas, the Miris, the Abors and the Mishmis.

Treaties and engagements of a sort bound these tribes to the British government. Thus the Charduar and Thengla Bhutias, the Akas, the Daflas, the Miris and the Abors received an annual allowance called *posa*, in cash or kind. Again, the Charduar Bhutias and the Akas had further pledged themselves never to join any group who were enemies of the British government but instead to oppose them in every way they could. Notwithstanding all this none of the tribes had definitely pledged themselves to refrain from intercourse with the foreigners.

Essentially, in its broad outlines, the policy with regard to the tribes had been one of non-interference, except in the case of outrages against British subjects or violations of the Inner Line to which regular administrative authority extended. Intervention was advocated in the event of proximity of the

---

[4] Chinese notes of protest were dated 14, 24 and 29 January 1911 respectively; the British note, 30 January (1911).
[5] Chinese note dated 12 February 1911. For a summary *supra*, n. 1.
[6] Jordan's note, 10 April 1911.

disturbance to the (British) border which might either endanger its peace or the interests of people dwelling in British-ruled areas.

Some measure of how British administration operated in the tribal areas in the closing decades of the 19th century may be gleaned from the duties outlined for Needham as Assistant Political Officer, Sadiya, in September 1882. *Inter alia*, he was

> to be chiefly employed on political work... but he should also take up such criminal work... and revenue work... (the Deputy Commissioner of Dibrugarh) should ordinarily issue through him orders upon all matters relating to affairs on the Abor, Mishmi and Singhbho-Khampti frontiers and the arrangements regarding the location of the frontier posts, their supplies, the patrolling between them etc. as well as the political relations with the Abors and Mishmis. His first duty will be to make himself thoroughly acquainted with the history of our relations with these tribes and their neighbours. His next should be to become personally acquainted with the leading members of the tribes, their chiefs, Katokis, etc.... He should endeavour to learn their languages, more especially that of the Abors.... [7]

It is not without significance that, despite Needham's induction into office in the eighties, knowledge of the tribes and their affairs remained meagre, at best, until 1910. This was particularly so with regard to the tribes beyond the 'Outer Line'; those between the Inner and the Outer were slightly better known.

The Inner Line, it may be recalled, was created by the Bengal Eastern Frontier Regulations of 1873. Its chief purpose was to define a territorial limit beyond which regular administration did not extend, nor were taxes realized. British subjects did not cross it without special permits. It also served to prevent friction between the tribes living beyond it and the plains people who went into these areas either to tap wild rubber or to catch elephants, thereby coming into contact, and sometimes conflict, with the tribesmen.

The 'Outer Line', which lay beyond the 'Inner', marked the limits of loose administrative control. Yet to confuse it with the 'international boundary of British India' or the 'frontier of India', would be straining both the facts as well as the imagination. The line of the Assam Himalayas was generally so well known and accepted as the frontier of India—both as a traditional fact and an historical legacy—that for the British to lay down 'the line of the foothills' as the international boundary would have been foolhardy. What the 'Outer Line' connoted was a limit beyond which British administration was so thinly spread that responsibilities that go with the conduct of day-to-day affairs were not readily assumed. That Calcutta regarded the tribal areas of Assam as falling securely within its orbit is clear from any textbook

[7] Elliott, Chief Commissioner, Assam, 28 September 1882 cited in *Reid*, pp. 183-84.

dealing with British India—the dots and dashes of the map or its yellow wash, as distinct from the pink that filled the rest, notwithstanding. For the Raj could scarce change the basic facts of Indian geography, or history.

A caveat, however, may be entered here namely that before the Chinese invasion of Tibet in 1910, neither the Government of India nor yet the Assam Government had turned their minds in a conscious or deliberate manner to the question at all. One would imagine that in Calcutta or Shillong, around 1900, if someone were asked where the international frontier of India lay east of Bhutan, he would have answered that while it had never been necessary to define the outer limits of the tribal areas north of the Assam valley, yet these tribes had political relations with the British government, *and not* with China or Tibet, and therefore must be regarded as lying within the orbit of the (British) Indian Empire.

What the Chinese occupation of Lhasa in 1910, with all its ramifications in the districts of southern Tibet, brought about was a new awareness of an hitherto dead, inactive, peaceable frontier which seemed suddenly to spring to life and activity. Before long the British awoke to the grim realization that Chinese troops had not only moved into Pome and Pemako but that even Zayul and Myitkyina, bordering on the eastern extremity, were not safe from Chao and his men.

Compared to Chao's, the British pace had been more deliberate, if far slower. It may be recalled that in December 1905, Noel Williamson took over as Assistant Political Officer, Sadiya, from J F Needham who, 'through his exploration and discoveries' over a period of a quarter century (1882–1905), had laid the 'foundations of the modern north-east' Assam. Until his gruesome murder in 1911, Williamson did a remarkable job of work in building up where Needham had left.

One of Williamson's first tours, in December 1907, was up the Lohit towards Rima, his object being to make himself 'acquainted' with the people and their country and 'to collect information' regarding the practicability of a trade-route towards south-east Tibet. Williamson did not reach Rima and, in fact, remained this side of Walong. His conclusions bordered on the optimistic. *Inter alia,* he noted that just then

> south-east Tibet has no industries because she has no incentive for the development of her resources . . . (but) once the Tibetan learns that every hide and every pound of wool has a marketable value in Assam, which can be reached quickly, comfortably and safely . . . commercial interchanges are assured and the expenditure on the route justified . . . there can be no objection to attracting the Tibetan to trade with us by constructing a good bridle path from the borders of Tibet to Sadiya, a place which in a short time will be in close proximity to the terminus of the Dibrugarh-Sadiya railway.[8]

[8]Williamson's letter, No. 233-G, dated 27 February 1908, cited in *Reid*, p. 211.

Meantime, under the impact of developments in Tibet, the government of East Bengal and Assam—Bengal had been partitioned in 1905—had come out openly against the then accepted policy of non-intervention. Dacca argued that the extortions demanded by the Abors from timber-cutters and traders in British territory, should cease. Besides, non-intervention had been barren of results, except in terms of 'interference' with the 'development of trade'. What was worse was that

> half a century of proximity to civilisation has failed in any way to redeem the tribes from their native savagery.[9]

While the Lt.Governor advocated a firm abandonment of the policy of non-interference, he refused to endorse Williamson's two specific recommendations of pushing the 'Inner Line' forward or relaxing the restrictions on crossing it. Nor did he agree with the Assistant Political Officer's recommendation that the line of police posts should be advanced to the foot of the hills, i.e. to the then 'Outer' Line.

The government in Calcutta was not easily persuaded on abandoning a time-honoured policy; all that it agreed to therefore was to allow Williamson to undertake a tour between the 'Inner' and the 'Outer' Lines in order to ascertain the actual state of affairs. Accordingly, in March 1908, such a tour was undertaken from Pasighat, through the foothills, south-west to Ledun and then on through the Pasi Minyong and Galong country to the Sinyong river at Dijmur.

In February 1909, Williamson penetrated to Kabang, a village not hitherto visited by any European. He noticed that there was no Tibetan influence in the area. A logical deduction made was that insofar as the tribal people recognised that the country up to the foot of the hills was British territory, a settlement with them would be easier to work out. The tribals were also found to be amenable to the influence of money.[10]

In 1909-10 Williamson repeated his earlier Lohit tour of 1907-8 and went as far as Rima, partly with a view to constructing the Digaru-Miju bridle path but more towards establishing contacts in that area. He described Walong as 'a hovel with five inhabitants', found no trace of Tibetan influence there and advanced as far as a stream, Tatap Ti by name, where this influence seemed to start. Here the Tibetan Governor of Rima visited him on 4 February 1910. Williamson gathered the impression that in Rima the authority, either of Tibet or of China, was very slight nor could he find any trace of a conflict between the two.

Later that year, however, disturbing news of Chinese penetration poured in. In its letter of 26 May (1910), the Government of East Bengal and Assam

---

[9]Ibid., p. 213.
[10]East Bengal and Assam to India, 29 June 1909, in *IOR*, P & E F 1910/13.

reported that a large force of Chinese troops had occupied Rima, demanded taxes and issued orders to the Mishmis to cut a road to Assam. Presently, the Lt. Governor was to confirm that the Chinese had effectively occupied Rima and planted flags at the river Yepuk, 2 miles to the west of Walong or 30 miles to the west of Rima.

Early in 1911, Williamson again penetrated into the Mishmi hills and repaired to Walong. He noticed that the Chinese had put up flags outside Tibetan territory. Even if Walong were to be considered a part of south-east Tibet, Williamson argued, it was clear that Peking had no business going as far south as Menakrai or Menilkrai where its flags had been planted. The Assistant Political Officer also noted that the fact that the Chinese were in full possession of Rima did not appear to 'arouse any resentment' on the part of the Tibetans.[11]

Whatever Lhasa's reaction, Assam was very worried. The latter felt, and strongly, that Chinese influence should not be allowed to extend up to the Outer Line: ' that would overawe the hill-tribes of our border and dominate ' all the tea-gardens north of the Brahmaputra. Besides, it argued, the Mishmis should be brought ' definitely ' under British control.

A few months later the foot-loose Bailey, on his long intercontinental odyssey, arrived at Sadiya travelling all the way from China, via Batang and Rima. *En route* he had noticed not only large numbers of Chinese troops in that twilight region but evidence of their growing influence. He discovered too a great deal of friendliness for the British among the Miju Mishmis.

Even as Bailey was on his way, Williamson, accompanied by Dr Gregorson of the tea-gardens around Tinsukia, in Lakhimpur district, had set out from Pasighat on 8 March (1911) with a view to ascertaining the extent of Tibetan influence in the Abor country. The tour—the two reached Rotung on 20 March—was expected to last about six weeks. On 30 March, however, Gregorson was murdered at Pangi and, a day later, Williamson at Komsing. Three of their companions who escaped, reached an Abor village near the mouth of the Dibong, from where tidings of these ghastly murders were broadcast.

The news aroused a veritable hullabaloo, both in India as well as in Whitehall. While the Assam Government made it clear that in crossing the Outer Line Williamson had acted contrary to instructions, it admired his enthusiasm in the quest of better and more detailed information.[12] Calcutta endorsed this view and underlined that his

fault was that of a zealous officer anxious to obtain information which he believed would be valuable, and willing to run a certain amount of risk in getting it.[13]

[11]*Supra*, n. 1.
[12]East Bengal and Assam, Report No. 197-CG, 22 April 1911, cited in *Reid*, p. 220.
[13]India, No. 850-EB/dated 8 May 1911, Loc. cit.

In the larger whole of India's tribal policy, the murder of Noel Williamson marked the end of an epoch. Before it took place, the general problem of Chinese encroachments was already causing anxiety. Thus early in July (1910) the Lt. Governor of Assam had asked Calcutta as to the degree of recognition that was to be extended to the Mishmis and the attitude to be adopted *vis-à-vis* the Chinese occupation of Rima. Later, the Governor-General, Lord Minto, confided to the Secretary of State that as a result of the ' proceedings of Chinese in Rima and vicinity of tribal tracts on the North East Frontier ', the question of ' future relations ' with these tribes was a cause for concern. Additionally, the military authorities considered that, *vis-à-vis* the Chinese, ' the existing position is strategically unsound ', that it would be unwise in any case to surrender the Mishmis to China more so as they regarded the British to be their protectors. Again, Minto argued, was it advisable to allow ' a possibly hostile power ' to thrust itself in upon the Indian frontier ' nearer than we can legitimately ' prevent?[14]

Whitehall's reaction was tepid if only because of the impending change in the incumbency of the Governor-General in Calcutta.[15] After Hardinge took over, the Lt. Governor of Assam broached the subject afresh, explaining at length the policy that prevailed at the time and the change that he now advocated. A personal interview with the new Viceroy followed, but failed to carry conviction.[16] Refusing to be brow-beaten, the Governor expressed himself in forceful prose. He pin-pointed the major difficulty of having outposts which were not located on the Outer Line because ' such a string of positions ' on the foot of the hills would be ' too unhealthy ' to occupy. If, however, the posts were pushed up and located ' on the spurs of the hills and above malaria height ' it would necessitate establishing British suzerainty, apart from obtaining the consent of the hill people. This seemed desirable for

> in view of the possibility of the Chinese being pushed forward it would be a mistake not to put themselves (the British) in a position to take up suitable strategic points of defence.

Hence the need for taking a ' more active ' line. The latter was to take the form, *inter alia*, of tours in the hills bordering the frontier, improving trade routes to the principal villages and making presents to the neighbouring tribes ' for friendly service and information.' It was necessary too to maintain the existing position, thereby preventing the Chinese from further encroachments. For ' if China presses forward, we must forbid ' its further progress, and the sooner the better. Broad policy apart, of immediate moment, however, was the fact of Chinese intrusion into the Mishmi country and here the Governor felt strongly,

[14]Governor-General to Secretary of State, 23 October 1910, *supra*, n. 1.
[15]Secretary of State to Governor-General, 25 October 1910, *supra*, n. 1.
[16]The interview took place in Calcutta on 22 November 1910, *supra*, n. 1.

We should be well-advised to take our stand here—to allow the Chinese to intrude here would make the defence of the Lakhimpur district difficult and would not be in agreement with the accepted Burma frontier line. I have already advocated this view in my official representation, and I wish to make it clear that I do not recede from that position.

Lord Hardinge, however, was not easily persuaded:

We do not see our way at present to recommend the more active policy... we recognise that the action of the Chinese may ultimately compel us to fix a line beyond which no further advance can be permitted. But we see no necessity at present of incurring the risks and responsibilities entailed by a forward movement.... Should it be possible to obtain further information about the country beyond the Outer Line without risk of complications, we should be prepared to authorise explorations for the purpose.....[17]

On this debate, Williamson's murder made a powerful impact. That it could not be allowed to go unavenged was obvious enough. What the provincial government proposed was to make the punitive military expedition, which normally followed such outrages, an occasion for achieving a number of objectives, the most important of which was the extreme urgency of obtaining an adequate knowledge of the country for determining a suitable boundary with China. This, in turn, entailed the despatch of a number of exploration parties. One such was to go to the Mishmi country with a view not only to prevent that tribe from joining the Abors but to obtain information as to the nature of their land and the limits of their authority. Further this party was enjoined to erect cairns and boundary stones which would be useful in the event of future negotiations with China for frontier demarcation. A mission was also to be despatched to the country occupied by the Miris.

Between December 1910, when Lord Hardinge's government turned down, without qualification, the 'more active' policy advocated by his predecessor,[18] and endorsed by the Assam provincial authorities, and September 1911 when it completely reversed itself, certain important changes were readily discernible. Thus, in the earlier instance, while it recognised that Chinese action may 'ultimately' compel it to fix a line beyond which no further advance could be permitted, it refused to accept the necessity, 'at present', of incurring the risks, and responsibilities, entailed by a forward movement into the tribal areas which then lay beyond its control. Again, while Calcutta wanted more information about the country beyond the 'Outer Line', it felt that it was important that in doing so there should be no 'risk of complications'. Understandably, it was unwilling to permit 'any general increase of activity' in the

---

[17] D O letter from Sir Lancelot Hare to Lord Hardinge, *supra*, n. 1.
[18] India to Secretary of State, 22 December 1910, *supra*, n. 1.

direction of further explorations, nor would it be a party to 'any promise' being held out to the tribes, for help or support, in the event of Tibetan or Chinese aggression.

Williamson's murder took place in March (1911). By June, Lord Hardinge was advocating, in the interests of 'general peace and security' of the frontier, an armed expedition. That, however, was to be the thin end of the wedge for advantage was to be taken 'to survey and explore' the tribal area as far as possible with the ultimate objective of gathering enough information for determining a 'suitable boundary' with China. The Mishmi mission, as has been noticed, was charged with erecting cairns and boundary stones 'on a suitable frontier line'—a fact that would strengthen the Indian position when negotiations with China did eventually take place. It was nonetheless clear that it

> was not proposed to advance our administrative frontier . . . and, in the event of our demarcating our external limit we should explain that we regard it as the line within which no Chinese officials should come and that we should periodically send a small police column.[19]

'Recent events' on the Burma frontier, Calcutta further reminded the Secretary of State, had shown the urgent necessity of coming to an understanding with China, of preventing Chinese intrigue in India and of keeping that country removed, 'as far as possible', from 'our present administrative' area.

Before many months passed, on 21 September (1911), India, in a comprehensive despatch, listed 'further developments in the Chinese policy of expansion' which it found 'impossible to ignore.' *Inter alia*, it referred to the fact that no sooner had Hertz's expedition on the Burma-China frontier withdrawn, than the Chinese attempted to assert their influence in that region. Besides, in April (1911), a party of Chinese had appeared in the Aka country, close to the administrative frontier of Assam, while Chinese officials at Rima had sent summons to Mishmi headmen to appear before them, with the result that an annexation of the territory was feared. There was the additional news that, to put down disturbances in Pomed and Poyul, Peking had approved the despatch of a force down the Dibong river and towards the Abor country. From all this, Calcutta concluded, a complete reversal of the policy pursued hitherto was called for:

> Circumstances have thus forced us to revert practically to the original proposal of Lord Minto's government that endeavours should be made to secure, as soon as possible, a sound strategical boundary between China and Tibet and the tribal territory from Bhutan up to and including the Mishmi country, and this should, we consider now be the main object of our policy.

[19]Hardinge to Secretary of State, 29 June 1911 in *IOR*, P & E F 1910/13.

As long as such tribal territory lay between us and our peacefully dormant neighbour Tibet, an undefined mutual frontier presented neither inconvenience nor danger. With the recent change in conditions, the question of a boundary well-defined and at a safer distance from our administrative border admits of no delay.

Elsewhere in its despatch, India refered to the advent ' of a new, aggressive and intriguing neighbour ', affirmed that it rejected the idea of a ' third or intermediate line ' between the existing ' Inner Line ' and ' the new external boundary ', and refused to approve of the boundary being regularly demarcated until the limits of locally recognised Tibetan territory were correctly established. As for an interim policy towards the tribes, it was to be one of loose political control, the objective being a ' minimum ' of interference compatible with the necessity of protecting the tribesmen from ' unprovoked aggression ' and of preventing them from ' violating ' either British or Chinese territory.

It is important however to underline the fact that there was no intent to do anything behind the back of China. For, as the despatch made clear,

as soon as the boundary has been roughly decided, a formal intimation should be made to China of the limits of the country under our control.[20]

The tasks assigned to General Bower, leader of the Abor Expedition, included, apart from exacting severe punishment and reparations for the murders of Williamson and Dr Gregorson, the establishment of British military superiority in the estimation of the tribes, visits to as many Minyong villages as practical, and a survey of ' as much of the country ' as possible.

It would be obvious that the political objective of the Abor expedition and its confluents, the Mishmi and the Miri missions, was to establish friendly relations with the tribesmen so as to bring them under a measure of ' loose political control '. Its geographical objective was to explore and survey as much of the country as possible and, on that basis, to submit proposals for a boundary between India and Tibet, although no such boundary was to be marked on the ground. Tentatively the basis for the boundary was to be the line approximately determined in 1911.[21]

Despite the fanfare of publicity that surrounded it, and on General Bower's own admission later, the achievements of the Abor expedition were not very impressive, unless, of course, the decision to sub-divide the whole frontier into three parts be reckoned as one. A subsidiary of the Abor venture was the Mishmi mission placed under the political control of Dundas.[22] The objective here was Rima, or as far as the place where the Chinese had planted flags

---

[20] Hardinge to Crewe, 21 September 1911, Ibid.
[21] India to Major General H Bower, 25 September 1911, Ibid.
[22] India to W C M Dundas, 5 October 1911, Ibid.

between Menilkrai and Walong. Eventually, however, the mission was subdivided into two—one group undertaking a survey of the Sisseri and the Dibang valleys, another of the Lohit. The major objective was to enter into friendly relations with the Mishmis who were to be persuaded to accept an exculsive British political control. This did not present any difficulties, for Dundas who took charge of the Lohit group found the Mishmis well disposed, despite the fact that the Chinese had been making repeated overtures to win them over. The Dibang exploration party, however, was not able to go beyond Shingging and thus could not achieve much by way of examining the proposed boundary. In much the same manner, the Lohit group had to be withdrawn early in the season before anything could be done to determine a boundary in the north-westerly direction. The Miri mission too, owing to its own slow advance added to the tribe's hostile attitude (culminating in an attack on the party at Tali), was unable to get closer to the proposed new frontier.[23]

Based on the findings of the Abor expedition, and in consultation with General Bower, Assam, in February 1912, made certain preliminary recommendations for the future control of tribal territory. In essence, a three-fold division was recommended: a central section, comprising the Abor country; an eastern, embracing the Mishmis and Hkampti Long; and a western, comprising Tawang.[24]

To catch up on what had been left over, in 1913-14, Assam put forth an ambitious programme for survey and exploration work. Calcutta, however, over-ruled large segments of it and finally sanctioned: a 'promenade', on a small scale, to Walong; a short tour into the Dafla hills and a friendly visit by Captain Nevill, unaccompanied by an escort, to Tawang.

The Walong promenade with Captain O'Callaghan, then Assistant Political Officer, Sadiya, as its leader visited Rima. Among its recommendations it stressed the importance of carrying the Lohit valley road up to the frontier and of establishing a post as near to it as possible. In forwarding O'Callaghan's report, the Chief Commissioner expressed the hope

> that the Government of India will agree in his view that the impossibility of recognising a Chinese boundary in the neighbourhood of Menilkrai has been finally established and as regards Mr O'Callaghan's action in removing the boundary posts as thoroughly justified. He has all along held that our boundary should begin at the junction of the Tho Chu stream with Lohit, and that the road should be continued upto this point.[25]

In the case of Burma too, timely action by the Indian government helped to avert a major crisis. For, from reports received of the concentration of

---

[23]India to G C Kerwood, 5 October 1911, Ibid.
[24]A Bentinck, ' Political Report on the Abor Expedition ', 23 April 1912, in *IOR*, P & E F 1910/14.
[25]Chief Commissioner to India, 6 May 1914, cited in *Reid*, p. 250.

Chinese troops at various centres all along the frontier, it may as well have happened that Peking would have occupied positions west of the boundary line claimed by the British. In sum, a general forward movement of the Chinese was checked in time and a boundary, based on the watershed principle, was sought to be established. That the British were sold on the idea was no secret.

PART III   TOWARDS A TRIPARTITE CONFERENCE IN INDIA

Chapter 9

The October (1911) Revolution and the 'Outer Dependencies'

ON THE 10th day of the 10th month of the year 1911, the chance discovery, before its time, of a secret plot at Wuchang set the tumbrils of the revolution rolling in China.[1] Before many months had passed, the C'hing dynasty, badly shaken by the Boxer rising of 1900–1901 and the death of the Dowager Empress Tzu Hsi in 1908, seemed destined to be on the way out. By early in 1912, the Manchus called it a day and handed over to Yuan Shih-kai who, as leader of the New Army in North China, had, by December 1911, manoeuvred himself into a strong position. Later he was called upon to head the new Peking regime and seemed a rallying-point for all that could be salvaged—in the then prevailing situation, perhaps the only choice. As the Imperial Edict of February 1912 declared:

> Yuan Shih-kai, having been elected sometime ago President of the National Assembly at Peking, is, therefore, able at this time of change to unite the north and south, let him then with full powers so to do, organise a provisional Republican Government, conferring thereon with the representatives of the Army, of the people, that peace be assured to the people whilst the complete integrity of the territories of the five races, Chinese, Manchus, Mongols, Muhammadans, and Tibetans, is at the same time maintained making together a great state under the title of the Republic of China (Chung Hua Ming Kuo).[2]

Apart from the internal strains to which it was exposed, the Republic faced a situation in the 'Outer Dependencies' that was none too comforting. In December 1911, Mongolia, under the Urga Huthukhtu (who was crowned

---

[1] Ho Kan-chih, *A History of the Modern Chinese Revolution* (Peking, 1959), p. 7, compares the Revolution of 1911 to that of the Taipings' viewing it as ' most important in scope and influence' and an event that dealt ' heavy blows ' to both feudalism and imperialism.
  An interesting study of the Chinese revolution is in Wu Yu-chang, *The Revolution of 1911: A Great Democratic Revolution of China*, Third Edition, (Peking, 1964). Another recent study is Mary C Wright (Editor), *China in Revolution* (Yale, 1967). Also see V P Dutt, ' The 1911 Revolution of China', unpublished thesis, Delhi University, 1961.

[2] H F McNair, *Modern Chinese History: Selected Readings* (London, 1927), pp. 722–26.
  The Imperial Edict, dated 12 February 1912, is a remarkably comprehensive document laying down, *inter alia*, in seven articles, the terms accorded to the Manchus, Mongols, Muhammadans, and Tibetans as to their future status in the new Republican regime which Yuan was likely to head.   [n. contd. overleaf

'Khan of all Khalkha, the ruler of Mongolia and the Great Khan of the Empire'), proclaimed his country

> an independent state under a new government endowed with authority to manage its affairs independently of others...Mongols shall obey neither Manchu nor Chinese officials, whose administrative authority is being completely abolished.³

As would be noticed presently, the situation in Tibet was no whit better. Briefly, by the end of November (1911), Chinese garrisons in Yatung and Gyantse were becoming mutinous; by December, troops in Lhasa had deposed the Amban Lien Yu and replaced him by the ambitious General Chung Ying, commander of Chao Erh-feng's flying column to the Tibetan capital. Meanwhile the rebellious Chinese soldiery in Pomed, ill-clad and ill-fed and badly mauled in the fighting, began its slow trickle back into Lhasa. The news of the October Revolution released them from the few restraints of discipline and orderly conduct that they had hitherto accepted. What was more, Lhasa's political climate, with Amban Lieu Yu besieged by Chung Ying's men and an unfriendly, if not a hostile, Tibetan Government in power, acted as a further spur in unleashing them to indulge in an orgy of loot and pillage.

If the Czar's government had actively assisted the Bogdo Khan in his revolt, the hand of the British behind the Dalai Lama's attempt to return and defy Peking was tacitly, if not overtly, discernible. In the net result, on top of the civil war that raged fiercely in China, Yuan, on the morrow of his induction into office, found himself, *vis-à-vis* the Empire's 'Outer Dependencies', completely at his wit's end.

In Mongolia, the new Chinese President was keen that the Huthukhtu retrace his steps. Unable to use force, he now engaged in an animated correspondence with the Bogdo Khan, an exchange that throws an interesting light on the character of the two men and the stakes for which they were fighting. Driven to the wall, the Huthukhtu revealed his hand asserting that

> the declaration of independence and autonomy was effected before the abdication of the Manchu Emperor. Such proclamation has been made to the world, and I am not at liberty to make any alteration. If you insist on doing so, please consult with the neighbouring country to prevent any objection that might arise.⁴

For details of how the abdication was brought about 'at a time when the structure of the state was still undecided', and the role that Yuan Shih-kai played in the crisis see Pu Yi, *From Emperor to Citizen* (Peking, 1964), 2 vols., I, pp. 33–38.

³Cited in Peter S H Tang, *Russian and Soviet Policy in Manchuria and Outer Mongolia, 1911–31* (Durham, 1959), pp. 299–300.

⁴Cited in Aitchen K Wu, *China and the Soviet Union* (London, 1950), p. 42. Reference may also be made to Michel M Pavlovsky, *Chinese-Russian Relations* (New York, 1959), pp. 89–90.

Undeterred by this rebuff, and Russia's clear involvement as 'the neighbouring country' was patent, Yuan Shih-kai issued 'Orders' which were a clear indication of his determination, at least in word, to stop the rot before it was too late. Thus in a most solemn and 'unchangeable oath', he pledged himself to put an end to 'all the apprehensions and irregular measures' of the preceding regime and affirmed that he would treat the dependencies 'on a footing of equality' with China proper. Even as he did so, he entreated both the Bogdo Khan and the Dalai Lama—'who used to be a buttress on our north-west frontier'—to follow the wishes of the people as a whole.[5] As though anticipating the rumblings of a not-too-distant storm, Yuan declared:

> Now that the five races are joined in a democratic union... the term 'Dependencies' as used under the monarchy must, therefore, cease to be used.... For the future all administrative matters in connection with these territories (Tibet, Mongolia and Turkestan) will come within the sphere of internal administration.... Until the local politics have all been brought into harmony, all matters in Mongolia, Tibet and Turkestan should be dealt with in accordance with existing procedure.[6]

'Local politics' was no doubt a euphemism for the independence movements in these countries. As for the rest, it was apparently a holding brief—'until' these politics had 'all been brought into harmony'. Clearly the President was prepared to stay his hand till such time as he had a firmer grip over the then somewhat uncertain pulse of his country.

Yuan died half-way through the first decade of the Chinese Republic (1911–21), a period of great turmoil marked by three principal characteristics. To start with, the central power of the dynasty was gone, with nothing even half as effective to take its place. It followed that there was a lessening of efforts at reform from the top, a development that afforded widespread opportunity for local change and innovation. Applied to the concrete situations in the peripheral regions, which is a matter of some relevance to this study, the extinction of a central authority in Peking meant the emergence of an 'independent' Outer Mongolia and of a Dalai Lama in Lhasa who paid only lip service to the Presidential 'mandates' from Peking.

As briefly noticed, before the end of 1910 the Po-bas in Pomed had been partly successful in repulsing General Chung Ying's troops sent from Lhasa. By the first half of 1911, the tide had turned decisively and a Chinese battalion in Kongbu, deputed to put down the revolt in Pomed, had to be reinforced. Not that it worked, for the expedition was a failure, severe losses were incurred,

---

[5]For the full text of the Presidential 'Order' dated 25 May 1912, see Jordan to Grey, 31 March 1912, No. 28 in *Foreign*, October 1912, Proceedings 12–45.

[6]For the Presidential 'Order' of 21 April 1912, see Jordan to Grey, 27 April 1912, Sub Encl. 2 in No. 36 in Ibid.

and the defeated troops, with their morale and discipline at a low ebb, gradually trickled back into Lhasa.

In sharp contrast to his shaky hold in Pomed, Chao's success in the districts of East Tibet had been, on the surface at any rate, phenomenal. He had been successful in setting up a nominal Chinese administration over the entire country from Tachienlu to Chamdo. The tribesmen for their part were content with a change that left them as much as ever to their own devices while the newly-inducted Chinese magistrates were tactful and refrained from any interference in their (tribes') day-to-day affairs.

As an earlier chapter has spelt out at some length, certain factors had militated against these apparent Chinese successes. The first related to the lamaseries which, understandably, were not able to reconcile themselves to the threat posed by Chao and his policies. Thrown out from their lands, and gompas, they were waiting in their thousands, across the border, for a favourable opportunity to regain their lost influence. The lamas apart, a greater threat to Chao's empire came from his own troops. Long disaffected, but kept under control with ruthless severity, they were now becoming openly rebellious. Mutinies among them had not been unknown—viz. at Lamaya in 1908 and Hsiang Cheng in 1910—but on each occasion the mutineers had been completely wiped out.[7]

Chao, who for a few months in 1908 had acted as the Viceroy of Szechuan, handed over his charge in the Marches in the summer of 1911. It was clear that the Viceroyalty at Chengtu was a well-deserved tribute to the success of his mission—a Chinese administration over the entire March country. The Warden had even mapped out a blueprint to carve a new province of Hsi-kang comprising parts of Szechuan and of Tibet, and extending to Giamda, not far from Lhasa itself! It turned out, however, to be an academic exercise, for Chao's proposal ' never received ' Imperial assent nor, so far as Tibetan territory was concerned, could it ever be put into effect. And yet the frontier, according to Chao's ' abortive blueprint ', was transplanted into Chinese maps; what was more, British map-makers, accepting the ' fictions of Chinese cartography', showed a similar line![8]

As has been remarked, in Tibet the news of the October Revolution was a signal for the mutiny of Chinese troops who killed some of their officers, deposed the Amban at Lhasa and looted several towns. These depredations had aroused the Tibetans to reprisals against Chinese officers and men who were gradually driven out or killed while the force in Lhasa found itself surrounded by a hostile populace.

The revolutionary fever proved highly infectious for, by the beginning of 1912, the insurrection had spread to eastern Tibet and the Marches where a large force of Tibetans, controlled from Lhasa, assisted in the revolt. By June,

[7] Report from Louis King on ' Chinese Administration in the Tibetan Frontier Region ', in *Foreign*, March 1912, Encl. in No. 219, Procs. 1–251.

[8] Richardson, *History*, p. 100.

Chinese posts at Hsiang Cheng, Sangai, Gonjoh, Draya, Sampa, Kantse, and Litang were captured. At Shobando, another body of troops was disarmed and permitted to return to China. Early in July, the Tibetans attacked Holiou but were repulsed and, in September, the Chinese garrison in Zayul was annihilated.

Chao Erh-feng, who had barely taken over at Chengtu, fell a victim to this incipient rebellion that now engulfed the land. A protégé of Chao, Yin Chang-heng, was responsible for his execution—it is believed he did it with his own hands.[9] Yin, young in years, appeared to have a goodly measure of confidence both in his own capacity as also the ability of his troops to put a disorderly house in order.

To start with, however, his prospects looked bleak. There was a Chinese army beleaguered in Lhasa; Hsiang Cheng, the nerve-centre of a good deal of trouble to Chao, had broken away from the Chinese hold; at Chamdo, the Chinese garrison, under the command of General Peng Jih-sheng, found itself under a fierce attack from about 3,000 monks of the large gompa in the town. Apart from these isolated pockets, China's line of communication in the Marches was exposed to raids by armed nomads and it was clear that until the roads were safe, no troops could be moved.

To place Chao, and developments in east Tibet in 1910-12, in their proper perspective, it may be useful to catch up with the Dalai Lama's Tibet during these eventful years. It may be recalled in this context that with the arrival of General Chung Ying's flying column in Lhasa, early in 1910, the Dalai Lama had taken flight. In contrast to 1904, he had on this occasion headed towards the south, seeking refuge and shelter with his former adversaries. After a singular, if vain, endeavour to seek active British support and intervention, he reconciled himself to the inevitable. At Whitehall's behest, Calcutta had made it clear to the Lama that there could be no question of restoring him to his throne or of ending Chinese oppression in Tibet which, to Morley, would be synonymous with interference in the internal administration of the country.[10] All that the British could do was to recognise the *de facto* government with whom they would deal.

[9] S C Yang, 'The Revolution in Szechuan, 1911-12', *Journal of West China Border Research Society*, VI, 1933-34, pp. 64-90, gives an eye-witness account of Chao's murder. This happened after Chao had given up the Chengtu governorship and was getting ready to go to the Tibetan border with his men and was allegedly involved, along with his deputy Fu Song-wu, in 'a revolutionary counter-attack'.

Richardson, *History*, p. 102, refers to Chao falling 'an early victim to Republican vengeance'.

[10] No. 532 in *Foreign*, June 1910, Procs. 276-550.

Years later Bell recorded:

When I delivered the message to the Dalai Lama, he was so surprised and distressed.... He could not...realise the extent to which we were tied and the attitude of the Home Government.

Bell, *Tibet*, p. 113.

From Tibet and the Dalai Lama's standpoint, it was far from being a satisfactory position. The Lama's subsequent efforts, through a meticulous listing of Chinese breaches of their solemn pledges, their manifold acts of oppression and usurpation of his administrative power in Tibet, their conversion of large areas of the Marches into a new province (Hsi-kang) of China,[11] one and all failed to move the British. Years later Bell recalled that when the letter embodying government's decision not to intervene on his behalf was delivered, the Lama read it 'three times' and 'couldn't speak' for some time afterwards. His ministers too were 'surprised' as well as 'distressed.'[12]

Nor did the Lama derive much satisfaction from an attempt, ingeniously contrived behind the back of his Indian hosts, to appeal to the Czar to come to his rescue. For the innocuously-worded, non-commital, Russian reply was, to the Lama's great embarrassment and chagrin,[13] routed through the British!

Even as the Lama wrestled with the problem of British/Russian intervention on his behalf, throughout 1910, and the greater part of 1911, Chinese influence in Tibet had grown steadily. Not only were the country's principal towns—Gyantse, Shigatse, Phari and Yatung—garrisoned by Chinese troops; what was more, Tibetan officials were systematically stripped of all power, and some were even superseded by their Chinese counterparts. Another characteristic of Chinese domination was the intensity of the anti-British campaign. Remonstrances and protests from Calcutta evoked repeated affirmations of a scrupulous regard for the terms of the treaties while evasive, and even untruthful, replies were returned to specific complaints of these breaches or infringements.[14] Nothing seemed to avail, as the intensity and rigour of the stranglehold continued to grow.

It was at this stage that the news of the October Revolution on the mainland shook the rickety Chinese superstructure in Tibet to its very foundations. Reports from Yatung, and Gyantse, suggested that Chinese officials, afraid of the mutinous conduct of their men (now reduced to a mere rabble which refused to obey orders), were seeking refuge with the British Trade Agents located at these outposts. As has been briefly noticed, before the year was out, General Chung at Lhasa had deposed the Manchu Amban (Lien Yu) and later made him a prisoner in the Yamen. In his place, Chung proclaimed himself to be Lien Yu's successor, declaring at the same time his adherence to the cause of the Revolution. Chung was popular with the soldiers and through them, it seemed, was making a bid to consolidate his position.

The situation, however, was fluid and soon got completely out of hand. A major contributory factor was the rebellious soldiery that now began to trickle back from Pomed and Po-yul. As briefly noticed, it was ill-fed and ill-clad,

---

[11] No. 133, in *Foreign*, August 1910, Procs. 58–246.
[12] Bell, *Tibet*, pp. 114–115.
[13] Ibid., p. 115.
[14] Para 17, Memorandum on 'Situation in Tibet', in *Foreign*, March 1914, Procs. 1–251.

badly beaten in battle, and with a sizeable part cruelly slain. No wonder its morale was at a low ebb. The news of the Revolution on the mainland now acted as a further spur to its lawless and disorderly conduct and, on their way to Lhasa, the troops indulged in large-scale arson and loot. Thus, apart from his own men in the Tibetan capital, Chung now found himself saddled with a disorganised rabble that may either refuse to accept him as its commander, or having accepted him refuse to be amenable to his discipline.

Nor was that all. For the rebellious troops apart, there was another powerful factor to reckon with: the ingrained hostility of the Tibetans to Chinese rule. While it is true that, on the morrow of the deposition of Lien Yu, General Chung had, under a threat of looting the Potala, extorted nearly a quarter million rupees from his Tibetan hosts, this had only served to add fuel to the fire. For the unruly conduct of the Chinese army in Lhasa, re-inforced by the arrival of troops from Pomed, led to an orgy of indiscriminate looting and arson in the capital itself where the hideous tales, indubitably exaggerated, of what the troops had done on the way, helped to exacerbate an already tense situation. In March 1912, large-scale fighting broke out in the Tibetan capital.

As it progressed, Chung Ying's position, never very strong, became increasingly untenable. This was partly because the small Chinese garrisons in Gyantse and Yatung soon surrendered their arms, accepted passage money and got ready for their long, arduous journey back home. Nor did fitful negotiations in Lhasa on their behalf yield any results, for what Chung Ying demanded—withdrawal of his forces, through the advanced Chinese positions in the Marches—the Tibetans were not prepared to concede. Besides, the Chinese would not accept Tibetan promises at their face value as, understandably, each side suspected the other for the worst. With negotiations falling through, Chung's troops besieged the Sera monastery, then known for its pronouncedly anti-Chinese leanings. The siege proved abortive but, in the process, the Chinese found themselves prisoners in the barracks at Trapchi with a hostile Lhasa populace, fanned no doubt by the Dalai Lama's clandestine emissaries, crowding around and demanding blood. The Chinese troops too were 'worn down' by the overwhelming mass of the 'untrained yokels' attacking them.[15] Before long fighting spread, outside Lhasa, to Shigatse and Gyantse. Nor did the Tengyeling monastery in the capital itself,[16] notorious for its pro-Chinese leanings, escape notice.

Chung Ying's position, bad as it was, became much worse when his own soldiery, apart from a hard core of loyal bodyguards, turned rebellious. What was disturbing (to Chung) was their inadequate supply of food and funds, nor could his depleted ammunition have borne the brunt of a protracted siege. To contend, therefore, that he was, 'in theory', more than a match for 'the monk

[15] Bell, *Tibet*, p. 120.
[16] Ibid, pp. 120–21.

army' that opposed him,[17] would be to fly in the face of harsh realities. To be candid, Chung's position was, both in theory and in fact, increasingly difficult—with every day that passed, it became worse; towards the end it was almost impossible.

There was, however, a solitary string to his bow that might yet bear results and this was the possibility of help reaching him from his compatriots in East Tibet. It is true that the situation there, in the initial months of the Revolution at any rate, had threatened to get completely out of hand, for the young, and impetuous, General Yin's execution of Chao Erh-feng, briefly referred to, had proved to be a signal for widespread disorder. What was worse was that all through the March country, large armies of disgruntled lamas, long threatened by Chao's revolutionary reforms, stood in battle-array, supported by their superstition-ridden and ignorant laity, made up mostly of local tribesmen. Thus at Chamdo, 3,000 of the monks, helped by a still larger number of the local populace, besieged the Chinese garrison under General Peng Jih-sheng. The latter, however, soon rallied and though the cost was heavy—the gompa at Chamdo was completely razed to the ground—appeared to weather the storm.

Even as Lhasa and the March country were seething with revolt, in far-off Peking President Yuan Shih-kai proclaimed Tibet to be one of the five races, now 'joined in a democratic union', with its administration a part of the internal administration of the country.[18] That sentiment was dutifully echoed by Yin Chang-heng, Chao's successor in the Marches, and General Peng, the commander of the Chinese garrison in Chamdo. Tibet, declared the latter, was a 'buttress on a national frontier' and as it was of 'most vital importance' to China, there was an element of urgency in despatching a relief column to Lhasa. It was with this (relief) column that the hopes and aspirations of Chung Ying, as no doubt of the deposed Amban Lien Yu, were closely intertwined.

To this much-talked-of reinforcement, India was resolutely opposed and for good reason. Any change in the *status quo* in Tibet, it argued, especially one brought about by forcing the country to enter into the Chinese fold, would be undesirable. As it turned out, Chinese control in the trade marts (1907–11) had brought matters to a head for the British, no less than for the Tibetans. With fresh reinforcements all along the border, there would be a further serious threat to the north-east frontier, no less than to the independence of Nepal, Bhutan and Sikkim. Accordingly, Calcutta urged a strong protest in Peking with a special emphasis on countermanding the proposed expedition.[19] When the protest was actually lodged, Yuan Shih-kai maintained that the expedition in question was authorized to deal only with the state of disorder in the Marches and, without specific orders, would not proceed further. Asked to give a

---

[17] Lamb, *McMahon Line*, II, p. 373.
[18] *Supra*, n. 6.
[19] Nos. 273, 289, 339 and 348 in *Foreign*, July 1912, Procs. 70–336.

categoric assurance that it would not cross the Tibetan frontier without previous consultation with the British Government, the Chinese President prevaricated. He did, however, disclaim any intention of making Tibet an integral part of China or of instituting any change that would conflict with his country's treaty obligations.[20]

From Lhasa, the expedition seemed distant and the promise of relief that it held out equally illusory. Less a visionary and more a pragmatist, General Chung Ying was, therefore, more interested in coming to terms with the Tibetans who laid siege to his fastness where his position had progressively continued to deteriorate. By May (1912), the Tengyeling monastery, in which part of the Chinese remnants had now sought refuge, came within range of Tibetan fire. What was more, barring a small number of his trusted bodyguards, Chung Ying had lost control over his own men. No wonder he preferred a direct settlement.

Even as Chung sought out a compromise, the Tibetans too had been driven to much the same conclusion. It was well-known that the monks were sharply split—and right down the middle. Lhasa's largest monastery, Drepung, openly sided with the Chinese and later, even after some of its leading monks were executed, gave only half-hearted support to the cause of the Dalai Lama. Tengyeling's loyalty to the aliens was no secret either, nor the fact that its monks 'fought openly' for the Chinese.[21] Thus among the principal four, Ganden and Sera alone had supported the cause of Tibet and of its absentee ruler.

There were other factors too. At the outset was the well-known anxiety of the Dalai Lama to end his years of exile in India and repair home. Again, the Panchen, who in the Dalai Lama's absence had played a somewhat compromising role, was keen to mediate between the Chinese and the Tibetans, hoping thereby to ingratiate himself with the master of the Potala. Besides, the Nepalese who had borne the brunt of the disturbed state of affairs in Lhasa, in terms both of loss of goods and trade, were keen that peace return to the Tibetan capital. In a viable compromise, the British too had a stake if partly because a flourishing colony of Ladakhi Muslims in Lhasa, including its leaders, had found themselves besieged in their mosque by a none-too-friendly Chinese soldiery.

With both sides feeling their way towards a settlement, a truce of sorts was arranged, early in May. Unfortunately it proved to be still-born—lasting, as it did, less than three days! What undid it was the mounting distrust that gnawed at both ends; an air of mutual suspicion, a lack of faith in each other's bona fides.

It was at this stage that the British began to weigh seriously the possibility of mediating between the two sides in the person of the Sikkimese Police Officer, Laden La. The latter's qualifications for the job were impressive. Son of

[20] No. 372 in Ibid.
[21] *Supra*, n. 16.

Lama Ugyen Gyatso, Laden La, as India's liaison officer with the 13th Dalai Lama during his two years (1910–12) of exile, had done a good job of work and inched his way close to the Tibetan ruler. His new mission was to ensure that the Chinese, should they lay down their arms as a result of a settlement with the Tibetan government, would not be molested. Their peaceful withdrawal from Tibet, India argued, was a goal for which any price was worth paying. This was the more desirable in that Nepal was known to be intransigent, and had insisted that it would use its army to exact reparations if the situation worsened. It was thus evident that the longer the fighting continued, the harder it would be to restrain the Gurkhas.

Earlier, in June (1912), after a good deal of cogitation, the Dalai Lama decided to cross over into Tibet. The situation was difficult and Lord Hardinge argued, with a measure of reasonableness, that if the Lama were attacked by the rebellious Chinese soldiery, the British position would become untenable. It followed that the latter could scarce remain indifferent and yet the slightest modicum of intervention on the Lama's behalf could lead to trouble with the Russians who would be quick to point to a clear breach of the covenant of 1907!

Again, it was patent that once the Dalai Lama set foot on Tibetan soil such voluntary restraints, as worked on him while he was in India, would no longer hold good.

Bits and pieces of news from Tibet lent further credence to British fears. For, at Phari, present to greet the Tibetan ruler was Dorjieff, fresh from his travels in Mongolia and St. Petersburg! Was the ghost of Russian intrigue in Tibet, through the person of the Buryat, being revived all over again? Later, at Ralung, 30 miles from Gyantse, the Dalai Lama met the Panchen and, to all appearances, patched up with him. That the Tibetan ruler was keen about the earliest possible evacuation of Chinese troops was apparent from the fact that he told the British Trade Agent at Yatung that, should his efforts to settle with the Chinese at Lhasa fail, ' he would ask Mr Bell to mediate '.[22]

Even as the Dalai Lama was on his way to the capital and, by reason of increased lawlessness in the country, his progress had been deliberately slow, the Chinese garrison at Lhasa was in a perilous state. About the same time Peking had informed the British Minister that to relieve the Lhasa garrison it had ordered the immediate advance of a combined expedition from Yunnan and Szechuan. It maintained that the rescue of the garrison was demanded by a strident public opinion and that, if countermanded, the Chinese position in Tibet would become untenable, and may later have to be retrieved by use of *force majeure*. Pressed to state his own opinion, Jordan made it clear (to Peking) that if an attempt were made to solve the question by force, it would precipitate a crisis that might well prove fatal to the Chinese Government.[23]

[22]Bell, *Tibet*, p. 121; *Portrait*, p. 134.
[23]No. 210 in *Foreign*, October 1912, Procs. 59–282.

A few days later, Yuan Shih-kai resiled from the stand taken up earlier by his minister. He affirmed that though pressed into making an advance into Tibet, he had no intention of sanctioning one. Nor did he intend incorporating any portion of Tibetan territory into China; instead, he preferred to work through the Dalai Lama.[24]

[24]No. 219 in Ibid.

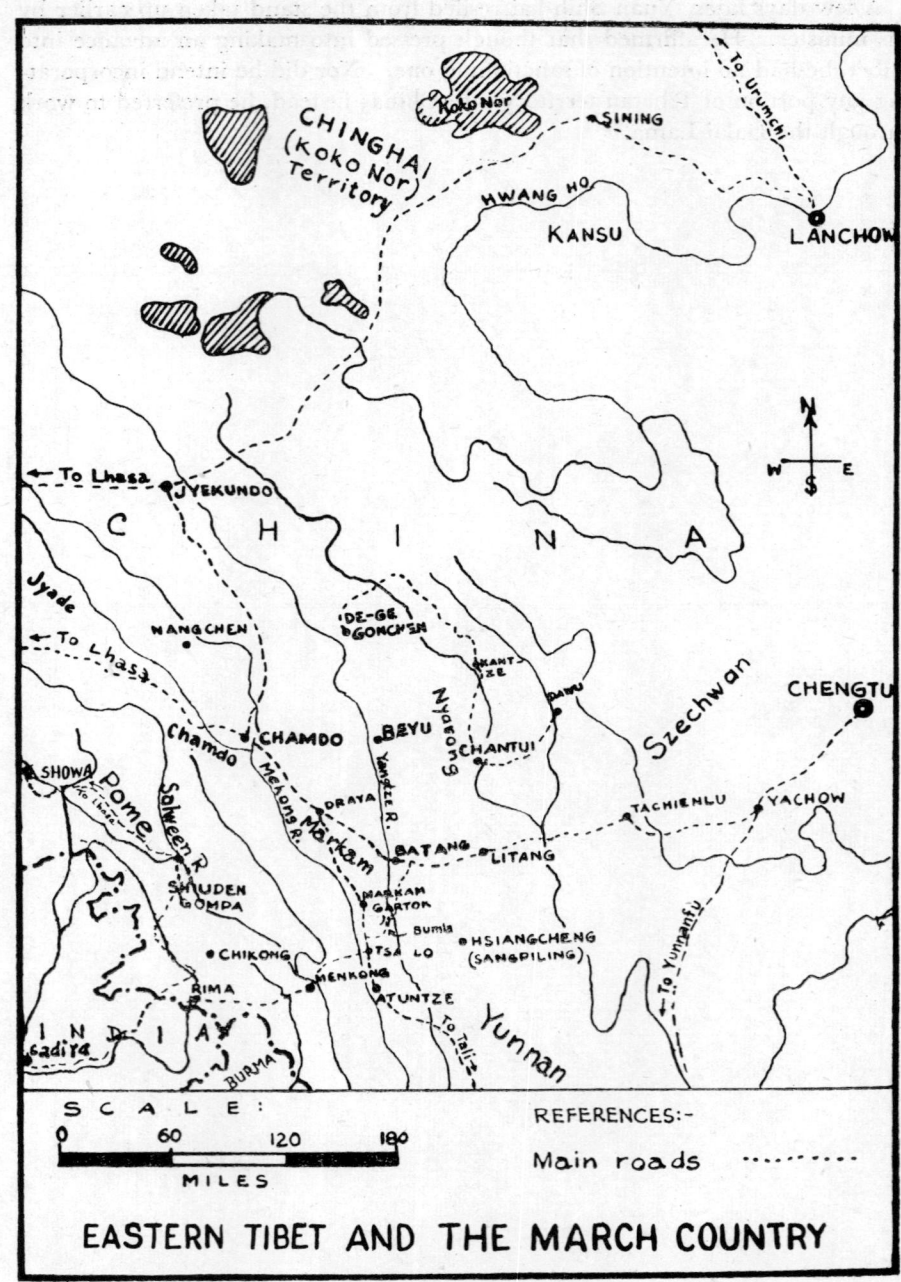

MAP 1: EASTERN TIBET AND THE MARCH COUNTRY

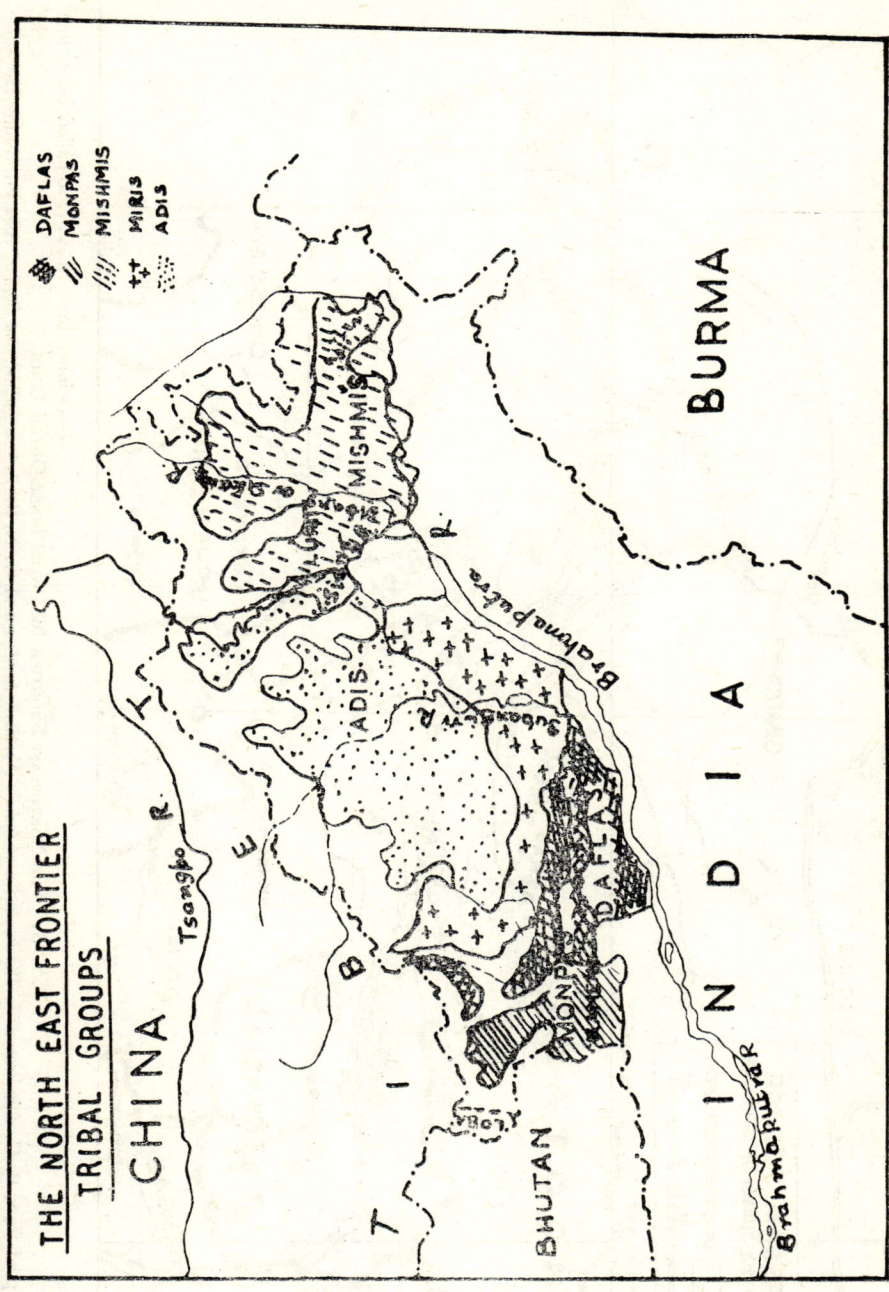

MAP 2: THE NORTH-EAST FRONTIER TRIBAL GROUPS (© Government of India, 1969)
Based upon Survey of India map with the permission of the Surveyor General of India.

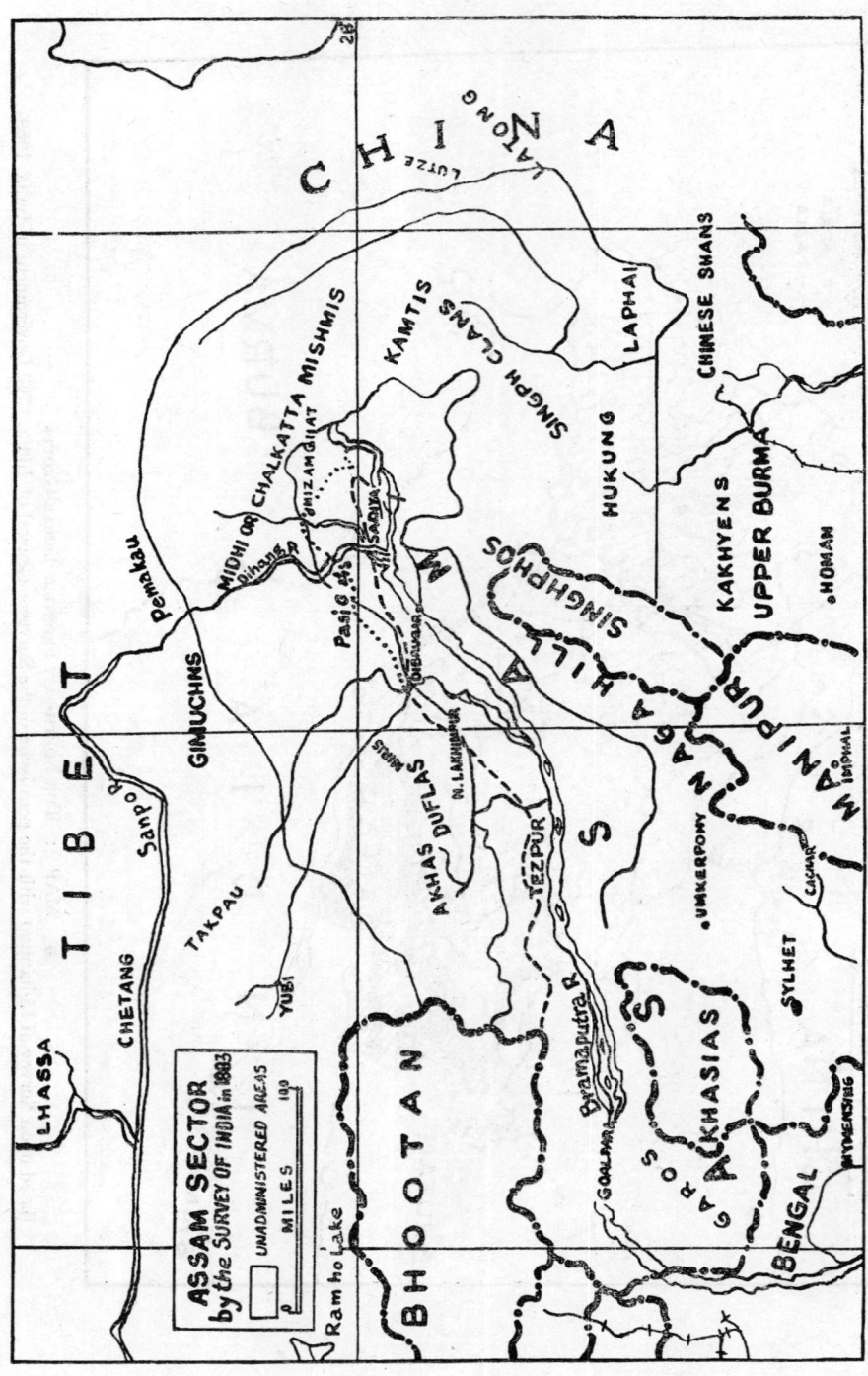

MAP 3: The North-East Frontier 1883 with Inner/Outer Lines

Adapted from P. C. Chakravarti's *The Evolution of India's Northern Borders* and G. N. Rao's *The India-China Border*, Asia Publishing House,

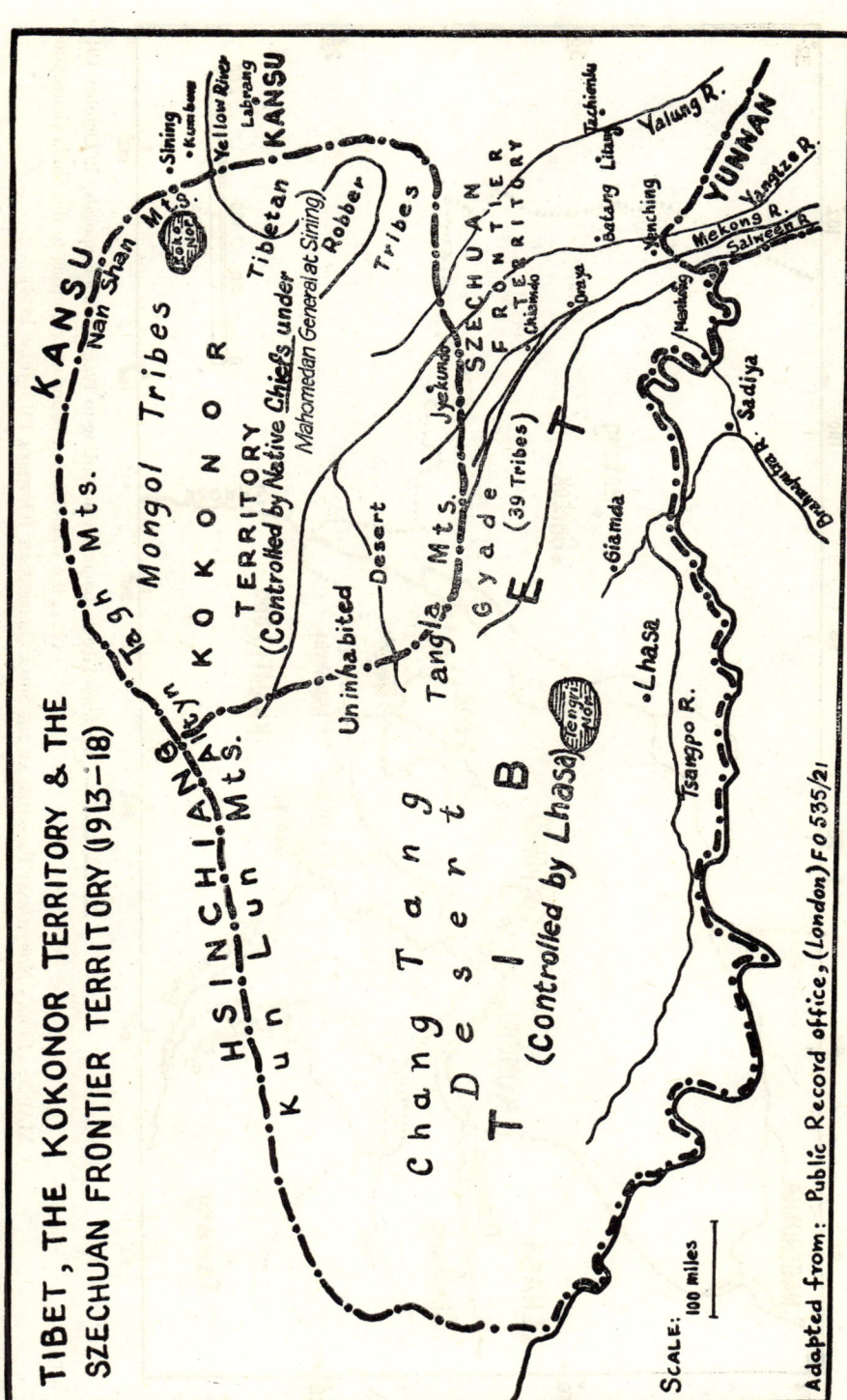

MAP 4: TIBET, THE KOKONOR TERRITORY AND THE SZECHUAN FRONTIER TERRITORY (1913–18)

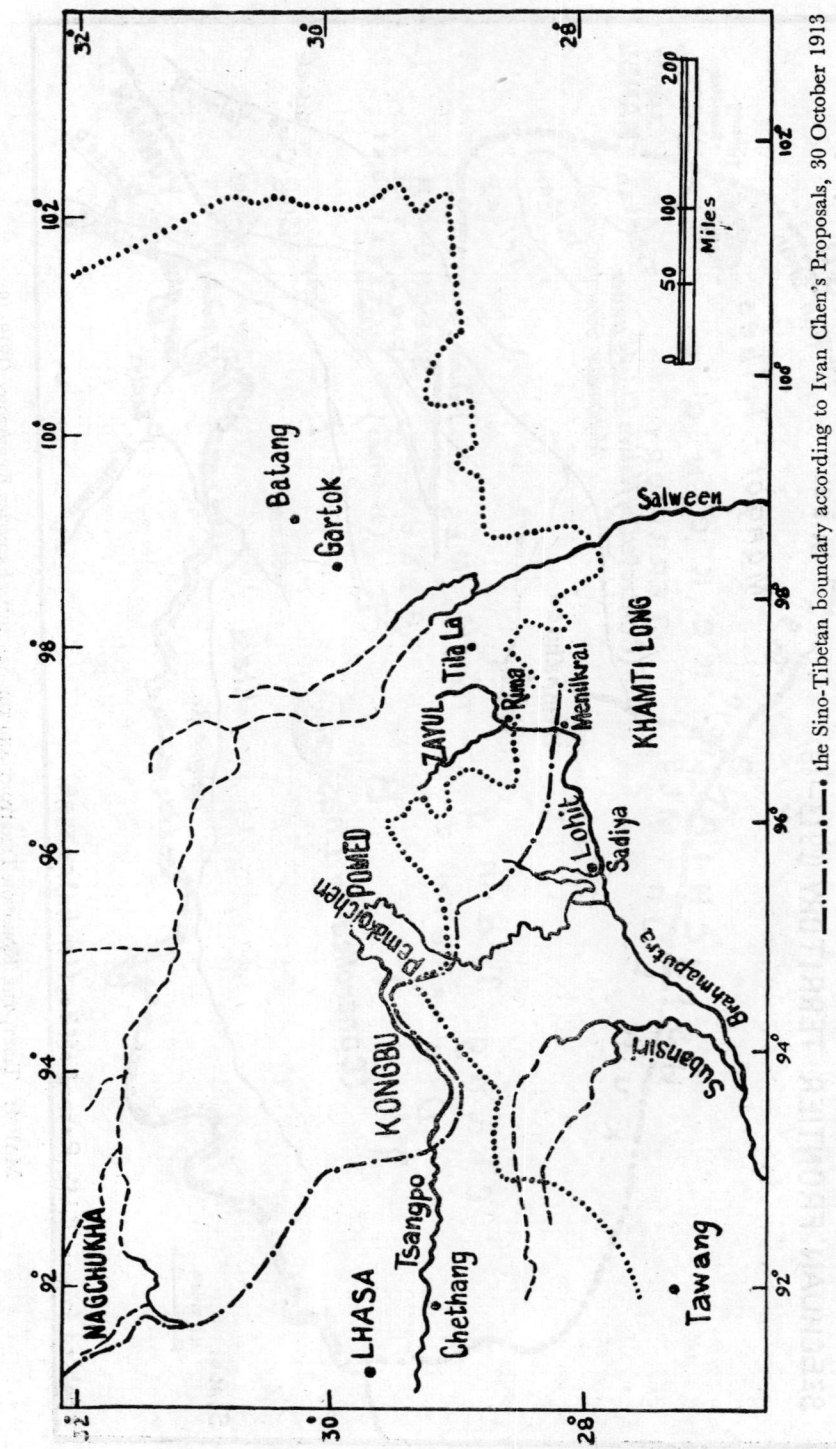

MAP 5: INDIA'S NORTH-EAST FRONTIER AT THE SIMLA CONFERENCE (OCTOBER 1913–JULY 1914)

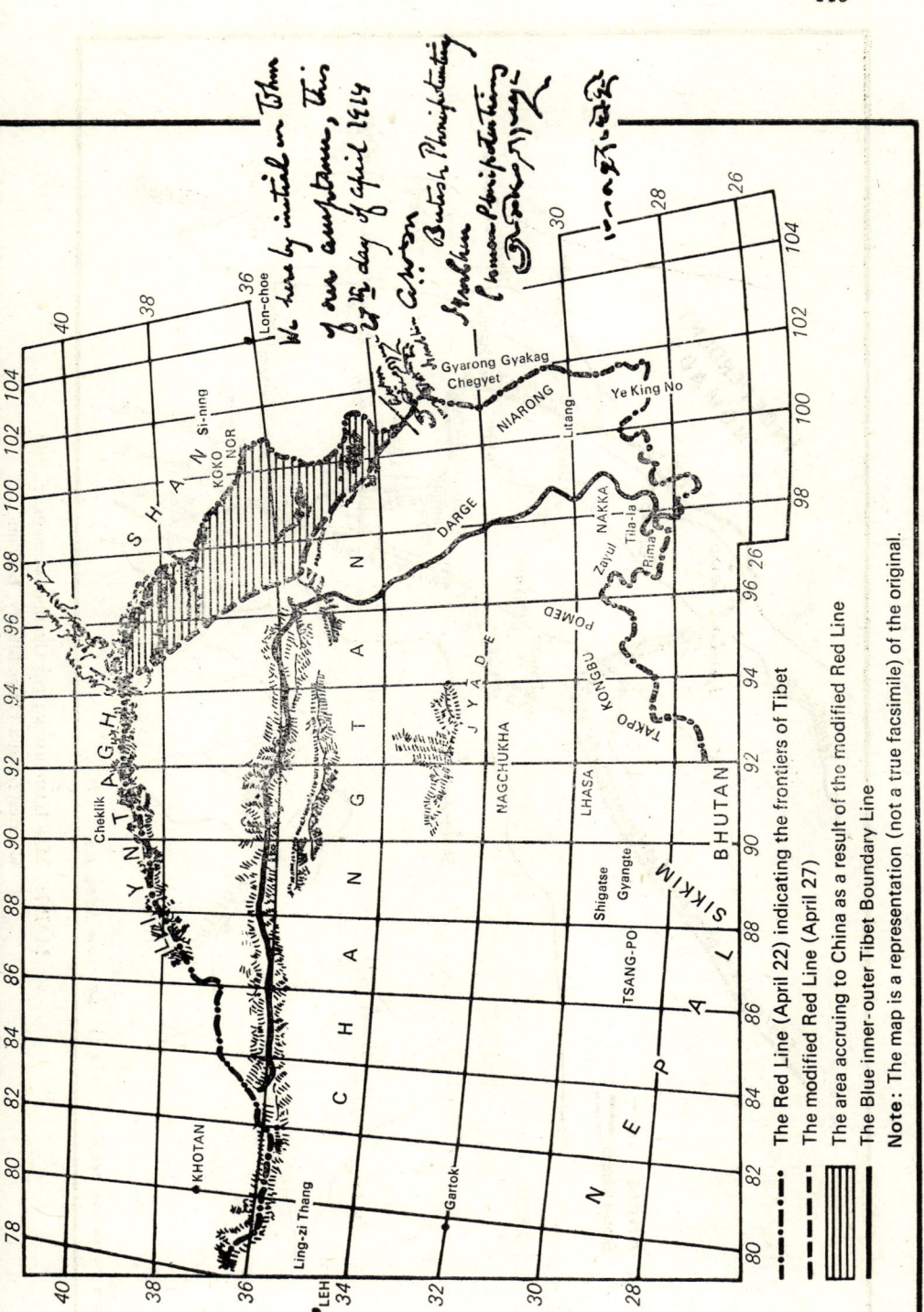

MAP 6: THE RED AND BLUE LINES OF THE SIMLA CONFERENCE

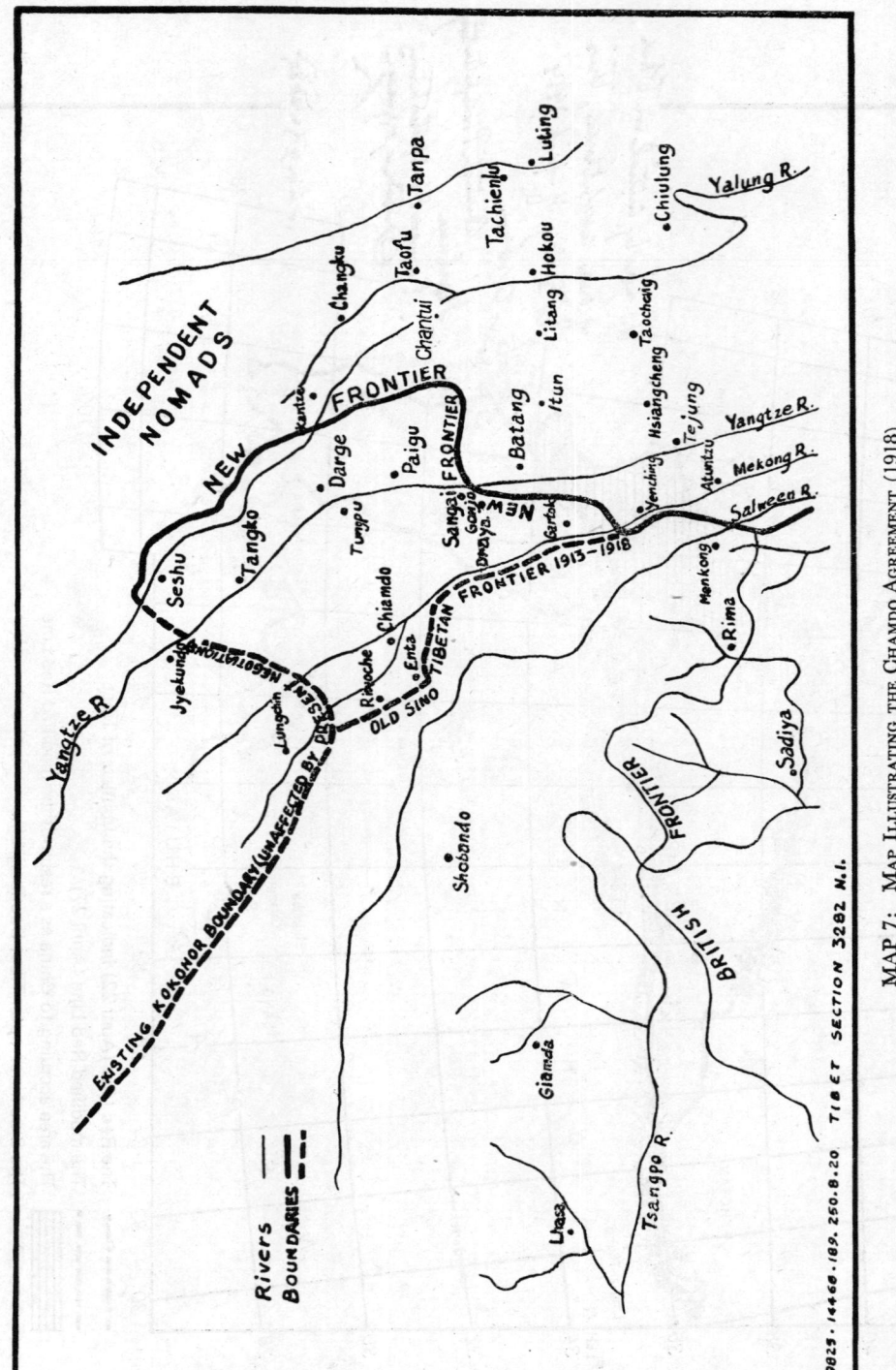

MAP 7: Map Illustrating the Chamdo Agreement (1918)
Courtesy: India Office Library, London

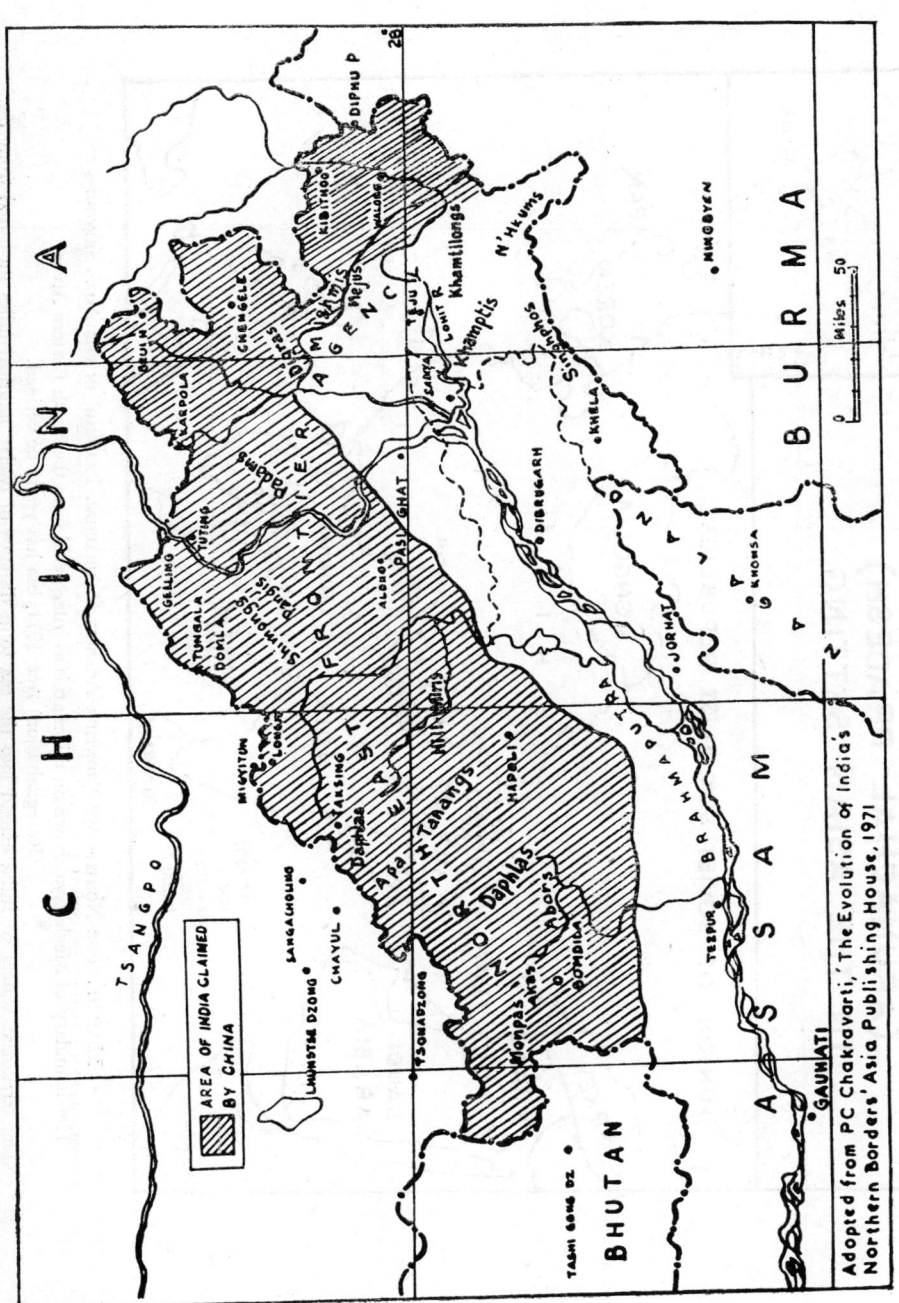

MAP 8: THE MCMAHON LINE: CHINESE CLAIMS

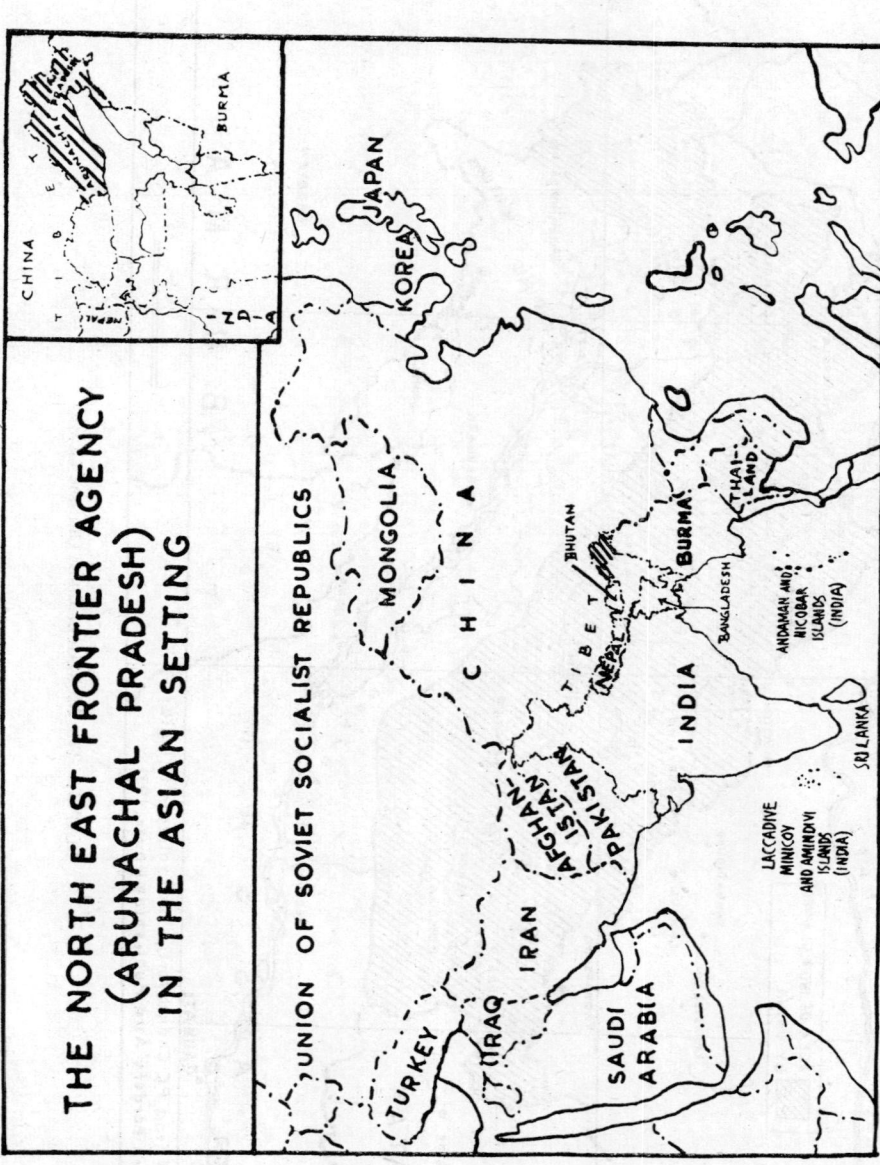

MAP 9: THE NORTH-EAST FRONTIER AGENCY (ARUNACHAL PRADESH) IN THE ASIAN SETTING

The boundary of Meghalaya shown on this map is as interpreted from the North Eastern Areas (Reorganisation) Act, 1971, but has yet to be verified.

The territorial waters of India extend into the sea to a distance of twelve nautical miles measured from the

Chapter 10

Chinese withdrawal and Tibet's 'Independence'

THE OCTOBER (1911) Revolution had a profound impact, and not only on the internal politics in China. Mongolia's declaration of independence followed almost immediately. It helped, if only indirectly, in a gradual erosion of Peking's authority over large parts of western China. Szechuan itself was in the throes of a rebellion and in no position to reverse the gears in Tachienlu, or Chamdo for that matter. Before long the infection had spread to Lhasa and, to Peking's discomfiture, could not be arrested.

The Dalai Lama, it may be recalled, had left Kalimpong on 24 June (1912), on his way back to Lhasa. His exile of a little over two years had brought about a complete metamorphosis in the situation, as evidenced by a considerable change in the British attitude towards Tibet. From a curt refusal, in 1910, to entertain his repeated pleas for restraining the Chinese, there was now a welcome realisation that his authority needed to be buttressed. Thus the tone of the Governor-General's farewell message to the Lama was in such welcome contrast to the earlier attitude when the 'leading idea' was to refuse him 'all political encouragement'.[1] Now, as Hardinge spelt it out, his great 'desire' was

> to see the internal autonomy of Tibet under Chinese suzerainty maintained without Chinese interference so long as treaty obligations are duly performed and cordial relations preserved between Tibet and India.[2]

This change in the British position synchronised with an easing of tension all along the frontier as Chinese power, and capacity for trouble and intrigue, vanished overnight. Instead, anxiety now was riveted on the Lama's return and installation in the Potala so that he may well prove a rallying centre for the forces of order and check thereby the fissiparous and divisive elements, unhappily very powerful. Another desideratum was the evacuation of the mutinous Chinese soldiery, and possibly without any mishap.

It was this latter consideration which was responsible for the slowness of the Lama's pace. Early in July, he and his entourage had reached Phari, at the head of the Chumbi valley. Later that month he reached Gyantse. From then on, however, his progress came to a dead-halt as he settled at Sam-ding, on the placid shores of lake Yamdrok. He entered Lhasa in January (1913),

---

[1] Bell, *Tibet*, p. 122.
[2] No. 357 in *Foreign*, July 1912, Procs. 70–336.

by which time the problem of Chinese troops had been solved reasonably satisfactorily.

A reference has been made earlier to a truce between Tibetan and Chinese forces in Lhasa in May (1912) which soon broke down owing to their mutual distrust. Since the British had refused to mediate—Laden La was recalled and his mission countermanded—for fear of offending the Russians, the Nepalese representative in Lhasa, Lieutenant Lal Bahadur, was pressed into service. After a great deal of acrimonious discussion, an agreement was finally wrought in August. According to its terms, the Chinese were to store their arms in a warehouse which was to be guarded jointly by their men, as well as the Tibetans and the Nepalese. Besides, unarmed Chinese troops were to be guaranteed safe passage to the Indian frontier, and provided for on the way by Tibetan authorities, while Chinese traders or businessmen who remained behind in Lhasa, were to receive protection from Tibetan authorities.

The Lhasa agreement was welcome news to the Indian government. For Peking had been anxious about the safety of its troops and Yuan Shih-kai had specifically asked Jordan that Indian authorities lend a hand in effecting their evacuation. It was finally decided that the British Military Attache in Peking, Lt Colonel Willoughby, should supervise the operation. The Colonel, who had a first-hand understanding of the organisation of the Chinese army and some knowledge of the language, did a fairly successful job. By October, nearly 1,000 officers and men, besides 180 women and children, had been evacuated; by March (1913), barring some stragglers under General Chung Ying, the bulk of the Chinese had been repatriated.

Broadly, Chinese troops in Lhasa fell into three categories. There was the old Amban Lien Yu and his bodyguard, then there was Chung Ying and his supporters, and finally the left-overs of the men who had arrived from Pomed and entrenched themselves in the Trapchi barracks and in the Tengyeling monastery. For fear their own arms be used against them by their enraged, yet unscrupulous captors, the Chinese troops had resisted their surrender to the very end, and when they finally did, took away the bolts of their rifles so as to make the weapons useless! And yet, despite their initial resistance, by September as has been noticed above most of the troops had left Lhasa and travelled over to Chumbi; by mid-October, a majority had crossed over to India.

Thanks to their own factional rivalries and the hostility of the Tibetan populace, what would normally have been a peaceful evacuation of disarmed troops became a tortuous operation. Republican China's overweening ambitions, evidenced by Yuan Shih-kai's not infrequent Presidential 'Orders', complicated an already difficult situation. Recognising that Chung Ying alone wielded the sceptre in Lhasa, and that Lien Yu did not, Peking in September (1912) appointed the former to be its Amban in place of the latter. What was more, Chung was asked to stay put.

When Chung Ying notified the Tibetan authorities about Peking's new directives they, not unnaturally, accused him of a breach of promise, and worse. What had been decided on 12 August seemed to be undecided again. Luckily for Chung, a powerful bargaining counter that came handy was the capture by his men of the premises where Chinese arms in Lhasa had been stored. On the debit side though was the uncomfortable fact that, since the closing down of the Indian frontier in August to any ingress or egress, his links with Peking had been snapped, for the only other route, through Eastern Tibet, was now completely inoperative. It was this fact above all which made it impossible for Chung Ying to keep his masters posted with the actual situation obtaining in Lhasa. The black-out of news was bad enough, what was worse was that this divorce from reality in Peking proved disastrous both for him personally as well as for the Chinese position in Tibet.

Consequent upon Chung Ying's deciding to stay back, fighting broke out afresh in Lhasa and threatened to be interminable. Meanwhile Basil Gould, then British Trade Agent in Gyantse, was able to persuade Lien Yu, the deposed Amban, to quit the scene. He did finally, early in December. This left behind only Chung Ying, with the rump of his bodyguard. An attempt to bring in the British as mediators in the person of Laden La, had proved, as briefly noticed earlier, infructuous, a fact that was sorely disappointing to the Tibetans. The Nepalese, being pressed in again, brought about a fresh truce signed on 14 December. This time, the (Chinese) arms dump was to be exclusively in Nepalese custody until Chung and his men had been evacuated safely to Chumbi; Lhasa, in turn, undertaking to provide the necessary commissariat in terms of transport and food. The latter also pledged not to mount any reprisals against such Chinese traders as may be left behind or, for that matter, against the rabidly pro-Chinese monks of the Drepung monastery. Additionally, the Amban's yamen was to be sealed until such time as a settlement was arrived at. An undertaking was also given that Chung Ying and his men would not be molested[3]—an assurance that, in the then tone and temper of Tibet, was doubly necessary.

Five days after the truce, Chung Ying left Lhasa. On the way, he stopped over briefly at Gyantse where he had an opportunity to meet Basil Gould. Reminiscing about this meeting nearly half a century later and referring to Chung as the ' last of Chinese to leave ', Gould recorded:

He was a mountain of a man, several inches over six feet and broad and thick in proportion. Two days out from Gyantse, I invited him to dinner. Christmas was near and I had with me a large turkey and the usual trimmings. Our appetites were healthy, but three times I carved him a helping twice as large as any of ours. Finally I handed to him what remained of the bird on its dish. Next day it was reported that he had enjoyed the hospi-

'Basil Gould records that the Tibetans treated the Chinese, on their way back to India, ' with courtesy and with ample supplies'. Gould, *Jewel in the Lotus*, p. 24. Also see Bell, *Tibet*, p. 122.

tality we had been able to offer and that on returning to his camp he had sat down to a proper meal.[4]

Nor was this the last of Chung Ying. His progress was slow, far slower than what the Tibetans had wanted or even the British in India desired. A major difficulty was the endless intrigue of which, right on the other side of Nathu La, he became both the focus as well as the instigator. On the one hand, he seemed to be encouraging the Nepalese to play a greater, and more active, role in Tibet and its affairs. On the other, he had established a close, if secret, liaison with the Panchen Lama who was at once pro-Peking and, pronouncedly anti-Lhasa. Meanwhile, through the notorious Lu Hsing-chi, of whom much more will be heard presently, Peking uninterruptedly, and emphatically, impressed upon Chung the desirability of remaining inside of Tibet.

Two things, however, finally weighed heavily against him. The first was a growing concentration of Tibetan troops in Chumbi where Chung Ying seemed to settle down in a manner of semi-permanent residence. At one time the Tibetans numbered 250 or thereabouts, a fact that made the Chinese General increasingly uncomfortable. What appears to have been a decisive factor against Chung Ying's continued stay was the disturbing news that Lien Yu, the ex-Amban in Lhasa whom Chung had deposed, had arrived in Peking and was actively engaged in undermining the latter's position. More than most, Lien Yu appeared to lay all of China's misfortunes in Tibet at Chung's door. And apart from this general charge there was the more specific, if serious, one of his being responsible for the murder of Lu Ching-chi, the Chinese commander of the ill-starred Pomed expedition. Evidently Chung must either vindicate himself or face the prospect of going down into oblivion in Republican Peking's then uncertain political milieu.

The long and short of it was that on the fateful 14 April (1913), Chung with his motley remnant of a half-starved, and demoralised, bodyguard crossed over the Nathu La into Sikkim. With his departure ended, for many a long summer, the last vestiges of whatever had been left of Chinese authority in the Dalai Lama's domain.

It is not without significance that the Lama himself did not step into Lhasa until Chung Ying and his retinue had withdrawn completely not only from the Tibetan capital but even from Gyantse. Chung, as has been noticed, left the Tibetan capital on 19 December—five days after the second truce, negotiated through the Nepalese. As for the Lama, he did not enter Lhasa until the third week of January (1913), by which time Chung had reached Chumbi and was thus safely out of harm's way. It is evident that there was an anxiety to avoid an ugly confrontation, should a clash unfortunately take place.

[4]Gould, op. cit., p. 25.

What was more, it was imperative that there be a clear demonstration that the Lama's return to his seat of authority should signify a great victory, all the more necessary as his flight, two years earlier, had been viewed as an unmixed debacle.

On the morrow of his return, the Dalai Lama set about mending his fences. Some of the monks of Drepung, the largest of Tibet's monasteries, were executed for their openly pro-Chinese affiliations. Even so a measure of how powerfully entrenched this group was, may be gauged from the fact that despite this weeding out of undesirable elements, Drepung's loyalty to the Lama's cause remained dubious, if also half-hearted. Tengyeling, too, was subdued. Later its monks were expelled and its large landed estates declared forfeit to the Tibetan government.[5] It was clear that the Dalai Lama must, with as great a show of force as possible, curb the activities of those elements in the body-politic who had always, in moments of crisis, revealed their extra-territorial loyalties. What was more, it was necessary to demonstrate that in Lhasa, that maelstrom of rival factions and internecine jealousies, the Dalai Lama's authority alone was supreme.

It has been noticed that in July 1912, the Dalai Lama had been greeted at Phari by the Buryat Mongol Aguan Dorjieff who had earlier, as a confidante of the Lama, played a decisive role in the crisis of 1903–4. Later, while still encamped on the banks of the Yamdrok Tso, not far from Lhasa, the news of the Russo-Mongolian agreement must have filtered through to the Lama. Concluded on 3 November 1912, the four-clause agreement had pledged Russian support to the 'autonomous regime' which the Mongols had established. Besides, Urga was to have its own 'national' army and to admit 'neither the presence of Chinese troops on her territory nor the colonisation' of its land by the Han.

A year earlier, on 30 October 1911—barely three weeks after the rising at Wuchang—the Mongol princes had declared their independence, forsaken their allegiance to China and elected the Hutukhtu as their grand Khan.

A month later, on 1 December 1911 to be precise, Urga had proclaimed its independence couched in a language that was at once clear and unequivocal:

> ....Our Mongolia in its original founding was an individual state—Mongolia proclaims itself an independent state under a new Government endowed with authority to manage its affairs, independently of others....Mongols shall obey neither Manchu nor Chinese officials, whose administrative authority is completely abolished.[6]

The Mongol 'declaration' followed what Professor Lattimore has called

---

[5] Bell, *Tibet*, pp. 120 and 122.
[6] Cited in Tang, *Russian and Soviet Policy*, pp. 299–300.

many 'preliminary debates' before this 'final plunge' into the unknown.[7] This is borne out by the fact that while the Mongol princes had declared their 'independence' and forsaken allegiance to China on 30 October, the formal declaration itself came on 1 December. Another four weeks were to elapse before the Hutukhtu was crowned 'Khan of all Khalkha' and the 'ruler of Mongolia and the great Khan of the Empire', at a largely attended assembly at Urga.[8] These dates would make it clear that Mongolia's 'independence' owed little to the 'collusion, common action or even consultation' with the authors of the October Revolution in China, which preceded it.[9] A lot, however, was due to the Russian (Tsarist) regime which had fully backed, and buttressed, the intrigues and seditionist (*vis-à-vis* China) moves of the Mongol princes. Thus early in December 1911—before the Hutukhtu was crowned —Russia's Irkutsk headquarters had delivered to him, and the Mongol princes, a sizeable quantity of firearms: 15,000 rifles, 75 million cartridges and 15,000 sabres.[10]

The four-clause Russo-Mongolian Agreement of November 1912, briefly alluded to above, made explicit what had been apparent all through, albeit below the surface. This was the fact that Russia's solemn undertaking to assist in maintaining the autonomous regime in Urga was to be buttressed by Mongolia's own 'national' army.

The impact of these developments in Mongolia on neighbouring Tibet, and the usually well-informed Buryat Dorjieff must have brought the Lama up-to-date on the shape of things, was far-reaching. Mongolia apart, the Lama's interests were sufficiently broad-based and, as the Indian authorities noted in 1912, 'seemed to include anything that was happening anywhere' in the world.[11] It is thus significant that in October 1912, with the Dalai Lama still out of Lhasa, the Tsongdu wrote to Lord Hardinge that the country had broken off its relations with Peking and would like all Chinese troops to be withdrawn. Whether this communication could be regarded as a declaration of Tibet's 'independence' is debatable for, on the surface at any rate, it was devoid of all the trimmings that go with a formal proclamation.[12] Clearly it lacked the seal of authority of the head of state, the Dalai Lama. More appropriately perhaps, it could be viewed—since Chung Ying, with his hold on the Chinese arms dump in Lhasa, still held his ground—as an attempt at seeking British intervention to throw out the Chinese, in much the same manner as the Mongols had sought Russian good offices to eliminate the Han from Urga.

[7]Owen Lattimore, *Nationalism and Revolution in Mongolia* (Leiden, 1956), pp. 51–52.
[8]*Supra*, n. 6.
[9]*Supra*, n. 7.
[10]*China Year Book, 1919–20* (London, 1920), p. 588.
[11]Gould, op. cit., p. 24.
[12]Lamb, *McMahon Line*, II, p. 398, while maintaining that it was not easy to interpret Tibetan attitudes towards their international status 'at this period', regards the Tsongdu's communication as 'tantamount to a declaration of Tibetan political independence'.

Meanwhile in Calcutta, several communications had been received from the Dalai Lama to the effect that the Chinese government be asked to withdraw all their troops and officials from Eastern Tibet and send their delegates to India to discuss matters. Later, writing to the Governor-General, the Lama is said to have announced the ' independence ' of his country and categorically asked to be helped in securing its autonomy.[13] Since Chung Ying had not so far left Tibetan soil, the British debated whether the Lama may not be well-advised to inform him that a delegate would be sent to discuss terms of peace with him, if he (Chung Ying) should retire.

Another version of Tibet's independence relates to Yuan Shih-kai's efforts to woo the Lama and the latter's categorical refusal to fall into the trap. It may be recalled that as early as March 1912, Yuan had issued a decree promising a complete change in the earlier Chinese policies *vis-à-vis* the Dependencies:

> Our people of Mongolia and Tibet, followers of the old religion, used to be a buttress on our North-west frontier, contented and loyal. But of late years the frontier officials have ill-performed their duties and have subjugated these pontiffs... to grievous oppression....But now that the form of Government has been changed to a Republic, and the five races ... have been placed on a footing of equality the President, do take a most solemn and unchangeable oath that all the oppression and irregular measures of the past will be abolished and done away with. Mongolia and Tibet should therefore all the more follow the wishes of the people as a whole and should maintain peace and good order.[14]

A few weeks later the President went a step further. He promised a new deal—hoping, it would seem, to stem the adverse tide that had begun to flow so powerfully with the declaration of Mongolia's ' independence '. *Inter alia*, he affirmed:

> Now that the Five Races are joined in a democratic union, the lands comprised within the confines of Mongolia, Tibet and Turkestan all become a part of the territory of the Republic of China and the races inhabiting these lands are all equally citizens of the Republic of China. The term ' dependencies ', as used under the Monarchy, must therefore, cease to be used and henceforth as regards Mongolia, Turkestan and Tibet complete scheme must be devised to arrive at a unified system of administration, and so promote unity in general among all races of the Republic. The reason why the Republican Government did not create a special ministry to deal with dependencies was that Mongolia, Turkestan and Tibet are regarded on an equal footing with the provinces of China proper. For the future all

[13] Para 40 in Memorandum on ' Situation in Tibet ', in *Foreign*, March 1914, Procs. 1–251.
[14] For the text see Jordan to Grey, 31 March 1912, No. 28 in *Foreign*, October 1912, Procs. 12–45.

administrative matters in connection with these territories will come within the sphere of internal administration. Now that the establishment of a single united Government is an accomplished fact, let all matters formerly dealt with by the Ministry of Dependencies be forthwith transferred to the control of the Ministry of the Interior, and all matters which belong to the province of other Ministries be handed over to the Ministries respectively concerned. Until the local politics have all been brought into harmony, all matters in Mongolia, Turkestan and Tibet should be dealt with in accordance with existing procedure.[15]

Yuan followed this by restoring the titles of the deposed Dalai Lama. Actually, as early as August 1912, after the Lama had been in Tibet for some time, he had informed the British Minister in Peking to this effect. Not long after, when the Lama was on his way to Lhasa and the Chinese position in Tibet seemed to be clearly lost, Yuan sent a telegram expressing regret for the excesses of the C'hing dynasty and announcing that he was restoring the Lama's official rank. This Presidential Mandate, of 28 October (1912), gave back to the Lama his former position and titles 'in the hope', Yuan declared, that he may prove 'a support to the Yellow Church and a help to the Republic'. The dismissal of the old Manchu Amban Lien Yu was confirmed, as also the appointment of the new incumbent, General Chung Ying. Blame for all the misdeeds of the past was saddled squarely on the Manchus and Lien Yu, their Amban. Chung, who was planning to leave, was ordered back and exhorted to stay put.[16]

The Lama responded to the Presidential overture by making it clear that he wanted no rank from Peking and had merely resumed what he thought to be rightfully his, namely the country's supreme spiritual and temporal authority. This message of the Dalai Lama is regarded by the Tibetans to be a formal declaration of their independence.[17]

President Yuan's effort to restore the badly-shaken Chinese position in Tibet was multi-pronged, a mixture at once of a great deal of diplomatic manoeuvring and finesse and, to sustain it, an armed expedition. Symptomatic of the first were deliberate attempts at placating the Lama's injured feelings. Thus the 'decrees' of March and April, alluded to above, were designed to demonstrate the new spirit of camaraderie, of equality, that was to prevail among the five races—a spirit in which the Tibetans, and the Mongols, would forget their past grievances against the predominant Han, and against all the oppressions and irregular measures of the past. Later, the President, realizing that the situation was fast deteriorating and threatened to get completely out

---

[15]For the text see Jordan to Grey, 27 April 1912, Sub Encl. 2 in No. 36 in Ibid.
[16]Teichman, *Travels*, p. 39, gives the full text.
[17]Richardson, *History*, p. 105.
Thus the god-king, Bell wrote, 'made clear his declaration of Tibetan independence.' *Portrait*, p.135.

of hand, restored the Lama his official rank, his former position and his titles—in the hope that he may yet cast his lot on Peking's side.

The diplomatic effort apart, the President had hinted at something sterner. Thus the April (1912) decree while conferring on (Mongolia, Turkestan and) Tibet the same status, on ' an equal footing ', as the provinces of China proper, had unmistakably referred to ' local politics ' being brought ' into harmony '. So far as Tibet was concerned an effort in this direction no doubt was the Szechuan expedition which was designed not merely to succour the beleaguered Chinese garrisons in Lhasa but to restore Peking's lost position in the Dalai Lama's domain.

The leader of the Szechuan expedition was General Yin Chung-heng who had been appointed ' Commander-in-Chief ' of the ' Chinese Western Expeditionary Forces '. Yin, young and flamboyant, and known in the Marches as the slayer of Chao Erh-feng, now headed a force of 100,000 men and openly proclaimed his resolve of proceeding to Lhasa to help re-establish Chinese sovereignty there.[18]

In retrospect, as the succeeding pages bear out, General Yin's loud boasts remained, at best, idle threats. But the fear they inspired, and the danger they posed to such respite as the Lama had belatedly won for himself and his harassed land, was enough to nullify all the pious platitudes about the Republic's noble intent. What was worse, the actions of Yin's ' plundering soldiery ' and the ' oppressive and unjust ' rule of (his) ' rapacious and unjust ' officials,[19] were clear enough demonstration of what the Republic meant, not so much in theory, but in practice.

As has been briefly alluded to, the in-fighting among the Chinese at Lhasa had led to the intrepid Chung Ying deposing the Manchu Amban Lien Yu and holding him a prisoner, along with his close bodyguard, in the Yamen at Lhasa. Since Tibetan authorities refused to accept Chung Ying as the new Amban—as a matter of fact, he too was besieged by a hostile Tibetan populace in the Trapchi barracks—Lien Yu played his cards with consummate skill. Starting with the premise that an Amban at Lhasa must be an essential feature of any eventual settlement, he visualised himself as the only choice. Subsequently, he told his captors that if they accepted the proposition that a Chinese representative, with a suitable escort, would be stationed in Lhasa, he would lay down his arms. It was much later and only when he realised that the Republican regime in Peking would rather have Chung Ying than himself as its nominee, that he gave up all pretence of coming to terms with it. It has been noticed earlier that eventually, through the persuasion of Basil Gould, Lien Yu did leave Lhasa and later crossed over into Sikkim.

Nor, in its essentials, was Chung Ying's approach any whit different. There

---

[18] *Yao-ting Sung*, pp. 84–85.
[19] Teichman, *Travels*, p. 41.

is no doubt that he regarded himself as the logical successor of Lien Yu and was keen that the authorities in Lhasa should accept him as such. It is significant too that in his decree restoring the titles and position of the Tibetan ruler, Yuan Shih-kai designated Chung as the new Amban, the successor of Lien whose dismissal he now confirmed. It is also worth noting that Chung remained in Lhasa to the very end, leaving only when his position there had become untenable. After Lhasa he hung on to the slender thread of hope that Chumbi proffered for he realised, as did Yuan Shih-kai in Peking, that his departure from the scene would be a calamitous, an almost fatal blow to all pretence of Chinese authority in Tibet.

Just before Chung Ying left Lhasa, President Yuan despatched a mission of pro-Chinese Lamas headed by one Yang Feng to help persuade the Dalai Lama to swear loyalty to the cause of the Republic. One of its members, a brother of Yang Feng, had earlier met the Dalai Lama in Darjeeling in 1910 in an attempt to persuade him to return to Tibet and accept the *fait accompli* of a Chinese administration running the affairs of his country. The Lama, as one may deduce, had proved stubbornly unyielding. Yang Feng's own mission, though well-disguised, was found out and the Indian Government refused it permission to cross their frontier into Tibet.

Denied direct access to pursue the Lama into Tibet, Yang Feng tarried on in Darjeeling until May (1913) and made a herculean effort to negotiate a settlement, over the telegraph lines! Among the principal terms that he offered the Tibetan ruler was an assurance that the whole question of Tibet's 'independence' would be open to discussion with his representative, that Lhasa would accept a Chinese Amban in the person of Chung Ying, and finally, that he would recognise the new Republican regime—in which case, the latter would be prepared to compensate him for such losses as its rebellious soldiery may have inflicted on his people. Should the Lama, however, still remain adamant, the threat of the Szechuan expedition marching in to subdue him was brandished in no uncertain terms. It is significant, that while Yang Feng's terms were being secretly communicated to the Dalai Lama Peking publicly announced that the Lama's titles had been restored and that Chung Ying had been formally appointed its new Amban!

Just about this time, Peking also announced the appointment of one Fu Shin-yen, charged with the mission of bringing about 'harmony' among the leaders and people of Tibet. So enthusiastic was Fu about the high ideals of his mission that he is said to have offered to bear the entire expense of his travels to Lhasa and back! Unfortunately for him, the mission proved still-born, for Fu never left Peking! Meantime another more romantic, if also elusive, character emerged who took upon himself the responsibility of restoring China's well-nigh lost position.

A nondescript Chinese trading firm in the populous 'Chinatown' of Calcutta was Thinyik and Company. What exactly its business was, or its trade, is not quite clear; a lot more though is known about its master, Lu Hsing-chi, or in its more anglicised version, S C Loo.[20] Finding how perilous the position of his country in neighbouring Tibet was, Lu decided to do something about it. And during 1913–14, to the extent determined effort, organisation and low intrigue could do the trick, he left no stone unturned to achieve his end. His ability was recognised by President Yuan with whom he was in direct communication and who appointed him first as the Amban-designate in Lhasa and, later, as Chinese Consul in India. Lu revealed himself a master of detail and had a clear grasp of the essentials of his country's policy towards Tibet, more especially as he conceived that policy ought to be.

In the initial stages, in the autumn of 1912, Lu advised Chung Ying to hang on in Lhasa as long as he could. Later, in Chumbi, Lu counselled Chung not to evacuate at any cost. He it was who urged him (Chung) to hold discussions with Nepal and persuade that country to affirm its allegiance to the new Republican regime in Peking. This would, Lu argued, help keep the Dalai Lama in his place.

Lu Hsing-chi's policy towards Tibet was a clever admixture of holding out the olive branch as well as brandishing the naked sword: due consideration for the Lama's known preferences, while repeatedly emphasising the despatch of the armed expeditions then being mounted from Szechuan and Yunnan. If partly, it was a hark-back to the Assistant Amban Wen Tsung-yu who had been partial to Tibetan susceptibilities and resigned rather than compromise on what he regarded a clear breach of a solemn undertaking. This related to the number of troops Chung Ying marched into Lhasa in the opening months of 1910.

Lu Hsing-chi's anxiety, as no doubt that of Yuan Shih-kai in Peking, was to coax or cajole the Dalai Lama into accepting the new Republican regime. The Lama's response, however, and this despite Lu's animated epistolary exchanges,[21] was cautious to a degree and, at best, an uncertain quantity.

After Chung Ying's forced withdrawal, Lu Hsing-chi, in a message to Peking, had strongly urged the restoration of the old Manchu title—'Resident in Tibet, administering Great Minister'—in his own person. This, he felt, was necessary to 'restore' China's 'sovereign rights' in Tibet.[22] Peking complied almost immediately and President Yuan, in a message to the Dalai Lama on 18 May

---

[20]In a D O letter, No. 6396 C, 29-30 July 1913, the Commissioner of Police, Calcutta, informed the Director of Criminal Intelligence, Simla that Captain A M L Vonck VD (Volunteer Decoration) had accepted the appointment of Private Secretary to ' Mr S C Loo, Amban-designate at Lhasa ' and proposed to accompany him there. Loo who had established his office in the premises where Captain Vonck resides ' and goes there daily', was awaiting the arrival in Calcutta of two Chinese officials. Correspondence in *Foreign*, March 1914, Procs. 1–251.

[21]An excellent source for these exchanges is the *IOR*, L/P & S/10/393, called ' Intercepted Telegrams ', which start as from 7 May 1913 and continue through February 1914. These afford an interesting sidelight into Lu's ' secret diplomacy ' to help restore China's position in Tibet.

[22]Lu Hsing-chi to Peking, 11 May 1913, No. 2350/13 in Ibid.

(1913), while announcing Lu's appointment as 'Administrator in Tibet' directed the Lama to send his officers to the Sikkim frontier ' to meet and escort' him to Lhasa in state,

> where he will be able to discuss and carry out all measures for future reform and for the restoration of the old system of administration... all contention will thus be allayed (and) general prosperity reign.[23]

Five days later, Lu followed up by announcing to the Tibetan Ministers that unless a Chinese officer ' enters ' their country and there ' discusses personally everything needing explanation', there would be mistrust and suspicion on both sides. For his part he promised—' on my arrival in Tibet '—to enquire ' minute(ly)', show ' no partiality ' and in every way ' promote ' the ' true union ' of the five races.[24]

To these fervid appeals, the Dalai Lama's reply, in a message to Lu, was brief: any venue for a meeting inside Tibet would ' present difficulties', for the misconduct of Chinese troops had roused suspicions. But if

> the troops were recalled and the Conference held at Darjeeling, matters would be more easily settled and peace more speedily attained.

To Yuan Shih-kai, the Dalai Lama was franker. While reminding him forcefully that Chinese depredations in Tibet were 'greatly at variance' with the ' tenor of your communications', he confessed that the latter had aroused ' grave ' doubts in Tibetan minds.[25]

On the very day the Lama telegraphed his reply, Yuan sent the Tibetan ruler another message in the reverse direction. It broadly sketched out the Republic's three-pronged policy. To start with, it intimated that ' Chiamdo and the other places mentioned', were included in Szechuan under the Manchus (and now constituted the new Republic's 8th ward) and since these had ' now devolved upon the Republic', their ' status *cannot* be altered'. Two, as to Darjeeling as a meeting place, no agreement had yet been worked out and therefore the President had ' directed' Lu to ' cooperate with you'. Three, the Lama should ' first discuss ' all outstanding questions with the Administrator (Lu) who would ' then communicate ' with the Central Government.[26]

It was evident that as between the two sides, there was no meeting ground, a fact that resulted in a complete breakdown of communications. Lu, however, was a man of considerable resource. Thus on 28 May (1913), while

---

[23]Peking to Lu Hsing-chi, 18 May 1913, loc. cit. The message was for transmission to the Dalai Lama.

[24]Lu Hsing-chi to Tibetan Ministers, 23 May 1913, loc. cit.

[25]The message to the President which bore the same date was an enclosure in Lu's letter. For the text No. 2572/13 in Ibid.

[26]President to Lu Hsing-chi for transmission to Dalai Lama, 4 June 1913 in Ibid.

reiterating his request to Peking for half a million dollars which he proposed to use 'solely in connection with my entry into Tibet', he told Yuan:

> Fortunately the Dalai Lama has not hitherto categorically disclaimed allegiance to the Central Government; the British also continue to regard Tibet as a dependency to China, we must cling to these threads of opportunity.[27]

To 'threads of opportunity', however tenuous, Lu did cling. One of these, besides those listed, was his secret contacts with the Panchen Lama who was the recipient of special favours and titles from Peking. In the early months of 1913, he was hailed as the 'Most Loyal Exponent of Trans-migration', an honour which the Panchen is said to have received in a 'kneeling posture' after making 'nine prostrations' and rendering thanks for 'this mark of celestial favour'.[28]

Besides Lhasa and Tashilhunpo, in Peking too Lu constantly urged that he must go to Tibet in order to score a 'distinct advantage' in the impending negotiations with Britain. Should the Dalai, however, prove recalcitrant,

> we can settle the question by force of arms (for) the Tibetans will be able to blame the Shachas (a corruption for Shapes?—the Cabinet Ministers) and we shall retain some foothold from which to restore our status in Tibet.[29]

It is significant that Chung Ying, the deposed Amban, had advised Lu to much the same effect namely, that the Tibetan question could 'only' be settled by 'use of force', direct or indirect.[30] Later Lu advocated that Pome should be divided into three parts which would become 'outposts' for an eventual Chinese advance into Tibet.[31]

But much more important than Pome was the restoration of Chinese control in East Tibet. For, in more ways than one, Lu argued, it held the key to developments in the Dalai Lama's domain. East Tibet's 'permanent occupation' and 'protection', he further emphasised, would mean that the whole of Tibet could be 'dominated', nor would the country then 'dare harbour' thoughts of 'revolt', much less the 'foreigners' be able to indulge in their 'ambitious' schemes.[32]

---

[27]Lu Hsing-chi to Liang Yen-sun, Private Secretary to President, 28 May 1913, No. 2671/13 in Ibid.

[28]Calcutta to Teng-yueh, 6 June 1913 enclosing letter from Tashi Lama, No. 2884/13 in Ibid.
In his covering letter, Lu bemoaned the fact that because of the surveillance exercised by the Dalai Lama's men, the Tashi Lama and others 'do not venture to send their correspondence freely'. This also helped to explain 'the great dearth of news' from 'Ulterior' Tibet.

[29]Lu to Peking, 13 May 1913, No. 2350/13 in Ibid.

[30]Lu to Teng-yueh, 25 May 1913, No. 2572/13 in Ibid.

[31]Loc. cit.

[32]Lu Hsing-chi to Cabinet, 9 June 1913, No. 2884/13 in Ibid.

In August (1913), the British closed the Indian frontier, making it impossible for Lu, or anyone from China for that matter, to cross into Tibet. This placed the 'Administrator' at a grave disadvantage, for he could never exercise the functions of his high office in Lhasa by being kept scrupulously in quarantine—a thousand miles away, in Calcutta! Failing with the Dalai Lama, Lu next turned his attention to his most senior Minister who had succeeded Tsarong Shape. Conscious that Shatra was 'extremely hostile' to China and had distinct leanings towards the British (Lu's 'foreigners'), he mapped out his new strategy. As he informed his principals in Peking, he would send a Tibetan messenger 'secretly' to persuade the Lonchen to come to India and have a 'personal' interview with him (Lu). Should he fall into line, there would be no problem but

> if his demands are excessive, there would be no difficulty in orders being passed from China, directing him to return to Tibet.[33]

Later Lu informed the Lonchen that the latter had been appointed one of the officials in Peking's Bureau of Tibetan and Mongolian Affairs and albeit his nomination had been notified in Peking a long time back, it was not certain if the Lonchen had received the intimation. Would he be prepared to accept the appointment, Lu queried.[34]

In his reply a few days later, the Lonchen evaded a direct answer to the question and instead branched off at a tangent.[35] Meantime, as the record makes it fairly obvious, the British Government were determined to frustrate Lu's efforts to exercise his functions as the 'officiating Chinese Resident in Lhasa'.[36]

Lu Hsing-chi did not stop there, nor did he take these warnings too seriously. His activities continued unabated and, as it happened, he was destined to play a most significant role in the events leading to the Simla Conference and later in ensuring that Ivan Chen did not sign the resultant convention. This fascinating tale of Lu's back-stage intrigue in sabotaging the conference will be recounted in subsequent pages.

[33] Lu Hsing-chi to President and Cabinet, 23 June 1913, No. 3096/13 in Ibid.

[34] Encl. 5 in No. 2, *Foreign*, March 1913, Procs. 12–51.

The letter was dated 1 August 1913 and Lu styled himself as 'Tangkwam', Administrator of Tibet. It referred to a telegram which Lu had received from Kunzang Norbu, Chief of Tsen-ni-yon, intimating him of Shatra's appointment.

[35] Encl. 6 in No. 2 in Ibid.

Lonchen Shatra referred instead to the proposed conference in Darjeeling, besides his own arrival in Chumbi and expressed the hope that Chinese delegates will arrive soon. 'It will be a good thing' if they did, he added.

[36] No. 34 in Ibid.

F O to *I O*, 28 July 1913, concurring in the proposal of H M Charge d'Affaires in Peking that Lu be warned of 'deportation from India' if he carried out the duties of his appointment.

Chapter 11

China and the British Memorandum of August 1912

IN SHARP contrast to Mongolia's, Tibet's declaration of independence was not as unequivocal, nor its severance of links with the 'great Motherland' as sharp and clear-cut. Part of the answer may perhaps, with justification, be attributed to the difference between Russian and British support to their respective protégés; yet whatever the reasons, the results were most revealing. Chung Ying's long-sustained, and heroically fought out, rear-guard action in refusing to leave Tibetan soil to the very end and Lu Hsing-chi's desperate battles in straining every nerve to gain admittance thereto, have been briefly touched upon. Another interesting facet was the complicated skein of events in which the British started by seeking a solution through a bilateral Tibet-China conference, while keeping themselves scrupulously out for fear their participation attract any unwanted responsibilities. Later, however, the compulsion of events added to the temptation to help secure a safe buffer for India's north-eastern frontier slowly, yet surely, brought them in.

No sooner did the October Revolution break out and the Chinese soldiery in Lhasa rebel, than the old structure of Manchu authority crumbled to the ground. As the news spread, Lhasa, and indeed the whole of Tibet, presented a state of considerable confusion. In the capital, as we have noticed, Lien Yu, the Amban, and his men were besieged in the Yamen, while Chung Ying and his cohorts were surrounded in the Trapchi barracks and in the Tengyeling monastery. All the while, the Dalai Lama was still far away from his seat of authority.

With Chinese power in Tibet thus seriously threatened, the new government in Peking lost no time in staking its claims. It was soon clear that the subjugation of Tibet was a priority item in the Republican programme. To be sure, President Yuan Shih-kai's declaration alluded to earlier, that Tibet was an integral part of China and indeed one of its provinces,[1] was disturbing to the British for its implications were far-reaching and considerably in excess of any claim which the Manchus had ever wagered.

For the British, three vital questions were posed. At the outset, were they justified, by their treaty rights, in opposing the inclusion of Tibet in China

---

[1] For the text of the Presidential ' Order ' of 25 March 1912, see Jordan to Grey, 31 March 1912, Sub Encl. 3, No. 28, *Foreign*, October 1912, Procs. 12–45.
For the text of the 21 April ' Order ' see Jordan to Grey, 27 April 1912, Encl. 2, No. 36, in Ibid.

proper? Two, if the opposition were sustained, might it not take the shape of anti-British demonstrations and help in the further dismemberment of other outlying parts of the Chinese Empire? And finally, what steps were to be taken to give shape and content to this policy?[2]

Calcutta's answer to the above queries, on which its opinion had been sought by Whitehall, was spelt out on 23 March 1912. It was a direct reply and admitted little by way of qualification. Tibet, it maintained, had been an autonomous state under the suzerainty of China. Its conversion, therefore, into a province could only be at the cost of its administration whose separate identity had been safeguarded in a number of treaties and trade regulations concluded since 1890. Further, insofar as Chinese treaties with foreign powers were not held to be valid in Tibet, it would follow that even China did not consider her to be an integral part of the mainland. Again, Britain's own interests, as indeed those of Nepal, Bhutan, and Sikkim, which it had pledged to safeguard, would be best served by opposing the inclusion of Tibet into China proper. Geographically too, India argued, Tibet's position was such that its political isolation was most desirable.

Significantly, the Indian Government did not anticipate any anti-British outbreaks in China. Nor perhaps was military action deemed necessary, for a change of regime in China had rendered it superfluous. In sum, India suggested that a satisfactory settlement with China in regard to Tibet, should be a condition precedent to the recognition of the new regime in that country.[3]

The views of the British Minister in Peking were a variant on the same theme. While Sir John Jordan conceded that with the incorporation of Tibet as an integral part of China, which the Republican regime now avowed as a fixed aim in its political programme, Tibetan suzerainty tended to be diluted, he was quick to point out that Britain had acquiesced in, if not encouraged, the consolidation of Chinese influence in Tibet. To that extent, it followed that her protests would lose much of their force. He advocated, therefore, a demand for the maintenance of the status quo as stipulated under treaty.[4]

HMG approved Jordan's course of action. On 24 May 1912, the latter had an interview with the Chinese Foreign Minister who tried to explain away the presidential order regarding the inclusion of Tibet into China proper. Earlier, news about the proposed Szechuan expedition injected an element of urgency into the situation. The Indian government, as briefly noticed earlier, was visibly upset, recommended a strong protest for fear the expedition should re-create the old, 1910–11, unsatisfactory situation along its frontier and constitute a threat to the independence of Nepal, Bhutan and Sikkim.[5]

On 12 April 1912, when, under instructions from London, the British Mini-

[2] *F O* to *I O*, 13 January 1912, and Secretary of State to Viceroy, 31 January 1912 in Ibid.
[3] Viceroy to Secretary of State, 23 March 1912, No. 16 in Ibid.
[4] Jordan to Grey, 12 April 1912, No. 18 in Ibid.
[5] Nos. 273, 289, 339 and 348, in *Foreign*, July 1912, Procs. 70–386.

ster sought a clarification from the Chinese President himself, the latter asserted that the Szechuan expedition was authorised to deal only with the state of disorder in the Tibetan Marches and would not, without definite orders from the Central Government, proceed further. Pressed to state categorically that the expedition would not, without previous consultations with the British Government, cross the frontier into Tibet, Yuan Shih-kai demurred, maintaining that he would have to confer with his Cabinet on this point. He affirmed nonetheless that he had no intention of incorporating Tibet into China, or of affecting a change in her status that would conflict with existing treaty obligations.[6]

Later, in August, the Chinese Vice-Minister for Foreign Affairs declared that the President had sanctioned the 'immediate' advance of a combined relief expedition from Yunnan and Szechuan into Tibet, ostensibly to afford relief to the beleaguered (Chinese) garrison in Lhasa. When the British Minister warned against such a step, the Wai-wu-pu maintained that the expedition was demanded by a clamorous public opinion and that, if countermanded, would imply the abandonment of China's position which may later have to be regained through use of superior force. Pressed for his own reaction, Jordan expressed the view that while the re-establishment of Chinese suzerainty on the basis of treaty stipulations, and recognised usage, could form the subject of subsequent friendly negotiations, any attempt to solve the question by force 'would precipitate a crisis that may prove fatal' to the Chinese government.[7]

Later, Yuan Shih-kai was to resile from the stand taken by his Vice-Minister at the Foreign Office. He denied that instructions had been given to the expedition to advance into Tibet, averred that, though pressed to make such an advance, he had no intention of sanctioning it, much less of incorporating any portion of Tibetan territory into China. His own preference, he confessed, was to work through the Dalai Lama.[8]

Professions to the contrary notwithstanding, what bothered the British in India, and worried the Tibetans, was news of continued Chinese activity in the Marches. It may be recalled that on 16 June 1912, General Yin Chang-heng with the support of Hu Ching-i, then acting Military Governor of Szechuan, had proclaimed, at Chengtu, his decision to launch a military campaign designed to save Chinese forces in Lhasa. Further, Yin who, as has been noticed, claimed to be responsible for the death of 'butcher' Chao, pledged to pursue this objective with firm determination. Besides, did not the Tibetans who dared betray China in its hour of trial by an act of open rebellion, deserve an exemplary punishment as traitors?—and Yin proposed to rectify previous errors by taking Tibet back into the family of the five races.

By the end of July, Yin had reached Tachienlu with about 4,000 troops,

---

[6]Jordan to Grey, 23 June 1912, No. 372 in Ibid.
[7]No. 210 in *Foreign*, October 1912, Procs. 59–282.
[8]No. 219 in Ibid.

while General Peng Jih-sheng, commanding at Chamdo, had been able to put down mercilessly a large rebellion there albeit, in the process, he had razed the monastery to the ground.[9] If only Yin could clear the road between Tachienlu and Chamdo, his objective of marching on Lhasa would not be difficult to realise. With this end in view, he had split his men into two parts. The first group, under General Liu Jui-heng, was to advance on Chamdo along the northern road through Dawa, Kantze and De-ge; the second, under Yin himself, was to march along the southern road through Litang, Batang and Draya. Thus, in what appeared to be a clever, tactical move, the two columns would converge on Chamdo for the final assault on Lhasa. This bold plan was sanctified by the fact that Chao Erh-feng himself had employed it, and successfully, during his campaigns in 1908-10. By early in September, Yin announced that he had cleared the main road east of Batang and that the territory to the west of it would soon be in his hands.[10]

It is against this background of President Yuan Shih-kai's categorical disavowal of any move to incorporate Tibet into China, coupled with General Yin's plans to bring about the very consummation his political superiors disowned, that the British Memorandum of 17 August (1912) should be studied.

As Whitehall viewed it, the Memorandum was designed to lay down a clearcut policy vis-à-vis Tibet in the interest of harmonious relations between Britain and the new Chinese Republic. It started by recalling Jordan's earlier talks with the President on 23 June; the Foreign Minister, Lu Cheng-hsing, on 29 June; the Vice-Minister, sometime in August; and finally, the President again a day prior to the presentation of the Memorandum. Jordan's emphasis on 'friendly negotiations', use of force 'prejudicing an amicable arrangement', or of 'grave' complicationst hat might ensue should the Chinese expedition cross the frontier into Tibet, underline a reference to these talks. Peking's assurances were catalogued too: on 23 June it had affirmed that there was 'no intention' of incorporating Tibet into China and that treaties would be 'scrupulously observed'; on August 16 'the most emphatic' assertion had been made that the expedition would not cross into Tibet, nor would the latter be merged into or made a 'province' of China.

The 'definite statement of policy', which formed the body of the memorandum, fell into five parts. The *first* was perhaps the most pivotal and deserves citation:

HMG while they have formally recognised the suzerain rights of China in Tibet, have never recognised and are not prepared to recognise, the right of China to intervene actively in the internal administration of Tibet which should remain, as contemplated by the treaties, in the hands of the

[9]Teichman, *Travels*, p. 38.
[10]Major D S Robertson (British Military Attache in Peking), ' Report on the Chinese Military Situation in the Tibetan Marches', 3 January 1913, No. 45 in *F O* 535/16.

Tibetan authorities, subject to the right of Great Britain and China, under Article I of the Convention of 27 April 1906, to take such steps as may be necessary to secure the due fulfilment of treaty stipulations.

The *second* paragraph laid down that the British government took exception to the conduct of Chinese officers in Tibet who, during the preceding two years (1910-12), had assumed 'all administrative power' in their hands. The doctrine 'propounded' by President Yuan, that Tibet was to be regarded on an 'equal footing with the provinces of China proper' and that 'all administrative matters' connected with the country 'will come within the sphere of internal administration', was stoutly repudiated, for

HMG formally decline to accept such a definition of the political status of Tibet and they must warn the Chinese Republic against any repetition by Chinese officers of the conduct to which exception has been taken.

The *third* paragraph made it clear that while China's right to have a representative, with a suitable escort, was unquestioned, HMG were not prepared to acquiesce in the maintenance of an unlimited number of Chinese troops either at Lhasa or in Tibet generally.

The *last two* paragraphs dwelt on the urgency of concluding 'a written agreement' on the foregoing lines, which was to be a 'condition precedent' to the British extending diplomatic recognition to the new Republic. Besides, until such agreement had, in fact, been concluded, 'all communication with Tibet, via India', must be regarded as absolutely closed. Later, however, the frontier might be re-opened 'on such conditions as HMG may see fit to impose', although this stipulation was not to apply to the withdrawal of the Chinese garrison at Lhasa which was 'at liberty' to return, via India.[11]

What did the memorandum imply?

At the outset it was clear that Whitehall was unwilling to condone all that the Chinese had been guilty of, in the preceding years, in terms of extinguishing an independent Tibetan administration. Nor, for that matter did it approve of the new dispensation of President Yuan whereby Tibet was to be treated as a province of the mainland and its affairs relegated to the sphere of internal administration. Additionally, Tibet's 'political status' was re-stated in terms of the old, pre-1904, formulae viz, Chinese suzerainty exercised through an Amban, with a suitable escort, stationed at Lhasa. The escort was not to be stretched to cover an unlimited number of troops either at Lhasa or in Tibet generally.

What of the sanctions? Here, as has been noticed, two weapons were employed: denying diplomatic recognition to the new regime and closing the Indian frontier to any communication with Tibet. Not that there was any-

[11] For the text No. 184 in *Foreign*, February 1913, Procs. 170-509.

thing unusual in these measures. Diplomatic recognition has always been the attribute of a sovereign state and in the then climate of international opinion was regarded as a legitimate weapon for extorting concessions. It may be recalled here that both Russia and Japan were then engaged in a similar exercise in regard to what they deemed to be their legitimate interests in Mongolia and Manchuria respectively. Britain's action in regard to Tibet, therefore, was more typical than exceptional.

Recognition apart, what was likely to hurt the Chinese most was the embargo placed on movement into Tibet across the Indian frontier. This was more so in that conditions in the Marches were far from settled and had brought all communication with Lhasa, through this channel, virtually to a dead-end. Evidently, and for good reason, the British were not prepared to be a party to allowing the Republican regime to regain its lost position in Tibet, except on their own terms.

While the Chinese Foreign Office had, understandably, shown no precipitate anxiety to reply to the British Memorandum, Russian activity in Mongolia and Kashgar assumed serious proportions. It was clear that whereas Britain was pledged to non-interference in Tibet, in terms of the Anglo-Russian Convention of 1907, Russian action, both in Mongolia and Sinkiang, was unfettered by any such commitment. On 5 December 1912, Whitehall asked India if it sought compensation in Tibet in case the Russians occupied Sinkiang or Kashgar.[12] Predictably, Calcutta replied that St. Petersburg should renounce all interest in Tibet subject to the British guaranteeing the country's integrity and recognising the well-worn religious connection between Tibetan lamas and Russian Buddhists. Should the Russians however fail to agree, the British should ask specifically for the right

(a) to have an Agent at Lhasa;
(b) to communicate direct with the Tibetan authorities;
(c) to occupy the Chumbi valley, if found necessary, to protect British interests and maintain order;
(d) (of Nepal) to exact redress to the extent of asking for a rectification of its boundary (with Tibet).[13]

Apart from the danger of Russian action in Sinkiang, to which it is proposed to revert later, there was persistent talk too of a Chinese advance on Tibet permeating into such districts as Zayul, sensitively close to the Indian frontier. Jordan, in Peking, was of the view that to counter such a threat, a force should be placed on the frontier between Sadiya and Rima which may act as a powerful deterrent to any Chinese adventure. Further, should it prove

---

[12]Secretary of State to Viceroy, 5 December 1912, *Foreign*, February 1913, Procs. 1–67.

[13]Viceroy to Secretary of State, 11 December 1912 in Ibid. Also office notes by McMahon and Hardinge, 9 and 10 September 1912, pp 3–4 in Correspondence, Ibid.

insufficient, it may be necessary for this force to advance on Rima, or even beyond.[14]

With Jordan's viewpoint, as spelt out in the preceding paragraph, India was not in agreement. The feeling here was that the threat most likely to prove effective in Peking was a categorical warning that agreements regarding Tibet would no longer hold good should China enter that country. Further, it was to be made clear that assistance would be furnished to Tibet to resist such an advance and that Russia too would be ivited for a joint effort in the same direction. It was also necessary that Zayul should be specifically mentioned in the communication, for there had been persistent reports of its conversion into a civil district. Its close proximity to the Assam border, and the fact that it was regarded as an integral part of Tibet, underlined, as Calcutta viewed it, both the urgency and the gravity of the situation.[15]

Even as these exchanges between Peking and Whitehall were taking place, disturbing news from Eastern Tibet continued to pour in. Thus in November (1912), the British Consul General in Chengtu reported that the project for converting the Marches, and a part of East Tibet, into a new Chinese province of Hsi-kang had made considerable headway. Chamdo was to be the capital and the headquarters of a 'Pacificator'. News poured in too that the expedition from Yunnan had occupied Chungtien, Atuntzu, Yenching and Weihsi, while the force from Szechuan had, by October (1912), recoverd Litang, Draya and Chamdo.[16]

What with the Chinese threat to Zayul and the advance of the Szechuan expedition to Chamdo, Whitehall proposed to ask the Chinese Government for an immediate reply to its Memorandum of 17 August, failing which it was to regard the Anglo-Chinese Convention of 1906 as being no longer valid. At the same time it was to hold itself free to enter into direct negotiations with Tibet, and give the latter active assistance in establishing, and maintaining, its independence.[17]

It may be useful to underline here the fact that at this stage the India Office was keen that advantage should be taken of this opportunity to make Peking accept a Sino-Burmese border settlement along the line of the Salween-Irrawaddy divide and renounce all territorial claims to Pienma and Hkampti Long. It was also imperative that, to counter known Chinese tactics of procrastination and delay, some time-limits should be set: 14 days for a reply and 'three months' to carry the negotiations through.[18]

While Sir Edward Grey at the Foreign Office supported Lord Crewe's principal conclusions as spelt out above, he was chary of attracting Russian

---

[14]Jordan to Grey, 29 October 1912, No. 311 in *Foreign*, February 1913, Procs. 170–509.
[15]Viceroy to Secretary of State, 7 November 1912, No. 357 in Ibid.
[16]Louis King to India, 17 September 1912, No. 304 in Ibid.
[17]Grey to Jordan, 12 December 1912, No. 425 in Ibid.
[18]Loc. cit.

attention under the provisions of the Anglo-Russian Convention of 1907. It was obvious too that Russia would not make a concession in Tibet without demanding a *quid pro quo* in Afghanistan, even though Nicolson, in St. Petersburg, felt that the latter might be more amenable if faced with a British *fait accompli* in Tibet.

Jordan's own reaction to proposals emanating from Whitehall was two-fold. While expressing himself broadly in agreement with its policy of pushing the Chinese into a corner to make them reply to the British Memorandum, he was averse to tying up too many things—the Burma-China frontier, for instance—with the fundamental question of Tibet. He discouraged too the continued use of threats of force, fearing these would provoke strong resentment which Britain could ill-afford in view of its vast commercial interests in China.[19]

On 14 December (1912), before Jordan could take an intiative, the Chinese Foreign Office invited the British Minister for an exchange of views on various points raised in the (August) Memorandum. Peking's Vice-Minister, Dr Yen, who was a member of the Young China Party and held pronouncedly radical views on the question of Tibet, was the principal spokesman. An exchange followed in which diametrically opposite positions were taken by the two sides. To start with Peking maintained that it had never undertaken not to interfere in Tibet. Not that it intended exercising that right, but, under the terms of the treaty, it was indeed free to do so. Jordan countered by arguing that Tibet had always been an autonomous country, that China had never had any right of active intervention in its internal administration, and that the claim now put forward was entirely inconsistent with repeated pledges given both verbally, and in writing, by the Ch'ing dynasty. Since the Republic had taken over the commitments of the previous regime, it followed that these pledges were still valid.

Dr Yen denied that Chinese officers had assumed all administrative power in Tibet and, as to the Presidential order, was prepared to renew the assurance that there was no intention of incorporating Tibet into China as one of its provinces. The British Minister retorted by asserting that the Presidential order was a direct violation of earlier pledges and that assurances were of no avail when a part of Tibet had already been merged into the new province of Hsi-kang.

Peking, in turn, took exception to Whitehall's use of the expression ' unlimited ' number of troops, maintaining that, in normal times, about 2,000 were kept in Tibet principally to discharge obligations imposed by the Convention of 1906 and the Trade Regulations of 1908. Jordan countered by pointing out that Chinese activity in recent years had been disturbing to Tibet's southern neighbours and as to the number of troops to be stationed, this could form the subject of later negotiations.

[19] Jordan to Grey, 13 December 1913, No. 428 in *Foreign*, February 1913, Procs. 170–509.

The Vice-Minister further maintanied that his government considered the existing agreements concerning Tibet adequate and did not deem it necessary to negotiate a fresh one, more so as the new Republican regime had not yet been recognised. Jordan warned against what he thought to be perfunctory disposal of a grave question, and repeated that the Republic, in announcing that Tibet was to be incorporated as a province of the mainland, had gone back on, and indeed violated, all previous treaty commitments.

Finally, Peking let it be known that it viewed the closing down of the frontier between India and Tibet as an 'unfriendly' act. In reply, Jordan asserted that the British had shown great consideration in allowing this route to be used for the evacuation of Chinese troops. Winding up, he counselled acceptance of the Memorandum which he thought helpful to Chinese interests insofar as it was drawn up at a time when there was still a modicum of Chinese authority in Tibet. By December the situation had changed for the worse and if China did not accept what were favourable terms, HMG would be free to act in a manner that best suited its interests.[20]

China's formal reply to the (August) Memorandum was handed over on 23 December and was, to all intents and purposes, a variant on the points made in the preceding paragraphs. *Inter alia*, reference was made to a British note of 17 January (1911) wherein HMG had recognised the interests of China in Tibet and pledged not to intervene as long as treaty stipulations were observed. The conclusion sought to be drawn was that China had full, and uninhibited, administrative powers in Tibet. Various pronouncements regarding that country's future were alluded to and stress laid on the fact that the objective was to complete the union, into one family, of five races—a view, which Peking maintained, was in harmony with HMG's thinking. It was also pointed out that closing of communications with Tibet, through India, was a measure that may have been resorted to only in the event of war and hope was expressed that it would be discontinued before long. Touching Whitehall on a soft spot, the Chinese reply referred to the traditional ties of friendship, and commerce, which had subsisted between Britain and China and expressed the hope that British recognition of the Republic would not only be a gesture of friendship, but prove mutually beneficial.[21]

Despite its outward suavity, the Chinese reply, it was evident, was tantamount to a complete rejection of the British Memorandum. Peking questioned the need for a new agreement, existing treaties being regarded as adequate. While any intent of converting Tibet into a province of the mainland was stoutly denied, emphasis was laid on the objective of completing the union of the five races into one family. And, by a quixotic logic, not easily intelligible, it was sought to be shown that HMG endorsed this standpoint! No wonder that when Jordan was approached for a reply, he made it clear that the tone,

---

[20]No. 433 in Ibid.
[21]No. 471 in Ibid.

and substance, of the (Chinese) note was so unsatisfactory as to warrant none.[22]

The ball being thus squarely put back into the Chinese court, its Foreign Minister, on 30 January 1913, expressed a desire to resume negotiations. Peking maintained that one of its major difficulties in regard to Whitehall's memorandum related to the expression 'suzerain rights', for it had found no place in any of the earlier treaties. The Minister reiterated that an exchange of notes would meet the requirements of the situation and that no new formal agreement or treaty was called for.[23]

Two developments which, at this stage, powerfully influenced the course of subsequent negotiations may be briefly mentioned. The first related to the Russo-Mongol agreement of November 1912 which marked a clear break-away of the latter country from the Chinese Republic. This, one would suspect, led, towards the end of the year, to a good deal of re-thinking in the Wai-wu-pu. The second, more disturbing to the British, related to the Tibet-Mongol agreement of January 1913. With Russian influence in Mongolia firmly established, thanks to the earlier November (1912) agreement, the British argued, opportunities for its spread to Tibet, through Mongolia, would multiply. Consequently, British anxiety to draw Tibet out of the Russian orbit now increased.

Meantime the Chinese thought of another way out of the impasse. Much of the bargaining with the British over the August Memorandum—and no Chinese regime would have relished its stiff terms—could be avoided, Peking calculated, if only it could establish a direct pipe-line to Lhasa. It was with this object in view that the Lama's titles had been restored in the fall of 1912 and he was hailed as a buttress of strength to the Republic! Again, since conditions in the Marches were disturbed and, inside the Dalai Lama's domain, Chinese forces beleaguered by a hostile Tibetan populace, a Chinese Mission led by Yang Fen and comprising a good many Buddhist leaders was despatched to Tibet by way of India. If it failed in its objective, as it did (for the British did not permit its crossing the frontier), the fault was not of Peking's making. To be sure, what little foot-hold the Chinese possessed in Tibet was put to its maximum use, and it may be recalled that both Lien Yu, the old Manchu Amban, and Chung Ying, his successor, made a desperate bid to find some bit of ground to hang on to, after conditions had become virtually untenable. It is evident that Peking viewed the Amban's physical presence inside Tibet, and the retention of his office, as of pivotal importance; and it was with the utmost reluctance that it surrendered these vantage points.

---

[22]No. 505 in Ibid.
[23]No. 302 in *Foreign*, May 1913, Procs. 261-502.

Chapter 12

A Tripartite Conference in India

IN THE fall of 1912, the broad outlines of a British policy towards Tibet begin to take shape and form. In this context, and strictly from India's point of view, two questions were of importance; the first related to the physical boundaries of Tibet, the second to the degree of control which China was to exercise in its former dependency.

As for the first, para 3 of the memorandum of 17 August had referred, *inter alia*, to HMG's refusal ' to acquiesce in the maintenance of an unlimited number of Chinese troops ' either at Lhasa, or ' in Tibet generally '. India had expressed the view that what was known as Tibet proper included the districts of Markham, Zayul, Chamdo, Draya, Gyade and Nagchuka but excluded San-ugai, Batang and Derge—although the latter three, prior to being brought under Chinese administration, were under the religious authority of the Dalai Lama. Unless their recent conquest by Chao Erh-feng rendered it unavoidable, the Indian government deprecated their cession to China for this would, besides much else, bring the latter into a dangerous proximity to Lhasa. As for Draya and Chamdo, there were ten to twelve difficult passes to be negotiated before they were reached, a fact which underscored the importance of their being included into Tibet proper. Further, not only Zayul but Markham may also be left in Tibet, for it would help keep the Chinese away from the Assam Himalayas and, what with their recent experience of Peking's infiltrations, the British had undoubtedly felt sore and bitter. Finally, the retention of Markham and Draya was rated as more important than that of Chamdo, the latter being viewed as expendable.

As India saw it, within the limits of Tibet thus defined, no Chinese troops were to be allowed. This precluded, of course, the stationing of an escort, not exceeding 300 men, for the Amban at Lhasa. Should Chinese garrisons be maintained in other parts of the country outside Lhasa, Delhi argued, the old story of Peking superseding Tibetan administration and obstructing trade and personal contacts with the British would repeat itself. Any plea on China's behalf that a small number of troops (viz. Amban's escort) would not be adequate to enable it to discharge its responsibilities could be countered by the argument that the treaties were never so little observed as when the Chinese were in control of Tibet.[1]

A further refinement of the preceding arguments was contained in a draft agreement drawn up by HMG, early in 1913. It laid down, *inter alia*, that China was to refrain from all interference in the internal administration

---

[1] No. 495 in *Foreign*, February 1913, Procs. 170–509.

of Tibet and to ensure this all Chinese troops, or officials, who happened to be in the country at the time of the conclusion of the treaty, were to be withdrawn within a month. The embargo, of course, did not apply to the Republican counterpart of the Amban or his escort of 300 men. Again, Tibet, which was to include all territory to the south and west of the Tangla range, and *not* China, was to be responsible for the administration of trade marts, protection of trade routes and regulation of commerce.[2]

On these draft proposals, the British Minister in Peking made some significant comments. He expressed serious doubts about China accepting an autonomous Tibetan administration or even agreeing to leave unmanned its posts on the lines of communication with Tibet, through the Marches. Again, while the British regarded the status quo *ante* 1904 as pivotal, from the Chinese standpoint the year 1910 seemed more relevant. Jordan's views, however, found little support in Delhi which felt that HMG's draft provided a good basis for negotiations and maintained instead that, as an interim measure, China should be released immediately from its obligations under the Trade Regulations of 1908. The Regulations, it was argued, had hitherto given Peking an excuse for interference in the internal administration of Tibet. Another suggestion, on the analogy of the Russo-Mongolian agreement, sought to preclude colonisation in Tibet proper by Chinese, or British subjects. This was deemed necessary to prevent Chinese ingress into such neighbouring districts as Zayul.[3]

It would be apparent from the above, that the earlier British policy of sterilising Tibet had to be abandoned for, with the elimination of Chinese influence —and Lhasa, it was axiomatic, could not stand on its own—there would be an inevitable gravitation towards Russia. To counter this, closer relations with the Lama seemed necessary. Again, the British argued, in return for a guarantee against Chinese encroachments on his eastern frontier, may not the Lama be persuaded to accept the reinstatement of a Chinese Amban, with a suitable escort, at Lhasa? Jordan was of the clear view that the best solution would be a tripartite arrangement among Great Britain, China and Tibet and that negotiations, in India, among the three might serve as a useful preliminary to its consummation. Even their failure, he felt, would leave the British in a better position to negotiate with Tibet, independently of China.[4]

Whether the suggestion for a tripartite conference first emanated from India is not clear. What is, is the fact that as early as October 1912 Delhi was pressing for

---

[2]The final article in HMG's six-point draft visualised that Britain and China were to use ' their good offices ' with Lhasa ' to secure the due fulfilment ' of the agreement. For the text No. 322 in *Foreign*, May 1913, Procs. 261–502.

[3]No. 327 in Ibid.

[4]No. 374 in Ibid.

(a) an exclusive right to have an Agent at Lhasa—'though we should not exercise this right unless circumstances compelled us to do so';
(b) right of communicating direct with the Tibetan authorities;
(c) right to occupy the Chumbi valley.

India had also made it clear that the threat most likely to prove effective with China, should it enter Tibet in force, was to denounce all existing agreements with her. Such an adventure, Peking was to be clearly warned, would be opposed by giving active assistance to Tibet in establishing and maintaining its independence.[5]

Whether, in the early stages, Delhi favoured direct British participation in the talks is not certain, albeit the Indian Government was undoubtedly averse to any negotiations taking place between the Dalai Lama and the Chinese *inside Tibet*—a viewpoint which the Lama fully shared. And yet direct talks with the Tibetans, either at Chamdo or at Lhasa, was a goal on which the Chinese had set their hearts. Since the Lama spurned every such overture and the British helped, if partly, by refusing admittance to Peking's delegates into Tibet, via India, Chinese efforts in this direction were often frustrated. It is at this stage that, contrary to the views of HMG who initially had sought to control the bipartite Sino-Tibetan negotiations *from outside* and fought shy of direct participation, that the British Minister in Peking came out openly in support of tripartite talks.[6] He it was, and Jordan wielded considerable influence in the Foreign Office, who finally persuaded Whitehall to accept the logic of a tripartite conference, to be convened *in India*.

A recent thesis that the Dalai Lama's vague proposals of holding talks with the Chinese in India 'offered the chance' to convert two sets of bipartite, Sino-Tibetan and Sino-British, discussions into a single tripartite negotiation, smacks of misplaced emphasis. So does any reference to the Indian authorities' extreme reluctance to see a matter 'as important to its frontier security as was Tibet' taken up in London or Peking.[7] As the preceding paragraphs make abundantly clear, a major factor in giving to the talks their tripartite character, and in choosing India to be the venue, appears to have been Sir John Jordan's powerful advocacy. This is not to gainsay the fact that, in the light of its own unhappy experience about the 1906 Peking Convention, Delhi must have welcomed the prospect of negotiations taking place in India, as no doubt of Tibet's full participation.

It is interesting to note that despite Jordan, HMG was a reluctant convert. While agreeing that, 'with a view to controlling the negotiations', they should take a direct part in them, they were still unwilling to accept its logical outcome as a tripartite agreement. This, it was argued, would involve responsibility

[5]No. 10 in *Foreign*, February 1913, Procs. 1–67.
[6]*Supra*, n. 3.
[7]Lamb, *McMahon Line*, II, p. 465.

from which the British clearly shrank. As Whitehall spelt it out, its attitude should be one of 'benevolent assistance '—making the Chinese accept the main points of the 17 August Memorandum 'direct with Tibet, but to our satisfaction', and at the same time to persuade the Lama, with whom closer relations were to be established, ' to accept an Amban at Lhasa ' with a suitable escort. Should an agreement on the above lines be concluded, it was argued, ' its formal communication to HMG might suffice ' for the time being, while the question of a separate agreement with China could be left over for subsequent consideration.[8]

It is revealing that while India concurred in the views outlined above,[9] the British Minister in Peking was strongly opposed. Jordan felt that the procedure outlined would, at best, prove to be a temporary palliative for the immediate difficulties, and offered no permanent settlement of the Tibetan question. Again, he thought it extremely unlikely that the Chinese Government would consent to negotiations being controlled by a third party that was not to sign the agreement. Besides, even if Peking agreed, Jordan argued, it would be difficult, ' if not impossible ', for Whitehall to exercise any effective control over the negotiations. The Minister, therefore, reverted to his earlier suggestion for a tripartite arrangement citing the precedent of the 1908 Trade Regulations, and maintained that this would involve the British Government in less responsibility than if it had followed its original course by first coming to an arrangement with China and then getting Tibet to accept it.[10]

At this stage, India fell in line with Sir John Jordan's reasoning. While recognising that his proposals would increase its responsibilities, it felt that a tripartite treaty which would recognise, ' under strictly defined Chinese suzerainty', the autonomy of Tibet would be a natural consequence and a safeguard against encroachments from the north. Besides, through such an agreement the British should obtain the exclusive right to send a mission to Lhasa, without the obligation of doing so, while in the interim there would be no difficulty in maintaining direct and close relations with the Dalai Lama through a Sikkimese or Nepalese representative stationed in the Tibetan capital.[11]

For the rest, the earlier draft, now revised, followed the pattern already outlined: China was to recognise Tibet's integrity, refrain from domestic interference, maintain an escort in Lhasa and be released from the obligations imposed by the Trade Regulations of 1908.[12]

Even as the British were debating these issues, the Chinese came down a peg or two from their earlier stance. On 27 March 1913, their Foreign Office formally accepted the Memorandum of 17 August (1912) as a basis for

---

[8] No. 410 in *Foreign*, May 1913, Procs. 261–502.
[9] No. 438 in Ibid.
[10] No. 462 in Ibid.
[11] Viceroy to Secretary of State, 15 April 1913, No. 470 in Ibid.
[12] Encl. in No. 446 in Ibid.

bipartite discussions which, they now proposed, should be held in London. Their representative for the talks was to be Wen Tsung-yao, one-time Assistant to Lien Yu at Lhasa. Wen was known to be sympathetic to the Tibetan cause, having resigned in 1910 over what he thought a clear breach of the solemn Chinese promise in regard to the number of (Chinese) troops to be stationed in Lhasa.[13]

It was in reply to this offer from the Wai-chiao-pu that Grey intimated his acceptance of the principle of *tripartite* talks with the British as equal, and active, participants. The venue was to be Darjeeling, *not* London.[14]

A principal reason for the earlier (British) Foreign Office reluctance to accept tripartite negotiations had been the self-denying clauses of the 1907 Anglo-Russian convention on Tibet. As has been noticed, as early as September 1912, HMG had sought India's opinion as to the compensation to be demanded from Russia in the event of the latter's then likely occupation of Sinkiang and Kashgar. Predictably, Delhi asked for a complete renunciation by Russia of all its interests in Tibet, subject to the British Government guaranteeing that country's integrity. Failing this, the exclusive right to have an agent in Lhasa and of communicating direct with the Tibetan authorities were its minimum demands. By January 1913, however, the conclusion of the Russo-Mongolian agreement as well as the Mongol-Tibetan treaty altered the picture completely. Although the British endorsed the Russian view that the latter treaty had no political significance in the absence of an agreement as to the legal rights of the signatories,[15] they still took the fact of the treaty fully into account in all their calculations. Thus it is clear that in accepting tripartite negotiations, an important factor that weighed was the fear of increased Russian control in Tibet, exercised through Mongolia. So too a growing emphasis on fostering closer relations with the Dalai Lama. HMG, however, was not easily persuaded and Grey had Russia very much on his mind when, early in 1913, he minuted:

> It may fairly be argued that we are entitled to become a party to a Tripartite Agreement with China and Tibet without violating the Anglo-Russian Agreement. Under that Agreement we are entitled to negotiate with China about Tibet and we are entitled to the fulfilment of our pre-1907 agreement with Tibet. We have, therefore, a locus standi for being a party to negotiations with China and Tibet.

And yet:

> We should have to be careful that under the tripartite agreement we acquire no rights and undertake no responsibilities that infringed the Anglo-Russian

---

[13] Jordan to Grey, 27 March 1913, *F O* 371/1610.
[14] No. 37 in *Foreign*, September 1913, Procs. 1–271.
[15] Office note by Archibald Rose, 28 November 1913 in Correspondence, *Foreign*, June 1914, Procs. 151–57.

agreement. We should therefore be bound to explain to Russia what we are doing and the limits which we intend to keep. I do not mean that we should be bound to inform Russia of all that passed which affected only the relations of Tibet with China, but we should have to keep her informed of the scope of our action.[16]

It is thus evident that, for Whitehall, its participation in the proposed tripartite negotiations was far from being that of a free agent; in fact, its role was to be severely restricted within the limits set by the Anglo-Russian Convention. This was evident from the decision taken to inform Russia of the reasons which made negotiations necessary and of communicating to her the text of the revised draft. Additionally, if and when a suitable tripartite agreement was concluded, Russian consent was to be sought for such freedom of action as the British may desire to obtain in Tibet.

No sooner, however, had Whitehall agreed to the tripartite basis in principle, than Jordan was instructed to inform Peking and to impress upon it that such a conference in India, would offer 'the only plan possible' for effecting a mutually acceptable arrangement. For, in the alternate, an agreement between Great Britain and China would face the principal hurdle of lacking Tibetan consent. China was also informed that a similar invitation had been sent to the Dalai Lama. Finally, to obviate traditional Chinese procrastination, Jordan was to specify a date, ' say July 1 ', by which Peking's delegates were to arrive in India. Further details of the proposed draft agreement, then under discussion, were to be withheld until negotiations actually commenced.

The initial Chinese reaction to the British proposal was cold, if not hostile. Jordan noted that the Minister for Foreign Affairs ' showed a dislike to the idea of a Tibetan delegate taking part ' but promised submission of the proposal to his political superiors.[17]

Meanwhile, on 26 May, there appeared in the Peking Government Gazette a Presidential ' Order ' of the preceding day which cited conciliatory messages to the Governor of Yunnan by Tibetan frontier authorities. *Inter alia*, it incorporated instructions to the army, then operating in the Szechuan Marches, that their dealings with the native tribes should be of a peaceful character. The ' Order ' also stipulated that the ' boundaries ' of the Marches, existing during the last few years of the Manchu regime, be accepted and the country occupied by the army may not extend west of Chiang Ta (Giamda).[18]

Innocent though it may have appeared on paper, the ' Order ' had far-reaching implications in that it excluded from Tibet large parts of its territory. Under instructions, Jordan impressed upon the Foreign Minister, as also the President, its real significance. In reply, Yuan Shih-kai confessed his igno-

[16]Minute by Grey, Encl. in Jordan to Grey, 10 April 1913, *F O* 371/1610.
[17]No. 39 in *Foreign*, September 1913, Procs. 1–271.
[18]No. 40 in Ibid.

rance of the geography of the frontier. Nor was he opposed to tripartite negotiations being held in India and mentioned Chang Yin-tang as a possible choice for delegate. Jordan intimated that Chang was not a success as Commissioner (at the time of the revision of the Tibet Trade Regulations of 1908), and would, on that account, be unacceptable. On his own bat, the British Minister suggested as an alternative Ivan Chen, more correctly Chen I-fan, lately Counsellor of the Chinese Legation in London.[19]

China's acceptance of the August (1912) memorandum as a basis for negotiations, coupled with its agreement to a tripartite conference in India, marks a major watershed in the post-Revolutionary era. It may, therefore, be useful at this stage to tie this up with parallel developments in Tibet and the Szechuan Marches consequent upon the return of the Dalai Lama, the collapse of Chinese authority and the proclamation of Tibet's 'independence'.

---

[19]No. 59 in Ibid.

Chapter 13

'Negotiations' in East Tibet, 1912-13

IT HAD taken the Chinese the best part of a year to accept the British Memorandum of August 1912; more significantly, it had taken the British almost the same time to realise that what they sought—peace on their frontier—could best be achieved not indeed through a two-tier bilateral set of negotiations, but a tripartite confrontation among the countries directly involved. Complicated as the negotiations had proved in making Peking accept the new bases in principle, the sequence to give them a practical shape was even more frustrating. This was disappointing though, in British experience, by no means exceptional. What was more disconcerting was the discovery that, having accepted the tripartite principle, the Chinese were making every endeavour to sabotage it, either through Lu Hsing-chi's back-stage intrigues, or by holding independent negotiations with the Tibetans in Chamdo behind the back of the British. In the sequence, they proved abortive, albeit not for want of trying on the part of the Chinese. Nor for that matter, in these mysterious goings-on, did Lhasa's, and the Dalai Lama's, role appear to be straight, or above board.

In an earlier chapter, a brief reference has already been made to the activities of General Yin Chang-heng and the fanfare of publicity with which he launched his military expedition in the Marches in June 1912.[1] Part of Yin's self-proclaimed mission was to relieve the beleaguered (Chinese) garrison in Lhasa and, by scoring a resounding military victory, fulfil his over-weening political ambition—overlordship of the whole of the north-west. By early in September, he claimed to have cleared the main road to Batang;[2] on 1 October (1912) he had formally inaugurated a new administration of the Marches at Tachienlu![3]

What is interesting about Yin's new administration was its revival of Chao Erh-feng's blueprint for the new Chinese province of Hsi-kang. It may be recalled that Chao's immediate successor as Warden, General Fu Sung-mu, had submitted similar proposals to Peking just before the October Revolution swept him, and a lot else, into the limbo of oblivion. Now, less than

[1] *Supra*, Chapter XII.

[2] Yin's claims were seriously disputed by Louis King, then stationed at Chengtu. For details see Jordan to Grey, 17 October and 3 December 1912, in *F O* 371/1329.

[3] For a summary see 'Annual Report on China, 1912' (portion on Tibet), Encl. 4 to No. 122-A in *Foreign*, March 1914, Procs. 1–251. Also see Major D S Robertson, 'Report on the Chinese Military situation in the Tibetan Marches, 3 January 1913', No. 45 in *F O* 535/16.

a year later, in August 1912 to be precise, Hu Ching-yi, acting Governor of Szechuan, formally proposed to President Yuan the creation of the new province. Chamdo was to be its headquarters, Yin its first Governor, in rank equal to the Tutu who reigned at Chengtu.[4]

The significance of Hu Ching-yi's fresh initiative is two-fold. One in that, as he conceived it, the territorial limits of Hsi-kang were to embrace a larger chunk of territory than Chao or his deputy had originally intended. Thus the new province was to include the south Tibetan districts of Pome and Zayul, while its western frontier was to be at Giamda or Chiangta, a little less than a hundred miles to the east of Lhasa.[5] It is indeed revealing that, as though anticipating the birth of the new province, the Szechuan authorities had, early in 1912, despatched two teams of inspection to Zayul,[6] a development which predictably frightened Calcutta out of its wits. The latter argued that while

> the extension of Chinese administrative ambitions in the direction of Chiamdo can have but a distant and indirect interest we cannot be unmoved by the establishment of a Chinese military centre in the Brahmaputra basin within easy reach of Assam. Should such a position become permanently established, it would leave one vulnerable point in the North-east Frontier line, which now gives promise of providing a strong natural boundary along the whole of the line where India marches with China and Tibet.[7]

Another point that bears emphasis about the Szechuan Tutu Hu's proposal is the fact that, by October (1912), it had received the formal consent of President Yuan Shih-kai in Peking. The only caveat the President entered was that while he saw no objection to the inclusion of Chamdo and Shobando within the proposed administrative frontier of the new province of Hsi-kang, he thought it well to await the delimitation of the Szechuan-Tibet boundary before attempting to advance the line as far west as Lali or Chiangta.[8] This, however, was essentially a matter of detail. More significantly, Yuan's seal of approval to the Hsi-kang blueprint would clearly demonstrate that the policy of the Republic *vis-à-vis* Tibet, and the frontier districts bordering Assam, differed from the strong-arm methods employed by Chao Erh-feng and Fu Sung-mu only to the extent that it was to be more methodically, if ruthlessly, pursued!

---

[4]Wilkinson (Consul General, Chengtu) to Jordan, 4 September 1912, *F O* 371/1329.
[5]Jordan to Grey, 23 October 1912, in Ibid.
One would presume that Yin's proclamation of the new administration of eight prefectures at Tachienlu on 1 October 1912 corresponded to the boundaries of Hsi-kang as envisaged by Hu Ching-yi.
[6]Jordan to Grey, 18 May 1912, in *F O* 371/1326.
[7]*Supra*, n. 3.
[8]Jordan to Grey, 17 and 23 October and 5 December 1912, in *F O* 371/1329. See also ' Annual Report for 1912 ', portion on Tibet, cited in *supra*, n. 3.

It was not for want of trying that Yin's ambitious plans to conquer the March country and to take Lhasa by storm did not work out in practice. Part of the answer lay in the intense personal rivalry between Yin and his one-time protégé, Hu Ching-yi. Professions to the contrary notwithstanding, Hu had kept Yin's expedition starved of supplies and much-needed funds. More important, while securing his own nomination as substantive Governor or Tutu of Szechuan, he got Yin a lower post—'Generalissimo or Administrator of the Marches'. The arrangement was viewed as distinctly unsatisfactory by Yin who, on receipt of the news, had rushed back to Chengtu, poised for a *coup d'état*. The worst, however, was averted by a compromise solution—a new title, 'Governor of the Marches', equal in rank to that of the Tutu, was conferred upon Yin, a gesture which, if only temporarily, assuaged his injured feelings. But the chasm was too wide to be easily bridged, the running sore of a personal rivalry bedevilled all possibilities of cooperation between the two men. The contrast with Chao's days when Chengtu had proffered all possible assistance to the Warden stood out in bold relief.

Another of Yin's difficulties lay in the unusually strong, and unexpected, opposition which the Tibetans offered to the Chinese advance. Symbolic of this sustained resistance was the Hsiang-cheng monastery which the Tibetans appear to have captured in January 1912, and where, week after week and month after month, the lamas fought valiantly, if ferociously, to stem the Chinese tide. Frustrated in his efforts, and yet unable to face upto it, Yin perpetrated the subterfuge of forging the signatures of his commanders to prove that he had, in fact, taken the stronghold. Not that it worked. For in spite of it the much hoped for funds from Chengtu did not arrive. This was not only because the realisation had dawned at the Szechuanese capital that Yin's whole venture had proved to be a complete, indeed expensive, failure but also because the Generalissimo had failed to account for a sum of £125,000, already advanced to him.[9]

A word, if only in parenthesis, about what Yin had been unable to do and what Chao had achieved, may not be out of place here. The latter, Jordan tells us

> was mainly concerned with the formation of a buffer State between Western China and the zone of British activity; that his real energies were directed to the strengthening of the frontiers and the extension of Chinese administration as far west as the col of Tanta, and as far south as the Indian border; that the Zayul valley was to have been included in Kham; and that he was determined to secure a strong political position at Lhasa, as the simplest and surest method of controlling the fortunes of the country through the agency of the Lama Church.[10]

[9] For a summary see 'Tibet: Memorandum from Ist January to 30th August 1913', Encl. 4 in No. 122-A in *Foreign*, March 1914, Procs. 1–251.
[10] Jordan to Grey, 2 April 1913, in *I O R*, L/P&S/10/150.

This was something which Yin was 'unlikely' to achieve even though he was 'determined' to establish himself at least 'as far west' as Batang. Yet the stark awareness of the strategic importance of what was at stake is nowhere better revealed than in Hu Ching-yi's appendix, written in September 1912 by way of an introduction to General Fu Sung-mu's 'History of the Creation of Hsi-kang province':

> More complete knowledge of this country has long been desired by patriots anxious for the safety of the Marches.... Its area has widened, it is situated on an important highway, and it is largely inhabited by Chinese.... A new heaven and a new earth were created when this dominion was incorporated in China proper; a new policy becomes necessary to deal with a changed situation....[11]

Actually the 'changed situation' in the Marches, to which Hu referred, was for the worse. For despite the new and more vigorous policy promised, and the imprint of Presidential approval accorded it, by early in March (1913) Chengtu was both sadder and wiser, and so was Peking. Funds for which Yin had clamoured but in vain, were not released while President Yuan announced the appointment of two 'Conciliators'. Coupled with his policy of placating the Lama by restoring him his titles, the conciliators—Wang Chein-ching and Kuo Chang-kuan—were charged with the duty of making Lhasa abandon its idea of parleys in India and instead negotiate a separate peace with the Chinese at Chamdo.[12]

An interesting facet of the situation in the Marches, in the latter half of 1913, revolves around this sustained Chinese effort to negotiate a deal *direct* with Lhasa, without the British coming in. Thus in a letter written on 21 September 1913, the Tibetan Chief Ministers had informed David Macdonald, then British Trade Agent at Yatung, that the two Chinese officials had arrived at Nagenda and written to the Kalon Lama; the Tibetan commander in Kham, of their desire to come to Shobando, where he was stationed, and to have talks with him there. Earlier they had demanded the surrender not only of Hsiang-cheng, but of other gompas located in the provinces of Markham and Derge, failing which they threatened that Chinese soldiers would be despatched to expel the Tibetans.[13]

Growing Chinese frustration, if also rank suspicion of Tibetan bona fides, was evident from the contents of their communication to the Kalon written on 1 August 1913:

---

[11]Extracts from the 'History of the creation of the Hsi-kang Province' by General Fu Sung-mu, encl. in *supra*, n. 10.

[12]Consul General, Chengtu to Minister, Peking, 12 August and 8 October 1913, Nos. 95 and 119 in *Foreign*, March 1914, Procs. 1–251.
See also Alston to Grey, 8 September 1913, Encl. 4, No. 122-A in Ibid.

[13]Macdonald to India, 4 October 1913, Encl. 1 in No. 126 in Ibid.

Formerly we were of one mind, but you appear to have doubts on us. Why are you doubting? You know very well that the five races belong to one family and we are very anxious to re-establish friendly relations with the Tibetans and to see the work of the Government prosper as heretofore. Now we must abandon the evil deeds and act according to the good customs of other foreign powers.[14]

This is interesting as far as it goes, what is far more revealing is that the 'Conciliators' did not give up these efforts long after their principals in Peking had agreed with the British to participate in a tripartite conference in India! Thus as late as 27 September 1913, when Ivan Chen, the Chinese Plenipotentiary, was on the high seas on his way to Simla, Wang Chein-ching one of the conciliators who styled himself as 'Administrator of Lhasa and all Tibet', issued an 'order', under 'telegraphic instructions from the great President', in which he explained that he had

> come towards Tibet via Chiamdo with a view to acquaint the people of Tibet with the ways and customs of the Republican Government and to establish a friendly understanding between us and those people to the best of my ability.... With this end in view, I will leave Chiamdo on the 4th of the 10th month (4th October 1913) and come to Shopado, passing through Riwoche and Gyade in the hope of meeting the Kalon Lama and coming to a clear and definite understanding with him whereby we might restore peace and prosperity to the country and the people...you, the people falling on the route whether of better class or common people should bear in mind that if you misunderstand the purport of my mission and regard me with fear and suspicion, you will be rendering my purpose abortive which may lead to dreadful results.[15]

Lhasa's attitude to these clandestine, if under-hand, goings-on may be gauged from two facts. *One*, that the Dalai Lama made a clean breast of all that the Chinese were trying to do—negotiating independently with his officials in an area where some contact between the two sides still existed. The fact that he did so would seem to suggest that he was not very willing to fall into Peking's trap. *Two*, he assured the British that, so far as he was concerned, he had instructed his officials 'not to allow' Wang to cross into Tibetan-held territory.[16]

The climax to the Conciliators' efforts was a treaty which they allegedly signed with the Kalon Lama sometime during these confused, if event-filled months. The terms make interesting reading and may be reproduced here:

[14]For the text see Encl. 2 in No. 126, *supra*, n. 13.
[15]Wang to Kalon Lama, 27 September 1913, No. 149-A in Ibid.
[16]Viceroy to Secretary of State, 1 November 1913, No. 153 in Ibid. See also Bell to India, 7 October 1913, Encls. 1–2, No. 114 in Ibid.

1. Dalai Lama to retain his position as supreme head of the Church;
2. Tibet to enjoy favoured-nation treatment;
3. Tibet to enjoy right to levy taxes and duties;
4. Tibet to have right to raise troops to defend her territory;
5. Tibet to have right to restrict cultivation (i.e. colonisation) and trade;
6. China to give increased annual grants to lamaseries;
7. China to assist Tibet to revise her education system;
8. China to refrain from appointing additional officials in Tibet;
9. China not to send troops into Tibet except in case of internal disturbance;
10. China to help Tibet in the reconstruction of her Government.[17]

When confronted with the above text, Lonchen Shatra, the Tibetan Plenipotentiary at Simla, professed complete ignorance. Further, he viewed it as a clever Chinese ruse to encourage Szechuan in giving larger financial assistance to Yin's military venture and to inspire the latter's soldiery in making renewed efforts in the same direction.[18]

Harold Porter, the British Consul General in Chengtu, however, was not so easily convinced. While forwarding the text of the 'treaty', he expressed the view that though lacking confirmation

> of this news from other sources and (I) have no means at present of ascertaining whether the information is correct or the document quoted authentic, but it would appear to be not unlikely that actual or attempted negotiations are taking place at Chiamdo independently of the conference in India.

In sitting in judgement on the Lonchen and the Consul General, two facets of the question need scrutiny. In the first place, unless the Dalai Lama and his advisers were playing a double game—and well they might—there is no gainsaying the fact that their attitude of refusing any intercourse with Lu Hsing-chi in Calcutta, despite the latter's unceasing activity and tempting baits, could only have been repeated in the Kalon Lama's dealings with 'Administrator' Wang in Chamdo. There is the additional fact that while Harold Porter regarded the situation in the Marches as a 'little difficult to follow', he was quite clear that the Chinese 'are now scarcely in a condition to oppose' a really determined Tibetan advance.[19]

Again, why should the Tibetans have entered into negotiations when the Chinese position was visibly weakening—there were persistent reports that

---

[17]Consul General, Chengtu to India, 28 October 1913, No. 148 in Ibid. Porter had indicated that according to his information the terms 'were presented to Chinese Plenipotentiary by Tibetans'. For the text see extract from 'Szechuan Kung Pao' of 27 October 1913, Sub-encl. in No. 200 in Ibid.
[18]Viceroy to Secretary of State, 1 November 1913, No. 153 in Ibid.
[19]Porter to Jordan, 28 October 1913, Encl. in No. 200 in Ibid.

General Yin himself was being recalled to Peking—[20] is not easy to explain. Hence a certain difficulty in accepting these rumours at their face value.

Another aspect of the question deserves to be noticed too. It may be recalled that just about this time, fag-end of October 1913, at the initiative of the British Minister in Peking, India asked the Lama to return a 'categorical refusal' to 'any future' Chinese invitations to attend a Conference at Chamdo.[21] It may not be unreasonable to argue that the Lama needed the warning and that his communications to the British regarding Peking's overtures to him, and his officials, were part of a deliberate effort to establish his own bona fides in their (British) eyes.

Whatever the truth, the rumours about the treaty only served to illustrate what seemed obvious enough namely that, on the eve of the Simla Conference, the situation in the Marches was complicated, if not completely confused. The much-talked-of military offensive under General Yin had petered out, as also Peking's clever diplomatic manoeuvre to persuade the Tibetans to a separate conference in, or around, Chamdo. If by contrast, the Tibetans, to an extent, had succeeded in holding back the Chinese and in organising powerful pockets of resistance in their rear.

It has been noticed earlier that the Dalai Lama and his Ministers were keen to discuss matters with the Chinese—but outside of Tibet. The fear that they would be intimidated, and forced to accept the Chinese bidding, was paramount with them. For both past experience, and mounting distrust of Chinese bona fides, made Lhasa circumspect—and suspicious. What the Dalai Lama had gone through during his stay in Peking, and on his return home, was too recent to be forgotten.

The alacrity with which Lhasa accepted HMG's invitation to a Conference in India is revealing in this context. The decision to invitet he Tibetans and the Chinese to a joint conference was taken by HMG sometime in May (1913) when a communication to this effect was made to the Dalai Lama. A formal invitation, however, was kept pending until the Chinese reaction was known. Later, in informing the Lama of Chinese acceptance, Bell was told

> that all communications from the Chinese Government unless these were received through HMG should, pending the results of the Conference, be ignored by him (Dalai Lama) but that he should inform HMG of them at the time of their receipt[22].

---

[20] Porter had pointed out that it was 'rumoured' that Yin 'had been called to Peking' and was to be 'brought to book' for complicity in the Chungking insurrection. For details *supra*, n. 19.

[21] Secretary of State to Viceroy, 22 October 1913, and Viceroy to Secretary of State, 24 October 1913, Nos. 135 and 138 in Ibid. *Inter alia*, the Viceroy intimated that the Lama had in fact 'already been advised to reject' all such proposals of the Chinese.

[22] No. 115 in *Foreign*, September 1913, Procs. 1–271.

Three days after the message had been received at Lhasa, the nomination of Lonchen Shatra as Tibetan delegate to the proposed conference was made. The Lonchen, it would appear, arrived in Chumbi not long after, although he was to keep kicking his heels there for months before the conference eventually convened in Simla, in October.

Self-evident from the above, Tibetan anxiety is further underlined by a recent (Tibetan) writer who has expressed the view that

> while exerting military pressure on the Chinese (in the March country), the Dalai Lama continued to press the British into arranging a tripartite conference...the (Chinese) hoped to delay the conference for some time, but the presence of the Tibetan troops under Chamba Tender (viz. Kalon Lama) in Kham made them reconsider their position.[23]

---

[23]*Shakabapa*, p. 251.

Chapter 14

China and Tripartite Negotiations (June–August 1903)

TIBETAN KEENNESS, and indeed anxiety, for an early settlement was matched, if in the opposite direction, by notorious Chinese procrastination. It may be recalled that sometime in the middle of June (1913), the Chinese accepted the August (1912) Memorandum as a basis for negotiations, agreeing at the same time to participate in a tripartite conference in India. Having cleared the ground on these major premises, a few preliminaries remained to be settled—the respective negotiators, their status as also the date for convening the conference. It is significant that the Chinese dragged their weary feet so successfully that months elapsed before these details were worked out; the Conference itself did not convene until 13 October.

After his interview with President Yuan Shih-kai on 4 June, referred to in an earlier chapter, Jordan gathered the impression that the Chinese accepted both the tripartite basis of the talks as also the nomination of Ivan Chen as their delegate—Yuan had initially suggested Chang Yin-tang, to which choice Jordan had demurred. To British surprise, however, on 15 June the Peking official gazette published a Presidential Order nominating Ivan Chen and Hu Han-min, then Tutu of Canton, as 'Commissioners for the Pacification of Tibet'.[1]

Normally, Peking employed the term 'Pacificator' for appointments made to provinces in China proper; its use, therefore, in the context of Tibet indicated an obvious assumption of control over that country. Noticing this Jordan informed Whitehall that, in his view, Ivan Chen could not be received as a negotiator while holding the title of 'Pacificator' and that Hu Han-min's previous record did not inspire confidence in his bona fides. He therefore sought, and obtained, his government's authority to seek cancellation of the order of 15 June as a condition precedent to any further negotiations on the basis of the August Memorandum.[2] In reply, Peking indicated that while it was reluctant to cancel the June order, it was more than willing to issue another clarifying the position.[3]

Without losing much time, Whitehall asked Jordan to inform the Chinese Government of its proposal about a conference in India and to demand an immediate suspension of hostilities in Eastern Tibet. Additionally, any

[1] No. 86 in *Foreign*, September 1913, Procs. 1–271.
[2] No. 101 in Ibid.
[3] No. 109 in Ibid.

further Chinese advance was to be stayed until Tibet's geographical limits had been defined by the Conference.[4]

At his interview with the President on 29 June, Jordan sought clarifications and definitive commitments on the points at issue. Yuan assured him that the title ('Pacificators') used for Ivan Chen and his deputy carried no territorial powers and promised that the Wai-wu-pu would furnish a statement in writing to that effect. The President now definitely accepted the invitation to the conference but felt that the designation of the delegates must be agreed to before Ivan Chen's appointment could issue. As for the cessation of hostilities in Eastern Tibet, the Chinese Foreign Office furnished Jordan a copy of the Presidential Order of 2 June. Among other things, the latter had directed the Chinese Commander-in-Chief at Litang to remain at Enta and other places occupied some 75 miles west of Chamdo, but allowed him a free hand in dealing with the country of 39 Banners, and with Po-med, on the plea that these districts were never subject to Tibet. Jordan protested that the 'order' implied a recrudescence of Chinese activity in the neighbourhood of the Indian frontier and an advance on Lhasa by roads north and south of Chamdo. The President recalled his previous assurances on the subject and pledged that the Chinese Government had no intention of ordering an advance into Tibet.[5]

Meanwhile the British Minister asked his political superiors about the designation of the respective negotiators, intimating that Peking's intent was that its representative should occupy the same status, *vis-à-vis* his Tibetan counterpart, as at the time of the 1908 negotiations for Tibetan Trade Regulations. On his own, Jordan expressed the view that the three representatives should be designated Plenipotentiaries and that, in the present circumstances in Tibet, any formal subordination of the Tibetan to his Chinese counterpart, as in 1908, would be premature.

On 30 June, the Chinese Foreign Office handed to the British Minister copies of fresh Presidential 'orders' to the Chinese commanders on the Szechuan and Yunnan frontiers intimating that, in view of the impending talks, all troops should adhere strictly to their present positions and forego any advance.[6] Later, a memorandum from the Wai-chiao-pu stated that the 'Pacificators' had no connection with the internal administration of Tibet and were only appointed to announce the peaceful intentions of the Chinese Government.[7]

---

[4]No. 93 in Ibid.

[5]No. 138 in Ibid.

[6]No. 139 in Ibid.

[7]No. 168 in Ibid.

A word here about the nomenclature of the Chinese Foreign Office. Initially, in 1861, an Imperial Decree had set up the Tsungli Yamen—a bureau for dealing with the 'foreign devils', various powers conveniently grouped as well as naval matters; in the aftermath of the Boxer rising, in 1901, the Yamen became a full-fledged ministry and was christened the Wai-wu-pu; under the Republic, after 1911, it acquired a new name, the Wai-chiao-pu. For details

A couple of weeks later, HMG informed Jordan that if the title 'Pacificator' implied no territorial, administrative or juridical powers over Tibet, he need not insist on the withdrawal of the President's 'order' of 15 June. Nonetheless he (Jordan) should take steps to ensure that the representatives of Great Britain, China and Tibet were placed on an equal footing. The question of actual designation, however, was held up, pending details being available of the powers vested in the Tibetan representative. As to 1908, it was to be pointed out that whereas at the time the interests of China and Tibet were, or were assumed to be, identical, in the present instance negotiations were taking place against the background of actual hostilities between the two countries. The Presidential 'order', directing Chinese troops to stand their ground, was considered sufficient compliance with Whitehall's demand for a cessation of hostilities. Finally, it was imperative that the departure of the Chinese Plenipotentiary should be expedited and his status and powers scrutinised—*before* he started.[8]

China in the meantime was playing a double game. Thus while evading the formal appointment of its delegates for the proposed conference it was trying, through the appointment of Lu Hsing-chi as the Amban-designate at Lhasa, to keep up the fiction of supervising Tibetan administration. Delhi, as no doubt Jordan himself, viewed this manoeuvre with stern disapproval and, on 6 August (1913), Lu was informed that any attempt to carry out the duties of his appointment would lead to his being deported from India.[9]

At Peking, the Chinese continued their well-worn delaying tactics. When informed on 14 July that British and Tibetan representatives were ready to meet at Simla, the (Chinese) Foreign Office again cited the precedent of 1908 regarding the Tibetan delegate's subordinate status and refused to yield ground. To gain time, it now sought the exact wording of the commission issued to the British delegate and threw out a discreet enough hint that one way out of the difficulty would be for the Chinese representative to reach an agreement with his Tibetan counterpart before negotiating with the British. This was taking things back to where they belonged and the British refused to accept the position.[10]

When later on 28 July Alston, Jordan's temporary replacement in Peking, communicated to the Wai-chiao-pu the full text of the powers granted to Sir Henry McMahon and Lonchen Shatra, the Chinese reiterated the objections they had raised earlier in regard to the equal status of the Tibetan delegate. The British Minister countered by pointing out that the declared objective of the Conference was to decide the position of Tibet *vis-à-vis* China and that

---

see L. Tung, *China and Some Phases of International Law* (London, 1940), pp. 105–10 and Y C Cheng, 'The Organisation of the Wai-chiao-pu', *Chinese Social and Political Science Review*, I, 1916.

[8] Grey to Jordan, 12 July 1913, No. 175 in *Foreign*, September 1913, Procs. 1–271.
[9] No. 236 in Ibid. Also see Nos. 154, 164, 178 and 225 in Ibid.
[10] No. 183 in Ibid.

this could best be achieved by treating the three delegates on a footing of perfect equality.[11]

To obviate the ' indignity ' of having to sit at the conference as ' the mere equal ' of a Tibetan, the Chinese reverted to their earlier suggestion of having separate negotiations with the Tibetans—a position which the British politely declined. Later it was suggested that questions of procedure might be left over till the Conference opened. This too Alston regarded as an attempt at delaying matters, for an interminable procedural wrangle could blight the prospects of the conference when it eventually convened. He, therefore, insisted on a copy of Ivan Chen's full powers before he reported back to his principals.

On 2 August a Presidential Order was issued broadly conceding the British position. It read:

For Tibet negotiations Ivan Chen is appointed, as special officer with plenipotentiary powers.

The ' Order ' itself was communicated on 5 August, with an explanatory note two days later. Herein, for the first time, Peking accepted the Plenipotentiary status of the Tibetan delegate and the tripartite nature of the talks. Ivan Chen, it declared, was ordered to proceed to India ' as speedily as possible ' with a view to

open negotiations for a treaty jointly with the Tibetan Plenipotentiary and the Plenipotentiary appointed by the British Government and to sign articles which may be agreed upon for the purpose of removing all difficulties which have existed hitherto in regard to Tibet.[12]

In the light of all that had gone before, Alston viewed the Chinese note as satisfactory. He was clear, nonetheless, that any further attempt by Peking to raise the question of status must be met by a categorical refusal to reopen an issue which was regarded as closed. For assuredly, he argued, the Chinese Government were fully acquainted with the conditions attached to the invitation to attend the Conference before 7 August, the date of their note.

Meanwhile Whitehall asked Peking to set a date for its representative to reach India, failing which it ' will commence negotiating ' with the Tibetan representative alone. A warning was also sounded that any attempt, before or during the conference, to alter the status quo in Eastern Tibet or the Marches would result in an immediate breakdown in negotiations and necessitate the adoption of ' such other measures as may be required for the protection of British interests ' in Tibet.[13]

When Alston named 6 October as the date for the Conference to convene,

[11]No. 238 in Ibid.
[12]No. 252 in Ibid.
[13]Grey to Alston, 21 October 1913, No. 16 in *Foreign*, March 1914, procs. 1–251.

President Yuan expressed satisfaction and hoped Ivan Chen would be able to leave immediately. The British Minister noted that

> His Excellency's attitude was very friendly throughout and he said that he would be glad to receive Mr Rose before his departure.[14]

This 'friendly attitude' accounted for the British Minister holding over, for a later occasion, the warning which he had been directed to sound regarding the disturbance of the status quo in Eastern Tibet and the Marches, although he had made the point in a formal reply to the Chinese Foreign Office while acknowledging their note of 7 August. As he viewed it, Alston was happy that the four principal issues, raised during the negotiations for a conference, had now been satisfactorily settled. In sum

1. The fact that the Chinese representative had also been appointed a 'Commissioner for the pacification of Tibet' had no connection with or relation to the Conference;
2. The status quo on the frontier shall be maintained before and during the Conference;
3. The representatives of the three countries shall enter the Conference on a footing of equality;
4. Negotiations at the Conference shall be tripartite in character.[15]

On 27 August the Political Officer in Sikkim was directed to inform the Tibetan Plenipotentiary of the communication made to the Chinese Government that the Conference would definitely convene on 6 October 'whether the Chinese delegate arrived or not' and that, during its pendency, no attempt to alter the status quo in Tibet or the Marches would be countenanced. In the meanwhile, Lhasa was 'to decline firmly' any proposals put forward by China for negotiations at Chamdo, and keep Bell

> rapidly and fully informed of any indication of advance into Eastern Tibet on the part of the Chinese.[16]

This sounded like another hurdle. For, on the basis of letters which he had received from Lhasa, Bell noted 'repeated breaches of faith' by the Chinese in respect of their undertaking to suspend hostilities, pending the Conference at Simla. He noted that the Dalai Lama was

> afraid that before the Conference at Simla takes place, the Chinese troops may break through to Lhasa.[17]

[14]Alston to Grey, 25 August 1913, No. 26 in Ibid.
[15]Alston to Grey, 30 August 1913, No. 48 in Ibid.
[16]India to Bell, 27 August 1913, No. 29 in Ibid.
[17]Bell to India, 19 August 1913, No. 14. in Ibid.

HMG, therefore, directed the British Minister to address an appropriate warning to the Chinese President to the effect that

> negotiations in India must obviously remain abortive unless such proceedings are stopped once for all, and in that case there will be no other alternative for HMG but to safeguard, by other measures, British interests.[18]

Nor was that all. For the unwilling Ivan Chen soon appeared in Peking with a strong ' personal ' appeal to the British Minister to have the Conference postponed to 20 October '—alleging want of time to collect staff, obtain money, clothes etc'. The request was strongly supported by the Chinese Foreign Office. In private, Ivan Chen confessed that he had ' never intended to take up the appointment ', nor for that matter, Alston argued, did any Chinese official want to accept a post ' in the nature of a leader of a forlorn hope '.[19]

Meantime when Alston brought to the President's notice reports of Chinese attacks in Eastern Tibet coupled with attempts at bilateral negotiations at Chamdo, Yuan was visibly embarrassed. He assured the British Minister that the incidents listed, and of which he disclaimed all knowledge, 'could only . . . (be) due to the officials having got out of hand during the recent disturbances'. As to Ivan Chen

> His Excellency said that he had urged Mr. Chen to lose no time, and hoped that the Conference would not begin without him.[20]

As if this were not enough, a great deal threatened to be unsettled by a Memorandum delivered to the British Legation on the afternoon of the 29th. It purported to be a reply to Alston's own letter of four days earlier and, after placing on record HMG's understanding of the settlement reached, spelt out the Chinese version. Peking, it alleged, had consented to the proposal for tripartite negotiations in view of Jordan's twin undertakings. The first, held out at his interview of 30 January (1913), that a new agreement was called for in order to enable China to regain its former position in Tibet; the second, on 4 June, that tripartite negotiations were necessary in order to enable the existing treaties between Great Britain and China, in regard to Tibet, to become effective once more.[21]

From what has been said above, it would be clear that while the first statement was factually correct though misleading, when torn out of its context, the second was an even more grotesque inference from the actual words used. These were to the effect that in the then prevailing conditions in Tibet, the existing treaties were of no use. The aim of the Chinese Memorandum appeared

[18] Alston to Grey, 30 August 1913, No. 48 in Ibid.
[19] Alston to Grey, 9 September 1913, Encl. 1 in No. 122-A in Ibid.
[20] *Supra*, n. 18.
[21] Alston to Grey, 30 August 1913, No. 49 in Ibid.

to be to place on record an alleged undertaking on the part of the British to the effect that the objective of the Conference was to re-establish China in her old position in Tibet and to maintain the existing treaties, including the Trade Regulations of 1908. This, the British realised, would amount to 'a very material and entirely unacceptable' addition, to what had become an agreed basis for negotiations, namely the Memorandum of 17 August.

Predictably, the British Charge d'Affaires was profoundly upset. He let the Chinese Foreign Office know that he would not receive the document, protested to the Vice-Minister against this device to reopen a settled question and warned that, if the attempt were persisted in, 'serious consequences' would ensue. In reply, the Vice-Minister disclaimed any intention of altering the conditions agreed upon and withdrew the Memorandum.[22]

Not to give the Chinese Foreign Office another opportunity to revert to the subject, the British Minister deferred, for the time being, any mention of the incidents in Eastern Tibet to which he had referred earlier. It was clear to him that the latest reports from Chengtu indicated that the Chinese had again lost control of the north road (to Chamdo) and thus the threat posed by their garrisons may be no more than a 'bluff' to conceal the precarious nature of their own position.

With Ivan Chen's departure from Peking the stage seemed to be set, at long last, for the tripartite conference to open in Simla.

---

[22]*Supra*, n. 19.

PART IV   THE SIMLA
CONFERENCE 1913–14

Chapter 15

The Simla Conference: Some Preliminaries

DESPITE PEKING'S persistent prevarications, and Lhasa's over-zealous solicitations, added to a strong admixture of alternate coaxing and cajoling by the British, the Plenipotentiaries for the tripartite conference did not assemble in Simla until the very eve of 6 October. It was a far cry from the meetings first envisaged between the Dalai Lama's representatives and Lu Hsing-chi, the Amban-designate to Lhasa (temporarily resident in Calcutta) in Darjeeling or between Wang, the 'Administrator of Lhasa and all Tibet', and the Kalon Lama in far away Chamdo. Simla was British India's summer capital and October with its bright, crisp sun, though slightly cold, is particularly pleasing.

And yet the venue and the weather notwithstanding, a certain mystery, an odd jumble of fact and fiction, surrounds the Simla Conference. Even the date it convened has not been properly stated, not to mention the fact that the men who negotiated continue to remain, at best, shadowy figures. Another interesting facet is that the Simla Conference, despite the name that sticks, did not convene at Simla alone, nor for all the time. For some of its important meetings, more specifically those related to a settlement of the India-Tibet boundary, took place in Delhi.

A word about the day the conference held its first formal session. Jerome Chen, the biographer of Yuan Shih-kai, and lately of Mao Tse-tung, mentions it, if only indirectly:

> The ensuing Simla Conference, which began in October 1913.... But here was a tricky point of timing. Yuan recognised the autonomy of both Outer Mongolia and Tibet simultaneously on 7 October 1913—the day on which Britain conferred her recognition upon Yuan's Government.[1]

Alastair Lamb is more categorical:

> The formal opening of the Simla Conference took place on 6th October and its first working meeting was held on 13th October, when Sir Henry McMahon was elected President of the Conference.[2]

Actually in the records of the Conference, and its detailed proceedings, the meeting of 6 October, formal or otherwise, does not find any mention. It is

---

[1] Jerome Chen, *Yuan Shih-kai: 1859–1916* (London, 1961), p. 175.
[2] Lamb, *McMahon Line*, II, p. 477.

true though that Ivan Chen had arrived in Simla just in time—on the afternoon of 5 October—and expressed himself in readiness for the meeting.³ In reply, Sir Henry stated:

> With reference to your letter of 6th October, I have the honour to suggest that the Tibet Conference should open at 11 o'clock on Monday 13th October at Wheatfield House.⁴

Additionally, in a telegram to the Secretary of State, the Viceroy noted that the 13th instant had been fixed for the opening of the Conference.⁵

Again, there is on record the regret, expressed by Alston, then acting British Minister in Peking, that despite the earlier emphasis both from Delhi and Whitehall he could not

> help regretting, after what has passed here, that at least *formal* meeting of Conference did not take place on 6th October.⁶

From the above, it should be plain that no meeting of the Conference, formal or otherwise, took place on 6 October. Why then has the general impression persisted?

A close study of the records seems to offer a clue and reveals that the myth concerning 6 October was perpetuated by the man who presided at the Conference. In his periodical Memoranda on the Conference—there are four such—as well as in his 'Final Memorandum', McMahon repeats 6 October as the date the Conference convened. Thus the first Memorandum under the heading, 'Tibet Conference' is entitled 'Memorandum regarding progress of negotiations from 6th October–20th November 1913' and contains the following passage:

> On the appointed day (October 6) all the representatives had assembled at Simla, and after an exchange of visits and the customary ceremonial, the first meeting of the Conference was convened on 13th October.⁷

To the unwary, 6 October would seem the obvious starting point and yet it was not. In contrast to the 'First', McMahon's 'Final Memorandum' is more explicit on the date:

---

³Ivan Chen to Sir Henry McMahon, 6 October 1913, Correspondence, n. 1, *Foreign*, October 1914, Procs. 134–396.

⁴McMahon to Chen, 8 October 1913, Correspondence, n. 2, in Ibid.

⁵Viceroy to Secretary of State, telegram, 8 October 1913, Correspondence, n. 3, in. Ibid.

⁶Alston to Langley, telegram, 9 October 1913, No. 122-A in *Foreign*, March 1914, Procs. 1–251.

⁷' Memorandum regarding progress of negotiations from 6th October–20th November, 1913', in *Foreign and Political Department Notes*, October 1914, Procs. 134–396; cited et seq. as *Foreign, Notes*.

Invitations to a Tripartite Conference in India were therefore issued... and on their acceptance...plenipotentiaries representing the three governments assembled at Simla on 13th October, 1913.[8]

The date apart, the fortuitous link-up between Peking's attendance at the Conference and British diplomatic recognition to the Chinese Republic needs careful scrutiny. From the above it should be evident that the Conference did not meet until the 13th, although Ivan Chen had arrived in Simla a week earlier, and British recognition had been accorded to Yuan's government on the morrow of his election to the presidency by a ' National Assembly ' in Peking.

Again, as has been demonstrated earlier, the issue of recognition was mixed up with certain other inter-related questions of which Chinese acceptance of Tibet's (or Mongolia's) autonomy was not very relevant. Besides, although Britain along with Russia, France and Japan had held out in the hope of extorting some concessions, they were all outmanoeuvred by other powers, more particularly the United States. In the end, they delayed matters on the pretext, plausible as it was, that before they acted Yuan's regime be regularised through his own election as President. And no sooner did the National Assembly elect him, and Li Yuan-hung as Vice-President, recognition was accorded by thirteen powers together. The conclusion, therefore, that it is more than probable that the dates of the opening of the Simla Conference and of British recognition to the Republican regime have but a ' coincidental relationship ' to each other, appears to be quite valid.[9]

A word about the three principal plenipotentiaries at Simla. The British representative, Sir Arthur Henry McMahon,[10] was then Foreign Secretary to the Indian Government and had to step down so as to take up his new appointment. He brought to his assignment a rich experience of the frontier, more particularly in the north-west.

Of boundaries, and boundary-making too Sir Henry McMahon had acquired first-hand knowledge—he had demarcated the boundary between Baluchistan and Afghanistan in 1894–96, and acted as an arbitrator on the boundary dispute between Persia and Afghanistan in Seistan. Again, as Foreign Secretary

---

[8]' Final Memorandum ', Section I, in *Foreign*, May 1915, Procs. 36–50, Appendix to Notes.
[9]Lamb, *McMahon Line*, II, p. 477, n. 1.
[10]Sir Arthur Henry McMahon, who was born in 1862, had joined the Indian Political Department in 1890. In 1891–93, he was Political Agent, Zhob; later he accompanied the Durand Mission to Kabul as Political Officer. In 1894–96, he demarcated the boundary between Baluchistan and Afghanistan, and from 1899-1901 acted as Political Agent, Dir, Swat and Chitral. He was British Commissioner, Seistan Mission, 1903-5 and Agent to the Governor-General and Chief Commissioner, Baluchistan, 1905–11. After the Simla Conference, McMahon became Britain's first High Commissioner in Egypt, 1914–16. At the Peace Conference in Paris, Sir Henry was the British Commissioner on the Middle Eastern International Commission. A keen Mason, Sir Henry was among the founders and the first MWS of the McMahon

since 1911, he had to deal direct, and at the highest level, with the problem of Chinese incursions into the Assam Himalayas and the aftermath of the October Revolution in Tibet. No wonder his grasp of detail and understanding of the varied ramifications of British and Chinese policy was unrivalled.

Ivan Chen, or more correctly Chen I'fan, the Chinese representative, had a varied, and rich, experience. It has been noticed earlier that his name was suggested by Jordan, the British Minister in Peking. He had, before 1911, a long innings as Secretary Counsellor of the Chinese Legation in London where, apart from a good knowledge of the language, he had acquired among his British colleagues a reputation for sobriety and reasonableness. Rated an adept diplomat, on his return to China he took part in the closing stages of negotiations leading to the Opium agreement. Later, he was appointed Taotai on the Burma-Yunnan frontier with a view to fostering a better understanding with the British: there had been, as noticed earlier, frequent frontier clashes there. As it happened, he could never reach his outpost, for the outbreak of the October Revolution seriously interrupted his progress.

Under the Republic, Ivan Chen became Commissioner for Trade and Foreign Affairs at Shanghai. It was from this post that reluctantly, and perhaps against his own better judgment, he was persuaded to go to Simla where, long before he set out, the British Minister in Peking had rated his prospects as a ' forlorn hope '.[11]

The Tibetan delegate to Simla was Shatra Paljor Dorje Kalon, more simply Lonchen (viz. Minister) Shatra. Shatra had been to Darjeeling towards the

Chapter Rose Croix No. 161, established in Quetta in 1908. A small booklet, published in London on 11 April 1961, gives a ' Short History ' of the Chapter.

In 1907, Sir Henry developed very close personal relations with Amir Habibullah of Afghanistan, then on a state visit to India, part of the reason being the Amir's induction into Freemasonry. In a note written in January 1936, McMahon expressed the view that the Afghan Amir's ' faithful friendship ', which was an important factor in the ' successful issue ' of World War I—when Afghanistan remained benevolently neutral—was helped by Freemasonry ' in creating and cementing ' that bond.

It may be noted here that Sir Henry was the last of the Foreign Secretaries who held the combined charge of the Foreign and Political Department of the then Government of India; after him the Political Department became a separate charge.

No biography of Sir Henry exists nor are his ' papers ', if there are any, easy to locate. For a brief sketch, and a portrait by John Collier, see Lt Col E H Cobb, ' A Frontier Statesman ', *The Piffer* (London), V, 6 May 1963. Also see *Dictionary of National Biography*, *Who Was Who* and Sir Ronald Storrs, *Orientations* (London, 1943).

[11]Encl. 1, No. 122-A in *Foreign*, March 1914, Procs. 1–251.

Dr. Li's assertion, *Historical Status of Tibet*, p. 135, that it was because of his opposition to India ' as a meeting place ' that Wen Chung-yao, formerly Deputy Amban in Lhasa, refused to accept appointment as the Chinese delegate, seems misplaced. The fact is that Wen's name was never accepted by Jordan; the question of his refusal, therefore, becomes superfluous. In support, Li relies upon the *Times* of 29 March 1913 and the *North China Herald* of 20 July 1912—n. 22, p. 267, in Ibid. Actually, as we know from the records, the question of nominating a Chinese Plenipotentiary did not arise until June 1913. For details see No. 29 in *Foreign*, September 1913, Procs. 1–271.

close of the century where he acquired a shrewd understanding, and at first-hand, of British power and authority.[12] Later promoted a Kalon and a member of the Kashag he is said to have been a strong advocate of a peaceful settlement with the British in regard to the Sikkim frontier and other trading rights. This was largely because he realised Tibet's lack of military prowess. The Tsongdu, at once ignorant and bigoted, had, however, advocated a fight to the finish, and suspected Shatra of being a British protégé.[13] Nor was that all, for the British on their part suspected him of being the Dalai Lama's principal adviser in the latter's pro-Russian policy.[14] Consequently, when Younghusband advanced into Tibet, Shatra and his three other colleagues in the Kashag found themselves prisoners in the Lama's Summer Palace.[15]

Later, in 1907, in the course of his 'wanderings' far from home, the Dalai Lama, while at Sian-fu in China, is said to have written to the authorities in Lhasa to appoint Shatra as Lonchen so that he, in close liaison with the Regent, may look after the country's administration. He is said to have been confirmed in his new post by the Lama personally when the latter eventually returned home towards the end of 1909.[16] The Lonchen accompanied the Dalai Lama to India during his second exile, 1910–12, where he came into close personal contact with Bell who formed a high opinion both of his intelligence and grasp of detail.

The Lonchen's powers, as Tibet's Plenipotentiary at the Simla Conference, were wide-ranging for the Dalai Lama had authorised him

to decide all matters that may be beneficial to Tibet and (I authorise him) to seal all such documents.[17]

Between 13 October 1913, when it formally convened, and 3 July 1914, when it dispersed, the Simla Conference held eight formal sessions. The first two took place at Simla on 13 October and 18 November respectively; the next three at Delhi, on 12 January, 17 February and 11 March (1914); and the last three again at Simla, on 7 and 22 April (re-convened on 27 April) and 3 July. Thus the Conference met both at Simla and in Delhi.

Nor did the formal meetings by themselves exhaust the scope of the work

---

[12]Shatra had been sent to study the situation arising out of the Trade Regulations of 1893 but his reports did not find favour with his own government who felt that too close a contact with the British would damage the Tibetan way of life. *Shakabapa*, p. 203.

The Tibetan title 'Lonchen' may be regarded as equivalent to the British 'Minister'.

[13]Ibid., pp. 208–9.

[14]Bell, *Tibet*, p. 64. *Kawaguchi*, pp. 502–3, mentions Shatra's pronouncedly pro-Russian leanings.

[15]*Shakabapa*, p. 209.

[16]Ibid., pp. 221 and 223.

[17]No. 238 in *Foreign*, September 1913, Procs. 1–271. Also *Shakabapa*, p. 251.

of the conference, for a number of informal sessions were held too. Thus the negotiations pertaining to the boundary settlement between India and Tibet took place in Delhi between 17 January and 25 March (1914). So too were a number of sessions convened in private, between Ivan Chen and McMahon's China expert, Archibald Rose. A member of the (British) Chinese Consular Service, 'Archie' Rose had served in Tengyueh as Consul General and possessed an unrivalled knowledge of the language and of China's frontier diplomacy through a first-hand acquaintance with the intricacies of the Burma-Yunnan frontier dispute. At Simla, and later in Delhi, it fell to him to smooth over a number of ticklish questions in regard to laying the boundary between China and Tibet in the east.

At the end of the second meeting of the Conference at Simla, on 18 November, McMahon concluded that a major watershed had been reached in the discussions. So, in fact, it had. And this related largely to the intractable problem of laying down a boundary between China and Tibet and settling their respective territorial claims against each other. Meantime, and much more vital to the discussions at Simla, was hammering out the terms of a draft convention that would meet the urgent needs of Tibet, the peremptory requirements of the Government of India in regard to the frontier in the north and the tender susceptibilities of HMG, more specifically in regard to the provisions of the Anglo-Russian Convention of 1907.

It may be recalled that the Memorandum of 17 August 1912 had broadly sketched the outlines of an arrangement within whose frame-work HMG visualised an eventual settlement of the Tibetan question. The fact that the Chinese had accepted the Memorandum as a basis for discussions at Simla was viewed by the British as a satisfactory beginning. Yet long before the three Plenipotentiaries assembled, a great deal of behind-the-scenes consultations had taken place between Whitehall, the Governor-General in Delhi and the Minister in Peking, with a view to hammering out a draft that may be presented to the other two parties. One of the very first drawn up in London, early in 1913, reflects British thinking at the time and may be briefly spelt out here.

Three themes were uppermost. The first related to the territorial integrity of Tibet which was to be ensured both through Peking abstaining from 'interference' in the country's 'internal administration' and engaging not to send troops nor yet station 'civil or military officials'. An exception, however, was made in regard to the posting of a Chinese representative at Lhasa who may advise in regard to the country's foreign relations, but whose escort was in no case to exceed 300 men.

Since this objective could only be achieved by China being released from its obligations under the Trade Regulations of 1908, in regard to the administration of trade marts, protection of trade routes and regulation of commerce, the draft stipulated that such a release be effected.

And finally, short of defining Tibet's physical boundaries, the districts which constituted it were severally enumerated.[18]

It is obvious that, at the time the draft was prepared, the British visualised a bilateral arrangement with China, which Lhasa was later to be persuaded to endorse. This would ensure, the British argued, a return to the status quo *ante* 1904. Nor was it deemed necessary to insist on the specific cancellation of the Presidential Order regarding the inclusion of Tibet in China proper, provided limitation of Chinese troops and prevention of Chinese interference in the country's internal administration were secured.

Jordan's observations on the draft were interesting. To start with, he was not sure if the Chinese would accept the proposition that Tibet's internal administration was its own business. He recalled that the nomination and selection of civil officials, although made by the Tibetans themselves, always required Chinese confirmation. Similarly, argued the British Minister, the Chinese were certain to ask for the re-establishment of posts between Lhasa and Szechuan to maintain their lines of communication without which the garrison at Lhasa would be isolated and in no position to obtain requisite supplies.[19]

Delhi's comments on Whitehall's draft were cast in a different key. In principle, it deplored any reference to treaty stipulations, for fear this might lead to prolonged discussions. As to Peking pressing for the re-establishment of posts between Szechuan and Lhasa, India was confident necessary supplies could be arranged in an adequate measure by the Tibetans and that, provided treaties were observed, the route via India could be made use of for purposes of sending relief. Furthermore, denunciation of the 1908 Regulations was deemed necessary in order to deprive China of any excuse for interference. Delhi also suggested an additional article, on the analogy of the Russo-Mongolian treaty, precluding colonisation in Tibet proper by Chinese, or British, subjects. This was viewed as a necessary safeguard against the ingress of Chinese settlers into Zayul.[20]

It would be obvious that the British draft was soon outpaced by developments in Tibet, the conclusion of the Russo-Mongolian Agreement and of the Mongol-Tibetan Treaty. In Tibet itself, by the middle of 1913, there was a complete erosion of Chinese authority which, it was apparent, could only be regained either through conquest, or by negotiation. These factors had powerfully influenced HMG towards accepting the idea of a tripartite convention instead of their earlier resolve of lending their ' benevolent assistance ' towards making China and Tibet reach an agreement on their own. The result was that on 7 March 1913, a modified version of the earlier draft agreement emerged. The latter gave an interesting definition of Tibet's status as being ' *under the suzerainty but not the sovereignty* ' of China, a *mantram* which in years to come was to acquire considerable significance. It took the place

---

[18] For the full text see No. 322, in *Foreign*, May 1913, Procs. 261–502.
[19] For Jordan's comments see No. 327 in Ibid.
[20] For Government of India's observations on the British draft see No. 355 in Ibid.

of treaty stipulations to which the earlier Whitehall draft had referred and to which Delhi had raised strong objections. Reference was also made to China being debarred from establishing colonies, a stipulation which Delhi had specifically sought.[21] It is interesting that the March draft still retained its bipartite character, eloquent testimony to the fact that for long HMG stoutly resisted any broad-basing of the negotiations so as to embrace all the three countries.

A word here about the distinction between the suzerain and the sovereign, based essentially on European feudalism and now sought to be injected into the relationship of powers in this part of Asia. The basic bond between the Ch'ing Emperor and the Dalai Lama, it may be recalled, was that of the Patron and the Priest, a sort of extension of the *chela-guru* idea which does not yield easily to a precise definition nor allows itself to be put into a strait-jacket. Like most Asian concepts, it is neither rigid nor legalistic, but elastic and flexible and subject to change. While there is the right of the *chela* to temporal ' supremacy ' and the duty of the *guru* to tender ' subordination ' in the higher interests of the state, there is also the spiritual supremacy of the *guru* and his right to demand protection and the moral subordination of the *chela* and his duty to render help when required. The nearest analogy to it in European history is that of the relationship between the Holy Roman Emperor and the Pope. The Pope acknowledged the Emperor as his superior in material things; the Emperor regarded the Pope as his *guru* and agreed to the autonomy of the Papal states in Italy. In all this, one is powerfully struck by a certain naiveté on the part of the British in transplanting from its feudal European origins and background to the heart of Asia the suzerain-sovereign concept which, at its best, is woefully inadequate to describe the relationship between the Manchu Emperors and the Dalai Lamas. More, it could hardly survive the replacement of the ' Son of Heaven ' by an ordinary mortal as the head of a godless Republic!

From Whitehall to the Potala. What ideas, if any, did Lhasa have on a settlement? On 23 July (1913) Bell reported what appeared to be the Dalai Lama's principal terms. *Inter alia*, Tibet was to

1. manage its external affairs, after consultation with the British Government on matters of importance;
2. control its internal administration;
3. include Batang, Nyarong, Litang, Derge and, in fact, the entire area up to Tachienlu;
4. have Chinese traders but neither an Amban, nor other (Chinese) officials, much less any soldiers.[22]

---

[21] For the text see No. 446 in Ibid. The draft was proposed by the India Office in its note to the Foreign Office on 7 March 1913.

[22] No. 208 in *Foreign*, September 1913, Procs. 1–271. Also see Bell, *Portrait*, p. 205.

Lonchen Shatra who was in the Chumbi valley, ready for the Conference that had been promised, and about which he and his country were so keen, had told Bell that under Lhasa's dispensation—barring the provision for consultations with the British ' on matters of importance '—his country would occupy the same position *vis-à-vis* China as it, in fact, enjoyed during the reign of the Fifth Dalai Lama (1616–80). It was a position which, he argued, Lhasa had been striving to attain during the previous three years (1911–13). A somewhat discordant note, however, was struck by the Tsongdu which, in sharp contrast to the position thus taken by the Dalai Lama and the Tibetan Government, favoured the stationing of a Chinese Amban—' who would not, however, have power to intervene in the internal administration ' of the country.[23]

Delhi had serious reservations on the position taken by the Lhasa authorities which, it made clear, ' could not be supported '. Nonetheless it saw no disadvantage in the Tibetans putting forward claims of a more extensive nature, in the first instance at any rate. This, it was argued, would make it possible for HMG to assume the role of an arbitrator and demonstrate that it was using its influence with a view to the curtailment of Tibetan pretensions. ' Naturally ' the same reasoning, Delhi insisted, applied to the ' excessive pretensions ' on the part of China.[24]

Insofar as access to their archives pertaining to the Simla Conference is denied, what may be regarded as Chinese drafts for a bipartite settlement with Tibet in the first instance, or later tripartite negotiations, are conspicuous by their absence. Some straws in the wind, however, may be taken note of for they afford a useful clue to Peking's thinking. Thus, as has been noticed, the Gazette notification of 12 June (1913) designated Ivan Chen, as also Hu Han-min, as ' Commissioners for the Pacification of Tibet '—the terminology being the same as employed for appointments made to provinces in China proper and smacking strongly of an assumption of control over a dominion. It is true that Peking later wriggled out of this position and maintained that the ' title ' carried ' no territorial powers '. Nonetheless the fact remains that the Presidential order of 15 June was not revoked and that in the final count it was HMG which dropped its opposition to it.[25]

Another pointer was Peking's unswerving insistence that the Tibetan representative at Simla could not occupy the same position as his Chinese, or British, counterpart. Here the Wai-chiao-pu cited repeatedly the precedent of the Regulations of 1908 where, it maintained, the Tibetan representative ' had signed after, and as adjoint ' to his Chinese counterpart. Later, on 7 August, when the Chinese Foreign Office relented and accepted the principle

---

[23]No. 208 in *Foreign*, September 1913, Procs. 1–271. Bell, *Portrait*, p. 13, mentions 1680 as the date of the Dalai Lama's death; Richardson, *History*, p. 46, gives it as 1682.

[24]No. 213 in *Foreign*, September 1913, Procs. 1–271.

[25]Nos. 86, 168 and 175 in Ibid.

of 'a treaty jointly' with the British and Tibetan Plenipotentiaries, the British Minister in Peking noted that this

> did not necessarily prevent the Chinese delegate from re-opening the question of the status of the Tibet delegate at the Conference.[26]

Towards the end, when all seemed to have been settled, the Chinese threw in another spanner. This was their Memorandum of 30 August, alluded to earlier, which made out that Peking had accepted tripartite negotiations on Jordan's twin assurances that the new arrangement was necessary to enable China to regain its former position in Tibet and would make existing treaties between Great Britain and China effective again.[27]

To put it mildly, the British, the Tibetans and the Chinese argued their respective positions from assumptions which ran directly counter each to the other. As between them, on the eve of the Conference, a meeting-ground, if any, seemed hard to discern.

[26]Office note, ' Situation in Tibet ', in *Foreign*, March 1914, Procs. 1–251.
[27]No. 49 in Ibid.

Chapter 16

The China-Tibet Boundary and the Birth of Inner-Outer Tibet

BEFORE NOVEMBER was over, it was clear beyond the shadow of a doubt that the three Plenipotentiaries at Simla were pulling separately, each in a different direction. Ivan Chen's major preoccupation was a political settlement whereby Lhasa accepted, and without qualification, China's sovereign status; the Lonchen, on the other hand, sought an explicit recognition of the boundaries of an ' independent ' Tibet; while the British were, for a time, content to play a waiting game. Before many weeks were over, they hoped to be called upon to act the ' honest broker '.

McMahon's ' strategy ' at the Conference had been broadly sketched out by the Governor-General in a ' Very Confidential ' telegram to the Secretary of State a week ahead of the actual day of its first meeting:

> After usual scrutiny of credentials of delegates McMahon proposes to open the proceedings by presenting to plenipotentiary of Chinese Government the statement of Tibetan demands which will be embodied in a draft agreement prepared for purposes of convenience on skeleton lines of draft agreement of HMG. The statement puts forward claims very much in excess of what McMahon understands Tibet is willing eventually to agree to and it will therefore serve as a useful preliminary basis of discussion. It will, in McMahon's opinion, elicit statement of demands of Chinese Government on lines equally exaggerated and will facilitate subsequent mutual settlement on desired lines.

The Governor-General added that the ' procedure proposed ' had his ' concurrence '.[1]

Lord Crewe, while he entered no known objections, entertained serious doubts as to the Chinese reaction and warned the Governor-General to

> remember that invitation was issued to Chinese to negotiate on basis of Memorandum dated 17th August...and Chinese delegate may decline any other. If Chinese delegate follows this line, McMahon will not be able to insist on making statement of Tibetan requirements the formal basis of

---

[1]Viceroy to Secretary of State, telegram, 8 October 1913, Correspondence, *Foreign*, October 1914, Procs. 134–396. The first sentence read: ' The 13th instant has been fixed for opening of the Tibet conference.'

discussion....Do you not think it would be preferable that Tibetan delegate should himself produce his statement?[2]

This is precisely what happened at the first meeting. For, after the preliminaries of his own election as Chairman, mutual self-congratulation by the three delegates and expression of a pious hope for an 'early' and 'successful conclusion' of their deliberations,

> Sir Henry McMahon on learning that the Lonchen Shatra had prepared a statement of Tibetan claims which he wished to present, invited him to lay it on the table. This was done and a copy given to the British and Chinese Plenipotentiaries.[3]

The 'statement of Tibetan claims', duly sealed by the Lonchen and date-lined 10 October, was divided into six parts. The *first*, though a long and laboured repetition of Chinese excesses against Tibet in the recent past, concluded on an affirmative note:

> Tibet and China have never been under each other and will never associate with each other in future. It is decided that Tibet is an independent state....
> Tibet repudiates the Anglo-Chinese Convention concluded at Peking on the 27th April, 1906...as she did not send a representative for this convention, nor did she affix her seal on it. It is, therefore, decided that it is not binding on the three Governments.

Whatever Tibet's 'declarations' in the previous year, nothing could be a plainer or more unequivocal statement of its independence.

The *second* part defined the boundaries of Tibet thus:

> On the north the Kuen Lun range, the Altyn Tagh with the Ho Shili range, the Ba-kang Poto range...thence in a southerly and south-easterly direction including the country of Go-lok, Har-kog, Nya-rong...thence in a southerly direction of the boundaries of Szechuan and Yunnan and thence along the boundary of Tibet to Rima.

As if the physical contours were not explicit enough, the Lonchen underlined the fact that the

> above countries all form part of Tibet, being inhabited by the Tibetans and included in Tibet. It is decided that the revenue of these countries of the past years shall be returned to the Tibetans.

---

[2] Secretary of State to Viceroy, 11 October 1913, No. 138 in Ibid.

[3] 'Proceedings of the 1st Meeting of the Tibet Conference held at Simla on the 13th October 1913', No. 139 in Ibid.

The rest of the statement on Tibet's ' claims ' was more matter of fact. Thus in the *third* part, the Trade Regulations of 1908 were sought to be revised by Britain and Tibet ' in mutual consultation and agreement '—China ' having no longer any concern ' with them.

The *fourth* part of Tibetan ' claims ' sought China's exclusion by stipulating that in future

> no Chinese officials and troops will be allowed to stay in Tibet. Their staying there ... (is) a source of constant friction.... In order ... to ensure peace between the two countries ... no Chinese Amban or other officials and no Chinese soldiers or colonists will be permitted to enter or reside in Tibet.

Political exclusion notwithstanding, Tibet did not want its religious ties to be snapped, for the *fifth* sub-head laid down that the

> people of Mongolia and China send monks to the different monasteries in Tibet and also pay vast tribute to the monasteries. The Buddhist monasteries and other religious institutions in Mongolia and China recognise the Dalai Lama as their religious head. All these facts will be continued to be recognised as at present.

And *finally*, Lhasa claimed damages

> for all the forcible exactions of money or other property taken from the Tibet Government, for the revenue of Nyarong and other districts which they kept in their possession by force, for destroying houses and property of monasteries ... and for the damage done to the persons or property of Nepalese and Ladakhis.

Nor did the claims enumerated represent the final count-down for, as the Lonchen indicated, more such lists ' are coming '—from Kham.[4]

The inevitable happened. Ivan Chen could not long be idle. On 30 October, he sent his reply containing ' the views of my Government in regard to this question ', and sought ' another meeting ' of the Conference to ' consider ' his draft. The battle royal had been joined.

The Chinese ' counter-proposals ' were prefaced by a brief, if tendentious account of the relationship between the two countries. For the 'misunderstanding ' that ' now ' exists, Chen argued,

---

[4]For the full text, in English, see Annexure IV, No. 139 in Ibid.

In his telegram to the Secretary of State, the Viceroy referred to these ' claims ' as a ' draft agreement... .presented by the Tibetan Plenipotentiary '. In a subsequent telegram, of date, the Viceroy summed up the draft succinctly.

it is not China that can be blamed, but it is entirely due to the conduct of His Holiness... the intractability... and his ignorance of the international situation.

Indicating that the claims presented by the Lonchen were 'inadmissible', the Chinese Plenipotentiary went on to list his own 'demands' which, he noted, offered 'the only basis for the negotiations' of the Tibetan question:

1. Tibet was to be 'an integral part' of China and no attempts by Britain, or Tibet, to interrupt 'this territorial integrity' were to be tolerated. China however, 'engages not to convert' Tibet into a Chinese province and Britain not to annex the country or any part thereof;
2. A Chinese Resident was to be stationed at Lhasa enjoying 'all such privileges and rights' as he had done hitherto. His escort was to number 2,600 men—1,000 posted at Lhasa and another 1,600 at such places as the Resident thought fit;
3. Tibet was to be guided by China in its foreign and military affairs and was not to enter into negotiations 'except through the intermediary' of the Chinese government. Exception, however, was made for direct relations between British 'Commercial Agents' and Tibetan authorities as provided under article V of the Lhasa Convention and confirmed by the Adhesion Agreement of 1906;
4. Tibet was to grant an amnesty to all those, officials and non-officials, who had been punished by reason of 'their well-known sympathy' for the Chinese and to restore their property;
5. China was willing 'to discuss' the continuation of religious ties which Tibet had sought;
6. A revision of the Trade Regulations of 1893 and of 1908, 'if found necessary', must be made by 'all the parties concerned' on the basis of Article III of the Adhesion Convention of 1906;
7. The frontier boundary between China and Tibet which the latter was to endorse was indicated on a map and conformed largely to the then prevalent Chinese notions on the subject.[5]

While Tibetan and Chinese claims and counter-claims appeared to occupy the stage, McMahon was frantically busy in behind-the-scenes moves to hammer out a draft agreement to which he could persuade the two sides to agree. Thus on 10 November, the Viceroy telegraphed to the Secretary of State an

---

[5]For the text see Proc. 149 in Ibid.

The Governor-General summed it up in a long telegram to the Secretary of State on 31 October 1913, No. 153 in Ibid. As for the map: 'the Kuen Lun range is left at about longitude 84°. Then south-east in almost a straight line to Giamda (not Chiamdo) leaving Nagchuka and Tangla range in China. From Giamda it runs south to Tsang-po and follows river as far as Gyala and thence runs almost in a straight line to Nmaikha river through Menilkrai'.

amended draft agreement on which the British Plenipotentiary had laboured hard.[6] HMG, however, was circumspect and refused to be hustled into a decision. Besides it warned that

> without previous concurrence of Russia it would not be possible to negotiate anything resembling draft presented by McMahon. HMG conclude ... that right of representation at Lhasa should rest exclusively with us. Is a British or native agent at Lhasa contemplated by Government of India?[7]

Obviously there was many a rough edge yet to be rounded. No wonder McMahon, outwardly at any rate, got busy on the rival, if contradictory, 'claims' of Tibet and China. Besides he did want to avoid the slightest suspicion of an intentional delay on his part.[8] Thus the day the Secretary of State's reply was received, the British Plenipotentiary wrote to Ivan Chen enquiring 'if 11 a.m. on the 18th instant' was a convenient date and time for the next meeting of the Conference. As for the agenda,

> I propose to bring forward ... certain questions relating to the frontier of Tibet; the compensation of losses claimed by Tibet; the amnesty claimed on behalf of those who have suffered in the cause of China, and also certain questions relating to our future procedure.[9]

When the second meeting did convene on the appointed day, there was a wrangle and not only over procedure.

McMahon started by putting forth the view that the 'first and most important' question related to a 'definition of the limits' of Tibet; 'among minor ones' he listed the Tibetan claim for 'compensation of losses' and the Chinese for an 'amnesty' and 'restoration of confiscated property'. He proposed discussing them 'informally' in order 'to facilitate business' and to bring them to the Conference 'only when the issues had been cleared'.

While the Lonchen agreed with this procedure, Ivan Chen enquired as to the order in which the various items would be discussed and, more specifically, whether 'the frontier question would be taken first'.

To McMahon's rejoinder that until some agreement was reached on the 'limits of Tibet' he was unable to take up other points or form any opinion on them, Ivan Chen countered by suggesting that the political status of Tibet should be 'the first point and the most important'. A decision on the issue, he felt, would 'help to solve' the frontier question.

When the Lonchen lent his support to the position taken up by the British Plenipotentiary, Chen revealed that he had 'definite orders' from his princi-

---

[6]Viceroy to Secretary of State, telegram, 10 November 1913, No. 159 in Ibid.
[7]Secretary of State to Viceroy, telegram, 13 November 1913, No. 160 in Ibid.
[8]Viceroy to Secretary of State, telegram, 18 November 1913, No. 166 in Ibid.
[9]McMahon to Chen, letter, 14 November 1913, No. 161 in Ibid.

pals to have the first two clauses of his statement settled first, and not to discuss the question of compensation at all. McMahon thereupon ruled that 'the limits of the country' to be defined should receive priority and proposed taking up this question with the Lonchen 'until their Chinese colleague' was authorised to join in the discussion.

'In the circumstances', Chen announced, he would telegraph to his government for instructions. Meanwhile could not other clauses in the Chinese statement be considered? McMahon's rejoinder was a firm negative for he

> did not think this could be done until the main question of the limits of Tibet was settled.

And on this note the second meeting of the Conference adjourned.[10]

A postscript may be appended here. On 23 November, five days after the Conference had adjourned, the British Plenipotentiary was informed by Ivan Chen that his government had authorised him '*to enter into negotiations* regarding Tibet's territorial limits.'[11] There was a rider however, namely that as soon as there was a prospect of some settlement, other clauses of the Chinese statement of counter-claims would be taken up. Before initiating a discussion on the boundaries, however, Chen indicated that he was awaiting 'a despatch map' from Peking.[12]

The Chinese game, McMahon concluded, was clear for they

> will in any case devote their full energies to obtain their first two demands (i.e. political status of Tibet and the re-instatement of a Chinese Representative at Lhasa) and ignore all other proposals with a view to retaining somewhat intangible rights in Tibet without limitation or definition.

He cautioned, however, against falling into their trap and trusted that no

> recognition or prospect of recognition of these claims will be accorded to the Chinese Government, until we have secured a suitable *quid pro quo*, and the acquiescence of China in our own demands.[13]

McMahon's conclusions, it seems, were based on a note recorded by Archibald Rose after an informal meeting with Ivan Chen on 21 November when the latter

---

[10]For details 'Proceedings of the 2nd meeting of the Tibet Conference', No. 165 in Ibid; for McMahon's report, Viceroy to Secretary of State, 18 November 1913, No. 166 in Ibid.

[11]In his 'Memorandum regarding progress of negotiations from October 6 to November 20', McMahon had anticipated this: *supra*, n. 7, 'the disadvantage of our ex-parte enquiry will elicit this permission,' he had remarked.

[12]Viceroy to Secretary of State, telegram, 24 November 1913, No. 172 in Ibid. Also see Ivan Chen to McMahon, letter, in *Foreign, Notes*, October 1914, Procs. 134–396.

[13]*Supra*, n. 11.

said that his Government stipulated that, as soon as the question (of the frontier) appeared to be reaching finality, the questions of the political status of Tibet and the reinstatement of the Amban should be discussed concurrently. He understood this to mean that there should be no actual acceptance of a frontier line before the other points had received due consideration.

In private, Chen confessed to Rose that the frontier question 'had been exploded' upon him and his government 'rather unexpectedly', for all that he was prepared for was the Memorandum of 17 August 'on the strength of which' his Government had been invited to the Conference. Rose countered by arguing that it was Chen who had 'pushed this question to the front' by outlining a boundary which severely restricted Tibet, and then proposed stationing within it 'a body of 2,600 men'. This it was that made it imperative for McMahon to come to 'some decision' as to the domain in which these men were to function.[14]

The long and short of it all was that as soon as the Conference moved to Delhi, early in December, a series of informal discussions took place in which the Chinese and Tibetan Plenipotentiaries presented their respective claims and counter-claims with a view to evolving an agreed procedure, if not an agreed frontier.[15]

At the first of these meetings, on 5 December, Ivan Chen proposed that no minutes of their discussions be kept, nor any decisions held to be binding unless so confirmed by a formal meeting of the Conference. On this there was general agreement. Later, after some discussion, in which the Lonchen's opposition was sufficiently pronounced, it was agreed that the main question be taken up on 'broad and general lines', the difficulties of detail revealing themselves as they proceeded. The Lonchen favoured bilateral discussions, of a preliminary nature, between himself and Bell as also between Ivan Chen and Rose. To this the Chinese delegate was opposed for fear it may 'complicate' the 'frank exchange of views' between the parties. The meeting adjourned on the Lonchen agreeing to convene as soon as his archives arrived from Simla.

Though superficially frustrating, McMahon concluded that these discussions had served a useful purpose

in focussing the ideas of the Chinese and Tibetan Plenipotentiaries as to the best method of dealing with the intricate question of the frontiers.[16]

[14]Note by Archibald Rose, 21 November 1913, in *Foreign Notes*.
[15]Minutes of the 'Informal Discussions' were recorded by Rose and Bell. These are to be found at Serial 45 in *Foreign, Notes*.
[16]Office note on 'Informal Discussions' held on 11 December 1913, in Ibid.

At their second informal meeting, a week later, the two Plenipotentiaries read out statements of their general case for the boundary as claimed by their respective governments. In brief, Ivan Chen asserted that China had exercised a virtual sovereignty over Tibet since the time of the Yuan (Mongol) dynasty, a fact signalled by the appointment of Chinese officials in Tibet. Further, China had maintained an effective occupation of the country during the time of the Manchu dynasty and this constituted a substantive right in international law. The Chinese occupation, Chen alleged, reached as far west as Giamda (Chiangta), included the districts of Pomed, Zayul, Markham, Drege, Draya and Gyade. Besides, Peking's claims on Kokonor, Batang and Litang, were 'generally' recognised.

To the above the Lonchen replied by maintaining that Tibet had always been 'an independent country', that at one time a Chinese princess had been given in marriage to a Tibetan ruler, at another a boundary pillar had been erected at Marugong (Kokonor-Kansu border). Again, even though in the eastern region the Chinese had given titles to some of the border princes, the collection of taxes and the administration of the country had always remained in Tibetan hands.[17]

In the discussions that took place on 12, 15 and 19 December the boundary problem got no nearer solution. As may be clear, the two Plenipotentiaries showed a persistent tendency towards defining 'the political status' of the border country with the result that the issues relating strictly to the frontier were soon forgotten. Nor did Chinese evidence in regard to 'a boundary pillar erected 300 li west of Batang, in 1727' prove very convincing to the Lonchen:

> Could Mr. Chen give him any satisfactory documentary proof that this pillar existed, that it was a boundary mark between China and Tibet, and that it had been acknowledged by the Tibetans?

Ivan Chen did not know all the answers but the Lonchen did for he

> proposed to prove by authentic documents that the lands of the monasteries east of the pillar were held from the Lhasa Government and that the Lhasa Government held full administrative rights in all the country inhabited by Tibetans east of Batang and as far as Tachienlu.[18]

When the Chinese delegate returned to the subject of the Batang boundary pillar on 15 December it was already clear that his ground was shaky. For evidence on the pillar, he fell back on Jordan's interview at the Foreign Office in Peking on 30 January 1913—where the Minister had, in fact, invoked the

[17] Office note on 'Informal Discussions' held on 12 December 1913, in Ibid.
[18] Office note on 'Informal Discussions' held on 15 December 1913, in Ibid.

authority of Sir Alexander Hosie, a British officer who had first-hand knowledge of this frontier. Nor did China's territory end with the pillar—it had been extended by Chao Erh-feng. With the sharp, seasoned eye of an attorney, the Lonchen pounced upon the innumerable holes in the arguments adduced by Chen. Chao's campaigns, he asserted, were in the nature of ' illegal raids ' rather than recognised conquests. As for the pillar:

> If (it) ... really existed, and if it really had been erected as a frontier mark, there should be no difficulty in producing documentary evidence of the fact. Failing this he was unable to admit its existence or validity... many pillars had been erected in Tibet from time to time, but they had never been intended as territorial boundaries.

The Batang pillar vanished into thin air. Ivan Chen had nothing much to adduce as documentary evidence. When his turn came, the Lonchen mentioned three identical monoliths, erected about a thousand years earlier—in Lhasa, at the Chinese capital, and on the frontier—recording a Chinese-Tibetan treaty and outlining the frontier between the two countries. He produced copies, in Tibetan, of the inscription on the pillars and a reference thereto in the ' History of Tibet ', compiled by the 5th Dalai Lama.[19]

The last meeting on frontier discussions was held on 19 December, this time on British initiative, for Sir Henry wanted ' to push on the work ' as far as possible. As the Lonchen's translations of the inscription on the boundary pillars were not ready, discussion reverted to individual districts. Here too a difficulty cropped up for while the Lonchen was ready to discuss Nyarong and Derge, Chen wanted to take up Gyade and Gyamda. As the argument seemed to be leading nowhere in particular, Chen proposed a compromise to the effect that

> he and the Tibetan Plenipotentiary should each prepare a written statement embodying his complete evidence on the whole case regarding the frontier and should hand such written statement to the British Plenipotentiary at a full Conference.

The British representative kept his counsel, undertook to examine these statements and let his two other colleagues know the result. The latter position, it would seem, Ivan Chen was not prepared to accept for an office note recorded that he

> does not agree necessarily to abide by the opinions of the British Plenipotentiary on the frontier question.[20]

---

[19] Office note on ' Informal Discussions ' held on 19 December 1913, in Ibid.

[20] ' Memorandum regarding Progress of Negotiations from 21 November to 24 December 1913 ', Serial 45, in *Foreign, Notes*.

Summing up the results of the second phase of the Conference, during which no formal meeting as such was held, the British Plenipotentiary made some interesting points:

One, his proposal to institute 'an enquiry into the limits of the Tibetan territories' with the Lonchen alone, elicited from Peking 'immediate instructions' to their representative to take part in these frontier discussions;

Two, at the informal meetings—at which 'I considered it well to take no active part in the proceedings'—his aim was to elicit from both parties 'the fullest information in regard to their rights and claims' (meantime he had directed both Bell and Rose to refrain from any expression of opinion as to the value of the evidence produced much less with the initiation of any proposals for a settlement);

Three, Ivan Chen had, initially, resisted any discussion of the territory east of Batang on the plea that the Batang pillar, erected in A.D. 1727, furnished incontestible evidence that the March country was beyond the limits of Tibet. The British countered by suggesting that as boundary lines had been indicated on the skeleton map both by the Chinese and Tibetans, any country lying between the two lines was clearly within the scope of their discussion. The aim was 'to acquire all possible information and to produce all available evidence' concerning any portion of the disputed territory;

Four, 'it was evident from the outset' that the Tibetans were in a more favourable position than the Chinese as far as documentary evidence was concerned. While Chen had relied chiefly on the pamphlet of General Fu Sung-mu, recording the campaigns of Chao Erh-feng and on the published works of authors like Holditch, the Lonchen had refused to accept these as conclusive evidence. On his own, he had produced a large number of original archives from Lhasa, tomes of delicate manuscripts, the official history of Tibet compiled by the 5th Dalai Lama, the text of the Chinese-Tibetan Treaty of 822. He promised to produce the original records of each Tibetan state as far east as Tachienlu proving that the lamaseries and tribal chiefs had exercised a continuing administrative control over the country for many centuries;

Five, under the powerful impact of this relentless pressure, for some days Chen showed evident signs of panic; he protested that his Government would never consent to the production of evidence in regard to the country east of Batang or the discussion of Kokonor; he telegraphed to Paris for an official copy of the 'Institutes of the Manchu Dynasty', and stated that he relied on China's position in international law, by which Chao Erh-feng's effective occupation of the country cancelled any earlier Tibetan claim.[21]

[21]Viceroy to Secretary of State, telegram, 18 December 1913, No. 179 in *Foreign*, October 1914, Procs. 134–396.

Nor was it Chen alone who reeled under the Lonchen's weighty tomes, for Sir Henry panicked too. 'The available documents', he noted, 'showed signs of becoming so voluminous and feeling was running so high' that for a time he contemplated 'intervention'. Luckily, Chen's proposal for written statements by either side came to his rescue. When these were presented, 'on or about 2nd January', McMahon proposed to summon a meeting of the full Conference and explain his own views which had in the meanwhile, as we would notice presently, undergone a complete metamorphoses.

The first known mention of the expressions 'Inner' and 'Outer' Tibet, in the context of a territorial settlement between Tibet and China, may be found in a telegram from the Viceroy to the Secretary of State on 18 December. For the British Plenipotentiary a factor of some importance to cope with, as has been noticed in the preceding paragraphs, was the voluminous documentary evidence adduced by the Tibetans in support of a frontier including Kokonor and all the March country as far west as Tachienlu, to counter which the Chinese had nothing comparable to offer. Another was the fact that 'it will be necessary to take cognisance' of the whole area in one treaty. 'The best way' out, McMahon now suggested, was

> by treating Tibet in two zones, i.e. an Outer Tibet comprising Tibet proper and an Inner Tibet including Kokonor and the country between (but excluding) Chiamdo and Tachienlu. Autonomy would be restricted to the former zone.

There were advantages in so doing for

> it would—(*i*) facilitate negotiations with both Tibet and China; (*ii*) safeguard and perpetuate Tibetan (and indirectly British) interests in Inner Tibet; and (*iii*) prevent the possible future inclusion of any portion of Tibetan territory within the still undefined frontiers of Outer and Inner Mongolia.[22]

That the British Plenipotentiary had not fully worked out all the details is evident from the fact that he confessed he was 'not yet in a position' to say whether it would be necessary to define any specific rights of the Lhasa authorities in Inner Tibet, in the body of the treaty. Nor, for that matter, could he 'show more definitely' the limits of the two zones. It is nonetheless clear that McMahon's proposal had the support of the Government of India who were keen that 'until we are in possession of more definite information', nothing further was to be said to Russia 'regarding limits of Tibet'.[23]

That the idea did not come to him a day earlier is evident from the fact that in his draft agreement of 10 November, briefly alluded to, no mention is made

---

[22] Loc. cit.
[23] Viceroy to Secretary of State, telegram, 10 November 1913, No. 159 in Ibid.

of the two zones.²⁴ Again, even on 11 December, Delhi in commenting upon HMG's fears of a possible Russian refusal to revise the Tibetan clauses of the Agreement of 1907 without a corresponding *quid pro quo*, did not come up with the concept of Inner/Outer Tibet as a possible way out.²⁵ Less than a week later the British Plenipotentiary had spelt it out!

In suggesting the two zones McMahon, it seems, was impressed not only by the Lonchen's weighty evidence and his 'well-supported claim' to a frontier including Kokonor but also the fact that, in first-hand reports emanating from Louis King, then stationed in Tachienlu, it was clear that the Chinese 'hold' on the Marches was 'more substantial' than had been generally realised. What was more, a Chinese force of 3,000–5,000 men, equipped 'with modern rifles and artillery', was still garrisoned in this area. Additionally, despite their earlier occupation and their far-flung garrisons, the Chinese had not been able 'to effect any material change' in the Tibetan administration of the tribal states. Hence it appeared

> necessary to recognise in our Treaty an extended Tibetan territory covering the whole area in the Lonchen's claim. The only solution...would be the recognition of two zones...it appears in the interests of the three contracting parties to take cognizance of the whole of this country, but to limit the autonomous area to Outer Tibet. This would possibly satisfy China...it would prevent the absorption of Inner Tibet as a Chinese province, and so perpetuate and safeguard existing Tibetan (and indirectly British) interests there, and it would prevent the inclusion of any portion of the country within the undefined frontiers of Outer and Inner Mongolia, in which other Powers have now acquired spheres of political interest, it would also tend to the creation of an effective Chinese zone, between Tibet proper and the encroaching spheres of foreign influence on the north and east, a result which is generally desirable in view of the recent changes in the balance of power in Asia.²⁶

There was another reason why McMahon wanted 'to facilitate' such an arrangement and it stemmed from his conviction that 'some understanding' existed between Tibet and Mongolia in regard to the Kokonor border. The Lonchen, he noted, had shown the 'greatest reluctance' to define any frontier line which 'can possibly create friction' with Mongolia. He (Lonchen Shatra) had also 'refused to include on his skeleton map' a large tract on the north-east which had always been shown as Tibet on European maps. Could this, McMahon argued, be due to pressure from the direction of Urga? In any case, all this forced upon him (McMahon) a recognition of the fact that

---

²⁴Viceroy to Secretary of State, telegram, 11 December 1913, No. 178 in Ibid.
²⁵*Supra*, n. 20.
²⁶Loc. cit.

Kansu and Eastern Tibet belonged to a belt of Chinese territory which separated Mongolia from any portion of Tibet.

It is significant that while he could not as yet define the two zones with any precision, the inclusion of Chamdo within the limits of autonomous Tibet was important enough to make McMahon ' consider any reasonable *quid pro quo* ' to secure the acquiescence of China.

Another fact to which the British Plenipotentiary devoted a great deal of attention was the reported conclusion of the Mongol-Tibetan Treaty of 11 January 1913. Here too he had strong circumstantial evidence to suggest that it had, in fact, been signed and sealed and that as a result the

> new interests which have been acquired by Russia over a large tract of Eastern Asia have completely altered the *status quo* of Tibet since the conclusion of the Anglo-Russian Convention. New responsibilities have been forced upon us both as regards our Indian frontier and our broader imperial interests, and I see no possibility of avoiding an even heavier responsibility in the future.[27]

The 'heavier responsibility', to which McMahon was alluding, was the stationing of ' a recognised British representative ' at Lhasa which, he argued, was already ' a centre of foreign intrigue '. While it is proposed to revert to the subject of the Mongol-Tibetan treaty, and of a British representative at Lhasa a little later, for the present it may suffice to say that the concept of Inner and Outer Tibet and of laying down a boundary between the two zones was powerfully influenced by both these developments.

Before long HMG accepted, in principle, the ' proposed division ' of Tibet, albeit with reservations. Whitehall noted *inter alia* that it

> will be necessary... when the time comes carefully to define Tibetan rights etc. in the ' Inner ' zone, which...is not to be regarded as autonomous, and in which therefore it will presumably be open to China ... to make good her position by all the means at her disposal. Unless there is a clear understanding on this point, the action of the Chinese...is likely to give rise to constant Tibetan appeals for British intervention which cannot but be embarrassing to HMG, and which may seriously compromise their future relations with the Tibetan Government. It may also be desirable to obtain from both parties an undertaking to refrain from acts of reprisal for past outrages in the ' Inner ' zone.[28]

[27] Secretary of State to Viceroy, 6 January 1914, No. 182 in *Foreign*, October 1914, Procs. 134–396. Also *I O* to *F O*, 23 December 1913, No. 188 in Ibid.

[28] For the minutes of the third meeting see No. 184; for the text of the ' Chinese Statement on Limits of Tibet ', see Appendix in No. 184; for the Lonchen's Statement, Encl. 2, No. 184 in Ibid.

The Lonchen's statement ran into 25 typed pages, followed by a list of 90 documents as ' documentary evidence to prove the boundary of Tibet '. Appended were 62 enclosures containing English translations of various texts, treaties, abstracts, running into another 27 typed pages.

At the third meeting of the Conference on 12 January, at Delhi, the Tibetan and the Chinese Plenipotentiaries laid on the table their respective statements of evidence in regard to the frontier claimed by each. Ivan Chen's, running into about seven pages in type, comprised answers to two specific questions: what were the territorial claims of the Chinese government in regard to the question of the limits of Tibet and on what 'rights' were these claims based.

In answer to the first, he listed the following districts as constituting a part of China: Gyade, Dam, Zayul, Chamdo, Enta, Markham, Po-yul, Pema-koi, Chen, Derge, Lho-jong, Shobando and Tenke.

As for Chinese rights, these were derived, Chen argued, from the 'historic connections' of all these places with China and what in international law would be called 'effective occupation', of which he now furnished some details.

Appended to Chen's statement was the 'translation' of a Bill passed, in 1912, by the 'House of Senators of the National Assembly in Peking' giving new names to the old districts or places in the March country—each place, in its new garb, being designated a 'Lien', or 'Fu'. The Chinese statement ended by stipulating that all these 'Lien' and 'Fu' now constituted the 'eighth division of the Parliamentary election district of Szechuan'.

Predictably, the 'Tibetan statement on Limits of Tibet' was a study in contrast. The Lonchen started by maintaining that 'though a great deal can be written justifying the claims of the boundary', he was giving only 'an abstract of the case'. Among the chief points made in the 'abstract', the following may be highlighted.

Gyade (or '36 districts') in East Tibet 'has been and forms part of Tibet' ever since the time of King Strong-tsang-gampo, for the inhabitants were all Tibetans 'by race, manners, customs, language' and, what was more, Buddhists 'by religion'.

The Lonchen took Ivan Chen severely to task for his statement that the territory east of Batang belonged to China and queried

> whether the Chinese could produce any original document stating that the Dalai Lama had ceded the said state to the Chinese Emperor or whether the Chinese had made war on Tibet and conquered it.... The Chinese Plenipotentiary said that he was not sure whether the pillar he mentioned bore inscriptions alongside those of the Chinese. As regards original documents, for the present he had only the extract from Sung's book and the books written by European authors, as well as the statement made by the British Minister at Peking.... I beg to say if the Chinese side had any reliable original documents they would produce them according to the laws and customs of every country... so the inability to produce any authentic documents... in itself proves that their claim over the lands in question is not lawful.

The Lonchen took up each of the districts in turn and adduced seemingly convincing evidence to show that they were part of Tibet. These included

Gyade, Tsai-dam, Kokonor, Amdo, Tongkor, Nyarong, Derge, Markham, Zayul, Chamdo—and scores of other names. In each case, his evidence was detailed and based on what one might call authentic records. He pointed out that Chamdo was under Lho-jong and Draya under Markham Gar-jong; that the monasteries in Chamdo were branches of the Sera monastery in Lhasa just as the Draya monasteries were branches of the Drepung; that the appointments of head Lamas were made, and their titles and ranks conferred, by the Tibetan Government.

The Lonchen ridiculed Chen's argument that in the final analysis Peking's claims were based on the conquests of Chao Erh-feng. And here he had a mouthful to say both of the man and his methods. Chao, said the Lonchen, was

> well-known to everybody as a most unscrupulous adventurer whose acts cannot be justified or condoned... out of mere thirst for blood (he) attacked and demolished the Chartin (Hsiencheng) and other Buddhist monasteries... and butchered many innocent men, both high and low. He destroyed several temples and villages by setting fire in them.... He plundered gold, silver and rare bronze images.... He cast the bronze and copper offering vessels of worship into bullets and small coins... he had paper rolls of shoes made out of the leaves of sacred Buddhist scriptures...(he) had been guilty to such glaring misdeeds that even if he had a hundred lives he should forfeit every one of them to the law.

Could the 'conquests' of such a man be accepted as legal?

> It would be an instance of international encouragement to similar lawless acts.... It would be like a murderer and a robber being allowed to enjoy his booty and remain unpunished.

And yet, argued the Lonchen, instead of owning the truth, the Chinese

> descend so low as to base their claims on his raids as conquests and call it incontrovertible proof of just claim, it is like trying to swallow a living person.[29]

Five days after the formal session of 12 January (1914), where the claims and counter-claims of China and Tibet had been presented, the Viceroy in a telegram to the Secretary of state outlined a boundary for Tibet along with a dividing line between 'the inner and outer' zones. For the Tibet-China frontier he based his line on

(a) the limits of Tibet as shown in Chinese maps;

[29]Viceroy to Secretary of State, telegram, 17 January 1914, No. 190 in Ibid.

(b) the terms of treaty pillar of 912 A.D.;
(c) the fact that the country is occupied by people of Tibetan race, language and religion; and
(d) the absence of regular Chinese administration in any of the included areas.

For the frontier itself he had shown,

> a line along watershed of Kuen-Lun, Altyn Tagh and Humbolt ranges, thence north of Kokonor and along crest of Nau Chau to about longitude 101. Then to the south running just west of Donkyr to a point where Hwang Ho rounds east corner of Machin range and along eastern limits of Gyarong, Gyakog, Chagyet to Tachienlu which remains in Tibet. Line then runs to corner of sharp bend of Yalong Ho, longitude 102, and thence up the Yalong and Litang rivers to point where latitude 28 cuts latter river for the second time. Thence it follows latitude 28 to crest of Mekong-Salween divide and runs southward along the watershed to about latitude 27°30′ where it crosses Salween to its Western watershed and follows it to Isu Razi pass, which thus becomes the trijunction point of the Tibet-China-India frontiers.

As for Outer Tibet,

> watershed of Kuen Lun, Marco Polo and Shuga Ula ranges to about longitude 96, thence skirting west corner of Tsaringnor and crossing Yangtse river at about longitude 97 to Jyekundo, which should remain in Outer Tibet. Along Mekong-Yangtse divide (except where departure from watershed in an easterly direction may be found necessary in order to include whole of Draya and Markham within Outer Tibet) passing Chinese boundary pillar at Pamotang west of Batang to a point abreast of Yakalo. Thence across Mekong valley just north of Yakalo to crest of Mekong-Salween divide and southward along the divide to a point abreast of Mekong. Here it crosses river just south of Mekong to Salween-Irrawaddi divide thence along the divide to Tilla La and from that pass along northern watershed of Taron valley to nearest point on the Tibet-India frontier.[30]

There was one major lacuna in this boundary, of which McMahon was not unmindful, and this related to the fact that it excluded Derge and Nyarong from Outer Tibet. But even though these were two of the richest districts and Tibetan evidence as to their possession, and administration, ' was very strong ', the British Plenipotentiary intended to use them as bargaining counters to make the Chinese agree to the inclusion, in Outer Tibet, of Chamdo and Draya,

[30]Loc. cit.

which are now similarly held by Chinese troops, but are strategically more important to Tibet.[31]

Meantime McMahon was working on the problem of Tibetan rights in 'Inner Tibet' which, the Secretary of State had urged, needed clearer definition so as to avoid incurring of unnecessary responsibilities.[32] His dilemma was obvious:

> I not only am unable, at the present moment, to define what should be the Tibetan position in that zone, but I think the more we attempt to define it, the greater our responsibilities may become.

On the advantages of constituting this non-autonomous Inner Zone, however, his mind was clearly made up—'Tibet gains and so indirectly, do we'—for

> it cannot be converted into a Chinese province, its territorial integrity and safety from outside exploitation are assured and it comes within the scope of the various safeguards which apply to all Tibet under the 1904 agreement.[33]

Lhasa's gains, however, were more of a sentimental, than substantial, nature. But once the situation had settled down through an agreement, and with it Chinese fear of the British annexing Tibet was removed, the former may 'give up their expensive and unprofitable' attempts to subdue and administer the Marches.

Understandably the Secretary of State had been informed that the position in Inner Tibet would differ from that of Outer Tibet in that

> China can station officials, establish colonies and send troops there. In other words, the Government of China can, to any degree short of converting it into a Chinese province, administer the Inner zone.

As for Lhasa, some provision for the continuance of the right of the Dalai Lama to confer on the head lamas their customary ranks and titles and issue their appointment orders, would suffice to maintain in that zone the 'present privileges' and material advantages, of the Tibetan government.[34]

---

[31]Secretary of State to Viceroy, telegram, 6 January 1914, No. 182 in Ibid.
[32]McMahon's note, 19 January 1914, Serial 57 in *Foreign, Notes*.
[33]Viceroy to Secretary of State, 21 January 1914, No. 192 in *Foreign*, October 1914, Procs. 134–396.
[34]Loc. cit.

Chapter 17

The Conference gets Underway: October 1913–January 1914

BY JANUARY 1914 the Simla Conference had already moved from the snowy discomfort of a winter in the hills, to the warmer, more bracing milieu of old, imperial Delhi. But apart from this change of venue, the delegates had not much to show by way of concrete results. Behind the scenes, McMahon had, it is true, evolved the Inner/Outer Tibet concept but as to the boundaries between the two, and the respective jurisdictions of Peking and Lhasa, a wide chasm yawned between the Lonchen's claims and Ivan Chen's counter-claims. For all that, nothing much had happened since they convened in October, for the three Plenipotentiaries had yet to come to grips with the essentials of their problems. At best they had touched them, and skirted around.

In the draft agreement which he submitted for the consideration of HMG on 10 November, and which has been briefly alluded to in the preceding chapter, McMahon had suggested some major changes. It may be recalled, *inter alia*, that article 3 of the earlier India Office draft had stipulated that a Chinese representative ' with suitable escort ' (which shall ' in no circumstances ' exceed 300 men) was to be stationed at Lhasa. McMahon now proposed that the additional rider, ' with authority to advise the Tibetans as to their foreign relations ', be omitted and the following substituted in its place:

> The Government of Great Britain shall have the right to maintain in a similar manner a representative at Lhasa to discuss and settle with the Government of Tibet matters relating to their mutual interests.[1]

The British Plenipotentiary justified the above on the plea that the historical claim of the Chinese Amban to intervention in Tibet's foreign relations was misplaced, that the claim as such was confined only to Nepal, Bhutan, Sikkim and Chumbi and that the deletion he now suggested was with a view to removing a potential danger.[2] The provision for a British representative came in the context of the one concerning the Chinese Amban. Apart from

---

[1] For the text, Viceroy to Secretary of State, telegram, 10 November 1913, No. 159 in *Foreign*, October 1914, Procs. 134-396. Also see Appendix to Notes, ' Tripartite Treaty in reference to Tibet: Draft proposed by British Plenipotentiary ', in Ibid.
[2] Peking despatch, 8 March 1913, Encl. 4, cited in note under Article 3 in No. 159 in Ibid. Also see Mayers, *The Chinese Government*, pp. 102–3.

the escort, the former's general status, McMahon argued, was sufficiently 'safeguarded' by the expression, 'in a similar manner'.[3]

Another interesting addition in McMahon's draft was the appearance of Article 6 which recognised that

> Great Britain, by reason of her geographical position has a special interest in the external relations of Tibet...(and the Governments of Great Britain, China, and Tibet) hereby engage that Tibet shall not form the subject of any negotiations or agreement with any state without the consent of the Government of Great Britain.

In justifying the new article, McMahon argued that it was desirable to control the foreign relations of Tibet even with regard to China or Nepal, thereby completing the safeguards provided for in Article 9 of the Lhasa Convention of 1904. He found 'an analogous precedent' in Article 3 of the Russo-Mongolian Agreement of 1912 and suspected that 'the unusual wording' of that article appeared to indicate some provision for the subsequent treaty of January 1913 between Mongolia and Tibet.[4] Essentially, however, he felt that the 'main principle' on which his draft agreement was based was the stationing of a British Representative at Lhasa.

Predictably, Whitehall's reaction to McMahon's draft centred principally on the theme of the Agent. A decision, it was pointed out, 'must rest partly' on the view taken of the treaty *en bloc*. Besides, India 'doubtless' realised that 'without previous concurrence of Russia' such a provision could not be inserted. Alluding to Delhi's earlier (September 1912) view, that HMG should press for 'exclusive right to have an Agent at Lhasa',[5] Whitehall now enquired whether a British 'or native Agent' was contemplated.[6]

Delhi's reply to HMG's urgent demand for its views, 'by telegraph', on McMahon's draft Memorandum, started by strongly advising that Russia be asked to agree to a modification of Articles II, III and IV of the Convention of 1907. This, it felt, was necessary with a view to providing for a British Representative at Lhasa and 'for freedom of industrial and commercial enterprise in Tibet'. The former was of pivotal importance for

> it will not be possible for us without a representative of our own to detect or frustrate foreign intrigue and that if Tibetans are to maintain the integrity

---

[3]*Supra*, n. 1

[4]Article 3 of the Russo-Mongolian Agreement read:
> If the Mongolian government finds it necessary to conclude a separate treaty with China or any other foreign power, the new treaty shall in no case infringe the clauses of the present agreement and of the protocol annexed thereto, or modify them without the consent of the Imperial (Russian) government.

[5]No. 10 in *Foreign*, May 1913, Procs. 261–502. Also No. 470 in Ibid.

[6]Secretary of State to Viceroy, telegram, 13 November 1913, No. 160 in *Foreign*, October 1914, Procs. 134–396.

of their country it will necessitate the constant advice and moral support of a British Officer. Provision for this in agreement is most essential since it may be difficult later on when Tibet and China have achieved their main objects to obtain their consent.[7]

While agreeing 'generally' with McMahon, Delhi suggested a small textual change so as to 'cover the right to provide our representative with an adequate escort'.[8]

Earlier, in behind-the-scenes activity, McMahon had strongly urged on the Viceroy the need for a British representative. A telegram of 4 November, addressed to the Foreign Secretary at the Viceroy's Camp, lays bare his whole thinking on the proposed draft and merits a summary reproduction. Among its principal points the following may be of interest:

(a) That it would be dangerous to allow either the Chinese or the Tibetans the great latitude in the fulfilment of their international obligations which the absence of a British representative would involve;

(b) That it was absolutely futile to expect Tibetans to be able to maintain the integrity of their country without Britain's advice and moral support owing to a fatuous lack of cohesion among themselves;

(c) That the main objective of the Tibetans was autonomy and of the Chinese the re-establishment of their Amban at the Tibetan capital. It should be his (McMahon's) endeavour to make the two sides acquiesce in a British representative at Lhasa before each had obtained its main objective in the coming treaty;

(d) That a stage had been reached when 'in the interests of safety' there must be a provision for carrying on direct communications with Tibet and of obtaining reliable information about events in that country;

(e) That the present juncture—owing to the conclusion of the Russo-Mongolian and the Mongol-Tibetan treaties—was 'peculiarly favourable' for a settlement with Russia on the Tibetan question. Since conditions—'political, geographical and otherwise' of Tibet and Mongolia vis-à-vis Russia, China and India, in that order—were so identical, Britain should have the right to exercise the same freedom in Tibet as Russia had obtained in Mongolia. Thus, without necessarily reopening the general question of the Anglo-Russian Convention of 1907, the opportunity presented by the impending completion of the Russian agreement (with China) regarding Mongolia should be taken advantage of to arrive at an understanding with Russia about Tibet;

(f) That recognition of a British representative in Tibet will imply both freedom to regulate trade and freedom of direct relations with Tibet. What it left open was freedom of industrial enterprise and, McMahon

---

[7]Viceroy to Secretary of State, telegram, 25 November 1913, Proc. 173 in Ibid.
[8]Loc. cit.

argued, the agreement accepted by Russia regarding Mongolia ' necessitates our demanding a free hand ' in this respect also.[9]

That the British Plenipotentiary saw an extreme urgency in the situation is evident from the fact that on 6 November he asked the Foreign Secretary to telegraph the Viceroy's reaction.[10] A day later he reverted to the subject:

> I feel more and more strongly... that alternative proposal put forward by me that British Trade Agent, Gyantse, should...pay occasional visits to Lhasa will not adequately meet our requirements and that it is absolutely necessary to have a Resident in Lhasa. Our Gyantse Agent will be unable to compete in effect or influence with permanent Chinese Resident... and will also be unable to counteract intrigues of foreign powers in Lhasa.[11]

McMahon's promptings[12] notwithstanding, the Viceroy's telegram to the Secretary of State viewed the question of the Resident at Lhasa ' from a more general point of view ' arguing that

> if we obtain a Resident at Lhasa, I am not at all sure that the sterilisation of Tibet is not the best policy, since it would be impossible for us to obtain a monopoly of commercial and industrial enterprise.[13]

The Viceroy's telegram thus shifted the ground considerably from that which McMahon had urged, albeit the necessity for a British Resident was now the greater, for

> Russia has created a new situation on our northern frontier and it does not need the gift of prophecy to foretell Russification of Tibet unless countermeasures are taken in time.

Unlike McMahon, the Governor-General was also averse to reopening the question of the Anglo-Russian convention for fear any Russian interference in Afghanistan should involve the British in difficulties on the North-West Frontier. And yet, he argued, may not the opportunity offered by the com-

---

[9]Foreign Department to Foreign Secretary, Viceroy's Camp, telegram, 4 November 1913, Office Notes in *Foreign*, March 1914, Procs. 1–251.
[10]McMahon to Foreign Secretary, Viceroy's Camp, telegram, 6 November 1913, in Ibid.
[11]McMahon to Foreign Secretary, Viceroy's Camp, telegram, 7 November 1913, in Ibid.
[12]In forwarding McMahon's telegram of 7 November, the Foreign Secretary (J B Wood) in a note of date, *supra*, n. 11, pointed out that Lord Crewe had foreseen the argument (No. 468 in *Foreign*, May 1913, Procs. 261–502) that since ' Tibet cannot stand alone ', a British Agency at Lhasa was the only effective means of ensuring that it will fulfil its obligations. He also referred to a later exchange of views between the India Office and the Foreign Office—Nos. 52 and 73 in *Foreign*, September 1913, Procs. 1–271.
[13]Hardinge's note, 8 November 1913, in Office Notes in *Foreign*, March 1914, Procs. 1–251.

pletion of the Russo-Chinese Agreement regarding Mongolia be used 'for revising our understanding' with Russia, regarding Tibet?[14] However, the necessity to come to an agreement with the Russian Government 'must not deter us' from considering, on its own merits, each of the questions involved. Thus, Hardinge argued, without the 'vigilance and advice' of a British Agent, would not a settlement with China, in regard to Tibet, be 'so much wastepaper' under existing conditions?

Again, there were 'grounds for belief' that while Tibet would welcome a British representative at 'this stage', later, after both Tibet and China had obtained what they wanted, the former's consent may not be easy to obtain. Besides, in the changed context of the Russo-Chinese Agreement regarding Mongolia, 'it may be impossible for us' to prevent indirect representation in the form of a Dorjieff or any other Russian Buryat. As to a native agent, he

> would not be able to compete with the intrigues of a Chinese Amban or with the above-mentioned class of Russian Agent and we, therefore, do not contemplate the appointment of a native but that of a British representative at the Tibetan capital.[15]

Further, Delhi argued, the presence of a British Agent would also help in the economic development of Tibet, upon which the Dalai Lama seemed to lay considerable stress. This necessitated that China forego the monopoly which had accrued to her under Article IX (d) of the Lhasa convention, enabling it, *inter alia*, to negotiate Trade Regulations direct with the Tibetans. Once the monopoly was done away with, there would be an open door for commercial and industrial enterprise for British subjects. Later, 'to prevent foreign intrusion', Britain could rely on the political influence exerted by the presence of its 'representative' at Lhasa.[16]

McMahon's views, as modified by the Foreign Department in Simla, were summed up in the Viceroy's telegram of 25 November, referred to earlier in the narrative. The long and short of it all was that a British representative was necessary both 'to detect or frustrate foreign intrigue' as also to help Tibet maintain its 'integrity'.[17]

---

[14]Viceroy to Secretary of State, telegram, 8 November 1913, Ibid.

Originally marked 'official', Lord Crewe later directed that the telegram be treated as 'Private'. *Inter alia*, the Viceroy had desired that, pending a decision on his telegram, 'the question of according favourable reception to Russo-Mongolian and Russo-Chinese agreements ...be held in abeyance'.

[15]Foreign Department to Foreign Secretary, telegram, 17 November 1913. This was a draft reply to the Secretary of State's telegram of 13 November. For the text *Foreign, Notes,* October 1914, Procs. 134–396.

[16]Foreign Department to Foreign Secretary, Viceroy's Camp, telegram, 20 November 1913, in Ibid.

[17]*Supra*, n. 7.

To all that Delhi-Simla stood for, and advocated, Jordan, at Peking, was strongly opposed. It was clear to him that in agreeing to any modifications of Articles II, III and IV of the Convention of 1907, Russia would demand some compensation in Chinese Turkestan. Besides

> any attempt to come to a settlement of the question at the expense and without the consent of China is earnestly deprecated by me. China is suspicious ... of our acting in concert with Russia regarding Tibet and deep resentment would be aroused throughout the country by any agreement come to independently with third power affecting a part of Chinese territory.[18]

Besides Jordan, who contradicted and confuted, Whitehall too appeared singularly unresponsive. For in his telegram of 3 December, Lord Crewe was emphatic that all that HMG would agree to was

> the right of Trade Agent at Gyantse to proceed when necessary to Lhasa. They will not agree to a permanent British Representative at Lhasa.[19]

Two other premises were underlined: *One*, that the Russian Government 'will not accept the revision of Tibetan arrangement by itself' and *two*, that HMG were 'not prepared to risk' reopening questions of Afghanistan, Persia or even Chinese Turkestan. As the Secretary of State viewed it, ' it would be useless ' to hope that these assumptions could be modified.

In the matter of industrial concessions too Whitehall anticipated 'serious difficulties'. Here while it was necessary to cancel Article III of the Anglo-Chinese Convention of 1906 which 'closed the door', a revision or modification of Article IV of the Anglo-Russian Convention of 1907 also became imperative. One substitute for the latter was a division of Tibet into British and Russian spheres of commercial influence; another, a provision that 'without previous consent' of each other, 'no concession anywhere in Tibet' would be sought for or obtained by either Power.[20]

In its reply to Whitehall, India stuck to McMahon and his draft for, it argued, this offered ' the only method ' by which it could be hoped ' permanently ' to solve the Tibetan question.

As the position in Tibet had undergone ' a complete change to our disadvantage ', Delhi reasoned, and as it was Russian action in Mongolia which

---

[18]Jordan to Viceroy, telegram, 27 November 1913, No. 176 in *Foreign*, October 1914, Procs. 134–396.

[19]Secretary of State to Viceroy, telegram, 3 December 1913, No. 177 in Ibid.

[20]Loc. cit.

Inter alia, the Secretary of State had asked the Viceroy to propose ' a definite British sphere... a belt, say two hundred miles as the crow flies from the borders of India or the land adjoining '. The ' desirablity ' of ' excluding the Japanese ' was also to be borne in mind.

had brought about this change, there was 'surely a great deal of justification' in claiming 'some *quid pro quo*'. This was to be effected

> on the strength of the Mongolian agreements, and as the price of our recognition of them... without reopening other questions of the Anglo-Russian Convention.

Any concession to Russia in Tibet was most earnestly deprecated, for

> it would bring within easy reach of our extended line of the Indian frontier a sphere of intangible and loosely defined Russian political influence.[21]

Besides, the fact that the Chinese provinces of Turkestan and Kansu intervened between Tibetan and Russian territory, the 'recognition in Tibet of a Russian sphere' would be all the more galling to China.

The Agent was still important, if only because Lhasa was 'already beset with foreign intrigue' and without a Representative there

> infringements of agreements... which might at an initial stage be checked may in time so develop as to render our obligations as a signatory more grave than we are now willing to contemplate.

And then there were the Japanese too—to be kept out. All in all, it followed that a British representative was 'absolutely essential' and seemed 'the only effective means' of checking these activities.

Even as Delhi was arguing its case, Whitehall's own thinking began to crystallise and took shape in what has been called Arthur Hirtzel's draft Convention. It is true it had not yet been formally approved in London and that the Russian Government had yet to be approached, but the draft was to form the basis of future telegrams,[22] and quite plainly had superseded McMahon's own. In Hirtzel's version, Article 8 laid down that the British Agent

> who resides at Gyantse, or other duly authorised Agent of the British Government, may visit Lhasa with his escort whenever it is necessary to consult with the Tibetan Government regarding such matters of importance (whether or not arising out of this treaty) as it has been found impossible to settle at Gyantse by correspondence or otherwise.

---

[21]Viceroy to Secretary of State, telegram, 11 December 1913, No. 178 in *Foreign*, October 1914, Procs. 134–396.

[22]Hirtzel to Wood, 28 November 1913, covering note in forwarding four copies of the draft Tibetan Convention. For changes proposed by McMahon see Viceroy to Secretary of State, telegram, 18 December 1913, No. 179 in Ibid.

Hirtzel's draft was received by McMahon on 17 December 1913, vide Office note dated 17 December 1913, in No. 91, *Foreign*, September 1915, Procs. 76–101.

As January advanced and the third formal session of the Conference, at Delhi, saw rival memoranda presented by the two sides on their respective geographical and territorial limits, McMahon found his position in the negotiations increasingly difficult. He argued that the 'main obstacle to progress' was HMG's unwillingness to agree to a British Resident in Lhasa as also its 'natural disinclination' to discuss any Tibetan question with Russia. The situation is well summed up in a note he recorded on 23 January 1914:

> It is now over six weeks since they (HMG) received our telegram of 11th December ont his and other principles at issue in our draft agreement.... It is over $3\frac{1}{2}$ months since the Conference began and I have so far succeeded in evading a single expression of opinion or policy to my colleagues without giving them any tangible pretext for protest, but further procrastination threatens to be dangerous as far as our mutual confidence, relations and subsequent negotiations are concerned.[23]

The result was the telegram of 24 January to the Secretary of State which had been intended as a 'gentle reminder of the desirability of expedition'. McMahon's fervid plea, that the 'continuance of my non-committal and detached attitude' would no longer be possible without prejudicing the 'mutual confidence' which then characterised his relations with the Chinese and Tibetan Plenipotentiaries,

> was fully endorsed by the Viceroy who urged a satisfactory settlement of pending issues, now under consideration.[24]

In his reply, the Secretary of State expressed the view that while Russia was being addressed separately 'on other points at issue', McMahon could, in the meantime, proceed with the 'question of boundary and zones'. He could also go ahead on the issue of the political status of Tibet and the stationing of a Chinese representative at Lhasa, with an escort which shall 'in no circumstances exceed 300 men'.[25]

The procedure suggested by Whitehall McMahon found to be extremely galling and, in private, dubbed it as 'unwise' and even 'undesirable'. He was opposed to the idea of 'concurrent negotiations' at St. Petersburg and Delhi (and Simla) with all its attendant 'disadvantages and dangers' and visualised a situation in which

> while Russia is being addressed on some points, I am to commence negotiations on the others and in doing so must play our best trump card and concede a

[23] Note by McMahon, 23 January 1914, in *Foreign, Notes*, October 1914, Procs. 134–396.
[24] Viceroy to Secretary of State, telegram, 24 January 1914, No. 194 in *Foreign*, October 1914, Procs. 134–396.
[25] Secretary of State to Viceroy, telegram, 29 January 1914, No. 195 in Ibid.

Chinese representative at Lhasa, on which depends largely the attainment of our own requirements.

He was also far from clear on the issues on which the Russian Government were being approached—' whether they are going to press for a whole-time Resident' at Lhasa or only 'the peripatetic Gyantse Agent' suggested in Hirtzel's draft agreement. Again, if the latter draft had been generally accepted—' as seems the case '—may not an approach to St. Petersburg be deferred ' until more is known ' of the result of his own negotiations?[26]

McMahon's official communication, which the Viceroy now forwarded to Whitehall, made it clear that his objective would not be attained by laying down a draft agreement ' forthwith on the Conference table', to which there would be little chance of obtaining the consent of the Chinese and the Tibetans. More appropriately, he should ' guide discussions ' in a direction leading to the formulation of specific articles in terms indicated in his draft. He also sounded a note of warning against delay

because the information of Chinese activity received from Tibet during the last few days is causing my Tibetan colleague the gravest anxiety while pressure for the hastening of negotiations has suddenly been released by my Chinese colleague which appears to indicate some marked improvement in the Chinese position in Tibet.

India, however, still seemed to cling to the slender thread of a British representative at Lhasa and, on its own, queried

whether it is intended to adopt the alternative provided in Article 8 of Hirtzel's draft agreement (Gyantse Trade Agent's visit to Lhasa) or to press for a British Resident in Lhasa.[27]

The die had, however, been cast against Delhi's proposal for, as amended by the Secretary of State on 14 February, Article 8 of Hirtzel's draft now read as follows:

The British Agent who resides at Gyantse may visit Lhasa with his escort whenever it is necessary to consult with the Tibetan Government regarding matters arising out of convention between Great Britain and Tibet of September 17th, 1904 which it has been found impossible to settle at Gyantse by correspondence or otherwise.

[26]Note by McMahon, 2 February 1914, *supra*, n. 23.
[27]Viceroy to Secretary of State, telegram, 3 February 1914, No. 196 in *Foreign*, October 1914, Procs. 134–396.

From the above, it should be clear that on the eve of his bout of intensive negotiations, in mid-February, McMahon had been authorised by his principals to demand not a British Agent at Lhasa, but the visits to the Tibetan capital of the ' peripatetic ' Trade Agent at Gyantse. What was more, he was informed that agreement on this article ' must ' be ' provisional '.[28] It is thus clear that in the first round, and on a vital issue, Delhi and its principal negotiator had lost the battle, and well-nigh completely.

The ' peripatetic ' Trade Agent at Gyantse may have been a little elusive but surely, argued the British Plenipotentiary, Tibet's physical boundaries were more tangible. Before he got back to the Agent, McMahon therefore reverted once more to the boundaries.

---

[28]Secretary of State to Viceroy, telegram, 14 February 1914, No. 200 in Ibid.

Chapter 18

A Territorial Settlement in East Tibet

IN A STATEMENT on the 'limits of Tibet', which he communicated to his other colleagues at the fourth meeting of the Conference on 17 February, Sir Henry made the following points:

That authentic records, both Chinese and Tibetan, including the China-Tibet treaty of 822 and the Chinese maps of the Tang dynasty, indicated historic Tibetan frontiers. These 'geographical and political frontiers' of Tibet, he now showed by a red line on a skeleton map which he laid on the Conference table.

That in the 18th century under Manchu emperors Kang H'si and Chien Lung, some measure of Chinese control was established in parts of Tibet. At that time a certain pillar was erected in the neighbourhood of Batang and it was clear that, together with the watershed on which it stood, it marked 'a well-defined line' between the sphere of 'periodical Chinese intervention' in Tibet and the sphere in which Chinese dictation was of a 'purely nominal' character. Indicated by a blue line on the map, he called the two parts, Inner and Outer Tibet.

That the military campaigns of Chinese officials during the last half a century had considerably modified the historic status of Inner Tibet. At various times, semi-independent states which had come under the more direct control of China had reverted to the Lhasa government, while other states which were the scene of Chinese military operations temporarily lost their independence. Eventually, however, the people, rising in revolt, drove out the Chinese not only from the outer zone but the whole of Tibet.

That when the tripartite Conference was summoned, the position in the two countries was somewhat uncertain: the historic limits of Tibet had not been respected by the Chinese, and the historic rights of the Chinese had, in consequence, been ignored by the Tibetans. A state of war existed and the common objective of the three Plenipotentiaries now was to find a way out which will restore to the whole country both prosperity and peace. That his solution of the problems of geography were the red (indicating Tibet's political limits) and blue (indicating the division between zones) lines on the map. As regards the 'political difficulty', it could best be met by recognising the 'established autonomy' of Outer Tibet while in Inner Tibet permitting the Chinese 'to re-establish' such a measure of control as would restore and safeguard their historic position 'without in any way infringing the integrity of Tibet' as a geographical and political entity.¹

At the formal meeting of the three Plenipotentiaries, where the above outline was spelt out, Sir Henry had made it clear that his statement represented the conclusions at which he had arrived. Further he had asked his two assistants, Bell and Rose, to reply to any questions which the two Plenipotentiaries might ask or receive any suggestions they may proffer. If both of them accepted the general principles laid down, he would soon be able to proceed with the formulation of a definitive treaty.

Not unexpectedly, McMahon's enunciation of the two zones and their physical demarcation on a map evoked strong reactions. The Lonchen was the first in the field. On 5 March, he communicated to Sir Henry a 'Verbal Statement' firmly reiterating his earlier stand both on the territorial and the political issues involved. Among the points made by him, the following may be mentioned:

> That both Batang and Litang should form part of Outer Tibet. He (Lonchen) had earlier adduced 'convincing (and) authentic documentary evidences' showing the appointment of local officers, and the collection of rents and taxes by the Lhasa government. The same applied to the Hor-ser tribes from whom he had produced an oath of allegiance to Lhasa.
>
> That, in many places, included in Inner Tibet, the Chinese had 'no control whatever of any kind' and since the inhabitants were principally Tibetan, all Chinese influence should be excluded from these areas. Or else, 'a prolific source of all future troubles' would be left, for past outrages still rankled in the hearts of people. He feared lest incessant raids and invasions from the adjoining Chinese province become a source of incessant trouble.²

Concluding, the Lonchen appealed to the 'wisdom' of the British Plenipotentiary to declare that the Chinese should have 'no power' of 'interfering' in Tibetan affairs. For that, he argued, was the only way of securing 'permanent peace'.

All that the Lonchen said, and more, was vigorously contested by Ivan Chen. In his 'verbal statement', communicated two days after that of the Tibetan Plenipotentiary's, he questioned the entire basis of McMahon's premise. Among the principal points made by Chen were the following:

> That the territorial limits of Tibet in the times of the Tang dynasty ' could not be admitted as evidence of any value' for her present claims to the

---

¹ 'British statement on the limits of Tibet', Annexure 1 in No. 200 in *Foreign*, October 1914, Procs. 134–396.

² 'Verbal Statement by Lonchen Shatra: communicated on the 5th March 1914, handed to Mr Ivan Chen on the 7th March 1914', No. 214 in Ibid.

provinces of Chinghai, Batang, Litang and Tachien-lu. Further that between the end of the reign of Kwang Hsu (1908) and the beginning of the reign of Hsun Tung (1909), the Manchu Government took these areas back and restored them to the province of Szechuan. Further, the Republic had 'no right to alienate' any part of the territory which it had inherited from the Manchu dynasty.

That as for the two zones, in the ' Inner ' control had been exercised by the Szechuan administration since the time of Yung Cheng while in the ' Outer ', there had been the direct administration of the Lhasa Amban. Besides, from the ' Anterior ' Tibet to the limits of ' Ulterior ' Tibet, Chinese military garrisons had been stationed at various points together with civil officials. It followed that the ' whole Tibet ' was the sphere in which China had ' actually ' exercised its authority.

That his government could not agree to the designations of ' Inner ' and 'Outer' Tibet as suggested by Sir Henry. Firstly, there had never been such designations ' known in any public record and official documents '; secondly, their acceptance would be fraught with 'very grave consequence to China'; and thirdly, all the areas could not be considered ' otherwise than Chinese territory '.

That Sir Henry's contention that in Tibet ' the inhabitants rose and drove out the Chinese ' not only from the Outer zone but the whole of Tibet was ' not exactly the fact ' for the Chinese military forces were ' not driven out but were withdrawn ' on the advice tendered ' to my Government by the British Minister '. Again, on the same advice, they had been ordered not to make an advance to the west after they had reoccupied Enta.

That while his Government would be prepared to consider the question of the autonomy of Tibet, their decision will rest on ' how the whole Tibetan question ' is going to be discussed. His government, however, could not recede from the claims made in his earlier statement of 12 January.

The Chinese Plenipotentiary also took the opportunity to repudiate the remarks made by the Lonchen earlier in regard to ' His late Excellency ' Chao Erh-feng; the stone pillar at Merugang; the Dalai Lama's spiritual authority which ' should not be confused ' with the temporal; the taxes paid to the Tibetans by the various tribes in Hsi-kang which were merely contributions to the monasteries—' rather charity, than tax '. At the same time he refused to accept any claim for payment of an indemnity to Tibet.[3]

With the Lonchen and Ivan Chen tearing each other apart, the ball lay once more, and squarely, in McMahon's court. On 9 March, in a 'verbal statement' communicated to Ivan Chen, yet significantly omitting the Lonchen, the British Plenipotentiary assumed his role of the honest broker to perfection. He maintained that the two ' verbal statements ' of his colleagues tended to take

[3] ' Verbal statement by Mr Ivan Chen communicated on 7th March 1914, handed to the Tibetan Plenipotentiary, 8th March 1914', No. 215 in Ibid.

the Tibetan question right back to where it was before the conference commenced its work, hence the need for ' some decisive step ' towards a settlement. *Inter alia*, he made it clear that the red line on his sketch map ' included ' the country occupied by people of Tibetan race, language, customs and religion ' from the earliest recorded delimitation of Tibet ', in A.D. 822, ' without a break, until the present time '. Again, Fu Sung-mu, whose authority had been repeatedly invoked by Ivan Chen, had admitted that, in 1906, the Chinese had no right of interference in the administration of either Batang or Litang, which were under their own Tibetan chiefs. Hsiang-Cheng then was in the hands of the Tibetans, nor was Chiangta under Chinese control.

McMahon took the opportunity to reiterate his arguments in regard to the constitution of Inner and Outer Tibet. In 1904, he reminded Chen, there had been no Chinese administration in either zone. Now, he was willing

> under certain conditions to see the Chinese placed in the best possible position to maintain the integrity of Tibet as included within the geographical limits of China and to consolidate a buffer state, described as the Inner zone of Tibet, which will safeguard the internal interests of Kansu, Turkestan, Szechuan and Yunnan.

Again, the ' constant aggression ' of the Chinese frontier officers in Eastern Tibet had convinced him that, to ensure peace, the zone of Chinese military influence should be clearly marked by some natural barrier. Hence the blue line between the Inner and Outer zones had chosen ' watersheds ' and ' deserts ' which would afford to both sides ' the best and safest natural barrier ' against periodic acts of aggression.

While handing over McMahon's ' verbal statement ', Archibald Rose had been directed to give Chen an *aide memoire* containing information regarding Chinese activities in Eastern Tibet. Besides, he (Rose) was to warn the Chinese delegate that as a result of Chinese activity, his (McMahon's) restraining influence on the Lonchen had become virtually nil for the

> Tibetans are hardening in their refusal to accept any representative of China and any reinstatement of Chinese influence either in Inner or Outer Tibet.

As to the British, all they wanted was ' some ' agreement which will record the ' integrity ' of Tibet as a part of the ' integrity ' of China.[4]

The fifth meeting of the Conference, which convened in Delhi on 11 March, was a variation on the theme of Sir Henry's ' verbal statement ' outlined

---

[4] ' Verbal statement by Sir Henry McMahon, communicated by Mr A. Rose to Mr Ivan Chen on 9 March 1914 ', No. 216 in Ibid. There is no recorded evidence to suggest that this statement was communicated to Lonchen Shatra.

in the preceding paragraphs. The British delegate started by expressing his ' grave' concern that the settlement with which they had all been charged ' was being postponed too long'. At the same time he was convinced that ' the only solution' which would meet the 'just' requirements of the case, and provide ' honourable satisfaction' to both Tibet and China, was the one which he had put forth. Since news of renewed fighting between the two countries had been received, he thought the time had come to lay upon the table the draft of an agreement that would be ' satisfactory' to all the three parties. He appealed to both his Tibetan and Chinese colleagues for ' a broad and statesmanlike spirit of compromise' so that their labours could be brought to a speedy and successful conclusion.

The Chinese response was not particularly enthusiastic and Chen wondered how progress in the drafting of an agreement could be made insofar as the general principles laid down by Sir Henry in the earlier meeting of 17 February had not yet been accepted by his (Chen's) Government. Was it 'not premature', consequently, 'to proceed with the consideration' of the draft convention? McMahon retorted by underlining the need to expedite business and ' thus avoid' the evil consequences of further delay, albeit he conceded that the agreement was dependent on Peking's acceptance of his general principles.[5]

British cards, so far as a territorial settlement was concerned, were now on the table. No wonder, when news of what McMahon had proposed in Delhi reached Peking, there was a noticeable flutter. It was widely believed that on the advice of Lu Hsing-chi, the self-styled Amban-designate to Lhasa, the Chinese would stiffen their attitude. *Inter alia*, Lu appears to have suggested that Peking should maintain its military posture in Eastern Tibet, reject the proposals made by McMahon in Delhi and, if possible, make a forced march on Lhasa after seizing Gyade and Pomed.[6] Nor was it difficult to appreciate his line of reasoning. Convinced that China's relations with other powers would be affected as a result of the Conference in India, Lu further held that, as opposed to the pro-Tibetan faction of the Lonchen, feeling in Tibet was gravitating towards China. Since militarily India was in no position to intervene in Tibet, he argued, the British would find it impossible to force an agreement on Peking that was patently distasteful to her.

Acting on Lu Hsing-chi's cue, Peking despatched to Delhi a telegram on 6 March couched in ' most vigorous terms '; next day, a gist thereof was communicated to Sir Henry.[7] Nor is it unlikely that Ivan Chen's ' verbal '

---

[5] ' Proceedings of the 5th meeting of the Tibet Conference held at Delhi on the 11th March 1914', No. 217 in *Foreign*, October 1914, Procs. 134–396. Handing over to both delegates copies of his draft agreement, Sir Henry expressed the hope that, with its acceptance, an adjournment to Simla ' may not be necessary '.

[6] See for instance Lu Hsing-chi to Military Governor Hu (Chengtu), 28 December 1913, and 21 January 1914, and Hu (Chengtu) to Lu Hsing-chi, 6 January 1914, in *IOR*, Political and Secret, 2350/1913, ' Tibet: Intercepted Telegrams '.

[7] Viceroy to Secretary of State, telegram, 14 March 1914, No. 224 in Ibid.

statement of 7 March was a reflection of the Peking telegram's uncompromising stance.[8] There is the interesting fact that a day later Chen confessed to Rose that as a result of the appointment of Chang Yin-tang (the negotiator of the 1908 Trade Regulations) as Special Adviser to the President, his own position had become 'increasingly delicate and dangerous'.[9] The new broom in Peking had begun to sweep rather fast.

Public postures notwithstanding, the British had not been taken unawares, thanks to the 'intercepted' telegrams. In Peking meanwhile a Wai-chiao-pu functionary had met Jordan twice to reiterate China's 'right' to Kokonor as also to the frontier marked approximately by the river Salween. He specifically mentioned Enta, where Chinese troops had been stationed, and maintained that Chamdo and Gyade must be included in the Chinese domain. If a 'neutral' zone were to be an integral part of McMahon's proposals, Peking argued, it would have to be west of the line China now proposed. Jordan's conclusions were significant:

> Line of thought of the Secretary indicated that the Chinese wish to retain their present military position in Eastern Tibet which approximately represents Chao Erh-feng's conquests and it appears not improbable that these views are the result of Lu Hsing-chi's telegram dated the 5th March. From the Secretary's tone I conclude that though the Chinese at present appear unwilling to accept Sir Henry McMahon's decision, they are anxious to continue the negotiations as regards the boundary line nevertheless.[10]

On 18 March, the Chinese Foreign Office telegraphed to Ivan Chen a message that was tantamount to a virtual 'rejection' of McMahon's boundary line and indeed his 'whole draft'. *Inter alia*, Peking now proposed that all places east of the Salween shall be administered by China 'absolutely' while for places west of the river, up to Giamda, it was 'prepared to make a declaration' that they would not be converted into Chinese districts. The proposal was termed 'a great concession' by Peking, and was intended to demonstrate its 'high appreciation' of McMahon's work as also its 'genuine readiness' to cooperate with him.[11]

The 'great concession', however, left the British Plenipotentiary singularly cold, for presently he informed Chen that he had received the communication 'with astonishment' and 'with regret'. Besides, he emphasised, its transmission to the Lonchen would only show that Chen never had 'any real desire' to effect a settlement. Sir Henry, therefore, asked his Chinese

---

[8]*Supra*, n. 3.
[9]Office note by Rose, 9 March 1914, *Foreign*, *Notes*, October 1914, Procs. 134–396.
[10]Jordan to Viceroy, telegram, 17 March 1914, No. 225 in *Foreign*, October 1914, Procs. 134–396.
[11]For the text of the telegram 'communicated by Mr Ivan Chen on the 19th March 1914' see 'Notes' in *supra*, n. 9.

colleague to 'consider once more' the grave consequences that would follow, should the latter adhere to the 'uncompromising attitude' indicated in his reply.[12]

Elsewhere, McMahon had indicated that he did not regard China's preliminary reply 'too seriously', and that his own rejoinder amounted practically to a 'refusal' to consider it in its present form. Meanwhile he hoped that the situation would crystallise about 24 March, until which time the proposed communication to Russia was to be held over.[13]

Portents from Peking, however, boded ill for McMahon's guarded optimism. On the appointed day, the Wai-chiao-pu telegraphed to Ivan Chen, while its Foreign Minister told Jordan that no alteration in the administrative system was contemplated in the area between Giamda and the Salween. East of the river, Chao's conquests were to remain intact. The only redeeming feature of the Chinese rejoinder, Jordan remarked, was that Peking 'appeared anxious' to avoid breaking off the negotiations.[14]

By this time, third week of March (1914), it would appear that the British Minister had already started the sell-out on Kokonor, and India learnt that Jordan was prepared to recognise that this region had 'no connection with Tibet'. Asked specifically whether he had mentioned Kokonor at his interview with the Chinese Foreign Minister,[15] Jordan was wary:

> I said that I might feel justified (in) telegraphing any reasonable suggestion that they desired to make with regard to a rectification of the frontier in the region of Kokonor if the objection referred only to Kokonor and the Government of China were prepared to accept the rest of the frontier arrangement as you laid down.[16]

Meanwhile the Chinese, partly it would seem as a diversionary tactic and partly with a view to keep the negotiating pot boiling, complained of Tibetan 'depredations' in the March country. McMahon countered by pointing out that it was becoming 'increasingly difficult' to restrain the activities of Tibetan troops when Peking laid claims to a frontier line in the heart of

---

[12] For McMahon's 'draft' reply to Ivan Chen, dated 20 March 1914, see Ibid.

[13] Viceroy to Secretary of State, telegram, 20 March 1914, No. 226 in *Foreign*, October 1914, Procs. 134–396.

[14] Jordan to Grey, telegram, 20 March 1914, No. 227 in Ibid. Jordan's interview with the Chinese Minister took place on 18 March.

[15] McMahon to Jordan, telegram, 20 March 1914, in 'Notes', *supra*, n. 9.

McMahon had marked the telegram 'Private' and 'Confidential' and indicated that his information was based on a 'secret, reliable channel'—a euphemism, one would suspect, for the Intelligence Department.

[16] Jordan to McMahon, telegram, 21 March 1914, in Ibid. Jordan underlined the fact that the Chinese Minister 'laid great stress' on the fact that McMahon's proposals assigned the whole of Kokonor to Tibet whereas it had been recognised as 'under Chinese jurisdiction'.

Tibetan territory. Conscious of China's weakness and by no means averse to putting pressure on her, he informed Chen on 27 March that

> the offer of settlement on the map attached to his statement of 17th February cannot remain open indefinitely. Should his Chinese colleague be unable to discuss that map in a spirit that is likely to lead to a settlement in the near future, Sir Henry feels that there will be no alternative but to withdraw the map and to lay before the Conference proposals of a different nature.[17]

A day previously, McMahon had informed the Secretary of State that ' confidentially ' he had learnt that the Chinese were going to ' reiterate ' arguments ' brought forward ' by them earlier in support of a frontier running through Chiangta and at the same time propose various amendments and alterations —' some of (a) sweeping nature '—to the other articles of his draft. He was sanguine, however, that through ' continued patience and firmness ' he would be able to bring them around and conclude negotiations ' successfully '. His ' strategy ' was to decline to consider other terms ' until settlement of limits and extent of country ' were first determined. On his own, he confided, he would adhere to the two zones, be prepared to exclude Nyarong and Derge from Outer Tibet yet stick out for Kokonor. In all this he could claim the support of the Governor-General who urged adherence to the proposed limits of Outer and Inner Tibet and felt that any change would be ' politically unsound ' and ' unjust ' to Tibet.[18]

On 30 March Chen met Rose and sought his ' private opinion ' in regard to the contents of a telegram which he had received from Peking that day. *Inter alia* the message had underscored China's ' unutterable difficulty ' in accepting McMahon's proposed boundaries, due to the ' great regard ' that had to be paid to the feelings of the general public, especially of people in Szechuan and Yunnan. Among the ' further concessions ' Peking was now willing to make, it indicated that in places west of the Salween up to Tanta Col (instead of Giamda, as suggested in a previous telegram) the status quo would be maintained in that these areas would not be converted into Chinese administrative districts. For the rest (viz. districts east of the Salween), the country was to be ' administered absolutely ' by China while Dam and Gyade were to be treated as areas west of the Salween.

There was not really much to talk about but Rose put on airs, refused to express ' even a private opinion ' and asked for time to formulate ' in my own mind the consequences ' of Peking's latest move. No wonder there was an element of drama in the situation, for Chen, Rose noted, was ' greatly disturbed ' and begged him ' to communicate as quickly as possible '.

[17]McMahon to Ivan Chen, ' verbal communication ', 27 March 1914, in Ibid.
[18]Viceroy to Secretary of Sate, 26 March 1914, No. 229 in *Foreign*, October 1914, Procs. 134–396.

This Rose subsequently did. Chinese claims, he told Chen, were 'exaggerated' and in bringing these forward again, he (Chen) was inviting certain definite consequences, the most important being that

> in view of the negotiations and correspondence which had already passed, and of the critical situation in Tibet itself... you (McMahon) would feel bound to withdraw your proposals of 17th February with the accompanying map.[19]

From the evidence ready to hand, it would appear that at this stage Ivan Chen telegraphed furiously urging his superiors for such concessions as could possibly be made. The result was the telegram of 3 April, which Chen presented to a formal meeting of the Conference four days later.[20]

The 'five-point proposal' which Peking now put forward may be reproduced here for convenience:

1. That the river Nonkiang, or the Salween, shall be the boundary line between Szechuan and Tibet;
2. That all the territory east of the Salween shall be under the absolute jurisdiction of China;
3. That all the territory west of the Salween shall be within the limits of the autonomy of Tibet, provided it is agreed that Tibet forms a portion of the territory of the Republic of China just the same as Outer Mongolia;
4. That Chinghai shall remain, as a matter of course, under the absolute jurisdiction of China;
5. That Gyade shall remain under Chinese administration as before but it was understood that China will institute no new district in this area.[21]

In Peking, Jordan was told that the five points, retailed above, represented 'the extreme limit' of concessions which China was prepared to make. In reply, the British Minister expressed his 'surprise' and 'pain'. The President's step, he felt, was 'unwise', for China was pursuing a 'fatal' policy in Tibet, nor did he (Jordan) see any chance that these conditions would be accepted. The net result, he feared, would be merely to perpetuate the border troubles of recent years. Essentially, Jordan argued, the Tibetan question would admit of easy adjustment if, instead of pursuing 'barren conquests', China showed the same magnanimity as the British had in 1904.[22]

Even as these exchanges were taking place, McMahon learnt that the Chinese

---

[19]Office note by Rose, 30 March 1914, in 'Notes', *supra*, n. 9.

[20]'Proceedings of the 6th meeting of the Tibet Conference' held at the Foreign Office in Simla on 7 April 1914, No. 223 in *Foreign*, October 1914, Procs. 134–396. At this meeting, Lonchen Shatra was absent, being indisposed, and Tibet was represented by Bell.

[21]Appendix to No. 233 in Ibid.

[22]Jordan to Viceroy, telegram, 5 April 1914, No. 232 in Ibid.

had been encouraged to believe that his proposals need not be taken ' too seriously ', that insofar as they ran counter to the integrity and advancement of China, outside powers may intervene and entrust the final settlement to China and Tibet alone, thereby excluding the British Plenipotentiary from the *pourparlers*. Again, while Britain may be interested in an early settlement, Peking had concluded, it was in no position to adopt a ' forcible ' attitude.

Two clues are of relevance, in the context of the above report. One, that on 1 April, for the first time, Ivan Chen was instructed to secure an interview with the Lonchen. Two, that the boundary now suggested by China was the same as put forth by the Russian Minister for Foreign Affairs in 1906 in the course of negotiations leading to the Anglo-Russian Convention of 1907!

To bring matters to a definitive conclusion—and McMahon had, after the Conference adjourned on 7 April, indulged in some plain-speaking with Chen— the British Plenipotentiary proposed to hold a formal meeting of the Conference on 14 April, ' in order to withdraw ' the draft convention and the accompanying map.[23]

While exerting pressure on Delhi, the Chinese had been diplomatically active in London too. Thus on 11 March, their Minister had presented to the Foreign Office, on ' urgent ' and ' anxious ' instructions from his government, a note to the effect that Tibetan negotiations were not proceeding ' satisfactorily', and that in resisting the ' extravagant demands ' of the Tibetan delegate, Peking had not received that 'measure of support ' from the British to which its reasonable attitude entitled it. All that Peking desired was that ' instructions' be telegraphed to the British delegate to give such 'friendly assistance' to the Chinese as would lead to a reasonable and satisfactory settlement.[24]

The reply which the Foreign Office had initially wanted to return was stiffened by a dose of strong language supplied by the India Office. Here McMahon's proposals were powerfully supported for, based on a full consideration of available evidence, they represented, ' in the opinion of HMG ', the broad outlines of a compromise which alone could form the basis of a settlement.[25]

In Simla, McMahon was now going ahead with preparations for convening a meeting of the Conference on 15 April, and the Secretary of State had given him the green signal to withdraw both the map and the draft convention.[26] Suddenly, however, Ivan Chen showed himself ' extremely anxious ' to secure a ' postponement'. Even though he had ' no instructions ' from his government, he confided, either to discuss the frontier ' in some such definite way '

[23]Viceroy to Secretary of State, telegram, 7 April 1914, No. 235 in Ibid.

[24]Chinese Minister to Foreign Office, 11 March 1914, Encl. 1 in No. 242 in Ibid.

[25]Encl. 2 in No. 242 in Ibid, gives the ' draft Memorandum ' for communication to the Chinese Minister. To this, the India Office, vide its letter of 25 March, No. 243, Ibid., suggested some material modifications. *Inter alia*, it suggested that opportunity might be taken, ' to mention orally ' that HMG suspected that misleading accounts of their attitudes and intentions were reaching Peking. It expressed the hope that the latter will not be so ill-advised as to pay any attention to such reports.

[26]Secretary of State to Viceroy, telegram, 14 April 1914, No. 246 in Ibid.

or indeed any part of the proposals made by Sir Henry, he undertook to telegraph on the subject 'in the strongest possible terms', should the British Plenipotentiary in return agree to a postponement 'for even a few days'.[27]

McMahon obliged by a week's postponement while at the same time he made it clear that on the stipulated 22 April, there 'will have to be' a final decision; either the Plenipotentiaries will 'initial the documents', or he 'would feel bound' to withdraw them.

Chen viewed the proposal as 'reasonable', sought 'some indication' of McMahon's final attitude so that he might 'formulate it definitely' in a telegram to Peking, and promised to do his utmost to secure an 'unconditional reply'.

For the first time since the Conference convened, Chen seemed to be unbending. On the afternoon of the 14th, he asked Rose if the terms of the draft Convention could be discussed threadbare between the two of them. Besides, on the more specific issue of Tibet's territorial limits, he was 'extremely' anxious to ascertain the 'final' attitude of HMG. In reply, Rose made it clear that, consistent with the maintenance of 'general' principles, he would endeavour to meet the Chinese viewpoint on questions of detail. *Inter alia*, he

> pointed out the advantages of the watersheds which had been utilised in defining the frontier lines, and repeated your (McMahon's) earnest desire that these watersheds should be used as frontier limits wherever possible as they were permanent and intelligible to the mind of the local tribesmen whilst they avoided the necessity for elaborate frontier commissions.

As to the frontier, Chen sought a cancellation of the two zones. 'His government', Rose noted, 'appears to dislike the idea very much'. Besides, Chen

> could not understand the zone theory at all and he could only suppose that we were bent on ignoring the position which the Chinese had made and still held in the districts of Inner Tibet.

More specifically, the Chinese Plenipotentiary was of the view that the watershed frontier between the two zones should follow the mountain range on the west of the Yangtze, thereby 'leaving Derge and Nyarong' in Inner Tibet.

Chen had also sought the deletion of a clause, in Article IX of the draft,

[27] Office note by Archibald Rose, 14 April 1914, in 'Notes', *Supra*, n. 9. In a telegram to the Secretary of State, McMahon reported that 'under instructions' from his government Chen had 'earnestly' requested for a postponement which he (McMahon) had granted 'as a personal concession' and that, as he saw it, there were 'distinct signs of weakening' in the Chinese attitude. For details, Viceroy to Secretary of State, telegram, 14 April 1914, No. 245 in *Foreign*, October 1914, Procs. 134–396.

about the government of (Outer) Tibet issuing 'appointment orders to Chiefs and local officers' and collecting all 'customary rents and taxes'. Further, would Peking, the Chinese Plenipotentiary queried, be given a free hand in the consolidation of its position in Inner Tibet?

The British position, as outlined by Rose, on the various issues raised by Chen was familiar. On Derge and Nyarong, where Tibetans had brought 'very strong' evidence,

> it would be extremely difficult, he told Chen, to obtain Tibetan assent to any realignment of the frontier.

Nonetheless, he assured the Chinese delegate that the points raised, which he promised to report to McMahon, would 'receive consideration'.

On the two zones however, Rose was emphatic, the British attitude was quite firm, for any suggestion to abandon them 'could not be entertained for a moment'.

As for Lhasa issuing 'appointment orders' to Chiefs and local officers in Inner Tibet, Rose promised 'to do his best' to secure the 'deletion' of the clause. Insofar as the question of Peking consolidating its position in Inner Tibet was concerned,

> I replied in the affirmative, with the proviso that such consolidation did not infringe the integrity of Tibet as a geographical and political entity.

Specific clarifications and assurances apart, Rose left little doubt in Chen's mind that the purpose of the postponed meeting, now to be held on 22 April, was to withdraw the draft proposals and that the only way to avoid this was their unconditional acceptance. Unfortunately, there had been no 'reasonable response' from Peking and while he (Rose) would do his best to secure such modifications as he had promised, he 'begged' Chen to make the situation 'absolutely clear' to his government and to leave 'no loophole for a misunderstanding' of the British attitude. This Chen agreed to do.[28]

Reporting to his political superiors in London on all that had transpired between Chen and Rose, McMahon pointed out that

> in regard to the frontier lines, slight modifications have similarly been accepted, so as to include in China the towns of Atuntse and Tachienlu and the lake of Kokonor, whilst the Mekong-Yangtze watershed has been reintro-

---

[28] 'Note on an interview between Mr Ivan Chen and Mr Rose on 15th April 1914' in 'Notes', *supra*, n. 9.

It is interesting that on 16 April, Rose and Chen exchanged letters on 'notes of yesterday's interview' and that Chen informed Rose that 'after having carefully read them', he found the 'notes' to be 'correct'. Rose noted too that at the interview on 15 April, which lasted ten hours, Chen debated his points 'with skill and tireless persistency'.

duced as the boundary between the zones in accordance with my original proposal, which was approved by HMG.[29]

Despite all that had preceded it, at the seventh meeting of the Conference on 22 April, Ivan Chen presented on behalf of his government, five new ' demands '. These, McMahon noted, ' showed no signs of a conciliatory attitude '. Nor were things any the better after the adjourned meeting ' re-assembled ' five days later. As McMahon pointed out, the five ' demands ' were

> vague and elusive, expressing general acceptance of the main principles... but demanding further unspecified concessions to the frontier before any settlement was possible, and appearing to convey no authority for the acceptance of our draft.[30]

Since Chen ' categorically refused ' to initial the draft, McMahon persuaded the Lonchen ' to make ' some ' last concession '. This was with regard to the

> tract of country in the neighbourhood of Lake Kokonor to which the Chinese appeared to attach importance, although neither the Chinese nor the Tibetans had any definite information in regard to its nature or inhabitants.

As a ' last ' concession, this tract was excluded from ' Inner ' Tibet and included into China proper. It was this territorial settlement on the map to which Ivan Chen eventually appended his signatures, *not* initials, on 27 April.[31]

The map and the proceedings of the Conference on the fateful 27 April would thus demonstrate, and beyond the shadow of a doubt, that with the modifications in the Kokonor region, all the three Plenipotentiaries including Ivan Chen, accepted the Red and Blue Lines defining Inner and Outer Tibet as delineated (on the Convention map), on behalf of their respective governments. This despite earlier Chinese and Tibetan reservations, the former's with regard to the nomenclature and of both in respect of the allocation of districts each coveted of the other.

---

[29]Viceroy to Secretary of State, telegram, 16 April 1914, No. 247 in *Foreign*, October 1914, Procs. 134–396.

[30]McMahon had made it clear that he proposed to continue the fiction of adjournment ' as late as noon on 27th April, if this should be found necessary '. Viceroy to Secretary of State, telegram, 22 April 1914, No. 262 in Ibid.

[31] ' Proceedings of the 7th meeting of the Tibet Conference held at the Foreign Office on the 22nd and 27th April 1914 ', Annexure II, No. 257 in Ibid. Also ' Memorandum regarding the progress of Negotiations from 25th December 1913 to 30th April 1914 ', in 'Notes ', *supra*, n. 9.

Chapter 19

Negotiating the India-Tibet Boundary

By 27 April, with the map signed and the Convention initialled, a great deal of the work of the Conference seemed to be over. The weary months in Simla and the interminable formal/informal discussions in Delhi appeared to have borne fruit at long last and a compromise of sorts, acceptable to all, worked out. As a matter of fact, a great deal more had been achieved than was apparent for, apart from the Inner/Outer Tibet zones, a settlement of the India-Tibet boundary, part of McMahon's Red Line on the map, had also been effected.

In his Memorandum of 30 April, summing up the third phase of the Conference, McMahon had referred to the 'difficult' problem of the India-Tibet frontier which had been settled after 'prolonged discussions' between Bell and the Lonchen and his own exchange of notes with the latter on 24–25 March. He regarded the achievement as truly heroic, for

> the acceptance by the Tibetans of a recognised boundary, will so lighten our responsibilities, so materially strengthen our position, that I cannot but regard this definition as not the least important and valuable of the results which have been achieved by the work of the Conference.[1]

Born of a certain seemingly deliberate misrepresentation, a great deal of misunderstanding persists in regard to the settlement of this boundary and it may, therefore, be useful to enquire how the problem came up at the tripartite conference and the manner in which it was finally resolved.

Just about the time the Simla Conference convened, the Foreign Office in London wrote to the India Office that

> it (would) be necessary before a definite agreement is concluded to consider whether any settlement of the Indo-Tibetan frontier should not be communicated to the Russian Government and at what stage of the negotiations the communication should take place....[2]

---

[1] 'Memorandum regarding progress of negotiations from 25th December 1913 to 30th April 1914', *Foreign, Notes*, October 1914, Procs. 134–396.

[2] *F O to I O*, 21 October 1913, No. 180 in *Foreign*, March 1914, Procs. 1–251. In the light of this to suggest—Karunakar Gupta, 'The McMahon Line 191–145: The British Legacy', *China Quarterly* (London), 47, July–September 1971, pp. 521–45 (cited, et seq, as *Karunakar Gupta*)—that the delimitation of India's border was not, 'so far as the Government in London was concerned', among the purposes of the Simla Conference would be to fly in the face of known facts. The author clearly forgets that HMG had this very much in mind

In the light of Russia's known penchant for keeping nothing secret—a fact to which, among others, McMahon was later to make pointed references on more than one occasion—the charge that Tibet negotiated a 'sell-away' with Britain, behind the back of the Chinese, needs examination. This is the more important in view of the fact that the India Office did not object to the Foreign Office proposal about a communication being made either in a formal or an informal manner. Thus on 23 October 1913, Lord Crewe told Sir Edward Grey

> that by a definition of the boundary between Tibet and India he (Crewe) understands the Government of India to mean an agreement as to the spheres, at present undefined, of the two countries in the tribal territory east of Bhutan. He agrees that such an agreement, if reached, must be communicated to the Russian Government, but is inclined to think that it will suffice if this is done in the course of the ordinary communication of information regarding the proceedings of the conference which has been promised to M. de Etter. If any question arises of rectifying any well-recognised frontier, it will no doubt be necessary to make a formal communication.[3]

With this view, the Foreign Office concurred and a communication to the Russian Ambassador was postponed until he was to be informed, 'in the ordinary course' of the proceedings of the Conference.[4]

Meanwhile in Simla and Delhi, as no doubt in Shillong, a lot of attention had been given to the problem of working out a boundary alignment. On 26 September 1913, in an office note on the Assam Chief Commissioner's recommendation regarding the proposed frontier, Delhi recorded the following observation:

> The Secretary of State expected the frontier to be one not open to doubt in view probably of Chinese susceptibilities. If, however, the forthcoming (Simla) Conference is successful, China will drop out and the question will be for settlement between ourselves and Tibet. In these circumstances there would perhaps be no objection to securing a frontier to our advantage.[5]

Again, in an annotation on the boundary proposals emanating from Shillong, which he viewed as 'generally suitable', McMahon made two observations both of which are pertinent here:

long before the Simla Conference was thought of; more particularly, since the Chinese take-over of Tibet (1910). Again, as the record bears out, more than the India Office, the Foreign Office had been worried by Chao Erh-feng, and later Fu Sung-mu's, territorial as well as cartographic encroachments on what were sensitive areas on, or along, the North-East Frontier.

[3] *I O* to *F O*, 23 October 1914, No. 181 in Ibid.
[4] *F O* to *I O*, 28 October 1914, No. 186 in Ibid.
[5] Office note by ' TW ' (T G B Waugh), Acting Secretary to the Simla Conference, in *Foreign*, September 1915, Procs. 761–01.

In place, however, of making a small river boundary...the Tho Chu etc., it is always preferable for not only demarcation but administrative and jurisdictional purposes to take the watersheds of these rivers....I would therefore suggest the adoption of the outside watershed in each case....

Later:

It is desirable to come to an early decision in general terms regarding the boundary line we require, in order to enable us to come to an understanding on the subject *with China and Tibet* before the Tibet Conference closes.[6]

In his 'Confidential Note' of 1 June 1912, the Chief of the Army General Staff in India, while summing up the political-cum-geographical information gathered as a result of the various missions into tribal territory following Williamson's murder, submitted a 'rough definition' of the 'proposed frontier line'. Named after the various tribes and the exploratory missions, the frontier was broadly divided into four sections—the Miri, the Abor, the Mishmi and the Hkampti Long, the last clearly falling outside the scope of these pages.

The Miri section was the starting point, touching the frontiers of Bhutan in its western extremity and embracing the watersheds of the Subansiri and its tributaries, the Kamala and the Khru. It was pointed out that from about Long. 94°-93° and Lat. 28° 25'/20' there was a high range which formed a well-defined barrier. Two principal passes crossed it, while the rivers, the Subansiri and the Kamala, rose south and east of the range. There was the additional fact that the northern Miris were in no way under Tibetan influence. The obvious conclusion sought to be drawn was that the mountain barrier was a 'suitable frontier line', albeit more information was necessary regarding the Khru river and the pass from the Subansiri in the eastern part of the section.

Part of the problem in regard to the Miri section was the frontier above Tawang which required 'careful consideration' for, as the 'Note' put it,

the present boundary...(allows) a dangerous wedge of territory...between the Miri country and Bhutan. A comparatively easy and much used trade route traverses this wedge from north to south by which the Chinese would be able to exert influence or pressure on Bhutan, while we have no approach to this salient from a flank, as we have in the case of the Chumbi salient. A rectification of the boundary here is therefore imperative.

The 'ideal line', it was pointed out, would be from the knot of mountains near Long. 93°, Lat. 28° 20' to the Bhutan border north of Tsona dzong, in a direct east and west line with the northern frontier of Bhutan. There was also a convenient watershed for this line to follow.

[6]Office note by McMahon, 24 October 1913, in Ibid.

In the Abor section, near the Tibetan district of Pemakoi, there was a high peak, at an altitude of 25,700 feet. At the eastern end of this peak, the Dihang or Siang (later the Brahmaputra) breaks through in a deep gorge. A continuous mountain range running east to south-east from the gorge and joining the Mishmi hills, which in turn formed the watershed between the Rong Thod chu and the Delei, was to constitute the boundary in this section.

The geographical frontier in the Abor section was further sanctified, for

> ethnological evidence also supports the choice. The Tibetans and the Abors both recognise the Pemakoi range as the boundary, while Abors state that to the north-east of their country is a region of uninhabited, inhospitable mountains. North of the Pemakoi range the people are called Menba ... the people are Abors as far as Jido on the left bank of the Dihang, and pure Abors extend nearly as far on the right bank.

The Mishmi section comprised the valley of the Lohit and its tributaries, an ' exceedingly sensitive ' area:

> The Chinese are reported to be increasing their garrison and building more barracks at Rima. The Taroan and Miju Mishmis trade freely between Assam and Tibet, acting the part of middlemen. The Chinese made a determined effort in 1911 to bring the Taroans of the Delei and the Dou valleys under their sway ... they demanded that the Taroans should plant the dragon flag at the confluence of the Delei and the Lohit rivers. This is eloquent testimony to Chinese ambitions.

Nor was that all. For on the one hand the Tibetans of Zayul were ' desirous of exchanging the Chinese for the British yoke ' while on the other the attitude of the Mishmis, heavily ' tinctured with caution ', was ' non-committal'.

As to drawing the frontier in the Mishmi section, Menilkrai, where the Chinese had planted their flags to mark their southernmost limits, afforded ' no indication ' of a frontier line, the intent being to deny to the British the only suitable site, Walong. The frontier crossing therefore, the note recommended, should be ' a few miles ' to the north of Walong. The latter, initially a Mishmi settlement where Tibetan herdsmen maintained cattle for their (Mishmi) owners,

> was an ideal site, in an elevated situation, commanding the valley to the north on either bank, lending itself to the construction of defensible post and offering little difficulty in the matter of water-supply.

All in all, the frontier line proposed by the Army top brass from west to east, was to follow the watersheds of the Subansiri, with its tributaries the Kamala and the Khru, the Dihang as far as its major gorge and all its tributaries south of that point, the Dibang and its confluents and the Lohit and its tributaries. The proposed line, it was pointed out, 'corresponded very closely' with the one suggested by the Government of India in its letter of 1911.[7]

Somewhere in the middle of 1913, the Army Department in India submitted a 'Note on the Military Frontier on the North-east' wherein it endorsed, for most part, the Chief of the General Staff's earlier recommendations. Opportunity, however, was taken to stress, *inter alia*, the maxim that a mountain-barrier is a 'satisfactory' military frontier, that owing to the Chinese disposition to expand in the direction of Burma and Assam, the frontier to the east of Bhutan was more important than to its west. Again, the 'ideal' to be aimed at in determining a frontier in mountainous country, was that

> the line chosen should follow some prominent geographical feature, preferably the main watershed of the mountain system and... to facilitate effective occupation if necessary, the communications upto the frontier should be such as to afford reasonable access to the line selected. A lateral communication running parallel to and a short distance to the rear of the frontier is also a considerable asset.

The ideal apart, the limitations known to be operative in the case of the North-East Frontier were easily recognised. Thus there was no intention of 'administering' the country 'within the proposed frontier line', much less of undertaking 'military operations' in the area in question. And yet, as Chinese incursions at Hpimaw had demonstrated, it was 'desirable' to maintain some semblance of authority that could be backed by force, 'if necessary'. Again, it was obvious that, with a delimited frontier, there was the obligation to eject 'unwelcome intruders'. Realising how expensive road-building was and yet refusing to lose sight of the fact that the principal objective was to deny the Chinese access to the valleys of Upper Burma and Assam, the Army Department was confident that if its proposals for establishing posts in Hkampti Long and the Lohit valley were to receive official sanction, there would be 'little difficulty' in maintaining a sufficient influence as far as the boundary now being suggested. Nor was theirs a 'final recommendation' of the line the frontier should follow.[8]

A lot of emotional hang-over surrounds the question of Tawang and it may be useful to bring out an essential aspect of the question here. It may be recalled that at an early stage in the discussions, in 1910, Tawang was excluded from the tentative boundary proposed. Later, in 1912–13, the General Staff as well as the Army Department suggested a rectification and yet Delhi

---

[7] 'Confidential Note by Chief of the General Staff', *IOR*, Political and Secret, 1910/1918, part 2.

[8] The Army Department's note on 'The Military Frontier on the North-east' is to be found in 'Notes' in *Foreign*, September 1915, Procs. 76–101.

decided to let it stand over, as its Foreign Department was not sure if it could make out 'any sort of case' for its inclusion. Even as late as 12 November 1913, McMahon had pointed out that there was no accurate information regarding the southern limits of Dhirang dzong, which lay to the south of Tawang and allegedly belonged to Tibet. It followed, he argued, that any attempt

> to define more definitely the limits of Tibetan possessions around Tawang is, under present conditions, impossible. The Tibetan representatives had no knowledge on the subject and would not commit themselves to anything definite. It followed that the question of the investigation and determination of the actual boundary between Tibetan and Indian occupation in this section must be left to subsequent opportunities. It will be easy for us to recognise Tibetan rights to any area south of the line on which their claims may hereafter be established.

This would be the easier, for all that was contemplated in the tripartite agreement was

> merely defining the boundary by a line drawn on a map. This has obviously many advantages and is preferable to a verbal definition.[9]

From the above, two points emerge clearly. One, that the proposals of the General Staff, drawn up in June 1912, and the 'note' of the Army Department almost a year later, underwent considerable changes in the course of the months that elapsed until the 'Red line' appeared on the map, in March 1914. It is significant that even as late as November 1913, McMahon's draft showed the alignment, in the Kameng division, on the Se-la, with Tawang placed securely on the Tibetan side. It was clear to him that the matter needed further investigation; what was more, the Tibetans themselves had no accurate knowledge and would not commit themselves to anything definite.

Another point worth remarking is that in the Abor section, the inclusion of Pemakoichen south of the proposed alignment, as suggested by the General Staff, the Army Department and, albeit with slight modifications, by Neville and Dundas in 1913, had been countermanded by the time the Red Line was drawn up in Delhi, early in 1914. The moral is, and it is something that needs considerable emphasis, that in drawing the 'Red Line' on the map, McMahon and his advisers were laying down a boundary with the greatest deliberation and were not hustled into decisions taken for them either by the top echelon of the Army or the highest political authorities in London, much less in India.

[9] Office note by McMahon, 12 November 1913, in Ibid.
Hardinge, who saw McMahon's note on 20 November, initialled it, clearly implying his acceptance, and approval, of its contents. Ibid.

While the tripartite conference was convening in Delhi, Bell, on behalf of McMahon, conducted a number of informal discussions with the Lonchen on the question of the boundary. The first such meeting took place on 15 January when Bell showed the Lonchen the 'proposed Indo-Tibetan boundary' on map sheets of the Survey of India.

The Lonchen appears to have raised two principal objections, the first of which related to the extreme western part of the Subansiri section, the country around Tawang. The 'Lopas' (a loose term for Abors, Miris and Mishmis), he argued, paid taxes to the Tibetan Government, to Chayul Jong and to Tawang. Besides, there were individual Tibetans viz., Pokanam Deba, chief of the Po country, the Lhalu family and certain landlords of Chamdo and Sanga-cho dzong, who owned land in Pemakoichen.

The Tibetan Plenipotentiary also disputed the alignment near Menkong. The (Tibetan) frontier, he maintained, extended five stages beyond Menkong, whereas the line on the map presented to him showed the distance to be less.

Bell's reply to the Lonchen was couched in diplomatic language. The boundary as drawn on the map, he told the Tibetan Minister, was based on the reports of British officers and surveyors who had gone carefully over the ground in the areas under discussion. The proposed line, therefore, appeared to represent ' an equitable frontier ' between Tibet and India. As to Menkong. it might be that the road from it to the frontier was circuitous and difficult, Since relations between the British Government and Tibet were friendly, Bell argued, it was 'in the interests of (their) continued friendship' that a clear boundary should be arranged and friction avoided.

The Lonchen recognised this friendly attitude and, ' for the purposes of the present treaty', accepted the proposed boundary line. He did, however, stipulate that if it subsequently transpired that any territory belonging to the Lopas or under individual Tibetans fell on the British side of the line, questions relating to them might be settled directly by Lhasa with the (British) Indian authorities. Furthermore, if it were later found that any Lopas, under the direct control of the Tibetan Government, had been transferred to the British, the latter would waive all claims in regard to them.

Nor was that all:

> I (Bell) similarly waived all claims in respect of the lands of the Lopas, mapped on the Tibetan side of the frontier....I informed the Lonchen that I accepted this position....

Later Bell informed McMahon of the success of his first informal discussions with the Lonchen:

> The Tibetan Plenipotentiary, without suggesting a reference to Lhasa has agreed to the frontier you (McMahon) desire. Near Menkong we wish to

draw back the boundary line in any case and we shall thus give Tibet the territory she claims between Menkong and the frontier.[10]

A few days later, in a detailed note, Bell spelt out the problems thrown up by the western section of the Tibet-India frontier. Certain landed estates in the area south of Se-la belonged to the Lhalu family of Lhasa and some other unspecified individual Tibetans and he proposed to tell the Lonchen that the British would give 'favourable treatment' in respect of these estates. 'On these lines', he noted, he was confident of effecting a settlement.

Additionally, there was the problem of the route followed by the Tsari pilgrimage, to which the Tibetans attached a great deal of importance. Bell was conscious of the fact that to claim places which were occupied by the Tibetans along this route would be to invite the hostility of Lhasa and its three great monasteries, who wielded powerful influence. He, therefore, planned to inform the Lonchen that the proposed boundary line left the highest mountain ranges before reaching the Tsari heights thereby placing the latter, and the short pilgrimage route, in Tibetan territory. But a part of it did perhaps come within British domain. The country here, however, was essentially low-lying, 'uninhabited and unsuitable' for Tibetan colonisation. In any case, India would avoid all interference with the rights of pilgrims. Besides, 'any representations' from Lhasa would receive 'careful consideration'.

Nor was Bell unmindful of the 'military and commercial' advantages that would accrue from the new frontier-line:

of easy access to the rolling uplands and broad valleys of Tibet by placing our frontier at the end of a difficult valley country. The inhabitants between the Menlakathong and the Se-la ranges are more akin to the inhabitants south of the Se-la than they are to the people north of the Menlakathong La. A few miles north... is Chukang, where the Lhasa authorities maintain, or used to maintain, a toll-house levying duties on all goods from the south. All indications go to show that north of this range the inhabitants are typical Tibetans and that the administration is controlled by Lhasa.

Bell was also conscious of the great value of the strip between the Menlakathong La and the Se-la which was akin to the Chumbi valley or the northern Sikkim valleys of Lachung and Lanchen. He felt that, after the conclusion of the Conference, 'it may be advisable' to create a North-east Frontier Agency to conduct the 'political work' connected with Sikkim, Bhutan, Tibet, and the tribes between Assam and Tibet. As he visualised it, the head of this agency may be stationed at, or near, Tawang and would be

nearer Lhasa than is the Political Officer in Sikkim at Gangtok. The road between Tawang and Lhasa is easy. In due course, a trade mart should be

[10]Office note by Bell, 17 January 1914, in *Foreign*, September 1915, Procs. 76–101.

opened at Tsetang.... Our British Trade Agent there would only be 60 miles from Lhasa along an easy road and could reach Lhasa easily on the second day.... Tawang is much nearer the Assam frontier tribes and nearer the residence of the Maharaja of Bhutan than is Gangtok.

Finally, Bell touched upon two problems—according favourable treatment to the Tawang monastery and withdrawing the proposed frontier line south of Menkong, thereby giving Tibet the territory she claimed in its neighbourhood.[11]

The next meeting between Bell and the Tibetan Plenipotentiary took place on 28 January, at the latter's initiative. Discussion centred chiefly on the pilgrimage routes in Tsari and Kongbu. There were three such pilgrimages: ' Tsari Nyingpa ' (' old Tsari '), which took place once in 12 years; ' Tso Karpo ' (' white Tsari '), which took two days going around a lake; and ' Tsari Sarpa ' (' New Tsari '), which was an annual feature and took three days. All along these routes there were a number of monasteries, each having 10–15 monks; larger ones, on the Tsari Nyingpa, had 40 each. Besides the monasteries, there were houses all along the route where alms were distributed to the pilgrims, who came from Tibet as well as Mongolia and Kham. Of particular importance was Migyitun where Tibetan officials and pilgrims, numbering about 20,000, assembled every 12 years so as to arrange matters with the Lopas, through whose territory the pilgrimage route passed.

Bell, on his part, undertook to ensure that the frontier would be so laid as to leave Migyitun on the Tibetan side. Such monasteries and other sacred places as fell into British territory, he had already assured the Lonchen, would be protected and put to no harm.

In return, the Lonchen told Bell that he was awaiting instructions from Lhasa where he had sent a map indicating the proposed frontier, as well as a report ' explaining the circumstances ' in detail. He was sure that there would not be any great difficulty in coming to a ' satisfactory settlement ' on the lines proposed by him (Bell).[12]

At their meeting on 30 January, more details were filled in. *Inter alia*, Bell informed the Tibetan Plenipotentiary that any land on these pilgrimage routes that might lie on the British side of the frontier (and being no more than one day's march from the present frontier line), would be placed in Tibetan territory and the frontier modified accordingly. Again, Migyitun would be placed in Tibet as also Shangamla and Po-trang. Since grazing grounds would be required near these places for the use of pilgrims, they would be situated somewhat deep into Tibet. Later, Bell promised to send the Lonchen detailed maps showing the modified boundary.[13] The position was further

[11]Office note by Bell, 23 January 1914, in Ibid.
[12]Office note by Bell, 30 January 1914, in Ibid.
[13]Office note by Bell, 3 February 1914, in Ibid. [n. contd. overleaf]

spelt out in his letter to the Lonchen on 6 February, which recapitulated that, in regard to the Western section, Shatra had undertaken to make a reference to Lhasa and that McMahon, to whom he (Bell) had reported, ' approved ' of the arrangement.[14]

The Lonchen's reply, three days later, underlined his lack of any ' accurate knowledge ' of boundaries. All the same he had referred to Lhasa which, he hoped, in view of the 'kind' help rendered by the British Government, would settle the matter ' satisfactorily '.[15]

In an office ' note ' of 10 February, Bell recorded that the Lonchen's reply indicated ' a fair chance ' of the Tibetan Government agreeing to the boundary settlement. This was endorsed by McMahon who pronounced the results, ' so far ', to be ' very satisfactory '.[16]

The thread of negotiations was taken up again on 17 March when the Lonchen informed Bell that he had heard from Lhasa on the question of the India-Tibet frontier. *Inter alia*, the Tibetan government now agreed to surrender all revenues on the British side of the frontier, and requested that the income and estates of private individuals and monasteries might be given to them. Besides providing a sufficiently exhaustive list of such claims the Lonchen reserved the right of supplying ' fuller information ' later about the revenue and expenditure of lands south of the frontier, in which the Tibetan government might be interested.

Bell saw the Lonchen on the 20th, and told him that, pending receipt of fuller information, he could assure him that all property rights ('dak-tops ') of individual Tibetans on the British side would be respected. When the Lonchen mentioned his government's right of appointing the Head Lama of Tawang monastery and the taxes which the Monpas paid on such items as rice and chillies, which they brought for sale to Tsona dzong, Bell countered by pointing out that these were matters of detail which could wait. Later, when more information was forthcoming, he assured the Tibetan delegate, they would be settled ' in a friendly spirit '.

To give their agreement shape and form, McMahon and the Lonchen exchanged formal letters, and copies of maps showing the boundary. This was done at Delhi on 24–25 March. The British Plenipotentiary's letter reiterated Bell's assurances about Tibetan ownership in private estates which was ' not to be disturbed '. The earlier concession about the sacred places of Tso Karpo and Tsari Sarpa being included in Tibet, ' if they fall within a day's march ' of the British side of the frontier, was also confirmed. Details regarding dues collected by the Tibetan Government at Tsona dzong and in Kongbu and Kham, from the Monpas and the Lopas, were to be settled ' in a friendly

The maps, Bell noted, were sent on 31 January; the Lonchen's official, the Nyendron, he recorded, ' left for Lhasa last night ' (i.e. 2 February 1914).

[14]Bell to Lonchen, 6 February 1914, in Ibid.
[15]Lonchen to Bell, 9 February 1914, in Ibid.
[16]Office notes by Bell and McMahon, 10 and 11 February 1914, in Ibid.

spirit'. Concluding, McMahon expressed the hope that a 'final settlement' of the Indo-Tibetan frontier would be of 'great advantage' to both governments.

The Lonchen's reply was dated 25 March, and may be reproduced in full:

> As it was feared that there might be friction in future, unless the boundary between Tibet and India is clearly defined, I submitted the map, which you sent to me in February last, to the Tibetan Government in Lhasa, and I accordingly agreed to the boundary as marked in red in the two copies of the maps signed by you, subject to the conditions mentioned in your letter dated the 24th March, sent to me through Mr. Bell. I have signed and sealed the two copies of the maps. I have kept one copy here and return herewith the other.[17]

Bell was satisfied. 'The Tibet-India frontier', he noted 'may now be regarded as settled'.

In his 'Memorandum' to the Secretary of State, McMahon explained the delineation of the boundary which

> follows, except where it crosses the valleys of the Taron, Lohit, Tsangpo, Subansiri and Njamjang rivers for a short distance near Tsari, the northern watershed of the Irrawaddy and Brahmaputra rivers.

Near Tsari, it left the watershed so as

> to include in Tibet the course of the sacred pilgrimage route known as Tsari Nyingpa ('old Tsari') which is used every year in large numbers by Tibetans...(also) the village of Migyitun to which the Tibetans attach considerable importance.

As for Tso Karpo and Tsari Sarpa (mentioned in his note to the Lonchen),

> it is probable that both places are either on the main watershed which forms the boundary or to the north of it, but should they be found to be within a day's march on our side of the boundary as now shown, it has been agreed that the boundary line will be altered so as to include them in Tibet. No difficulty should be found in doing this because our evidence tends to prove

---

[17]At the interview, when Bell presented McMahon's letter, the Lonchen remarked that his government had sent 'mounted officers to the eastern part of the boundary and that if their reports showed that the actual boundary differed greatly from the map, he would wish to report matters afterwards to us.'

Bell, in reply, indicated that the matter had been 'definitely settled' and counselled the Lonchen to scrutinise the maps and have McMahon's note translated.

'In the evening,' Bell recorded, 'the Lonchen wrote his reply, which he sealed in the usual way and signed maps as well as sealing them.'

that there is a wide continuous tract of uninhabited country, along the south side of the main watershed.

Reverting to the extreme western strip above Tawang

> the boundary line... follows the crest of the mountain range which runs from peak 21431 through Tu Lung La and Menlaka-thong La to the Bhutan border. This is the highest mountain range in this tract of country. To the north of it are people of Tibetan descent, to the south the inhabitants are of Bhutanese and Aka extraction. It is unquestionably the correct boundary.[18]

As for undisturbed Tibetan ownership in private estates, referred to in his note, it was necessary ' to safeguard ' such rights for the same principle had been followed on the Sikkim-Tibet frontier—' with advantage ' to the inhabitants of both countries.

---

[18]For the text of the Memorandum, to which the exchange of notes was appended, see No. 231(a) in *Foreign*, October 1914, Procs. 134-396.

Bell, it would seem, scored out all references to Tawang in McMahon's draft, noting that it would be ' safer ' to do so: ' It is not in any sense a district: the district, if any, would be Tsona'. Again, McMahon's draft referred to the delineation as based on the survey reports of Bailey and Morshead. Bell modified it to the extent that the range alone was referred to: ' Captain Bailey informed me (Bell) they did not see this range and this is no doubt why he (Bailey) at first doubted the desirability of making the frontier when I first suggested it. We are perhaps on safer ground in putting it on the fact that the inhabitants are not Tibetans'. Office note by Bell, 1 April 1914, in *Foreign*, September 1915, Procs. 76-101.

It has been suggested, *Karunakar Gupta*, that at the time of the Simla Conference the Foreign Office in London had 'no clear intimation' of the incorporation of the Tawang tract into India— an assertion that betrays colossal ignorance of known, and available, records. Thus it is a truism that all the despatches to and from India were cleared with the Foreign Office, with copies endorsed to Jordan in Peking. Again the Memorandum, cited in the footnote, makes specific references to Tu Lung La and Menlakathong La even as it did to Tsona dzong as well as to Tibetan ownership in private estates on this side of the frontier. But if indeed the Foreign Office were kept in such complete ignorance, as is implied, it may be recalled that early in May (1914) it was responsible for despatching to its envoy in St. Petersburg both the India-Tibet boundary agreement as well as the accompanying maps. What is possible to concede is that the Foreign Office did not know the true significance of this cession (but then who did?), yet of the cession *per se* it certainly did know. For details, *infra*, Chapter XXI.

Chapter 20

The First Simla Convention, 27 April 1914

LONCHEN SHATRA was a tough negotiator, but given a measure of mutual confidence in his relations with the British, the 'Red Line' on McMahon's map did not take more than two months to work out, part of the delay having been occasioned by a reference to Lhasa, which the Tibetan Plenipotentiary had thought desirable. Essentially, it was a give-and-take deal. Thus the British yielded ground on the pilgrimage routes, compromised the watershed principle by which they swore and placed these areas securely, and deep, into Tibet. Lhasa too had given way over the private estates, and religious privileges which the Drepung monastery, and important members of its lay community, owned, and exercised, on this side of the Thagla ridge.

The long and short of it was that by 25 March, the 'Red Line' on McMahon's map had been settled, but not so the 'Blue'. In sharp contrast to the former, the latter proved to be a gruelling, and a tortuous, operation and a good deal of the ground pertaining to it has been covered already in a preceding chapter. The boundaries apart, the first round of truly earnest, and business-like negotiations on the British Plenipotentiary's draft convention took place on 15 April (1914), a little over six months after the Conference had convened in the previous October. Even so these serious parleys were brought about largely by McMahon's threat to withdraw his proposals, and his maps, owing to a lack of agreement among the parties.

The meeting was an informal one between Archibald Rose and Ivan Chen, and took place at the latter's initiative. To start with, the Chinese Plenipotentiary 'strongly objected' to the status of equality accorded to Tibet, *vis-à-vis* Great Britain and China, as spelt out in the Preamble.[1] When it was pointed out to him that the British Charge d'Affaires in Peking had underlined this fact in his note to the Chinese Foreign Office on 25 August (1913), Chen countered with the remark that the reference was to the 'course' of the Conference. The convention, he maintained, would be signed only after the Conference was over and any recognition of equality between China and Tibet in signing it was 'out of the question'. The British representative retorted with the argument that the convention would necessarily be a part of the Conference and that until Tibet signed it, her status was that of 'an independent nation recognising no allegiance' to China.

---

[1]For details a reference may be made to 'Note on an interview between Mr Ivan Chen and Mr Rose on 15th April 1914', in *Foreign, Notes*, October 1914, Procs. 134–396.

In Article II of McMahon's draft, Chen objected to the phrase ' but not the sovereignty ' of China (' The Governments of Great Britain and China recognising that Tibet is under the suzerainty, *but not the sovereignty* ' of China). He also demanded the addition of a clause recognising Tibet to be ' a portion of Chinese territory '. Additionally, he was keen that the limits, political *not* geographical, of ' suzerainty ' should be defined in a separate agreement—a claim the British were not willing to entertain, if only because the term itself was ' vague '. They did, however, agree to a slight textual change from ' including the selection and *appointment* of the Dalai Lama ' to ' including the selection and *installation* of the Dalai Lama '.

Chen was anxious about some formal recognition of China's role in the investiture of the Lama. Rose partly accepted this and later incorporated it in a note, appended at the end of the Convention, which referred to the Chinese government communicating to the newly-installed Lama ' the titles consistent with his dignity ' which had been conferred upon him.

Peking's Plenipotentiary also took exception to Tibet being debarred from representation in the Chinese Parliament, a demand strongly resisted by Rose. The British, however, agreed to take this clause out of Article II and place it in the notes to be exchanged, and lumped together, at the end of the Convention.

In Article III, relating to Britain's ' special interests ' in the existence of an effective Tibetan government, Chen objected to the expression ' adjoining states ' (' and in the maintenance of peace and order in the neighbourhood of the frontiers of India and *adjoining states* '). In reply Rose, specifically pointing to Chinese activity ' during the last eight years ' in areas comprising the north-east frontier of India, refused to yield ground. Two concessions, however, were made—the expression ' Chinese colonists '[2] was deleted while the period of withdrawal of Chinese troops, and officials, from Outer Tibet, was extended from one to three months.

Article IV, relating to the stationing of a Chinese representative at Lhasa, proved another hard nut to crack. After a good deal of contention, the earlier version of ' a Chinese representative with suitable escort...maintained at Lhasa ' was altered to ' a high official with suitable escort...maintained at Lhasa by the Chinese government '. On two other inter-related points, however, Rose refused to give in. The first was Chen's insistence on a clause laying down that the Chinese dignitary ' receive the respect and consideration due to his rank '; the second related to ' the right of the Amban ' to guide the Tibetans in their foreign policy. The British also resisted Peking's desire to appoint officers to keep a watch on its commercial interests in Tibet.[3]

[2]Chen had asked for an assurance, which Rose gave, that 'bona fide traders, merchants and priests ' would not be considered colonists. He was also assured that the British ' would not establish (in Tibet) colonies of native subjects of British India, or of the adjoining states '. For details, loc. cit.

[3]Rose reminded Chen that Britain's ' past experience ' of these officers had been ' so unfortunate ' that there was no question of the request to station them ' being considered '. Loc. cit.

In Article V, Chen desired that in place of ' Governments of China and Tibet' being debarred from negotiations or agreements concerning Tibet—the phrase should read ' the high contracting parties '. This, he argued, would make the self-denying clause equally binding on all parties. Rose resisted this, and successfully.

Article VII of McMahon's draft related to the cancellation of the Trade Regulations of 1893 and 1908 and provided for new ones to be negotiated directly between India and Tibet. Chen wanted a rider introduced to the effect that the regulations contemplated should ' in no way ' effect any ' commercial rights or interests ' which the Chinese enjoyed. In reply, Rose pointed out that the earlier regulations were based on a recognition of Chinese administrative control in Tibet which had now ceased and that the wording of the new article took account of the changed situation.

Clause (c) of Article VII was the subject of a good deal of wrangling. Originally, in McMahon's draft, it read:

> The Government of China is hereby released from its engagements under Article III of the Convention of 1890[4] between Great Britain and Tibet to prevent acts of aggression from the Tibetan side of the Tibet-Sikkim frontier.

Chen maintained that the question involved was a political one and by no means related to, or dependent upon, a recognition of Tibetan autonomy. In any case, the Chinese delegate insisted, his government could not agree to this clause. Rose countered by arguing that now that China did not maintain any garrisons in Tibet, for it to accept any responsibility on the Sikkim frontier was out of the question. The best he could do was to transfer this clause to the notes, proposed to be appended at the end of the Convention.

Article VIII of McMahon's draft had provided for the visits to Lhasa of the Trade Agent at Gyantse and proved to be another serious bone of contention. Chen made it clear that he was opposed to discussions at Lhasa of ' any questions ' of a ' political, territorial or international ' nature by the British Agent. Rose countered by pointing out that the subject was covered by the Convention of 1904, accepted by Peking in 1906. Later, Chen demanded that the right of proceeding to Lhasa should be limited to the Agent at Gyantse, a point which Rose appeared to concede.

The Chinese Plenipotentiary also desired that the (British) Agent's ' travelling escort ' should be limited in number. Rose, sure that it was ' unlikely ' that a British official would travel about with a large escort, thought it ' inadvisable ' to impose a limit, for that, he argued, would destroy the ' practical utility ' of this provision.

[4]The article in question had stipulated that the two governments (Britain and China) undertook ' reciprocally to respect the boundary as defined in Article I, and to prevent acts of aggression from their respective sides of the frontier '. Loc. cit.

Article X[5] of the draft Convention related to such compensation as China was to pay for 'losses incurred' by the government and subjects of Tibet, the Nepalese and the Ladakhis as a result of Chinese depredations following the October revolution. Chen's reaction to this was most uncompromising: 'he could not consent' to the inclusion of this clause in 'any form', not even as a note. Rose pointed out that the claims had been 'most carefully' assessed, that if China did not pay India was bound to compensate the traders. Chen, however, was unmoved and refused to relent. As Rose later put it, he

> was very firm on the point, and said that China was not in a financial position to recognise claims of this indirect nature. He refused to accept any responsibility for payment, and he was sure that HMG would regard his refusal with understanding and not as an obstructive move.

Finally, the Chinese delegate was agreeable to an additional article (for which, Rose informed him, the Tibetan Government too was anxious) stipulating that in case of a difference of opinion between China and Tibet on questions arising out of the Convention, the two would refer them to the British Government for 'equitable adjustment'. If Article X, relating to compensation, were deleted Chen argued, he was prepared to recommend the new article to the 'favourable consideration' of his government; it might indeed be inserted in its place! Besides, Chen pointed out, the new article would make the original provision regarding the English text being authoritative as 'superfluous'.

Before concluding—and the interview had lasted a whole ten hours—Chen enquired whether the embargo on the entry of accredited Chinese representatives into Tibet, by way of India, would be lifted when the agreement in question became operative. To this Rose replied in the affirmative; when the convention was signed, he informed Chen, the embargo would 'automatically cease'.

The Rose-Chen parleys were of a momentous character. As McMahon told his political superiors on the morrow, the 'voluminous demands' of the Chinese were 'hurriedly revealed' and submitted to negotiation 'as a whole'. While he resisted them for most part, the British Plenipotentiary was nevertheless willing to accept some. Of the latter, the important ones were: (a) the elimination from Article II of the words 'but not the sovereignty' and (b) the cancellation of Article X, relating to compensation by China. Two other concessions related to references in Article II to Tibetan representation in the Chinese Parliament and, in Article VII (c), to China's release from the obligations of the Convention of 1890. McMahon was prepared to take these from the main

---

[5]Article IX which related to the boundary between Inner and Outer Tibet was strongly disputed by the Chinese delegate. For details, *supra*, Chapter XVIII.

body of the Convention and incorporate them in subsidiary notes to be placed at the end.

The British Plenipotentiary's conclusion was that although the Chinese had maintained an aggressive and vigorous posture throghout, they were truly afraid ' lest ' his present proposals ' should be withdrawn '.[6]

An important problem that McMahon was still up against concerned the procedure for the ratification of his draft convention. He was of the view that it would be much to their advantage if, on the date of its signature, the convention should come into force ' immediately '. This was the more important because of the ' vacillation and weakness ' of Tibet,[7] and the ' now evident ' determination of the Chinese to resist ratification on a tripartite basis. Peking, he argued, might be tempted by the thought that with the convention signed and sealed, it would be ' formally reinstated ' as the suzerain power in Tibet. But what of St. Petersburg? Should negotiations with Russia present difficulties, McMahon told Whitehall, he would provide specially for tripartite ratification after a lapse of three months.[8]

Between 15 April, when Chen held his first serious talks on McMahon's draft convention, and 22 April, when the Conference convened for its seventh session, two major developments intervened. The first related to a widely-circulated report that immediately the agreement was concluded, Peking would despatch a representative to Lhasa. This made the Tibetans a great deal anxious, for what they feared most was that once China had attained its principal objective by the reinstatement of an Amban, the withdrawal of its garrisons from Outer Tibet might be 'indefinitely' delayed. To counter this, McMahon proposed the insertion of a note, to be appended at the end of the Convention, stipulating that the Chinese Amban would be free to enter Tibet only after the terms of Article III, relating to the withdrawal of all (Chinese) troops, had been fulfilled to the satisfaction of the representatives of the three signatories.[9]

Whitehall's reaction to McMahon's proposed changes was conveyed in the Secretary of State's telegram of 21 April which, *inter alia*, made the following points:

1. In Article II the following was to be deleted:
' The Governments of Great Britain and China recognising that Tibet

---

[6] Viceroy to Secretary of State, telegram, 16 April 1914, No. 247 in *Foreign*, October 1914, Procs. 134-396.

[7] On 26 March, McMahon had reported that although the comments of the Tibetan government on his draft convention ' were awaited', he understood that the Tibetan Plenipotentiary ' if pressed (would) be willing to sign convention as it stands '. The same held true of the Trade Regulations while, as for the boundary, it had already been satisfactorily settled. Viceroy to Secretary of State, 26 March 1914, No. 227 in Ibid.

[8] *Supra*, n. 6.

[9] McMahon had underlined the urgency of implementing Article III by pointing to the constant ' counter-complaints of aggression ' by the Tibetans. For details, Viceroy to Secretary of State, telegram, 21 April 1914, No. 249 in *Foreign*, October 1914, Procs. 134-396.

is an autonomous State under the suzerainty *but not the sovereignty* of China '; while the expression ' and recognising also the autonomy of Outer Tibet ' was to be added.
2. The subsidiary notes at the end were to be treated as though forming an integral part of the Convention.
3. The signing of the Convention was to be deferred pending a reference to Russia, albeit the draft would be initialled in the meanwhile.
4. As to the note relating to Article III, the India Office had no objection and the same held true of the arbitration clause. But it was pointed out that the latter clause may have to be withdrawn, under protest from Russia, in which case it would be safer to stick to the original Article XI—providing for the English text to be authoritative.[10]

Meanwhile, the Conference convened, as scheduled, on 22 April. One of its first tasks, on which Ivan Chen had been very keen, was to receive a ' message ' which had arrived late on the evening of 20 April, listing the ' several points ' on which Peking would *never* give in:

1. That Tibet shall not be represented in Parliament or other similar body;
2. That the number of escort of the British Agent shall under no circumstances exceed that of the escort of the Chinese Amban in Lhasa;
3. That the Chinese Amban shall have the right of appointing deputies to all the places where there are British Trade Agents;
4. That the new Regulations, to be negotiated between Great Britain and Tibet, shall be submitted to the Chinese Government for its approval.
5. That briefly with regard to the ' frontier question ' all places west of the Salween shall be placed within the autonomy of Tibet.[11]

Endorsing the proposals of his Government, the Chinese Plenipotentiary put forth the view that their points of difference were gradually decreasing— ' they were now reduced to five '. He was hopeful that, with patience and care, they would minimise further until all differences ' would disappear '.

McMahon was not that easily convinced. Chinese proposals, he felt, were unacceptable as they were ' entirely inimical ' to the principles on which his own draft agreement was based and, although the differences might be fewer in number, they were ' more serious ' in character. To reopen discussions on the basis of Peking's proposals would, he argued, be tantamount to cancelling

---

[10] Secretary of State to Viceroy, telegram, 21 April 1914, No. 250 in Ibid.

[11] Wai-chiao-pu to Ivan Chen, telegram, 20 April 1914 (' and received in Simla at 11 o'clock p.m. the same day '). Annexure II in No. 257 in Ibid. *Inter alia*, the Chinese Foreign Office had pointed out that since questions relating to ' territory and rights of sovereignty ' were involved ' we cannot make any compromise in order to bring about a settlement '. Besides, it was not prepared to accept ' any blame ' if negotiations came to ' a premature end '.

all the results of their previous work, in which every point of view had been 'carefully weighed', discussed, 'and decided'.[12]

The Lonchen too was lukewarm about the proposed convention even though, as McMahon was to point out later, this was due not so much to his rejecting the British draft as to his desire 'to impress' the Chinese Plenipotentiary.[13] *Inter alia*, he felt 'bound to state' that

> any draft which provided for the inclusion of Niarong and Derge in Inner Tibet, would be unacceptable at Lhasa. In the circumstances he must withhold his consent to the convention.

This provided the occasion for McMahon—'unable to conceal his disappointment'—to withdraw the draft and the accompanying map, 'with as much ceremony as possible'. It was a dramatic moment and the reaction was instantaneous. This incident, he noted,

> gave me an indication of the real situation. The tension had become very marked and when the documents were actually removed, the usually placid and inscrutable faces of my colleagues showed for a moment the most intense astonishment and agitation.[14]

Determined not to call it a day (viz., neither to close the meeting 'formally' nor yet change its 'conclusive character'), McMahon decided upon what he later aptly described as 'a fiction of adjournment'. Initially he was for a 'temporary' adjournment—'say until 5 o'clock, the next afternoon'—but Chen pleaded for an opportunity 'once more' to consult his government whom he wanted to leave in no doubt about the 'finality' of the British attitude.[15]

Meanwhile, on 20 April, the Chinese told Jordan in Peking that in the negotiations at Simla and Delhi, McMahon had adopted an 'exacting, aggressive and unfriendly' attitude, that the proposals they had telegraphed to Chen that day represented the 'final concession' which the President would make, or which would be 'tolerated' by Chinese 'public opinion'. The British Minister who clearly saw that it was an attempt to place the blame for any 'rupture' of negotiations on HMG reminded Peking that it

> had paid dearly in the past for asserting 'these shadowy claims' and warned of 'serious consequences'—which would not be 'confined to Tibet'—

---

[12] 'Proceedings of the 7th meeting of the Tibet Conference' held at Simla on 22 and 27 April 1914, No. 257 in Ibid.

[13] Viceroy to Secretary of State, telegram, 22 April 1914, No. 252 in Ibid.

[14] For details see 'Memorandum regarding progress of negotiations from 25th December 1913 to 30th April 1914', Encl. 3, No. 36 in *Foreign*, May 1915, Procs. 36–50.

[15] At Chen's insistence it had been arranged that the meeting of 22 April 'should not be held to have terminated' until 'noon on Monday, 27th April'. *Supra*, n. 12.

that might follow the rupture of negotiations.

Besides:

> As for public opinion on Tibet, there was none and if there were, the President had 'by his recent policy' shown that he could 'afford to disregard' it.[16]

Despite Jordan's plain-speaking, it was obvious that Peking was not likely to change its stance. And by the time the adjourned meeting convened on 27 April, Chen received a message from his government, the gist of which was contained in its penultimate paragraph:

> with the exception of Article 9 of the draft convention, we are prepared to take the main principles embodied in the other articles, into our favourable consideration, which is again a further great concession from us.[17]

As it was, Article IX, relating to the Inner-Outer Tibet boundary, was pivotal. McMahon made it plain that acceptance of the Chinese position would be difficult, as it would upset the 'delicately weighed' balance among the three parties, which he had achieved with great difficulty. The primary aim of the conference, as he saw it, was to put an end to the state of war that had existed between China and Tibet; more, it was to ensure that there was no recrudescence of hostilities between them. He was confident that the draft convention achieved these objectives, for it

> held promise of a very real gain to all concerned, it contemplated the reestablishment of Chinese suzerainty over a vast tract which had seceded from the Republic and the formation of an effective buffer state to the provinces of China proper, it formally recognised the autonomy of the territory under control of the Lhasa Government...the draft had been drawn up in a spirit of compromise and mutual loyalty.

When Chen announced that he was in no better position now than he was on the 22nd and that he was without authority from his government to initial the draft, the Lonchen took the position that since he (Chen) would not agree, 'it was useless for him (Lonchen) to say whether he agreed or not'.

At this stage, with Chen withdrawing from the chamber, McMahon and the Tibetan Plenipotentiary appended their initials. The two also resolved that, unless Chen was able to cooperate with them, it might become necessary to eliminate the clause recognising the suzerainty of China, as also the privileges accruing to it therefrom.

---

[16] Jordan to Viceroy, telegram, 21 April 1914, No. 251 in *Foreign*, October 1914, Procs. 134–396.

[17] Wai-chiao-pu to Ivan Chen, telegram, 25 April 1914 ('and received in Simla the following day at 2-15 p.m.'), Annexure III, No. 257 in Ibid.

Later, informed of what had transpired between his two colleagues, Chen persuaded himself to initial the draft but

> on the clear understanding that to initial and to sign... were two separate actions. He also said that he must wait for express instructions from his Government before the formal signature of the convention... he would telegraph to his Government what had taken place at the Conference and would communicate their reply....

In concluding the meeting, McMahon expressed the view that although the convention had been initialled and any further modifications thereby rendered impossible, the fact of settlement should not be disclosed, for the 'time and circumstances of its publication' would rest with their respective governments. Until then it was their duty to maintain 'absolute secrecy' in regard to the results of their negotiations.[18]

Much as he may have congratulated himself on the results achieved, in terms of a joint initialling of the draft convention, the British Plenipotentiary was not unaware of certain inherent weaknesses in the situation. Thus there was the uncomfortable fact that Peking's 'final instructions' to its Plenipotentiary on the 26th were

> vague and elusive, expressing general acceptance of the main principles... but demanding further unspecified concessions in regard to the frontier before any settlement was possible, and appearing to convey no authority for the acceptance of our draft.

McMahon was conscious too that it would be 'useless' to accept any finality from the Chinese, that their attitude throughout had been 'entirely destructive'; more, they had 'brushed aside' all his constructive efforts. What was worse was that Ivan Chen's position was far from enviable:

> on the one hand, his government though fully informed of the conclusive nature of the meeting (on April 27) had given him no indication of its willingness to accept our terms; on the other hand he saw the possibility of losing the Chinese seat in the Tripartite Conference and the danger of the conclusion of an agreement between Great Britain and Tibet alone.

Pressure had been mounted on Chen from another direction:

> Mr. Rose had communicated to him (Chen) the results of my interview with the Lonchen (just preceding the final initialling on April 27) and had now left him with the doubly initialled documents for a brief period of quiet consideration.

[18]*Supra*, n. 12.

McMahon, therefore, was not far wrong in concluding that it was only with the 'greatest difficulty' that Chen's consent to initial the convention was obtained. Hence his plea ' in the circumstances ' then obtaining

to hasten the date of signature, and so to avoid the possibility of any further obstruction on the part of China.

There was the additional reason that ' any lengthy interval ', before formal signature, ran the risk of ' premature disclosures ' which ' might create embarrassment '. Hence the twin need for

an early signature and of securing, by a provision for ratification, any interval that may subsequently be necessary.

He favoured too the retention of Article X, which underlined Britain's role as a mediator,

and which in regard to the future of Tibet leaves us in the most advantageous and least responsible position.[19]

In this context, Article IV of the Russo-Chinese compact on Mongolia, McMahon argued, appeared to contemplate a similar provision for Russia to act as an arbitrator between the suzerain power (viz. China) and Mongolia.[20]

As events were to demonstrate, McMahon's anxiety had not been in vain, nor misplaced. On the 27th, the Chinese in Peking handed Jordan a Memorandum listing the 'successive' concessions which they had made at the Tibet Conference and deprecating any threats ' to break it up '. The President, Jordan was assured, was ' sincerely anxious ' to settle the question amicably and, barring Article IX, was willing ' in principle ' to accept the rest of the terms. Nonetheless the Minister noted that it

was vaguely hinted that our claims in Yangtse valley may be affected if we insisted on our demands.[21]

The bombshell exploded on the 29th. That morning, Ivan Chen called at the Foreign Department in Simla and handed a message from his government:

We learn with great astonishment that the British Plenipotentiary only consents to make a concession to us of a small portion of territory to be delimited to Chinghai and has pressed us to accept.

[19]Viceroy to Secretary of State, telegram, 27 April 1914, No. 260 in Ibid.
[20]Article IV of the Russo-Chinese Agreement had stipulated that China was ready to accept the ' good offices ' of Russia for the establishment of its relations with Outer Mongolia.
[21]Jordan to Viceroy, telegram, 27 April 1914, No. 261 in Ibid.

> The Central Government disapprove the action you have taken, under the pressure of circumstances, in initialling the draft Convention, and you are instructed to inform your British colleague to that effect and that your action of initialling is null and void.
>
> If the British Plenipotentiary is willing to continue the amicable negotiation, we will continue it, we have no desire to break it off abruptly.[22]

McMahon refused to give a reply to 'so unusual' a message but, in his 'report' to Whitehall, laid stress on two points. At the outset, he repudiated the insinuation (as 'the message from Peking suggests') that the Chinese Plenipotentiary 'was coerced'. He had no doubt that Chen

> signed rather than leave an agreement on the table to which China had not been a party and from which the elimination of the clause relating to Chinese suzerainty was foreshadowed....[23]

Answering the all-important question, why China was behaving the way it was, McMahon made two guesses. One, that Lu Hsing-chi on learning (from a spy on the staff of Chen) that the draft had been initialled, had at once telegraphed to Peking to disavow Chen's action. Two, there was the 'proverbial disinclination' of the Chinese to meet final issues.[24]

At the same time the British Plenipotentiary was quite emphatic that no further concession could be made 'without injustice' to Tibet and 'detriment' to the British. It followed that HMG must adhere to the 'accomplished' fact of the initialled convention as the 'only satisfactory' settlement on a tripartite basis that was possible.

A day later he was still not 'without hope' that the Chinese

> may withdraw from the somewhat unusual position of disavowing a settlement which has been formally agreed upon by their Plenipotentiary.[25]

The settlement itself had been advantageous to Peking and he had

---

[22]Wai-chiao-pu to Ivan Chen, telegram, 28 April 1914 ('and received in Simla at 6 a.m. the following day'), No. 263 in Ibid. The telegram was 'personally' communicated to the Foreign Department by Ivan Chen.

[23]Viceroy to Secretary of State, telegram, 29 April 1914, No. 265 in Ibid.

[24] 'Memorandum regarding the progress of negotiations from 25th December 1913 to 30th April 1914', *supra*, n. 14.

McMahon had pointed out that the issues involved in the Convention had been under discussion for many years—ever since the Adhesion Agreement of 1906—'the eighth anniversary of which was celebrated by the initialling of the present convention'. Cited in 'Memorandum', *supra*, n. 14.

[25]Loc. cit.

endeavoured to meet the views of the Chinese in every possible way, to safeguard their prestige, to restore to them an honourable position in Tibet and an effective buffer state for the provinces of China proper.

Weeks later, McMahon, in a more chastened, mellower mood and in a position to view the situation in a larger perspective, concluded that

> when the Chinese Plenipotentiary initialled the convention on 27th April, there can be no doubt that he did so with a feeling of great relief. He admitted that he had obtained more favourable terms than could reasonably have been expected in view of the actual position in Tibet and the complete collapse of Chinese power and prestige in the country. His Government, however... (had) their traditional dislike of finality and concluded agreements.[26]

---

[26] 'Memorandum regarding progress of negotiations from 1st May to 8th July 1914', Encl. 4, No. 36 in *Foreign*, May 1915, Procs. 36–50.

PART V   FAILURE AT
SIMLA: NEGOTIATIONS
WITH RUSSIA AND CHINA

Chapter 21

Negotiations with Russia: Mongolia and Tibet

WITH THE signing of what later came to be called the first Simla Convention, on 27 April 1914, a major watershed had been reached in the tripartite negotiations. The 'Red' and 'Blue' Lines had been accepted and the three Plenipotentiaries agreed to McMahon's draft convention, with only minor changes. To the superficial eye, the work of the Conference had drawn to a close. And yet before it could, or did, Whitehall had to persuade St. Petersburg to accept the alterations, necessitated by the new agreement, in the earlier Anglo-Russian Convention of 1907, especially insofar as it related to Tibet. This was by no means an easy task; as a matter of fact, it proved to be a most difficult one. For Sazonov, the then Russian Foreign Minister, was a hard, tough bargainer, the more intractable because his political standing at home was singularly weak and shaky. Additionally, he was keen to retrieve his country's position in strategically important Afghanistan as a bargaining counter for any concession he might be called upon to make to the British in Tibet.

Long before the three Plenipotentiaries convened in Simla, both Delhi as well as Whitehall were alive to the varied ramifications of negotiating with the Russians in regard to the proposed convention on Tibet. A brief historical resume of what was involved may help to put matters in proper perspective.

At the very outset it may be recalled that following the British withdrawal from Lhasa in the wake of the Younghusband expedition, the British Foreign Office had embarked upon a policy of cutting down its losses. Thus, as an earlier chapter spells out at some length, even before the Adhesion Agreement of 1906 had been concluded in Peking, the British started earnest negotiations with the Russians for a mutual hands-off policy in different parts of Asia, including Tibet. Concluded in 1907, three of the five clauses of the Anglo-Russian Convention pertaining to the 'arrangement' (concerning Tibet) may be reproduced here to facilitate continued reference in the narrative. Thus Article I provided that:

> The Two High Contracting Parties engage to respect the territorial integrity of Tibet and to abstain from all interference in the internal administration.

Article III laid down that:

> The British and Russian Governments respectively engage not to send Representatives to Lhasa.

Article IV stipulated that:

> The Two High Contracting Parties engage neither to seek nor to obtain, whether for themselves or their subjects, mines, or other rights in Tibet.[1]

This phase in Britain's withdrawal from Tibet resulted, as has been noticed, in the gradual, yet powerful, assertion of Chinese authority; by 1910, Peking had secured complete control over the internal administration of the country and virtually reduced it to the position of a province of the Empire. Soon, however, with the October 1911 revolution, followed by the revolt of Chinese garrisons in Lhasa, a complete change came over the situation. Distracted by rebellion and civil strife at home, China found itself powerless to regain its lost position in Tibet or for that matter in other outlying parts of the newly proclaimed Republic. On the other hand, the Dalai Lama and his people, by throwing out the Chinese, regained effective independence. After a good deal of effort, as the preceding pages reveal, a tripartite conference convened in Simla in October 1913 to sort matters out.

In determining policy in the new situation created by the expulsion of the Chinese, developments in Mongolia, discussed at length in an earlier chapter, were of great relevance. So was the Anglo-Russian Convention of 1907 which had taken no objective account of a conquering, or of a receding, China, and was utterly unsuited to conditions following the break up of the Ch'ing empire. The problem was to persuade Russia that a realistic assessment rendered that part of the 1907 Convention, relating to Tibet, out of date and that a fresh look was urgently called for. Surely, the very arranging of the Tripartite Conference was contrary to thes pirit, if not the letter, of the Convention so far as the latter bore on Tibet.

As early as October 1912, India's view had been that an ideal compensation for Whitehall in return for all that St. Petersburg had gained in Mongolia would be for Russia to renounce all interest in Tibet, subject to the British guaranteeing not to violate its (Tibet's) integrity. Failing this, HMG should press for:

(a) Exclusive right to have an Agent at Lhasa—' though we should not exercise this right unless circumstances compelled us to do so ';
(b) Right to communicate direct with the Tibetan authorities—' assuming that HMG adhered to the view that the Government of India were debarred from doing so '; and
(c) Right to occupy the Chumbi valley—should it become necessary—' in order to protect British interests and maintain order '.[2]

India's plea for an Agent at Lhasa, however forcefully argued, did not,

---

[1] For the text see P L Mehra, *Basic Documents*, 2 vols., I.
[2] No. 10 in *Foreign*, February 1913, Procs. 1–67.

as has been noticed, carry conviction in London. What was grudgingly vouchsafed, as embodied in Arthur Hirtzel's draft of November 1913, was the visits to Lhasa of the 'peripatetic' Trade Agent stationed at Gyantse. Whitehall had expressed the view that the question of the Agent, of trade and industrial concessions, required prior consultations with Russia in terms of the stipulations made in 1907. Early in February 1914, McMahon, then on the threshold of delicate negotiations in Delhi with the Chinese and the Tibetan Plenipotentiaries, had requested for, and obtained, a six-week moratorium on a reference to St. Petersburg for fear any leaks there might jeopardise the success of his own efforts.³

A few days earlier, on 28 January (1914), the Foreign Office in London had communicated to the India Office the draft of a letter which was proposed to be sent to Buchanan, then British Ambassador in St. Petersburg. This was in fulfilment of an earlier assurance to Russia to keep her posted with all that was happening at Simla. After alluding briefly to what had transpired at the various sessions of the Conference since it convened on October 13—the disputed territorial limits of Tibet and the decision about Inner and Outer Tibet—the draft letter drew pointed attention to some 'further questions' to which a solution must be found, 'before a permanent settlement' could be effected.

Among these was one of industrial, commercial and financial concessions in Tibet, regulated by Article III of the (Anglo-Chinese) Convention of 1906 and Article IV of the (Anglo-Russian) Convention of 1907, both of which conferred upon China a monopoly of such concessions. Since Tibet was keen, Whitehall argued, to break out of the 'practical sterilisation' which had been foisted upon it and since, owing to developments following the October (1911) revolution, there had been a complete erosion of confidence in Peking's own bona fides, a way out had to be found.

Two suggestions were made. One, that Article III of the Adhesion Agreement of 1906, which enabled China to obtain concessions in Tibet, denied to any other Power, be cancelled; two, that the treaty then being negotiated at Simla should stipulate that the term 'foreign power' in Article IX (d) of the Lhasa convention of September 1904, did not include China, thereby permitting the latter country to use any concessions which Tibet might choose to give to Chinese subjects. Of relevance to Russia was HMG's proposal that Article IV of the Anglo-Russian Convention of 1907 should be cancelled for, in the event of its being operative, both Great Britain and Russia would be placed at a disadvantage, when compared with other powers, in respect of concessions in Tibet.⁴

---

³Viceroy to Secretary of State, telegram, 3 February 1914, and Secretary of State to Viceroy, telegram, 14 February 1914, Nos. 196 and 200 in *Foreign*, October 1914, Procs. 134–396.
  The Secretary of State was quite categorical: 'no communication to Russia will be made for six weeks i.e. till March 24th in deference to your (Viceroy's) wishes'.

⁴ *F O* to *I O*, 28 January 1914, No. 211 in Ibid.

Debate proceeded, and the contents of the proposed communication to Russia continued to be discussed,[5] even though the communication itself was held back in deference to McMahon's express wishes.

It had been evident for sometime that both McMahon and Hardinge, as no doubt Whitehall itself, wanted to make use of the altered Russian position in Mongolia as a bargaining counter to wrest concessions in Tibet. The Russians, however, were not easy to persuade and the British were painfully conscious of this fact. Thus on 7 November 1913, on the morrow of the Russo-Chinese agreement concerning Mongolia, the Foreign Office informed the India Office that it had

> taken into account the possibility of making terms with Russia with regard to the Tibetan question in connection with the Russo-Chinese agreement,[6] but is of the opinion that it would be unwise to do so at present in view of the declared attitude of the Russian Government and the views expressed by M. Sazonoff in his interviews with Sir Edward Grey and Lord Crewe.[7]

There were some obvious snags. Thus, if Whitehall asked for the open door for British trade in Mongolia and for direct dealings with the authorities in Urga, might it not lead to a demand by Russia for similar direct negotiations with the authorities at Lhasa?[8]

The 'declared attitude' of the Russian government had come out clearly during Sazonov's conversations with the British Ministers in London, in September 1912. More, they had served as a curtain-raiser to the Russian Foreign Minister's capacity for tough bargaining. When Grey explained how a Chinese invasion of Tibet would seriously upset the British and that

> unforeseen trouble might arise that might make it desirable for us to send some agent to Lhasa to keep us informed...M. Sazonoff said he would be ready to listen to this (some relaxation on his side of the 1907 agreement about Tibet) but he would require some *quid pro quo* for Russia. Mongolia was outside the Anglo-Russian Agreement, and he could not regard that

---

[5] *I O* to *F O*, 30 January 1914, No. 212 in Ibid.

[6] The Russo-Chinese agreement was signed in Peking on 5 November 1913; the Russo-Mongolian, at Urga, on 3 November 1912.

In a telegram to the Secretary of State, 8 November 1913, No. 348 in *Foreign*, July 1914, Procs. 341-391, the Viceroy had suggested that, pending the tripartite Convention, then being negotiated, the question of according favourable reception to these agreements be 'held in abeyance'.

[7] *F O* to *I O*, 7 November 1913, No 359 in Ibid.

[8] *I O* to *F O*, 13 November 1913, No. 361 in Ibid.

as in *pari materia* with Tibet. He assured me that Dorjieff had no mission from Russia and was in Tibet on his own adventure.[9]

The visiting Russian leader was more outspoken in the course of his talks with Lord Crewe, when Afghanistan was specifically mentioned. The latter noted that

> he (Sazonov) thought it better to deal with any matter effecting Tibet as it naturally arose and not to attempt a formal revision of any points. At the same time if he (Crewe) were to give material assistance in smoothing things with Afghanistan, he (Sazonov) would be able to face opinion in Russia more easily in connection with other questions.[10]

The British entertained their own serious misgivings as to whether, in reality, the Russian public took such keen interest in Tibet as Sazonov indicated that it did. Was it so sensitive

> as to render it difficult for the Russian Government to negotiate a complete revision of the Anglo-Russian Convention of 1907, should such a step prove desirable?[11]

While oftentimes the Russian Foreign Minister's 'clean departure from truth' were annoying to the British,[12] the latter were anxious not to do anything that might be misinterpreted by their ally. Thus early in February (1913), Grey had specifically asked the British Ambassador in St. Petersburg not to receive the Mongolian mission then visiting the Russian capital, a move with which the India office did *not* agree. The latter, in a note to the Foreign Office on 25 March 1913, had argued that by its hands-off policy *vis-à-vis* Mongolia, Whitehall might lose an advantage

> which is probably unlikely to recur, of obtaining a footing in Mongolia which might prove of great value in future dealings with the Russian Government (more so those regarding Tibet).... Lord Crewe cannot but fear that, if Russia and its subjects came to enjoy by treaty or practice a predominating influence in Mongolia as compared with other foreign states and their

---

[9] 'Note on conversations between Sir Edward Grey and M. Sazonoff', 24 September 1912, No. 55 in *Foreign*, March 1913, Procs. 54–62.

[10] 'Note on conversations between Marquess of Crewe and M. Sazonoff', 29 September 1912, No. 56 in Ibid.

[11] *F O* to *I O*, 9 October 1912, No. 57 in Ibid. The Foreign Office felt that Sazonov had exaggerated the interest taken by the Russian public.

[12] Grey to Claude Macdonald (British Ambassador in Tokyo), 10 October 1912, No. 60 in Ibid.

subjects, a revival of Russian influence in Tibet which it has been the policy of HMG for the last 10 years to counteract, must inevitably follow.[13]

The Foreign Office, however, was far from convinced. It reasoned that while it may be possible to establish Britain's right to equal commercial treatment in Mongolia, it ' cannot hope ' to compete ' effectively ' with Russia at Urga.

Whether it could compete effectively at Urga or not, Whitehall was nonetheless determined to use the political situation arising out of the Russo-Mongol agreement to its advantage. The result was that on 24 January 1914, before Russia was approached on McMahon's draft Convention, Grey had written to Buchanan that he was anxious that

> there should be no unnecessary delay in acquainting the Russian Government with the fact that the changes which have been effected in the political and commercial situation in Central Asia merit serious attention...explaining verbally to M. Sazonov that the alteration in the status of Mongolia which has had an indirect but important effect on the position of Tibet.[14]

The British Ambassador in St. Petersburg joined issue with the Russian Foreign Minister on the lines indicated. The resultant exchange is well summed up in Buchanan's own words:

> he (Sazonov) virtually admitted our right to ask for the open door but contended that Russia had acted well within her rights in helping Mongolians and had done nothing to change the situation as regards Tibet...(Buchanan) that our respective positions in Asia were materially altered by the veiled protectorate which Russia was assuming over Mongolia and as above changes might react on Tibet it was natural we should wish to safeguard our interests there...(Sazonov) but...were he gratuitously to renounce all rights secured to her under convention, Russian public opinion would accuse him of sacrificing Russia's interests. Mongolia, he trusted, would not be quoted as a reason for asking concessions in Tibet as the two questions were entirely separate and ought not to be mentioned in the same breath....

Sazonov was a formidable bargainer, and Buchanan was not too sanguine:

> but I (Buchanan) propose to continue to argue that we are entitled to expect consideration in Tibet for our recognition of Russia's privileged position in Mongolia.[15]

[13] *I O* to *F O*, 25 March 1913, No. 274 in *Foreign*, October 1913, Procs. 44–301.

[14] *F O* to *I O*, 15 January 1914, No. 371 in *Foreign*, July 1914, Procs. 341–91. See also Grey to Buchanan, 24 January 1914, No. 379 in Ibid, and *F O* to *I O*, 29 March 1913, No. 276 in *Foreign*, October 1913, Procs. 44–301.

[15] Buchanan to Grey, 1 February 1914, No. 380 in *Foreign*, July 1914, Procs. 34–191.

Similar exchanges took place in February-March 1914.¹⁶ All through the Russian Minister stuck to much the same position: in assisting the Mongols to secure ' autonomy ' under Chinese ' suzerainty ', he maintained, Russia had acted well within her rights and, in fact, but for her ' moderating counsels,' the Mongols would have opted for ' complete independence '. As for ' compensation ', he retorted, Russia might as well ask for it ' in the event of our extending our sphere of influence ' in South Africa. Was it any wonder then, that even as early as 3 February (1914) Buchanan in a despatch to Grey had concluded that it would be ' difficult ' to persuade Sazonov that the British were entitled to claim in Tibet ' compensation ' for the rights that Russia was acquiring in Outer Mongolia.¹⁷

To meet an apparent impasse, Buchanan proposed what he called ' his own strategy ' for the impending negotiations. Since it would not be easy, he argued, to get what the British wanted ' without ' bargaining

> it would be advisable for us to begin by asking for more than the irreducible minimum of our requirements. If, when Monsieur Sazonov has shown his hand, we find that the price is more than we care to pay, we should have a margin for bargaining, as we could always withdraw some of our original demands.... Should he (Buchanan) on the contrary, begin by putting forward our minimum claims we might have to choose between paying the price asked for or renouncing our claims altogether.¹⁸

India Office was not very happy about the way Buchanan had presented his brief, for the argument, it maintained, was

> not that the predominance acquired by Russia in Mongolia ought to be accepted by her as an equivalent for any concessions, which she might make to us in Tibet, but that it has materially altered, to the detriment of Great Britain, the status quo in Tibet on which the Anglo-Russian Agreement of 1907 was based, and that it has consequently become necessary to provide further safeguards for British interests in order to meet the needs of a situation differing entirely from that contemplated by the Agreement.

Two points on which Russia's assent was necessary were Article IV of the 1907 Agreement (under which the two governments had engaged not to seek concessions in Tibet) and the right of the British Trade Agent at Gyantse to visit Lhasa which touched Article III. As for the former, it was in the nature of a mutual ' self-denying ordinance ' from which Russia may also want to be released. Was there any need, therefore, for a *quid pro quo*? In regard to

---

¹⁶*F O* to *I O*, 12 February 1914, No. 381 in Ibid, and Buchanan to Grey, 4 March 1914, Encl. in *F O* to *I O*, 14 March 1914, No. 384 in Ibid.
¹⁷Buchanan to Grey, 3 February 1914, No. 388 in Ibid.
¹⁸Buchanan to Grey, 4 March 1914, Encl. in *F O* to *I O*, 14 March 1914, No. 384 in Ibid.

the British Trade Agent's visits to Lhasa, and to allow for Buchanan's plea for a 'margin for bargaining', may not HMG, in the first instance, ask for a permanent British representative at the Tibetan capital? If, in return, Russia demanded its own representation, a difficult situation may result. It followed, the India Office argued, that to start with, no commitment should be made until Russia's counter-demands were known.[19]

All through March 1914, the 'strategy' for negotiating with the Russians continued to be planned with the India Office oftentimes finding itself completely out of step with the Foreign Office, or more specifically its men on the spot. Argument was met by counter-argument, one line of reasoning by another. The pace nonetheless was slow—even leisurely. No sooner, however, was the draft convention initialled on 27 April, McMahon, for fear the Chinese wriggle out, pressed strongly for early signature. HMG, clear in its mind that it 'cannot agree' to signature pending conversations with Russia, undertook nevertheless that these would be 'hurried as much as possible'.[20] On 8 May, Buchanan communicated the text of the Convention, with its accompanying maps, to the Russian Government and explained that

> the document which I (Buchanan) had given to him (acting Minister for Foreign Affairs) about the Indo-Tibetan frontier, the two Tibetan Zones, the Trade Regulations had no practical interest for Russia,[20a] but that the friendly relations existing between the two Governments made us anxious to keep them informed of all that had taken place during the tripartite negotiations.[21]

Neratoff, the Russian Deputy Foreign Minister, even though he had promised 'to expedite' a reply, felt helpless until Sazonov returned. Later, on 17, 18 and 19 May, Buchanan had fairly prolonged talks with the Russian Foreign Minister who made it clear that the British proposals constituted an 'abrogation' of the 1907 agreement and 'established' a British 'protectorate' over Tibet. Albeit

[19] *I O* to *F O*, 26 March 1914, No. 385 in *Foreign*, July 1914, Procs. 341–9.

[20] Secretary of State to Viceroy, telegram 4 May 1914. No. 380 in *Foreign*, October 1914, Procs. 134–396.

[20a] It has been maintained, *Karunakar Gupta*, that the exchanges between McMahon and Shatra were kept secret—'and not only from the Chinese'. This is incorrect. It is true that the Chinese were not *officially informed* about these exchanges, but there is enough circumstantial evidence to suggest that they did know if not the text of the letters (unimportant in any case), at any rate their substance. They certainly knew the maps which clearly, if on a small scale, showed the new boundary. In any case, the secret was kept '*only*', and *not* 'not only' from the Chinese; for the Russians had been taken fully into confidence.

[21] Buchanan to Grey, 8 May 1914, No. 204 in *Foreign*, April 1915, Procs. 204–23.

Also Grey to Buchanan, 4 May 1914, *F O* 371, 1929/18917 and *F O* 535, 17/112. The papers which were to be communicated to Sazonov were listed thus: Tripartite agreement, Indo-Tibetan boundary agreement, Trade Regulations, Maps accompanying the two agreements.

personally (he) did not care what we did with Tibet but that, if he (Sazonov) did not obtain a quid pro quo he would be accused more especially by his Nationalist colleagues of being the dupe of England, just as he had been accused of having been duped by Germany at Potsdam....

More specifically, Sazonov was opposed to Articles VI, VIII and X of the Simla Convention. Before discussing his objections, it may be useful to spell out briefly their text. Article VI, it may be recalled, provided that the term 'Foreign Power' (used in Article IX of the Lhasa Convention of 1904) did not include China and that 'no less favourable' treatment shall be accorded to British commerce than to the commerce of China ' or the most-favoured nation'. Article VIII laid down that the British Agent at Gyantse could visit Lhasa 'with his escort' whenever it was necessary to consult with the Tibetan government on matters which could not be settled ' by correspondence or otherwise'. Article X stipulated that in case of a difference of opinion between China and Tibet, as to the terms of the Convention, the British would be called upon to make 'equitable adjustment'.

More than anything else, the Russian Minister was dead-set against Article X which, he maintained, was tantamount to the establishment of a British protectorate over Tibet. Articles VI and VIII too, he would have suitably amended so as to secure for Russia rights similar to those which the British had acquired.

In reply to Sazonov's insinuation about British control over Tibet, Buchanan argued that by virtue of the position Russia had obtained at Urga, it practically exercised a veto over Britain's commercial relations with Outer Mongolia. Russia, he pointed out, had no interest in Tibet and if it now thought of establishing an Agent there, its motives were likely to be suspect.

It was Sazonov's turn now. Russia's economic interests in Afghanistan, he maintained, were 'of a far more important kind' than Britain's in Tibet. It followed that Russian agents should be allowed to go there—for there were such problems as irrigation which needed to be looked into. If the British objected to concessions in Afghanistan, they might suggest other areas in which these were feasible. Buchanan's counter-argument that Russia had established a protectorate in Mongolia and that what the British did in Tibet was a direct consequence of what had been done at Urga did not carry conviction with the Russian Minister. He was willing nonetheless to accept

all our proposals if we could keep the convention secret...that we should not mention them in the Convention and that Russia would give us a secret undertaking to raise no objections when the occasion arose.

In return, Sazonov demanded, the British were to give a similar undertaking allowing Russia to send 'occasionally' a native agent to Herat.

Buchanan's conclusion was unmistakable: Sazonov was 'so afraid' of the criticism of his colleagues that he wanted to 'save his face' by getting something which he could represent as a ' counter-concession '.[22]

On 18 May, the British Ambassador asked the Russian Minister if the latter would agree to Articles VI and VIII of the Simla Convention should the British substitute Article X by merely providing that the English text of the convention be deemed authoritative. Sazonov's reply was that while the substitute Article X would be 'very agreeable', in regard to Article VI he would have Britain and Russia exchange 'notes' undertaking not to ask for concessions for their respective subjects ' without a previous mutual understanding'. Buchanan noted that he (Sazonov) seemed

> almost prepared to give us a secret assurance that he would not support, or at all events encourage, requests for such concessions by Russian subjects, and oppose those which we might put forward.

As to Article VIII, Sazonov suggested that if Russia's right to send an Agent to Lhasa were conceded, he would give a secret assurance that he ' would never send one'. If, however, the article were to stand, he would demand an exchange of notes, to be made public, that it would not be put into force without a previous agreement with Russia. He

> might then give us a secret assurance that he (Sazonov) would not withhold his consent from visits of our Agent to Lhasa when the time came for his giving it.[23]

Russia's price for the above was a declaration to the effect that

> His Majesty's Government engage not to support any demand for irrigation works, railways or industrial enterprises in northern Afghanistan, on the part of British subjects.

Buchanan noted that the Russian Foreign Minister had made it clear that, in his view, the British were ' tearing up ' the agreement of 1907, that Russia was getting nothing in return and that the proposals outlined above were ' his last word'. On his own, the British Minister had come to much the same conclusion:

> It is not, I fear, possible for me to obtain better terms and if they are not acceptable to HMG the only alternative is to find some counter-concessions, outside Tibet, to offer Russia.[24]

[22]Buchanan to Grey, 17 May 1914, No. 205 in *Foreign*, April 1915, Procs. 204–23.
[23]Buchanan to Grey, 18 May 1914, No. 206 in Ibid.
[24]Secretary of State to Viceroy, telegram, 20 May 1914, No. 287 in *Foreign*, October 1914, Procs. 134–396.

Besides the 'Note' on Afghanistan, Buchanan wrote, Russia was also to ask Britain to recognise its 'predominant interest' in northern Persia more fully, albeit it had been stated that this was not to constitute part of the new arrangement regarding Tibet.[25]

Elsewhere the British envoy, who had been impressed by the 'friendly attitude' of the Russian Foreign Minister, explained that

> M. Sazonoff's term of office is not very secure and there are again rumours of the approaching appointment of M. Krivoshein—a confirmed Nationalist —to the post of President of the Council...should it prove to be correct it would render it still more difficult for M. Sazonoff to make concessions to us....[26]

After consultations with Delhi, there was fresh thinking in the Foreign Office. Summing up, Grey telegraphed to Buchanan on 22 May that

1. HMG agreed to deletion of Article X and the substitution in its place of the English text being regarded as final;
2. in regard to Articles VI and VIII, HMG would address a note to the Russian Government to the effect that it (HMG) would not act on these until Russia's acceptance had been forthcoming;
   Should the tripartite Convention be published, the above note would be made public too;
3. pending the conclusion of an understanding with Russia, HMG would not require any secret understanding that was now being proposed and thus, in fact, would treat the 1907 agreement as being both valid and binding.

As he viewed it, the position was that

> HMG would by the Tripartite Convention obtain the consent of Tibet and China to seek concessions in Tibet and to send the British Trade Agent from Gyantse to Lhasa, but they recognise that, owing to the Anglo-Russian Agreement of 1907, the consent of Russia also is required for these things and they would undertake not to do them till that consent had been obtained.[27]

[25] On 18 May, Sazonov had complained that the British were not behaving 'properly' in Persia and that British policy was being more and more 'anti-Russian'. Buchanan to Grey, 18 May 1914, No. 207 in *Foreign*, April 1915, Procs. 204–23.

[26] Buchanan to Grey, 19 May 1914, No. 208 in Ibid. Buchanan had warned that even though Sazonov had 'dropped' the question of Afghanistan for the moment, it may be 'reopened' any time.

[27] Grey to Buchanan, 22 May 1914, No. 213 in *Foreign*, April 1915, Procs. 204–23. See also Buchanan to Grey, 19 May 1914, Proc. 212 in Ibid., and Viceroy to Secretary of State, telegram, 21 May 1914, No. 288 in *Foreign*, October 1914, Procs. 134–396.

Before Whitehall's telegram was received in St. Petersburg, Sazonov had shifted his ground. For, on 24 May, Buchanan informed Grey that the Russian Minister

> would prefer arrangement of 19 May.... He eventually agreed to Convention being signed at once.... Article X, as agreed, and VI and VIII not (to be) operative until understanding with the Imperial Government.

The Convention, however, was not to be published until a full understanding of the whole question had been reached with the Russian Government, for there

> could be no object said he (Sazonov) for immediate publication of convention, and he hoped, in the circumstances, that we would consent to keep it confidential for the time being, while he would keep confidential the note which we were to address to him.[28]

A day later, however, Sazonov appears to have had second thoughts, for Buchanan telegraphed to say that he now insisted that the convention was not to be signed until 'a definite agreement' (with Russia) on the whole question had been reached.[29] Grey countered by remarking that even if an arrangement between HMG and the Russian Government were not reached before the signature of the convention, the official note, formally recording the assurances of HMG in regard to Articles VI and VIII, would 'safeguard and cover' all Russian interests, pending a definite understanding between the two governments.[30]

More than anything else, it was the Afghan question, however, that worried the India Office most, as it no doubt did the government in Delhi.[31] It was the more embarrassing insofar as Sazonov appears to have set his heart on it. On 26 May, Lord Crewe had telegraphically informed the Viceroy that he was *ab initio* 'most reluctant' to consent to the proposed Afghan deal; if, however, an alternative *quid pro quo* could not be arranged, there was no help. For his part, he (Crewe) would consent to a declaration to the effect that

---

[28]Buchanan to Grey, 24 May 1914, in Secretary of State to Viceroy, 26 May 1914, No. 290 in *Foreign*, October 1914, Procs. 134–396.

[29]Buchanan to Grey, 25 May 1914, No. 215 in *Foreign*, April 1915, Procs. 204–23.

[30]Grey to Buchanan, 26 May 1914, No. 217 in Ibid.

[31]In a marginal comment, dated 22 May 1914, on the proposed Russian demand in Afghanistan, S H Butler, then Education Member in the Governor General's Executive Council, noted:

> I was afraid of this. The condition as to Northern Afghanistan, may lead the Amir to suspect a secret treaty between us and Russia. The condition is clearly designed to make trouble between us and the Amir.

Foreign, Notes, October 1914, Procs. 134–396.

Russian Government reaffirm their adherence to the principle that Afghanistan is outside the sphere of Russian political influence. HMG engage not to support demands by subjects of British Government for irrigation works on Hari Rud or for irrigation works, railways or preferential rights for commercial or industrial enterprise in Afghanistan north of Hindu Kush. Hindu Kush is understood to be main ranges or watershed stretching from Chinese frontier towards Persian frontier at Hari Rud and to include Band-i-Baba ranges for purpose of this declaration.

Further, the Secretary of State expressed his fear that the Russian Government 'may insist' on the omission of the opening sentence of the above declaration for it had just then asked for HMG's 'good offices' to secure from Afghanistan an irrigation concession on the Oxus, near Tarmez.[32]

Delhi's views on Whitehall's proposed changes were spelt out in a telegram on 28 May. If an Afghan concession was 'not possible' to avoid, it

> would urge most strongly inclusion of Russian re-affirmation suggested in first sentence of your draft Declaration.... Such re-affirmation would go a long way to dispel Afghan suspicion and would greatly facilitate explanation to Amir of Afghanistan.

As to defining northern Afghanistan

> not only is the definition proposed somewhat vague... but any definition would inevitably create impression that Afghanistan was being partitioned into definite spheres of influence as obtains in Persia.[33]

On 6 June, Grey informed Buchanan that HMG were agreeable to the exchange of notes—both public and secret—proposed by Russia with regard to Articles VI and VIII. As for Afghanistan a note, to be made public, was to stipulate that

> The Russian Government reaffirms its adherence to the principle that Afghanistan is outside the sphere of Russian political influence.

> The British Government engages that it will not support any application by British subjects for irrigation works, railways or preferential rights for commercial or industrial enterprises in Northern Afghanistan.

---

[32]Secretary of State to Viceroy, telegram, 26 May 1914, No. 290 in *Foreign*, October 1914, Procs. 134–396.

[33]Viceroy to Secretary of State, telegram, 28 May 1914, No. 292 in Ibid. Also see note by A H Grant, Foreign Secretary, dated 28 May 1914, in 'Notes', *supra*, n. 31.

A secret agreement was to define 'Northern Afghanistan', so as to scrupulously exclude from its territorial limits both Herat as well as the plains of the Afghan Hari Rud.[34]

Sazonov's reaction was along expected lines. To start with, he insisted that any definition of northern Afghanistan should be made public, nor would a definition that excluded the valley of the Hari Rud have any meaning for him—after all, so far as Russian irrigation was concerned, it was the most important river. The Russian Minister also demanded that the Indian Government allow Russian subjects, who were on pilgrimage to Buddhist holy places, to enter Tibet from British India; there had been specific instances where this had been denied and which had resulted in protests by the Russian Consul General in Calcutta.[35]

It was at this stage that negotiations in St. Petersburg were abandoned. Actually, as would be evident, there was hardly any meeting-ground between the two sides, for in the final analysis Sazonov insisted on making public all arrangements regarding Afghanistan—a course to which the Government of India were strongly opposed. Besides, no mutually agreed definition of northern Afghanistan could be found, while the British were understandably sensitive both on Herat and the Afghan Hari Rud. But above all, by the second week of June it was clear in Simla, as no doubt in London, that the Chinese may not after all agree to the Tripartite Convention. Was it, therefore, worthwhile to pay the price Sazonov demanded to secure Russian agreement to the terms of a Convention to which one of the parties had raised serious objections?

---

[34]Grey to Buchanan, telegram, 6 June 1914, No. 219 in *Foreign*, April 1915, Procs. 204–23.
[35]Buchanan to Grey, 10 June 1914, No. 220 in Ibid.

Chapter 22

Negotiations with China: Peking and London

WHITEHALL HAD bent over backwards as it were to obtain Russia's consent to the terms of McMahon's Tripartite Convention initialled at Simla. Before long, its fond hope that the advantages St. Petersburg had gained at Urga could be made use of as a bargaining counter over Tibet, proved singularly unavailing. Sazonov was a difficult negotiator and insisted on his pound of flesh. What was worse, not only did the pound itself continue to inflate but the flesh he demanded inched nearer to the heart of the Empire: in Afghanistan, in Persia and last, but by no means the least, permitting Russian pilgrims to cross over into Tibet across India's frontiers. It was quite a mouthful and one would suspect that the apparitions of Dorjieff and Tserempil, across Tibet's barren wastes, and a turbulent north-west frontier to boot, would have awakened afresh in British breasts!

By mid-June, negotiations in St. Petersburg had reached a dead-end. Not only was Whitehall unwilling to pay the price which the Russians demanded, but China's own intractability and refusal to accept the Convention was now sufficiently patent. What was more, the political situation in Europe had deteriorated to a degree where a major clash of arms seemed imminent. No wonder in London, if also in Simla, discussions on the Tripartite Convention appeared to be seemingly incongruous, if not irrelevant.

Peking, however, was differently placed for this part of the world did not appear to be directly involved in, and if so only marginally, in Europe's internecine conflicts and rivalries: in the Balkans, on the high seas, in Africa. Besides, here it was not only the major European powers but their satellites, who called the tune. Asia stood outside the ring and China was determined to eke out what advantages it could from this situation. There was too, what McMahon had so aptly called, the traditional Chinese reluctance to accept firm conclusions or finality—more so when neither the conclusions, nor finality itself, suited the Chinese book.

Immediately after the initialling of the Convention at Simla, the Chinese Foreign Office in Peking had, as has been noticed, publicly repudiated the action of its Plenipotentiary. Peking's version of what transpired had implied that Ivan Chen was, in fact, coerced into putting down his signatures and its note had repeatedly referred to his 'individual and informal initialling'. In his report to his superiors, Chen maintained that McMahon further informed me (Ivan Chen) that the proposed draft convention had already been initialled by himself with the Tibetan delegate: and that if I did not initial the document today (April 27) then Articles 2 and 4 of the draft convention would be deleted, the Convention would be made with Tibet and no further negotiations carried on. I mentioned to the British delegate that the initialling of a document was different from its signature, and that I could not sign the convention without the instructions of my Government, to which the British delegate agreed. I then initialled the convention, as the best thing to do under the circumstances.

Peking maintained that as Chen had received no instructions

his act was an informal initialling by himself as an individual. Instructions were thus at once sent to him to cancel his initialling of the document.[1]

Nor was his action valid, for the Chinese government

cannot regard the initials of Delegate Chen as binding, because he initialled it entirely on his own initiative without first receiving instructions from them, and further he did so through being compelled by force of circumstances.[2]

The British were quick to react. The implication that Chen had been ' coerced ' was too much to go unchallenged:

HMG cannot refrain from expressing surprise at such a suggestion....The British delegate has been consulted in the matter and has reported that not only is the suggestion entirely unfounded but that it was not even made by Mr. Ivan Chen....[3]

From a careful perusal of the proceedings of the meeting of 27 April—and Chen had raised no objection to its minutes—as also of the Memorandum which McMahon wrote a few days later, it is difficult to deduce that Chen was forced into appending his signatures. McMahon's explanation that the Chinese Plenipotentiary initialled—actually he had put down his full name—for fear that the British go it alone with Tibet and that his country may thereby be deprived of the benefits that accrued to it from the Convention's terms,[4] appears to be more reasonable.

[1] Jordan to Grey, despatch, 2 May 1914, Encl. 1, No. 337 in *Foreign*, October 1914; Procs. 134-396. For the text of the Memorandum, Encl. 2 in Ibid.

[2] ' Translation of a telegram received by the Chinese Legation from the Wai Chiao Pu ' (communicated by Chinese Minister, 29 April 1914), No. 354 in Ibid.

[3] ' Note communicated to Chinese Minister (in London) ' on 1 May 1914. For the text No. 356 in Ibid.

[4] For details *supra*, Chapter XX.

It is significant that the Chinese, while repudiating the action of Ivan Chen, were deeply concerned lest the initialling of the Convention imply ringing down the curtain on the 6-month old negotiations. They made out that McMahon had suggested that the conference 'terminated' on 27 April and had, so far as China was concerned, 'cancelled' Articles II and IV of the Convention. Since, 'apart from the question of boundary', other articles were 'generally speaking' acceptable, Peking argued, why may not negotiations be allowed to continue, for

> the Chinese Government's willingness to reach a friendly decision...with the British Government is the same as before. The negotiations should, therefore, be continued and cannot be interrupted because of cancellation of Mr. Chen's individual and informal initialling of the Convention.[5]

Simultaneously, the Chinese Minister in London was asked to 'approach' the British Government and 'request' them to 'telegraphically instruct' their delegate to continue the negotiations.[6]

Soon there was another string to Peking's bow. Having never taken kindly to McMahon, of whose combative disposition it had always complained, it now suggested shifting the venue of the talks. Ground was carefully prepared. In blaming McMahon, Peking drew a distinction between his 'aggressive' and 'unfriendly' attitude and that of HMG which was more accommodating. Failure at Simla, it argued, was due to the 'uncompromising adherence' to the 'impracticable terms' formulated by Sir Henry. What was more, he had refused to see China's 'difficulties', used 'unconciliatory language' and shown 'strong partiality' towards Tibet. This came out clearly in his 'unfriendly' attitude to China in the matter of demarcating Tibet's boundaries, as also in laying down that the Amban's escort should not exceed that of the British Agent's by some seventy-five per cent.[7]

On 11 May, under instructions from his government, the Chinese Minister presented a Memorandum placing on record his desire for peaceful negotiations 'with a view to settlement', and opposing McMahon's alleged refusal for

---

[5]*Supra*, n. 1.

In London, the Chinese Minister was directed to 'approach' the British government and request them to 'telegraphically' instruct their delegate to continue the negotiations.

[6]*Supra*, n. 2.

[7] 'Telegram from the Wai Chiao Pu', (communicated by Mr Lew Yuk-lin, Minister in London), 22 April 1914, No. 352 in *Foreign*, October 1914, Procs. 134–396.

On 12 March (1914), the Chinese Minister had complained about the 'unsatisfactory' progress of talks in India and specifically mentioned that Ivan Chen was not getting that 'measure of support' from the British delegate to which he was entitled. For the text, Encl. 1 in Proc. 242 in Ibid. Also Jordan to Grey, letter, 24 April 1914, Encl. 1 in No. 313 in Ibid., wherein Jordan indicated that a 'Secretary to the President' had complained to him about the conduct of negotiations in Simla.

'further negotiations'.[8] Earlier, on 1 May, the Legation in London had communicated a Memorandum couched in much the same language deprecating, *inter alia*, that the draft tripartite agreement should be 'dropped altogether' and that the 'labours of several months' be thrown to the winds. And all this, 'just because' a complete agreement on one of the articles had not been reached on a date 'specified' by the British delegate! If the latter had indeed decided not to negotiate further in India, Peking would be willing

> either (to) send Mr. Ivan Chen to London to continue the negotiations or negotiate in Peking with the British Minister, Sir John Jordan, through the Wai Chiao Pu.[9]

In its rejoinder, Whitehall forcefully upheld the stand taken by McMahon. On 27 April, it explained, primarily with a view to accommodating the Chinese, the British delegate had made a 'further considerable' concession of territory. Besides, 'every point' in China's favour that could be allowed, 'without injustice' to Tibet, had been conceded, and without demur. Again, insofar as it knew, there was every reason to believe that the agreement, as initialled, would be signed 'in due course'. As for reports about McMahon terminating the negotiations these must have been based, HMG maintained, on 'some misapprehension',[10] nor yet could there be any question of changing the venue—to London or to Peking.[11]

Failure in its efforts either to drive a wedge between McMahon and his political superiors or in persuading the British Government to reopen negotiations with a change in the venue, did not overly discourage the Chinese. For on 13 June, the Chinese Minister handed to Jordan in Peking, a memorandum containing his detailed proposals regarding the boundary settlement as also the administrative arrangements envisaged in regard to Inner Tibet. The British Minister viewed this as an attempt at 'reopening' the whole question already thrashed out at Simla and revealed that the Chinese Minister for Foreign Affairs

> repeatedly pressed me to submit proposals to you and evidently not anxious to break off negotiations although he did not recede from his original attitude.[12]

---

[8] *F O* to *I O*, 15 May 1914, No. 321 in Ibid. Encl. 1 gives the text of the telegram from the Wai-chiao-pu presented to the Foreign Office on 11 May.

[9] 'Memorandum communicated by Chinese Legation (in London)', 1 May 1914, No. 355 in Ibid.

[10] *Supra*, n. 3.

[11] 'Note to Chinese Minister', 20 May 1914, No. 324 in *Foreign*, October 1914, Procs. 134-396. Also see Encl. 2, No. 321 and No. 322, both in Ibid.

[12] Jordan to Grey, telegram, 13 June 1914, No. 318 in Ibid.

Delhi was not unaware of this aspect of the question, and the Viceroy informed the Secretary of State that the Chinese government interpreted the transmission of their proposals of 13 June as an 'expression of willingness' on Britain's part to reopen negotiations in Simla, a course that threatened further procrastination and to which McMahon was clearly averse.

Between 27 April, when the three Plenipotentiaries initialled the Convention, and 3 July, when McMahon and the Lonchen signed it, the British made one major concession and were willing to make another. The first related to a recasting of Article X, due largely to St. Petersburg entering strong objections to its original version which it had equated to the establishment of a British protectorate over Tibet. McMahon, it may be recalled, had resisted the change not in that he was opposed to it *per se* but in that he felt that any alteration in the initialled version would give the Chinese an excuse for renegotiating the entire deal *de novo*. Once, however, it was clear that HMG had made up its mind to cave in, Delhi changed its stance. May not the revised version, it now argued, be used as a bargaining counter to impress upon Peking that

> in deference to the susceptibilities of China and in order to remove from the Convention any undue suggestion of British tutelage they (HMG) are willing to modify Article X of the Convention...but they can make no further alteration in the map or in the text....[13]

Jordan did not agree with this reasoning. He was clearly of the view that 'no impression' was likely to be produced by the proposed modification of Article X, as the Chinese had 'probably' heard of it already, and would know in any case that it had emanated from Russia.[14] Over-ruling Jordan, however, on 5 June the Foreign Office in London presented a slightly altered version of the Indian note to the Chinese Minister.[15] What impression, if any, this communication had on the Minister, or his principals, is debatable.

The nub of the problem, so far as Peking was concerned, was the territorial settlement. This had been evident from the very beginning and more so after January when McMahon presented his maps and proposed boundaries for Inner/Outer Tibet. At the time the draft was initialled at Simla on 27 April, Ivan Chen's instructions still related principally to what Peking regarded as its legitimate demesne. Later, both in London and Peking, the gravamen of the Chinese charge against McMahon's 'unfriendly' attitude was that he did not pay due heed to China's territorial claims, that he was 'partial' towards the Tibetans not only insofar as he listened to them but also that he lent counte-

---

[13]Viceroy to Secretary of State, telegram, 17 June 1914, No. 325 in Ibid. Also Viceroy to Secretary of State, telegram, 27 May 1914, No. 291 in Ibid.

[14]Jordan to Grey, telegram, 31 May 1914, No. 296 in Ibid.

[15]Foreign Office 'Memorandum', 5 June 1914, presented to Chinese Legation in London, No. 361 in Ibid. Also see Nos. 358, 359 and 360 in Ibid., relating to correspondence between the India Office and the Foreign Office regarding the Memorandum.

nance to their claim for territory. Again, it is significant that the concession which McMahon made to the Chinese at the formal meeting on 27 April, with a view to persuading the reluctant Ivan Chen to append his signatures, related to territory—it was the proposal to take Kokonor out of Inner Tibet and place it within the bounds of mainland China. It was territory, therefore, that dominated Chinese thinking almost to the exclusion of other issues.

It is important to bear in mind here the fact that China's eagerness on the territorial issue was confined exclusively to the boundaries between China and Tibet, while the boundary between India and Tibet, McMahon's 'Red Line', (and later India's McMahon Line), was never raised at all as an issue. In other words, the 'boundary question' in Chinese minds did not extend to the boundary between Tibet and India; it related only to the so-called Inner and Outer Tibets.[15a]

To complete this catalogue of repeated Chinese insistence on territorial issues, it may be recalled that at his interview with Jordan on 25 April, two days before the initialling of the convention at Simla, Wellington Ku, then a Secretary of the Wai-chiao-pu, made two points. One, that President Yuan Shih-kai was 'sincerely anxious' to arrive at an amicable arrangement and 'deprecated' the idea of breaking off negotiations. Two, that he (Yuan Shih-kai) was ready to accept 'in principle' all the provisions of the draft agreement, with the exception of Article IX, relating to the boundary question. Here too the President

> had made successive concessions all of which had met with no response from the British side and he felt that the time had now come when HMG should modify the boundary stipulations of the Agreement in the interests of an amicable settlement.

> In the course of conversation, another unmistakable hint was dropped namely that

> insistence upon our (British) claims with regard to Tibet might hamper the Chinese government in its desire to facilitate the settlement of our claims in the Yangtse valley.[16]

The memorandum presented by Wellington Ku on this occasion was an interesting document. It summed up the Simla negotiations, from the Chinese viewpoint, and admirably. To start with, while the British delegate was

---

[15a] A recent authority, *Karunakar Gupta*, has doubly underlined McMahon's 'abortive diplomatic sleight of hand' with regard to showing the agreed India-Tibet boundary on the Convention map which Ivan Chen signed (*not* initialled) at two places. It is necessary to emphasise in this context that while the Chinese were raising such a hue and cry about the Inner-Outer Tibet boundary, they were scrupulously silent about this part of the alignment. Surely for weeks, if not months, Ivan Chen and his principals in Peking had time enough to scrutinise it!

[16] Jordan to Grey, despatch, 30 April 1914, No. 312 in *Foreign*, October 1914, Procs. 134–396.

'anxious that the boundary question should first be discussed', China was 'strongly opposed' albeit it eventually 'gave way'. Later, when the Lonchen presented claims 'affecting the sovereignty and territory of the Republic' China, unable to agree, had yet hoped that the British delegate would help a 'just conclusion'. This, however, did not come about. 'Unexpectedly', the Tibetan claim having been presented first, became 'the dominant factor'. Again, 'suddenly' the idea of 'Inner and Outer' Tibet was brought forward and the two boundaries marked on a map which the Chinese Government

> much regrets that it was impossible for it to recognise...and considers that the original intention of the British Government in offering its mediation was very different from this.

Peking then listed a whole series of 'concessions'—five in number—which it had made at Simla. Relating to 'government and territory', these were 'sufficient' proof of China's desire for reaching a 'friendly settlement'. Referring to McMahon's specific demand regarding the 'conclusive' nature of the meeting of 27 April, Peking made it clear that to a proceeding of 'this sort' it found it 'impossible' to agree.

Despite failure, the memorandum continued, negotiations must continue both because it would not be a 'difficult matter' to reach an agreement by 'mutual consultation' as also because the final goal of a 'friendly conclusion' must be attained.[17]

In regard to the territorial settlement, much of the ground has been covered already. One point alone needs emphasis namely, that in a private communication to Langley, Under Secretary at the Foreign Office, Jordan had urged the cession of Kokonor. Langley, reminding Jordan of McMahon's concession of 27 April, had telegraphed on 18 June:

> Presume this meets your criticisms and that you do not recommend any further modification of boundary of Inner Tibet.[18]

Earlier on 1 May, in Peking, Jordan received Wellington Ku who had told him that

> the President's main objections to the boundaries now defined, was the inclusion in Outer Tibet of Chiamdo and of the southern portion of the Kokonor territory. The latter extended, he said, to the Tang La range and had always been Chinese. It was moreover barren waste country.[19]

McMahon's objections to China's new demands were weighty. He was of the 'firm opinion' that by conceding them, the disturbed state of the Marches would be perpetuated and the safety of Tibet imperilled. Besides the

[17] For the text of the Memorandum, Encl. in No. 312 in Ibid.
[18] Foreign Office to Jordan, telegram, 18 June 1914, No. 380 in Ibid.
[19] Jordan to Grey, despatch, 2 May 1914, Encl. 1, No. 337 in Ibid.

exclusion of Niarong and Derge was only agreed to by the Tibetan Plenipotentiary on the understanding that Chiamdo remained in Outer Tibet and that China would not be given any further territorial concessions.[20]

In other words, the Chinese game was that having secured Nyarong and Derge, they would now press their claims to Chamdo!

Before the curtain was finally rung on the Simla confabulations, two attempts were made to reach a conclusion on the territorial question. The first, briefly alluded to, was on 13 June, when Jordan was handed a Memorandum whose principal points were:

1. Boundaries of Inner Tibet were to be so modified as to include areas west of Litang and Batang and the region between the Yangtse and the Menkong. Kokonor was to be a part of China although the latter country was prepared to agree to include the south-western part of it in Inner Tibet; as for Derge and Niarong, China would engage to create no new military posts there;
2. China was to have ' a free hand ' in the administration of Inner Tibet so as to consolidate its position while civil and military officers stationed there, ' shall continue to exercise their rights and carry on their duties ';
3. The Dalai Lama was to continue to enjoy rights of appointing high priests and retain full control in all matters affecting religious institutions;
4. China would recognise as autonomous ' Outer Tibet ' that portion of the country which lay west of the boundary line from Menkong.

Jordan's conclusions about his interview were significant. He noted that it had

> lasted nearly two hours and was marked by great earnestness on the part of the Minister for Foreign Affairs who, while appearing to realise the grave responsibility of his position and displaying an evident anxiety not to break off negotiations was unwilling to recede from his original attitude.

As for Chinese proposals, Jordan concluded, these represented ' practically no advance ' beyond what had been put forward at Peking or Simla on 21 April —the only difference being that the buffer zone of Kham and a portion of what was claimed as Chinese Kokonor now made up ' Inner Tibet '. Had these proposals

> been confined to the inclusion of Batang and Litang and that part of the Kokonor north of the Kunlun range... I should have been inclined to

[20] Viceroy to Secretary of State, telegram, 2 May 1914, No. 275 in Ibid.

submit them for your favourable consideration.... It seems to me, however, to be important that the areas through which the northern and southern roads to Lhasa pass from Jyekundo and Chiamdo, respectively should remain within autonomous Outer Tibet.[21]

Delhi's reaction to Chinese proposals was a firm negative. Later it explained that the

> situation at present appears to be that Government of China think that British Government are bluffing but that, if they are undeceived on this point by a decisive reply to their last proposals, they will consent to sign.[22]

The above conclusion was strongly disputed by Jordan who questioned the validity of McMahon's assumption that the Chinese interpreted the presentation of their proposals of 13 June as 'willingness on our part' to reopen negotiations and that his (McMahon's) firmness in rejecting these as 'impossible' had caused 'anxiety' in Peking. He noted that

> no anxiety and no indication of any change of attitude on the part of Chinese is detected by me here. I am informed that decision conveyed (proposals of 13 June)...is that of President who himself is handling the question.[23]

Just about this time Jordan appears to have staged a complete *volte-face*, and intervened strongly on the Chinese side. He pooh-poohed the much-trumpeted concession made to Peking by McMahon at the meeting on 27 April. What the latter had described as a tract of country in the neighbourhood of lake Kokonor, Jordan pointed out, was 'only' the north-eastern portion thereof. Since, according to Rockhill, 'politically speaking' Tibet begins at Tangla range, and the latter formed the southern boundary of Kokonor, was it not fair—Jordan did not quite say it—that the whole of Kokonor should form part of China?

As though the implication were not clear, he dug out the Chefoo convention to drive home the point that its 'separate article' had provided that passports for Kokonor should be issued by China. Nor was that all, for exclusion of Litang and Batang 'will also be objected to strongly' by Peking.[24]

Jordan's change of stance is reflected more fully in the Viceroy's 'private'

---

[21] Jordan to Grey, telegram, 13 June 1914, No. 318; for details, Jordan to Grey, despatch, 16 June 1914, Encl. 1, No. 373, both in Ibid. Also Jordan to Grey, telegram, 11 June 1914, No. 317 in Ibid.

[22] Viceroy to Secretary of State, 14 June 1914, No. 319, and Viceroy to Secretary of State, 18 June 1914, No. 327, both in Ibid.

[23] Viceroy to Secretary of State, telegram, 17 June 1914, and Jordan to Grey, 18 June 1914, Nos. 325 and 328 in Ibid.

[24] Jordan to Grey, telegram, 19 June 1914, No. 331 in Ibid.

telegram to the Secretary of State on 22 June. Significantly, it does not find a mention in the Conference proceedings but is tucked somewhere in the official correspondence. The Viceroy started by asking if the Foreign Office reluctance to the Convention being signed between the British and Tibet, ' independently ' of China, was due to

> considerations...based entirely on Sir John Jordan's doubts as to prospects of concessions and mining leases in China being compromised by such action....

If this were so, the Viceroy emphasised, he

> would like to bring to your Lordship's notice that Tibetan situation is a purely Indian question which closely affects the defence of our frontier, and that HMG should not allow British commercial concessions to weigh in the balance....

In regard to Jordan's plea for a new territorial adjustment,

> I do not understand how Sir John Jordan's views have changed so materially since his telegrams of 5th April and 21st April when he knew that Sir H McMahon was proceeding to conclude a definite settlement of the question....

And finally the Viceroy underscored what he deemed important namely

> that Inner Zone of Tibet while defined geographically as Tibet becomes politically Chinese, appears to have been forgotten by Government of China.[25]

Despite the vigorous fight put up by the Viceroy to resist Jordan's pressure on the Foreign Office, India on its own did some rethinking. A day later the Viceroy telegraphed again:

> if it would materially assist present situation, ensure without further question immediate signature of Convention, and propitiate Chinese feelings he (McMahon) might be able to get the Tibetans to consent to Kuen Lun being substituted for Altyn Tagh as the northern boundary of Tibet. There would then be no tract of Inner Tibet on the north.[26]

---

[25]Viceroy to Secretary of State, telegram, 22 June 1914. Inscribed ' Private ', the telegram is in *Foreign, Notes,* October 1914, Procs. 134–396.

[26]Viceroy to Secretary of State, telegram, 23 June 1914, No. 332 in *Foreign,* October 1914, Procs. 134–396.

McMahon's revised territorial deal, as spelt out, formed part of the Memorandum which was handed in Peking on 25 June. *Inter alia*, it stated that Chinese proposals, vide their memorandum of 13 June, which would bring the boundary ' within 200 miles ' of Lhasa were ' wholly unacceptable ', that a substantial concession had already been made in Kokonor (on 27 April)—and was ' the utmost ' which Tibet could be asked to make. All this notwithstanding

> if instead of trying to re-open the whole boundary question again, the Chinese government had confined themselves to asking for such a modification as the substitution of the Kuen Lun range for the Altyn Tagh in the north....

In return, Peking was to withdraw ' all other demands ' and sign the Convention ' immediately ' while, for its part, HMG would persuade the Tibetans to this ' further substantial ' concession.[27]

On 29 June, China's reply was handed over to Jordan in Peking. The issue that stood out above all else was still the ' boundary ' to which China was ' unable ' to agree. In fact, the

> very last concession which they (Chinese) made on this head is the inclusion of the country south of Kuen Lun range in Inner Tibet.

Again, Peking had yielded ground and undertook that

> Chinese troops would merely hold the places in which they were quartered and would not cross to west of Chiamdo. But it is absolutely impossible to transfer territory which historically belongs to China and which Chinese troops now occupy to map of Outer Tibet.

The above notwithstanding, Peking was willing to make another bid— ' as further evidence of her exceptional friendliness towards Great Britain '. To remove the ' objectionable ' feature of Gyade's close proximity to Lhasa, China

> will make that region a doubtful area of Inner Tibet where no large bodies of troops will be stationed but only civil officials with reasonable number of troops for their protection.

This apart, ' no further concession ' was possible and even though the Chinese Government

---

[27] Jordan to Grey, telegram, 25 June 1914, No. 335; for the text of the Memorandum, Encl. 2 in No. 377, both in Ibid.

do not sign convention, it is nevertheless urgently necessary to declare that they have absolutely no desire to terminate present negotiations and that they are unable to regard unauthorised initialling of convention by their representative as effective. They earnestly hope that HMG will still continue to act as mediator between China and Tibet....[28]

The 'finality' of the Chinese position was underlined in no uncertain terms and the hope expressed

that HMG will be able to take this fact (that 'no further concession' is 'possible') into consideration, and it is consequently impossible for it (China) to be coerced into signing the convention; the reason is that it has no option in the matter.[29]

Here then matters rested on the eve of the final round at Simla. Peking had made it clear that it had 'no option' except to refuse to sign; Whitehall, that it would be prepared to make 'a substantial concession' on the territorial question, if China would sign 'immediately'. Since Peking refused to oblige, the British turned to the only alternative now left to them—viz. to sign alone with Tibet. It is to Simla then one has to turn for those eventful, if fateful, days preceding 3 July.

---

[28] Jordan to Viceroy, telegram, 30 June 1914, No. 338 in Ibid., gives a summary of the Chinese (written) reply handed over to him the previous day.

[29] For the text of the Memorandum, Encl. 2, No. 386 in Ibid.

According to Dr Sung, the Chinese proposal of 28 June was made after President Yuan had ordered a 'special committee for the study of Tibetan Affairs' to work out a compromise solution on the basis of the draft presented at Simla. *Yao-ting Sung*, p. 106.

THE Government of India have drawn attention to an order dated the 18th March last, issued by the ambans at Lhassa, which directs the cancellation of a grant of land to the late Shabdung Lama, a former Thibetan employee of the British trade agency at Gyantse, and forbids the Thibetan Government and all lamas of Tashi-lhunpo, from the Tashi Lama downwards, from holding any communication with foreigners, whether on state or private affairs.

Mr. Max Müller has been instructed to bring to the notice of the Chinese Government this action on the part of the resident at Lhassa, and to point out that the prohibition imposed on the Thibetan Government and the lamas of Tashi-lhunpo from holding intercourse with foreigners appears to be in violation of article 12 of the Trade Regulations of 1908. Further, that neither the Anglo-Thibetan Convention nor the Anglo-Chinese Convention provide for the interposition of the Chinese Government between His Majesty's Government and the Thibetan authorities upon any subject whatever.

His Majesty's Government have observed the strictest neutrality in regard to recent developments in Thibet, and they have certainly never given the Chinese Government reason to believe that they wished to be other than friendly neighbours. They have a right to expect that this friendly attitude should be reciprocated, but the present and other instances already brought to the notice of the Wai-wu Pu show that the representatives of the Chinese Government in Thibet are not animated with a similar spirit of conciliation. Since the avowed purpose of the Chinese Government's intervention in Thibet is the pacification of the country and the carrying out of its treaty obligations, Mr. Max Müller is instructed to represent that that purpose might be better served by the appointment of a resident more sympathetic to the inhabitants and less unfriendly to the friends of his Government than the present Chinese commissioner at Lhassa. Failing this, stringent orders should be dispatched to Mr. Lien to adopt a more conciliatory attitude in matters affecting the interests of His Majesty's Government and British subjects.

The favour of an early reply is requested for the information of His Majesty's Government.

(In the absence of His Majesty's chargé d'affaires),
ERNEST SCOTT.

Peking, August 27, 1910.

1. Max Müller to Grey, August 1910 (see p. 92)

(Private and Confidential.)

THE political conditions here are puzzling, and severely try the temper of patient Christians like myself. The country west of Tachienlu to Batang has been conquered, and some attempt is being made to govern it. The Thibetans are undoubtedly better off now than before, and Chinese education, civilisation, and moral ideas are improving the Thibetan outwardly; but it is impossible to understand what China intends to get out of the country. If his Excellency Chao was the head of a missionary board, and his officials and staff of Chinese poorly remunerated but self-denying missionaries, the efforts and results might become famous; but when one realises that the reforms which are influencing the moral, religious, mental, and physical life of the people are emanating from Peking—conservative, utilitarian, and unsympathetic—the puzzle becomes decidedly Chinese. The country is far too high to produce cereals, and the Chinaman has little use for beef, mutton, wool, hides, milk, butter, and cheese. In fact the country only produces what he values slightly. Again, even if it did produce cereals, no one would think of sending them to the coast, especially viâ Tachienlu, Chungking, and Shanghai. It seems to me that the day is coming when all the products of Eastern Thibet will go down by Talifu and out by Burmah. And so good-bye to Tachienlu and all theories which depend for success from that centre. The situation is something like this: his Excellency Chao says, "the region is eminently suitable for agriculture, therefore parcel out the waste uplands, between 13,000 and 16,000 feet, among good and industrious husbandmen." But two factors are at work interfering with this fundamentally important requirement: his Excellency can neither command nature nor induce good husbandmen to leave the fertile plains of Chengtu for the bleak uplands of Asia. Hence failures which would be amusing were they not so pathetic. So much for the country conquered.

His Excellency is busily engaged, after having pacified Derge in establishing the supremacy of China in the Chamdo region, as well as territory between that and Assam. So far the regions north and west of Batang are being quietly, but surely forced to tender in reality allegiance long tendered in theory. Just how it is being done is a mystery; but this conquest of Eastern Thibet is being accomplished with little or no bloodshed. The fighting force under the Warden is miserably inadequate, perhaps 4,000 men being a liberal estimate. There is no doubt before very long a great part of Thibet will be recognising the authority of China. But two questions arise: Can China do anything with the conquered country? and is the alleged subjugation a policy on the part of the Thibetans to avert the vengeance of the one invulnerable Chinaman? "Wait," they say, "Chao will go some day, and then our turn will come." And there is probably something in such rumours, for has not China's conquest and reconquest in this land been the wearying tale of the ages? Conquer a turbulent country at great expense, hold it at great inconvenience, and at the same time get nothing from it, and what happens? The fact, however, that Thibet is such

2. PRIVATE LETTER FROM BATANG, SEPTEMBER 1910 (see p. 76)

3. MINUTE BY RITCHIE/CREWE, JULY 1911 (see p. 97)

'I am in accord with Sir A Hirtzel's view and think that his emendations are all improvements. The passage beginning "I fully concur" should stand—which the G[overnment] of I[ndia] will fully understand the force of. It is clear that where you cannot have a single frontier line you must be prepared to deal with frontier incidents as they arise, on the mertis of each case.'

C. 24.8.11

'Lord Crewe
The draft, as concluded by Sir A Hirtzel seems to me an improvement on the FO suggestions while securing the points on which Sir E Grey insists.
'The point of difference not composed is the mention of the sentence "I fully concur in Your Excellency's decision not to advance administrative frontiers" which it'

3 (A). MINUTE BY RITCHIE/CREWE, JULY 1811 (see p. 97)

'such is that in question cannot be established. The question is whether to take the risks involved in an outer frontier or to fall back on a frontier up to which we do effectively administer.'

R.R. 22.7.11

I have it on good authority that in one of the President's telegrams on the subject of Yin's dismissal there occurs a remark to the effect that that official's dilatoriness at a most critical period in the history of Sino-Tibetan relations has done irreparable harm to China's position in Tibet. This can only mean that if Yin had recovered all that part of the frontier which lies west of the Mekong before Great Britain intervened, China's position at the Conference would have been immensely strengthened. Unfortunately for China Yin's energies were from first to last directed to regaining his position at Chengtu instead of to re-establishing China's authority over the Tibetans. It would be safe to surmise that a very large portion of the two million taels found its way into the coffers of his political party at Chengtu.

I have the honour to be,

SIR,

Your most obedient, humble servant,

LOUIS KING.

Sir John Jordan, G.C.I.E., K.C.B., K.C.M.G.,
      His Majesty's Minister,
            Peking.

4. LOUIS KING TO JORDAN, FEBRUARY 1914 (see p. 156)

We have the honour to refer to your telegram, dated the 24th July last, regarding the punitive operations against the Abors, and explorations and policy on the north-east frontier of India.

2. We have issued instructions for preparations for the expedition against the Abors, and the Mishmi Mission, to be taken in hand, and an estimate of the cost will be telegraphed to Your Lordship as soon as the information is available. In the meantime, we desire to place before His Majesty's Government our views as to the policy to be followed in future on the north-east frontier, together with a selection of correspondence on the subject.

3. The frontier to be considered extends eastwards from the Bhutan State (which has, we trust, been secured from Chinese interference by the treaty* concluded on the 24th March 1910, under which the State vested the control of its foreign relations with the British Government), up to and including the Mishmi country, and then southwards to the Myitkyina district of Upper Burma. The latter portion of the frontier, that is, between the Mishmi country and the Myitkyina district is being separately considered, and need only briefly be mentioned here in order to co-ordinate the evidence which we have of what appears to us to be China's general policy of aggression along the whole of the north-east frontier. The Chinese Government were definitely informed by His Majesty's Government in 1906 that, from the end of the demarcated Burma-China boundary at Manang Bum (or as it should now be called Pangseng Chet) in latitude 25° 35′ N. to the confines of Tibet, the Irrawaddy-Salween watershed was the boundary between the two Empires, and that, failing acceptance by China of their terms, the Government of Burma would be instructed to occupy and administer the country without further

---

* Secret despatch to Secretary of State for India, No. 47 (External), dated the 17th March 1910.

Events of 1910.
Erection of flags at Menilkrai.

1. Chinese activity on the Mishmi border (extreme N.E. of Assam) first excited notice in May 1910, when information was brought to Sadiya by the Chief of Pangum (lat. 28°, long. 96° 38'), in the Miju section of the Mishmi country, to the effect that two Tibetans had come to his village with the news that 1,000* Chinese soldiers had arrived at Rima and had demanded taxes from the Tibetan Governor. The Governor refused to comply with this demand, and was imprisoned.† The Tibetans also brought orders from the Chinese to the Pangum Chief to cut a track from Tibet to Assam broad enough for two horsemen to ride abreast. The Chief refused to obey, saying that he was a British subject, and that he declined to take orders from anyone except the Assistant Political Officer at Sadiya. (Pol. 1093/10.) From a statement made by a Miju named Halam to the Assistant Political Officer, Sadiya, in July 1910, it appeared that the Chinese had established a firm control over Rima, and had planted flags near the River Yepuk, a tributary of the upper Lohit‡, but that they had not attempted to assert sovereignty beyond what might be argued to be the limits of Tibet. (Monthly Memorandum of Information received, &c., September 1910, paragraph 15.)

It was further reported in October 1910, on the authority of certain Mishmis who had come into Sadiya, that the Chinese had prohibited all trade between the Miju Mishmis and Tibet.

Captain Bailey's Journey.
Viceroy's telegram, dated 18th August 1911.
P. 1372/11.
Captain Bailey's Report, dated 19th September 1911.
P. 1822/11.

2. Further information on the subject of Chinese intrigues with the Mishmis was furnished by Captain F. M. Bailey, who travelled from China to Assam *via* Rima and the Mishmi country in the summer of 1911.

Captain Bailey reported that on the 15th June 1911 he met two Mishmi headmen at Tin-ne or Tini (two days south of Rima and three miles north of

---

* The number is evidently an exaggeration. Captain Bailey, who passed through Za-yul in the summer of 1911 (*see* paragraph 2), found 20 Chinese troops at Rima and 320 at Chikung,

1. A suitable military frontier should follow the principal watersheds and include on our side the tributaries of the lower Brahmaputra, the Lohit and Irrawaddy rivers. A mountain chain is from every point of view the most advantageous strategical frontier.

2. It is realised that other questions, such as the determination of the limits of habitation of tribes, originally under Tibet on the one hand, and independent frontier tribes on the other, will largely affect the question of our frontier *vis à vis* China, but the military aspect should be prominently kept in view.

3. We are already precluded from obtaining the best military line on this part of the border; the Tsangpo alone decides this point. Besides this instance, the Chinese, by their effective occupation of Tibet, control many of the ranges and passes, and have established themselves at the head-waters of several of the rivers which flow down into Assam.

4. From east to west, the more important are :—

    The Lohit; the Nagong Chu, or Dibang; possibly the Yamne; the Tsangpo, or Dihang; the Nia Chu, or Kamla; the Tawang Chu, or Dangma.

The approximate line of frontier proposed by the Government of India is shown by red chain-dotted line in the accompanying sketch map. Roughly speaking, this line divides Tibet and the tribes originally under the Tibetan Government from the independent frontier tribes, and it will be seen that all the above-mentioned rivers cut through this line.

5. Such information will, therefore, be required from the expedition, missions, and survey parties as will enable the General Staff to determine the best military line under the circumstances.

The information already possessed, and that which is required is given below :—

(1) *The Lohit*.—This river is formed by the combined waters of the Zayul Chu and Rong Thod Chu, both rising high in the uplands of Tibet and uniting at Shikha, a few miles above Rima in Zayul.

A range of snowy mountains divides the waters of the Rong Thod Chu from those of the Lohit, and also divides the Tibetan district of Zayul from the Mishmi country.

The waters of the Zayul Chu and Lohit are divided from those flowing into the Irrawaddy by a continuous mountain range known successively throughout its length by the names Rirapphasi, Namkiu, and Phungan range. This range divides Zayul and the Mishmi country from Hkamti Long and Chiu tzu. Along these two ranges a suitable boundary seems indicated, but it will be necessary to find a convenient point at which the line should cross the Lohit river.

The Chinese are now in effective occupation of Zayul, and in 1909 planted flags, presumably to mark the boundary, at Manekrai or Menilkrai, a big boulder in the valley of the Lohit. This point is believed to be the ancient boundary between Tibet and India.

(2) *The Nagong Chu, or Dibang*.—Both the explorers A...k and Kinthup, and the Mishmis and Tibetans who were with Mr. Needham on his journey to Rima in 1886, stated that the Nagong Chu runs westwards from its source north of the Ata Gang La, through Po-med, and falls into the Dihang, north of the Abor country. If this statement is correct, the conclusion

IN my telegram No. 171 of the 14th instant I had the honour to inform you that Dr. W. W. Yen, the Vice-Minister of Foreign Affairs, had stated to me, under instructions from the President of the Republic, that in view of the perilous position of the Chinese garrison at Lhassa, Yuan Shih-kai had decided to sanction the immediate advance into Thibet of the combined military expedition fitted out in Szechuan and Yünnan, and now operating in the Szechuan marches. Dr. Yen had prefaced this statement by reminding me that the President had promised to inform me of any measures contemplated against Thibet. I reported to you fully by telegraph the language I held to the Vice-Minister in reply. It was evident that this was the first step in the process of again bringing the country entirely under the control of Chinese officialdom, and I had no hesitation in expressing the most unqualified objection to a line of conduct which was not only designed to bring about a political situation which would be a contravention of solemn treaty engagements, but could not fail to plunge Thibet again into turmoil and disorder. The only reason given me, namely, the necessity for rescuing the Chinese garrison, was no justification, for their withdrawal could be arranged for, as the President knew. I asked Dr. Yen to convey my reply to Yuan Shih-kai, and to say that I should be glad to see his Excellency before I left for a short holiday on the 17th August.

I called on the President yesterday by appointment, and to my amazement he said that he had not authorised the Vice-Minister to make the statement he had delivered to me. All that he had authorised him to say was that although the Chinese Government did not interpret the treaties as prohibiting an advance into Thibet, no such advance was contemplated. How the misunderstanding arose I cannot say. Yuan Shih-kai professed to be almost as much perplexed as I was, and there may be something in his suggestion that the Vice-Minister had confused his instructions with the views held by the Wai-chiao Pu. Even so, it is still difficult to account for the President's action in deliberately sending an official to deliver such a message which either was meaningless or, if intended to provoke a discussion, could have only drawn from me a repetition of our objections to anything in the nature of a military expedition entering Thibet.

However this may be, the President assured me yesterday more than once in the clearest possible terms that there was no intention whatever of ordering the troops to advance into Thibet. Several of the provincial generals had pressed him for permission to lead their men across the frontier, but he had telegraphed his entire disapproval of all such proposals. The operations, he told me, would be confined to the borders of Szechuan in the neighbourhood of Litang, Batang, and Tachienlu. His Excellency went even further and spontaneously assured me that there was no intention of incorporating Thibet in the provinces of China. He added that the natural authority over Thibet was vested in the Dalai Lama, and that he would much prefer to arrange matters by amicable agreement with him. I had the honour of telegraphing the gist of this conversation to you last night in my telegram No. 173.

Although the result of this exchange of views was to place a different complexion on the present state of affairs, I did not consider it desirable to suggest to you that the communication which you authorised me by your telegram No. 128 of the 15th instant to make to the Chinese Government should be deferred. I have therefore to-day addressed to the Wai-chiao Pu the memorandum of which I have the honour to enclose copy. After reminding the Chinese Government of the verbal assurances which, in spite of the presidential order of the 21st April, I have now on two separate occasions received from the President himself, I have indicated in the terms of your instructions the policy of His Majesty's Government in the Thibetan question. At the conclusion of my interview yesterday I told Yuan Shi-kai that this communication might be expected, and I asked him to be good enough to give his personal attention to it. The attitude which it embodied was, I said, eminently reasonable and fair, and

8. JORDAN TO GREY, AUGUST 1912 (see p. 139)

WITH reference to my despatches Nos. 493 of the 16th December, 1912, and 102 of the 8th March, on the subject of the position of the Chinese in Thibet, I have the honour to enclose a series of translations from the book published at Chengtu in November last, entitled "History of the Creation of the Province of Hsi Kang (Western Kham)" by General Fu Sung-mu the successor of Chao Erh-feng in the office of warden of the marches. They present an interesting and consecutive narrative of the events of the past few years in the border country between Szechuan and Thibet, and urge the formation of a border province under a regular Chinese Administration.

The book is convincing in its frankness, and may well come from the pen of a man who is introduced by the provincial Governor as a representative of an old martial stock who can "spend the day on horseback, chasing rebels, and dismount to indite a brilliant despatch." It deals mainly with period of Chao Erh-feng's campaigns from 1905–1911, when the Chinese position was established more firmly than ever before in the tribal country, and when the formation of a march province was within the bounds of practical politics. Recent events have led once more to the destruction of the Chinese power, but the book will be of value as a work of reference in the event of any readjustment of the boundaries of Thibet.

General Fu Sung-mu has set himself the task of defining the area of the province of Kham, which he describes as the territory lying between the Kokonor district of Sining on the north and the town of Wei-hsi in Yünnan, whilst it stretches from Tachienlu on the east to the Tanta Range on the west, a territory considerably larger than Szechuan, and, indeed, equal in size to the remaining area of anterior and ulterior Thibet. He is at pains to demonstrate that this territory cannot be considered as Thibet proper, though he reluctantly admits that even Chinese travellers have been prone to describe the Thibetan Dominion as commencing with the Ching-ning Range immediately to the west of Batang, and he advocates the transformation of Kham into a regularly constituted province of China under the name of Hsi Kang.

The author endeavours to trace a vague historic link between China and Kham for some 2,000 years, claiming that Tachienlu was Chinese territory as early as B.C. 140; that the country has been lost and won time after time by succeeding dynasties; that the troops of Kang-hsi forced their way through to Lhassa; and that the boundary-stone just west of Batang was erected in 1727. He deplores the fact that the principalities of Kham were allowed to fall away from their allegiance during the declining years of the Manchu dynasty, but urges the importance of a consolidation of Chinese power up to the limits of Chao Erh-feng's control.

The author admits his lack of historical evidence, but there can be little doubt that the true history of Kham commences with the campaigns of Srong Tsan Gyalpo in the seventh century. King Srong Tsan appears to have reigned over the whole of Kham, and to have gained a victory over the Chinese in the neighbourhood of Sining. He claimed a Chinese princess as his bride, and subsequently founded the city of Lhassa, thus establishing the kingdom which is now generally known as Thibet. The men of Kham belong to the original Thibetan stock, and to this day they possess a civilisation and skill in many arts and crafts which has not been attained in Thibet proper, whilst they are, admittedly, men of fine physique and of tried martial courage.

In about the year 1730 the Chinese succeeded in establishing a post road through Kham and on to Lhassa, with a line of courier stations and a number of commissary officers who exercised, however, no administrative functions, and whose jurisdiction extended only to their Chinese subjects. The natives have remained throughout under the sole control of their own officials, the sway of the princes being closely bound up with the spiritual power of the great lamaseries. Any control which may have been exercised either by Lhassa or Peking in the eighteenth century has certainly been largely modified in the course of the last fifty years, and the congeries of little states

10. MINUTE IN THE INDIA OFFICE AND TELEGRAMS FROM SECRETARY OF STATE TO GOVERNOR-GENERAL, 1, 2, 3 JULY 1914 (see p. 288)

'That the Secretary of State's instructions of 3rd July reached Sir H McMahon "too late to affect the proceedings of the conclusive meeting" was not due to any delay on the part of this office, but primarily to the fact that no one of sufficient authority to deal with the question arrived at the FO on Friday last until after 1 P.M.
'In the circumstances, Sir H McMahon appears to have acted most judiciously, and it is submitted that his action be approved by H.M.'s Govt.' [*Contd.*

This telegram has no doubt crossed ours of 2nd July; but, even so, our telegram of 1st July (to which the Viceroy refers) ought to have made it clear to Sir H. McMahon that separate signature with the Tibetan delegate was ruled out by H.M.'s Gov't.

The attached draft has been approved by F.O. (Sir W. Langley) Sir E. Grey is away.

'This telegram has no doubt crossed ours of 2nd July; but, even so, our telegram of 1st July (to which the Viceroy refers) ought to have made it clear to Sir H McMahon that separate signature with the Tibetan delegate was ruled out by H. M.'s Govt.
'The attached draft has been approved by FO (Sir W[alter] Langley). Sir E. Grey is away.'

The question itself is not merely one of giving arms to Tibet for her protection against unprovoked attack, it involves a multitude of other issues, e.g. (1) the desirability of sending a representative to Lhasa, either temporarily or permanently, (2) the effect of such a step upon our treaty obligations and position (3) the application of the Arms Convention (4) the frontier situation as between Tibet and China (5) our relations with China (6) the attitude and policy of Japan. Upon all these subjects the most diverse views are expressed.

Broadly speaking the India Office and the Government of India are in favour of sending a representative to Lhasa, (whether temporarily or permanently I am not quite clear), of authorising him to offer arms to the Lhasa Government and generally of taking a strong line to safeguard the autonomy and territorial integrity of Tibet.

The Foreign Office are rather aghast at the apparent indifference to treaty obligations which this may be held to involve; they are disposed to think that the perils of the local situation have been exaggerated, and they do not want to raise the question in a form that might on the one hand alienate China and on the other give a handle to Japan.

Sooner than do this, arbitration (on the frontier issue) has been proposed.

The only way out of these difficulties is I think to have a conference at which they shall all be thrashed out; a sort of Far Eastern Committee. I am quite agreeable.

Something turns on the local situation. At an earlier date the India Office were rather afraid about this. They feared the activities of the Kansu mission at Lhasa, and the expected aggression of the Chinese frontier forces.

11. CURZON'S MINUTE, JUNE 1920 (see p. 342) [*Contd.*

The Kansu Mission has retired, as it is thought, re infecta, and the Chinese frontier troops are reported to be required for the internal situation in China, rather than for external advance.

To this extent the situation is alleviated.

On the other hand the negotiations with China re Tibet are indefinitely suspended, and are not likely for the moment to be resumed.

There are several possible solutions. (a) the bold India Office solutions viz. an envoy at Lhasa, arms guns and the like (for which the justification appears to be hardly sufficient, (b) the arbitration solution which I do not quite like – for I would sooner settle it ourselves, (c) some intermediary plan. If action of some sort be indispensable, I am rather favourably impressed with Sir J. Jordan's suggestion, which I understand to be this. Tell both the Chinese, and, if we like, the Tibetans, that if the Chinese attempt to cross the frontier as accepted by them when they proposed to re-open the negotiations in 1913, we will arm the Tibetans to resist. Whether this policy could or should be mixed up with the question of a British representative at Lhasa I am not quite clear, nor can I find in these papers a discussion of the latter point either on its merits or on its compatibility with Treaty stipulations.

I would suggest that we send to the India Office a copy of the Foreign Office memorandum giving the history and the arguments, and of this Note from me, and that we invite them to a Conference at an early date, at which Sir J. Jordan should assist.

I agree generally with Mr Bell. The policy of 10-15 years ago - that of "sterilising" Tibet - became both wicked & foolish when Tibet showed a desire to establish relations with the outside world. The tripartite negotiations of 1913-14 were a step in the right direction, but our relations with Russia, perhaps more than Chinese unwillingness to ratify the agreement, blocked it. Then came the war, & now the situation is different. Russia is for the moment knocked out, but will shortly re-enter the ring, more dangerous than ever. China is largely dominated by Japan, & Japan is her willing to negotiate greatly interested in Tibet; it is a serious question in China that prevented the Chinese Gov.t from resuming her bound by our previous negotiations with us a year or two ago. We cannot prevent

12. HIRTZEL'S MINUTE, APRIL 1921 (see p. 364)

'I agree generally with Sir A Bell. The policy of 10-15 years ago—that of "sterilising" Tibet—became both wicked and foolish when Tibet showed a desire to establish relations with the outside world. The tripartite negotiations of 1913-14 were a step in the right direction, but our relations with Russia, perhaps more than Chinese unwillingness to ratify the agreement, blocked it. Then came the war, & now the situation is different. Russia is for the moment knocked out, but will surely re-enter the ring, more dangerous than ever. China is largely dominated by Japan, & Japan is greatly interested in Tibet: it was a Japanese agitation in China that prevented the Chinese Govt from resuming negotiations with us a year or two ago. We cannot prevent Tibet from getting help from Japan, or from the Bolsheviks if they succeed in penetrating, as they threaten to do. [Contd.

'It seems to me that everything is in favour of recognising the de facto autonomy of Tibet.

'If the Chinese had been willing to negotiate we should no doubt have been bound by our previous admissions as to the Chinese position. They

Is there any sense in liberating Tibet from China only to let it fall under the influence of one or other of two powers irreconcilably hostile to Gt. Britain's position in Asia? & can we afford to do so?

'I do not under-rate the formal difficulty to which Mr. Wakely refers, but it does not seem to me insuperable. It is true that we have recognised that Tibet is part of Chinese territory & under Chinese suzerainty. But since we first did so, the Tibetans have ejected the Chinese & the Chinese have been unable to restore their authority. It is true, again, that the tripartite agreement reflected our recognition of the Chinese position. But have not been willing & for ten years the Tibetans have maintained de facto autonomy, practical independence. Surely that is good enough for us. If we are longer bound by what seems a mere formal scruple in all probability it will not be China—in whose interests we profess to respect it—but Japan and Russia who will profit.'

[Contd.

Ferrard 8.4.21

the essence of the present position is the refusal of the Chinese to ratify that agreement or even negotiate a new one. They cannot have it both ways. It is open to us, it seems to me, to recognise Tibetan independence at any moment, & at least people who believe in the foolish catch-word "self determination" could not complain.

'The objection to resuming negotiations with China lies in the present condition of the country. The Chinese Govt exercises no control over the Govts of Yunnan & Szechuan. The Chinese Govt might ratify the tripartite agreement tomorrow, but that wd. not ease the situation on the Sino-

[Contd.

situation on the Sino-Tibetan frontier, & there wd. be a risk that the Tibetans wd. round on us.

We shall presumably soon receive the views of the F. of I. There are signs that the Foreign Dept. favours the laissez aller policy of Sir H. Grant, & it is perhaps unfortunate that Reading sd. have to take up this question so soon after his arrival. For that reason I do not suggest that we telegraph for the G. of I.'s views, though it is desirable to arrive at a decision soon.

R[...]

A. H. 7.4.21

Tibetan frontier & there wd. be a risk that the Tibetans wd. round on us.
'We shall presumably soon receive the views of the G[overnment] of I[ndia]. There are signs that the Foreign Dept. favours the *laissez faire* policy of Sir H Grant, & it is perhaps unfortunate that Lord Reading sd. have to take up this question so soon after his arrival. For that reason I do not suggest that we telegraph for the G of I's views though it is desirable to arrive at a decision soon.'

Your Excellency,

The National Assembly of Tibet, including representatives of Drepung, Sera, Ghetan Monasteries and the monk and lay officials of the Government and of the people of Tibet beg to inform Your Excellency that with reference to the settlement of the Sino-Tibetan boundary question the Chief Ministers of Tibet had fully put our case before Lieut. Col. J.L.R. Weir, Political Officer in Sikkim, during his recent visit to Lhasa and as asked in our previous note shall be much obliged if Your Excellency could arrange the following :-

(1) The Simla convention of 1914 between China and Tibet to be immediately concluded.

(2) Convene a meeting of the representatives of China and Tibet and the British Government act as an intermediary power.

(3) Lieut. Col. J.L.R. Weir be appointed as one of the representatives of the British Government to sit on the conference as he is acquainted with the full facts of the case.

Please assist us by representing the above matter very strongly to His Majesty's Government so as to bring about the immediate fulfilment of our desire.

Sending herewith a scarf of greeting, dated 9th of the 10th Tibetan month of the Water Monkey year.

Seal (of the three great monasteries and that of the officials and people of Tibet).

According to official reports from Lhasa, the paymaster attached to the advance party of the Chinese mission wished to present a seal and title to the late Dalai Lama from the Chinese Government. The Tibetan National Assembly considered the offer but declined it on the ground that the seal might suggest that Tibet was subordinate to China and that the title was in any case of doubtful value since the Dalai Lama was dead.

The Assembly may also have had in mind the rather similar favours conferred by Chinese Imperial decree in 1908 immediately before the invasion from Szechwan leading up to the occupation of Lhasa.

"ENSURER OF COMFORT"

The present mission was not deterred by the refusal, however, and, on its arrival in Lhasa, Huang Mu-sung, its leader, placarded the streets with the following notice:—

"The precious Dalai Lama, Ruler of the Kingdom, immeasurable in mercy, omniscient ensurer of comfort of all sentient beings, having departed from this world, I, Tron Hri, have been specially deputed to make religious offerings for his benefit and am at the same time empowered to issue the following notification on behalf of my Government:—

"In every respect the relations between the five nations of the Empire are like those of the members of a family. The thirteenth incarnation of the Dalai Lama, who was the dispenser of mercy and the efficient ruler of the Snowy Kingdom, had appeared among us. The effects of his 3,000 different kinds of good deeds had spread among all living beings. He was the protector of the kingdom and the saviour of all sentient beings—gods and all human beings bowing down before him and offering oblations. The Government, taking all the good qualities of the Dalai Lama into consideration, made everything prosperous and happy in the West. The five nations unanimously desired that comfort, prosperity, happiness, and glory should be secured to the Empire.

"While this was going on the precious being took his departure from this world, an event which has brought mourning to all. But the actual personality of the protector and omniscient one has not disappeared. It is still visible, like the dewdrops of the Yen Tara flower. It is therefore most fervently hoped that his reincarnation should appear very soon and that he should again guide the destiny of the Buddhist faith. This should be borne in mind by all the Tibetan people, lay and clergy. In deference to the wishes of the Chinese Government, all possible religious ceremonies should be performed. Reliance should be placed on the Chinese Government, who can ensure the comfort and happiness of all for ever."

THE FIVE NATIONS

This reference to the five nations—Chinese, Manchus, Mongols, Mohamedans, and Tibetans—has renewed memories of China's repeated insistence on the equality and unity of this "family" at a time when unity is being impressed by unequal and unfamilylike methods. Nor has it escaped notice that the terms of Huang Mu-sung's proclamation and his gentle hint of Chinese authority over Tibet are faintly reminiscent of the language applied to the same Dalai Lama in the Imperial decree of 1908, 15 months before the Chinese temporarily deposed him in another proclamation which called him "proud, extravagant, lewd, slothful, vicious, perverse without parallel, violent, disorderly, and disobedient towards the Imperial commands."

14. REPORT IN THE *Times*, SEPTEMBER 1934, (see p. 404)

A Mission to Lhasa

The Chinese have long and deservedly enjoyed a high reputation for tact and courtesy, those social virtues which are currently described as diplomatic, and adorn the best professional diplomatists. It is true that, like HOMER, Mandarins sometimes nodded; that the dignity of their attitude towards the representatives of barbarous foreign Powers, or of ungrateful subjects, was sometimes marred by fatuity, as when envoys of independent States were bidden to perform the "kowtow," and when regions which had long passed out of Chinese control were blandly claimed as provinces of the Celestial Empire. Still these errors could be ascribed to the defects of the defunct Imperial régime, and it was believed that the diplomatists of the Republic would always imitate the best European and American models. The latest news from Lhasa, however, will disappoint these expectations. Undeterred by the effects of a similar error during the negotiations which followed the close of the European War, HUANG MU-SUNG, Chinese Special Commissioner to Tibet, has appealed to the Tibetan people over the heads of the National Assembly, their *de facto* Government since the DALAI LAMA'S death. He had been sent by Nanking to attend the memorial services for the late pontiff and to negotiate for the resumption of the diplomatic relations between Tibet and China which were broken off in 1911. The strange story of his recent efforts to influence the Tibetans to accept Chinese authority over their country is told to-day by our Simla Correspondent. The paymaster attached to his mission offered to present the deceased DALAI LAMA, who, his followers believe, is watching spiritually over them between his reincarnations, with a Chinese seal and title. The National Assembly declined the offer, which savoured of a claim to Chinese sovereignty. Undeterred by their refusal, HUANG MU-SUNG caused a proclamation to be published in which a panegyric of the late DALAI LAMA was artfully compounded with an invitation to the Tibetans to join the family of "five nations"—Chinese, Manchus, Mongols, Moslems, and Tibetans—and rely upon the Chinese Government, " who can ensure the comfort and happiness of all for ever."

The notables of Tibet, however, had not forgotten their history. They remembered that the Chinese Government described the same DALAI LAMA in similar terms in 1908 and not long afterwards accused him of being "lewd," "slothful, . . . disorderly and disobedient towards the Imperial commands," after which they sent a military expedition to Lhasa, and drove him to seek refuge in India. But in 1911 the Chinese Revolution broke out, the Chinese troops in Lhasa were expelled, the DALAI LAMA returned from India, and British intervention prevented further Chinese attacks. The British Government, which had undertaken not to annex Tibetan territory, urged the Chinese Republic to come to an agreement on the Tibetan question, and tripartite negotiations were opened at Simla in the autumn of 1913. The British attempted to bring about a compromise between the political and territorial claims of Lhasa and Peking. A draft convention was initialled, only to be repudiated by the Chinese Government, and so until last month Chinese and Tibetans cut one another dead diplomatically and occasionally cut one another down on their disputed frontier. The Chinese envoy's attempt to induce the Tibetans to play "happy families" has invited a rebuff, but it would be regrettable if his failure in tact revived border warfare on the Sino-Tibetan marches.

The boundary between India and Tibet was laid down in 1914 at the Simla Conference between the British, Chinese and Tibetans during that year: please see the Convention of 3rd July, 1914, and the map attached to it (flagged at the bottom of the file).

Just on the Indian side of the line and adjoining Bhutan is the district of Tawang. Paragraph iv(4) of Sir H. McMahon's Memorandum on the Tibet Conference (see Flag 'A') refers to this district.

In that paragraph Sir H. McMahon refers to the desirability of putting the Tawang district, now that it was definitely inside India, on a satisfactory basis. This was never done; principally, it appears, because the Chinese never ratified the Convention and it was desired not to draw too much attention to its existence for fear of embroiling ourselves in a/unnecessary controversy with the Chinese. Indeed, there is a very large tract of unadministered territory between the administrative border of Assam and the international frontier with Tibet. (There is also a similar tract between the administrative border of Burma and the international frontier with the Chinese Province of Hsi Kang).

At Tawang there is a Tibetan Monastery. The Monastery collects various kinds of revenue for religious purposes from the surrounding country, and there can be no question of interfering with this arrangement. In addition, however, to the dues collected by the Monastery, it appears that the Tibetan Government carry on some sort of administration in the district and collect revenues for purely civil purposes. It is obviously undesirable that this should happen on the British side of the line, and it is proposed

15. MINUTE BY CLAUSON, AUGUST 1936 (see p. 417) [*Contd.*

by the Government of India that Mr. Gould should raise the matter with the Tibetan Government during his present visit to Lhasa.

At the same time it is suggested that he should obtain from the Tibetan Government a written reaffirmation of the 1914 frontier. It appears from the second and third enclosures to the Government of India letter of 17th August now submitted (see Flags 'B') that there is no question but that the Tibetan Government still recognise this frontier, as they specifically said so in connection with a recent protest which they made against Mr. Kingdon Ward's illicit expedition into Tibet, and it is perhaps doubtful whether it is really essential to secure a written reaffirmation from them. There would obviously be advantage, however, in doing so if Mr. Gould can do it without serious difficulty.

A draft telegram approving the Government of India's recommendations is submitted. The telegram is worded in such a way as somewhat to tone down the recommendations. Mr. Gould has rather delicate business to transact with the Tibetan Government while he is in Lhasa, and it seems undesirable to encourage him to be aggressive with the Tibetans over this frontier question as to which we know they see eye to eye with us.

There is a further suggestion in the Government of India's letter for a protest to the Chinese Government in connection with the Indo-chinese part of the frontier, but this is of no immediate urgency and may be left over for the moment. It is desirable to clear up the question affecting Mr. Gould's conversation with the Tibetans as he has already arrived in Lhasa.

MY DEAR TWYNAM,

Many thanks for your demi-official letter No. 23, dated the 3rd April 1939, on the subject of Tawang, which I read with much interest. As I told you in my letter of the 24th March, I was already considering the matter when your letter of the 17th March reached me and I had arrived at conclusion very similar to your own on the matter of Tawang. I have since then had the various points raised in your letter of the 17th March examined in the External Affairs Department and although I do not think that there is any reason to suppose that we are on insecure ground with regard to our Treaty rights, I fully agree with you that from the practical point of view there is no advantage and considerable risk in pressing the matter further with the Tibetan Government. The Secretary of State has shown some interest in the matter and I have therefore found it necessary to address him on the subject before a final decision is reached as to our future course of action. I trust, however, that he will agree with me that we should not take any further action at present to press the Tibetan Government with regard to Tawang. You will of course be informed officially in due course of the decision made in consultation with the Secretary of State.

2. You have recommended in your letter of April 3rd that we should attempt to establish a control area up to the Tawang Digien river in order to protect the Monbas from the depredations of the Akas who live on their borders. I realise that there would in ordinary times be much to be said for this proposal, but in present financial and world circumstances, I do not feel justified in committing the Government of India to any course of action which does not involve interests of really vital importance. I cannot therefore agree to any such scheme at present. I have also considered your proposal to allow Lightfoot to undertake a tour in the Dirang Dzong area with a small escort of Assam Rifles. This also I have been compelled to negative, because I feel that a very small force of this kind would be able to effect nothing of permanent benefit and might become involved in operations, which would be a serious embarrassment at the present time. I hope that you will not feel that I have been unsympathetic towards your proposals or unmindful of the responsibilities which we have in that area.

Yours sincerely,
LINLITHGOW.

16. LINLITHGOW TO TWYNAM, APRIL 1939 (see p. 444)

17. The reason why no reference was made to Twynam's proposal, which you mentioned in paragraph 15 of your letter of 25th July, to establish the frontier ultimately in the neighbourhood of the Se La and the Digien River was that he has not yet put it forward officially. My view is that there is much to be said for his proposal both on general and financial grounds, particularly as he thinks that a boundary on the Se La line would only cost about one-fourth of the expenditure estimated to be necessary, if we were to decide eventually to go right up to the McMahon Line and include Tawang. The present position is that following your Express Letter of the 13th July, we have asked Twynam to hold his hand for a year after which the whole matter will be reviewed. Meanwhile from subsequent reports received from Twynam it seems possible that it is more urgent to push forward further east on the line of the Lower Siang River (the Brahmaputra), where Tibetan influence shows signs of extending into areas which are purely tribal on an easy line of approach to the borders of Assam.

17. LINLITHGOW TO ZETLAND, 24 AUGUST 1939 (see p. 445)

Chapter 23

Towards a Second Simla Convention, April-June 1914

THE INTERVAL between the first Simla Convention of 27 April and the second on 3 July was, if partly, filled up by two major developments. All through May, and the early part of June, there were the hectic, if fevered, negotiations in St. Petersburg to make the Tsar's government accept modifications in the Anglo-Russian Convention of 1907, necessitated by a now completely changed political situation. Sazonov, however, demanded too high a price and, unwilling to oblige, the British, by mid-June, abandoned the *pourparlers*. In the meanwhile, after repudiating Ivan Chen, the Chinese were making a herculean effort to debunk McMahon and persuade his principals to agree to a change of venue—to London or Peking. The British Plenipotentiary, however, hoping against hope that he may still succeed in carrying Peking with him, was willing to make the Lonchen accept a major territorial concession by substituting the Kunlun for the Altyn Tagh as Tibet's northern boundary.

It did not avail. The Chinese, never easy to deal with, proved singularly unyielding on the boundary question. What was more, a broad enough hint was dropped that if the British did not give way, the railway and mining concessions which they were then feverishly negotiating in the Yangtse valley may prove abortive. Jordan, hypersensitive to what he deemed the copingstone of a lifetime, and supremely indifferent to Indian interests, was shaken and staged what looked like a complete *volte face*. McMahon, strongly backed by Hardinge, however, stood his ground and basing himself upon such intelligence as was garnered by intercepting Lu Hsing-chi's exchanges with Peking or his own conversations with Ivan Chen (who after 27 April appears to have been at a discount with his own government), concluded that the Chinese were playing at a game of bluff. The best way to call it, he argued, would be to sign with Tibet. Peking would then fall in line, and sooner than expected. The key to the final round of the Simla Conference thus lay in McMahon's persistent demand that the Convention be concluded by a definite date—*with* China and Tibet, if possible; *without* China, but with Tibet, if necessary.

As has been noticed, on the day the Convention was initialled at Simla, in the teeth of what McMahon had called Ivan Chen's 'most vigorous resistance to any final settlement', the British Plenipotentiary had strongly urged upon Whitehall to hasten 'the date of signature'. This would not only accord with the wishes of the Lonchen, who understandably dreaded the heat of India's plains, but avoid any risk of 'premature disclosures' that might cause 'embarrassment ', more so as conversations with St. Petersburg were likely to prove ' somewhat prolonged '. He did, therefore, press the ' advantage ' of an early signature, and of bridging the interval, between signature and enforcement, through a provision for ratification. For his part, there would be no delay, for the triple texts ' could be made ready for signature ' by 7 May, followed by ratifications on a tripartite basis in London ' as early as may be convenient '.[1]

His zeal notwithstanding, there was a fly in the ointment, for McMahon had presumed too much. It may be recalled that on 29 April—two days after the initialling—Peking disavowed the action of its Plenipotentiary which it declared ' to be null and void ', albeit it was willing to continue the ' amicable negotiations '.

It is true that Peking's disavowal did not come as a surprise to McMahon and yet it made an early signature impossible; as it happened, more than eight weeks were to elapse before the draft Convention, modified in some details, was signed by the British and the Tibetans, to the exclusion of the Chinese. And all this while China, and the Chinese, dominated the scene.

McMahon's explanation for Chinese action was two-fold. Primarily, he suspected, it was Lu Hsing-chi's spies, on Chen's staff, who had prevailed upon Peking to disavow the Chinese Plenipotentiary's action. Secondly, and of greater import, was Peking's ' proverbial disinclination ' to meet final issues.

The British Plenipotentiary's mind, however, was made up. Everything that could be abandoned, he noted, ' without injustice to Tibet and detriment to ourselves ', had been conceded to propitiate Peking. Moreover he had

reason to believe that the Chinese have, as a result of the Conference, obtained everything which they really require and far more than they had originally expected.

In the circumstances, therefore, he ' most earnestly ' hoped that HMG will stick to the accomplished fact of the initialled convention as ' the only satisfactory ' settlement on a tripartite basis that was really possible.[2] Two things, however, were by now abundantly clear. One, that the Chinese accepted without much ado the whole Convention barring Article IX, relating to the boundary settlement between Inner and Outer Tibet. Two, they were not prepared to take the responsibility for bringing the negotiations to an end.

In Whitehall, where Chinese delaying tactics were not unknown, some formula was being devised whereby the notes at the end of the Convention would be treated as integral parts of it.[3] McMahon had suggested that the Convention and the schedule be followed immediately by the notes which, in

---

[1] Viceroy to Secretary of State, telegram, 27 April 1914, No. 260 in *Foreign*, October 1914, Procs. 134–396.

[2] Viceroy to Secretary of State, telegram, 29 April 1914, No. 265 in Ibid.

[3] Secretary of State to Viceroy, telegram, 4 May 1914, No. 277 in Ibid.

turn, were followed by the initials themselves.⁴ This view was later endorsed by the British Foreign Office which, even though it would have preferred the addition of a clause that the notes ' shall be regarded as an integral part of the Convention ', presumed nonetheless that ' if exchanged ' these would be considered equally binding and treated as ' annexes '.⁵ Just about this time, early in May, McMahon had learnt from ' confidential channels ' that the Chinese were showing ' signs of alarm ' at the impasse, feared lest the British should make some arrangement with Tibet ' independently ' of them and, after ascertaining ' the actual situation ', were determined to prolong the negotiations.⁶

A great deal of controversy has centred around the fact that on 27 April, the Convention was initialled, *not* signed. It may be useful to recall in this context that, on 16 April, McMahon had suggested that it

> would be much to our advantage if on the date of signature, the Convention could come into force immediately....I think it would be wise to provide specially for tripartite ratification after a period of three months, should it not be possible to instruct me to make provision for the operation of the Convention as from the date of signature.⁷

This view was endorsed by Lord Crewe at the India Office. It was Grey, however, who put his foot down and insisted that

> the Convention shall only be initialled now if an agreement is reached and that the signature should be deferred until the Russian Government have been informed and have signified their assent to such portions of the Convention as affect the Anglo-Russian Convention of 1907.⁸

Accordingly, on 21 April, Crewe told the Viceroy that

> signature to Convention must be deferred pending reference to Russia, but Sir H McMahon may initial it as amended whenever his colleagues are prepared to do the same.⁹

⁴Viceroy to Secretary of State, telegram, 6 May 1914, No. 278 in Ibid. McMahon was in favour of retaining what had already been done 'because Tibet and China might be tempted to suggest redrafting of other articles ' if any alterations were made in the text.
⁵*F O* to *I O*, 19 May 1914, No. 323 in Ibid. Also *I O* to *F O*, 11 May 1914, No. 311, and Secretary of State to Viceroy, telegram, 22 May 1914, No. 289, both in Ibid.
⁶Viceroy to Secretary of State, 10 May 1914, No. 279 in Ibid. Should Ivan Chen ' on his own ' raise the issue, the Viceroy told Whitehall, McMahon proposed to keep his own counsel and ' be particularly reticent concerning Tibet.'
⁷Viceroy to Secretary of State, telegram, 16 April 1914, No. 247 in Ibid. McMahon had good reason to suggest this owing to ' the vacillation and weakness of Tibet' and China's ' evident determination ' to resist ratification on a tripartite basis.
⁸*F O* to *I O*, 21 April 1914, No. 284 in Ibid.
⁹Secretary of State to Viceroy, 21 April 1914, No. 250 in *Foreign*, October 1914, Procs. 134–396.

Thus it was in deference to Whitehall that the initialling took place on 27 April. And once this happened, McMahon stoutly resisted any alteration in its text. As has been noticed earlier, he was opposed to altering Article X, and for much the same reason: it would afford China an opportunity to reopen negotiations *de novo*.

Delhi's objections to the cancellation of Article X were, it may be recalled, over-ruled in London which suggested that its altered version be commended to the Chinese as ' more favourable ' to their Government and ' less suggestive ' of British ' tutelage '. In India, however, the problem was much more intractable for Ivan Chen's confidence had been shaken by the strictures of his Government while the disclosure of British negotiations with Russia added to his ' embarrassment '. In no position to take ' any further decisive step ', he

> informed the British Plenipotentiary confidentially that the Chinese Government are awaiting some definite indication of policy from London before issuing further instructions to him and without receipt of these in a categorical form he will take no further action; he added that the Chinese Government were evidently alarmed by the evasive answers of the Foreign Office and by the prolonged delay and evidently suspected that the British Government were concluding an independent arrangement with the Tibetan authorities.

Hence, in a telegram to the Secretary of State on 27 May, India argued that the proposed communication regarding the modified Article X must be made in London—not in Simla. A draft reply was spelt out which laid stress on the finality of conclusions already reached, and made it clear that no ' further alterations ' could be made either in the text or in the map—barring Article X. The best the Chinese could do, therefore, was to sign the Convention, as initialled. Or else, the British and the Tibetans would do so ' independently ', in which case the text would ' necessarily ' be modified to meet the requirements of a ' dual arrangement '. Should Peking, however, prove recalcitrant and

> decline to participate in the signature of the document which in itself will conclude the Conference and persist in their dissentient attitude the Chinese will naturally be debarred from the privileges contemplated by the Tripartite Convention.[10]

Two things are significant. One, a deadline—1 June, in this case—was introduced for the first time. This is the more remarkable in that the telegram suggesting it could not have reached London before 28 May. Two, the threat of signing without China, and of barring it from privileges that accrued to her under the Convention's terms, as also the finality of the agreement already reached, were heavily underlined. With minor modifications here and there, India persisted in this course of action and finally made HMG agree.

[10]Viceroy to Secretary of State, telegram, 27 May 1914, No. 291 in Ibid.

The first to enter a protest, however veiled, against going it alone with Tibet was Jordan. He stressed the fact that Chinese objections applied 'exclusively' to adjustment of 'boundary arrangements' and

> rather than face prospects of an independent arrangement between us and Tibetans they will probably agree to sign, but they will do so with a bad grace and resultant feeling of soreness will tend to impair efficacious settlement and is certain to react *very unfavourably on our negotiations regarding railway and mining concessions*.[11]

Here then was the problem: Jordan's eyes were set less on the Himalayas and the defence of India's frontiers, on Chamdo and of maintaining the integrity of Tibet against Chinese onslaughts as on *railway and mining concessions* which he was then negotiating. As has been pointed out earlier, Hardinge did, in the final stages, protest strongly against this attitude, but to no apparent purpose.

Around 1 June, McMahon had gleaned some useful information from 'confidential sources'. He learnt *inter alia* that the Chinese Plenipotentiary's departure from Simla was being postponed to demonstrate that, 'from first to last', it had not been China's intention to 'break off' negotiations. He (Ivan Chen) had also been directed to spy out if an 'independent' agreement had been reached by the Tibetan and British Plenipotentiaries.

McMahon, even though he had viewed Jordan's reports from Peking as 'unsatisfactory', held out no hope, for he had

> no further boundary concession to propose...(besides) the evacuation of Chiamdo by the Chinese is regarded by the Tibetan Government indeed as the direct *quid pro quo* for readmission of Amban to Lhasa and they consider that it affords the only hope of finality to the present chaotic situation in Eastern Tibet.

Apart from early signature by Britain and Tibet—' say, by 4th June '—he would ' warn ' China

> that we are prepared to give active assistance to Tibet in maintaining the integrity of her frontier and her autonomy.[12]

Here was a significant addition to what McMahon had proposed a few days earlier, and it is not without nothing that, in its reply, Whitehall forbade any 'further action'. In any case, 4 June was ruled out as the deadline and the

---

[11] Jordan to Grey, telegram, 31 May 1914, No. 296 in Ibid.
[12] Viceroy to Secretary of State, telegram, 1 June 1914, No. 298 in Ibid.
' In view ' of what was impending, McMahon used his ' personal influence ' to make the Lonchen postpone his departure, initially set for 1 June, ' for a few days ',

Viceroy's comments were invited as to the form 'active assistance' to Tibet was to take.[13]

Meanwhile in London, the Secretary of State was fighting the Viceroy's, and McMahon's, battles. On 3 June, the day he telegraphed to India, he urged upon Sir Edward Grey

> that no settlement of the Tibet question, compatible with the interests of HMG and the just claims of Tibet, is likely to prove otherwise than unacceptable to the *amour propre* of the Chinese. In these circumstances, Sir J Jordan's apprehensions may, in his opinion, be to a large extent discounted, as inherent in any satisfactory solution of the present difficulty....But in view of the fact that, after four years of grave disturbance in Tibet, a settlement is at last within sight, and having regard to the strong objections to which all alternative courses are open...(the proposed communication to the Chinese Government) should be made without further delay.[14]

Grey concurred and undertook that if the Chinese still refused to sign, he would approach the Russian Government again and obtain their consent to signature by the 'British and Tibetan Plenipotentiaries alone'.[15]

The Memorandum enclosed in the Foreign Office note of 8 June to Peking made slight textual modifications in the one proposed by the Viceroy on 27 May. Two omissions, however, are important. One, no deadline was laid for the proposed signatures on the Convention, although the Tibetan Plenipotentiary was expected to leave 'in a few days'. Two, no warning about the proposed 'active assistance' to Tibet, in the event of the Chinese holding out, was sounded.[16]

Instructing Jordan to present the proposed note 'as soon as possible', Grey intimated that as the Chinese seemed to be under 'some misapprehension' both as to the exact terms of the Convention, and as to the boundaries laid down at Simla, he

> may, if you see fit, give further explanations and show them, if necessary, with the map, the large concessions which were made at the last moment with a view to meeting their objections.[17]

[13]Secretary of State to Viceroy, telegram, 3 June 1914, No. 299 in Ibid.

[14]On 28 May, on receipt of the Viceroy's telegram of the preceding day, the Secretary of State appears to have written to the Foreign Office, urging the action proposed. Referred to in *I O* to *F O*, 3 June 1914, No. 358 in Ibid.

[15]*F O* to *I O*, 3 June 1914, No. 359 in Ibid.

[16]India Office concurred in the proposed modifications and the amended memorandum was presented to the Wai-chiao-pu on 7 June, and to the Chinese Minister in London on 5 June 1914. For details see *I O* to *F O*, 4 June 1914, No. 360; Encl. in *F O* to *I O*, 8 June 1914, No. 361; and Jordan to Grey, 7 June 1914, No. 302, all in Ibid.

[17]Grey to Jordan, telegram, 5 June 1914, No. 367 in Ibid.

Jordan did not 'see fit'. He had already explained the 'boundary concession' and felt that any 'further explanation' would be 'open to misconstruction', apart from being regarded as an invitation to discuss the whole question *de novo*.

It is interesting to note that on the day the above directive was issued to Jordan, George Buchanan in St. Petersburg was informed too about HMG's willingness to accept an exchange of notes, 'both public and secret', with Russia regarding Articles VI and VIII of the tripartite Convention, for

> Your Excellency (Buchanan) may immediately proceed to an exchange of notes embodying this arrangement, if it proves satisfactory to the Russian Government.[18]

As it turned out, negotiations with Sazonov proved barren of results while Sun Pao-chi, his Chinese counterpart in Peking, dragged his weary feet before any conclusive step could be taken. Yet, in the first week of June at any rate, HMG appeared to be determined to bring matters to a head.

Jordan, as has been briefly noticed, was reluctant to broach the subject with Peking. In his reply to Grey on 9 June, he expressed the view that a repetition of 'verbal explanations' would detract from the force of a written declaration made under the authority of HMG and would be construed as an 'indication' of weakness:

> the result would be either a repetition of request for the continuance of negotiations in India or a demand for a rectification of frontier, as a condition of signature.

In either case, his 'intervention' would not have 'improved' the situation.[19]

Jordan, it is thus clear, was not willing to oblige. Yet in Simla the Lonchen, who dreaded the heat of India's plains and was 'urgently wanted' at home, was becoming 'restless'. McMahon, therefore, pressed for an early date, 'say the 15th instant'—his telegram was dated 12 June—on which, 'in default' of Chinese cooperation, Britain and Tibet would 'sign the Convention'.[20]

It was at this stage, 13 June, that the Chinese presented Jordan their memorandum containing fresh proposals. Apart from the boundary, China's position in Inner Tibet, as the Dalai Lama's in Outer Tibet, was sought to be defined. At the interview at the Wai-chiao-pu it was emphasised that even though

---

[18]Secretary of State to Viceroy, telegram, 8 June 1914, No. 363 in Ibid. The Secretary of State intimated that Buchanan 'was instructed' on 6 June whereas the telegram to Jordan had been despatched a day earlier (viz., 5 June).

[19]Jordan to Grey, telegram, 9 June 1914, No. 314 in Ibid. *Inter alia*, Jordan had intimated that, 'if it was still desired', he was ready to do 'his utmost' to remove Chinese objections.

[20]Viceroy to Secretary of State, telegram, 12 June 1914, No. 316 in Ibid.

no Parliament existed at the moment it was still necessary to consider Chinese public opinion and the President did not wish to give a handle to the party of disorder in China.

The text of the Memorandum itself made it clear that the 'concessions' now proffered were 'really' the outcome of 'great hardship and intense bitterness' under which China had been compelled to suffer in her desire to compromise.

Jordan's considered view was that, contrary to the fanfare of publicity, the so-called concessions represented 'practically no advance' beyond those of 21 April, and that he was *not* prepared to recommend them for HMG's 'favourable' consideration.[21] These views were fully shared by India which felt strongly that HMG 'should decline' to accept 'any' of 'the present' Chinese proposals. Further, it sought authorisation to sign the Convention on the 18th *with*, or *without* China, for

> position of affairs regarding Convention in Peking appears exactly similar to that obtaining in Simla during the week preceding the initialling of Convention on 27th April and appears to require similar treatment to ensure settlement.[22]

The Secretary of State lent countenance to India's suggestion, declared Chinese proposals 'wholly unacceptable', and endorsed 18 June as the date for the signature of the Convention. He was nonetheless keen that Peking be assured that while the Convention would leave it 'free' to maintain and consolidate its present position in Inner Tibet

> the condition imposed by Article 2 viz., that the area shall not be converted into Chinese province does no more than secure the continuance of the status which it has always enjoyed, and which the Chinese Government has in the past disclaimed any intention of altering.[23]

On 17 June, McMahon informed Whitehall that the Chinese viewed the transmission of their proposals of 13 June as an 'expression of willingness' on the part of HMG to reopen negotiations. And this despite the fact that he had informed Chen

> on the 16th June, in reply to his urgent enquiries, that such a course was impossible and that instructions to sign on 18th June were expected by me.

---

[21] 'Translation of a telegram from Wai-chiao-pu to the Chinese Minister in London', 14 June 1914, No. 390 in Ibid. For the interview with Sun Pao-chi, Jordan to Grey, telegram, 16 June 1914, Encl. 1, No. 373 in Ibid.

[22] Viceroy to Secretary of State, telegram, 14 June 1914, No. 319 in *Foreign*, October 1914, Procs. 134–396.

[23] *I O* to *F O*, 15 June 1914, No. 362 in Ibid.

I, therefore, pressed him to obtain explicit orders from the Chinese Government. This message has apparently caused anxiety in Peking and I consider the moment for definite action is opportune.

To McMahon's plea, Hardinge added his own powerful endorsement and thought it ' most desirable ' to terminate what he called ' this policy of procrastination ' on the part of China.[24]

18 June, however, spent itself out quietly, except that in a fresh ' message ' McMahon proposed a new dead-line: 22 June.[25] It was a propitious day for the Tibetans, McMahon intimated, and one likely to impress the Chinese. From ' confidential sources ' he had learnt that Ivan Chen had received a telegraphic communication from his government stipulating that he was not to take responsibility for signing ' without fresh instructions ' which would be conditional upon a formal reply to Peking's proposals of 13 June. As has been pointed out, McMahon held the view that China thought the British were ' bluffing ' and that if it were ' undeceived ' on this point by a ' decisive ' reply, it would climb down and ' consent ' to sign. As for the Secretary of State's explicit warning ' not to sign ' unless China did too,

> no real necessity for dual settlement from which China would be excluded has ever been anticipated by me and my intention was to use it only as a stimulus.[26]

Jordan, as has been noticed earlier, had refuted the suggestion that there had been either any ' anxiety ' or ' change of attitude ' in Peking and underlined the fact that the President himself was handling the question. Further, he pooh-poohed McMahon's territorial concessions of 27 April, and suggested, if indirectly, that Kokonor should form part of China, as also Litang and Batang.

To pull any weight against Jordan, the all-powerful British Minister in Peking, would not have been an easy task at any time. It was rendered doubly more difficult when ' concessions and mining leases in China', then being negotiated with Yuan Shih-kai's shaky republic, were weighed heavily in the balance against the barren wastes of Kokonor, or Tibet or the defence of India's frontiers for that matter. The Viceroy's plea therefore, however strongly worded it may have been, could not have cut much ice or made any impact at the Foreign Office.[27]

Significant and perhaps eloquent of Jordan's strength, and to that extent of India's weakness, was McMahon's 23 June concession, on the territorial

---

[24] Viceroy to Secretary of State, telegram, 17 June 1914, No. 325 in Ibid.
[25] Viceroy to Secretary of State, telegram, 18 June 1914, No. 327 in Ibid.
[26] Secretary of State to Viceroy, telegram, 18 June 1914, No. 326 in Ibid.
[27] ' A glance at Major Robertson's memorandum will show that the region known as the Chang Tang and the country between the Kunlun and the Altyn Tagh to the west of the

question. This was designed partly to mitigate the Foreign Office opposition to a separate Convention with Tibet and the Secretary of State's apparent discomfiture in not being able to find any ' alternative suggestion '.²⁸ Nor could India think of one ' fair to Tibet or honourable ' to itself. As a consequence,

> if a decisive reply in the negative be given to the recent Chinese representation and they be confronted with the alternative of signing the Convention or of seeing us conclude it independently of them, I feel confident that the Chinese Government will be induced to sign.

While Hardinge did not rule out the possibility of the Chinese standing out—' until we have actually signed ' with Tibet—he was sure that they would not do it for long as

> the contingency of their allowing themselves to be excluded from the tripartite Convention seems so very remote that I trust full discretion may be allowed... to sign with Tibet, should this prove necessary, independently of China.

' Prolonged inaction ' at Simla, argued the Governor-General in his telegram of 21 June, had strengthened the Chinese in their belief that Russian objections were restricting Britain's freedom of action and that the latter was ' merely playing a game of bluff '.

Hardinge ended by pleading for an early date for the next, and ' conclusive ', meeting of the Conference.²⁹

Tsaidam are almost uninhabitable and little more than a barren waste of no present value to India, China or Tibet, either on strategic or economic grounds, and useful only as a neutral buffer zone '. Jordan to Grey, despatch, 16 June 1914, Encl. 1, No. 373 in Ibid.

Jordan added: ' the only portion reported by travellers to be inhabited has already been conceded to China by the decision of 27 April '. Loc. cit.

[28] Secretary of State to Viceroy, telegram, 20 June 1914, No. 329 in Ibid. Lord Crewe confessed that the F O were ' strongly averse ' to a separate convention with Tibet.

[29] Viceroy to Secretary of State, telegram, 21 June 1914, No. 330 in Ibid.

Chapter 24

The Second Simla Convention, 3 July 1914

TOWARDS THE end of June the territorial question was brought to the fore by Jordan referring again to the Conference proceedings of 27 April relating to Kokonor. It was clear beyond a doubt, although he did not state it explicitly, that he was far from satisfied with what had been done at Simla, both in regard to Kokonor as well as Litang and Batang.

The Viceroy's reaction to Jordan's opposition, both public and private, was, it may be recalled two-fold. On the one hand, he had protested strongly and argued cogently against Tibet being considered anything apart from a purely 'Indian' question; on the other, there was the offer of a substantial territorial concession to China viz., substituting the Kunlun for the Altyn Tagh as the northern boundary of Tibet. Two caveats were, however, entered. One, that this would 'materially assist' in breaking the deadlock and 'propitiate' Chinese feelings; two, that with no 'further questions' asked, it would lead to 'immediate signature' of the Convention.

That the Chinese were not propitiated was evident presently; whether Jordan was is questionable, although, on record, less evident. McMahon's concession of 23 June formed part of the Memorandum which Jordan handed to the Chinese Foreign Minister in Peking two days later. After spelling out the concessions made on 27 April, and the new one now proposed, the Memorandum made it clear that

> the patience of HMG is exhausted and they have no alternative but to inform the Chinese Government that, unless the Convention is signed before the end of the month, HMG will hold themselves free to sign separately with Tibet.

In this way a deadline, without specifying an actual date, was indicated for the first time; actually McMahon, and the Viceroy, had been continually pressing for it since early in May and had suggested, as the preceding pages bear out, specific dates all the time.

Besides, Delhi had argued that if Britain and Tibet signed and the Chinese did not, they

> will lose all privileges and advantages which the Tripartite Convention secures to them, including the recognition of their suzerainty and the return

of the Amban to Lhasa will be definitely postponed and HMG will render Tibet all possible assistance in resisting Chinese aggression.[1]

Here was endorsement, and to the hilt as it were, of McMahon's stand— of bringing things to a conclusion, promising Lhasa material assistance and calling a halt to the game of repeated Chinese procrastination.

On 29 June, the Viceroy specifically asked Whitehall if a date had been laid down ' for final action '. If not,

> we would advise that a date be fixed when the Chinese government would be informed that McMahon would be empowered to summon a final meeting of the Conference.[2]

On 30 June, Jordan telegraphed a 'summary' of Peking's written reply to the British memorandum reiterating

> its support to the majority of the articles of the Convention. The part which it is unable to agree to is that dealing with the question of boundary.

In the text of its reply, Peking made four points which were of considerable significance. *One,*

> inasmuch as the negotiations were opened between the three countries, it is still more impossible to recognise a signature of the Convention by Great Britain and Tibet *without* the concurrence of the Chinese Government.

Two, since no agreement had been reached on the territorial issue, and ' no further concession ' by Peking was possible

> it is consequently impossible for (Peking) to be coerced into signing the Convention, the reason is that it has no option in the matter.

Three,

> Although the Chinese Government does not sign the Convention...it has absolutely no desire to terminate the present negotiations....It is earnestly hoped that HMG will...continue in its original intention to act as mediator between China and Tibet.

---

[1] For the text of the Memorandum see Encl. 2 in No. 377 in *Foreign*, October 1914, Procs. 134-396.

[2] Viceroy to Secretary of State, telegram, 29 June 1914, No. 336 in Ibid. The Viceroy ' assumed ' that such a date had been ' prescribed ' in the Memorandum handed over by Jordan fn Peking and felt that matters would ' probably be accelerated by this procedure '.

And, *finally*, Peking

> has full confidence that, in view of the friendship between China and Great Britain, HMG will under no circumstances go so far as to assist Tibet, to the detriment of a friendly country.[3]

On 1 July, the Viceroy telegraphed the Secretary of State countering Chinese arguments retailed by Jordan. The main burden of his reasoning was that it would be impossible to reopen the territorial issue *de novo* and that the Tibetans would not consent to any change whatsoever, without a corresponding advantage. Since this reply summed up McMahon's position on the eve of his signing the Convention, a summary may not be out of place here.

On the territorial question, the British Plenipotentiary was emphatic that the Chinese claim conflicted with the testimony of its own officials—of Fu Sung-mu, the Chinese Warden of Marches, and of their Amban at Sining:

> The evidence of these two Chinese officers corresponds with that brought forward by the Tibetan Representative and is confirmed by a member of Lonchen Shatra's staff who has himself held office in Kokonor.

Again, the more relevant consideration was, and ought to be, McMahon argued, the 'actual conditions in Tibet'—not the historical case. The Lonchen had conceded, on behalf of his Government, the re-establishment of Chinese suzerainty, the reinstatement of a Chinese Amban at Lhasa and the cession of rich, revenue-producing districts of Nyarong and Derge—all 'valuable and material concessions'—in return for which the Chinese were required to evacuate Chamdo. More was not possible, for the Lonchen

> is convinced that the consent of his government to any further concession to China—without some corresponding advantage to Tibet—would never be obtained and he refused categorically to sign any document which contemplates any such concession.

Furthermore, the Lonchen, needed back home urgently, regarded the initialled Convention as binding and was content to place his reliance on it. However, for

> my confidential information he (Lonchen) adds...that his influence is being undermined and he fears that both his own position and the practical working of the new conditions contemplated by the treaty will be endangered by his long absence from Tibet.

---

[3]For Jordan's 'summary', see Jordan to Viceroy, telegram, dated 30 June 1914, No. 338; for the text of the Chinese reply, Encl. 2 in No. 386, both in Ibid.

Two alternatives offered themselves. One, to accept the fact that by the act of initialling 'a binding agreement' had already been concluded. Two,

> I should give to my Chinese colleague the option of signing, or of seeing conclusion of a dual agreement with the Tibetan representative.

Another suggestion McMahon made was that he himself should leave Simla as soon as the Lonchen did or else the Chinese

> would be encouraged...to hope for a dual agreement between China and Great Britain...a procedure which would directly play into their hands.

To McMahon's plea, the Viceroy added his own powerful support. Chinese 'frontier claims', he maintained, had no foundation in fact. He was also opposed to what he called 'these dual negotiations' in Peking as well as in Simla, as they offered no hope of 'finality', but only for 'interminable procrastination'. What was needed was to stress their tripartite character. Here it is important to remember that Russia too

> is now cognisant of the Convention as an initialled and accepted document and that it will, therefore, never be possible to destroy its status as a tripartite agreement. The Chinese will debar themselves from the privileges contemplated by the Convention so long as they fail to proceed to signature, but the text will be unchanged and even if the Convention remains only as initialled document, our own position will not be prejudiced in regard to Russia, whilst it will remain sufficiently satisfactory in regard to Tibet.[4]

On 2 July, the Secretary of State authorised McMahon to summon 'a final meeting' of the Conference the next day, making it clear that if the Chinese Plenipotentiary

> then refused to sign the Convention negotiations should definitely be terminated by Sir Henry. He (McMahon) should express to Tibetan Representative great regret at failure to arrive at a settlement and should also assure Lonchen Shatra that Tibet may depend on diplomatic support of HMG and on any assistance in the way of munitions of war which we can give them, if aggression on the part of China continues.[5]

---

[4] Viceroy to Secretary of State, telegram, 1 July 1914, No. 399 in Ibid.

[5] Secretary of State to Viceroy, telegram, 1 July 1914, No. 341 in Ibid. The Secretary of State referred to the Viceroy's telegram of 29 June in which the latter, without suggesting a date, had asked for authority to summon 'a final meeting' of the Conference. In his telegram of 1 July, *supra*, n. 4, the Viceroy had suggested a date—6 July—but this telegram crossed that of the Secretary of State bearing the same date.

Pursuant to the above, McMahon wrote to Ivan Chen about the proposed meeting next day emphasising that the proceedings will be of ' an absolutely conclusive ' character. He expressed the hope that Chen would sign but

> should you be unable to do so, the consequences of your failure to attach your signature have already been indicated to your Government in Peking.[6]

Even before the above communication reached him, Ivan Chen had received intimation from Peking about the final meeting of the Conference and his explicit instructions—' to attend...but to refrain from signing the Convention '. He nonetheless ' volunteered ', McMahon reported,

> on the ground that a tripartite signature would serve the best interests of China, to address a last plea to Chinese Government for permission to sign.

As for himself, McMahon had mapped out his strategy. He proposed to sign the Convention and the Trade Regulations with the Lonchen; in addition, he would sign

> a declaration to the effect that we regard the agreement as binding on us but that China will be debarred from privileges contemplated.... Purport of declaration will not be communicated to the Chinese Plenipotentiary although documents will be signed in his presence.

The objective was to ensure that the Chinese could participate in the Convention, ' as soon as they consent to sign ', and thereby preserve its ' tripartite ' character.

To the very end, McMahon was optimistic. Other things apart, Ivan Chen had ' confidentially ' informed him

> that even in the event of his (Ivan Chen's) signature being withheld tomorrow a favourable change in the attitude of the Chinese Government is likely to be produced by the actual conclusion of an independent agreement between Great Britain and Tibet.[7]

On 2 July, the Secretary of State repeated to the Viceroy the text of instructions which the Foreign Office had telegraphed to Jordan in Peking. These were, in essence, the same as contained in the Memorandum presented on

---

[6]McMahon to Ivan Chen, Simla, 2 July 1914, in *Foreign, Notes,* October 1914, Procs. 134–396.

[7]Viceroy to Secretary of State, telegram, 2 July 1914, No. 342 in *Foreign,* October 1914, Procs. 134–396. McMahon noted: ' In order to give him (Ivan Chen) every opportunity of receiving further instructions from China, I promised him that the meeting should not be held until 11 p.m.' Loc. cit.

25 June to the Chinese Minister in London. The text apart, there was an addendum marked 'Confidential':

> A broad hint will be given to Chinese by your memorandum and if they choose to ask for the modification referred to above (i.e. territorial concession regarding northern boundary of Inner Tibet) I (Grey) am, even at this late hour, prepared to try to secure it for them. You should not, however, propose it yourself or say more than that you will submit it to HMG if they (Chinese) propose it.[8]

Peking, however, had made up its mind, for its Minister in London had told the Foreign Office on 3 July that

> the Chinese Government regret very much that the proposals regarding the boundary question did not meet with their approval, and they are unable to sign the agreement as it stands.

Nor was his government willing to 'recognise' any deal that the British might enter into with Tibet, without its 'consent and approval'.[9]

On 3 July, the Viceroy received another telegram from the Secretary of State intimating that at the Conference that day McMahon should state that the 'status and boundaries' of Tibet were represented by the Convention 'as initialled' and that assurances contained with regard to Tibet (viz., diplomatic help and armed assistance) should be conveyed 'privately' to the Tibetan Plenipotentiary.[10]

Another peremptory message, which failed to influence the proceedings of the Conference, made it clear that 'separate signature' with Tibet could not be authorised by HMG.[11]

The 3 July telegram which arrived a little too late to affect the proceedings needs a word by way of explanation. Tucked somewhere in the records of the Simla Conference in the India Office in London is an interesting minute paper which reads:

> That the Secretary of State's instructions of 3 July reached Sir Henry McMahon 'too late to affect the proceedings of the conclusive meeting' was not due to any delay on the part of this office, but primarily to the fact that no one of sufficient authority to deal with the question arrived at the F O on Friday last until after 1 p.m. (approximating to 6.30 p.m. in Simla). In the circumstances, Sir Henry McMahon appears to have acted

[8]Secretary of State to Viceroy, telegram, 2 July 1914, No. 374 in Ibid.
[9]For the text of the Chinese note dated 3 July 1914, Encl. 1, No. 374 in Ibid.
[10]Secretary of State to Viceroy, telegram, 2 July 1914, No. 344 in Ibid.
[11]Secretary of State to Viceroy, telegram, 3 July 1914, No. 345 in Ibid. Also, Viceroy to Secretary of State, telegram, 4 July 1914, No. 347 in Ibid.

most judiciously, and it is submitted that his action be approved by H M's Government.[12]

It was. The lapse, it should be obvious, such as it was, did not lie at McMahon's door-step.

The Second Simla Convention, *initialled* by Great Britain and *signed* by Tibet with an accompanying ' declaration ', *signed* by the two countries, was different from the first only in respect of two textual details relating to Articles X and XI. For the rest there was no change. The terms of the declaration, however, are important as no doubt are the proceedings of this eighth, and final, meeting of the Conference.

The Conference convened at an ' unusually late ' hour—11.15 p.m.—mainly with a view to enabling Ivan Chen to receive his 'final' instructions. These, despite his best efforts, were not received in time. Those, which he had received earlier, however, were ' very explicit ' and had enjoined him ' not to sign ' the Tripartite Convention.[13]

In sharp contrast to the Chinese, the Lonchen was willing even though

> his Government did not consider the Convention satisfactory from their point of view, but as it had been accepted, there was no alternative but to sign. He was, therefore, prepared to conclude the Agreement.

McMahon made it clear that he was for ' conclusive action ', that in the absence of the Chinese, he would proceed, with the Lonchen, to sign it. This would place the document beyond the ' limits of discussion ' and ' no alteration '

---

[12]*IOR*, Political, 464/1913, parts 4-6, L/P & S/10/344. The minute paper bears no date, nor any signatures, nor initials.

Karunakar Gupta has maintained *inter alia* that on 3 July McMahon, in signing with Tibet, acted 'against both the letter and the spirit' of his instructions. This is tendentious and basically incorrect. The fact is that, on 1 July, McMahon had clearly spelt out his course of action: ' I should give my Chinese colleague the option of signing or of seeing the conclusion of a *dual* agreement with the Tibetan representative '. Again, the Viceroy's telegram of 2 July is even more explicit and sets out, in considerable detail, the procedure McMahon intended following. Besides, the instructions sent by the Foreign Office to Jordan, and repeated to India, underline the warning administered to Peking, namely that HMG would hold themselves ' free to sign the Convention separately with Tibet ', unless China followed suit ' before the end of the month'. The Secretary of State's telegram of 2 July (received on 3 July) acknowledges McMahon's earlier message of 1 July.

The fact is that it was the telegram of 3 July (received late in the evening of date) which withdrew the earlier authorisation—both explicit as well as implicit—about separate signatures with Tibet. McMahon had received it *before* he signed, but *late enough* (for him) to alter the arrangements he had worked out earlier.

For details see Nos. 339, 342, 343 and 345 in *Foreign*, October 1914, Procs. 134-396.

[13]According to Dr Sung, on 3 July both the British and the Tibetan delegates ' without consulting the Chinese Government at all' signed the draft Convention. In addition they signed the

would thereafter be possible. Meantime an additional declaration was to be signed, to which only Britain and Tibet would be parties, 'safeguarding' their respective 'interests'.

At this stage in the proceedings, Ivan Chen declared that his government would not recognise any treaty or similar document that might 'now or hereafter' be signed between Great Britain and Tibet. To which the Lonchen countered by saying that he 'deeply' regretted Chinese action and that in the light of it, his country 'felt bound' to take steps 'to defend' its interests.

When the Lonchen and Sir Henry proceeded to conclude the agreement, Ivan Chen was present briefly. He had made it clear, however, that his presence did not imply his 'recognition' of the conclusion of an agreement between Britain and Tibet. Later, however, he left the chamber.

After the Convention had been signed, Chen returned to the Conference room.

In concluding the proceedings, McMahon contrasted the Chinese attitude of 'opposition' and meeting all his proposals in an 'uncompromising spirit' with Ivan Chen's own 'unfailing courtesy', and a broad enough hint that

> should their Chinese colleague be in a position to sign the Convention and should he express a desire to reassemble this meeting for that specific purpose before their (McMahon and Lonchen's) departure, they would be willing to meet him once more on 6th July.

After Chen retired and the final session of the tripartite conference was over, McMahon and the Lonchen reassembled. Now, McMahon stated, he

> was authorised to inform the Lonchen that Tibet might count on the diplomatic support of HMG and on any reasonable assistance which they could give in supplying munitions of war.

The Lonchen's demands, however, were very far-reaching. He revealed that, in the event of the Chinese not signing, the Dalai Lama had instructed him to ask for

> assistance in arms and for the despatch of British troops and to conclude a separate agreement, without which Tibet would be powerless.

If such assistance were forthcoming, he assured McMahon, Tibet 'would see' that the British Government 'did not lose by it'.[14]

Indo-Tibetan boundary treaty and the New Trade Regulations. *Yao-ting Sung*, pp. 107–8.
  Interestingly enough, apart from this solitary reference, Dr Sung's study makes no mention of the India-Tibet boundary.
    [14]'Proceedings of the 8th meeting of the Tibet Conference held at Simla on the 3rd July 1914', and 'Proceedings of the 8th meeting of the Tibet Conference held at Simla on 3rd July 1914,

The sequence, however, belongs to another day—and another chapter. For the present we may revert, if briefly, to 3 July. To understand what precisely took place at Simla that fateful day, the following may help.

In the first place a declaration, appended to the Convention, was *signed* by McMahon and the Lonchen. *Inter alia,* it stated that the two

> acknowledge the annexed Convention as initialled to be binding on the Governments of Great Britain and Tibet and we agree that so long as the Government of China withholds signature to the aforesaid Convention, she will be debarred from the enjoyment of all privileges accruing therefrom.

In token thereof, the two Plenipotentiaries ' signed and sealed the Declaration '—two copies in English and two in Tibetan.[15]

In the second place, the Convention between Great Britain, China and Tibet was *initialled* by the Lonchen (actually his full signatures are appended) and Sir Henry McMahon (his initials ' AHM '), apart from their respective seals being affixed. The initialled Convention is the same in all respects, barring Articles X and XI, as the one initialled by the three Plenipotentiaries at the seventh meeting of the Conference at Simla on 27 April. For facility of reference, the two versions of these articles are reproduced below.

Article X, as initialled on 27 April:

> In case of difference, between the Governments of China and Tibet in regard to questions arising out of this Convention the aforesaid Governments engage to refer them to the British Government for equitable adjustment.

Article X, as initialled on 3 July:

> The English, Chinese and Tibetan texts of the present Convention have been carefully examined and found to correspond but in the event of there being any difference of meaning between them, the English text shall be authoritative.

Article XI, as initialled on 27 April:

(Ratification Clause)

---

continued'; No. 346 and Encl. 1, No. 346 in Ibid.

It may be recalled that the Secretary of State had specifically laid down that assurances of help or armed aid to Tibet ' should be privately given ' to the Lonchen. *Supra,* n. 10.

[15]The 'Declaration' forms Annexure 1, Encl. 2 in No. 346 in Ibid. Apart from the signatures, and seals of McMahon and the Lonchen, it bore the seals of the Dalai Lama, of the Drepung, Sera and Ganden monasteries and of the Tibetan National Assembly.

Article XI, as initialled on 3 July:

> The present Convention will take effect from the date of signature.

It may be noted that the Convention was initialled by Sir Henry McMahon and signed by the Lonchen, both at the end of its text of eleven articles as also at the conclusion of the schedule and the notes exchanged, which were the the same on 3 July as on 27 April.[16] Significantly enough, the map attached to the Convention bore the *signatures* as well as the seals of both the Tibetan and British Plenipotentiaries. It is the same as the one attached to the first Simla Convention bearing the *signatures* of Ivan Chen and of Lonchen Shatra, but only the *initials*, 'AHM', of McMahon—the signatures and the initials appearing at two other places on the map itself.

And finally, on 3 July, both Sir Henry and the Lonchen *signed and sealed* the new Trade Regulations between India and Tibet which earlier, on 27 April, had been merely initialled by them.[17]

The Tibetan Plenipotentiary was evidently fully aware of what was being done, though not his Chinese counterpart. McMahon reported that he (Chen) was

> in ignorance of the character of the documents executed at the meeting ...and I now believe that he is under the impression that we signed the Convention. I have not thought it necessary to disabuse him at the present stage.

It was not long before he *was* disabused.

---

[16]Encl. 3, Annexure II, No. 346 in Ibid.
[17]Encl. 5, Annexure II, No. 346 in Ibid.

PART VI   1919: CHINA
REVIVES THE SIMLA
PROPOSALS

PART VI: c. 1919: CHINA
REVIVES THE SIMLA
PROPOSALS

Chapter 25

Shatra, Tibet and Teichman's Memorandum of May 1917

NOT LONG after the Convention had been signed and sealed, Shatra left Simla for home—and a reception that was positively chilling, if not indeed hostile. So did McMahon and, a little later, Ivan Chen. The former was well received and for his labours rewarded by being designated his country's first High Commissioner in Egypt. Ivan Chen, however, remained under a cloud and, in Peking's then uncertain political climate, soon faded away into anonymity. With their departure, a major watershed in the story of a tripartite settlement of the Tibetan question now lay behind. Abortive as the Conference proved, a principal Indian objective in settling its north-eastern frontier with Tibet had been successfully worked out.

Yet Simla left a legacy that lingered long. For the Chinese disavowal of Ivan Chen's action, and their refusal to accept the Convention, cast a grim shadow which, in retrospect, proved forbidding. In the years immediately following the Conference, however, prospects for a resumption of negotiations did not look particularly depressing. Lhasa, conscious that China had kept out of the Convention, was anxious that it be persuaded to become a party. Peking, for its part, showed some interest and feelers were thrown to Jordan to pick up the threads. A major British effort, albeit in the nature of an academic exercise behind the scenes, was a consular official's memorandum of May 1917. A knowledgeable 'China hand', Teichman spelt out here, and at considerable length, the major lacunae, from Peking's point of view, in McMahon's handiwork and suggested a new basis for a settlement—on a scale 'more liberal' to the Chinese, and 'more in harmony' with what he termed 'existing facts'.

Throughout the period of the Simla Conference, Lonchen Shatra had played his rather difficult role with quiet dignity and, for a Tibetan, remarkable efficiency. In contrast to his Chinese colleague, he came fully prepared with his brief; the documentary material which he brought up to support his case was described by McMahon as 'overwhelming'. It was certainly very impressive and the fact that it was, for the most part, first-hand and authentic created a powerful impact. In his personal conduct and in the proceedings of the Conference, he revealed himself to be an astute negotiator who pounced upon every opportunity that came his way and made the best of it. Both in his formal, as well as informal encounters with Ivan Chen he was shrewd enough not to concede an advantage until he had obtained something in return. For that matter even on the question of what later came to be known as the McMahon boundary, he held his ground firmly and obtained a considerable advantage for his country before he gave in to British importunities.

To gain a clearer understanding of developments in Tibet in the wake of the Simla Convention, it may be useful to underline Shatra's role in the negotiations. In more ways than one he represented his own and his country's ambitions and hopes—and its fears. What was a personal tragedy was that his later career was marred by the grim shadow of his supposed failure at Simla. The story of this 'failure' is revealing and may be briefly touched upon to illustrate the tragedy of Shatra, and of Tibet.

In his first Memorandum on the progress of the negotiations, McMahon had formed a good impression of the Lonchen:

> as a diplomat he (Ivan Chen) has, I think, met his match in Lonchen Shatra, who is a remarkably shrewd and quick-witted old gentleman, more than able to hold his own in discussion, and full of resource.

Nor did he make any mistake regarding what the Lonchen's true intent was about:

> For the moment the energies of my Tibetan colleague are concentrated on securing the recognition of the autonomy of Tibet.

And again:

> The Tibetan Government is at present willing and indeed anxious to have a British representative in Lhasa but when once they have gained by treaty their desired autonomy, without any proviso regarding British representation in Tibet, it may be difficult to get them to agree to it.[1]

By the end of December (1913), McMahon's opinion of the Lonchen had become distinctly more friendly:

> It was evident from the outset that the Tibetans were in a more favourable position than the Chinese as far as documentary evidence was concerned. In support of the Tibetan claim he (Lonchen Shatra) produced a large number of original archives from Lhasa, tomes of delicate manuscripts bound in richly embroidered covers. He announced that he would lay on the table the original records of each Tibetan state as far east as Tachienlu....

The Lonchen's shrewdness in dealing with Mongolia, and the treaty which Tibet had concluded with that country, was brought out in his

---

[1] 'Tibet Conference: Memorandum Regarding progress of Negotiations from 6th October to 20th November, 1913', Encl. 1, No. 36 in *Foreign*, May 1915, Procs. 36–50.

greatest reluctance to define any frontier line which can possibly create friction with his Mongolian neighbour. It is impossible to estimate to what extent this may be due to pressure from the direction of Urga.

McMahon noted that the Tibetan Plenipotentiary was unduly wary on the question of that treaty, for he

> has avoided any categorical denial and there is reason to believe that he knows more of the treaty than he is willing to communicate and that he is simply endeavouring to evade reply by his reference to Lhasa.[2]

In his negotiations on the question of the Indo-Tibetan boundary, the Lonchen again revealed himself to be an astute judge of men and affairs and played his cards remarkably well. From his first informal meeting with Bell on 15 January, to the formal notes of 24–25 March (1914), while he yielded ground in some cases, his gains in others were sizeable. It is not necessary to recapitulate the story here except perhaps to emphasise that British assurances, and the Lonchen's own reservations, were to find their due place in the exchange of notes between the two Plenipotentiaries which took place in Delhi and are referred to in the preceding pages.

At the Conference meeting on 22 April when Chen, under instructions from his government, presented five new demands which showed no signs of a conciliatory attitude, the Lonchen reacted sharply. His government, he declared,

> was desirous of effecting an agreement, but they felt that the draft (presented by McMahon) demanded from them a very serious sacrifice... he felt bound to state that any draft which provided for the reinstatement of a Chinese representative at Lhasa, and for the inclusion of Niarong and Derge in Inner Tibet, would be unacceptable at Lhasa. In the circumstances he must withhold his consent to the Convention.[3]

At the adjourned meeting on 27 April when Chen, refusing to initial, had withdrawn, the Lonchen, on McMahon's initiative, agreed to make some 'last concessions'. His reaction, however, to China's later disavowal of Ivan Chen's initialling of the Convention was, predictably, bitter. All the previous treaties and agreements, he declared,

> were discussed and signed by Plenipotentiaries who were given full powers to do so but if the action of the Plenipotentiaries could be disavowed in this way, then those treaties and agreements could also be disavowed in a

---

[2] 'Memorandum Regarding progress of Negotiations from 21st November to 24th December, 1913', Encl. 2, Proc. 36 in Ibid.

[3] 'Proceedings of the 7th Meeting of the Tibet Conference on 22nd and 27th April, 1914', No. 257 in *Foreign*, October 1914, Procs. 134–396.

similar way.... He gave up Derge and Niarong, in spite of orders from his Government to the contrary.... The Chinese Government seem to think that the British Government would make further concessions if only they (the Chinese) were persistent in holding on.... The Tibetans always heard from Eastern Tibet that the Chinese were saying that this Conference was simply a pretence to gain time, as the Chinese army was not quite ready.

Bell counselled the Lonchen ' not to be anxious ' and promised to meet him oftener. Apart from being useful in their own right, these meetings, it was felt, might also rouse Chinese suspicions and thereby render them ' more inclined ' to sign the Convention. The Lonchen, Bell noted, agreed that ' this was probable '.[4]

Earlier, Shatra had told Bell that if the Chinese disavowed the action of their Plenipotentiary now, ' how could they be trusted ' to respect the Convention after it had been formally signed and sealed? What was more, Shatra revealed that after he

had initialled the Convention he had himself received instructions to press the claim for damages and also not to agree to the Convention, unless Derge and Niarong were included in Outer Tibet.... He had already reported the initialling of the Convention to the Tibetan Government who would be both surprised and disgusted at any such Chinese breach of faith.[5]

The Lonchen had been equally vocal against Chinese claims presented to Jordan in Peking on 29 June, on the eve of the final meeting of the Conference. McMahon noted that the Tibetan Plenipotentiary

categorically refused to consider it, or to sign any document which accorded fresh privileges to China without some corresponding concession to Tibet. He urged that he had met the views of China in every possible way, he had initialled a Treaty restoring the lost suzerainty of China over Tibet, recognising her right to reinstate an Amban at Lhasa and virtually ceding to her the rich revenue-producing provinces of Derge and Niarong. In return for these considerations Tibet had received only, by the terms of the initialled convention, a promise that the Chinese would evacuate the country lying to the west of Chiamdo and Markam and thus put an end to the state of war which had been in progress for the last three years. If the Chinese were unwilling to abide by that promise, he added, Tibet would prefer to continue fighting rather than consent to the unjust and unreasonable demands, now presented by Peking.[6]

[4]Office note by Bell, 19 May 1914, in *Foreign, Notes*, October 1914, Procs. 134–396.
[5]Office note by Bell, 9 May 1914, in Ibid.
[6]' Memorandum Regarding progress of Negotiations from 1st May to 8th July, 1914 ', Encl. 4, No. 36 in *Foreign*, May 1915, Procs. 36–50.

In his 'Final Memorandum' too, McMahon paid Lonchen Shatra a handsome encomium. He maintained that it was 'difficult' to do adequate justice to the Lonchen's personality and that his selection as Tibetan Plenipotentiary was 'most' fortunate, for he

> combines a simplicity and charm of manner with an unexpected knowledge of men and affairs... a man of very great shrewdness and capability (who) despite his want of diplomatic training... proved quite his (Ivan Chen's) match in debate and political acumen.[7]

Later, at a personal interview on 8 July, when McMahon complimented him on his conduct of the negotiations all through the Conference, the Lonchen was characteristically self-effacing and confessed that he

> had had confidence in the Sahibs and followed their advice throughout and to that was due any success which he had obtained.[8]

On his return to Lhasa, and despite the gloss put on it by a recent Tibetan writer, the Lonchen was under a shadow.[9] Bell records that the Dalai Lama's understanding of the Simla Convention was, until 1921, far from perfect. It is well-known that the Lama was at a loss to understand why Tibet had been divided into two,[10] and one would imagine that he saddled the blame squarely on the Lonchen's head. Bell records, with the characteristic British penchant for under-statement, that the

> Dalai Lama was not very sympathetic towards Shatra. Perhaps the latter's ability piqued him a little. Shatra on his side was thoroughly loyal to his master.[11]

At another place the Lonchen's political eclipse is again briefly touched upon by Bell:

> Towards the end of his life, Shatra was a lonely figure. He had climbed high, and as usually happens in eastern lands, many people wanted to pull him down.[12]

---

[7] 'Final Memorandum by the British Plenipotentiary', 8 July 1914, No. 36 in Ibid.

[8] 'Note on Farewell Interview between Sir Henry McMahon and Lonchen Shatra, the Tibetan Plenipotentiary on 8.7.14', in *Foreign*, External B, September 1914, Proc. 238.
The note is by Bell and is dated 14 July 1914.

[9] Shakabapa's commendation about Shatra having 'served Tibet so well at Simla... and his achievements as a Minister for the Tibetan Government will long be remembered' appears to be in the nature of a posthumous award. For, in his life-time, more especially after his return from Simla, the Lonchen was in evident disgrace. *Shakabapa*, pp. 208 and 262.

[10] Bell, *Portrait*, pp. 206–7.

[11] Ibid., p. 207.

[12] Loc. cit.

To be sure, after his return from Simla, the Lonchen was in disgrace, for his frequent bouts of 'illness', and refusal to take an active part in the affairs of state, appear to have been forced. Division of Tibet apart, the cession of Tawang, under the terms of the Simla Convention, was held specifically against him—Lhasa viewing the Convention as being conditional upon China accepting the terms of the Convention.[13]

Another aspect of the question is relevant too. At Simla, did Shatra have explicit authority to accept the terms of the Convention, without reservations? It may be recalled that in a personal letter to McMahon on 8 July, he had written:

> *Despite contrary instructions*, I took upon myself the responsibility of doing as the British Plenipotentiary proposed, viz. signed the draft Convention.

What was more:

> We rely earnestly upon the British Government for aid and protection to enable us to defend our territory and our freedom from foreign yoke. We are sure to do our best to secure those in our own interest....[14]

It may well be argued that insofar as he acted 'contrary' to 'instructions', and on the 'bidding of the Sahibs' (McMahon and Bell), was the Lonchen in any better position than Ivan Chen whose lapse in initialling the Convention, without express instructions, was viewed as unpardonable?

While still in Darjeeling, on his way to Tibet, the Lonchen's continuous refrain was the proposed British mission to Chamdo provided for in (Article III and note 7 of the Schedule) the Simla Convention to ensure the complete withdrawal of Chinese personnel from Tibet. He wrote to Bell asking, *inter alia*, for the 'immediate necessity' of deputing an officer to inspect the frontiers of Chamdo and Draya, for grant of arms and ammunition, and above all for 'despatch' of (British) troops 'as promised'.[15] Later in Gyantse, on his way to Lhasa, he asked David Macdonald, the British Trade Agent, that a (British) representative, 'with suitable escort', be sent to Chamdo to open negotiations between the Chinese and Tibetans at an early date.[16]

Meanwhile in the Tibetan capital itself, the Dalai Lama was playing a

---

[13]In his report to the Foreign Department in December 1915, the Political Officer in Sikkim wrote that 'after working for a brief period' in the Council, the Lonchen had again 'taken sick-leave'. Further, ' Shatra is blamed for the results of the Simla Conference and has lost power and to this his continued retirement is due '. Bell to India, 9 December 1915, No. 101 in *Foreign*, July 1916, Procs. 39–163.

[14]Office note, pp. 1–3, *Foreign*, June 1915, Procs. 135–220.

[15]Lonchen to Bell, 22 July 1914, in Correspondence in Ibid.

[16]Macdonald (Trade Agent, Gyantse) to India, 22 October 1914, No. 442 in *Foreign*, May 1915, Procs. 398–508.

shrewd game. On 4 January 1915, the British Consul General in Chengtu referred to persistent rumours, based 'probably (on) some truth', about independent negotiations having taken place between the Kalon Lama and the Chinese Commissioner at Tachienlu, or his representative nearer to the frontier in Chamdo.[17] At about the same time, the Dalai Lama's Chief Ministers were urging Bell how 'necessary' it was to have the tripartite treaty concluded 'as soon as possible'. This they viewed to be more pressing because 'people were of diverse minds' and 'great harm' might result if the question were left hanging.[18] Another string to the Lama's bow was a secret message that he had sent, sometime in October 1915, to St. Petersburg in which he

> testifies to the success of his efforts to consolidate his special powers and his administration and asks for advice on the possibility of a rapprochement (with Russia).[19]

Preoccupied with his own problems, and World War I had broken out, the Tsar was in no mood to fish in troubled waters. His reply, therefore, was non-committal and discreetly 'silent' on the question of a rapprochement (with Tibet). The Indian government, who viewed the Lama's overtures as 'distinctly underhand' and 'contrary' to the terms of the Convention, held them as an argument for refusing to assist his regime further with arms.[20]

About the time the Dalai Lama was seeking a reconciliation with the Tsar, a development of some significance was a Chinese initiative for a settlement of the Tibetan question. Thus on 2 August 1915, Jordan, who earlier had rejected these overtures as 'quite inadmissible', telegraphed to Grey that a Wai-chiao-pu official in Peking had submitted to him some 'informal and tentative' proposals for a settlement. Their burden was an implicit recognition, in the body of the Convention, that Tibet formed 'part' of 'Chinese territory' and that Chinese Trade Agents were to be stationed at Chamdo, Gyantse, Shigatse, Yatung and Gartok—'and other places'—which may be opened to trade in future. In return, China would agree to the retention of Chamdo in Outer Tibet, while boundaries in other respects were to remain as finally proposed by China at Simla. However nebulous, this initiative was welcome in Whitehall. Unfortunately, it proved still-born for the member concerned had left the Ministry before serious parleys could begin.[21]

---

[17]Consul General, Chengtu to India, telegrams, 4 and 5 January 1915, Nos. 469 and 470 in Ibid.
[18]Chief Ministers of Tibet to Political Officer in Sikkim, Encl. to No. 126 in *Foreign*, July 1916, Procs. 39–163.
[19]Buchanan to Grey, 8 October 1915, No. 74 in Ibid. The Lama's message was transmitted through Miller, the Russian Agent in Mongolia.
[20]Office note by A H Grant, 23 November 1915, in Ibid.
[21]Jordan to Grey, 2 August 1915, No. 60 in *Foreign*, July 1916, Procs. 39–163.

Incidentals apart, a primary reason why the Chinese move proved barren of results was the then chaotic political situation in Peking. To put it mildly, the last few months of Yuan Shih-kai's rule were stormy. The monarchist movement, sedulously opposed by Japan for ulterior motives, was responsible for a major schism between the north, predominantly pro, and the south, unmistakably anti. In between were the military leaders of Kiangsu, Chekiang, Shantung, Shansi and, in the south-west, of Yunnan, Kweichow, Kwangtung and Kwangsi. They were, for the most part, fence-sitters. Of particular moment, in the then political context, was Yunnan's declaration of 'independence' on 25 December (1915): 'since he has betrayed the Republic, Yuan Shih-kai naturally loses all claims to be the head of the state'. *Inter alia*, the anti-monarchist military junta in the province which spear-headed the movement, planned to seize Szechuan by force, threaten the adjacent provinces of Hupei and Hunan and thereby influence, into anti-Yuan action, the military leaders along the lower reaches of the Yangtse.

Nor was that the end. For soon, against heavy odds, the chief leader of the anti-monarchist, and anti-Yuan, movement, General Tsai' O, managed to capture Hsufu (31 January 1916), and Luchou (6 February). By the middle of February he was already threatening Chungking. Not long after, on 22 May (1916) to be precise, Chen Huan of Szechuan, a trusted lieutenant of Yuan Shih-kai, announced his 'independence' in a telegram to Peking. This was, as it proved to be, a fatal stab in the back. Yuan, already sick, inched his way to the grave—in less than a fortnight, he was a dead man.[22]

However feeble, and shaky, his hold in the last few months may have been, with Yuan Shih-kai's death passed away for many a summer to come the prospect of a settlement of the Tibetan question. While China's recalcitrance, and even obstruction, at Simla has been commented upon, two facts need to be underlined. One, that the basic questions at issue were territorial: in September 1914, the Wai-chiao-pu told Jordan, and not for the first time, that the principal hurdles were the 'inclusion of Batang and Litang in Inner Tibet and of Chiamdo' in the Outer.[23] Two, Peking's professed inability to enforce the Tibetan Convention upon the directly affected provinces of Szechuan and Yunnan may have been genuine. These facts emerge clearly from 'a long, private' conversation between Jordan and Yuan Shih-kai which took place in November 1914, and in the course of which the British Minister told the President that the latter's

> attitude in this matter (Simla Convention) has caused much dissatisfaction to HMG and no little personal disappointment to myself and that I (Jordan) could never understand his reasons for refusing to sanction the signature of the Simla Convention....

[22]Yuan died on 6 June after a brief illness. For a detailed study of the events immediately preceding his death see Jerome Chen, *Yuan Shih-kai*, pp. 219–35.

[23]Jordan to Grey, 25 September 1914, No. 167 in *Foreign*, June 1915, Procs. 135–220.

Yuan's reply was candid. Anxious as he no doubt was for a settlement, he

> had not under the present circumstances the power to enforce the Convention as it now stood upon the provinces of Szechuan and Yunnan. In both of these provinces the military authority was still largely vested in generals who had taken a prominent part in the Revolution and who, being politicians as well as military leaders, would keenly resent the transference of Chinese territory which was involved in the inclusion of Chiamdo in Outer Tibet and of Batang and Litang in Inner Tibet... he (Yuan) himself had always been opposed to a policy of expansion on the Tibetan borderland and as a member of the Cabinet under the (Ch'ing) dynasty had constantly formed one of the small minority who deprecated Chao Erh-feng's campaign. But he repeated that he could not consent to the alienation of places like Litang and Batang which had long been recognised as Chinese.[24]

Nor did Jordan, much less his Legation in Peking, view matters differently. In a long 'Memorandum on Tibetan Question', drawn up in May 1917, Eric Teichman, who was later to play an important role in bringing about a cessation of hostilities in Eastern Tibet, drew pointed attention to what he viewed as major lapses in the Simla Convention.[25] Briefly, his principal conclusions were:

1. With 'more than two years' having passed since the conference at Simla, it was now evident that 'no Chinese Government' would adhere to the Convention 'in its present form';
2. Lhasa could not 'indefinitely' stand the strain of maintaining a 'comparatively large force' on its eastern frontier against the Chinese. Nor could the influence of the pro-Chinese party in Lhasa be ignored;
3. 'Provided' the Chinese were free from 'domestic' troubles, the Tibetans could no more stand against them now than they could when Chao Erh-feng and Chung Ying carried out their 'successful raid' on Lhasa— in February 1910. And once the Chinese marched into Lhasa there would be an 'immediate reversion' to the state of affairs existing before the Revolution of 1911 and the opportunity for a 'satisfactory' settlement of the Tibetan question would be lost 'for good';
4. The 'radical defect' of the Convention was the arrangement whereby, 'in return for being allowed into Tibet to a very limited extent', China

---

[24] Jordan to Grey, 3 October 1914, No. 180 in Ibid.
Jordan had 'lunched alone' with Yuan on 24 September when the talks took place.
In a personal letter to Langley on Yuan's death, Jordan wrote: 'I could go on reciting indefinitely acts to the credit of my dead friend—for simply as a friend I shall remember him.... He fell in an unequal struggle and to me he was greater in his adversity, than he had been at the height of his power'. Jordan to Langely, 13 June 1916, cited in *Jerome Chen*, p. 234.
[25] Alston to Balfour, 19 May 1917, Encl. No. 31 in *Foreign*, October 1917, Procs. 1–51.
For the text of the Memorandum see Sub-encl. 2, No. 31 in Ibid.

was expected to sign away the Tachienlu-Batang portion of Szechuan and the Tsaidam part of Kokonor as Inner Tibet. The argument that these gains were a result of Chao Erh-feng's 'campaigns' and were 'note exactly' conquests of Tibetan territory did not cut much ice in Peking;

5. The 'insurmountable obstacle' to a settlement on the lines of the Simla Convention was the Inner-Outer Tibet division. It was 'difficult to see what anyone gains by the artificial creation of 'Inner' Tibet in which China is apparently at liberty to make what military dispositions she pleases...unless it be that China's irritation and loss of face is considered of advantage to Tibet';

6. Should the present waiting continue, there was an 'ever-increasing risk' of the Tibetans giving way and negotiating independently with China. This alone should make the British use the opportunity created by the elimination of Chinese power in Tibet, through the revolution of 1911, and create an autonomous Tibet while the time was still 'favourable'.

Elsewhere the Memorandum spelt out a new tripartite arrangement on a scale 'more liberal' to the Chinese and 'more in harmony' with 'existing facts'. *Inter alia,* this stipulated

(a) Complete autonomy of Tibet under Chinese suzerainty;
(b) The boundaries of Outer Tibet to follow roughly the lines fixed in the Convention map for 'Outer Tibet', the frontier itself being delimited later by a British-Chinese-Tibetan Boundary Commission;
(c) British and Chinese representatives of equal status, with escorts of equal size, to be stationed at Lhasa to advise on foreign relations. It was to be understood that autonomous Tibet would not violate China's suzerain rights;
(d) British and Chinese Trade Agents or Consuls to be stationed at trade marts which would include Chamdo;
(e) Apart from the above, no British/Chinese troops nor their civil and military officials were to be allowed into Tibet without the concurrence of all the three parties—neither Britain nor China interfering in Tibet's internal affairs, much less founding colonies of their nationals;
(f) Extra-territorial rights were to be enjoyed by British and Chinese nationals in Tibet, British subjects exercising the same rights of freedom and trade as the Chinese while the commerce of both countries was to enjoy most-favoured nation treatment;
(g) Tibet was not to be represented in the Chinese Parliament;
(h) Provisions of existing conventions which were inconsistent with, or repugnant to, the terms of the present Convention were to lapse;
(i) The new treaty was to be published at the trade marts throughout Tibet,

with Britain engaging to keep China fully informed of any negotiations or agreement which she may enter into with Tibet;

(j) China was to adhere to the new Trade Regulations which Britain had negotiated with Tibet;

(k) Religious rights of the Dalai Lama over monasteries in the Kokonor, as well as the provinces of Kansu and Szechuan were to continue;

(l) The English text of the Convention was to be accepted as authoritative.

The Memorandum concluded by suggesting that, in return for the 'final' Chinese concession on Chang Thang, 'Inner' Tibet should be abolished while the Kokonor territory and the March country of Szechuan should revert to China. India's objection to the stationing of Chinese Trade Agents—the Simla Convention had ruled them out completely—was to be met by stipulating that their functions were purely consular and indeed limited to Chinese nationals. Nor was the convening of a new conference deemed necessary for the whole question could be settled, it was felt, with a minimun of negotiations.

Teichman's Memorandum, which vowed that it looked at the problem strictly 'from the Peking point of view', made a powerful impact on the Foreign Department in Simla. Denys Bray, then Deputy Foreign Secretary, expressed the view that there was 'a great deal of force' in it and that India would have 'eventually' to modify its present 'intransigent attitude'. The Foreign Secretary, Grant, was more outspoken. He called it a

> very able review and to my thinking very reasonable. The truth is that Sir Henry McMahon adopted an extreme pro-Tibetan attitude throughout the Simla negotiations in 1914 and spoiled what might have been a very valuable settlement by asking far too much from the Chinese.

These views notwithstanding, India was not in favour of reopening the question and for two good reasons. One, there was 'no stable Chinese Government' with whom to negotiate; two, reopening the parleys on the lines of the Memorandum would excite the 'liveliest suspicion' in Tibet, 'estrange' the Dalai Lama and 'open the door' to Japanese intrigue at a time when all these contingencies were considered 'most undesirable'.[26] The Governor-General's private letter to the Secretary of State was a variant on the same theme. Sir Henry's 'pro-Tibetan' attitude throughout the Simla negotiations was such, Lord Chelmsford confided to his political superiors, 'as no Chinese Government were likely to accept in toto'. As to the Memorandum, the Viceroy made it clear that his objective was

[26]Office notes by Denys Bray and A H Grant, 27 and 28 July 1917, in Correspondence in Ibid.

not to suggest immediate action, but merely to ask you to bear the matter in mind and to realise that when the time comes we shall probably have to adopt towards China a much less compromising attitude than we did in 1914 if we are to obtain a working settlement with regard to Tibet.[27]

Whitehall, however, thought differently. It felt, even as Jordan did, that the Tibetan question should be settled while China was ' still weak and distracted' and before Japanese influence became 'predominant'. For the record, Jordan, ' in general agreement ' with the views of the Peking Memorandum, had made it clear that China would ' never accept ' the definition of ' Inner ' Tibet as laid down in the 1914 Convention.[28]

---

[27] Viceroy to Secretary of State, 7 August 1917, in Correspondence in Ibid.
[28] Secretary of State to Viceroy, 20 August 1917, No. 46 in Ibid.

Chapter 26

China and Fighting in Eastern Tibet, 1915–18

IN ITS essence, the Teichman Memorandum of May 1917 was a plea for knocking out the concept of Inner Tibet and thereby restoring to China its full authority in that region. McMahon's aim had been to treat it as a buffer; Teichman's to re-establish Peking's *amour-propre* by calling the area a part of China. What the Memorandum had failed to emphasise was the vital issue of imposing some sanctions against China's continued refusal to face squarely to the question of a disturbed frontier with Tibet. The joint McMahon-Shatra ' declaration ' of 3 July 1914 was an assurance that China would be debarred frome xercising its rights unless it was also prepared to shoulder some of the consequential duties and responsibilities. What bedevilled the years after the curtain had been finally rung on the Simla confabulations, was the running sore of intermittent fighting in Kham, with each side trying to score an advantage over the other and the British in the unenviable position of helpless spectators, both unable and, perhaps, even more, unwilling to intervene. The role of the honest broker in such cases is by no means an easy one.

Albeit the Indian authorities, as also the British Government, were determined to keep the Tibetan question in cold storage as long as World War I lasted, a number of developments drove it to the forefront. Of considerable importance in this context was the civil war which broke out in China on the morrow of Yuan Shih-kai's proclamation, towards the end of 1915, of a new ruling dynasty. It may be recalled that the last few months left to him until his death, early in June 1916, were largely concerned with the consequential crop of rebellions and ' declarations of independence ' in different parts of the country— a process that indubitably hastened his end. It has already been noticed that one of these numerous revolts broke out in Yunnan and cast its deep shadow all the way to Szechuan, which later proclaimed its own 'independence' from central rule, and that too before Yuan's death. Nor did the latter's disappearance from the political scene help to improve matters; actually things began to go downhill all the way and most of the southern provinces gradually broke away from the government at Peking. China was in the throes of a major civil strife.[1]

[1] 'On 25 December 1915, the Governor (Tang Chi-yao) declared Yunnan's independence. There followed six months of limited fighting, mainly in Szechuan, and intensive negotiations. By degrees eight southern and western provinces turned against Yuan while he (Yuan Shih-kai) first postponed his enthronement, then renounced the throne, and finally died a broken man '. Reischauer, Fairbank and Craig, *East Asia: The Modern Transformation* (London, 1965), p. 651.

To help size up the situation, it may be useful to sum up the years 1916–18, immediately following Yuan's death. All over China, and for the most part, it was the *tu-chuns*, literally 'directors of armies' or the warlords, who dominated the scene. The first phase, 1916–17, resulted in an almost complete control of the Peking Parliament by this new coterie of leaders, a development that drove the southern provinces farther away from the north. It may be recalled that Yuan was succeeded, in June 1916, by his Vice-President Li Yuan-hung. The latter, a sincere constitutionalist, sought to revive the Yuan–Sun Yat-Sen compact of March 1912 and, in consequence, reconvened the Parliament of 1913. In this, however, he had to contend with his Prime Minister, Tuan Chi-jui, the chief Peiyang militarist, whose close allies led by Liang Chi-chao constituted the 'Research clique', then dead-set against the Kuomintang. The Peiyang *tu-chuns*, who dominated a dozen northern and central provinces, formed an inter- provincial association under an old Manchu supporter, General Chang Hsun, ostensibly to maintain national peace and unity but in reality to control the government and parliament.

In May 1917, the Peiyang warlords made an abortive bid to pressurise parliament into a declaration of war against Germany. To forestall this, President Li forced Premier Tuan Chi-jui to resign and, in return, under pressure, sought the mediation of General Chang Hsun. The latter succeeded in obtaining the dissolution of parliament in June and, in a coup, announced the restoration of the last Ch'ing Emperor, Pu-yi. Nor did the Emperor last long, for other warlords soon joined in suppressing Chang's revolt and made Tuan premier again.

The second phase (1917–18) of the Civil War, which is relevant to our narrative of Sino-Tibetan fighting in Kham, was to witness a widening of the north-south split, a further fragmentation of political power and the resultant increased frustration of the civilian politicians. One of the features of this period was the re-emergence of Sun Yat-sen. In July 1917, with the help of his former Kuomintang colleagues (and most of the Chinese Navy, traditionally pro-KMT) Sun convened some 250 members of parliament and formed a military government with himself as the Generalissimo—even though real power rested with the southern warlords. By an interesting coincidence, Sun at Canton, trying to team up with the local men in power, was not unlike Liang Chi-chao at Peking endeavouring to provide a civilian component to the government of Premier Tuan Chi-jui. Both, however, were soon frustrated.

From the north, Tuan tried to take over Hunan and Szechuan for the Peiyang clique, but failed. He had resigned in November 1917, became Premier again in March (1918) and continued in that post until October of the same year. In August 1917, as has been noticed, he had been instrumental in forcing Peking to declare war against Germany, although the situation bordered on the semi-comic. For here, as a group of keen observers of Chinese affairs have observed, was a declaration of war abroad without fighting, and a fight at home without a declaration of war. China declared war against Germany and Austria on August 14, but during the last ten days of July troops had been sent to Hunan where there was no war.[2]

The subterfuge of a war with Germany had come handy to contract enormous loans from Japan. To be sure, there had been a covert military alliance with that country which additionally had also supplied Peking its military instructors. The result was the emergence of a new pro-Japanese group of politicians, aligned with a military clique called the An-fu. The latter was opposed by Feng Kua-chang who led the rival, Chihli, clique. With these two warring factions, the Peiyang militarists were thus rent apart right down the middle.[3]

In the south, Sun Yat-sen's Canton Parliament stood divided too. A rump thereof had cooperated with the warlords, who soon began to assassinate Sun's men and forced him, in May 1918, to retire to Shanghai. In consequence, a Kwangsi clique of militarists now dominated the south, even as the An-fu controlled the north. Meanwhile as World War I drew to a close, the north and the south were under considerable pressure to patch up and, in 1919, the two negotiated at Shanghai in an abortive 'peace' conference. During 1920, however, China's fragmentation entered a third phase when minority elements, both in the north as well as the south, seeking allies wherever possible, ousted the groups in power and yet, in turn, failed to stabilise their own control.

It is against the background of this civil strife, and of a complete breakaway of Szechuan and Yunnan from any vestiges of central control from Peking, that the problem of fighting in the Kham area has to be considered. It would perhaps be obvious that such government as there was in the Chinese capital was in no great anxiety to pull the traditional chestnuts out of the fire for the sake of those provinces whose allegiance to its own authority was dubious at best.

With conditions in China bordering on the chaotic, Delhi had concluded as early as July 1916, that any diplomatic intercession at Peking regarding possible Chinese aggression in Tibet, was practically impossible and could certainly not be effective. Similar representations, through the British Consul General in Chengtu, were 'equally hopeless' owing to the 'chaotic conditions' in Szechuan. What was significant was that while Chinese aggression in

---

[2] Li Chein-nung, Ssu-yu Teng and Jeremy Ingalls, *The Political History of China 1840–1928* (New York, 1956), p. 373.

[3] 'An-fu' is an abbreviation of An(hwei) and Fu(hien). As militarists, the clique were much haughtier and more overbearing than their predecessors whom they regarded as rascals. Ironically 'An' and 'Fu' stand for 'peace' and 'happiness'.

Tibet was rated ' most improbable ',[4] it was held that the Tibetans were raising an undue alarm over it in order to justify ' a little aggression ' of their own! This, Delhi concluded, would no doubt largely explain the almost continuous refrain from Lhasa for a supply of fresh arms.[5]

Meanwhile as prospects for a settlement with China seemed to recede into the distance, Tibet's anxiety to conclude one appeared to grow. For its part, India was duly alive to the strains to which Lhasa had been exposed by the ' constant menace ' of a fresh domination by China. There was also the awareness that behind the Chinese threat lurked Japanese intrigue. If Tibet was ' acquiescent ' and Peking ' responsive ', India argued, negotiations might be opened among the three powers in the Chinese capital. That relations with the former were rated important, and that India set great store by them, is revealed by its support—later overruled in Whitehall—to a visit to Lhasa by Charles Bell, its Political Officer, in response to repeated invitations from the Dalai Lama. Such a visit 'would show', the Foreign Department had reasoned, ' that we attach great importance ' to the Tibetan question and ' are as anxious as themselves ' for an early settlement.[6]

Nor was Tibet's anxiety entirely misplaced. The fact is that hardly had the Simla Conference drawn to a close, when Lhasa got seriously alarmed over the reported movements in East Tibet of the Chinese commander, General Peng.[7] In this context the British Agent Louis King's despatches from Tachienlu, towards the close of 1915, make interesting reading. Thus on 17 October, King reported that General Peng had received orders to fight his way to Lhasa and occupy that place ' forthwith '.[8]

Two days later:

General Peng was reported travelling ' night and day ' and was expected to arrive at Chiamdo by the 24th of October.[9]

Alarmed, on 30 October the Foreign Office in London directed Jordan to seek an ' explicit assurance ' that Peng and his troops would, ' in no circumstances', proceed beyond Chamdo, and to intimate that British objections to the despatch of a peaceful mission would apply ' with much greater force ' to a military expedition.[10] Peking countered with the plea that it was ' entirely

[4]Office note by A H Grant, 25 July 1916, in Correspondence in *Foreign*, November 1916, Procs. 1–65.
[5]Office note by A M Cardew, 28 September 1916, in Correspondence in Ibid.
[6]Office note by A H Grant, in Correspondence in *Foreign*, May 1918, Procs. 15–145.
[7]Trade Agent, Yatung to India, No. 86 in *Foreign*, July 1916, Procs. 39–163.
[8]Consul General, Chengtu to India, 23 October 1915, No. 45 in Ibid.
[9]Consul General, Chengtu to India, 25 October 1915, No. 47 in Ibid.
In a letter, in October 1915, the Chief Ministers of Tibet reported that Peng had with him ' a lot of money, 5000 troops, a large number of rifles and ammunition and one large gun '. Trade Agent, Yatung to India, telegram, 20 November 1915, No. 76 in Ibid.
[10]Foreign Office to Jordan, 30 October 1915, No. 98 in *Foreign*, July 1916, Procs. 39–163.

'ignorant' of the General's mission, although it did undertake to write to Tachienlu and enquire about his 'alleged movements'.[11]

Whatever its public professions, the regime in Peking had not been, despite serious preoccupations at home, altogether inactive in the Marches. Thus King noticed that in the matter of elections to Parliament from the Tachienlu region, then underway, no differentiation of any kind as between Chinese and tribesmen was being observed, either as regards the right of electing or of being elected. It followed that the border country was being treated as if it were an integral part of China, with both Chinese and 'natives' freely exercising their right to vote.[12]

Another development of some significance which Jordan reported, in November 1915, was abolition of the post of the Kokonor (more popularly the Sining) Amban and its conversion into that of 'Occupation Commissioner of Ning Hai', on the Kansu border. This brought it into line with that of the Occupation Commissioner of Szechuan Marches, resident at Tachienlu. The Sining Amban, who under the Ch'ing was a Manchu of high rank, represented the Emperor in all matters relating to the Tibetan and Mongol populations of Kokonor and controlled the region through 'native' (viz. tribal) princes and chiefs. Jordan expressed the view that the changes effected implied that the Chinese government 'intend strengthening their hold' and that the new incumbent, a 'prominent' Muhammadan leader of Kansu, was 'well qualified' to deal with the turbulent populations of these regions.[13]

Earlier, a change in the headquarters of the Chinese Commissioner from Tachienlu to Batang was viewed by Louis King as of no great significance,[14] even though it should have been obvious, except to the purblind, that the Chinese were pushing farther and farther into an area which had been a subject of serious dispute at Simla. This was the more important as Tibet was being made to realise that its 'independence' was an 'unattainable ideal' and that in throwing off its allegiance to Peking, it 'must inevitably' fall a victim to foreign aggression; that, in fact, Chinese sovereignty was the 'only protection' against worse things that might be in store.[15]

All through 1916 a veritable stalemate developed in the fighting in East Tibet, if partly because the 'Pien Chun', the Chinese Frontier Force, had become Tibetanised—living in 'native' style and taking 'native' wives; while

---

[11] Jordan to Viceroy, 4 November 1915, No. 56 in Ibid.

[12] Louis King to Jordan, 21 October 1915, Sub-encl. 2 to Encl. in No. 94 in Ibid.

[13] Jordan to Grey, 4 November 1915, No. 100 in Ibid.

The old post was abolished and the new one created by a Presidential mandate of 3 October; another, of 5 October, made the appointment of Ma Ch'i.

[14] Louis King to Consul General, Chengtu, Encl., No. 444 in *Foreign*, March 1915, Procs. 398–508.

[15] These remarks were made at a representative gathering of Lamas whom the Commissioner addressed at Tachienlu on 23 July 1914—on the morrow of the abortive Simla Conference. Louis King to Jordan, 27 July 1914, Sub-encl. 1 in No. 426 in Ibid.

the 'Lu Chun', the regular militia, had a poor reputation for courage.[16] By June 1917, however, a Tengyueh intelligence report retailed 'much talk' of a Chinese expedition to Lhasa, to be carried out by the combined forces of Szechuan and Yunnan. With General Yin Cheng-hsien at Tachienlu as its commander, the expedition appeared to be the concrete manifestation of the newly emergent confederacy of China's south-western provinces under the leadership of Yunnan, albeit financed by the riches of Szechuan. Mapped out in the months immediately following Yuan Shih-kai's death, these ambitious plans would have made the Yunnanese heirs to the frontier question.[17] Unfortunately for Yin and his compatriots, they miscarried for, in the summer of 1917, civil war broke out again in Szechuan, with the result that the Yunnanese were driven out of Chengtu.

The final *coup de grâce* to the Yunnanese adventure was delivered by the departure, in October 1917, from the frontier scene of General Yin himself.[18] Ambitious and clever beyond measure he had earlier drawn up, for the government in Peking, fairly comprehensive plans for the strengthening of China's military position on the border and the reduction of Tibet to subservience by 'force of arms'. Teichman, a close observer of the scene, later expressed the view that if only Yin had been provided with 'a good division of Yunnanese troops' and 'proceeded methodically' according to his scheme, he would have had no difficulty in subjugating Tibet, for

> the Plan outlined by Yin represents merely what the Yunnanese would have done on the frontier had they remained in power at the head of the south-western provinces and what they are likely to do if they ever rise to that position again in future.[19]

In retrospect General Yin, and his Yunnanese adventure, was a brief affair. Yet, contrary to expectations, Yin's departure brought no improvement in the situation. While there were other Chinese commanders located at Tachienlu and Batang, the real threat to peace was posed by General Peng Jih-sheng, then stationed at Chamdo, and in control of districts along the

---

[16]Coales' 'Report on Tibet Frontier', 21 March 1916, Encl. 1, No. 1 in *Foreign*, November 1916, Procs. 1–165.

Early in March 1916, Coales had succeeded Louis King as Assistant to the British Consul General, Chengtu. This possibly was his first report from Tachienlu.

[17]Extract from 'Tengyueh Intelligence Report for six months ending 30 June 1917', No. 18 in *Foreign*, May 1918, Procs. 15–145.

[18]Jordan to Balfour, 10 December 1917, Encl. No. 89 in Ibid.

Yin remained Military Commissioner for the Szechuan Frontier territory for a whole year, October 1916–October 1917.

[19]Teichman to Jordan, 21 November 1917, Encl. in No. 104 in Ibid.

Yin's paper, of which Teichman furnishes a detailed summary, was divided into six sections: I—Collation of Military Intelligence respecting the Frontier Territory, Tibet and India; II—A Detailed Plan for the Reduction of Tibet; III—Details of a Scheme for the complete re-

North road. Peng, who finds mention earlier in the narrative, was a 'big talker' with a well-known penchant for bellicosity, and was credited with the intent to advance and 'utterly destroy' the Tibetans.[20] Since he was to play an important role in the fighting in Kham, a word on him may not be out of place here.

General Peng had been on the frontier since the days of Chao Erh-feng's early campaigns and, not long after him, rose into prominence. He was rated an 'absolute autocrat' of the northern districts—appointing and dismissing civil and military officials and collecting and disposing of the revenues of the country as he pleased. Soon enough he acquired notoriety for his intolerant attitude towards the Tibetans who held him responsible for the destruction of the great monasteries of Chamdo, Draya and Yemdo in the earlier campaigns. After the death of Chao Erh-feng, the Tibetans looked upon him as an arch-enemy.

Towards the close of 1917, after Yin's departure, General Peng, chafing under continued neglect both of himself and his troops by the Central Chinese Government, and the authorities in Szechuan, conceived the grand design of breaking the truce by advancing on Lhasa. He had a dual objective in view: securing much-needed loot and supplies for his famished troops and obtaining the post of Frontier Commissioner, or of Resident in Tibet, by bringing off a resounding military victory against the Tibetans. In so doing, he gravely miscalculated, for it was soon evident that conditions had changed a great deal since Chao Erh-feng scored his early successes in the March country or his deputy Chung Ying sneaked, unnoticed, into Lhasa. There was also apparent, on General Peng's part, a complete lack of knowledge or understanding of the new Tibetan soldiery who, with a much augmented strength and better equipment, was in high spirits and indeed looking out for an opportunity to recover some of the country of which it had been deprived by Chao Erh-feng.[21]

---

organisation and training of Chinese troops in the Frontier Territory; IV—Foundation of Military Territories throughout the Frontier Territory; V—Reorganisation of Commissariat and Supply of Arms, Food and Clothing; and VI—Plans for reorganisation of Military Transport arrangements throughout the Frontier Territory.

Apart from the summary, Teichman provides a full-length translation of the paper, running into 12 pages of close print. The exact title of Yin's paper read: 'A Secret Memorandum submitted by Yin Cheng-hsien, Military Commissioner for the Szechwan Frontier Territory to the Central Government in December 1916 for the reorganisation of the Chinese military position on the border and in the Frontier Territory and the reduction of Tibet by force of arms'.

[20]Teichman to Jordan, 21 November 1917, Encl. in No. 105, in Ibid.
[21]For an account of General Peng's plans see Teichman, *Travels*, p. 52; also Richardson, *History*, p. 119, and *Shakabapa*, p. 260.

Two mis-statements in Richardson may be noted: one, Peng was *not* Governor of Szechuan but only one of the commanders of Chinese troops stationed on the frontier; two, Teichman had replaced Coales *before* the fighting precipitated by Peng's miscalculation, and his resultant defeat and debacle.

A pretext was soon to hand, an incident of a trivial character across the Tibetan frontier outpost beyond Riwoche. Here Peng's men acted in a provocative manner, seized a subordinate Lhasa officer and carried him a prisoner to Chamdo. In retaliation, the Tibetans attempted a rescue and some skirmishing did take place. This was enough for Peng to proclaim that the truce was at an end and that his troops would advance. The goal, he declared, was Lhasa itself.

It would appear that the Kalon Lama, the Tibetan commander in Kham, exerted himself strongly to avoid hostilities. His repeated pleas to General Peng, however, were either left unanswered or elicited insulting replies. Thus one of his communications to the General brought back a letter filled with dung; another, early in January 1918, extracted this for an answer:

> I (General Peng Jih-sheng) have received your letters. You must be aware that Tibet, which was formerly subject to the Emperor of China, is now subject to the President of the Chinese Republic. You Tibetans have rebelled, as servants revolting against their masters. Evil thoughts have entered your hearts and your lips have uttered falsehoods. The Chinese emperor can protect his own dominions and has no need of British mediation. The Chinese soldiers who have advanced from Riwoche are travelling in their own country and can go where they please. The Chinese forces are now about to advance on Lhasa, and you are ordered to make all the necessary preparations for their march.[22]

Nothing could have been more provocative! Brave words, however, did not match resolute action. What was worse, before many days were past, the Kalon Lama's men seized the upper hand and put the Chinese forces of General Peng to rout. News, however, of the Tibetans crossing the Mekong were to remain long unconfirmed and, in Peking, Jordan was disposed to play down the gravity of the situation. Plausibly enough he argued that frontier commanders, evidently 'very nervous', were exaggerating the true state of affairs with a view to securing much-needed supplies of ammunition and reinforcements from a central government which, understandably, was not very obliging.[23]

---

[22] Teichman, *Travels*, p. 53.
There is a slight textual change in the translation of General Peng's letter as provided by the Chief Ministers of Tibet. For the text see Encl. 2, No. 119 in *Foreign*, May 1918, Procs. 15–145.
The date of the letter, as mentioned by the Chief Ministers, is 4 January 1918; Teichman, who gives no date, mentions 'early' in January 1918.
According to Teichman, the Kalon wrote thrice; to his first letter, there had been no response from General Peng.
Also see *Yao-ting Sung*, p. 116. Sung holds General Peng squarely responsible for starting the war owing to his 'false calculations' of the 'tremendous strength' of the Tibetan forces gained 'through British aid'.

[23] Jordan to Viceroy, 18 February 1918, No. 122 in *Foreign*, May 1918, Procs. 15–145.

Peng's own plans were ambitious. Essentially, he had mapped out a three-pronged assault: by way of the North Road, from Riwoche; by the main road, from Enta; and by a road from Draya leading, across the Mekong, into the Tibetan district of Bashu. To start with, all the three columns registered an advance, but before long the first two were beaten and fell back on Chamdo. The Draya column, which crossed the Mekong and encountered the enemy, fled precipitately in such confusion that the Tibetans followed close on its heels and captured the province. In the bargain, two mountain guns and several hundred Chinese soldiers with their rifles fell into their hands.

By early in March 1918, David Macdonald, the British Trade Agent at Yatung, had received confirmation of the news that the Tibetans had recovered Enta as well as Draya.[24] The latter's fall had wide ramifications. *Inter alia*, it cut the main road in General Peng's rear and, with two important passes on the Derge road in the hands of the Kalon Lama and his men, Chamdo was soon invested. South of Draya, the Tibetans advanced into Markham, captured, or dispersed, all Chinese troops stationed in its neigbhourhood and extended their hold to the old frontier line on the Bum la.

Held at bay, and completely encircled, General Peng appealed for reinforcements. An outlying battalion was rushed to his aid; so was another small force, with supplies and ammunition, from Tachienlu. Unfortunately for him, neither proved of avail: the Kanze force was surrounded by the Kalon Lama's men in a monastery two marches short of Chamdo; the Tachienlu relief garrison had barely reached Dege Gonchen when, learning of Tibetan victories, it fled pell-mell.[25] Chamdo was thus completely cut off and fell back on its own resources, and reserves. The Chinese troops in the town fought back hard. At long last, after a siege lasting several months, and with nearly half his garrison killed or decimated by disease, Peng capitulated towards the end of April 1918.

The Tibetan rout of General Peng was impressive, Teichman's grim forebodings to the contrary notwithstanding.[26] What was more, as the Kalon Lama's men continued to advance against their adversaries, observers in the March country noticed a marked superiority in their equipment and training; no longer a disorganised rabble, they were now armed with modern rifles and led by officers in 'khaki'. There was widespread criticism too of the strange paradox whereby India provided the Dalai Lama with British rifles to attack the forces of China—a power allied to Great Britain in the European war![27] Another interesting development, consequent upon Tibetan

---

[24] 'Yatung Trade Agency News Report No. 1 of 1918', 12 March 1918, Encl. in No. 23 in *Foreign*, June 1918, Procs. 15–84.

[25] Teichman to Jordan, 27 March 1918, Encl. in No. 64 in *Foreign*, October 1918, Procs. 11–202.

[26] Jordan to Viceroy, 20 April 1918, No. 46 in Ibid. Also see Teichman to Jordan, 11 February 1918, Encl. in No. 49 in Ibid.

[27] Teichman to Jordan, 22 February 1918, Encl. in No. 63 in Ibid.

successes and the Chinese falling back, was a spate of frantic requests from Tibet's Chief Ministers that British and Chinese representatives be ' deputed to conclude a treaty ' and ' demarcate ' the Sino-Tibetan frontier.[28]

For its part, India was anxious that Lhasa's advance should be stayed, ' pending ' a settlement of the whole (Tibetan) question. It felt that the Dalai Lama's government should issue

> clear instructions to their local officers to refrain absolutely from further aggression and to cooperate whole-heartedly with Teichman... in Tibet's own interest.[29]

As the British viewed it, these ' clear instructions ' were necessitated by the Lama's seemingly overweening ambition. The latter, it appears, had asked the Kalon Lama to conquer ' all East Tibet upto Tachienlu ', a plan ' the wisdom or practicability ' of which the Kalon was, Teichman reported, ' secretly doubtful '.[30] Whatever the outcome of this clash of wills between Lhasa and its local commander, India's Foreign Department found itself completely helpless to influence policy. Denys Bray, then Foreign Secretary, noted that he could

> take no action more decided than exhortation and a refusal to supply Tibet with further ammunition.[31]

---

[28] Trade Agent, Gyantse to India, 23 May 1918, No. 76 in Ibid.

[29] India to Political Officer, 24 May 1918, No. 79 in Ibid.

[30] Teichman to Jordan, 20 May 1918 in Trade Agent, Yatung to India, 15 June 1918, Encl. in No. 27 in *Foreign*, October 1918, Procs. 11–202.

[31] Office note, 17 June 1918, in Correspondence in Ibid.

Chapter 27

Teichman, Tibet and China: The Boundary and Truce Agreements of *1918*

GENERAL PENG's discomfiture, and the capture of Chamdo in April 1918, brought matters to a head. With the momentum it had then acquired, the Tibetan advance seemed to sweep everything before it. Competent observers of the scene reasoned that, without much ado, the Kalon Lama's men could have overrun Batang, Litang and even Kanze, a development that would, without doubt, have precipitated a regular outbreak of hostilities between Tibet and China. Teichman who had stepped into the shoes of Louis King and of Coales, ostensibly as Assistant to the Consul General at Chengtu, but in reality as the British watch-dog on the frontier, considered the situation to be grave beyond measure. Completely cut off from Peking, except through circuitous, erratic and time-consuming channels, he braved odds with a resource and a persistence—and this despite his own physical disability—that would have done credit to younger men. To him more than anyone else, the Chinese and the Tibetans owed a temporary boundary settlement, followed by a one-year truce. Together, and for more than a decade and a half, they helped to stem the rival tides from sweeping across each other's domains and thereby preserve some semblance of peace in the twilight country that McMahon had called Inner Tibet.

By June (1918) Teichman, impressed by the urgency with which the situation required to be tackled, had written to Jordan at some length. On the one hand he wanted General Liu, the Chinese commander at Batang, invested with 'fullest authority' to act on behalf of Peking as also of Szechuan; on the other, he was no less keen that the impending Tibetan occupation of Chantui and of Derge be forestalled, for this could serve 'no useful purpose' beyond inciting Chinese authorities to further hostilities. Left to himself, Teichman viewed the Yangtse as a satisfactory and a stable boundary where Lhasa could 'tranquilly' wait until a permanent settlement with China had been effected.

Having arrived at Chamdo shortly after General Peng's capitulation, Teichman furnished intimate vignettes of life on the border. Chamdo, he noted, after a siege of some three months was not so much starved into submission as carried by assault. What was more, the Tibetans, who possessed no guns, had won the day with the help of British rifles, for

> amongst the miscellaneous collection of Russian, German, Chinese and Japanese rifles and carbines in use on this border . . . the remarkable success

attending to present Tibetan offensive is universally, and probably rightly, ascribed to the possession of these (British) rifles.¹

As for the Chinese debacle, Teichman viewed it as a 'natural culmination' of years of 'neglect' of the frontier garrison; a 'fitting punishment' for the 'foolish arrogance' and 'aggressive demeanour' of General Peng; and, what was more, 'a terrible tragedy' for the half-starved (Chinese) soldiers and civilians who filled the town. He noted that out of a garrison of 800 men, nearly 300 had been killed and that even in the month of May

> the stench of the wounded survivors and of the hundreds of dead, lightly buried in the half-frozen soil on the outskirts of the town, still poisoned the air.

His praise for the Chinese was the greater in that they had put up a good defence, despite a certain hopelessness in the position in which they were placed. 'From the very start' they suffered from a pronounced 'inferiority' in men, arms and ammunition. The credit for capturing the town belonged to a young battalion commander, Tsogo Depon who, Teichman noted, had visited India and 'knows a few words' of English. Apart from the Depon, however, there was only 'the smallest leavening' of training of any kind among the Tibetans and he wondered if they would stand up against modern Chinese troops.²

While able to build up a good *rapport* with the Kalon Lama and exercising a restraining influence on Lhasa, via India, Teichman found Peking difficult, intractable. After a long talk with the Chinese Prime Minister to whom he transmitted messages from General Liu, Jordan noted, early in July 1918, that the Central Government had

> practically no control over Szechuan, was out of telegraphic communication with authorities on Tibetan border-land, and could not in any case entrust negotiations to officers of the standing of Liu of whom they knew little or nothing.

Later, the British Minister was to conclude that

> the interest taken in question by Prime Minister was only lukewarm and conversation with him and similar informal conversations with Wai-wu-pu make it clear that Central Government was not very anxious to arrive at settlement at present. It is clear that they feel that time is in their favour

---

¹Teichman to Jordan, 20 May 1918, Encl. in No. 27 in *Foreign*, October 1918, Procs. 11–202. Also see Teichman to Jordan, 20 June 1918, Encl. in No. 40 in Ibid.
²Teichman to Jordan, 29 May 1918, No. 66 in Ibid.
This long despatch furnishes a vivid account of the siege and fall of Chamdo.

and they can let Tibetan question take its course until control over Szechuan has been regained.³

In an earlier assessment, in May (1918), Jordan had noted Peking's ' lack of interest ' coupled with a very ' obvious reluctance ' to discuss a subject in which it was ' insufficiently versed ' and whose settlement would expose it to the charge that the country's sovereign rights were being ' surrendered '.⁴

Lhasa was a study in contrast for the greater China's disinclination, or unpreparedness, to discuss the question, the stronger appeared to be Tibet's anxiety, ' at this very time ', to make a ' permanent settlement '. Nor was this difficult to understand. All through 1917–18, repeated messages poured in from the Chief Ministers entreating the ' great British Government ', Tibet's ' only hope and protector ', to intercede on its behalf. Their unending, tireless refrain was that China's debacle provided the ' most favourable opportunity ' for a settlement—which must be of a ' permanent ' character—and for which purpose British and Chinese representatives shoud be appointed ' at once '.

Another chorus that runs through these messages is the emphasis on the supply, ' at once ', of munitions of war.⁵ As the Indian Foreign Department viewed it, the Tibetan

> experience of the Simla Conference showed them that the Chinese were difficult people to negotiate with and the present disorder in China naturally appears to the Tibetans as a very good reason for pressing their claims.⁶

With Peking supremely indifferent and Lhasa eager to press home its advantage, Teichman's self-imposed task to negotiate a boundary settlement and thereby bring about a truce in the fighting then raging at white heat, was by no means an easy one. His only justification appears to have been that until such a settlement was effected, there was the danger of a recrudescence of trouble, with the Tibetans marching further into areas to which they had no legitimate claims. This, in turn, Teichman argued, would provoke the Chinese into retaliatory action that may push back the Kalon Lama across the Marches

---

³Jordan to Viceroy, 5 July 1918, No. 52 in Ibid.

⁴Jordan to Balfour, 10 May 1918, No. 63 in Ibid.

Jordan noted that the present moment was ' decidedly unfavourable ' for the reopening of the Tibetan question.

⁵Nos. 34 and 80 in *Foreign*, May 1918, Procs. 15–145; Nos. 15 and 31 in *Foreign*, June 1918, Procs. 15–84 and Nos. 18, 33 and 99 in *Foreign*, October 1918, Procs. 11–202 are some typical instances.

As for arms, so desperate was the position, that the Tibetans had sounded even Nepal for the supply, on payment, of 6,000 to 7,000 Martini-Henry rifles. For details, Bailey (then Resident in Nepal) to India, 18 July 1918, No. 76 in *Foreign*, October 1918, Procs. 11–202.

⁶Office note by A M Cardew, 10 August 1918, in correspondence, *Foreign*, October 1918, Procs. 11–202. Cardew argued that ' even if ' a temporary settlement were made, Peking would, ' as usual ', throw over anything ' unfavourable ' to the Chinese side.

into Tibet itself. Militarily, the Tibetans were the weaker party and, in the long run, bound to suffer serious reverses. All the more reason, therefore, Teichman debated, that they should favour a solution which, however unpalatable it may appear in the present, was bound to be accepted as correct in the long run.

The head-on clash of opposing arguments makes fascinating reading through a detailed study of the documents in this period. Thus the Tibetan viewpoint is summed up succinctly in a communication from the Chief Ministers towards the end of June 1918. Writing against the background of a large-scale military debacle suffered by the Chinese, Lhasa noted that if

> the British and Chinese governments cannot appoint their representatives to arrange the terms of peace in Kham until settled conditions are restored in China, once settled conditions are restored, the Chinese will despatch troops, and, if hostilities occur when both parties have recovered their strength, the greater power will encounter the less and we have great fear of losing territory....[7]

Understandably, any news from China that differences were being composed among its rival factions or unity fostered, frightened Lhasa out of its wits.[8] Equally, there was no yielding ground nor any

> question for us (but) to refer the matter to our protector... and we request that the agreement which was kept in India, may be formally sealed as quickly as possible, after reconciling the remaining arguments of the Tibetans and Chinese....If temporary boundary only (were made) matter will remain for future discussion (and lead to) later misrepresentations by the Chinese...(hence we) request the British Government to negotiate a permanent settlement at this very time.[9]

In the months that followed, the train of Tibetan thinking, as outlined in the preceding paragraphs, remained unaltered. In sum, as China was in a disturbed state, Lhasa argued, if pressure were brought to bear it ' will not be able to do otherwise than carry out the orders (i.e. the agreement) '. Hence the need ' to seal the agreement' and thereby settle the matter ' once for all '.[10]

The Chinese viewpoint has been alluded to earlier. Jordan noted that both

---

[7]Chief Ministers to Political Officer, 18 June 1918, Encl. in No. 81 in Ibid.

[8]On 8 July, the Shapes wrote to Major Campbell, then Political Officer, that news about Szechuan and Yunnan composing their differences frightened them and that they dreaded ' very much ' an ' un-expected ' (Chinese) advance. Encl. in No. 88 in Ibid.

[9]Chief Ministers to Political Officer, 20 July 1918, Encl. in No. 99 in Ibid.

[10]Encl. 1, No. 163, Encl., No. 164 and Encl. 1, No. 165 in Ibid., give texts of letters addressed by the Chief Ministers to David Macdonald, then Trade Agent, Gyantse and Yatung.

the Prime Minister, as well as the Foreign Office, showed no interest whatsoever. Worse still, they distrusted the activities of Teichman. For the matter of that, Jordan himself doubted if the British negotiator's continued presence in Tibet could serve any useful purpose. As to persuading Peking

> to come to a reasonable settlement I have already gone so far as I safely could, but, so far all my overtures have met with no genuine response though politely received. The Tibetan encroachments which they very well know can be checked easily as soon as some measure of order is restored in Szechuan, are not regarded by them in serious light.... I fear that an eventual settlement here (Peking) will not be facilitated by the conclusion of local agreement with a subordinate official against wishes of superior officer of his own Government. As long as it suits them, China will respect agreement and not longer.

Their present restraint, for what it was worth, was not difficult to explain, for it was

> regard for us and uncertainty as to the material support we may in the last resort extend to Tibetans added to prevailing disorder in Szechuan and not only any fear of Tibetans themselves that have, since the conclusion of the agreement of 1914, been guiding motive of Chinese policy towards Tibet and I am afraid that an attempt to come to a local arrangement with an unauthorised agent may seriously weaken this restraining influence....[11]

Was it any wonder then that Jordan's efforts to get the government in Peking involved into the goings-on in Eastern Tibet met with such poor response? To start with, in the latter part of June, his initiative was sought to be spurned through a perfunctory message from the Foreign Office, albeit finally he did succeed in getting an interview with the Prime Minister. The latter Jordan found to be 'much more conciliatory than his message'; yet evidently his pride had been touched by receiving ' such humiliating news ', as were now retailed to him by General Liu's communication, made through a ' foreign channel '—being forwarded by Teichman through the British Legation itself. While courteous, the Prime Minister displayed only a ' lukewarm ' interest. He ' knew nothing ' of Liu nor would he consent to ' delicate negotiations ' being entrusted to him (Liu). Writing to Balfour, then Foreign Secretary, on 6 July, the overall impression Jordan conveyed was that the Chinese

> having lost control of Szechuan are not at all anxious to relieve that province of the burden of the Tibetan question and that the Premier and his Cabinet are far too much occupied with matters effecting their own precarious tenure

---

[11] Jordan to Viceroy, 16 August 1918, No. 120 in Ibid.

of power to devote serious attention to Tibet. They doubtless realise that time is in their favour, that Tibetan aggression is not a serious matter in itself, and that they can afford to let it run its course until they have regained control over Szechuan.[12]

Lacking any support in Peking from his own Legation, and denied all encouragement by the Central Government of China, Teichman's task was by no means an enviable one. Paradoxically, what brought his negotiations to a successful conclusion was the fact of his being completely cut off from any direct contact with his political superiors for, at its quickest, no messages could get across to him in less than six to eight weeks, through channels which were far from dependable. The result was that by the time news reached him,[13] countermanding his action, or directing him to refrain from any particular initiative, his deals were already through.

Teichman negotiated two settlements: the first, a ceasefire, signed at Chamdo on 19 August; the second, a supplementary agreement enforcing a truce and troops' withdrawals, at Rongbatsa on 10 October. What he *did* achieve in the circumstances was doubtless of a limited and local character, but indeed remarkable. And this largely because he was a dedicated and persistent man.

Briefly, Teichman's territorial settlement stipulated: the Yangtse, from Kokonor to Yunnan, to form the China–Tibet boundary; Derge to be restored to its native chief (thereby creating a neutral buffer state between the opposing sides), and no Chinese troops to be stationed at Nyarong.[14] India thought the deal to be 'quite sound' and after all, it argued, Teichman was 'the man on the spot'.[15] Delhi, however, was far from enthusiastic about the 'idea of buffer states' although, in sharp contrast to Jordan, it was keenly desirous of a 'local settlement' that may 'give pause' to hostilities in the Marches and 'hold good' for some time.[16] It would appear that it was largely because of this helpful Indian attitude that Teichman was not recalled from his mission.

---

[12]Jordan to Balfour, 6 July 1918, Encl. in No. 154 in Ibid.

Jordan's earlier encounter with the Foreign Minister had been far from happy and when messages from General Liu had been relayed to the Premier, the latter had indicated that he was 'disinclined' to discuss the question 'at present'.

[13]There were three such channels; one, fast courier to Batang (ten days), thence by telegram to Chengtu (ten days), thence by telegram to Peking (time unknown); two, fast courier to Atuntzu in Yunnan (14 days), thence by telegram via Yunnanfu to Peking (time unknown); three, fast courier to Gyantse, via Lhasa (18 days), thence by telegram and cable via India to Peking. The last, Teichman thought, was 'the quickest and most reliable' method of communicating with the Legation in Peking. Teichman to Jordan, 1 August 1918, Encl. 1, No. 157 in *Foreign*, October 1918, Procs. 11–202.

[14]Teichman to Jordan, 16 July 1918, No. 93 in Ibid.

[15]Office note in Correspondence, pp. 14–15 in Ibid.

[16]Viceroy to Secretary of State, 21 August 1918, No. 126 in Ibid.

For his part, the British mediator all through underlined the *temporary* character of his settlement, a fact amply borne out by clause 2 of his proposed draft:

> This agreement is of a temporary nature only, but it is to remain in force until such time as the governments of China, Tibet and Great Britain shall have come to final settlement of the boundary and other questions at issue, or until such time as the contracting parties shall agree to its modification.[17]

But conscious of the overwhelming odds that beset him, Teichman continued to mount pressure on Jordan by way of messages which Liu wrote to the Chinese President, but transmitted through him (Teichman); or, in some such involved phraseology as ' Liu desires me to ask you (Jordan) to point out to Chinese Government, should you have a favourable opportunity '. Liu apart, his own emphasis on the gravity of the situation was unmistakable for, as he put it, a

> stage has been reached in Sino-Tibetan dispute when parties concerned must either resort again to arms or negotiate peace immediately, the boundaries of territories which the Tibetans over-ran this year are much too vague to permit of a continuation of state of passive hostility which reigned from 1913 to 1918.[18]

Support by Peking for his negotiations became the more necessary because even though the Chinese Commissioner at Tachienlu backed Liu and, in private, ' reaffirmed his willingness to our peace negotiations ', in public he denounced Teichman's work as ' cunning intrigue '.[19] Interestingly enough, the British Consul at Chengtu regarded the Chinese Commissioner of Tachienlu as an ' unreliable individual ' while, on his part, Teichman had developed great respect for General Liu. This was, if partly, because the latter too realised the seriousness of the situation and wanted to explain the ' whole matter ' personally to the highest authorities in Peking.[20]

To sum up, the ' tripartite ' talks between Teichman, General Liu, whom he had carried in his train, and the Kalon Lama opened in Chamdo on 11 August and drew to a close eight days later. Before they convened formally Teichman had, in considerable behind-the-scenes activity, hammered out the basis for a settlement. He had, as has been noticed, angled delicately, if desperately, for receiving due authority for Liu but, convinced that the one now presented was ' most favourable opportunity ' for securing a ' very

---

[17]Teichman to Jordan, 26 June 1918, in Correspondence, pp. 22–24 in Ibid.

[18]Teichman to Jordan, 2 August 1918, No. 136 in Ibid.

[19]Teichman to Jordan, 14 August 1918, in Trade Agent, Gyantse to India, 2 September 1918, No. 138 in Ibid.

[20]Teichman to Jordan, 3 August 1918, in Consul General, Yunnanfu to India, No. 149 in Ibid.

satisfactory settlement', stipulated that even if Liu did not receive instructions in time, the settlement could later be ' submitted ' to Peking for 'approval '.[21]

On 19 August, Teichman announced the conclusion of the tripartite agreement. The territorial compromise has been briefly alluded to. It may be recalled that during the course of the negotiations the idea of a ' neutral and independent ' Derge had been advanced if only for the reason that the Tibetans were most unlikely to abandon territories which they had conquered. The agreement had further stipulated that unless Chinese acceptance was forthcoming within four months, Lhasa was free to resume hostilities—a ' bluff ', as Teichman put it, to avoid ' indefinite procrastination ' on China's part. As for Lhasa:

> I have never received anything but the greatest courtesy from the Tibetans from the Kalon Lama himself to the lowest soldier . . . that the Tibetans, great and small, could not have been kinder had I been a blood brother.[22]

The crux of the matter, however, was ratification. Here, in sharp contrast to cooperation from Tibet, Teichman was up against a miasma of Chinese intrigue and back-slapping. Not only were there rumours galore that the British, intent on conquering Western Szechuan right up to Tachienlu, had equipped Tibetan troops with arms and loaned the Tibetan Government money, but what was more they were said to have despatched an Indian expeditionary force ' to follow up their (Tibetan) success '.[23] To cap it all, the Frontier Commissioner at Tachienlu was playing a double game—on the one hand, commending Teichman's efforts and giving General Liu authority to negotiate; on the other, writing to the Dalai Lama to withdraw Tibetan troops from the occupied districts to their original positions, before peace could be restored. These communications, Teichman ruefully concluded, were ' typical ' of the ' duplicity ' of Chinese officials in their dealings with the Tibetans on the frontier. Nor were the latter any the better behaved for they too had launched a heavy attack on Kantze during July (1918)—' after they had assured me ' that they agreed to a cessation of hostilities. For the record, this attack encountered stiff resistance as the Chinese were well-armed unlike the wretched ' Pien Chun ' whom, earlier, the Tibetans had so easily overwhelmed.[24]

Of the Tibetan stance at Chamdo, Teichman furnished a vivid account. At the outset, the Kalon Lama had told General Liu that unless his country ' immediately accepted ' the agreement, Tibetans ' would have no option '

---

[21]Teichman to Jordan, 1 August 1918, Encl. in No. 156 in Ibid.

[22]Teichman to Jordan, 6 August 1918, Encl. in No. 160 in Ibid.
Also see Teichman to Jordan, 19 August 1918, in Trade Agent, Gyantse to India, 9 September 1918, No. 151 in Ibid.

[23]Teichman to Jordan, 23 June 1918, Encl. in No. 161 in Ibid.

[24]Teichman to Jordan, 14 August 1918, Encl. in No. 162 in Ibid.

but to resume hostilities and advance on Batang. The Kalon also demanded that monasteries in Chinese-ruled territory should be under the ' complete control ' of the Dalai Lama and the inhabitants granted immunity from ' Ula ' and all other forms of Chinese taxation. More, the native chiefs (*tussu*) in Chinese territory should be restored a measure of their power. In sum, all that Chao Erh-feng had done, and which Liu had quoted ' unwisely ' as a ' precedent ', was to be repudiated, undone.

Later, Teichman adduced his own ten ' good ' reasons why the Peking government ' in their own interests ' should ratify the arrangement that he had worked out. *Inter alia*, he warned the Chinese to realise the

> utter absurdity and falsity of the idea (unfortunately current) that in surrendering districts to the Dalai Lama's rule they are ceding territory in some vague way to the British.

Furthermore, he pointed out that at the time the agreement was made all the districts of the 'so-called Szechuan Frontier Territory', which still remained with the Chinese, were ' at the mercy ' of the Tibetans. His agreement, even though ' purely provisional ', would not only help stabilise China's western frontiers and prevent raids, but held out a promise of resumption of commercial relations and friendly intercourse between Szechuan and Tibet—now all the more necessary because of the ' chaos still apparently reigning ' in China. Above all, while Chao had only to deal with scattered tribesmen lacking any cohesion, their place was now taken by

> well-trained and well-equipped Lhasa regiments (of today) who form rallying points for all the natives of Kham.

Understandably, in regard to the boundary settlement itself Teichman had to face a much greater difficulty with the Tibetans than with the Chinese. This was largely because Lhasa had a decisive territorial edge and had advised the Kalon Lama that Nyarong should be retained. Teichman noted that

> while admitting to the truth of my arguments he (Kalon Lama) showed for a long time that unreasoning obstinacy characteristic of a Tibetan or a Chinese, and it was only at the last moment, after threatening to throw up the negotiations and hinting at the displeasure of the Government of India, that I induced him to yield the point.

He justified his action in ceding eastern Derge to Tibet, for it

> entirely closes the North road beyond Kantze to most of Chinese troops, and this route rather than the more difficult southern road has of recent years been mainly used by the Chinese in communicating with the frontier.

Commending his handiwork for acceptance, Teichman felt it could be used 'as a lever' for obtaining 'a satisfactory permanent settlement' on the basis of creating an autonomous Tibet bounded on the east by the Yangtse. This would entail surrender of east Derge to China which, even though the Tibetans be unwilling, should be given up, the British mediator argued, in return for a rectification of the Kokonor boundary farther north.[25]

Nor was the frustrating finalisation of a boundary settlement the end of Teichman's difficulties. Two dangers lurked. One, as Liu had pointed out, was the possibility that Hsiung Ko-wu, then Governor of Szechuan, driven from his post by the northerners might seek to rehabilitate himself by means of an expedition against Tibet. The second eventuality was more serious, if also perhaps more immediate. To sustain the Chamdo agreement, it was necessary to separate the rival forces a reasonable distance from each other, through a truce agreement. But here the Kalon Lama would not allow Liu to leave Chamdo 'until' there was news from Peking regarding the latter's acceptance of the 19 August agreement. Yet, as Teichman pointed out,

> as long as Liu remains here my presence is necessary to act as intermediary between him and the Kalon, the latter still refusing to see him except in my presence or even to communicate with him except through me.[26]

Jordan was upset too, and expressed the hope that

> all influence of the Government of India will be used to move Dalai Lama to order the unconditional and instant release of General Liu and to facilitate Teichman's return. As long as the former is detained latter will feel naturally bound to remain...(what was more) I do not consider it advisable to approach the Chinese Government until I hear that General Liu has been released.[27]

A day earlier, on 24 September, he had told Teichman in no uncertain terms that there was

> no prospect of the Chinese Government ratifying the agreement come to at Chamdo....[28]

Fortunately for him, Teichman was beyond reach, having already shifted his scene of activity. With the Chamdo agreement now behind him, his next task

[25] Teichman to Jordan, 21 August 1918, Encl. in No. 189 in Ibid.
[26] Teichman to Jordan, 21 August 1918, Encl. 5 in No. 184 in Ibid.
[27] Jordan to Viceroy, 25 September 1918, No. 175 in Ibid.
[28] Jordan to Viceroy, 24 September 1918, No. 174 in Ibid.
Later the Chinese were to maintain that since they had not ratified the truce agreement, the frontier fixed under its terms was *not* 'legally binding'. *Yao-ting Sung*, p 116.

was to bring about a truce between the combatants. For this purpose, he convened a ' conference ', in a tent ' pitched between the opposing lines ', where two representatives of the Kalon Lama and two deputies of the Tachienlu-based Frontier Commissioner met. The conference site was the village of Rongbatsa, a long day's march west of Kanze, which, though held by the main body of the Commissioner's troops, had lately been seriously threatened by the more mobile Tibetan forces. Here, after nearly three weeks of hard bargaining and his own active intervention, a truce agreement was finally hammered out on 10 October.[29]

The Rongbatsa compact provided for a year's truce between the opposing sides and bound down the Frontier Commissioner at Tachienlu, General Chen Hsia-ling and, Teichman added, ' his successors', to a cessation of hostilities for that period. At the same time, the Tibetans were warned that if they continued their blind policy of aggression against a power which, though ' temporarily ' weakened, was ' so infinitely more powerful ' than themselves, disaster would result.

Liu and his men, Teichman noted, had been cordial ' partly... with a view to deceiving me in regard to their real thoughts and intentions ' but also because being on the frontier (' unlike the people in Chengtu '), they realised the hardships and difficulties involved in a renewal of their military campaigns. The British mediator had expressed the hope that with two high Chinese authorities—Generals Liu and Chen—bound to the truce by instruments to which a British official was a party, the Chinese Government and the Szechuan authorities would think twice over before breaking it. Indeed any such action would be tantamount to a 'gross breach of faith' with Great Britain. Nonetheless he was aware that

> at the worst our proceedings give time for something to be effected in Peking and it is only there that a suitables ettlement, whether on the lines of a ratification of the Chiamdo Agreement, or in other directions can be arrived at.[30]

In private, Teichman was critical of the Lhasa regime. Thus in a letter written on 12 October 1918 to Grant, then Secretary in India's Foreign Department, he expressed the view that the Tibetan offensive had been ' a mistake'; that the frontier would best be settled on the basis of the Mekong or the Yangtse-Mekong watershed; that the Chamdo agreement should be fully used to ' hold off ' a Chinese invasion which would be ' morally justified '. He favoured Lhasa's restoring Derge to its former chiefs, if the Chinese Government asked for such a modification of the Chamdo agreement and, in return,

---

[29]Teichman to Jordan, 11 October 1918, Encl. in No. 45 in *Foreign*, April 1919, Procs. 9–93. This despatch gives a vivid account of Teichman's journey from Chamdo to Kanze.
[30]Teichman to Jordan, 23 October 1918, Encl. in No. 45 in Ibid.

thought it necessary that the *British* should render Tibet all possible support in ' maintaining ' such a boundary.³¹

It was not long before Teichman discovered that Jordan regarded all his activities a ' mistake ' and called into question his entire work on the frontier. Driven to the wall, the mediator in him fought back:

> Do you not prefer a local truce even if unratified by the Chinese Government to a continuance of hostilities? It was absolutely a choice of two evils, either mediate and that very actively and without delay, or permit the Tibetans to sweep on over the ruins of Batang, Litang and Kantze, towards the borders of China proper, in which case there must have followed a regular war between China and Tibet, instead of frontier fighting in remote and unknown districts.... I submit ... whether the Chinese Government ... wanted me to mediate or not, my refraining from doing so would have been absolutely disastrous to Anglo-Sino-Tibetan relations.³²

Not that Jordan was altogether unappreciative of Teichman's handiwork. *Inter alia,* he conceded that the latter's despatches contained the ' most interesting' information regarding the state of affairs in the Tibetan Marches; that his efforts to effect a reconciliation between the conflicting elements had been ' most untiring '; that he had handled the matter with an ability and tact worthy of the best traditions of the Consular Service of which he was ' undoubtedly ' one of the ' most capable ' members. But a

> local armistice can provide no permanent solution of this question unless the agreement is fully endorsed by the Central Chinese Government.

But would that work? For, as he saw it, the

> real stumbling block to any agreement with Great Britain regarding Tibet (was) the hopeless infatuation of the Chinese for anything they consider to come under the heading of ' sovereign rights '.

What was worse, ' north ' as well as ' south ' China viewed the Tibetan rash with supreme ' indifference '

> being fully conscious that a re-united China will accelerate the retirement of the Tibetans within their own frontier.³³

---

³¹Teichman to Grant, 12 October 1918. The ' D O ' is marked ' secret ' and is to be found in Correspondence, p. 8, in *Foreign*, April 1919, Procs. 9–93.

³²Teichman to Jordan, 25 November 1918. This ' D O ' letter is in Correspondence, pp. 12–13 in Ibid.

³³Jordan to Balfour, 13 December 1918, Encl. in No. 74 in Ibid.

The Chinese Minister was Chen Lu and the interview took place on 6 December 1918. Chen Lu, who had been Head of the Political Department of the Wai-chiao-pu during the Simla Conference negotiations, had later served as Chinese Resident in Urga.

As to the boundary and truce agreements, Jordan emphasised that Peking ' could never accept ' the Simla basis for negotiations. Besides, it held Tibetan successes in the recent fighting as the direct result of Teichman's ' intrigues '. Nor could a settlement be made until China was unified and war in Europe had ended. Further, Peking argued, in this (Tibetan) question Great Britain ' must yield something ' before progress could be made and, like other states ' of the present day ', China regarded the preservation of reserve space as vital. A little later, the Chinese Foreign Office received from their Frontier Commissioner copies of the Chamdo and Rongbatsa agreements with the revealing title ' Agreement made by General Liu unauthorisedly with Mr. Teichman and not recognised '.[34]

The gravamen of Teichman's charge was that if Peking did indeed disapprove, it

> could have communicated with Liu through me or through Yunnan at any time during the past six months. If they disapproved of his making peace and desired him to sacrifice himself, his troops and Batang, why did they not send him instructions to that effect?[35]

While Teichman was hypercritical and Jordan only moderately optimistic, in the hope that a way for ' serious negotiations ' may soon be opened, both Lhasa as well as Whitehall were getting increasingly impatient. By the end of 1918, the former hoped that peace would soon return now that the ' big War in Europe ' had drawn to a close.[36] The India Office for its part was conscious of the inconvenience that would arise ' if the truce expires ' without an agreement having been reached, and hoped Jordan would ' lose no opportunity ' to effect one when conditions were ' more favourable '.[37]

---

[34] Jordan to Viceroy, 1 February 1919, No. 75 in Ibid.
[35] Teichman to Jordan, 26 December 1918, Encl. 1 in No. 84 in Ibid.
[36] India to Political Officer, 18 February 1919, No. 80 in Ibid.
[37] *I O* to *F O*, 24 January 1919, No. 80 in Ibid.
We are told that as between February and December 1918, Jordan made the ' same request ' (viz. for settling the Tibetan question) ' nine times ' which was a ' clear indication of the anxiety of the British Government ' and, one may add, that of Tibet. *Yao-ting Sung*, p. 118.

Chapter 28

May 1919: China Revives the Simla Proposals—and then Backs Out

THE CHAMDO agreement had provided for a 'provisional' boundary between China and Tibet while the one-year Rongbatsa truce of October 1918 had brought hostilities between the two countries to an end. As months sped by and Teichman's efforts, aided by Jordan's in Peking, to make the Central Chinese Government ratify these arrangements (to which its local officials had been a party) proved of no avail, anxiety mounted in Tibet, no less than in India. Lhasa, never too well-informed, was anxious for a 'permanent' settlement with marginal adjustments on the bases laid down in the 1914 Simla convention; Delhi, painfully aware that the Lama could not long sustain a war effort in Kham, wanted an early end to the stalemate and, in the interval, to buttress Tibet's strength. For its part, Peking, far too occupied with domestic squabbles, seemed oblivious, if not supremely indifferent, to what was happening in or on Tibet's borders.

It is to this period that a fairly detailed, and serious, Chinese initiative to settle the Tibetan question belongs. The May 1919 proposals spelt out the bases on which the Chinese were willing to settle; nor, barring some parts thereof which it intended using as bargaining counters, were the British averse to accepting them. Lhasa too, in the final analysis, may have been coaxed or cajoled into giving its assent. What undid the May proposals, however, was Peking's own complete repudiation of them. Who did it, and why, has remained an open question, albeit the Japanese were long regarded as the principal culprits. Nor did Jordan's later, and indeed desperate, efforts to breathe life into them bear any tangible results.

Towards the summer of 1919, as the one year time-limit for the Rongbatsa truce drew to a close, India Office, as no doubt Lhasa itself, was getting increasingly impatient in the matter of bringing negotiations with China to a firm conclusion. Whitehall felt unhappy at the thought that Tibetans should 'first occupy' and 'are later expelled' from Chinese territory,[1] while the Indian government had warned the Dalai Lama that 'scrupulous regard' for the letter and spirit of the provisions of the Chamdo and Rongbatsa agreements offered the 'best chance' for that permanent settlement for which he had been so very anxious.[2] Writing early in February 1919, Jordan had expressed the

[1] *I O* to *F O*, 24 January 1919, No. 89 in *Foreign*, April 1919, Procs. 9–93.
[2] India to Political Officer, 18 February 1919, No. 80 in Ibid.

hope that now that Peking knew what had happened in East Tibet, a way out for serious negotiations may shortly be opened.[3]

Teichman, much closer to the scene than remote Lhasa or Peking, was getting increasingly disillusioned. More than anything else he had been deeply upset by the ' duplicity and chicanery ' of the Chinese as evidenced by the conduct of the Frontier Commissioner who while he received him with ' effusive friendliness ' had been at once ' double-faced ' and ' mendacious '. Additionally, both in Szechuan and in Peking, the Commissioner had been responsible for ' libellous rumours ' about British motives in their mediation effort. Part of his wages, it seems, was a telegram from Peking intimating that the Kansu authorities would assist him 'with men, money and supplies ', a contingency which Teichman viewed as ' extremely improbable '.

There were certain other conclusions which the British mediator had drawn. *One*, that the Chinese Government in East Tibet, in the past six or seven years, had been a ' disgrace ' to China and all that it stood for. *Two*, that among the Tibetans in Kham, the British had become quite popular: given a free choice, they would probably vote for Tibetan rule ' under British protection '. *Three*, that the Chinese believed that they could recover Chamdo but were likely to meet an Indian army ' before reaching Lhasa '. *Four*, that now that a local peace had been effected, the next move lay entirely with Peking. But

> if the Chinese Government still refuse to accept the Chamdo treaty, it is exceedingly undesirable to delay the opening of negotiations for a final settlement a day longer than is absolutely necessary....[4]

This, however, was no easy task. A major hurdle was the complicated political mosaic, ' wheels within wheels ' as Teichman called it, which made up Peking's attitude towards the Tibetan question on the frontier. Thus, at the beginning of 1919, in western Szechuan alone he listed three semi-independent leaders whose jurisdictions overlapped: General Hsiung Ko-wu, Governor of Szechuan; Liu Yu-chiu of Yachau, appointed by the southern Chinese government to help restore peace on the frontier and take charge of Tibetan affairs generally; and Chu Hsia-ling, the Frontier Commissioner at Tachienlu. Besides, there were the Yunnanese and other groups who directly influenced the Tibetan situation. This seemed slightly odd for repeated declarations had been made by all political parties in China that Tibetan affairs were of national importance and, therefore, outside the scope of China's internal politics.[5]

Its political entanglements notwithstanding, Szechuan was still a far cry.

---

[3]Jordan to Viceroy, 1 February 1919, No. 75 in Ibid.

[4]Teichman to Jordan, 19 February 1919, Encl. in No. 47 in *Foreign*, July 1919, Procs. 15–96.

[5]Teichman to Jordan, 17 March 1919, Encl. in No. 67 in Ibid. Also see Teichman to Jordan, 21 February 1919, Encl. in No. 48 in Ibid.

The real difficulty stemmed from the situation that prevailed in Peking. As Jordan put it, the Chinese President was

> practically powerless to take any useful action ... until the dispute between the North and South has been settled and until he can obtain some measure of real authority over the military governors who at present govern China with their own armies and for their own purposes. Tibet is far from being the most important of the many difficult questions with which the President is confronted. The situation in Mongolia, which is much nearer Peking, is also very precarious. The conditions in Shensi are notorious, and many other provinces are little better. The Central Government therefore feel that they can well leave the Tibetan question to wait until they have solved more pressing matters nearer home.

There were two other aspects of the question to which Jordan drew pointed attention. One, that Tibetan successes in the March country, as Peking saw it, were largely due to the use of modern weapons supplied from India at a time when China, 'our ally', was suffering from serious internal troubles, and was in no position to pay attention to those remote frontier questions. This alone, Jordan emphasised, accounted for the

> indifference and sullen silence with which the Government here, so friendly to us in other respects, has received our representations in regard to Tibet.

The second arose from the

> obstinacy and pertinacity with which the Chinese cling to shadowy rights of suzerainty. It is idle to reason with them ... and futile to point out.....[6]

Convinced that it may not be possible to break through Chinese 'obstinacy', India urged that Lhasa stake a claim for self-determination, and press it at the Peace Conference in Paris. One wonders if it was to forestall such a claim being made that China, early in 1919, announced the formation of a Board for Tibetan Affairs? In any case, Delhi viewed the new Board as a 'piece of bluff', and argued that a demand for self-determination was such an 'obvious step' to take that the only reason for delay on Lhasa's part appeared to be that news of such possibilities had not yet 'filtered through".[7]

An important facet of the Tibetan situation was Lhasa's repeated requests, ever since 1914, for the supply of some machine-guns and munitions. During the years the war was being waged (1914–18) such requests had been completely ignored, but now that hostilities were over the British Political Officer was more sympathetic, convinced that

[6]Jordan to Curzon, 2 April 1919, Encl. in No. 79 in Ibid.
[7]Office note by A M Cardew, 8 May 1919, in Correspondence, pp. 9–10 in Ibid.

all that the Tibetan Government really want is that we should assist them to keep what they hold and to defend their country from Chinese aggression. If we can supply them with a reasonable quantity of military store, sufficient for defence but not for an active forward policy, we shall probably avoid the possibility of having to face the re-appearance of the Chinese on the North-east Frontier of India....[8]

In the Foreign Department, which the Political Officer served, two considerations were of over-riding importance. One, that a 'definite promise' to supply Tibet with ammunition at the end of the war[9] was long overdue; two, that if Britain rebuffed Tibet too often, and in all directions, there was the possibility that Lhasa would turn to Japan for assistance, 'either on her own initiative' or 'on a hint' from that country. In either case, it would make India's difficulties 'more serious still'.[10] A danger to be guarded against was that supplies made to Tibet may not be used for 'purposes of aggression'.[11] This was the more important insofar as Sir John Jordan's opposition to any supplies being made at all was no secret.[12]

Both these factors weighed powerfully with the policy-makers in Whitehall with the result that, at the end of June (1919), a final decision was postponed until there had been some move on the 'general question' of 'reopening negotiations'. It was clear that the conclusion reached was against the better judgment of India which feared a sudden Chinese attack on Tibetan positions in Kham and was painfully aware of the 'present weakness' of Tibet.[13] Jordan, who 'strongly deprecated' any suggestion that Tibet should continue to be supplied with arms and ammunition, was emphatic that no Chinese government would accept Tibet's 'conquests' in these frontier regions. What was more, a supply of arms would imply support to Lhasa's continued advance and thereby make Peking even more recalcitrant.[14]

A breakthrough in what appeared to be a veritable deadlock was the Chinese Foreign Office proposals of 30 May (1919). Presented to Jordan at a formal interview in Peking they stipulated *inter alia* that

1. The statement that Tibet formed a part of Chinese territory, now included in 'notes' appended to the (1914) Convention, was to be inserted in the treaty itself;

[8]Political Officer to India, 3 April 1919, No. 44 in Ibid.
[9]Bell's letter to the Chief Ministers contained this promise as did Major Campbell's. For details No. 48, Encl. 1 in No. 53 and No. 58 in *Foreign*, October 1916, Procs. 40–72.
[10]Office note by Denys Bray, 25 April 1919, in Correspondence, p. 5 in *Foreign*, July 1919, Procs. 15–96.
[11]Office note by Major Campbell, in Correspondence, pp. 15–16 in Ibid.
[12]No.167 in *Foreign*, October 1918, Procs. 11–202.
[13]Office note by A H Grant, in Correspondence, pp. 15–16 in *Foreign*, July 1919, Procs. 15–96.
[14]Jordan to Curzon, 2 April 1919, Encl. in No. 79 in Ibid.

2. Contrary to what had been laid down in the (Simla) Convention, Chinese Commissioners were to be stationed at the trade marts in Tibet;
3. A clause was to be inserted, in the treaty itself, that autonomous Tibet recognised Chinese suzerainty;
4. As to the boundary which had, in the final analysis, wrecked the Simla negotiations,

   (a) Territories under the jurisdiction of Chamdo, Riwoche, Gyade and Pashufat (to include Markham, Draya and Gonjo) were to form part of Inner Tibet;
   (b) Derge, Nyarong and that portion of Kokonor territory which lies between the Kunlun and the northern boundary of these areas, was to form part of Inner Tibet;
   (c) Tachienlu, Litang and Batang were to be included in Szechuan;
   (d) Original jurisdiction of Yunnan and Hsiangcheng was to remain unchanged.

In telegraphing the Chinese proposals home, Jordan made it clear that he regarded them as a basis for negotiations. Nor did he deem them to be Peking's last word—but even if it were

a settlement on these lines would fully safeguard our interest and would by no means (endanger) Tibet's.[15]

It would be evident that the British Minister's reaction was one of cautious optimism. The first and third propositions as listed, he felt, were unexceptional. As to the third viz., providing for Chinese Agents at trade marts in Tibet, he suggested that in lieu thereof, the British should ask for a Representative at Lhasa. In regard to the boundary now proposed, it seemed to Jordan essentially the old 18th century line, modified by transfer to Inner Tibet of Derge and Sangen. He thought it a great advance that the Chinese had offered to surrender Chamdo, Draya, Markham and Gonjo—the 'real crux', as he viewed it, of the boundary dispute.

Two other points were heavily underlined by Jordan. One, that a satisfactory settlement could only be concluded in Peking and here the presence of a Tibetan delegate was 'wholly undesirable'. Tibet, the British Minister felt, should 'merely be informed' of the fact of negotiations and 'not permitted in any way' to discuss the terms of a settlement. It followed that it was for

---

[15] Jordan to Viceroy, 31 May 1919, No. 1 in *Foreign*, February 1920, Procs. 1-208. The Minister for Foreign Affairs had formally invited Jordan to receive his 'new proposals'. Earlier, on 19 May, Jordan had urged the Minister 'to effect a settlement' of the Tibet question.

According to a Chinese scholar, the proposals were drawn up 'on the basis of the last proposal endorsed by the late President Yuan' in 1915. *Yao-ting Sung*, p. 118. Sung's date, '3 May 1919', is obviously wrong.

India to ram the terms, arrived at in Peking, down Lhasa's throat. Two, Jordan was averse to any territorial questions coming in the way of a speedy settlement of the dispute and strongly deprecated conflicting claims in the 'barren regions of Kokonor' from stalemating the parleys. What was pertinent was that the Chinese had 'always' been, and 'at present moment' were, in possession of this region and 'unlikely' to be thrown out by any means 'short of military force'.

Further, the British Minister underlined both the importance of the Chinese initiative and the extreme urgency of seizing the opportunity at once. If he were given a 'free hand', Jordan was confident a stable and fair settlement would result; understandably, he would be opposed to the necessity of 'constant reference home'. Above all, he was keen to avoid the 'risk' of breaking off formal negotiations now initiated, 'after months and years' of procrastination and delay, for if the opportunity somehow slipped away a 'united and stable' China would come into being, 'prepared and able' to advance on Lhasa.[16]

Chinese proposals sharply split the Foreign Department in Delhi. The hard-liners, the 'hawks' in current parlance, including the Political Officer Major Campbell, wanted Chinese adherence to the 1914 compact with a 'minimum of modifications'. More specifically, the proposal regarding the posting of Chinese Agents at the trade marts was bitterly opposed. Again, even though the desirability of a British representative at Lhasa was recognised, it did not seem 'worthwhile', Delhi argued, to secure this in return for the presence of the Chinese at the marts.

A matter of some significance which emerges even from a most superficial glance at the Chinese draft is the fact that there is no mention here of Tibet's frontiers with India and that the whole emphasis is on 'Inner' Tibet, Kokonor and the Marches. The territorial settlement, India pleaded, seemed good enough, even though far from fair for the area of Inner Tibet, where Lhasa claimed religious rights, had been reduced without any corresponding gains accruing to the Dalai Lama's domain. Nor was the 'cavalier' treatment of Tibet advocated by Jordan acceptable for this, it was feared, would make her (Tibet) unduly suspicious of Britain's aims and objectives, and imperil the friendly relations built up since 1904. There was also the danger of Lhasa turning to Japan, if it lost faith in the British.[17] Additionally, there was the possibility that an agreement reached with China may be rejected by Tibet. Hence, Delhi argued, 'constant consultation' with Lhasa must go alongside negotiations with China.[18]

---

[16]In a later, and more detailed, analysis, Jordan maintained that the new Chinese proposals, in conjunction with those of Wellington Ku, made in June 1915 (No. 61 in *Foreign*, July 1916, Procs. 39–163) constituted a very considerable advance when compared with earlier (Chinese) offers. Jordan to Curzon, 1 June 1919, No. 21 in *Foreign*, February 1920, Procs. 1–208.

[17]Office note, in Correspondence, pp. 1–6 in Ibid.

[18]Note by Major W L Campbell, 16 June 1919, in Ibid.

The end-result of discussions in the Foreign Department was summed up in the Viceroy's cable to Whitehall on 27 June. Broadly, proposals 1 and 3 were acceptable, but 2 (relating to stationing of Chinese Commissioners at the marts) was not, for it would mean Chinese 'intrigue and provocative action'. Delhi, however, was averse to demanding British representation at Lhasa as a counter-concession, even though it suggested that the Minister might find it a useful lever to induce China to abandon its original suggestion. Besides, Tibet was to be kept 'fully informed', albeit a breakdown of negotiations, in any case, was to be avoided.[19]

To Delhi's anxiety to consult with Tibet, Jordan was resolutely opposed, for it would, he reasoned, mean further 'prolonged delay'. There was another risk that gnawed on the British Minister's mind, and it related to Japan giving publicity to the 'most sensational accounts' of British demands, thereby vitiating the atmosphere for the (British-Chinese) talks.[20]

The fact that there was a grave risk of negotiations falling through may be gauged from persistent rumours in Peking—and the May 30 movement had just about got under way—about China's sell-away on Tibet and the diabolical machinations of British imperialists. This is borne out by a joint (Sino-British) statement, issued early in July, wherein Britain's role as a 'friendly middle man' helping Tibet and China to come to a 'stable settlement' of the boundary question was heavily underlined and the possibility of some modification of the frontier laid down in 1914, through British good offices, was duly stressed.[21]

As exchanges continued between Jordan in Peking and the Viceroy in Delhi, the former showed obvious signs of growing impatience. On 30 July, he telegraphed home to say that two months had elapsed since Peking made its proposals, while another two and a half remained for the truce agreements of 1918 to expire. Further, he feared that Chinese activity in Mongolia, if successful, would cause an unfavourable reaction in their attitude and expressed himself 'increasingly anxious' about the outcome of his impending negotiations, if their opening was further delayed.[22]

On 31 July, Whitehall showed some signs of movement for on that day the Viceroy was authorised to inform the Tibetan government that Jordan was initiating the parleys in Peking. While HMG shared Tibet's objections to the stationing of Chinese Trade Agents, as for a British representative at Lhasa, all that it was prepared to agree to was a modification of Article VIII of the 1914 Convention, the modified version reading as follows:

---

[19] Viceroy to Secretary of State, 27 June 1919, No. 9 in Ibid. On 24 June, Foreign Secretary Grant had noted: 'I am entirely against a British Resident at Lhasa'. Office note in Correspondence, in Ibid.

[20] Jordan to Viceroy, 1 July 1919, No. 16 in Ibid.

[21] Jordan to India, 6 July 1919, No. 15 in Ibid.

[22] Jordan to Curzon, 30 July 1919, No. 23 in Ibid.

British Agent at Gyantse may visit Lhasa whenever necessary for the purpose of communicating (with) Tibetan Government. Should British Government hereafter decide with consent of Tibetan Government to station a permanent Resident at Lhasa, Chinese will have no objection.[23]

The green signal from London came a day later. Very broadly, Jordan's line of reasoning was approved; nor was it deemed necessary to obtain Lhasa's prior concurrence. The frontier proposed by Peking was 'generally' agreed to—on the assumption that the new Kokonor border will leave Tangla range securely in Tibetan hands. The nub of the problem, as Whitehall viewed it, was the Chinese demand for the Trade Agents, and Lord Curzon, then at the helm of affairs in the Foreign Office, made it abundantly clear that it was 'unacceptable'. If at all agreed to, it was to be on the

> distinct understanding that their functions were (to) be strictly confined to questions of Sino-Tibetan trade and that they must in no circumstances concern themselves in administrative matters or attempt to interfere between British Trade Agent and local Tibetan authorities. We could in no case allow situation of 1906–10 to recur....[23a]

A couple of weeks later, Jordan intimated that at the outset of his negotiations, the Chinese attitude appeared 'reasonable'. His own 'strategy' was to underline three propositions. *Firstly*, to replace Article IX of the (1914) Convention (relating to Inner-Outer Tibet) which had been a major bone of contention by a new version laying down the boundary between China proper and Tibet and safeguarding the Dalai Lama's religious rights in the Chinese-controlled frontier region. He also proposed to

> omit all reference to Indo-Tibetan boundary unless instructed to the contrary since I understand latter to have been laid down in agreement between British and Tibetan representatives in March 1914.

Secondly, he proposed to leave Article VII (relating to regulation of trade between Tibet and India) unchanged in order 'to avoid raising new points'. The fact that new trade regulations had already been negotiated and were in force could be mentioned subsequent to the exchange of notes—'if indeed it was considered necessary'.

And *finally*, statements that Tibet formed part of Chinese territory and recognised Chinese suzerainty may be inserted in Article II, in return for a modification of Article VIII regarding the right of British representation at Lhasa. However, in the

---

[23] Secretary of State to Viceroy, 31 July 1919, No. 29 in *Foreign*, February 1920, Procs. 1–208.
[23a] Curzon to Jordan, 1 August 1919, Proc. 124 in Ibid.

event of Chinese insisting on right to station (their) Trade Agents at marts in return for latter (British representation at Tibetan capital) I will resist ... short of breaking off negotiations and as a last resort make my agreement thereto conditional on receipt of (assurance?) required by you.[24]

Jordan's approach was, so far as it went, sound enough and, put to test, may have yielded handsome dividends. However, as ill-luck would have it, hardly had some progress been made and parleys got underway when they drew to an 'abrupt and totally unexpected' end in circumstances which, the British Minister confessed, were, in his experience, 'quite unprecedented'. His own description of this sudden and dramatic anti-climax could scarcely be bettered. On the eve of a previous appointment with the Minister, when he hoped the boundary question would be settled, a Councillor put in an appearance

to inform me that in consequence of a change in public opinion Cabinet had decided to postpone negotiations and (to inform him) that today's appointment should be considered as cancelled.

Jordan's brave, and dogged, fight to get the decision reversed did not avail much. The Chinese Minister's 'long and halting explanation' was far from enlightening: insofar as the proposals had not been 'approved' by Parliament, he had argued, they would encounter 'much opposition' when the public would come to know of them. Driven into a corner, and 'speaking privately', he nonetheless conceded that the

Minister of a certain Power had received from his Government instructions to make enquiries about Sino-British negotiations and indirectly admitted that this was cause of their interruption which he personally regretted deeply.

The British Minister was profoundly upset, and told his superiors that the incident

is regretted by me as a direct challenge by Japan of our whole position in Asia and I venture to hope that the challenge will be accepted ... (he knew of) a bitter campaign against these negotiations which has been engineered by Japanese Legation.... Example of Persia has been set up as a warning to Chinese of what Tibet will become under British guidance and every conceivable weapon, even my impending retirement, has been used to induce Chinese to abandon the negotiations.[25]

[24]Jordan to Curzon, 14 August 1919, Encl. in No. 109 in Ibid.
  In an office note on 31 July 1919, the Indian Foreign Department expressed the view that for reasons given by Jordan and Teichman, 'a textual boundary line certainly seems preferable to a map line'. Correspondence, p. 10 in Ibid.
[25]Jordan to Curzon, 27 August 1919, No. 64 in Ibid.

What was more, the Chinese Minister, Jordan noted, 'hardly concealed' the fact that he was acting against his own conviction implying thereby that, left to itself, Peking would be glad to settle the question.[26]

It certainly was a grave charge: Tokyo's 'direct challenge', as Jordan put it, to England's whole position in Asia. The subject assumed added importance in the light of Japan's known interest, and intrigue, in Lhasa. Where precisely did the truth lie? Three facets of the situation deserve scrutiny in this context. One, that a former Chinese Minister in London, Wang Ta-sieh, had told a Secretary in the British Legation in Peking that Tokyo had directly threatened that unless negotiations were terminated

> Japan and pro-Japanese military party would bring into being an agitation which would result in transfer of popular feeling regarding Shantung to Tibetan question.

And this, Wang confessed, the Peking Government was unable to resist.[27]

Another sidelight is afforded by Jordan's talks with the Japanese Minister who, while conceding that he had made a telephone enquiry from the Chinese Foreign Office, maintained that this was in the nature of a 'routine' exercise with a view to keeping the Legation 'informed of current events'. As for anti-British pamphlets, these had been ordered from a Japanese firm, albeit for a 'Chinese principal'. For his part, the Japanese diplomat attributed the suspension of negotiations to 'evasion' on the part of the Chinese.[28] Interestingly enough, the Japanese Minister in London, when pressed on the point by Curzon, stoutly 'repudiated' the suggestion that China had broken off the talks under his country's pressure.[29]

Whatever the truth, a significant aspect of the question was Jordan's impressive marshalling of evidence to sustain his thesis. *Inter alia*, he cited an article from a Japanese journal which maintained that Chinese public opinion regarding Tibet had been aroused and that the British had not only made con-

---

[26]In the (Indian) Foreign Department, A M Cardew speculated:
   Is it not conceivable that the alleged Japanese Minister's intervention may have been invented by a perhaps pro-Japanese party in China which wanted to 'get back' at us for having supported Japan's claims to Shantung at the Peace Conference?

Office note, 28 August 1919, in Correspondence, pp. 19-20 in Ibid.
[27]Jordan to Curzon, 6 September 1919, No. 83 in *Foreign*, February 1920, Procs. 1-208.
[28]Jordan to Curzon, 19 September 1919, No. 96 in Ibid.
Jordan had told the Minister that it was the Japanese influence with a pronounced military element in government which had led to 'this unfortunate result'.
[29]Curzon to Jordan, 1 September 1919, No. 134 in Ibid.
Curzon had told the Chinese Minister that, whatever the reason, 'the procedure was one which, if accepted, would render the conduct of negotiations between friendly powers almost impossible'. The shock to him (Curzon) was the greater for at Paris he had been fighting China's battles over Shantung. Was this 'the sort of return I might expect to receive?'

cessions on the Tibetan-Chinese frontier but were prepared to discuss the issue on the basis of China's claims. While it was

> true that the two provinces (Manchuria and Mongolia) are nearer to Central Asia than Tibet, but the Tibetan question involves an issue which is scores of times more consequential than the preservation of Japan's special rights and interests in Manchuria and Mongolia. It will be extremely interesting to watch how the Tibetan question will be solved.[30]

On his master's cue, R H Clive, a junior official at the Legation in Peking, compiled a Memorandum that surveyed the anti-British press campaign instigated by the Japanese and concluded with the remark that without doubt the

> whole of this (anti-British) propaganda has been organised from Tokyo—and though we have no proof of it—almost certainly at the instigation of the Japanese Government, in order to justify their own action in Shantung and persuade the Chinese into believing that our (British) action with regard to Tibet is far worse than that of Japan in Shantung.[31]

Jordan's suspicions in the matter were further confirmed by his interviews with the Prime Minister and the President. While the former repeated stock phrases about 'popular and parliamentary' feeling and underlined the fact that the situation 'had changed' since the negotiations commenced in May,[32] the President enunciated three prerequisites which he deemed essential to their resumption. One, that representatives from Szechuan should be present in Peking for consultations during the negotiations; two, that Parliament would have to be kept informed about their progress; and three, that before signature the agreement would have to go before Parliament.[33]

Japanese 'stranglehold' apart, another situation was developing not far from Peking, which possibly made the Chinese shirk an early decision. The fact was that, by September 1919, China had recovered its well-nigh lost position at Urga and felt that a 'bold front' in Tibet might produce a 'similar result'. Besides, conveniently for it, Peking had never recognised

---

[30] Extract from 'Japan Advertiser', 23 August 1919, Sub-encl. 2 in No. 152 in Ibid.

Earlier, Jordan had sent Curzon the translation of a Japanese pamphlet accusing Britain of including in Tibet the provinces of Kansu, Kokonor, half of Szechuan and of Yunnan and 'cutting them off' from Chinese territory. For details Sub-encl. 1 in No. 125 in Ibid.

[31] 'Memorandum by R H Clive on anti-English press campaign instigated by the Japanese with regard to the Tibetan negotiations', No. 133 in Ibid.

[32] Jordan to Curzon, 29 August 1919, No. 70 in Ibid.

[33] Jordan to Curzon, 5 September 1919, No. 80 in Ibid.

Jordan noted that the replies given by the Prime Minister and the President were 'contradictory and confused' and remarked that while there would probably be no insuperable objection to continuance of negotiations, 'it is very unlikely that they would result in an acceptable settlement'.

[n. contd. overleaf

the 1918 Teichman-Liu-Kalon Lama negotiations in Eastern Tibet, much less the truce agreement that had resulted therefrom. It followed that, strictly from its limited angle, Tibetans were still 'rebels' against its authority and had to be dealt with as such.[34]

By December, when news of Mongolia's request for the 'cancellation' of its autonomy came through, Jordan expressed the view that Peking had

> now definitely decided to wait until Tibetans grow weary of situation and of our failure to obtain a settlement and then to endeavour to win them back to Chinese allegiance by assurances of autonomy and favourable treatment.[35]

Whatever the role of Japan, and of developments in Urga, in bringing to an abrupt, and abortive, conclusion the Sino-British effort to settle the question of Tibet, the latter's viewpoint both before and during the negotiations needs some scrutiny. Actually one is not too sure whether, even if the Japanese had not thrown in the spanner, Lhasa would have accepted the conclusions reached in Peking between the British Minister and the Chinese. For, from the very first, their suspicions had been aroused—and to the full. Thus it is significant that Tibet's reaction to the information that Jordan had, in fact, commenced the parleys was the convening of the Tsongdu which, in a resolution that bore the impressive, and weighty, seals of the three monasteries, requested that, if possible ', negotiations ' may be conducted at Lhasa or failing that at Gyantse or as last resort at Chamdo '. Nor was that all. For the Dalai Lama's government went a step further to state its 'unalterable stand' on four points stipulating that (1) Article II, relating to Tibet's autonomy and suzerainty, should remain unchanged; (2) no Chinese officials should be stationed at the trade marts in Tibet; (3) the Kunlun range should form the boundary for Outer Tibet while Derge and Nyarong should be included in Inner Tibet; (4) Lhasa's existing rights in Litang and Batang, as defined in Article IX, should be maintained.[36]

A Chinese writer has noted that while there was ' every indication ' that Peking ' seemed ready ' to accept the compromise solution, there was opposition from some of the provinces ' such as Szechuan and Yunnan ' and from the ' Chinese public as a whole '. *Yao-ting Sung*, p. 121.
[34]Jordan to Curzon, 9 September 1919, No. 152 in Ibid.
[35]Jordan to Curzon, 4 December 1919, No. 179 in Ibid.
A day earlier, the Foreign Minister had told Jordan ' definitely ' that a settlement was ' unattainable at present ' and alluded to the excited state of public opinion in the country and ' risk of an anti-British boycott '.
Sung maintains that there was a powerful anti-British movement in China fanned by an unpopular circular telegram which Peking had sent to the provinces, giving the background to its negotiations with the British. Popular opinion, we are told, denounced the regime as ' incapable, weak and with a particular lack of vision and interest ' in Tibet while British demands were condemned as ' practically amounting ' to the seizure of that country. *Yao-ting Sung*, p. 122.
[36]Political Officer to India, 27 August 1919, No. 63 in Ibid. [n. contd. overleaf

Two things may be noted. One, that on the terms stated by Lhasa there could have been no settlement of the Tibetan question, for it stands to reason that Peking would never have accepted the territorial arrangement made in 1914. Even Jordan at his first meeting with the Chinese, it may be recalled, had put forth his tentative ' counter-suggestion ' of abolishing Inner Tibet with a part going to Outer Tibet and another to China, thereby resulting in a clear-cut boundary separating the two countries.[37] Again, on the question of Chinese officials at the trade marts, the British, though determined to oppose the suggestion, were, as has been noticed, not prepared to carry their opposition to it to a point of complete break-down, a view which Lhasa may not have accepted.

It is significant that Major Campbell, the then Political Officer known for his pro-Lhasa leanings, regarded the Tibetan reply as ' uncompromising '. And this despite his having told the Lama, and his Ministers, that the alternative to a permanent settlement was a united China sending an army ' to conquer ' the country. Later, when the negotiations did, in fact, prove abortive, the Political Officer was hesitant to inform Lhasa lest the Tsongdu, ' sufficiently chauvinistic ' as it had proved without any ' encouragement ', view it as a triumph for their intransigence.[38] The plain, unvarnished truth was that Tibet still harked back to the terms of the 1914 Convention and the Rongbatsa truce concluded four years later and felt that all that was needed was to ' confirm ' these agreements. At the same time, Lhasa felt ' obliged to request ' that in any future negotiations, the representatives of its National Assembly must be fully associated.[39]

For its part, Delhi's Foreign Department rated the prospects of the Tibetan Assembly agreeing to anything as ' small ', and, in consequence, viewed the task of making Lhasa toe the line as ' none too easy '.[40] Nor was the consent of the National Assembly, and of the Lhasa government, a mere formality but, as

To put the record straight, it was on 31 July that the Secretary of State had authorised the Viceroy (No. 39 in Ibid.) to inform the Tibetan government that Jordan was ' opening negotiations '. This communication was received by the Political Officer on 6 August and it was not until some time later that Lhasa did, in fact, learn about the parleys.

[37] Bell doubted the advisability of abolishing Inner Tibet and felt that Lhasa would oppose it strongly, for
> they feel that Inner Tibet is still Tibet and the Simla Convention gives them the chance of establishing a fairly strong position in it. The Tibetan Plenipotentiary at the Simla Conference used to say: ' As regards Inner Tibet, the best men will win ', and since the Simla Convention, Tibetans had consciously done this.

Office note by Bell, 3 October 1919, Correspondence, pp. 30–31 in Ibid.

[38] Political Officer to India, 30 August 1919, No. 71 in *Foreign*, February 1920, Procs. 1–208.

[39] Chief Ministers of Tibet to Major Campbell, 23 August 1919, Encl. 1 in No. 81 in Ibid.

Also see Encl. 2, (No. 81) which is a communication ' From the Heads of the three monasteries of Sera, Drepung and Ganden and the clerical and lay officials of Tibet, being the National Assembly ' to Major Campbell.

[40] Office note, in Correspondence, p. 25 in Ibid. Also note by Bell, *supra*, n. 37.

Charles Bell noted, a necessary prerequisite. In all fairness, however, it may be remarked that the failure of the negotiations in Peking owed not an iota to Lhasa's opposition or churlishness on the question. Actually, a little later, as will be noticed presently, Tibet veered round to accepting a solution which it agreed might, in the first instance, be negotiated in Peking.[41]

[41]Political Officer to India, No. 81 in Ibid.

PART VII   BELL'S POLICY TOWARDS TIBET

Chapter 29

The Kansu Mission and the Question of Arming Tibet

CHINA'S ABRUPT repudiation of the May 1919 offer to re-negotiate the Simla Convention left the British cold and Lhasa jittery. Whether at Tokyo's behest, or as a result of compulsions of its own domestic situation, Peking forced a reversal of gears, and seemed singularly indifferent to all that was happening in or around Tibet's frontiers. And yet this was far from being the whole truth. On a pattern it had adopted earlier, China now made an effort to negotiate a bilateral deal with Lhasa. The British role as mediators, Peking argued, was superfluous; the best they could do, was to 'witness' an agreement which the other two parties had worked out earlier and on their own. As in the hectic months before the Simla Conference opened in October 1913, Lhasa refused to fall into line and the Chinese effort at a bilateral settlement, through the intermediacy of what came to be known as the Kansu Mission (January-April 1920), came to nought. The failure of the mission, however, made Peking disown its sponsorship and repudiate its proposals.

Irrespective of the results that emerged, the Kansu mission was a determined Chinese effort to go it alone with Tibet. Soon after it beat a retreat, debate raged in India, as in Whitehall and the Legation in Peking, over a change in Britain's Tibetan policy. An isolated Lhasa, it was argued, may become unfriendly, even hostile. To buttress its strength and help it regain its confidence, a modest dose of arms and ammunition was deemed necessary. Yet this was easier said than done. Besides, arming the country was only one facet of a changed policy towards the Dalai Lama's domain.

After Jordan had signally failed to make Peking revive its own offer of May 1919, British impatience with China grew, while the latter for a variety of reasons refused to discuss, much less settle, the Tibetan issue. Tuan Chi-jui, then acting as Foreign Minister, hinted that public opinion in China was excited and might erupt into an anti-British boycott—even as it had against Japan. Besides

> if Great Britain would stand aside China would settle matters directly with Tibetans... an arrangement might be reached on basis of a treaty signed by China and Tibet as principals and approved and witnessed by Great Britain.

Whether China could 'overawe' the Tibetans, even as it had the Mongols, or endeavour to win them back to Chinese allegiance by 'assurances of autonomy and favourable treatment', was not clear. What was, was the fact that Peking would play its game of procrastination until the Tibetans despaired of a settlement, convinced that the British were unable to bring about one. This was a situation that suited the Chinese book admirably.[1]

Whitehall's reaction to Chinese tactics was one of shock and indignation. It decided, *inter alia*, that to register its sense of outrage at the 'disingenuous character' of the negotiations and the 'discourtesy' of procedure in abruptly breaking them, Jordan be recalled. As to Peking, it may go it alone with Lhasa and hammer out a treaty that may be 'approved' and 'witnessed' by Great Britain.[2]

Unfortunately for the success of this procedure, Whitehall seemed to be taking the Tibetans too much for granted whereas, to men on the spot, it was evident that they could not 'possibly negotiate'—unless the British acted as mediators. Nor would Lhasa willingly accept the gratuitous role Great Britain mapped out for itself in merely 'approving' and 'witnessing' an agreement—'especially' if China regarded Tibet as 'irredenta country', to be recovered and incorporated into its larger whole at a favourable opportunity.[3]

None too keen as they seemed outwardly, the Chinese were, in behind-the-scenes activity, making their own cautious soundings at Lhasa. A conspicuous effort in this direction was the Kansu Mission (January-April 1920) which was led by Chu Hsien, an officer of the provincial government of Kansu, accompanied by a dozen lamas from the Kumbum monastery. It would appear that it had repaired to the Tibetan capital to persuade the Dalai Lama, and some of his men, to negotiate with the Peking regime but insofar as he proved unyielding, the Chinese quietly disowned it.

The first tidings came in an agitated telegram from the then Political Officer, Major Campbell, on 18 December (1919). While announcing the arrival of the Mission at Jyekundo, he pressed Delhi hard to heed Lhasa's demand for the 'immediate' deputation of a British officer. Campbell supported the request for, as he viewed it, any negotiations which were not tripartite in character would be 'undesirable' both for their ill-effects on the frontier, as also on Bhutan and Nepal.[4] While to outward appearances Peking disclaimed all responsibility for the (Kansu) Mission and called it an exclusive provincial effort, there were many who believed that once the Mission arrived at a settlement with Lhasa, the Central Government would claim its parenthood.[5]

[1]Jordan to Curzon, 4 December 1919, No. 179 in *Foreign*, February 1920, Procs. 1-208.
[2]Secretary of State to Viceroy, 13 December 1919, No. 184 in Ibid.
[3]Political Officer to India, 18 December 1919, No. 187 in Ibid.
  Major Campbell had written to say that the Tibetans had 'no objection' to a Chinese Mission visiting Lhasa provided that a British Officer 'accompanies' it.
[4]Foreign Secretary to Private Secretary to Viceroy, 19 December 1919, Correspondence, p. 48 in Ibid.
  Also see Political Officer to India, 18 December 1919, No. 195 in Ibid.
[5]Jordan to Curzon, 27 December 1919, No. 201 in Ibid.
  The Chinese Foreign Minister had affirmed that there were a number of Tibetan lamas offering to go with the Kansu mission but that 'their real object was to gather money'.

A lot of rumour-mongering enveloped the Mission not only through its three and a half months' sojourn in Lhasa, but in all that preceded its arrival and followed its departure. Cutting through a whole mass of irrelevance, two facts seem to emerge fairly clearly. One, that the Mission had come to Lhasa uninvited and was the effort primarily of the Kansu authorities to hammer out a solution of the seemingly intractable problem of Tibet. It was apparent that insofar as such prospects appeared singularly dim, Peking kept on the side-lines, and even feigned ignorance, albeit it may be pointed out that the despatch of the Mission had been advertised repeatedly in a prominent Chinese daily, the *North China Herald*.[6]

Another point that bears mention is the fact that between what the negotiators proposed and what Tibet was prepared to accept, there was no meeting-ground whatsoever. In its herculean effort—for two months of its stay there were intensive parleys between the parties—to wean Lhasa away from its southern neighbour, the Mission appears to have made liberal promises. Unfortunately for it, the Lama and his officials were not so easily persuaded, for the 1913–14 experience at Simla was a little too recent and disillusioning and had served as an eye-opener. Nor did Lhasa set much store by paper promises, however impressive they might appear.

It was revealing of their mutual distrust that all that the two sides finally agreed to was to postpone serious negotiations to a later date when, both as a result of the Kansu Mission's 'request' to the Chinese President and the Tibet Government's own independent approach, the British were expected to depute a representative to a tripartite meeting. Until these serious negotiations did come about, both the Chinese as well as Tibetan troops on the frontier were to observe a 'cease-fire'.[7]

The important thing about the Kansu Mission, it would seem in retrospect, was that it marked a decisive stage in British India's approach towards the Tibetan question. For once, the British were shaken by this open and deliberate Chinese attempt to woo the Dalai Lama. The shock was the more pronounced insofar as their own repeated efforts over many years to persuade Peking to reopen the Tibetan question had failed, and dismally. The failure

---

According to Dr Sung, the Kansu mission was the result of a 'special conference' convened in Peking in 1919 to find out 'ways and means' of establishing Chinese authority in Tibet. The leader was Chu Hsien, an officer of the Kansu provincial government. Sung refers to it as '*the* Chinese mission' which had 'no power' to deal with vital problems, but 'promised' to refer all questions (which the Dalai Lama had raised) 'to the Chinese Government for consideration except the one of continuing the truce which was accepted at its discretion'. *Yao-ting Sung*, pp. 124–25.

[6] Political Officer to India, *supra*, n. 4.

[7] Major Campbell believed that the Kansu Mission had been able to arouse 'anti-British' feelings, as 'invariably' happened with Chinese delegates at Lhasa. Political Officer to India, 30 April 1920, No. 5 in *Foreign*, November 1920, Procs. 1–102.

Also see Bell to India, 1 May 1920, No. 13 in Ibid, and Bell to India, 24 January 1921, No. 184 in *Foreign*, June 1921, Procs. 45–283.

too was significant in that the individual responsible for it was none other than Sir John Jordan who, for well-nigh a quarter century, was the most powerful, and influential, man in Peking's diplomatic corps. In reverse, in May 1919, having initiated the parleys on their own, the Chinese with a sudden abruptness that seemed insulting, shut up the lid and refused, despite threats of alternate coaxing and cajolery, to talk.

The stalemate in Peking had an important bearing on British thinking in regard to Tibet which largely resolved itself into three major propositions. To start with, there was the awareness that having made a solemn pledge to supply Lhasa with arms and ammunition in order that it be able to maintain its independence, Delhi had to break that promise because of the Arms Convention of 1919. Tibet, supremely ignorant of these compulsions of international diplomacy, could only view the British decision as a breach of trust and a refusal to honour a plighted word. In this respect, the Kansu Mission appears to have acted as a catalyst in making HMG realise that Tibet's case for a ridiculously modest supply of arms stood on a different pedestal and could indeed be viewed in a different light.

Another dimension to the Tibetan problem was the British government's long-postponed decision about their Political Officer, in the person of Charles Bell, accepting the Dalai Lama's often repeated invitation to visit Lhasa. Bell's intimacy and close friendship with the Lama, which had been sedulously fostered during the latter's exile in India (1910–12), could thereby be put to use not only in terms of cultivating Tibet but also in counteracting persistent Chinese intrigue in Lhasa. Here again it was the Kansu Mission which precipitated matters and brought them to a head.

Finally, there was a certain urgency in reviewing and, if necessary, revising the earlier policy. The whole issue of sterilising Tibet, of refusing to go beyond the undertakings of the Anglo-Russian Convention of 1907, and of waiting upon the convenience of China to come to firm conclusions came in for a thorough, if agonizing, reappraisal. Here too the apparently successful, and superficially effusive, welcome of the Kansu Mission at Lhasa played an important, if not indeed a crucial role. As a result, a process of re-thinking set in, fresh ground was broken and for once it seemed that Whitehall's Tibetan policy had got out of its hitherto all-too-familiar grooves.

In a preceding chapter, a brief mention has been made of the question of supply of arms to Lhasa. In the context of the Kansu Mission and discussions in regard to a changed policy on Tibet, the question needs further scrutiny. The fact that the Tibetans lacked ammunition was 'fairly well-known' and there was genuine fear that the Chinese might 'take advantage' of the situation to force issues. This apart, there was the strangely odd fact of the Tibetans having rifles but 'no ammunition',[8] a situation of whose gravity the India

[8] An extract from a letter of the Tibetan Chief Ministers, dated 5 April 1920, makes interesting reading:

Office was not unaware. Indeed, in May 1920, it viewed the question as one of ' most immediate urgency ' and felt that

> failing a solution of this difficulty, it seems evident that no useful purpose would be served by the deputation of a British officer to Lhasa ... and that the initiations of a new Tibetan policy ... would have little prospect of success.[9]

There were powerful arguments in favour of arming the Tibetans apart from the fact of the solemn pledges given in 1914 and reiterated since. For one, there was the danger of Tibet being overrun by adventurers on her eastern frontier over whom the Central Government in Peking exercised little, if any, control. Additionally, Peking's inability to ensure the maintenance of order on the frontier was in itself an argument in favour of arming the Tibetans to combat these ' forces of disorder '. Besides, as Delhi viewed it, there was little meaning in having a British Resident at Lhasa unless he was able to promise material support to the authorities there.[10]

The principal line of reasoning against arming Lhasa was that, with fresh supplies, it might be difficult to restrain the regime ' within the limits ' of the 1919 frontier. Again, there was the risk of ' forfeiting ' the goodwill of China, of pushing her reigning military junta further into the arms of Japan and of giving a powerful handle to the latter's propaganda offensive against the British. This is not to gainsay the fact that under the Arms Traffic Convention of September 1919, HMG, a signatory, was under an obligation 'not to allow the export of military arms and ammunition ' to non-signatory powers, among whom Tibet was one. Understandably, the British Foreign Office viewed the supply of such arms as a direct violation of the Convention's terms, and as tantamount to creating a ' highly undesirable ' situation.[11]

> Tibetans have got rifles but no ammunition. They are feeling very much perturbed at present, thinking that in the event of the Chinese assuming the offensive, the Tibetans will lose their territory. Therefore, consider this matter well.

Bell to India, 27 April 1920, No. 8 in *Foreign*, November 1920, Procs. 1–102. For an excellent summary of the arms and ammunition supplied to Tibet since 1914, see Office note in Correspondence, pp. 22–25, in *Foreign*, May 1920, Procs. 4–142.

[9] *I O* to *F O*, 10 May 1920, No. 49 in *Foreign*, November 1920, Procs. 1–102.
For ' a new Tibetan policy ', alluded to, see *Infra*, n. 17.

[10] In a Memorandum prepared by C H Bentinck, Under Secretary at the Foreign Office, nine arguments in favour of arming the Tibetans were listed. Among these was the urgency for such a supply as made out by the Government of India and the India Office. For the Memorandum see Encl. 1, No. 63 in Ibid.
Also see *I O* to *F O*, 15 May 1920, No. 50 in Ibid.

[11] Arguments against arming the Tibetans, as listed in Bentinck's Memorandum, *supra*, n. 10, were five.
For the Arms Convention, signed in Paris on 23 September 1919, see *F O* to *I O*, 23 September 1919, No. 9 in *Foreign*, May 1920, Procs. 14–142. In a later communication, the Foreign Office underlined its dilemma:

This Foreign Office reasoning, however, did not carry much conviction with the India Office who pointed out that the

> circumstances of the case are of a very exceptional character ... and it is the very inability of the Peking Government to control the aggressive tendencies of their own local officers that compels Tibet to put herself into a state of defence.

Furthermore, it was pointed out that Tibet did not lie within the ' zone of prohibition' as defined (in Article VI of the Arms Convention), nor was its 'technical inferiority of status' a bar to its receiving arms. Besides, its affairs were not likely to be of interest to any of the signatory powers ' except' Great Britain and China.[12]

Legal casuistry about the arms convention apart, in India the problem was viewed from a more practical angle. For, fundamental to the supply of arms and ammunition was the realisation, as Bell put it, that without such a supply ' our whole Tibetan policy must fail'. It was urged that the offer of material support against the Chinese had served as an inducement to Tibet adopting a ' friendly attitude' towards India. Besides, if a British officer took machine-guns and ammunition to Lhasa or brought permission for their purchase

> China will realise that Tibetan Government (are) able to defend (themselves) and that we (viz. British) are besides her and will negotiate ... (and) settlement of Tibetan problem may even result.[13]

Arguments were also pressed into service to view Tibet as equivalent in status to a ' self-governing dominion' of the British Empire thereby enabling her to join the arms convention in her own right.[14] It is significant that on this issue the views of the Political Officer in Sikkim, of the Foreign Department in Delhi and of the India Office in London were, for once, in the closest accord.[15] What

> Were it known that with the approval of HMG, arms were being sold to Tibetan government when China is not only the acknowledged suzerain of Tibet but herself a party to the Arms Convention in question, an untenable situation will arise.

F O to I O, 23 October 1919, No. 18 in Ibid.

[12] I O to F O, No. 11 in Ibid.

The note ended by suggesting that Lord Curzon ' may revise his views' on the question.

[13] Bell to India, 14 April and 13 March 1920, Nos. 117 and 93 in Ibid.

See also Office note dated 5 January 1920, in Correspondence, p. 3 in Ibid.

[14] India underlined:

China was prepared to recognise the autonomy of Outer Tibet even during the negotiations of 1913–14 and since then this zone has been fully and indisputably autonomous and appears to us clearly to have the status and position of a self-governing dominion.

Viceroy to Secretary of State, 23 April 1920, No. 137 in Ibid.

[15] On 12 March, Montagu had written to Curzon to suggest that ' if no expedient serves', Tibet may be invited, under Article I of the Arms Convention, to be supplied with arms

was more, reminders from Lhasa were now fairly sharply-worded. As one of these put it:

> The people of Tibet are taking all sorts of views of the question and this is sure to do great harm ... according to the requests we have been making for months and months and years and years, the case may become a matter of regret to the Tibetans and a disgrace to the good name of the British Government.[16]

Nor may the question be viewed in isolation. For the supply of arms was part of the larger whole involving a thorough revision of the previous policy *vis-à-vis* Tibet. Significantly, the initiative in this instance came from a totally unexpected quarter—the British Legation in Peking! In the light of the latter's known stance in the past, this represented a change symbolised by the departure from the scene of Sir John Jordan, well-known for his strong anti-Dalai Lama bias. Be that as it may, his successor, Sir Beilby Alston, in a telegram to the Foreign Office on 27 April 1920—the date on which the Kansu Mission left (or was made to leave?) Lhasa—spelt out the broad outlines of a new approach, including

> supporting and openly entering into closer relations with Tibet, informing China that we are doing so and continuing to invite China to come to a friendly settlement either by submitting matter to international arbitration or by negotiation. In pursuance a Resident be sent to Lhasa to remain there permanently with cognisance of Chinese Government and subsequently to the throwing open of Tibet to international residence and trade to such extent as may be desired by the Tibetans themselves.

The previous policy of ' sterilising ' Tibet

> only plays into China's hands and is now out of date. An opened Tibet would mean a Tibet strengthened and developed with our assistance, able to withstand external aggression and under our influence and friendly to and trusting in us.[17]

In an earlier and more comprehensive despatch, Teichman, the author of the Chamdo and Rongbatsa agreements and the Peking Legation's expert on Tibetan affairs, had argued the case convincingly against continuing the old

' for her own governmental requirements '. If this required Tibet to obtain admission to the League of Nations, this could be done too. ' These difficulties must be faced ', he stressed, ' otherwise Tibet will regard this as a betrayal '. *I O* to *F O*, 12 March 1920, No. 110 in Ibid.

[16] Chief Ministers to Political Officer, 26 March 1920, in Political Officer to India, 12 April 1920, No. 129 in Ibid.

[17] Alston to Curzon, 27 April 1920, No. 2 in *Foreign*, November 1920, Procs. 1–102.

policy. The pith of his reasoning was that if the Chinese were encouraged to procrastinate indefinitely, they will ' undoubtedly go back ' on the whole principle of ' tripartite negotiation '. In the final analysis, therefore, Teichman pleaded, the question resolved itself into a simple proposition: how could the British protect their interests against the dangers of indefinite delay without unduly offending Chinese susceptibilities? His answer was two-fold:

> By (1) entering openly into closer relations with Tibet, while at the same time (2) continuing to offer China a settlement on the basis of her own offer or, as an alternative, international arbitration.[18]

Certain factors were to help in an early decision on the new policy, the more important being the return of China's growing self-confidence in herself as a result of developments in Mongolia, briefly alluded to earlier. In a despatch to Curzon on 24 April 1920, after he had met the Vice-Minister for Foreign Affairs, Alston quoted the latter as saying that

> Mongolia having been recovered, China can make no treaty with Great Britain recognising the autonomy of Tibet and denying China's sovereign (as opposed to suzerain) rights in that country.

Nonetheless, if Lhasa were to

> beg for favourable treatment and a certain measure of autonomy, it will be graciously granted, Tibetans (being) members of a nation and no interference in Sino-Tibetan affairs by an outside party (such as the British) was to be tolerated.[19]

Besides Alston and Teichman in Peking, the Political Officer in Sikkim was a powerful advocate of change. Thus, in a despatch to the Foreign Department on 26 August 1920, he expressed the fear that, in the absence of a shift of stance, British influence

> may be lost and in course of time be succeeded by Tibetan hostility unless we

---

[18] These citations are from Teichman's ' Memorandum on Tibet ', dated 29 February 1920, and handed to Sir John Jordan when the latter left Peking on 1 March 1920. It may be worth mentioning that Teichman had been a relentless critic of the territorial settlement made at Simla which he dubbed as being ' not fair ' to China, besides smacking ' too much ' of Russia's former methods in Mongolia.

Teichman began his Memorandum thus: ' The Legation in Peking cannot make bricks without straw and we have never been authorised to do anything but beg the Chinese to come to a settlement....'

For the text, Correspondence, pp. 10–11, in Ibid.

[19] Alston to Curzon, 24 April 1920, Encl, No. 42 in Ibid. Alston stressed, *inter alia*, the ' markedly friendly ' attitude of the Chinese Minister at their meeting on 21 April.

can get into direct touch with the Tibetan Government without further loss of time. Tibet will turn to China again, there will be a resumption of Chinese intrigue in Bhutan, Nepal ... and the tribal areas on the Assam-Tibet border and Chinese pressure on the northern-most and eastern frontiers of India and Burma will become stronger than ever before.[20]

Without doubt, it was this ' risk ' of China regaining control over Tibet, ' as happened in 1910 ', that finally made the British reverse the gears, clinch the issue, and while for a time the question of supply of ammunition remained in the balance, a decision was taken to despatch Bell to Lhasa. Paradoxically, British hesitation on the question was, if partially, removed by the Chinese initiative over the Kansu Mission.

---

[20] Bell to India, 26 August 1920, No. 74 in Ibid.

Chapter 30

A New Tibetan Policy:
Bell's Mission to Lhasa, 1920–21

THE QUESTION of arming Tibet against a possible threat from China was, as may be evident, a matter of serious concern at the highest levels of government in Delhi, no less than in London. This was revealed by the vigour of debate and the seriousness of contention represented by the opposing schools of thought. As argument was set against argument, an interesting fact emerged namely, that the question could only be considered as an integral part of a larger problem: a radical change in the policy of isolating or insulating Tibet that had been pursued hitherto.

The changed policy, as envisaged, had as an essential part the question of sending Bell to Lhasa to make an objective, on-the-spot assessment of the situation in the Tibetan capital. The fact that relations between the superannuated Political Officer, now re-employed, and the Dalai Lama were the most intimate would make his visit doubly useful and thereby help in determining the new policy, then in the process of being formulated.

Among those who presistently beat their own drum, none could equal Sir Charles Bell. His advocacy of a mission to Lhasa in 1919 when he had retired from service has been alluded to earlier. In 1920, in the hope that such a mission would eventuate before long, Bell was temporarily re-employed and assumed his old charge in April that year. From the day he took over, through official communications, demi-official notes, private letters and telegrams, he untiringly advocated the new course. Thus in April:

> the establishment of closer relations with Tibet independently of China is the one thing she (China) fears. British official must, however, take some assurance as regards ammunition to relieve present dangerous situation of Tibetan Government.[1]

A week later, he viewed the deputation of a British Officer as 'absolutely necessary' on 'all grounds'.[2] Before another couple of days passed, he was asking the Foreign Secretary, in a demi-official letter, how the proposal was 'going on', adding that it was 'urgently necessary' to send an official.[3] A few months later, and despairing of delays, he wrote:

[1] Bell to India, 29 April 1920, No. 4 in *Foreign*, November 1920, Procs. 1–102.
[2] Bell to India, 8 May 1920, No. 16 in Ibid.
[3] Bell to Carter, D.O., 10 May 1920, Correspondence, pp. 4–5 in Ibid.

as the season is getting very advanced, I should be glad to know whether orders have been received yet about my going to Lhasa.[4]

When informed that a decision had been postponed, he confessed it was

a disappointment to me that neither this nor the new Tibetan Conference has developed though I realised the difficulties in the way of each.... I think that with a little more pushing we could make HMG see the necessity of despatching a British officer to Lhasa and that would help forward the Tibetan Conference also....It is evident that HMG do not quite understand the position of affairs.[5]

To be sure, the Government of India had done more than its usual quota of 'pushing' and the Viceroy had telegraphed frantically, both privately as well as officially. Thus on 27 May:

I should be grateful if you would expedite a decision ... the journey to Lhasa will take about a month each way and it is desirable that if an officer is to be deputed temporarily, he should ... start with as little delay as possible.[6]

Again, on 30 August, the Governor-General sent the Secretary of State a 'Clear the Line', private telegram:

Bell wires that his health precludes his continuing in service much longer and I think it very important that before he retires his special experience and friendship with Tibetans should be utilised by permitting him to visit Lhasa. The cold will make this impossible unless orders are received during the next fortnight.[7]

No one could have done more. Yet, on 8 September, London, in place of definitive orders, sent a lame-duck telegram imparting the precious information that HMG, 'in consultation with Alston', were 'still considering the question'.[8] Later, in the middle of October, when 'orders' did arrive, they were hedged in by all possible 'ifs' and 'buts'. Thus, in the first place, 'a written assurance' was to be obtained from the Chinese Government, 'which could be formally communicated' to Lhasa, to the effect that the latter

[4]Bell to India, 6 September 1920, No. 80 in Ibid.
[5]Bell to Dobbs, D.O., 14 September 1920, Correspondence, p. 19 in Ibid.
[6]Viceroy to Secretary of State, telegram, private, 27 May 1920, Correspondence, p. 6 in Ibid.
[7]Viceroy to Secretary of State, telegram, private, 30 August 1920, Correspondence, p. 17 in Ibid.
[8]Secretary of State to Viceroy, telegram, private, 8 September 1920, Correspondence, p. 18 in Ibid.

'would not be attacked' by China. Alston had thought such an assurance 'possible to obtain'. As for Bell:

> Provided latter (His Majesty's Minister in Peking) does not raise any objection and you concur in Bell's views (viz., a British Officer should visit Lhasa *without* authority to promise arms or ammunition) you are authorised to send him to Lhasa at once . . . with general instructions to treat Tibetan request for assistance etc. in a sympathetic manner, but without authority to promise arms or ammunition. . . .[9]

Thus was Bell's famous mission to Lhasa launched!

To understand fully the limitations under which Bell was to operate in Lhasa, a close analysis of the thinking that pervaded Whitehall on the eve of his departure may be helpful. Here the minutes of a meeting held on 22 July (1920) at which, apart from Hirtzel and Wakely from the India Office and Wellesley and Bentinck from the Foreign Office, Jordan, then recently retired from Peking, was present, make instructive reading. The venue was the Foreign Office and the objective was to sort out the sharp divergence in its views with its counterpart in regard to the supply of arms to Lhasa, a subject discussed at some length in an earlier chapter. Two things appeared to dominate the discussion. At the outset was Hirtzel's untiring plea that the Tibetans were fast losing confidence in Britain and therefore something in the nature of an assurance was required to convince them that China would not really attack. Another was the fear that an untenable situation might result at a later date if Russian intrigue were revived while the British persisted in operating in Tibet only through China. There was Jordan's confident note too that a Chinese government which was less under the influence of Japan would be friendly to Britain and more amenable to a settlement on the question of Tibet. Additionally, he expressed his fear that in supplying arms publicly to Lhasa, a situation would be created out of which both Japan and China would 'make capital'.[10]

The conclusions arrived at the meeting were summed up thus:

1. India Office was to enquire from the Government in Delhi whether it would be satisfied if assurances were obtained in writing from the Chinese, which could then be shown to the Tibetans, to the effect that the latter would not be attacked;
2. Mr. Clive, the Charge d'Affaires in Peking, was to be instructed to obtain such assurances 'bearing in mind the delicacy of his task';

[9] Secretary of State to Viceroy, 15 October 1920, No. 45 in *Foreign*, June 1921, Procs. 45-283. Bell arrived in Lhasa early in November 1920 and *not*, as stated by Dr. Sung, 'on 17 September 1920'. *Yao-ting Sung*, p. 126.

[10] 'Minutes of a Meeting held in Mr Wellesley's room at the Foreign Office on Thursday, 22 July 1920', Encl. 2, No. 111 in Ibid. Also see *F O* to *I O*, 6 July 1920, No. 63 in *Foreign*, November 1920, Procs. 1-102.

3. It was still an open question whether the assurances in question were to be delivered at Lhasa through (Louis) King (then stationed at Tachienlu) or Bell, the re-employed Political Officer in Sikkim.

In brief, Peking was to furnish written assurances to Tibet of its peaceful intent, through the agency of the British. A corollary to this was a warning to be administered to the Chinese that if they attempted to cross the (May 1919) frontier in East Tibet, the British would arm Lhasa to resist; even though the arms were to be delivered only after an actual ' act of aggression had been committed '.[11]

Oddly enough, late in October, when the Foreign Office finally approved the despatch of Bell's mission with all its in-built safeguards, the question of a written assurance from China was pushed into the background. At the outset, it was discovered that a verbal assurance had, in effect, already been held out to Alston by the Chinese as early as 21 April,[12] and as to a written one it was to await the Minister's return to Peking early in December or until such time as, ' in his opinion ', a suitable opportunity presented itself.[13] In retrospect, it may be added that even as late as March 1921, Alston was disposed ' to defer ' the question of reopening negotiations, or of obtaining written assurances, until the Chinese government's ' curiosity ' regarding Bell's visit to Lhasa was aroused. Yet, *pro forma*, he

> still adhere(d) to the opinion that written assurances should be asked for in the last resort . . . if (these were) useful in re-establishing Tibetan confidence in us. . . .[14]

Meantime in November (1920), Bell, whose patience at the India Office's continued delays had been tried to the utmost, started on his journey—'although the season is far advanced and the cold will be severe '. His brief, as has been noticed, was simple. While treating Tibetan requests for assistance sympathetically, he was *not* to commit himself in regard to the supply of arms and ammunition. Additionally, he was to acquaint his hosts with the problems inherent in negotiating with the Chinese, now rendered doubly more difficult insofar as the country was riven into warring factions. He was also charged with impressing upon Lhasa the desirability of preventing hostilities with China.

---

[11] This was the gist of a ' solution ' proffered by Sir John Jordan at his interview with the Secretary of State. For details see Encl. 1, No. 111 in *Foreign*, June 1921, Procs. 45–283.

[12] Alston to Curzon, 24 April 1920, Encl. No. 42 in Ibid.
Alston had stressed, *inter alia*, the markedly friendly attitude of the Chinese Minister at their meeting on 21 April, assuring him that Peking had ' no aggressive intent ' against Tibet.

[13] *F O* to *I O*, 8 October 1920, No. 111 in *Foreign*, June 1921, Procs. 45–283.

[14] Alston to Curzon, 5 March 1921, No. 201 in Ibid.
' In view of the continued quiet on the frontier ', apart from the fact that the (Chinese) Minister for Foreign Affairs was taking things quietly, Alston thought he had rather wait.

Keeping his eyes and ears open, he was to find out what took place at the time of the Kansu Mission and ferret out such information as he could, regarding Liu Tsan-ting's visit to Chamdo.

Reading between the lines it would be evident that, however well-disguised, a principal objective of Bell's visit was to find out if there was

> really any serious danger of the Tibetan Government making terms with the Chinese which would be harmful to our interests in the event of our not being able to insist on a renewal of the tripartite negotiations.[15]

As originally planned, Bell was to stay in the Tibetan capital for no more than a month; in actual fact, his visit lasted a whole year. The duration of his stay continued to be extended, largely, if not solely, because Alston in Peking lent it support and gave it his strong backing. This is not to gainsay the fact that Bell's own efforts in that direction were any the less conspicuous.

At the end of the first month, when his departure was impending, Bell sent in a fulsome report describing how the Dalai Lama, the Prime Minister, the Council and the National Assembly each had ' pressed him strongly ' to stay.[16] The Minister in Peking was no less insistent that Bell's visit to Lhasa would be useful in making the Chinese realise that the British were ' in earnest ' and that the effect will be the greater, the longer he remained.[17]

Oddly enough, it was India that was opposed, and strongly, for it argued that

> the longer he stays the more difficult will he find it to leave, and the greater the danger of the Tibetan Government trying to force our hands over permanent envoy at Lhasa and their taking umbrage at our refusal.[18]

In sharp contrast, in a despatch in April 1921, Alston was even more emphatic on Bell continuing to remain, for,

> in view of Bell's report (in which *inter alia* he had underlined ' how anxious '

---

[15]Office note by H R C Dobbs, Correspondence, p. 1 in Ibid.

[16] ' The Prime Minister ', Bell wrote to Bray, on hearing of his (Bell's) impending departure ' called ... (and said) that it would be like " rubbing my mouth in dust " ... that (Bell should not leave) until His Holiness, he (Prime Minister) himself, the Council and the National Assembly had fully considered the Kharita from H E the Viceroy ... he urged me to remain till the second or third Tibetan month (viz. April or May).... The following day the Council called in a body ... a day or two later the Prime Minister came again.... At my next interview with His Holiness, he pressed me strongly to stay.'

Bell to India, 14 December 1920, No. 125 in Ibid.

[17]Alston to Curzon, 5 January 1921, No. 145 in Ibid. ' As far as China is concerned ', Alston wrote, ' I recommend that fullest discretion should be given to Bell in the matter.'

[18]Viceroy to Secretary of State, 31 December 1920, Encl. in No. 2, *F O* 535/24,

Lhasa was for a settlement of the Tibetan question)[19] and impossibility with means at our disposal here of forcing China to an agreement while she has her own means of intriguing direct with Tibet, I would urge... the advisability of allowing Bell to remain at Lhasa until a decision on our future policy is arrived at....[20]

Meanwhile as the varied ramifications of a new, changed policy towards Tibet were being hammered out in seemingly interminable discussions between the Foreign Office, the India Office, the Governor-General in Delhi, the Minister in Peking, and Bell himself at Lhasa, the Indian Government's patience began to be visibly tried. On 10 May, the Viceroy wrote to the Secretary of State that if

it were proposed to keep Bell in Lhasa (and he had been there now for nearly seven months) till China begins to move, he might have to remain there indefinitely. We cannot compete with China in a waiting game....[21]

The fact is that the Foreign Department in Delhi had begun seriously to question the premise whether, not to speak of Bell's presence, even the posting of a permanent British Representative at Lhasa, would have ' any better effect ' upon the Chinese.[22]

To cut through Chinese procrastination, Whitehall finally persuaded itself to call it a day. On 17 August, Alston in Peking was directed that a

communication should now be addressed to the Chinese Government both here (in London) and in Peking inviting them to resume either in London or at Peking the negotiations of 1919 and informing them that unless such resumption takes place in the immediate future HMG in view of their

---

[19]On 19 January 1921, Bell had wired:
The whole of the Tibetan government from His Holiness the Dalai Lama downwards are extremely anxious for settlement of the Tibetan question....The Tibetans are weary beyond measure. They are sorely tried....
Bell to India, No. 132 in *Foreign*, June 1921, Procs. 45–283.
[20]Alston to Curzon, 14 April 1921, No. 241 in Ibid.
[21]Viceroy to Secretary of State, 10 May 1921, No. 281 in Ibid.
In actual fact, and despite Alston's strong advocacy, India informed Bell that ' he should cut his visit short, if possible'. India to India Office, Encl in No. 7, *F O* 535/24.
Bell stoutly contested this and reminded Delhi that ' when prior to my departure for England, the late Foreign Secretary required me to rejoin government service, it was with a view to my sharing in resumption of negotiations. To withdraw me now, when our plans seem likely to fructify would not only be a keen personal disappointment, but against public interest.' Bell to India, Encl. in No. 16 in Ibid.
[22] 'Policy towards Tibet ', office note, Correspondence, pp. 48–52, in *Foreign*, June 1921, Procs. 45–283.
Inter alia, the note pointed out that it had been hoped that Bell's visit to Lhasa will induce the Chinese to activity but five months had passed and there was ' no sign yet of China climbing down ',

commitments to the Tibetan Government arising out of the negotiations of 1914 and in view of the fact that the Convention of 1914 according autonomy to the Tibetans was (with the exception of the boundary clause) accepted in writing by the Chinese Government who subsequently confirmed in their offer of 1919 their willingness to grant autonomy to Tibet did not feel justified in withholding any longer their recognition of Tibet's status as an autonomous state under the suzerainty of China and intend in the future to deal with Tibet on that basis, but that at the same time HMG remain willing and anxious as heretofore to do all in their power to promote a tripartite settlement. . . .

The sting in the tail, however, was the penultimate paragraph which stipulated that if

after a reasonable time, say one month, has elapsed, it is clear that the Chinese Government do not intend to negotiate, the arms should be supplied to the Tibetans under strict guarantees without any further communication on the subject being made to the Chinese Government.[23]

The Memorandum was to be accompanied by some 'verbal' explanations. These included, *inter alia*, a statement of the British intent to treat Tibet as an autonomous state and its desire to enter into 'close relations' with her; to send a British Officer to Lhasa 'from time to time . . . whenever it is considered desirable'; to consult with Lhasa in order to open up intercourse between Indian and Tibetan trade marts to an increased extent and finally to afford the country 'any reasonable assistance' required by way of its 'development and protection'.[24]

While on the British side things seemed to be moving at long last, Peking, understandably, refused to oblige. After receiving the Memorandum and the verbal explanations, the Chinese Minister told Alston that the moment somehow 'did not seem . . . very opportune'. Apart from preparations for the Washington Conference, which then fully engaged his attention, he seriously disputed some of the premises on which Britain's new approach was based. Were Tibetans really 'capable of governing' themselves? Why, he queried, were the British 'anxious' about the Eastern Frontier of Tibet? Again, it was evident to him that the views adumbrated in the (British) Memorandum were a clear departure from Whitehall's previous policy. Besides, he noted, here was a subject on which the Japanese were sure to ask him inconvenient questions as to what was transpiring.[25]

A week or two later, the Chinese Minister was more specific, if also refreshingly candid. Peking, he confessed, exercised no control over Szechuan and Yunnan,

[23] India to Bell, 17 August 1921, No. 217 in *Foreign*, November 1921, Procs. 127–325.
[24] Curzon to Alston, 27 August 1921, No. 257 in Ibid.
[25] Alston to Curzon, 31 August 1921, No. 232 in Ibid.

both of whom were directly involved in any frontier settlement concerning Tibet. Besides, if 'strong men' like Yuan Shih-kai and Tuan Chi-jui were not able to bring about a settlement, the present regime was not likely to succeed either. For one thing, it was 'far too weak'. Even the life of the government, he confessed, was uncertain; it may not last 'another few weeks'.[26]

On 8 September (1921), the Chinese Foreign Office sent its official reply to the British Memorandum which listed the three principal reasons noted above: the impending Pacific Conference in Washington, the chaotic state of affairs in which China found itself and the precarious tenure of the then government. To these last two, Alston himself bore eloquent testimony:

> To deal with this Government which does not really govern, is practically waste of time. Neither President, Premier nor Cabinet possess authority individually or collectively. Their power over Tuchuns is nil and even in neighbourhood of Peking they cannot guarantee safety of foreigners' life or property.... So long as finances of China remain as they are, it is impossible for the tenure of any government to be secured.[27]

The strange, if cruel, irony of the situation was that it was this regime in Peking with whom Whitehall wanted to enter into serious negotiations to settle the seemingly intractable problem of delineating a frontier with Tibet! No wonder that all that Peking did finally commit itself to was the promise that 'immediately' the Washington Conference was over, it would sit down to sort out the problem. And this too after Alston had solemnly warned that HMG were not in a mood 'to accept any further trifling' over this question. After all, he argued, with goodwill three weeks 'would suffice' to settle the issue![28]

Bell's preliminary reports from Lhasa were enthusiastic and, understandably, highly complimentary to himself personally. His first visit to the Lama, on 19 November, 'an auspicious day', was memorable:

> When I entered he grasped both my hands in his and said then and once or twice afterwards during the interview how glad he was that I had come.[29]

A few weeks later, as has been noticed, everyone who mattered in Lhasa, from the Dalai Lama downwards—the Prime Minister and, 'twice over', the Council and the National Assembly—'pressed me strongly' to prolong his stay, which he did.

[26] Alston to Curzon, 8 September 1921, No. 248 in Ibid.
[27] Alston to Curzon, 8 September 1921, No. 249 in Ibid.
[28] Alston to Curzon, 20 October 1921, No. 207 in Ibid.
[29] Bell to India, 18 December 1920, No. 122 in Ibid.
Bell's first 'business interview' with the Lama took place on 30 November when he presented the Viceroy's 'kharita' and explained his instructions.

Apart from his routine reports—and he wrote one, it would seem, every week—Bell's first comprehensive survey of Lhasa's political landscape was made after a period of nearly three months in the capital. It largely revolved around three principal facets of the Tibetan situation: British policy to the extent it attracted considerable responsibility for the then state of affairs in the country; the achievements of the Lhasa regime in terms of a reasonably stable polity, and finally the varied ramifications of Peking's impact. The latter, it was no secret, if not positively hostile, was certainly far from being friendly and in any case waiting for a fit opportunity to strike and push the Tibetans back from the territory they had allegedly purloined. Thrown in between were the policies of Russia and of low petty intrigue epitomised by men like Aguan Dorjieff or his agents, of the Amban of Ili and last but by no means the least, the Japanese.

As to the British, Bell held them squarely responsible for most of the problems with which Lhasa was now beset. In the pregnant phrases of a Tibetan prophecy repeatedly recalled since the days of the Younghusband expedition of 1903–4, the British had proved to be the ' road-makers of Tibet '. Bell recited at length, nor for the first time, the advantages which had accrued from the Simla Convention, and feared that if the British delayed in holding out requisite assurances to Lhasa

> Japan and China combined will gain the power in Tibet. We, after having encouraged the Tibetans for so many years, will be regarded by them as their betrayers and we shall meet with the scorn that falls on those who do not fulfil their promises.

In such an event, should the northern frontier fall under hostile influences,

> in place of a 1500 mile barrier ... India will have a band of narrow mountain states, greatly liable to fall under the influence of Japan and China.... For Bhutan and Sikkim especially, the temptation will be very great. Nepal will find it difficult to hold aloof. In Burma, China will intrigue and stir up trouble....

Nor would he be disposed to wait

> for a China that does not intend to negotiate until she finds it definitely in her own interest to do so....

Bell's proposals, which are listed at length elsewhere, were largely concerned with arming Tibet adequately to meet this challenge, besides helping her in a number of other small ways to develop her own resources. After all, he argued

> we have no wish to dominate Tibet. That would truly be a foolish policy.

We wish Tibet to have internal autonomy, under the lightest possible form of Chinese suzerainty, a barrier for the northern frontier of India. We want her to be free to develop on her own lines....[30]

Weeks later, the Viceroy, Lord Reading, in a communication to the Secretary of State, summed up and 'endorsed' what he termed Bell's 'constructive' and 'admirably restrained' policy: ' the pith of it is that we should help Tibet to stand on her own '. To be sure, and he underlined this heavily, what

Tibet wants is either the acceptance of the tripartite Convention by China or assistance from us to enable her to develop her powers of self-determination as to keep China at arms' length.

Nor could the pace in Tibet—' and all she really wants is to live her own life '—be forced. For, as

long as Tibet wishes to keep her doors shut, we do not see any reason in self-defence or otherwise to attempt to force them.... If we did ... our influence upon her ... (which) springs largely from our forbearance to foist ourselves upon her would be shattered.[31]

In the context of a new policy towards Tibet, the question of arms supply was pivotal. Not long after he reached Lhasa, the dangers inherent in withholding such a supply were underlined by Bell. Thus on 21 January (1921) he had wired that he had 'just' been informed by a Tibetan friend

who is a member of Government that the latter are now considering whether it is advisable to import some thousands of rifles from Mongolia. He says that Mongolia is full of cheap and serviceable Japanese rifles.[32]

Eight days later:

A machine-gun said to be of Russian make, 7 Japanese rifles and a box of

---

[30]Bell to India, 21 February 1921, No. 209 in Ibid.
Bell thought his report provided ' an insight ' into the Tibetan situation. He noted, *inter alia*, a former Tibetan prophecy (in the context of growing Tibetan distrust of British intent): ' The sheep put their trust in the meadows and were hurled down the precipice '. He noted too that his views were closely in accord with that of the Legation in Peking:
When we agree on any points, such points are, I would submit, entitled to very special consideration.

[31]Viceroy to Secretary of State, 10 May 1921, No. 280 in *Foreign*, June 1921, Procs. 45-283.
[32]Bell to India, 21 January 1921, No. 173 in Ibid.

bombs arrived in Lhasa a few days ago from Mongolia. It is said that the machine-gun has been tested here and found satisfactory.³³

On 1 March:

Dalai Lama has written to his Agent in Mongolia to buy as many Mongolian rifles as possible.³⁴

These apart, there were those enormous quantities of Japanese arms, 'smuggled' into Mongolia to help save that country from the Bolsheviks. As if this were not complicated enough, there was the solitary Japanese monk Tada who, though studying ' very hard ' at the Sera Monastery for his Gy-she, may yet be involved, for the

Japanese, as a rule, find it difficult to abstain from politics.³⁵

As months rolled by, the importance of Bell's new approach became increasingly relevant, the more so as Peking seemed unwilling, if not indeed unable, to reopen the Tibetan question. Finally, as has been noticed, HMG did persuade itself that China should be told that unless it began serious negotiations, arms would be supplied to the Tibetans, 'under strict guarantees' and without ' any further communication ' on the subject being made to Peking.³⁶

In its final version, the note to Peking eschewed any open-faced reference to ' arms ', although the intent remained unmistakable. Thus the ' verbal explanation ', which was to accompany the note, made it clear that HMG—in case the Chinese did not respond within a period of one month—would deem itself free to

give Tibetans any reasonable assistance which may be required by them in development and protection of their country.³⁷

On 4 October—the ' notice ' to Peking had expired on 26 September—the Secretary of State authorised the Viceroy to direct Bell that he may communicate the decision ' regarding ammunition ' to the Lama's government.³⁸ Accordingly, a week later the British envoy told the Dalai Lama in a written communication that his government

---

³³Bell to India, 29 January 1921, No. 186 in Ibid.

³⁴Bell to India, 1 March 1921, No. 199 in Ibid.

³⁵Bell to India, 6 February 1921, No. 193 in Ibid.

³⁶*Supra*, n. 23.

³⁷*Supra*, n. 25.

³⁸Secretary of State to Viceroy, 4 October 1921, in *Foreign*, November 1921, Procs. 127–325.

will be allowed to import on payment munitions in instalments at adequate intervals provided . . . they will only use such munitions for internal police-work and self-defence. . . .

He was also to spell out the ceiling set for such imports: 10,000 rifles, 20 machine-guns and 10 mountain guns.[39]

With his mission fulfilled, Bell left Lhasa on 19 October (1921), almost eleven months after he had arrived for a brief, one-month stay. The Lama, he noted,

very emphatically (expressed) his personal regard for myself. My Indian and English address was taken by him in order that we may write direct to each other in Tibetan. To me ' I pray continually that you may return to Lhasa ' were his last words.[40]

' Nothing ', Bell concluded, ' could have exceeded friendliness of all classes ', at once lay and ecclesiastical. Nor was this the only mark of ' confidence ' and affection which Lhasa had showered on the British envoy and his entourage. For during his stay, he had been invited to visit many places and attend various ceremonies. At the Tibetan New Year reception he was accorded a place of honour: ' the longer we stayed in Lhasa, the more cordial our receptions became'. At a theatrical performance, he was given a place 'higher than that given to the Prime Minister ' nor was the performance allowed to commence ' until I arrived '. The mission's departure was

watched by the Dalai Lama himself from the roof of a neighbouring house.

It was ' generally believed ' that

in my last life, I was a Tibetan, who had prayed that he might be re-born in a powerful country so as to be able to benefit Tibet.

The contrast with earlier events could not have been sharper:

In 1904 the Dalai Lama refused to have any dealings with the British. Sixteen years later a British Political Officer is received as the guest of the Dalai Lama, allowed to see whomever and whatever he wishes, and pressed

---

[39]Bell to India, 12 October 1921, No. 296 in Ibid.

In addition to the figures mentioned there were to be 1 million rounds of small arms, ammunition (for the rifles) and ' a reasonable amount of ammunition ' for the machine-guns and the mountain guns. It is significant that Bell had suggested these figures as 'his maxima' in his report from Lhasa to the Foreign Secretary on 21 February (*supra*, n. 30) and that the Viceroy in his telegram to the Secretary of State on 10 May had called them ' not excessive' (*supra*, n. 31).

[40]Bell to India, 20 October 1921, No. 309 in *Foreign*, November 1921, Procs. 127–325.

to remain as long as he can....[41]

As Bell's mission drew to a close, the position of the three parties *vis-à-vis* each other could best be summed up as marking a definitive stage in the histroy of the frontier and of the Tibetan question. To start with, Tibet stoutly denied that it was under any obligation to the new Chinese Republic. It was certain that it desired complete independence from China with a frontier embracing all Tibetan-inhabited territory which made deep inroads into what Peking had long regarded as an integral part of its domain. For its part, China wanted to regain its control over Tibet and of a kind it had actually exercised during the years 1906–11. In other words, while prepared to permit the establishment of a nominally autonomous Tibet, under strong Chinese influence, it would have its limits confined to a comparatively small area around Lhasa, with the boundary between the two countries as it stood under Chao Erh-feng in 1910.

The (British) Indian role was the most important, even pivotal. Delhi had welcomed the events of 1910–12 in China and now worked for the permanent elimination of Chinese control in Tibet and yet

> not with any idea of wresting Tibet from China (as the Chinese always suspect) but merely in order to maintain friendly relations with the Tibetans, which experience had shown to be impossible when dealing with them through the Chinese as their nominal masters.[42]

In other words, what the Indian government hoped for was an autonomous Tibet under a nominal (Chinese) suzerainty, a regime with which Delhi could maintain direct relations without any overt interference from Chinese authority. Such a Tibet would serve as an ideal buffer, protecting the northeastern frontier of India from Russian and Chinese encroachments. It would be apparent that the Sino-Tibetan boundary was of no interest to the Indian Government except insofar as it affected its own position

> as intermediary and which in view of her (India's) obligations to the Tibetans arising out of the negotiations of 1914 and subsequent assurances, is committed to securing an equitable settlement for the Tibetan Government.

Since the Chinese had proved incapable of managing their own affairs while the Tibetans had, what Britain desired most was that Peking

---

[41] 'Final Report: Lhasa Mission, November 1920–October 1921', *Foreign*, File No. 393, External, Procs. 1–9.

Noting the permission he had been able to obtain for the Royal Geographical Society's proposed Mount Everest Expedition, Bell remarked: ' In fact, I never knew him (Dalai Lama) to refuse anything which I asked .'

[42] Memorandum by Teichman, 12 August 1921, No. 2 in *Foreign*, File No. 65, Part I, Procs. 1–56.

should recognise Tibet as an autonomous dominion bearing the same relation to China as a British dominion does to the United Kingdom and should agree to the frontier line they (Chinese) themselves proposed in 1919.[43]

The Chinese, however, were far from willing to oblige and when highly-coloured and over-exaggerated reports of Bell's 'treaty' with Lhasa began to gain currency, they were back at their old game. Thus, on the one hand there were reports that it had been 'finally decided' to introduce the Tibetan question into the Pacific Conference 'for disposal' while, on the other, Britain was officially informed that

> when the Pacific Conference is over, China and Great Britain must certainly take steps to concert an early and satisfactory settlement of the Tibetan question.

What was more, 'in order to obviate further misunderstandings', Peking made it clear that

> the Chinese Government will be unable to recognise any agreement of whatever nature into which Great Britain may at present enter with the Tibetans.[44]

At the other end, hardly had Bell turned his back, when the old entreaties, and embarrassing requests, from Lhasa began for the 'early conclusion' of a treaty between China and Tibet, through the intermediary of the British Government. For its absence

> makes us very anxious and we do not know what may happen in the near future as the conduct of the Chinese is wicked....[45]

Despite Bell, all seemed to be back to square one!

---

[43] This was according to an alleged report of Mr Sze, then Chinese Minister in London, attributed to the 'International News Agency'. Alston to Curzon, 9 November 1921, Encl. in No. 26 in Ibid.

[44] Memorandum, dated 4 November 1921, by Wai-chiao-pu, Encl. in No. 26 in Ibid.

[45] Tibetan Council to Bell, 13 January 1922, Encl. in No. 43 in Ibid.

Chapter 31

Tibet: Modernism vs *Conservatism*

IN THE euphoria attendant upon Bell's return from Lhasa and the apparent success of his mission, few seemed to realise how very short-lived his new policy of modernising Tibet would prove. Besides, one of the principal aims of his visit, namely to make Peking move out of its persistent refusal to resume negotiations on the Tibetan question, fell far short of realisation. For to British threats and blandishments alike, China proved to be singularly unresponsive. Compulsions of its civil war, which had reduced the country to near-chaos, added to Japan's creeping stranglehold, provided, between them, part of the answer.

In the early twenties, thus, the political situation in Tibet and its suzerain across the frontier, provided an interesting study in contrast. Lhasa was peaceful, the Dalai Lama's hold over his domain firm and unchallenged. Besides, a small army and the nucleus of a police force, which the British had helped to develop, lent his regime a measure of strength and stability it had rarely known before. In the process, however, these new-fangled importations generated a strong reaction, offended the powerful, monastic elements in the body-politic and culminated, in December 1923, in the flight of the Panchen Lama. Unable to resist the strains to which he was thus exposed, the Dalai Lama decided to call it a day and reversed the gears in all that had come to be known as modernisation.

In the bargain, Lhasa experienced a coup in which the Dalai Lama still remained at the top, though at the cost of severely compromising his policies. The situation was electric but Peking remained scrupulously indifferent, unconcerned; the British anxious, but unable and, even more so, unwilling to intervene.

The hope that Bell's presence in Lhasa, and even a prolonged sojourn—as it turned out, he stayed for a whole year—would make the Chinese solicitous for a settlement, was a hope soon belied, a view that stood discredited. Alston's firm belief that Bell's sojourn would make Peking realise that Whitehall was ' in earnest' and that its effect 'will be the greater the longer he stays'[1] was soon set against Delhi's own stark doubts. If Bell were to stay in Lhasa until the Chinese moved, India argued, ' he might have to remain there indefinitely' for no one could ' compete with ' Peking ' in a waiting game'.[2] In the final analysis, a ' one month ' notice was served on the Wai-chiao-pu to

---

[1] Alston to Curzon, 5 January 1921, No. 145 in *Foreign*, June 1921, Procs. 45–283.
[2] Viceroy to Secretary of State, 10 May 1921, No. 280 in Ibid.

'resume' the negotiations of 1919 or else the British would recognise Tibet's status 'as an autonomous state under the suzerainty of China', deal with her on that basis, and supply her with arms ' without any further communication ' being made. Past masters in the art of prevarication and supremely convinced that the present moment 'did not seem...very opportune', Peking succeeded in postponing the day of reckoning and undertook to sort out the problem ' immediately' after the Washington Conference.[3]

Before long 'immediately' was signified to imply ' when the Pacific Conference is over' while, ' to obviate further misunderstanding', it was made abundantly clear that Peking would be 'unable to recognise' any agreement which the British might enter into with the Tibetans.[4]

Whether at the Washington Conference, November 1921–February 1922, the Chinese delegate, Wellington Koo, was officially directed to raise the Tibetan question is not clear; what is, is the fact that he tried valiantly to plough it into the negotiations, however indirectly.[5] He asked Balfour for two categorical assurances—that there were no plans to control China's internal affairs and that Britain would not countenance Japanese efforts to increase the latter's influence in Manchuria—and broadly hinted that ' an unsatisfactory attitude' would be prejudicial to ' our commercial interests' and ' forthcoming Tibetan negotiations'. What was more, the Chinese Minister made it clear that the territories of the Republic, whose integrity was being guaranteed, did not signify China proper alone, ' but all the territories' which included Mongolia, Tibet and Kokonor. Balfour refused to discuss these 'suggestions', noted that they ' created a bad impression' on the Conference and feared that the Chinese ' contemplate' bringing up such questions as the status of Tibet.

The American Secretary of State, Elihu Root's reaction was equally sharp. ' It was outside the power of the Conference to determine " what is China?" ', he is said to have retorted.[6]

Even though Peking regarded the convening of the Pacific Conference as

[3]Curzon to Alston, 17 August, and Alston to Curzon, 31 August 1921, Nos. 217 and 232 in *Foreign*, November 1921, Procs. 127–325.

[4]Memorandum by Wai-chiao-pu, 4 November 1921, Encl. in No. 26 in *Foreign*, F. No. 65/1/1–56, 1922.

[5]An ' International News Agency' report, date-lined Peking, 1 November 1921, read:
Both the President and the Cabinet have now finally decided to introduce the Tibetan question into the Pacific Conference for disposal. Minister Yen has therefore been instructed to prepare the necessary data accordingly.
IOR, L/P&S/10/718.

Alston had however been assured that the news was not true. Alston to Curzon, 9 November 1920, in Ibid.

According to a Chinese scholar, although initially the Chinese government had the intention of ' thrashing out' the Tibetan question in the open, later the Shantung issue became ' so important' that it gave up the Tibetan bone of contention ' in order to get British support against Japanese claims for controlling Shantung'. *Yao-ting Sung*, p. 131.

[6]Balfour to Foreign Office, 15 and 19 November 1921, in *IOR*, L/P&S/10/718.
Inter alia, Balfour had told the Foreign Office that Elihu Root's idea was ' to avoid controversial topics and do something useful...something to help China '.

an exercise in diagnosing its ills and devising remedies for them, conditions inside the country continued to worsen. In his Annual Report for 1921, the British Minister in Peking noted that

> the country has continued to pass through a succession of crises and been rent by civil war, and plagued with riots of soldiers, large areas have suffered from floods and famine, and the depredations of armed bandits: the bane of 'militarism' with its concomitant, the revival of opium evil, has grown in force and misdirected pseudo-patriotic student agitation has spread its pernicious influence in many provinces....

What is more germane from our limited angle, the Chinese Foreign Office used the plea for an impending convening of parliament with a view to unifying the country, to postpone its promised discussions in regard to Tibet. To be sure the value of such parleys, as the British Minister viewed it, seemed dubious at best for

> as a capital it (Peking) has practically ceased to exist. It commands no respect and one begins to doubt whether any movement started in Peking will henceforward seriously influence more than a limited area of the North.[7]

Nor did matters seem to improve in the year following, when first-hand observers of the scene noticed 'increasing chaos and lack of government', a growing 'brigandage' and a 'lawless and unpaid' soldiery.[8] A measure of this lack of political stability may be gauged from the fact that in 1922 China had seven Prime Ministers or Acting Prime Ministers and, in a brief space of six months, as many as four Foreign Ministers.[9]

As Peking appeared in no position to ensure fulfilment of its plighted word, the British Minister, in September 1922, expressed the view that

> we should be justified in postponing our entry into formal relations with the new President (General T'sao Kun) until we had received definite assurances as to his attitude and that of his new administration towards the fulfilment of their responsibilities and treaty obligations to foreign interests....[10]

On Tibet's borders, the situation in Szechuan had continued to deteriorate to the detriment of the central authority. Nonetheless, China's new constitution, adopted in November 1923, noted that the territory of the Republic embraced not only the traditional twenty-two provinces but also 'Mongolia,

[7]*Foreign*, (A) Branch, F. No. 60–X/Pt.II, 1922.
[8]Clive (British Legation, Peking) to Curzon, 26 December 1922, in Ibid.
[9]Annual Report for China for 1922, in Ibid.
[10]Peking Legation, despatch 298, 18 September 1922, in Ibid. See also Hoare to Curzon, 17 October 1923, in *Foreign*, F. No. 60–X/Pt. III, 1923.

Tibet and the Kokonor '.[11]

Besides being weak and distraught internally, China was a prey to Japanese intrigue, both overt and covert. Understandably Tokyo appeared to

> think that a weak and bankrupt Government and a disunited country will be more amenable to pressure or cajolery, and that, if they can only obtain ascendancy by either means and secure the predominant role at Peking, the control of China's foreign policy and the management of its internal, financial and military affairs will ultimately fall into their hands and they will be in a position to oust all foreign competition.[12]

Japan's new policy of attaining its ends by ' subtler methods ' of ' pressure or cajolery ', was a substitute for an earlier approach, of the era of ' Twenty-one Demands ' (1915), to ' swallow up ' China by threat of force majeure and intimidation.

Nothing could be more conducive to Tokyo's unchanging purpose, its age-old objective than the fact that by 1923 China was split right down the middle. Briefly, the northern faction, the Chihli Military party, under the nominal leadership of T'sao Kun, was supported by Wu Pei-fu and controlled a solid phalanx of northern provinces. In the south, there was a triangular combination with the radical Kuomintang and the remnants of the once-powerful Anfu as the two principal partners. In Peking, the Chihli party ruled while its opponents, though unsubdued, were condemned for the most part to passive hostility. The situation in the border provinces with Tibet had continued to worsen, with Batang ' exposed ' to local attacks, the missionaries ' isolated and exposed ', and Lhasa in a strong position on the frontier.[13]

Anticipating a Tibetan settlement before long, and convinced that the primary issue was the definition of a boundary between Inner and Outer Tibet, India in 1922 was playing with the idea of ' carefully collating ' and working out a comprehensive report on East Tibet. *Inter alia*, it was designed to include a gazetteer of place-names, monasteries, detailed routes and a fresh map of the whole region.[14] In the same year, and despite a somewhat distracting

---

[11] A new Chinese constitution had been promulgated on 26 November 1923, in which Chapter III laid down that the territory of the Republic ' consists of all the dominions in the possession of China '. The British Minister noted, however, that although no specific reference had been made to Mongolia and Tibet,
  the corresponding articles of the National Constitution (which) defined the territory of the Republic as consisting, of 22 provinces, Mongolia, Tibet and the Kokonor.
Alston to Curzon, 26 November 1923, in Ibid.

[12] Macleavy (British Minister, Peking) to Curzon, 9 January 1924, in Ibid.

[13] Annual Report for China for 1923, in Ibid.

[14] O'Connor (British Resident, Kathmandu) to Howell, 19 July 1922, in *Foreign*, F. No. 1010-X, 1923.
  O'Connor made the suggestion in view of the ' apparently undigested and un-correlated information ' contained in the consular reports from Tachienlu.
  On 3 August 1922, Howell minuted: It seems to me hopeless to expect Chinese or Tibetans

internal situation in China, the British Foreign Office directed its Charge-d'Affaires not to delay a communication on the subject of Tibet, on account of the Wei-hai-wei Commission's impending report. Additionally, it expressed the view that the offer of May 1919 represented the most favourable settlement, from the Chinese point of view, which HMG could ask the Tibetan Government to accept. For their part,

> while anxious to tender their good offices to bring about an agreement, (HMG) are neither able nor willing to force on the Tibetan Government a settlement contrary to the interests of the latter, and that it is only with a certain amount of give and take that a solution will be possible at all.[15]

As briefly remarked, in sharp contrast to China in the early twenties, the political situation in Tibet was healthier, stabler. Bell's visit in 1920–21, and the policies he advocated including the decision to supply a limited quantity of arms and ammunition, had placed the country broadly on the road towards modernisation and development and, in turn, lent powerful support towards consolidating the Dalai Lama's regime. Acutely sensitive as he was to growing anarchy in China, and ambitious to a degree, the 13th Dalai Lama's principal goal was to stabilise his power on the basis of a viable, if permanent, settlement of his dispute with Peking. Unfortunately his experience, since the abortive parleys at Simla in 1913–14, had made it plain that there were limits both to Britain's diplomatic support and the pressures it could bring to bear on the Chinese. While this realisation took time to sink home, domestic developments of a more compelling nature had begun to exert themselves.

Among Bell's various recommendations, one that the Lama accepted unhesitatingly related to the organisation of a small, but efficient, armed force. Both at Gyantse in Tibet, where a small British escort was stationed, and a few other places in India, Delhi undertook to train young Tibetans who would later form the nucleus of an independent army. A small police force was to be organised too, and to this end the Lama borrowed the services of Laden La, the Sikkimese police official whom he had come to know, and trust, during his years of exile in India.

Added to the munitions that now began to arrive, the trained armed person-

---

to have any sort of ideas of accuracy or any comprehension of maps whatever....Later 'it is possible' that O'Connor might like to do the job himself 'but we need not consider that yet awhile'.

The General Staff Branch, on 4 August (1922), even considered asking Coales to do the job— Coales had already served for some years in Tachienlu.

[15]Foreign Office to Legation, Peking, 6 July 1922, in *IOR*, L/P&S/10/718. 'Whether it is advisable in the first instance... to propose the territorial status quo as the basis of discussion' was left to the Legation's discretion. Earlier, this had been suggested by the India Office at the instance of Sir Charles Bell both at a meeting at the Foreign Office on 13 February (1922) and later, in a private letter to L D Wakely at the India Office. For details see Ibid,

nel and the police injected a new, and hitherto entirely unknown, factor into the Tibetan Folity. For although, in theory, the Dalai Lama's authority was supreme and unchallenged, in practice, the three Lhasa monasteries—Drepung, Sera and Ganden—with their hordes of uncouth, if unarmed, monks always bridled and checked its unrestrained vagaries. They constituted a system of checks and balances that held the Tibetan regime together. The induction of the army and the police, it was clear, would challenge the traditional lamaist theocracy and the initial round in the battle had been joined while Bell was still at Lhasa. The latter's detailed account of what transpired on the eve of the New Year festivities makes it plain that it was the Dalai Lama's bayonets which, in the final analysis, cowed down the determinedly unruly among the monks and prevented an ugly situation from deteriorating further.[16]

A necessary concomitant to the new army, and the police, was an adequate financial provision to sustain them, and in this the Lama's dependence upon the monasteries for the success of his new policy was greater than he seemed to realise. In a land that has known no system of taxation, direct or indirect, the best of resources lay in the hoarded grain and treasure of these large gompas. Studded all over the land, the richest were, besides the three around Lhasa, Kumbum in Sining and the Panchen Lama's Tashi-lhunpo, near Shigatse. The Panchen, it may be obvious, was far from happy with the Dalai Lama's new passion for modernisation, if only because it meant a demand on him to contribute his share of the costs it entailed.

Traditionally, relations between the two Lamas had been far from happy. More recently, the 13th Dalai Lama suspected that the 9th Panchen had compromised his (Dalai's) position by his tacit, if not overt, support of Chinese authority both during his sojourn in Mongolia and China (1904–9) and his two years (1910–12) of exile in India. Differences, it is true, had to an extent been papered over by a meeting between the two Lamas in June 1912 when the Dalai was on his way to Lhasa from India. The ground-swell of suspicion however remained and the petty intrigues and machinations of the underlings over the years added their frightful quota to it. Besides his general distrust of Lhasa's new-fangled policies which were bound to undermine his own political, and therefore spiritual, authority, the demand for a sizeable financial contribution to implement them, presented in a tactless, if inept manner, made the Panchen flee from his monastery at Tashi-lhunpo. His ostensible objective was to collect large enough funds to meet Lhasa's imperious demands; his real aim was to escape from a situation wherein he found his position increasingly untenable.

The Panchen's flight, in December 1923, may be said to mark a watershed in Tibet's recent history and in more ways than one.[16a] On its morrow, and despite

---

[16] Bell, *Portrait*, pp. 288–90.

[16a] According to Dr Sung the Chinese government and the Panchen Lama ' worked together ' for the weakening of the Lhasa government. The Panchen was ' not only seeking Chinese help to rebuild his power, but was also allying himself with the Mongols in Kokonor, Inner

professions to the contrary, the Dalai Lama seems to have made up his mind to fall in line with the diehard, conservative, monastic no-changers, and to bid good-bye to modernisation and all that it implied. Thus it is noticeable that at the time of Bailey's visit to Lhasa, in the autumn of 1924, Tibetan authorities were already becoming increasingly indifferent to the new reforms. Tibet, the four Shapes then told the British Political Officer,

> was a poor country but very religious, and they were accustomed to spend large sums on their religion, and were finding it very difficult to maintain a large army on the Chinese frontier. The soldiers themselves wanted to get back to their homes.

The Dalai Lama told Bailey that as the British were not training men 'as quickly as they expected', Tibet would 'purchase no rifles this year', albeit it would take the other munitions.

The story on the police front was no whit different. On his own the Political Officer seemed self-complacent and, to an extent, perhaps self-congratulatory about its being a ' smart ' and ' very creditable ' force, which had 'reduced crime in Lhasa' considerably. Yet he noticed that

> some of the officials complain of the expense and the Dalai Lama told me that the police were apt to interfere with the duties of the magistrates in Lhasa. These reforms he (Dalai Lama) said must be brought in very gradually.

This is not to mention the English School at Gyantse. Bailey noticed that not only Tibetans ' as a whole ' were very ' lukewarm ' about it, but even the Prime Minister confessed to having ' great difficulty with the parents of the boys ' and in ' finding the money ' (for the school).[17]

The India Office assessment of the situation, as it emerged from Bailey's report, was somewhat superficial. *Inter alia*, it formed a ' strong impression ' of the personality of Tsarong Shape, then Commander-in-Chief and Master of the Mint. He and the Dalai Lama, it noted, were the ' most progressive ' forces in Tibet; the Shape was behind Ringang's electrical scheme, his interest in water-driven machinery was great, he played polo and tennis, owned a private cinema and—' can it be even indulges in the fox-trot?' Nonetheless Whitehall noted that the

> ' progressive ' party have great difficulties to face in the vast power of the fanatical lamas, but it is believed that their power is increasing.[18]

Mongolia, and the western part of Hsi-kang so as to form a second Buddhist centre in opposition to Lhasa '. *Yao-ting Sung*, p. 136.

[17] Bailey's conversation with the Dalai Lama took place on 15 August 1924.
[18] India Office minute, dated 3 December 1924, in *IOR*, L/P&S/10/718.

Actually, the reverse was true. Crudely put, of the two props of the 'Progressive Party', the more important, the Dalai Lama, withdrew his support and struck at the other, the Tsarong Shape. And all this before the ink on Bailey's report was dry.

True there had been rumblings of the approaching storm long before the Political Officer went to Lhasa in mid-July. Thus a report published in *Izvestia*, on 20 May (1924), despite its exaggerated and pronouncedly anti-British bias, was not without a modicum of truth:

> The Chief of the Police at Lhasa and the principal advisor of the Dalai Lama is a British Agent. The Tibetans are highly incited against the English, and the people are begging the Dalai Lama on their knees to drive out the English. The behaviour of the English soldiers towards the population is abominable. The Dalai Lama has at last realised the true position but is powerless to alter it. He has nevertheless refused the English demand for the exploitation of the mineral resources of Tibet....[19]

There were other reports too, mostly fanciful, in the Chinese press about the power and extent of British influence; of 300 British troops being stationed at Gyantse; of a British-built road all the way from the Indian border, across Tibet, to a point on the Chinese frontier near the junction of Szechuan and Yunnan, with 3,000 troops deployed all along; of 600 troops providing a personal body-guard for the Dalai Lama. It follows that the intriguing if interesting point about the crack-down on the westernising tendencies is that it was forecast well in time. Thus the (London) *Observer* noted on 23 November (1924) that the

> attempt to organise an army and a police has synchronised with these other efforts to introduce 'improvements'. Unfortunately neither the feudal nobility, the clergy, nor the peasants appreciate this policy, and the early effect of it has been a clash or two resulting in bloodshed.[20]

Again, in March 1925 Williamson, deputising briefly as Trade Agent in Gyantse, had written about the unpopularity of the Lhasa police.[21] News of the actual coup, marked by large-scale demotions, however came in April, and appears to have been a surprise. The victims included Tsarong Shape as well

---

[19]Translation of a report from *Izvestia*, datelined Peking, 17 May 1924, encl. in Hodgson (British Minister, Moscow) to Macdonald (Foreign Secretary), 21 May 1924, in *IOR* L/P&S/10/1088.

[20]Grover Clark (Editor, *Peking Leader*) to Eric Teichman, 28 July 1924, in Ibid.

[21]Williamson listed three reasons to explain why the police were unpopular: (1) *with the Government*, barring Tsarong Shape, because of 'their expense'; (2) *with the monks*, who regard them as 'an undesirable innovation'; (3) *with the army*, who say that the police are better paid and clothed than themselves and 'have no serious work to do'.
Williamson to India, 11 March 1925, in Ibid.

as officers trained at British military establishments. It was clear that 'all the officers' demoted were members of the so-called 'political and military party' and that the opposing group had struck when the Tsarong Shape was temporarily absent from the capital, thereby giving a clear field day to his adversaries.[22]

By the end of July, London's principal papers had carried the news under such headlines as 'Civil War in Tibet: Modernism *vs* Lamaism', the *Daily Telegraph;* 'Chinese Marching on Tibet: Troops to Attack Monasteries', the *Westminster Gazette;* and 'Trouble in Tibet: Reported Plot Against Lamaism: Generals Degraded', the *Morning Post.* A little later, *Izvestia* hailed the news as 'The East's New Success' and viewed 'the crash of British policy' as 'a very success' (sic) of the movement 'for national liberation'.[23] In the meanwhile, Bailey had compiled what he termed 'a useful summary' of the men removed from official positions and noted that, as a result, 'no officers trained in artillery work' were left serving. Besides, 'at present', the arms and ammunitions purchased (from the British) were 'lying idle' and although he did not view the coup as a general expression of the disapproval of the people with the Dalai Lama's policy, it was

> much more a personal move against the members of the Military party and more especially against the Tsarong Shape.[24]

For his part, the Political Officer was deeply upset over the news with all its varied ramifications. Its impact on the custody and use of the munitions supplied, on Tibet's military efficiency and its capacity to resist a Chinese attack was, he felt, bound to be considerable. No wonder he suggested that his Personal Assistant should go to Lhasa 'at once' and 'remonstrate with' the Dalai Lama over the turn affairs had taken. The India Office, however, viewed this as a 'somewhat daring' suggestion and 'disputable' advice and, in the event, accepted it in a very much watered-down version.[25]

---

[22]Bailey to India, 14 April 1925, in Ibid.

[23]All these reports appeared on 31 July 1925; the *Izvestia* report was dated 12 August. Earlier, on 28 May, the India Office had minuted:

Degradation seems to be the order of the day for offences varying from misappropriation to having the hair bobbed. Westernisation is not to be countenanced.

For details Ibid.

[24]Two other observations by Bailey may be noted:

'I don't think this move is a general expression of disapproval of the people with the Dalai Lama's policy' and 'there is no feeling against the Government of India in connection with these innovations. Nothing was in any way forced on the Tibetan government.'

Bailey to India, 18 July 1925, in Ibid.

[25]India Office minute, 13 August 1925. The minute regarded Bailey's suggestion as approaching 'perilously near' to 'unwarranted interference' in Tibet's internal affairs. IOR, L/P&S/10/1088.

Earlier, *supra,* n. 24, on 18 July, Bailey had expressed the view that *if* the efficiency of the Tibetan army was a matter of great importance, 'the situation created by the recent degradation of military officers must be considered as serious'.

Later when Norbu Dhondhup, Bailey's Assistant, did visit Lhasa, he was distressed in the extreme by the

> 'political naivete' of the Tibetan Government and Dalai Lama's attitude to the wholesale dismissal of trained military officers: 'he (Dalai Lama) laughed when the Rai Bahadur (Norbu Dhondhup) mentioned the subject'.

Norbu noted that enthusiasm for the hydel scheme of Ringang had evaporated, that the great effort of Laden La in the reorganisation of Lhasa's police had been callously thrown away. What was more the numbers, and emoluments, of the police had been severely reduced and an inefficient officer placed at their head.[26]

What is important about the Lhasa coup is that, by the end of 1925, the India Office had drawn the obvious conclusion that so far as the modernisation of his small army and police were concerned, the Dalai Lama had called it a day. Nor was it a temporary set-back. The monks had won and the Dalai Lama himself, essentially one of them, had swung to their side. Briefly, the 'great force of Tibetan conservatism' had scored a resounding victory. It may be noted, if only in parenthesis, that for the life-time of the 13th Dalai Lama there was no turning back; equally, that without his support no one in Tibet was strong, or powerful enough, to carry out such a far-reaching change. The die was cast, and irretrievably.

An important corollary to the Dalai Lama's repudiation of modernisation was a distinct cooling off in his relations with the British. It was not that he was hostile, but his attitude was markedly lukewarm, even studiedly distant, reserved. Could it be that he now began to see clearly that the British had failed in their attempt to make the Chinese accept the 1914 basis for a settlement with Tibet? Since the abortive Simla Convention, endless had been the appeals, requests, entreaties which he and his Ministers had addressed to the 'great British Government', innumerable the representations which they had made about the crushing burden of maintaining a large force on their eastern frontier with China.[27] Disillusioned, the alternative of trying on his own, and not 'through the intermediary' of the British government, may have crossed his mind. Before taking up these nebulous, vague and, as it proved, for most part unproductive yet strange goings-on, enshrouded in a mystery not unknown to the lamas, it may be well to sum up British endeavours in bringing about tripartite negotiations.

[26] Bailey to India, 4–6 October 1925, in Ibid.
[27] Typical of the genre was this letter from the Shapes, dated 7 August 1924:
The Tibetan government has been put to great expenditure by keeping troops to guard the frontiers for many years.... Thus the Tibetan Government and their subjects are in financial difficulties.... (They earnestly) approach the Government of India with a view to final conclusion of the Simla Treaty at Lhasa through the mediation of the British Government.
Encl., Bailey to India, 30 October 1924, in *IOR*, L/P&S/10/718.

PART VIII   THE TRIPARTITE BASIS VANISHES
1931–33

Chapter 32

The Tripartite Basis Vanishes: 1931–32

THE COUP in Lhasa, in 1925, was both interesting and revealing—and in more ways than one. To start with, the Dalai Lama retained his position at the top of the pyramid, even though he dropped his pilot, Tsarong Shape. Nor was that all. For Laden La, the organiser of the erstwhile police force, was packed off too, as was Ludlow, the British Headmaster of the Gyantse school. Not unexpectedly, relations with (British) India cooled off perceptibly and, as though to strike a balance, Lhasa warmed up towards Chiang Kai-shek and his Kuomintang regime—effective rulers of China after the Northern Expedition of 1928. After all, it argued, it may be possible to woo him into a settlement direct, instead of through the intermediary of the British whose record, all said and done, had been—particularly since the abortive Simla negotiations of 1914—one long stretch of unmitigated failure.

Outwardly, Chiang, the Kuomintang ruler, was not unresponsive to the Lama's overtures but in 1931 a dispute between rival monasteries, close to the Teichman Line of 1918, led to skirmishes in which the Lhasa's men were badly mauled. Scared to death lest his earlier gains be completely wiped out and convinced that the Chinese had tricked him, the Dalai Lama staged a virtual *volte face* and in the bargain made frantic efforts to persuade the British to intercede, and urgently, on his behalf. The Chinese, however, were in no mood to oblige. In the first place, they pointed out, there could logically be no *frontier* dispute in the same country. What was more, the British had no *locus standi* in a Sino-Tibetan quarrel which was of a purely domestic character. Their mediation, Nanking argued, was uncalled for; there could be no basis for tripartite negotiations!

By September 1922—the Pacific Conference was over in February that year—Sir Beilby Alston, the British Minister in Peking, was driven to the conclusion that the best chance of reaching a settlement with China was to treat the 1914 Convention, as modified by Peking's May 1919 offer, as a *fait accompli*. While he had viewed the presence of Wellington Koo as Foreign Minister in Peking to be a propitious augury for the success of his endeavours, the latter continued to drag his weary feet. He would, he told the British Minister, consult parliament albeit 'not officially', yet with a view to bringing its important elements around to his way of thinking.[1] Later attempts were frustrated more and more by the pronouncedly anti-British agitation among the radical elements in the towns, particularly the student community. Thus,

[1] Alston to Balfour, 15 September 1922, in *IOR*, L/P&S/10/718.

in March 1924, writing to Ramsay Macdonald, then Foreign Secretary, the British Minister in Peking noted that the Chinese Foreign Office

> have of recent years shown no desire whatsoever to raise the Tibetan question, since they fully realise that they are deeply committed to us in the matter, that we will not yield on the main principles involved and that any settlement arrived at is thus sure to lay them open to attack from the direction of the chauvinistic student element, of which they stand in such fear....[2]

By December (1924), the India Office too had reached much the same conclusion:

> The status quo is acceptable to us; the longer it remains undisturbed, the better chance it has of becoming permanent and negotiations with a stable Chinese Government are sure to be very difficult in view of the sensitiveness of Chinese opinion in regard to Tibet....[3]

One result of Chinese apathy was reflected in Tibet's own lack of interest in affairs on the mainland. This may be partly accounted for by the latter's decision to curb all tendencies that smacked of westernisation and, in consequence, to withdraw into the traditionally isolationist lama cocoon. The relative calm that descended on the Szechuan-Kansu frontier may also have fostered a certain smugness in Lhasa, a feeling that the 'Chinese menace' had perhaps been 'removed permanently'.[4] Understandably, therefore, such defence forces as existed began to be neglected. Thus in September 1927 Bailey reported that the

> troops in Lhasa drill daily but their uniforms are very ragged and some of them even appear on parade wearing only one boot and they openly beg for alms in the streets. The state of the police, who now number 100, is even worse. Recently five men deserted from the army and police but they were caught, flogged and imprisoned.[5]

Nor was that all. The general health of the polity was no better:

> His Holiness distrusts the Kashag (viz. the Cabinet). The Prime Minister is a nephew of His Holiness and is only 26 years of age ... is quite inexpe-

[2]Macleavy to Macdonald, 12 March 1924, in Ibid.
Early in 1924 an article in the *Times* by General Bruce, leader of the Everest expedition, created a good deal of stir in Peking where the British were accused of violating their treaty obligations with China in connection with their Tibetan policy.
[3]India Office minute, 3 December 1924, in Ibid.
[4]Bailey to India, 9 June 1927, *IOR*, L/P&S/10/1088.
[5]Bailey to India, 7 September 1927, in Ibid.

rienced.... Neither the Kashag nor the Prime Minister give any opinion at all, and when the Dalai Lama receives a case for orders, he usually calls in one or two monks who are in his confidence, or Lungshar, and consults them. The result of this state of affairs is general mistrust and suspicion....

Conduct of foreign affairs was particularly 'inefficient' and 'unsteady':

Relations with Nepal are bad. Relations with us are not always what they were a few years ago.[6]

While Lhasa was neglecting its defences during the late twenties, such Chinese energies as were not absorbed by domestic civil strife were devoted either to running down the British for their alleged 'designs' on Tibet or to working out paper plans for an eventual settlement. That the Dalai Lama was in league with John Bull was an accepted article of faith, a theme widely pubilcised, not least in pictorial posters. Perhaps typical among these were the four listed by the British Consul General in Chungking towards the end of 1927:

1. An Englishman with a sword in hand inviting the Tibetans to join him while a border Tibetan says: ' do not join the British, they are bad men ';
2. A rice-pulling mill grinding the skulls of lamas, the ox being the Dalai Lama and the driver British;
3. Lamas kowtowing to a figure on a cross;
4. Tibetans driving the Chinese across the border being represented as puppets on strings, which are held by an Englishman on a chair in the background.[7]

As for paper plans, one of these, discussed by the Nanking government in 1928, visualised Tibet being split into three provinces with their respective headquarters at Batang, Lhasa and Tashi-lhunpo. Another sought to convert the whole country into a province—' such as the Kokonor'. For obvious reasons, the ' plans ' came to nought for, even as Nanking confessed, the Tibetans ' show no enthusiasm '.[8]

For the British, matters came to a head over the issue of instructions with which Colonel Weir was to be armed on his visit to Lhasa. The year was 1930, and an invitation had been received from the Dalai Lama himself. Significantly, a year earlier, an attempt to obtain such an invitation had failed. But with the success of Laden La's mediatory role in the dispute between Tibet and Nepal, there was talk once again of 're-establishing' those cordial relations that had existed earlier between the Dalai Lama's government and Great Bri-

[6]Bailey to India, 20 November 1927, in Ibid.
[7]Consul General, Chungking to Minister, Peking, 10 September 1927, in Ibid.
[8]Consul General, Chungking to Minister, Peking, 28 November 1928, in Ibid.

tain. China, however, as always, loomed large and the question of a settlement with her came to the fore. After prolonged discussions in the Foreign Office and the Cabinet, the Secretary of State informed the Viceroy that

> HMG have constantly recognised Tibetan autonomy as subject to Chinese suzerainty, and, while Chinese attitude made progress with negotiations in 1921 impossible, they feel that it must be contemplated sooner or later when more favourable conditions present themselves, we should aim at regular settlement of Tibetan question. Until it is reached, maintenance of status quo is no doubt obligation of interest if not of honour, but we do not wish to give Tibet idea either that we are opposed to ultimate settlement with China or that we are anxious to encourage her to throw off Chinese suzerainty....

More explicitly, Tibet was to be informed that the present 'difficult internal situation' in China made a satisfactory settlement unlikely, and that until it regained control over Szechuan, Yunnan and Kansu, agreement would be difficult to come by. Additionally, while Tibet might secure better terms from a weak Central Government in Peking, there was the difficulty of binding a stronger, more powerful successor. HMG preferred this line of reasoning to New Delhi's which set much store on dissuading the Tibetans

> from pressing for resumption on ground of difficulty likely to be experienced in securing formal endorsement in a permanent settlement of the status quo in its entirety.[9]

True, in Whitehall there was a strong feeling against India's policy of leaving Tibet 'to stew in its own juice'.[10] Reports from Lhasa were viewed here as disquieting, and there was a distinct feeling that New Delhi had to be prodded into arranging Weir's visit.[11] Later it was deemed necessary to send an official telegram to India emphasising that such a visit was 'very desirable', both for establishing 'personal contact' as well as in arranging a discussion of 'outstanding questions'.[12]

Not only in 1930 but subsequently too, Weir's visits had, in fact, become essential for, as will be noticed presently, in the early thirties there was a recrudescence of trouble on the eastern frontier of Tibet. Here, in a see-saw of hostilities which lasted for the best part of a year, Tibetan forces were thrown back and this despite an outer facade of the Koumintang regime's goodwill towards the Lama and a fanfare of negotiations between China and Tibet to settle

[9]For the Cabinet Memorandum, C.P./280(30) dated 28 July 1930, see Ibid.
For Secretary of State to Viceroy, 31 July 1930, see *IOR*, L/P&S/10/718.
[10]India Office minute by Sir Arthur Hirtzel, 12 March 1930, in *IOR*, L/P&S/10/1113.
[11]Extract from a private letter, Walton to Howell, 28 March 1930, in Ibid.
[12]Secretary of State to Viceroy, 5 April 1930, in Ibid.

outstanding disputes. All through 1931 confused, if contradictory, reports continued to confound the lay observer. Thus the British Consul's 'Chungking Political Summary' for the quarter ending March (1931) noted that

> no progress has been made in the settlement of the dispute between the two lamaseries on the Sino-Tibetan border in which troops of the Lhasa Government are now participating. Reinforcements have been sent from Lhasa during the quarter and fighting is reported to have recommenced on 9 February.[13]

Six months later the situation was no better. It had been 'stagnant' during the preceding quarter and even though there

> has been no further fighting but no progress has been made in the peace negotiations. Both sides appear to be manoeuvring for position.[14]

By the end of 1931, however, there was talk of a *modus vivendi*,

> the principal provisions of which are that Kanze and Chantui remain under Tibetan administration and China pay Rs. 20,000 in respect of maintenance of prisoners taken by Tibetans.[15]

This, however, proved to be so much blowing of hot air for just the reverse was true. Despite promises of peace and goodwill, the Chinese had launched a vigorous offensive and rolled the Tibetan levies back. On 2 May (1932), they (Chinese) were said to have occupied Kanze and, less than a week later, poured into Chantui. In the beginning of July, Rongbatsa appears to have fallen into their hands and then Yu-lung. In August, Derge was captured necessitating Tibetan evacuation of all territory east of the Yantgse. Additionally, its fall posed a direct threat to Chamdo itself; what was worse, Tibetan troops had been compelled to raise the siege of Batang too.[16]

The Dalai Lama's clear conviction that Chiang Kai-shek, who emerged as the undisputed leader of Nationalist China after 1928, had completely tricked him, would be to put it mildly. He was frightened out of his wits and feared an attack on Chamdo to be imminent. On 19 August 1932, departing from

---

[13] Consul General, Chungking to Minister, Peking, in *IOR*, L/P&S/10/1228.
[14] Chungking Political Report for the half-year ending September 1931, in Ibid.
[15] Chungking Political Report for the quarter ending 31 December 1931, in Ibid.
  A Chinese confidential memorandum for presentation to the Executive Yuan had underlined the necessity for extension of Chinese influence to Tibet generally 'in order to counteract British influence at Lhasa and to prevent Soviet influence from becoming general'. Extract from 'Intelligence Report on Tibetan Affairs' in Ibid.
[16] Chungking Political Report for the quarter ending June 1932 in *IOR*, L/P&S/12/557. Also see India Office minute, 30 October 1932, in Ibid.

all known precedents, the Lama telegraphed the Political Officer directly proposing 'secret treaties' between India and Tibet. A day later he asked Weir to repair to Lhasa and 'render assistance' by discussing matters concerning China and the Tashi Lama.[17] On arrival, the Political Officer found the situation grave beyond measure with

> an undercurrent of panic prevalent in Lhasa. Except for the Dalai Lama and his immediate advisers, the truth regarding events in Eastern Tibet was known to nobody. Rumours of the wildest description were widely spread. Tibetan armies had been massacred wholesale, the Chinese were arriving in Lhasa in a fortnight, in ten days.

And there was good reason too, Weir argued, for this undercurrent of anxiety:

> The Tibetan troops were faring badly at the hands of the Chinese. Not only were they being defeated and driven back but many were surrendering. The reason given for the surrender was that they believed the Tashi Lama was helping their opponents.[18]

Deeply upset, Whitehall directed the British Legation in Nanking (capital of China under the KMT regime) to ask the Chinese to negotiate a frontier settlement with Tibet and refrain from all hostilities. With this end in view, the British representative (Holman) met a member of the Chinese Foreign Office on 31 August (1932). Before he could have his say the Chinese availed of the opportunity to register a strong protest over Britain's supply of arms to Tibet. In sum, their functionary (Hsu Mo)

> presumed that the government of India were under no contractual or legal obligation to complete the 1921 supply of arms if it were discovered that the Tibetan authorities were employing them for purposes other than those agreed upon. He then informed that information had reached the Chinese Government that some of the arms now being used by the Tibetan forces in the present hostilities with the Chinese on the Tibetan-Szechuan border were of British manufacture....

Placed on the defensive, Holman brought in the subject of a cessation of hostilities, proffered British good offices and

---

[17]Weir to India, 10 August 1932, in *IOR*, L/P&S/12/578.

A day earlier, the Lama had proposed 'secret treaties' between Tibet and India and asked Weir to 'let me know at once' his views on the matter. For details, Weir to India, 9 August 1932, in Ibid.

[18]Weir's report entitled 'Visit of Political Officer in Sikkim to Lhasa in 1932', dated Baroda, 1 March 1933, in *IOR*, L/P&S/12/36/12.

referred to the various occasions in the past when HMG and India had been of assistance to Peking in the matter of Sino-Tibetan frontier fighting and emphasised the fact that the latter could still rely on them on this occasion too.

Hsu Mo expressed appreciation

> but pointed out that, as Tibet was a part of China, there was really no question of a frontier. I (Holman) suggested tactfully that possibly an administrative frontier might be required. He assented. He then stated that the best way that HMG and the Government of India could assist in the dispute would be by refraining from supplying the Tibetan forces with further arms. In this way, Tibet would speedily give up the struggle, and fighting would automatically cease.

It was a cold douche and when the British representative suggested that the matter be brought to the Minister's notice, Hsu Mo countered by pointing out that he thought it 'too delicate' a subject to be broached with his superior.[19]

Supremely ignorant of the Chinese reaction, the Dalai Lama was driving Weir hard to press for immediate British intervention in order to restore peace on his borders. The Political Officer noted that the Tibetan ruler 'would not allow me to leave Lhasa' until he was satisfied 'that fighting had stopped'.[20] Hence the mounting pressure, both from New Delhi and the India Office, to impress on Nanking the gravity of the situation and to obtain a categorical assurance about a cessation of hostilities. The result was that despite Hsu Mo's cold reception of Whitehall's unsolicited good offices in restoring peace, Sir Samuel Hoare, the then Foreign Secretary, told the British Minister in Nanking that he was

> not without hope that a favourable opportunity may presently occur for renewing the offer, with a view to bringing about an armistice and a *modus vivendi* on the basis of the Teichman Agreement, or some other basis, or conceivably even a more permanent settlement of the boundary question in Eastern Tibet.

The India Office for its part had no doubt that if, as was rumoured, a further Chinese advance on Chamdo occurred, the question of 'taking strong diplomatic action' at Nanking, and even 'providing further assistance in munitions' to the Tibetan Government, would arise. China should therefore, it

---

[19] 'Minute of Meeting with Mr. Hsu Mo at Wai-chiao-pu on 31 August 1932', Encl. in No. 1, Ingram (British Charge-d'Affaires, Nanking) to Sir John Simon (Foreign Secretary), 24 September 1932, in Ibid.

[20] *Supra*, n. 18, para 7.

argued, be openly warned of the deep British interest, and of ' a certain degree of obligation ', in the

> maintenance of the integrity and autonomy of Outer Tibet and of an effective Tibetan Government, able to maintain peace and order in the neighbourhood of the frontiers of India and the adjoining states and free from the influence of any foreign power (excluding China from that term).[21]

It was soon apparent, however, that in Nanking, India's, or for that matter the Dalai Lama's known urgency did not carry any weight. This was evident when, on 24 October (1932), Lo Wen-kan, the Chinese Foreign Minister, informed Ingram, the British Charge-d'Affaires, that he was preoccupied with the Sino-Japanese crisis and had no 'personal knowledge' of the fighting on the frontier with Tibet. To Ingram's 'warnings' that a really serious situation might develop, and his repeated entreaties—'I begged Dr. Lo to lose no time in causing these hostilities, as far as the Chinese troops were concerned, to be abandoned '—all that the Minister vouchsafed was a promise to ' consult ' the Chairman of the Mongolian and Tibetan Committee and to 'see' whether 'anything could be done' to ease the situation. A few days later, a Foreign Office functionary informed the British Minister that 'instructions had been issued ' to the respective Chinese commanders on the frontier to cease hostilities and make no further advance. Nonetheless

> he wished, he said, to make it quite clear that these instructions had been issued by the Chinese Government independently, and before I had made my representations; the issue of the instructions had since been confirmed by reference to the Mongolian and Tibetan Committee (I, of course, made the necessary mental reservations).

When Ingram discoursed upon the necessity for a boundary settlement and, ostensibly off his own bat, suggested that the Yangtse was a good dividing line between Chinese and Tibetan forces in Eastern Tibet, while at the same time proffering HMG's good offices to bring about such a settlement, the response was along expected lines. He was informed, on the authority of the Minister for Foreign affairs, that the question was a 'purely domestic' issue. Nor did a reiteration of the nature of British interest, and 'the most serious' view that HMG might take should the autonomy of Outer Tibet be challenged or its integrity threatened, appear to have any effect. For the Foreign Minister informed him, after he had visited Chiang Kai-shek (by whom 'in

---

[21] *I O* to *F O*, 21 September 1932, in *IOR*, L/P&S/12/578.

Earlier on 16 September the India Office had made it clear that too much regard for the ' susceptibilities ' of the Nanking government would mean avoiding such matters ' as the existence of a legitimate British interest in the autonomy and integrity ' of Tibet. *I O* to *F O*, 16 September 1932, in Ibid.

the past' Tibetan affairs ' had been handled principally ') that

> any intervention on our part might have serious consequences, as the Japanese, in their usual way, were making capital of Colonol Weir's mission to Lhasa, and of our alleged designs on Tibet, and the Chinese press was beginning to get suspicious.[22]

There certainly was more to it, for Dr. Lo ' would not discuss ' Ingram's suggestion for an armistice, and as to his government being bound by the terms of the Simla Convention, ' there was a great deal to be said ' on the Chinese side.[23] When Ingram explained that what the British were proposing was ' not intervention, but mediation ', Dr. Lo retorted that while he understood this, ' it was difficult ' to get the Chinese people to see the matter in the same light. Nor was there any doubt as to what was implied, for in

> different words, and more polite phraseology, this was merely a reiteration of Mr. Liu's and Mr. Hsu Mo's words, that the Sino-Tibetan boundary question was a question of internal Chinese politics, and it seemed to me that we should not gain anything by pursuing the matter further for the moment. We had a definite assurance that hostilities were to cease, and all we could usefully do was to exert diplomatic pressure in the direction of having that assurance implemented.

Additionally, British relations with Tibet were receiving a ' very distorted and undesirable ' publicity in the Japanese and Chinese press and this, Ingram feared, might be exploited to ' our detriment '—should Nanking be driven a little too hard on Tibet.[24]

Reports of Ingram's interviews caused consternation in Whitehall, as no doubt in New Delhi. On 4 November 1932, Walton, a highly placed official at the India Office, minuted:

> There can be no question of acquiescing in the Chinese contention that the dispute is a purely domestic issue for China, and Mr. Ingram should continue to assert our position at every opportunity.[25]

---

[22] Ingram to Simon, 9 January 1933, paras 9, 11–12 and 15 in Ibid.
Ingram's reiteration that ' however much the Chinese attempt to ignore it now, the fact remained that the Indian government were also interested in Tibet ', was quietly ignored.
The Chinese official was Liu Shik-shan, then Head of the European Department of the Wai-chiao-pu.

[23] 'Minute of Interview respecting Tibet', encl. in Ingram to Simon, 26 October 1932, in Ibid.

[24] *Supra*, n. 22, para 16.
Inter alia, Ingram confirmed that he had a number of press clippings ' which would support this statement '.

[25] Minute by Walton, in *IOR*, L/P&S/12/578.

Earlier in September he had expressed himself in a more forthright manner:

> So long as there was a chance of the Chinese accepting our good offices there was some reason for avoiding controversy with them, but now that this chance has become remote there seems little reason for so much anxiety about Chinese reactions to what we might say or do.[26]

In January 1933, Ingram was broadly instructed along these lines, but the Chinese proved cleverer and took the matter out of British purview by directly informing the Dalai Lama that it would be 'absolutely impossible' to accept them (viz., the British) 'as an intermediary'.[27] With Whitehall thus out of the way, it may be useful at this stage to tie up the loose ends of this exercise at direct negotiations between the Dalai Lama and the Chinese authorities.

[26] Minute by Walton, 15 September 1932, in Ibid.
[27] Supra, n. 22, Ingram to Simon, Report, para 18.

Chapter 33

Bilateral Talks: Chinese Initiatives, 1920–33

NATIONALIST CHINA's stern refusal to accept the British as mediators in its dispute with the Dalai Lama's Tibet marked an important stage in the evolution of its policy on the question of tripartite negotiations. As Nanking viewed it, the quarrel with Tibet was a domestic issue between the Central Government of China and a recalcitrant, if rebellious, regime in Lhasa. The British in any case, it argued, had no *locus standi*.

A necessary corollary to spurning British good offices was for China to sort out its differences with Lhasa through bilateral 'negotiations'. These initiatives, for the most part, came from the mainland, as in the case of the 1920 Kansu mission. The Dalai Lama's response to such overtures, initially cool and even hostile, became warmer after his own decided break with modernisation—and Britain. Around 1930, with the visits of Liu Man-ching, a functionary of the Kuomintang's Committee for Mongolian and Tibetan Affairs, and of Yuggon Dzasa, an official of the Dalai Lama based in Nanking who came armed with a personal message from Chiang, there is a certain marked cordiality. Unfortunately not long after what began as a minor skirmish between rival monastic factions in far away Kanze soon developed into large-scale fighting in which, as has been noticed in the preceding pages, the Lama's troops were decidedly pushed back beyond the 1918 Teichman line on the Yangtse.

Keen to make use of his new-found friendship with Chiang Kai-shek, the Dalai Lama to his discomfiture, and utter disillusionment, discovered that the Chinese were not very responsive. And well they might, for the Lama's men had lost their advantage. Nor were the British any more effective. In the stalemate that ensued in the fighting, its edge blunted by civil strife in Szechuan, provincial Chinese commanders and the Dalai Lama's men negotiated a *local* settlement. The price, however, had been heavy, for the tender sapling of a direct Sino-Tibetan rapprochement soon withered away, and with it hopes of a bilateral settlement.

It may be recalled that as early as 1920, a four-man Mission from Kansu, which included two Chinese officials and two lamas, had arrived in Lhasa to negotiate with the Tibetan Government. *Inter alia*, it had sought a direct reply to the question whether Lhasa 'wished to continue hostilities or to conclude' peace.[1] The mission, as has been noticed, remained in the Tibetan

---
[1] Bell to India, 24 September 1920, No. 94 in *Foreign*, November 1920, Procs. 1–102.

capital for well-nigh three months, was received by the Dalai Lama and negotiated among others with five members especially deputed by the Tsongdu, Tibet's National Assembly. The Tibetan reply to its persistent demand for 'two to three representatives' to be sent to China to negotiate a settlement was that, in the light of what had happened in 1914 and 1919, this would serve no useful purpose. Briefly, if

> the (Chinese) President will arrange with the British Government to open negotiations either at Lhasa or in India, and when they have appointed and furnished their representatives with full (diplomatic) powers, then the Tibetan Government will also appoint their representative and that it is not convenient to send any representative to Peking for the present.[2]

It was rumoured at the time that the mission had held out a threat that if its demand for sending delegates to China was not accepted, 'there is no certainty' of hostilities 'not commencing'.[3] The Tibetan Chief Minister, however, had assured Bell when the latter was in Lhasa, that it had been arranged that 'both sides should keep the peace and remain on the defensive—pending a settlement'.[4] Bell's own view was that, as a direct consequence of the Kansu Mission, Chinese agents were steadily drawing over to their side 'influential members' of the Tsongdu. It may be recalled that it was with a view to counter this steady undermining of the Tsongdu, as also 'to strengthen the friendship and confidence' of the Tibetan Government, that Bell himself had been sent to Lhasa. An important result of his visit and of the new policy of helping Tibet, as he visualised it, was the

> probability of China negotiating a tripartite treaty with Britain and Tibet .... In fine, one may perhaps say without exaggeration that the Tibetan question has been settled as far as it can be settled at present. This settlement should last for several years and promote ... in the truest sense—the ultimate interests of China.[5]

To be sure, the Chinese thought otherwise and so did the Dalai Lama. It may be remembered that not long after Bell left, the Lama, thanks to strong monastic opposition at home added to the growing unpopularity of his new

---

[2]Dalai Lama to Bell, 7 May 1920, Encl. in No. 33 in Ibid.

Earlier, on 16 April, the Lama had told Bell that he had given the reply 'as coming from our own minds' and not in accordance with 'instructions received from the British Government'. Encl. in No. 13 in Ibid.

[3]Bell to India, 21 May 1920, No. 33 in Ibid.

Bell's informant had told him *inter alia* that the Tibetan government were feeling 'uneasy' in consequence of 'this threatening language'.

[4]Chief Ministers of Tibet to Bell, 1 May 1920, Encl. in No. 31 in Ibid.

[5]Bell's 'Final Report on Lhasa Mission, November 1920–October 1921', paras 8–9 & 27, *Foreign*, File No. 393, External 1–9.

army and police, turned his back on modernisation and, to him, its logical concomitant, Britain. This significant phase in his long reign, roughly dated around 1925, has been variously represented as 'Dalai Lama Turns Towards China', and strongly 'away from Britain',[6] but is largely concerned with a catalogue either of the demotion of individuals newly trained for the army or the police. At worst, it relates to the closing down of the Gyantse School, the shutting up of the proposed mint, the withdrawal of support from mine-prospecting and the refusal to employ a motor car for speeding the mail to Gyantse and beyond! The only tangible evidence of a pro-Chinese, if also anti-British, bias can be discerned in the refusal of the Tibetan Government to invite Colonel Weir to Lhasa in 1929 when such an invitation was indeed assiduously sought.[7]

This unmistakable 'rebuff' has been variously attributed to the influence of the 'anti-British' Lungshar, then Commander-in-Chief in place of the 'pro-British' Tsarong Shape;[8] a reported warning from a Bolshevik group that it would 'return in force' if 'any British Officer' came to Lhasa; the 'uncertainty' of Chinese movements in northern Tibet; and the 'desire' of some Americans and 'other foreigners' to visit the country.[9] The man directly involved, Colonel Weir, was of the view that the refusal to invite him was primarily due to a well-known Tibetan reluctance to accept responsibility and that if he had gone directly, without waiting for a formal invitation, all would have been well.[10] In retrospect, however, what is significant is not so much the refusal to invite Weir as the contacts which the Lama established about the same time with the Chinese through two important visitors from the mainland.

Liu Man-ching, an employee of the Nationalist Government's Committee for Mongolian and Tibetan Affairs, CMTA for short, was the daughter of a Chinese father and a Tibetan mother and reached Lhasa, through Szechuan, early in 1930. Her main objective appears to have been not so much to

---

[6]Bell, *Portrait*, Chapter LV: 'Dalai Lama Turns Towards China'; Li, *Tibet*, p. 148, sub-heading: 'The Dalai Lama Turning Strongly Away from Britain towards China'; Richardson, *History*, p. 128, calls it a 'reaction' against 'closer relations' which led to 'if not an estrangement, a marked coldness'.

[7]Weir, then Political Officer, had himself suggested such a visit. New Delhi, however, was cold, if not hostile. For, it argued, the advantages of such a visit were 'altogether insignificant' compared with the 'danger of China being baited' into action while there was 'any hope that she may otherwise not move seriously'. India to Weir, 9 February 1929, in *IOR*, L/P&S/10/1113. Weir, however, contested this and, with the support of the India Office and the British envoy in Nanking, who had 'no objections', sanction was finally given. For details Weir to India, 7 March 1929; Viceroy to Secretary of State, 12 April 1929; Lampson to Foreign Office, 20 April 1929; and Secretary of State to Viceroy, 17 May 1929, all in Ibid.

[8]This was Bailey's view as recorded by Walton in the India Office minute, 7 September 1929, in Ibid.

[9]These were the reasons retailed to Weir by the Tibetan Trade Agent at Gyantse. Weir to India, 22 July 1929, in Ibid.

[10]Weir to India, 13 August 1929, in Ibid.

engage in detailed negotiations as to establish, in the Lama's eyes, the *bona fides* of the new KMT regime in China. In his reply, the Tibetan ruler expressed himself in beautifully vague generalities: his 'appreciation and gratitude', for the message of sympathy she had brought; his faith in China, for, 'real unity and peace'; his realization of the 'importance' of guarding the 'national sovereignty'. The problem of the Tibet-Sikang frontier would be solved, he is reported to have underlined, the moment the central Chinese government consolidated its hold and placed 'honest and well-intentioned' men in positions of authority.[11] It has been maintained that despite Miss Liu's 'several informal approaches' to impress on her hosts the urgency for closer ties with China, she was given 'no encouragement' by the Tibetan Government.[12]

Yuggon Dzasa, also referred to as Kunchok Jungnay or Dzasa Tsetrung, was a confidante of the Dalai Lama who had been, since 1922, in-charge of the Lama temple in Peking. His choice as a KMT representative to straighten out matters of a 'political' nature was largely dictated by the fact that he was said to be very close to the Tibetan ruler. Arriving in Lhasa early in 1930, he is said to have been the bearer of a special letter from the Kuomintang and, on arrival, was the recipient of 'special favours' and great 'honours'.[13] What precisely he achieved is not clear but even if Dr Li's version of the Dalai Lama's answers to the questions posed to him be accepted without qualification, all that it boils down to is the underlining of fundamental differences between the two sides on important issues: the definition of Tibet's status, the demarcation of the boundary between Tibet and China proper, the readjustment of the relationship between the two great Lamas.[14] Two aspects of the matter, however, deserve notice. One, that the British were visibly

---

[11] Li, *Tibet*, pp. 151–52.

According to Li, Miss Liu arrived in Lhasa in February, had her last interview with the Dalai Lama on 25 May and returned to Nanking, via India, on 27 July 1930.

[12] Shakabapa, *Tibet*, pp. 266–67.

According to Shakabapa, Miss Liu 'was permitted' to enter Lhasa on an 'unofficial' visit and carried a letter from General Chiang Kai-shek.

On the testimony of Miss Liu, the Dalai Lama allegedly told her:

> The British Government did have the definite idea of drawing me to their side. Nevertheless, I acknowledged the importance of Chinese sovereignty and territorial integrity, which should never be surrendered by anyone. Moreover the Tibetans and the British have different religions as well as different customs and traditions. Therefore the dealings I had with the British were merely expedient. I have never conceded any right to them, nor will I do so in the future.

Liu Man-ching, 'My Mission to Lhasa' (Shanghai, 1932), p. 118, cited in *Yao-ting Sung*, p. 140. Also see C Y W Meng, 'Miss Liu's Mission to Tibet', *China Weekly Review*, no. 54, 6 September 1930, p. 22.

[13] Weir to India, 20 February 1930, in *IOR*, L/P&S/10/1228.

[14] Li, *Tibet*, pp. 152–55.

Shakabapa, *Tibet*, p. 266, is mixed up on the date which is 1930, *not* 1927, but is categorical that while the Dalai Lama 'welcomed' the possibility of friendly relations, he declined the suggestion that 'Tibet become part of China'.

upset by these goings-on and that the India Office not only expressed concern, and ' some disquiet ', but made it plain that an early visit of Colonel Weir, then Political Officer to Lhasa, would seem ' very desirable '.[15] There could, of course, be little doubt that the visit itself was hastened by Yuggon's presence. Additionally, Laden La, then in Lhasa to help tide over what threatened to be an outbreak of hostilities between Tibet and Nepal, was struck by

> how Chinese influence has so suddenly established here, probably owing to ourselves keeping away from Lhasa, while the Chinese seized the opportunity and pushed forward their policy.... Unggon Dzasa is trying hard to establish himself well with Dalai Lama and he associates Chinese lady (viz. Liu Man-ching) with Tibetan ladies....[16]

Another aspect of the matter that bears mention was a deliberate Chinese effort to play up the Yuggon's visit. Mr. Richardson sees in it

> certainly evidence of a thaw in the Dalai Lama's attitude towards China that he should be ready to discuss (Yuggon's) proposal without reference to the Government of India ... but ... the discussions for the Chinese were conducted by one of the Dalai Lama's own officials (Yuggon).... Moreover the tone of his (Dalai Lama's) replies suggests that he may have hoped to succeed where the British had failed.... It is clutching at straws to suggest that the Dalai Lama's reception of such missions showed a willingness to accept Chinese supremacy or that his attitude was running strongly towards China.[17]

Whatever the truth of the matter, typical of Chinese propaganda was the fact that the first issue of the ' Tibetan-Mongolian Weekly News ' highlighted the arrival of the Dalai Lama's representatives in Nanking who, the paper maintained, had been ' specially deputed ' to effect ' a rapprochement ' between the Tibetan and Chinese Governments.[18] A message sent by the Dalai Lama to Chiang Kai-shek pledging his support to the new regime evoked a response in which the KMT leader

> stressed the point that the relations between the two countries are funda-

---

[15]Extract from a private letter, Walton to Howell, 28 March 1930, in *IOR*, L/P & S/10/1113. Also see Secretary of State to Viceroy, 5 April 1930, in Ibid.

[16]Viceroy to Secretary of State, 7 May 1930, in Ibid.

[17]Richardson, *History*, p. 132.

[18]The ' Tibetan-Mongolian Weekly News ', which was very short-lived, was a propaganda journal issued from Nanking.
The article in question was entitled : ' Visit of Dalai Lama's Representatives to Nanking '. For details *IOR*, L/P & S/10/1228.

mentally most intimate and hoped that in future they would achieve complete unity.[19]

It is not without nothing that, in the autumn of 1930, Colonel Weir noticed that although the Dalai Lama did not think that the time was 'yet ripe' for resumption of negotiations with China or for the ratification or modification of the Tripartite Convention of 1914, there

> is without doubt a strong undercurrent of feeling among several officials that Tibet will not be able to retain her independence of China indefinitely and that steps should soon be taken to make friendly overtures to China. If such overtures are made, they anticipate that a semi-independence at least will be achieved for Tibet which would be preferable to complete absorption by China.[20]

The proof of the pudding, however, lies in the eating thereof and a concrete instance wherein the new rapprochement could have been put to a practical test was in bringing to an end the border warfare on the Hsikang-Tibet frontier. This had erupted, towards the end of 1930, from minor skirmishes between rival monastic factions in two lamaseries located across the (1918) boundary line. In the preceding pages mention has been made of British efforts to bring about a cessation of hostilities. These, as was noticed, were undertaken at the Lama's express request when his own endeavours in making a direct approach appeared to peter out. Highlights of what was a fairly confused situation may be briefly sketched out.

In December 1930, Ma Fu-hsiang, then Chairman of the CMTA, telegraphed to the Dalai Lama that

> Liu Wen-hui wired his soldiers stopped advancing but Dachi reinforced. Hope order Dachi stop fighting. Wait for pacification.[21]

There was, unfortunately, no waiting 'for pacification'. In a game where stakes were high, neither side was prepared to yield ground, professions to the contrary notwithstanding. Briefly, in the initial stages (summer 1931), with Tibetan troops receiving reinforcements, the Chinese were driven back from Kanze as far as Trango, a few marches from Tachienlu. But by April–May

---

[19]India to Weir, 29 September 1930, in Ibid.

Apart from Chiang, Ma Fu-hsiang, then Chairman of the CMTA, had also conveyed his 'greetings and assurances' to the Lama. For details Ibid.

[20]Weir's report on 'My Tibet tour and on my visit to Lhasa in 1930', para 12 in *IOR*, L/P&S/10/1113.

[21]This 'En clair' telegram addressed to the Dalai Lama passed through Gangtok and was evidently known to the Political Officer. Weir to India, 13 December 1930, in *IOR*, L/P&S/10/1228.

Liu-hui was the warlord of Szechuan.

1932, with fresh Chinese troops arriving and the Tibetans running short of ammunition, the former took the upper hand and drove the latter as far back as the 'Teichman Line' of 1918. Chinese pressure persisted and soon the Tibetans had to withdraw from Derge to the line of the Yangtse.

It would be evident that in the early stages, the Tibetans were keen to consolidate their gains. Thus the 'Consul General's Political Report' from Chungking for the half-year ending September 1931 noted that the

> Sino-Tibetan situation has been stagnant throughout the quarter. There has been no fresh fighting but no progress has been made in the peace negotiations. Both sides appear to be manoeuvring for position.[22]

A month later, although the air was still thick with rumours about negotiations, the British Consul-General appeared far from sanguine, for

> prospects of a meeting between Tibetan and Chinese representatives for negotiations ... (are) very remote ... an early resumption of hostilities (appears) as certain.[23]

In retrospect it would appear that, on the eve of the Chinese launching their well-planned offensive, the smoke-screen of an impending settlement of the frontier question was vigorously kept up. Thus the Chungking report for the quarter ending December 1931 suggested that

> negotiations regarding the trouble in the border regions have ultimately resulted in the conclusion of a *modus vivendi*, the principal provisions of which are that Kanze and Chantui remain under Tibetan administration and China pays Rs. 20,000 in respect of maintenance of prisoners taken by Tibetans.[24]

This, of course, was too good to be true and before many months passed, the Chinese mounted their offensive. By June (1932), Tibetan troops had been driven back from their earlier positions:

> There has been a recrudescence of warfare in the Kanze-Chantui area. The former town (was) occupied by the Chinese on 2 May and the latter on 6 May. Chinese intention (was) to re-occupy the whole territory up to Chiamdo. Kokonor troops (had been moved) to Jyekundo to co-operate.

Nor were Chinese successes confined to isolated instances. Darjye gompa and Rongbatsa fell to them at the beginning of July and Yu-lung, on the road

---

[22] Chungking Political Report for the half-year ending September 1931, in Ibid.
[23] Consul General, Chungking to Minister, Peking, 4 October 1931, in Ibid.
[24] Chungking Political Report for the quarter ending September 1931, in Ibid. Also see Extract from 'Intelligence Report on Tibetan Affairs' in Ibid.

from Rongbatsa to Derge, was taken by the middle of the same month. By August, it was reported, the Chinese had refused a Tibetan request for an armistice, convinced that it was no more than a bluff to allow reinforcements to come up from Lhasa. Derge was captured (in August) and Batang, where Tibetans had laid a seige in May–June, had to be abandoned.[25] Finally, what saved the Tibetans was not so much their own prowess in battle—in fact they had already run short of ammunition—but the in-fighting among the rival Chinese generals in Szechuan.

Frightened, even dazed with the inroads which the Chinese had made into his positions—and the avalanche of manpower that, in its wake, threatened to pour into his country—the Dalai Lama's earlier frigidity towards the British appeared to melt away. This is evident from the frantic messages which, as we have noticed, he sent to the British Political Officer in August 1932; his more than a broad hint for a 'secret treaty'; his insistence that Colonel Weir stay on in Lhasa until news of the cessation of hostilities could be confirmed. Pursuant thereto the British appealed to the Chinese, suggested an early settlement of the border conflict, and proffered their good offices. Nanking, at the highest level, received these initiatives with marked indifference and although the tone of its reaction may have varied, its essential content remained singularly unaltered. Since Tibet was an integral part of the mainland, it argued, anything that had to do with it was a domestic problem; the question of settling a Sino-Tibetan frontier did not arise because there was, and could be, no such frontier. At best, in the preliminary exchanges, offers of British good offices were coldly received; at worst, they were asked to mind their own business.

Later, due to growing pressures from New Delhi itself exposed to Lhasa's imperious demands, the Foreign Office in London changed its tune. Shedding for once its apologetic tone, Whitehall now reminded Nanking of HMG's direct interest in the integrity of Tibet, of its pledge to safeguard the latter's autonomy and its refusal to view the dispute as a 'purely domestic issue' of China.

---

[25] Chungking Political Report for the quarter ending June 1932, in *IOR*, L/P&S/12/577. Also see India Office Minute, 30 October 1932, in Ibid.

According to a Chinese scholar, for Nanking the 1931–32 war had great significance: Chinese frontier garrisons defeated Tibetan troops 'for the first time' since Chao Erh-feng's days; Chinese provinces lost to Tibet, since 1918, were now recovered; the 'anti-Chinese group' in Lhasa received a severe blow; the Kalon Lama committed suicide while the 'Conservative party' in Lhasa received a big boost. *Yao-ting Sung*, pp. 149–50.

Chapter 34

Bilateral Talks: Their Limitations, 1932–33

WHITEHALL'S CHANGE of stance from one of apologetic proffering of unsolicited good offices to a clearer, unambiguous, statement of Britain's close concern, if indeed direct involvement, in anything that touched Tibet and its autonomy marks an important watershed in our narrative during the inter-war years. Before long this interest was to show itself in a better, and in fact keener awareness of India's North-eastern frontier with Tibet, and even relations with China. That, however, was to be in the long run; in the short, to meet the British challenge, Nanking too changed its tune. The Chinese, acted on two fronts. On the one hand, the British were reminded that

> with respect to our contention that China had recognised our interest in Tibet (in the abortive Simla Convention of 1914) there was a good deal to be said on the Chinese side.

Old polemics apart, the hostility of the Japanese to British activity in Tibet, and growing Chinese suspicion of Tokyo's ulterior motives were heavily underlined. While refusing to yield ground on essentials, the Chinese Minister tried to soothe ruffled British feelings by conceding that, even though he understood that 'the essence' of their representations was not intervention but mediation,

> it was difficult to get the Chinese people to see the matter in the same light .... He repeated his earnest intention of bringing about a satisfactory settlement and asked me to explain to the Indian Government the difficulties with which the Chinese were faced.[1]

Meanwhile, there was another string to the Chinese bow and this was to administer, and directly, a stern warning to Lhasa which took the form of an exchange of messages between Chiang Kai-shek and the Dalai Lama in October-November 1932. The first, from the Chairman of the CMTA was dated 27 October and informed the Lama that

> Chiang Kai-shek has wired to Your Holiness, Szechuan and Kokonor asking each party to remain in their own territory pending negotiations.

[1] Ingram to Simon, 9 January 1933, *IOR*, L/P&S/12/577. Also see 'Minute of Interview respecting Tibet', encl. in Ingram to Simon, 26 October 1932, in Ibid.

As soon as a definite reply is received, negotiations for a just settlement of the case will be started.

A little over a week later, Yuggon Dzasa, the Lama's representative in Nanking, informed his master that the Chinese

> sincerely wish to establish friendly relations between China and Tibet—so that as soon as an intimation is received that orders have been issued for cessation of hostilities in Eastern Tibet, they have decided to send a representative (to Lhasa) to discuss terms of peace between China and Tibet and at the same time to present an honorific title to Your Holiness and offerings to the three great monasteries. Therefore they have asked me to wire and get Your Holiness' reply. At the present time there is a civil war between Liu Hsing and Liu Wen-hui and the latter got worsted but as the war is still in progress the above might be a ruse for fear of losing the territories that Liu Wen-hui won from us and please send instructions as to how to act towards the Chinese Government.

The Dalai Lama, shrewd and well-informed as he was, refused to fall into the Chinese trap. There could, he reasoned, be no question of starting *ab initio*. Acknowledging 'various telegrams' from Chiang Kai-shek he wired his representative on 9 November that it was

> two months since orders have been issued for our troops in Eastern Tibet to be withdrawn but so far the Chinese have been attacking us and thereby causing this estrangement. A treaty between China and Tibet alone would not be lasting and as an agreement was arrived at in the main at Simla in 1914 except in connection with the boundary the best course would be to resume and conclude the Simla 1914 treaty. Give the above reply to Chiang Kai-shek and send his reply immediately.

The Dalai Lama's hint of bringing in the British was explicit enough, but somehow Simla evoked memories which the new Chinese regime did not find very pleasant. In any case, even as the latter had earlier rebuffed Holman and Ingram in Nanking, and in no uncertain terms, there could be no question of obliging the Dalai Lama on that score. On 25 November, Chiang asked the Dzasa to inform his master that the

> Kokonor troops under Ma are being withdrawn. Knowing that Liu Wen-hui of Szechuan could not really spare troops to send into Eastern Tibet it is difficult to believe as represented (by His Holiness) that they are attacking and thereby causing estrangement. It is easy to see who is really to blame for this trouble. Keeping in mind the friendly and brotherly relations between China and Tibet every transaction should be dealt with in a straight-

forward manner without entertaining any suspicion and all matters settled between ourselves without the intervention of an outsider. Therefore to agree to the request for the treaty, with the British Government as an intermediary power, to be resumed and concluded would be absolutely impossible as it would be like agreeing to one's own body being dismembered.[2]

The preceding pages make it clear that, by the end of 1932, Chiang had unmistakably snubbed the British and at the same time told the Lama, in unequivocal terms, that all matters must be settled ' between ourselves '—and ' without the intervention of an outsider '. Lhasa, however, was not so easily persuaded and, in December 1932, using the Tsongdu as its mouthpiece summed up its position in the following three propositions:

1. The Simla Convention of 1914 between China and Tibet be immediately concluded;
2. A meeting of representatives of China and Tibet with the British government acting as an intermediary be convened;
3. Weir be appointed as one of the British representatives to sit on the three-power Conference as he was acquainted with the full facts of the case.[3]

Chiang's opposition, however, remained strong and uncompromising. He pointed out that he had already replied to the points raised and directed his appeal to the Lama's heart, *not* his head. China and Tibet, he maintained, had been ' united together ' for centuries, and, with China ' a Republic ', there was 'every opportunity' for free discussion 'of all matters between ourselves '. It followed that

it was ' most inappropriate ' to place ' another person of different nationality ' as intermediary as had been done heretofore.

The KMT ruler also proposed direct talks. To initiate the parleys, he asked the Lama to send some ' high official ', accompanied by ' one of the Tibetan representatives ' in China, so as to arrive at a ' permanent settlement '. Once ' friendly relations ' had been established, the boundary differences—' the Kham and Tibet question '—could be settled with ' ease '. As a preliminary, the Lama must agree to receive a Chinese representative, present China's case to his own people ' in a friendly spirit ', and above all inform ' the outsiders ' that they (China and Tibet) ' did *not* require ' an ' intermediary '.

The alternatives were spelt out too. Should the Lama fail to comply with Nanking's proposed course of action, the latter was likely to send Liu Wen-hui, who had been defeated in the civil war in Szechuan, to Kham

[2]The text of these telegraphic exchanges between the Dalai Lama and Chiang Kai-shek were given to Weir in Lhasa in the autumn of 1932 and are reproduced in *IOR*, L/P&S/12/578.

[3]The Tsongdu's resolution, dated 6 December 1932, was addressed to the then Governor-General, Lord Willingdon. For the text see Ibid.

while Ma Fu-hsiang's son Malcolm had already been despatched to Kansu and Nyingsha, 'in readiness' to attack.

To this clever admixture of entreaties and threats, the Lama's response was a reiteration of his earlier stand. While on the one hand he would ask the British to help ward off a Chinese attack,

> for the sake of permanency as per our representation ... we will persist asking Chinese Government to conclude Simla Treaty....[4]

To Yuggon Dzasa in Nanking, he had been more explicit:

> My intention is to press this point (viz., a settlement of the Sino-Tibetan, question with the British Government acting as an intermediary) until attainment of the object in view so hope they (Chinese) will concur as soon as possible....[5]

It is obvious that Lhasa was persisting in a seemingly self-stultifying course. Both from what the Minister for Foreign Affairs had told Ingram, and what Chiang himself had made explicit to the Tibetan ruler, the Chinese would refuse to have the British as an intermediary. Would it not be better, in the circumstances, for Whitehall to encourage the Lama to come to a direct understanding with Chiang Kai-shek? Opinion was sharply split.

Williamson, the Political Officer in Sikkim whose direct responsibility it was to keep in close, personal touch with Tibet and its ruler, was strongly opposed to such a course. For if

> the Chinese succeed in forcing him (Dalai Lama) to do so (i.e. negotiate direct) the policy as regards Tibet and China, which we have maintained since 1912, will be entirely stultified and our position in Tibet will be reduced to nothing.[6]

This was on 10 January 1933. Less than a fortnight later, the Political Officer reiterated the position while making it clear that it was 'in the interests of both India and Tibet' to put pressure on the Chinese not only for an 'immediate and complete cessation' of hostilities but also for a resumption of negotiations to bring about a 'permanent settlement'.[7]

New Delhi fully shared this viewpoint. In a long telegram to the Secretary of State on 14 February (1933), it recalled the major objectives of its Tibetan policy. The chief aim had been to

[4] Dalai Lama to Williamson, 8 January 1933, in Ibid.
[5] Dalai Lama to Yuggon Dzasa, 31 December 1932, in Ibid.
Inter alia, the Lama had asked the Dzasa to 'put the above matter very strongly and explicitly to Chiang Kai-shek' and to reply 'immediately'.
[6] Williamson to India, 10 January 1933, in Ibid.
[7] Williamson to India, 21 January 1933, in Ibid.

secure a friendly Tibetan Government which is strong enough to exclude external influences, including Chinese which are likely to cause trouble on the Indian frontier.

Over the last 20 years this had been achieved

> by supporting the Dalai Lama in his claim of integrity of Outer Tibet and to freedom from Chinese interference in that area....

The result was that

> in Lhasa (there was) a pro-British Government whose stability and friendship is to a large extent dependent on our continued support against Chinese aggression....

Should the Lama be now asked to

> make his own terms with China (there was a) possibility that Tibet will be forced to admit Chinese authority in Outer Tibet, or perhaps to seek assistance from Soviet (Government)....[8]

To this whole line of reasoning, Sir Miles Lampson, the then British Minister in China, was strongly opposed. To start with, he was definitely against

> giving Dalai Lama any encouragement... to think Chinese Government will ever agree to our mediation; for I feel sure they never will.

Sir Miles was 'also convinced' that it would be 'unwise' to provoke any controversy on the subject, for China's

> traditional attitude towards Tibet is that of a pre-occupied parent towards a naughty child which will one day return to the fold whether as a result of the parent's chastisement or of his own accord....

Nor did the Chinese care as to what happened

> in Tibet or on the frontier (unless we occupy the country as the Japanese have Manchuria) but they will never formally create any mental theory of Chinese rights over Tibet (in China theory counts far more than fact).

Hence the British should face facts and

> encourage, not discourage, Dalai Lama to come to terms with China by

[8] India to Secretary of State, 14 February 1933, in Ibid.

direct negotiation if he can, trusting to geographical propinquity of India to Lhasa to maintain our influence by promotion of free economic relations, *without this* official intercourse, across our frontier.[9]

At the receiving end in Whitehall, these opposing views of authorities who had the responsibility as also the benefit of direct dealings with both sides in the dispute, created a piquant situation. The initial reaction was to

adopt (temporarily at any rate) a compromise to cover the present period of Chinese intransigence, in the hope that, should the Chinese prove more amenable in the future, we may be able to revert to our earlier position of appearing as mediators, with a recognised status between Tibet and China and continue the negotiations on the same basis as was followed in the case of the tripartite Simla Convention of 1914.[10]

Less than twenty-four hours later, Walton minuted that what had been suggested in Nanking did not amount to a 'change of policy' and that the 'present trouble' was the same as had led to the breakdown of 1914 (viz., the eastern frontier dispute). Further, Williamson had clearly 'exaggerated' in suggesting that direct negotiations between the Dalai Lama and the Chinese 'would stultify' the previous policy. Since 'mediation in present circumstances' was 'not practicable', the Dalai Lama should be so informed

but we should frame our message in such a way as to avoid unnecessary discouragement; if in the circumstances he decides to enter into direct negotiations with China, we can play the part of friend and confidante behind the scenes; if he should be shy of direct negotiations, his position is not prejudiced, in the absence of renewed attacks by the Chinese Government or uncontrolled *condottiere* on the frontier; if he should suffer such attacks, we can consult together as to the best action to be taken in our mutual interests.[11]

For 'the substance' of the reply to the Dalai Lama, Walton argued, three alternatives were open:

1. to advise him to refuse the Chinese overtures (trusting to a *de facto* maintenance of the status quo on the frontier);
2. to tell him, as India had proposed, that he must decide for himself;
3. to give him some tentative and quite friendly encouragement ('while leaving the decision entirely to him') in accepting a Chinese offer for

---

[9]Lampson (British Ambassador, Nanking) to Simon (Foreign Secretary), 6 February 1933, in Ibid.
[10]India Office minute, dated 13 February 1933, by J P Donaldson, in Ibid.
[11]India Office minute, dated 14 February 1933, by J C Walton in Ibid.

direct negotiations, assuring him of 'our advice throughout' and 'our support' subsequently towards 'securing' a satisfactory settlement.

The third alternative he rated as the best, for it was

> difficult to see what harm could come of a Sino-Tibetan conference (perhaps at or near the frontier, perhaps at Lhasa) limited to the frontier question, and with the Dalai Lama turning to us for advice (as he doubtless would do) at each turn of the negotiations.[12]

Meantime, as Walton was arguing his brief, the Political Officer in Sikkim changed his stance, if only slightly. On 22 February 1933, Williamson told New Delhi that Tibet should be encouraged *not* to negotiate 'a permanent settlement direct' but 'merely a truce' on the frontier. Two things, however, were necessary prerequisites. One, that a 'definite assurance' be obtained that the Chinese will not renew their aggression on Tibet either from Kokonor (viz. Kansu) or from Szechuan. If this were forthcoming,

> the question of a permanent settlement of other outstanding questions can, owing to *China's refusal to negotiate with us and to Tibet's refusal to negotiate without us*, be left till a more favourable opportunity occurs.

Secondly, Williamson argued, the old policy *vis-à-vis* Tibet should not be abandoned, for 'no enemy is so bitterly hated as a former friend who is considered a betrayer'. Nor was there any prospect of a permanent settlement with China being concluded at an early date, unless the latter withdrew its 1919 insistence on posting Chinese representatives at the trade marts inside Tibet. The Dalai Lama, as was well-known, would have none of them. British or Chinese, but 'if he had a Chinese one, he must have a British one also'. Supporting Tibet did not however imply, Williamson reasoned, that the Lama was not to be restrained from his more adventurous courses, including an attempt to regain his lost territory.[13]

While the Lama's aggressive zeal, to which Williamson had alluded, was smothered by a polite enough hint, a communication on the lines of the India Office proposal was officially made to him. He was informed that he may discuss frontier matters with the Chinese and that British advice would be available to him in the course of these discussions, or after they had been concluded. Further, the British would help him by persuading the Chinese to clinch the agreement that may be reached between the parties.[14]

The Lama's reaction was friendly and helpful. He told Williamson on 27 March (1933) that although the Chinese had suggested 'direct' talks yet

---

[12] India Office minute, 15 February 1933, in Ibid.
[13] Williamson to India, 22 February 1933, in *IOR*, L/P&S/12/578.
[14] India to Williamson, 1 March 1933, in *IOR*, L/P&S/12/577.

so far no opening of negotiation has been possible although our representatives have been sent for this purpose. Moment their manifestation proves to be sincere and they lay their aim clearly before us so as to bring about a possible solution of difficulty, Tibetan Government hope that British Government taking a keen interest in the discussion will help to conclude an agreement as we feel that such an agreement would then be more permanent.

Additionally, the Dalai Lama accepted the British Government's 'kind offer' of 'friendly advice' while negotiations were in progress, and of 'diplomatic assistance' to induce China to conclude an agreement, if proposal 'acceptable to us' emerged from the talks.[15]

Even as communications to and from Lhasa continued, in the India Office there had been a virtual storm over Sir Miles Lampson's earlier telegram in which, *inter alia*, he had advocated that Tibet be induced to come to a direct understanding with China. An unfortunate textual error appeared to suggest that the British envoy had barred continuation of official intercourse with Tibet. In an office minute, Walton charged that Sir Miles had 'no special acquaintance' with the history of the Tibetan question and reminded the Foreign Office that

> HMG's policy and interests in relation to Tibet are not affected or diminished by the question whether or not the Dalai Lama should enter into direct negotiations with the Chinese Government on the isolated matter of the Sino-Tibetan frontier. It follows that there can be no question... of discontinuing our official relations with the Tibetan Government.[16]

The misunderstanding was finally cleared up in a personal exchange between Victor Wellesley of the Foreign Office and Sir Miles. This afforded the latter an added opportunity to explain his position more explicitly as also to lend his support to the decision to allow the Lama to negotiate direct. The British envoy deprecated

> our trusting to artificial barriers of our own creation in keeping Chinese and Tibetans apart. These barriers will break down one day—the traditional bonds between China and Tibet are too strong and long-standing—and if at that time we are still found trying to prop these barriers up, the result will be loss of face in Lhasa and a hostile China in Tibet.

If, however, things took their natural course and relations with Tibet were developed with 'full advantage' taken of the geographical position of Lhasa

---

[15] Dalai Lama to Political Officer, 27 March 1933, in *IOR*, L/P&S/12/578.
[16] *I O* to *F O*, 3 April 1933, in Ibid.
Also see India Office minute by Walton, 29 March 1933, in Ibid.

and Tibet proper—'which look out on India and turn their backs' on China —the British

should, I believe, stand a better chance of maintaining at the same time our influence in Tibet, and our friendly relations with China and I am sure we are all agreed that we do not want to purchase the one at the cost of the other.

He underlined too the 'futility' of encouraging the Dalai Lama to believe that China could be coerced into submitting to a course of action it did not relish. 'There are limits', Sir Miles emphasised, to what can be accomplished 'by diplomatic pressure on China'.[17]

Despite this clarification, the India Office continued to have a lurking suspicion that the attitude of the British envoy was far too pro-Chinese for its comfort. Earlier when asked if China may be sounded about a British observer's presence at any peace conference that may result from Sino-Tibetan negotiations, Sir Miles indicated that he would be opposed to making any such suggestion. The best he would do was to put it in a personal letter to the Chinese Minister for Foreign Affairs, so worded as not to offend Nanking. The India Office viewed this to be a 'timid and half-hearted' approach[18] and Walton minuted that

the *form* of the suggested communication (personal or official) could be left to Sir M. Lampson's discretion. But it will do little good for him to make it in too apologetic a manner, and in his efforts to soothe Chinese susceptibilities he might go too far in explaining away HMG's attitude. On the whole, therefore, it seems better that he should hold the suggestion in reserve for an opportunity when he may be able to make it with better heart and more effect.[19]

It had been evident that what was to be said to China by Whitehall, and the manner thereof, was not half so important as the outcome of a direct Sino-Tibetan confrontation across the negotiating table. That prospect, however, was to remain a pipe dream, receding farther into the distance with every month that rolled by. In September (1933), the Dalai Lama who, we are told, was 'very frank', confided to Williamson that the Chinese government

had appointed one person after another to come to Lhasa to discuss outstanding questions but that all had been afraid and had made excuses. In any case he did not want a Chinese official ever to visit Lhasa, as all

[17]Lampson to Wellesley, 2 June 1933, in Ibid.
[18]India Office minute by J P Donaldson, 4 April 1933, in Ibid.
[19]India Office minute by Walton, 6 April 1933, in Ibid.

that the latter would want to do would be to pave the way for the renewal of Chinese domination.[20]

Despite its failure to achieve a settlement of 'outstanding questions' with Nanking, Lhasa was successful in negotiating a reasonably satisfactory cessation of hostilities with the *de facto*, local, Chinese authorities. Thus we know that in Kokonor the Chinese Governor of Sining agreed to an armistice in June 1933. A Tibetan author would have us believe that Ma accepted the traditional boundary, which both sides undertook not to violate for fear of reprisals spelt out in the terms of the agreement itself.[21] Be that as it may, it is on record that a couple of months before his death (December 1933), the Lama had informed Williamson that the

terms have been carried out by both sides and that troops have been withdrawn accordingly.

What was more, the Lama had been 'encouraged' by this agreement to instruct his commander in Derge that the latter negotiate a 'peaceful return' of those parts of his territory which had earlier been lost to the Chinese.[22]

---

[20]This was on 21 September 1933. For details Williamson's 'Report on a visit to Lhasa in 1933', dated 6 January 1934, in *IOR*, L/P&S/12/36/12, p. 19.

The Political Officer noted, *inter alia*, that the Lama was 'more cordial and friendly than ever' and that he was 'very familiar in his manner and patted me on the back constantly'.

[21] Shakabapa, *Tibet*, pp. 269–70. Among the terms of the treaty were an exchange of prisoners and an undertaking by the Tibetans that they would hand over Riwoche and Chamdo etc. if they violated the truce. China was to hand over the '25 districts of Dimchi' if it did not observe the terms.

Shakabapa informs us that he accompanied the Tibetan negotiators as 'keeper of the seal' and 'took a number of photographs of the Chinese camp as well as of the signing of the treaty and other functions'.

[22]Williamson to India, 14 October 1933, in *IOR*, L/P&S/12/577.

PART IX   INDIA REDIS-
COVERS THE McMAHON
LINE: END OF BRITISH
RULE 1935-39

Chapter 35

India Rediscovers the McMahon Line, 1934-36

CHINA'S COMPLETE repudiation of the earlier British effort to revive the tripartite basis for a settlement of the Tibetan question, coupled with its own inability to come to a direct understanding with Lhasa left the Tibetan question where it had been all these years: hanging about in mid-air. Nor was a 'local' settlement, as Lhasa was soon to discover, an answer to its urgent need to stabilise the frontier. Additionally, as the 1931-32 exchanges between the Dalai Lama and Chiang Kai-shek demonstrated fairly conclusively, the latter's outer facade of goodwill was deceptive when it came to harsh, if grim, realities. Thus neither the effusive friendship of Yuggon Dzasa and Liu Man-ching, nor the pious platitudes of the CMTA functionaries availed when fighting erupted in East Tibet in the early 1930's. For the Dalai Lama's plaintive cries of a halt to the rapid advance of Chinese troops, across what he deemed his territory, went by the board, completely unheeded.

For Tibet, 1933 proved eventful for, in December that year, the 13th Dalai Lama 'retired to the heavenly fields'. His death marks a major landmark in Tibet's recent history for, with all his failings, he gave his country a strong and stable regime and a continuity of policy which it had rarely known before. The Chinese made the fullest use of this opportunity to stage a determined come-back in which, with a shaky regime in Lhasa, they came almost within an ace of success.

Just about this time, British India in the person of Olaf (later Sir Olaf) Caroe, then Deputy Secretary in the Foreign Department, suddenly awakened to the realisation that its frontier in the east was the Red Line, laid down at Simla in 1914! Nor need New Delhi alone be blamed for this lapse, for Whitehall's reaction to its belated demand for publishing the treaties and rectifying the boundaries was typical, if revealing. There was, the India Office reasoned, 'no strong balance' of argument in favour of this course, albeit later it gave New Delhi a grudging, half-hearted approval, hedged in by all the ifs and buts it could muster.

Despite the Dalai Lama's limited success in bringing the fighting to an end and his optimism in negotiating with the local Chinese commanders in Eastern Tibet, a successful return of lost Tibetan territory[1] remained a day dream. Here, apart from a traditional Chinese reluctance to oblige, the Lama's death,

---

[1] Williamson to India, 14 October 1933, in *IOR*, L/P&S/12/577.

in December 1933, intervened to prevent such a consummation. And, with his passing away, more than a boundary settlement with China was consigned to the limbo. Even at the best of times, a political system wherein succession to supreme authority in the state means a long wait for the discovery, installation and growing into manhood of a new ruler is far from ideal for stability. And Lhasa, on the morrow of the Lama's death, presented a somewhat sorry spectacle of a ruthless struggle for power and mastery with the Regent and the Kashag arrayed on one side and the Dalai's old favourites on the other. Nor was that all. For above them all hung the seemingly sinister shadow of the Panchen Lama whose absence from Tibet, known hostility to the regime in Lhasa and a profound fondness for Chiang's Kuomintang China visibly darkened the prevalent gloom.

Nor was Nanking slow in making capital out of this god-sent opportunity. Before long it announced the despatch of a high-power mission, headed by General Huang Mu-sung, then President of the CMTA. General Huang's ostensible purpose was to mourn the 13th Dalai Lama's death but, in reality, his aim was to coax or cajole the new regime in Lhasa into accepting Chinese hegemony. The wilful, errant, child who had defied his parents so long may yet be persuaded to return to the mother's fold.

Despite his six months (April–October 1934) of interminable negotiations interlaced with generous helpings of gold and liberal promises to buy any known recalcitrants, Huang Mu-sung's achievement was far from impressive. In the words of Norbu Dhondhup—the British official in Lhasa who, on behalf of Williamson, the Political Officer, kept a close watch on men and affairs while the Huang Mission was around—Tibet's admission of Chinese overlordship was to the following effect:

> On repeated pressure from Huang Mu-sung and in order to show the outside nations and as Tibet adjoins Chinese territory we admit that we are subordinate to China, but all our external relations and internal administration will be carried on by Tibet.[1a]

Here was a paper admission, however qualified, of Chinese suzerainty which the 13th Dalai Lama would perhaps have never accepted. Besides, however vague, theoretical, and face-saving a formula, Tibet's acceptance of its subordination to China was viewed by Nanking as a 'sufficiently definite', even meaningful, concession. Nor was that all. Fromt he point of view of the

---

[1a] Williamson to India, 20 January 1935, in *IOR*, L/P&S/12/36/12.

It has been held that among the recommendations made by General Huang the most important were that the Panchen Lama should go back to Tibet with a Chinese escort, for 'countering' British influence which was still prevalent, and that a new province of Hsi-kang be carved out of 'Szechuan Border Territory'. The latter would help consolidate Chinese rule there as well as safeguard 'national security' in Western China. Tung-hai Lin, 'Three Months in Lhasa', *China Critic*, 8, 8, 21 February 1935, pp. 173–74. cited in *Yao-ting Sung*, p. 160.

virtual independence it had enjoyed for more than a score of years now, the presence in the Tibetan capital of two members of Huang's mission, who were left behind with the wireless installation, as also of a Chinese official from Kansu, were compromises which were profoundly disturbing, not least to Tibet's southern neighbour. To meet what seemed a deliberate, high-powered Chinese offensive, Williamson, then Political Officer in Sikkim, suggested that he visit Lhasa, ' sufficiently supplied with money ', to offer the regime there

   (a) exemption from payment for munitions for three years in the first instance;
   (b) training of more Tibetan officers and troops at British expense;
   (c) permission to buy more arms.[2]

In addition, Williamson's brief stipulated that, should a permanent Chinese representative put in an appearance at Lhasa, the question of appointing his British counterpart was to be ' seriously considered '. Again, the desirability of ' becoming a party ' to any agreement reached between Tibet and China was to be kept in mind. Tibet was to be treated as completely autonomous and no negotiations were to be entered into with China, without Lhasa being fully represented, and ' on equal terms '.

It followed that every possible effort was to be made to buttress Tibet's morale in resisting Chinese pressures and to ' save her from domination ' by Nanking. For while, as New Delhi viewed it, the

re-establishment of Chinese control might not be an actual military danger (it) would be at least a source of constant irritation and annoyance along our North-East frontier.[3]

Out of the blue, the British became suddenly aware of the eastern frontier, which had, over the years since the Simla Conference, been largely neglected, if not forgotten. This awareness was now the greater in that the political vacuum in Lhasa created by the Dalai Lama's death boded ill for the stability of the new regime. It may be useful to summarise these intervening developments since 1913–14, if only in parenthesis, for they help to put in proper perspective the brief given to Williamson on his visit to Lhasa in 1935.

The agreement at Simla, including the terms of the Convention, the Tibet Trade Regulations, the maps showing the India-Tibet and the Inner-Outer Tibet boundaries, did not, for a variety of reasons, see the light of day for many a summer. Apart from the factt hat barely a month after they had been concluded, the onset of World War I put them completely in the shade, there was the fateful disappearance of McMahon from the Indian scene, and for good—

[2] Williamson to India, 20 January 1935, in *IOR*, L/P&S/12/36/12.
[3] Loc. cit.

he was appointed High Commissioner in Egypt. Besides, in the initial stages, the view held was that until an understanding with Russia had been arrived at, the latter could legitimately object to the terms of the Convention. Despite the more pressing preoccupations of World War I, there might have been an element of urgency to seek such an understanding, if the Chinese had agreed to sign the compact. Since they had refused, Russia was officially informed, and assured, that it would be consulted before the British acted upon any of the provisions of the 1914 Convention which came into conflict with the 1907 Agreement between the two countries. This happened on 11 July 1914, a little over a week after the Simla negotiations had broken down.[4] As the Chinese persisted in their refusal to sign all through 1915, the British Foreign Office held that the

> Tibetan question has since been modified so profoundly... that the acceptance by the Russian Government of its (Convention of 1914) provisions in the limited form proposed last summer would no longer seem to possess the same value as an off-set to a revision in their favour of the existing arrangement with regard to Northern Afghanistan, as it did when the negotiations were suspended.[5]

The above view was shared by Lord Hardinge, the then Governor General, who felt that India's interests in Tibet were

> safeguarded for the time being by the Anglo-Tibetan declaration and there appears no prospect of China signing the Convention in the near future. I therefore strongly deprecate any concession whatever to Russia as price of her prospective consent to Convention on the chance of its eventually being signed by China.[6]

There was a slight flaw in this line of reasoning insofar as Russia could, strictly speaking, object to the British availing themselves of the Anglo-Tibetan declaration of 3 July 1914, on the plea that, insofar as it conflicted with the 1907 Convention, it was 'invalid'. What was more, Russia could also refuse to amend the latter Convention 'except in return for (a) *quid pro quo*' in Afghanistan.[7]

---

[4]Grey to Buchanan, 10 July 1914, in *IOR*, L/P&S/10/455.

In a communication to the India Office on 14 July 1914, the Foreign Office made it clear that HMG 'can only act upon the initialled (Simla) Convention so far as it does not violate the 1907 Agreement'. For details *IOR*, L/P&S/10/344.

[5]*F O* to *I O*, 30 April 1915, in *IOR*, L/P&S/10/455.

Earlier, the Russian Ambassador in London had submitted a memorandum suggesting that questions relating to Afghanistan ' be settled in accordance with the wishes then (viz. 1914) formulated by the Russian Government'. Loc. cit.

[6]Viceroy to Secretary of State, 13 May 1915, in *IOR*, L/P&S/10/455.

[7]Secretary of State to Viceroy, 17 May 1915, in Ibid.

In the thick of World War I, with Russia on the brink of a mighty revolution, the India Office was playing with the idea of securing Russian consent to a revision of the 1907 clauses in return for the British accommodating them on a freer access to the Dardanelles. Thus, in 1916, India was to suggest that Russia might ' reasonably agree ' to

> our continuing the present practice, to which she has as yet taken no exception, and allow us directly to advise and assist the Tibetan Government—in despite of Article II of the Tibetan Agreement of 1907—and herself abstain from all interference in this country.[8]

Later in October 1917 this course of action was ruled out both by the British Minister in Petrograd, who held it to be a 'most inopportune moment',[9] and the forceful impact of events which intervened. By the close of the year, the Foreign Office deprecated any suggestion regarding British representation at Lhasa lest it should offer Russia an excuse for tearing up all agreements concerning Afghanistan, a contingency ' of which the disadvantages would be greater than any advantage ' accruing in Tibet.[10]

Later that year, while outlining the Indian ' Desiderata for Peace Settlement ', the Political Department of the India Office noted that it was necessary to

> wait until there is a Russian Government with which we can negotiate and then endeavour to get rid of the self-denying ordinance in Tibet without the embarrassing conditions that the Tsar's Government desired to impose in 1914.[11]

This, however, was not to be. Contrary to a good deal of wishful thinking, the Bolsheviks stayed on in power and, in the initial stages at any rate, scrapped all treaties and agreements—at once secret and open—to which Tsarist Russia had been a party. Later, in 1921, the British Foreign Office ruled that the Anglo-Russian agreement of 1907 may no longer be regarded as valid and, therefore, such restrictions as it imposed on British action in Tibet would not operate any more.[12]

Release from Russian anxiety was but short-lived. Soon enough the beginnings of a new phase were discernible in which China took the place of Russia as far as British sensitivity regarding the frontier was concerned. Initially, it may

[8] Extract from secret letter, No. 85, from India, 29 September 1916, in Ibid.
[9] Buchanan to Balfour, 2 October 1917, in *IOR*, L/P&S/10/3260/1917, Parts 1-3.
[10] *F O* to *I O*, 21 December 1917, in Ibid.
[11] Indian ' Desiderata for Peace Settlement ' (Note by Political Department, India Office), para 23 in Ibid.
[12] The Anglo-Russian Convention of 1907 was formally cancelled by Article I of the Anglo-Russian treaty of 7 August 1924. It was under the terms of this treaty that England accorded diplomatic recognition to the new Soviet regime.

be recalled, the publication of the 1914 Convention had been kept in abeyance in the hope that China might, at some stage, accept it—albeit in a modified form. There was also a lurking suspicion that if it were to be published in its entirety, it would not only ruin such chances as there were of reaching an accommodation with China but give the latter a handle to mount a strident anti-British campaign of 'imperialist designs' on Tibet.

As early as February 1920, the Foreign Office in London, desirous of including the texts of the Simla Convention and the joint Indo-Tibetan declaration of 3 July in the forthcoming issue of 'State Papers', asked the India Office about the 'expediency' of publishing them.[13] In reply, the then Secretary of State for India, Mr. Montagu, ruled that

> so long as there remains any prospect of a final settlement of the Tibetan question by negotiations with the Chinese government it will be better not to give unnecessary publicity to the provisional arrangements of 1914.[14]

Publication was accordingly withheld.

Five years later, in 1925, the India Office informed the Foreign Office that although the India-Tibet Trade Regulations of 1914 might be regarded as being in force between the two countries, their publication may be held up for fear it

> have the effect of arousing in China renewed public interest in Tibet, and anti-British comments.

Publication, however, was to be permitted if the Government of India thought it 'desirable' or attached 'importance to it'.[15] Delhi, of course, did neither.

Three years later, in 1928, when the Tibet chapter of Aitchison's *Treaties* was being revised, India omitted any explicit reference to the Trade Regulations of 1914 lest

> publication now of the facts of the Declaration of 3 July 1914, (though it seems unlikely that China is still unaware of its existence) may force her to take overt notice of it, and so afford a fresh handle for anti-British propaganda.[16]

---

[13] *F O* to *I O*, 26 February 1920, No. 134 in *Foreign*, External B, May 1920, Procs. 134–35.

It would thus be evident that the question of publishing the Simla Convention had been raised as early as 1920, if not indeed earlier. To suggest therefore—*Karunakar Gupta*—that the question 'came up again in official correspondence' only in 1928 would not hold water.

[14] *I O* to *F O*, 8 March 1920, No. 135 in Ibid.

[15] *I O* to *F O*, 3 July 1925, in *IOR*, L/P&S/10/857. Also *I O* to India, 13 August 1925, and *F O* to *I O*, 27 July 1925, both in Ibid.

[16] India to *I O*, 22 May 1928, in *IOR*, L/P&S/10/1192.

The result was that Aitchison's new edition carried a colourless narrative that eschewed not only all mention of the Trade Regulations, but also of the Convention itself and the Joint Declaration by Britain (for India) and Tibet! Significantly, this was a position in which both the India as well as the Foreign Office concurred.[17]

In 1934, the question presented itself in yet another form, for a Declaration in Council was deemed necessary in regard to the British Trade Agents' entitlement to exercise of foreign jurisdiction in Tibet. Since the Trade Regulations of 1914, from which this authority was derived, had not been agreed to by the Chinese Government, it was felt that if they were now specifically cited in the 'Declaration' in question, the Chinese might conceivably take exception to it. As Walton at the India Office pointed out,

> it has been our policy in recent years to avoid raising questions relating to Tibet with China as far as possible and to let sleeping dogs lie.

Two alternatives presented themselves: one, to cite in the proposed Order-in-Council the authority of the Trade Regulations of 1914 (and the fact that these were not published 'could not matter'); two, to mention the Trade Regulations of 1908, to which China had agreed, and which appear to be 'just as extensive'. But so far as the latter were concerned,

> a possible disadvantage of referring to them might be that China, on 9 October 1928, had addressed a note to His Majesty's Minister, Peking, which China might represent as constituting the demand for revision referred to in Art. XIII of the Trade Regulations.

As it happened, the 1928 'note' had been ignored. But, it was now argued, a reference to the 1908 Trade Regulations 'might conceivably' bring the Chinese back into the field.[18]

The long and short of it was that 'a general recital of treaty rights' in the Order-in-Council, in place of any specific mention of the Regulations of 1908 or of 1914, was deemed adequate for the purpose, a view with which India concurred.[19]

A footnote may be added here. Repeated references in the preceding

---

[17] India Office approved of the Government of India's suggestion, as did the Foreign Office. For details, *I O* to *F O*, 19 June and *F O* to *I O*, 5 July 1928, both in Ibid.

[18] India Office minute, Walton to Legal Adviser, 28 September 1933, in *IOR*, L/P&S/10/575.
Also see Foreign Department, Simla to Chief Secretary, Punjab, 1 July 1933; Punjab to Foreign Department, 27 June 1933; Chief Secretary, U P, to Foreign Department, 19 June 1933, and *F O* to *I O*, 18 August 1933, all in Ibid.

[19] The Legal Adviser in the India Office was of the view that the Trade Regulations of 1914 'being completed and operative' between India and Tibet 'would be sufficient foundation' for an Order-in-Council. Minute, 29 September 1933, in Ibid.
Also see Viceroy to Secretary of State, 16 January 1934, in Ibid.

lines to the Trade Regulations is borne out by the nature of the documentary evidence alone. This should not, however, lead to any loss of perspective. For what is patent is that for nearly two decades after 1914, the dubious risk of attracting hostile Russian, and later Chinese, attention continued to be the principal reason for the non-publication of the Simla Convention and its adjuncts, the Trade Regulations and the India-Tibet boundary agreement.[19a]

In 1935, the Foreign and Political Department in New Delhi seemed suddenly to awaken to the realities of the situation. Part of the explanation may perhaps lie in the fact that the travels of W F Kingdon-Ward, the botanist, brought into bold relief the question of the McMahon Line. In 1934–35, Ward had traversed Monyul in Balipara, and caused New Delhi considerable embarrassment[20] by his highly critical views on the ' casual way ' things were being done. *Inter alia*, he revealed

> that while the main (Himalayan) range might be *de jure* frontier, there would be no doubt that the *de facto* frontier lay much further south since the Tibetan Government, through Tsona dzong and Twang, was actively ... administering the whole of Monyul, while the influence of the Tibetan Church extended almost to the edge of the Assam plains—that is, into territory which had nothing to do with Monyul except propinquity.

The solution he proffered was ' direct ' administration and

> effective occupation by 1939, or at the latest, 1940 .... The alternative is complete retreat.

[19a] Even though the Government of India, as well as Whitehall, had scrupulously avoided any *public* references to the India-Tibet boundary after the Simla Convention, Sir Charles Bell's *Tibet, Past and Present*, published in 1924 (whose manuscript had been scrutinised and approved in the India Office), was both categorical and illuminating on the whole question. The Simla Conference, Bell averred, afforded an

> opportunity ... to negotiate the frontier to be established between Tibet and North-eastern India ... over eight hundred and fifty miles of difficult and dangerous country. We have thus gained a frontier standing back everywhere about a hundred miles from the plains of India.

It is interesting to note that not only did Bell discuss (and who could do so with greater authority?) the frontier, he showed it clearly on the end-map of his book. For the citation, Bell, *Tibet, Past and Present* (Oxford, 1924), pp. 155–56.

It may also be mentioned in this context that while Vol. XIV of Aitchison's *Treaties*, in its 1929 edition, did not specifically refer to the Trade Regulations of 1914 *per se*, it did mention the fact that ' certain modifications ' were made (in the Trade Regulations of 1908) as a result of the Simla Conference. Aitchison, *Treaties* (1929), p. 20.

[20] Gould noted that as a result of Williamson's visit to Lhasa, in August-November, 1935,

> the attitude of mind engendered ... facilitated a friendly settlement of the Kingdon-Ward escapade which otherwise might have tended to prejudice this year's Everest Expedition.

Gould's report on ' British Mission to Lhasa, 1935 ', in *IOR*, L/P&S/12/36/12.

He forecast the future with a grimness that sounds almost frightening:

> Sooner or later India must stand face to face with a potential enemy looking over that wall into her garden—or fight to keep her out of the Tsanpo valley. With Monyul a Tibetan province, the enemy would already be within her gates.[21]

For the record, it may be mentioned that Captain Nevill, then Political Officer, Balipara, had, after a visit, sounded a similar note of admonition as early as 1928: 'Should China gain control of Tibet, the Tawang country is particularly adapted for a secret and early entrance into India.'[22] The botanist's warning, however, was to prove more effective.

Not long after Kingdon-Ward, the astounding 'discovery' was made that in Assam there had been 'considerable misunderstanding' as to where the international frontier between India and Tibet lay. In a letter to Shillong on 28 November 1935, New Delhi asked whether it would

> accept the latter (the India-Tibet frontier 'as delimited by Sir Henry McMahon and accepted by Tibet') as a correct presentation of the position as regards the frontier between Assam tribal areas and Tibet.[23]

At the same time, India had told its Political Officer in Sikkim what it thought of Assam's ignorance of its territorial limits in the context of the boundary dispute with Bhutan. The matter, New Delhi argued, was complicated by a likely claim that Tibet might stake

> to the area in the foothills between the Deosham and the Dhansiri Rivers and his (Williamson's) recommendation is apparently coloured by the thought that it might be expedient to cede to Bhutan, whose foreign relations we control, an area in these hills before Tibet, a less controllable neighbour, can present an effective claim.

Since, in the Kingdon-Ward case, Tibet was said to have reaffirmed the Red (viz., McMahon) Line, it appeared that it

> could not in any case put forward a claim to sovereignty over any territory in the foothills east of Bhutān.

---

[21] W F Kingdon-Ward, 'The Assam Himalaya: Travels in Balipara', *JRCAS*, XXV, 4 October 1938, pp. 610–19, and Ibid., XXVII, 2 April 1940, pp. 211–20.
Kingdon-Ward's two addresses to the RCAS, reproduced in the *JRCAS*, were based on his earlier (1934–35) travels referred to in the text.
[22] *Reid*, p. 291.
[23] Caroe to Hutton (Chief Secretary, Assam), 28 November 1935, in *IOR*, L/P&S/12/36/23, Part I.

But even if it did, neither the 'presentation' nor the 'acceptance' of such a claim by Tibet was to cloud the issue of the 'inviolability' of the Indian frontier.[24]

On 6 February 1936, New Delhi categorically informed Assam that it was

> now clear that the whole of the hill country upto the 1914 McMahon Line is within the frontier of India and is therefore a tribal area under the control of the Governor of Assam acting as Agent for the Governor-General.

At the same time Shillong was asked if, in the course of the last 20 years, it had exercised 'any measure of political control' in this area; and whether, to its knowledge, the Tibetan government honoured the frontier, more particularly in the vicinity of Tawang.[25] To all this Assam's reply was that in order to ascertain the correct situation, it had asked the Political Officer, Balipara, to tour the tribal area south of the McMahon Line.[26]

On 9 April 1936, New Delhi communicated its 'findings' to London and underlined the fact that the matter was deserving of urgent attention for

> there is a real danger that important matters of this kind may go wrong if we refrain any longer from publishing our agreements with Tibet.... The Government of India think that there would be advantage in inserting in their published record copies of the 1914 Convention, the exchange of notes on the boundary between Sir Henry McMahon and the Tibetan Government and the Trade Regulations.[27]

Three arguments were adduced. One, that failure to publish might well be used by the Chinese 'in support' of their argument that 'no ratified agreement between India and Tibet' was in existence. Two, in the context of India's new (1935) constitution it was necessary to define the tribal areas in the North-east which were to be placed under the political control of the government of Assam. And, finally, the impending separation of Burma, which was responsible for a part of the frontier, made such a definition imperative.

Nor should any more time be lost, India reasoned, for failure hitherto to show the correct frontier had meant that such atlases as the *Times* delineated it wrongly—along the foot-hills of Assam.

---

[24]Caroe to Battye (Trade Agent, Gyantse), 28 November 1935, in Ibid.
[25]Caroe to Dawson (Chief Secretary, Assam), 6 February 1936, in *IOR*, L/P&S/12/36/12.
[26]Dawson to Caroe, 28 February 1936, in Ibid.
[27]Caroe to Walton (India Office), 9 April 1936, in Ibid.

A few days later Caroe, now aware that Bell's book in 1924 had treated the matter fully and frankly, insisted that 'we should not delay any longer in getting this frontier into our Treaty Publications and on to our maps'—a course which, he averred, Gould too supported, and to the hilt. Caroe to Walton, 16 April 1936, in *IOR*, L/P&S/12/36/23, Part I.

Reaction in Whitehall was far from enthusiastic. Walton noted that the proposal was not 'free from doubt', and that the arguments advanced were 'unconvincing'. The 'only thing' that went in its favour, he remarked, was the 'not improbable' assumption that the Chinese, aware of the Indo-Tibetan declaration of 3 July 1914, would view its non-publication as indicative of the fact that 'we doubt' the agreement's validity. Walton's conclusion, therefore, was that there was 'no strong balance' of argument 'either for or against' publication and that *if* the Foreign Office were willing, ' we *might perhaps* decide to publish '.[28]

Denys Bray, then a Member of the Secretary of State's Council in London, while generally agreeing with Walton, put in a rider. *Inter alia*, he stipulated that

> ostentatious publication would be unwise and unless the Government of India are contemplating a re-issue of the Aitchison volume, they should ... wait for it. But the maps might be corrected in any case, in the absence of any special objection.[29]

The Foreign Office concurred and India was informed accordingly. Writing to Olaf Caroe, then Deputy Secretary in the Indian Foreign Department, on 16 July 1936, Walton, however, queried:

> Would it not suffice to arrange for publication when the next edition of Aitchison's treaties is produced in normal course?

Besides, he warned, it was 'most desirable' to avoid 'unnecessary publicity' and therefore the subject was to be kept from the press or news agencies. Additionally, the text of the declaration of 3 July 1914 was not to be published, its place being taken by an explanatory note. All this notwithstanding, the Survey of India ' could show the frontier correctly forthwith '.[30]

In the process of formulating its policy in this case, Whitehall was not unaffected by developments in Outer Mongolia. It may be recalled that the conclusion, on 12 March (1936), in Ulan Bator of a 'Protocol of Mutual Assistance' between the Soviet Union and Mongolia had provoked a strong protest from China. The latter maintained that insofar as Mongolia was 'an integral part' of the Chinese Republic, 'no foreign state' could conclude with it any treaty or agreement. It followed, Nanking contended, that the Protocol was 'illegal' and that China could, 'in no circumstances', recognise it nor in any way be 'bound' by it. Understandably, the Chinese protest was categorically rejected by the Soviet Union[31] but the India Office felt concerned

---

[28] India Office minute by Walton, 4 June 1936, in Ibid.
[29] India Office minute by Denys Bray, 8 June 1936, in Ibid.
[30] *F O* to *I O*, 9 July 1936, in Ibid. Also see *I O* to *F O*, 13 June 1936, and Walton to Caroe, 16 July 1936, both in Ibid.
[31] For the texts of China's protest, 7 April 1936, and of Soviet rejection thereof, 8 April 1936,

lest Nanking should take a similar line in respect of any treaty 'between us' and Tibet. Mercifully, these considerations did not modify the 'tentative support' which Whitehall now gave to India's 'desire to publish'.[32]

Nor did New Delhi take long in reaching its own conclusions. It resolved to take 'immediate steps' for showing the international frontier in this sector in the Survey of India maps while, and 'with as little delay as possible', a revised edition of Vol. XIV of Aitchison was to be brought out. To have waited for an overall revision of the series as suggested by the India Office 'would take', it calculated, '15–20 years'.[33]

IOR, L/P&S/12/36/23, Part I.

The Soviet Union maintained that the new protocol did not change the 'formal or actual relations' between China and Outer Mongolia, nor did it affect the 'sovereignty' of China 'in the slightest degree' for the Peking agreement of 1924 still 'retains its force'.

[32]India Office minute by Rumbold, 9 July 1936, in Ibid. This was just a week before Walton wrote to Caroe according Whitehall's approval to India's proposal.

[33]Viceroy to Secretary of State, 17 August 1936, in Ibid.

Chapter 36

Tibetan Encroachments South of the McMahon Line

NEW DELHI's rediscovery of the McMahon Line was not without its lighter side. A significant fact that emerged was that Assam had been kept completely in ignorance both of the terms of the Convention and of the actual frontier marked on the map! Burma, however, had been informed, though not of all the details. Again, the reaction of the India Office to New Delhi's decision to publish seemed characteristic of the period: do nothing unless you have to and are driven into a corner. Interestingly, it emerged that Denys Bray, then acting as one of the Advisers of the Secretary of State in London had, as Foreign Secretary in New Delhi, never known of the existence of the McMahon Line! Again, if the India Office view had prevailed—to wait for the next edition of Aitchison's *Treaties*—the Convention may never have been published, at any rate not before 1947.

India's rude awakening to the harsh realities of the situation was marked by the discovery of Tibetan encroachments south of the McMahon Line, more particularly in the area around Tawang. In re-establishing its claims to the frontier delineated on the Convention map, a veritable difference of emphasis developed between the Assam Governor and his local advisers on the one hand and Basil Gould, India's Political Officer (and New Delhi's Agent *vis-à-vis* Tibet) and his man in Lhasa, Norbu Dhondup, on the other. The context was the visit to Tawang of Captain Lightfoot who, as a result of his ' exploratory mission,', was to advise government on the actual policy to be pursued. Briefly, Lightfoot, and Assam, advocated immediate steps leading to the taking over of Tawang and, in the process, making short shrift of the local Tibetan functionaries, the Tsona Dzongpons; Gould and Norbu were against all precipitate action. And, characteristically for its part, the Lhasa administration dragged its feet and stalled all decision!

Even as conclusions regarding rectification of maps and publication of treaties were being reached in New Delhi, and implemented, actual physical encroachments across the boundary were taking place. An age-old, running sore was the frontier between Tehri-Garhwal and Tibet in what is now known as the Middle Sector. The dispute, which could be traced as far back as 1921, concerned the ownership of a tract of territory which included the valleys of Jadh Ganga, the villages of Nilang and Jadhung and some adjoining forests. A boundary commission's findings supported Tehri's claims but Lhasa was unwilling to accept these and remained stubbornly recalcitrant. And even though the subject figured high on the agenda of every Political Officer on his visit to Lhasa, discussions were interminable, and the dispute was no nearer solution in 1936 than it had been 15 years earlier.

A minor boundary adjustment, however, is a case apart; actually, something much more serious was in the offing. For by the time New Delhi awakened to the long-forgotten existence of the McMahon Line, it became painfully aware of some other inconvenient facts.

It has been noticed earlier that, in June 1935, the Political Officer had recommended that the Bhutan-Assam boundary conflict might be settled by awarding the tract in question—' east of the Deosham river and west of the Dhansiri '—to Bhutan and that

> no action should be taken on the boundary which might draw the attention of the Tibetans to the matter. If Tibet is once brought into it, the question will drag on for years without any settlement as has been the case in the Tehri-Tibet boundary dispute....[1]

Soon, however, something more serious than the tract involved in the case of Bhutan was brought to notice. The neighbouring district of Tawang, south of the McMahon Line, and the seat of a large lamaist monastery became a subject of concern,[1a] although Captain Battye, Williamson's temporary replacement (after the latter's death while on a visit to Lhasa), thought otherwise. Writing to Government in December 1935 he noted, *inter alia*, that the

> Tibetans have no villages or vested interests there at all.... Tibetan Government informed me categorically in connection with Kingdon-Ward's recent escapade that the ' Red Line ' had in no way been modified.[2]

Despite Battye, New Delhi felt far from reassured and, as has been noticed,

---

[1]Williamson to India, 10 June 1935, in *IOR*, L/P&S/12/36/23, Part I.

[1a]This was in the context of the Kingdon-Ward case referred to in the preceding chapter. On 5 November 1935, in a telegram to its Political Officer in Lhasa, New Delhi had made its position *vis-à-vis* the McMahon Line clear beyond dispute:

Are you sure that Kingdon-Ward actually went or is alleged by Tibetans to have gone to Tibetan side of Red Line referred to above or have you any reason to suppose that agreement come to in 1914 has been modified by practice or otherwise since that date. It is important that you should not in any way compromise with the Tibetan Government validity of international boundary agreed to in 1914.

India to Williamson, telegram, 5 November 1935, in *IOR*, L/P&S/12/36/29.

[2]Battye to India, 13 December 1935, in *IOR*, L/P&S/12/36/23, Part I. Elsewhere, Battye had told New Delhi that ' so far as Tibet is concerned there appears to be no cause for concern '. For the full text, loc. cit.

Earlier, on 14 November, Battye had told his political masters:

Tibetan government allege that Kingdon-Ward went far beyond the Red Line.... They maintain that Red Line has not been modified.

Battye to India, 14 November 1935, in *IOR*, L/P&S/12/36/29.

in February (1936) asked Assam whether Tibet honoured the international frontier, 'more particularly in the Tawang area'.[3] By August, however, it was painfully aware of the fact that, in Tawang, the Tibetan Government were 'collecting revenue and exercising jurisdiction'. This the Indian Government viewed as dangerous, for it

> might enable China, or other Power in a position in future to assert authority over Tibet to claim prescriptive rights over a part of the territory recognised as within India under the 1914 Convention.[4]

It was the realisation of this threat which necessitated the inclusion of Tawang in the Political Officer's brief during his visit to Lhasa in 1936. New Delhi's initially blunt tone, however, was later considerably mellowed by Whitehall's distinct feeling that it was 'undesirable' to be 'aggressive' on a question in which the Tibetans 'we know... see eye to eye with us'.[5] Unless, therefore, Gould

> anticipates serious difficulty he should make friendly representations in such manner as appears to him best regarding the collection of civil as distinct from monastic revenues in the Tawang area and regarding a written reaffirmation of the McMahon Line.[6]

At about the same time, New Delhi asked Assam to make sure whether, apart from Tawang, there were any other parts south of the Line wherein Tibet was 'collecting revenue' or 'exercising other powers of administration'.[7] Confident that such 'encroachments' were not unlikely, it asked Gould

> that when discussing the Tawang case with the Tibetan Government it should be left in no doubt that the objections of the Government of India are not only to encroachments in the Tawang area but in any part of India to the south of the McMahon Line.[8]

[3]Caroe to Dawson (Chief Secretary, Assam), 6 February 1936, in *IOR*, L/P&S/12/36/12.
On 13 November 1935, Assam had maintained that
Tawang is more or less independent territory but holds some indirect allegiance to Tibet.... So far as information goes, there has been no change in recent years in the attitude of the Tibetan government in respect of their part of the frontier.
Assam to India, 13 November 1935, in *IOR*, L/P&S/12/37/28.
Better informed, a few weeks later it was even more categorical:
We have always in these late years taken the McMahon Line to be the Tibetan boundary and we are not aware of any claim to the area south of the line since 1914.
Assam to India, 7 December 1935, in *IOR*, L/P&S/12/36/23.
[4]Viceroy to Secretary of State, 17 August 1936, in *IOR*, L/P&S/12/36/23, Part I.
[5]India Office minute by M J Clauson, 31 August 1936, in Ibid.
[6]Secretary of State to Viceroy, 15 September 1936, in *IOR*, L/P&S/12/36/29.
[7]Caroe to Dennehy (Chief Secretary, Assam), 8 October 1936, in Ibid.
[8]Caroe to Gould, 8 October 1936, in Ibid.

Later, on Gould's advice from Lhasa, the actual implementation of steps—such as ' tours in this area ' or ' collecting of the revenues ourselves '[9]—was stayed, albeit the decision ' to exercise ' these ' rights ' stood and Gould was to explain ' our intentions ' to the Tibetan authorities ' in general terms '.[10]

In his report on the Lhasa Mission, Gould revealed himself to be a believer in a ' firm line ', so far as territorial encroachments were concerned, more so as there were serious dangers inherent in a situation in which China became dominant in Tibet. Basically, he felt, Lhasa must be told

> that since 1914 everything to the south of the McMahon Line has definitely been British, and that if there were a matter of *quid pro quo*, Tibet has had value in the form of support both in arms and in the field of diplomacy.[11]

His own considered view, of course, had been: ' We must know how we intend to act before we talk '.[12]

While Gould was emphatic that among the principal results of his Mission one was that the ' Tawang position ' had been ' ventilated ',[13] Lhasa's case had been no less frankly stated. Briefly, the latter had underlined the fact that ' upto 1914 ' Tawang was ' definitely ' Tibetan and that they

> regarded the Indo-Tibetan frontier as part of the settlement of all Tibetan frontiers by the Convention and that if they secured a definite Sino-Tibetan frontier they would be glad to accept the McMahon Line.... They understood from the Government of India's action in not asserting their authority at Tawang that they agreed with this interpretation of the situation.[14]

In order to effectively assert its authority in a part of the country which indubitably lay to the south of the McMahon Line, New Delhi decided to send Captain Lightfoot, then Political Officer, Balipara, for an exploratory mission to Tawang. A certain urgency was injected into the situation by the Government of India withdrawing its reservations to the International Slavery Convention in respect of its tribal areas which, *inter alia*, committed it *ultimately* to the exercise of a certain degree of control in these parts. It was the more keen therefore that, before he set out, Lhasa be informed of Lightfoot's visit

---

[9]Menon (Foreign Department, New Delhi) to Dawson (Chief Secretary, Assam), 2 September 1936, in *IOR*, L/P&S/12/36/23, Part I.
[10]India to Gould, 7 February 1937, in *IOR*, L/P&S/12/36/29.
[11]Gould's report, ' Lhasa Mission 1936–37 ', in *IOR*, L/P&S/12/36/27, Para 30.
[12]Gould to India, 31 January 1937, in Ibid.
[13]Gould's report, *supra*, n. 11, para 42.
[14]Gould to India, 15 November 1936, in *IOR*, L/P&S/12/36/29.
Gould stated, *inter alia*, that the Kashag ' were fully aware of the terms of the (1914) Convention ' as also of the fact that ' at no time since the Convention and the Declaration of 1914 had the Indian Government taken steps to question Tibetan, or assert British, authority in the Tawang tract '. Loc. cit.

and its 'acquiescence or, if possible, active goodwill' be secured to ensure the success of his mission. To this course of action both Gould and Norbu (the latter then incharge of the residue Lhasa Mission of 1936–37) were strongly opposed. They argued cogently that instead of India being on the defensive and having to explain its action, Tibet should be made to raise the issue and lodge its complaint *after* Lightfoot had arrived in Tawang. In other words, Assam's action in sending Lightfoot ' should precede ' conversations in Lhasa.

Between Norbu and Gould there were, however, slight shades of difference of approach. In the modern idiom, Norbu was a ' hawk' who suggested that Assam ' annex the area *immediately* or as soon as possible'; that if the issue were raised ' now ', Tibet will rake up ' the old question ' of the British helping to settle the Sino-Tibetan boundary dispute before they would talk of Tawang.[15] Gould, a hawkish 'dove', put it slightly differently. ' Politically ', he wrote,

> it does not seem desirable to have to admit that (if such is indeed the case) we have upto the present been acquiescing in the continuance of a Tibetan regime not only in Tawang but in Abor limits also; while practically it is doubtful whether even if a protest were lodged and orders issued accordingly by the Tibetan Government, any actual effect would be produced unless some local resistance were offered to the Tibetan activities complained of.[16]

In much the same context, Norbu suggested that instead of lodging protests against Tibetan officials collecting taxes in the Abor country—very much on the lines of what Assam's Governor had proposed—' the best course ' would be ' to prevent armed Tibetans from crossing our frontier ' at any point.[17] The difference, of course, was that whereas Assam would seek to do this ' through the Tibetan Government ', Norbu would not.

New Delhi's approach was far from clear; at moments, it looked even confused. As reports poured in from Lightfoot about the details of how the Tibetan administration functioned, Assam demanded ' firmest treatment ' and urged the establishment of ' a permanent post ' at Tawang.[18] Yet the Foreign Department, less precipitate and more deliberate, would only authorise that Lightfoot, while intimating to everybody that Tawang was ' Indian ' and ' *not* Tibetan ', should

> not demand their (Tibetan officials') withdrawal and should give no assurance to the local inhabitants but should simply inform them that he has been sent to make enquiries into local conditions and that Government will decide after his return whether to take any further interest in them or not.[19]

[15] Norbu to Gould, 12 December 1937 and 12 February 1938, in Ibid.
[16] Gould to India, 18 May 1938, in Ibid.
[17] Norbu to Gould, 13 May 1938, in Ibid. Also see Governor, Assam to Viceroy, 5 May 1938, in Ibid.
[18] Assam to New Delhi, 6 May 1938, in Ibid.
[19] New Delhi to Assam, 16 May 1938, in Ibid.

The India Office thought this 'an odd way of putting' things,[20] while New Delhi felt that even this step 'may create difficulties' for Lightfoot.[21]

Admittedly, his brief was far from satisfactory. Lightfoot reported that people 'lived in dread' of the Tsona dzongpons, and that the latter's removal would be the 'biggest boon' that could be conferred upon them.[22] Besides the town itself, elsewhere too conditions were far from happy:

> There is almost a panic in the district. Traders (are) selling goods as they are afraid Tibetan Government might send troops who would loot all their possessions... (they) fear everywhere that retaliatory action by the Tibetan Government (will take place) after our departure.

He had been 'as reassuring as possible', but felt that

> very quick action is necessary to be carried out as soon as possible this cold weather.[23]

Even as Lightfoot tarried on at Tawang, Norbu at Lhasa had bent over backwards to obtain a categorical commitment but, by the end of August 1938, confessed to a feeling of disappointment:

> So far I have seen the Kashag nine times and the Regent three times about Tawang. All of them are afraid to come to a decision in the matter and the explanation given by them regarding the possible delay in going through the question is merely a pretence. As they said definitely that they want time to come to a decision... it means that the matter will be delayed for many months or years....

The only way to treat with Tibet, Norbu suggested, was: (a) to depute the Political Officer, Balipara, to visit Tawang every year, accompanied by a personal body-guard; (b) to stop the annual 'posa' of Rs. 5000/- 'forthwith'; and (c) to make known 'in the widest possible way', that Tawang is within British India.[24]

By September 1938, Assam had received, and digested, Lightfoot's long and

---

[20]Marginal comment by Peel, on India Office minute, in Ibid.
[21]*Supra*, n. 19.
[22]Lightfoot to Assam, 16 May 1938, in *IOR*, L/P&S/12/36/29.
[23]Lightfoot to Assam, 19 June 1938, in Ibid.
On 15 August the India Office minuted:
Until some decision is taken by the Government of India as to their future policy in the Tawang area, the position of the unfortunate inhabitants will be very awkward and unsatisfactory since at present they do not know under whose authority they are and fear reprisals from the Tibetan government as a result of their relations with the British expedition.
For details, Ibid.
[24]Norbu to Gould, 26 August 1938, in Ibid.

fairly detailed report on his visit.[25] In forwarding it to New Delhi, the Governor described the existing situation in Tawang as 'intolerable' and demanded that it be terminated 'as soon as possible'. Among his major recommendations, the following may be listed:

1. A 'control area' around Tawang was to be established. It was to pay a nominal tribute, thereby acknowledging British supremacy, and from it Aka raids were to be barred, as also vestiges of Tibetan administration;
2. The Tawang monastery was gradually to discard Tibetan religious officials, their place being taken by the Monbas;
3. Existing monopolies in salt and rice were to be abolished while a tribute of Rs. 5/- per household was to be imposed throughout the area.[26]

The India Office viewed the Governor's recommendation in regard to the 'control area' sympathetically and thought it to be 'on the right lines'. It had no doubt that, in the last resort, 'it might be necessary to take over' Tawang. Whitehall, however, was a little less sure as to whether the monastery's officials should be Monbas, and not Tibetans.[27]

In December (1938), Assam again reminded New Delhi that if a permanent occupation were 'not immediately practicable', a second expedition would be necessary

as there were signs that Tibetan officials were reverting to their previous practices since our people had left.

Despite Shillong's urgency,[27a] it was not until April 1939 that New Delhi informed the Governor that the proposed second tour could not be allowed as it might result in

---

[25]Captain Lightfoot's report, entitled 'Report on the Tawang Expedition 1938', was in two parts, the first giving a comprehensive background of the area, its people, its communications, its social milieu including the role played by the Tawang monastery, a description of Tibetan administration and of how oppressive it was for the Monbas. Part two dealt with 'recommendations and suggestions'. For the full text see *IOR*, L/P&S/12/36/29.

[26]Assam to New Delhi, 7 September 1938, in Ibid.
In his letter, the Governor revelaed that, apart from the 'Report', he had had the opportunity of 'discussing personally' with Lightfoot 'the deplorable state of the inhabitants of the Tawang area under Tibetan administration'. Further, he was of the view that a state of affairs existed which bordered on 'virtual slavery' and was 'incompatible' with commitments to the League of Nations:
  His Excellency therefore ventures to trust that the Government of India will now place on record a decision that it is their intention to assume full responsibility in this area....
For a summary see *Reid*, pp. 299–300.

[27]India Office minute by Peel, 23 November 1938, in *IOR*, L/P&S/12/36/29.

[27a]In a personal, and 'confidential', letter to the Governor-General on 3 January 1939, Sir Robert Reid put forth the view that in regard to Tawang three alternatives presented themselves. *One*, 'to wash our hands of the whole thing' which would be tantamount to 'abandon-

having to undertake permanent occupation in order to fulfil their (Government of India's) obligations towards the Monbas.

This initial cold douche on Assam's, and Lightfoot's, enthusiasm was followed by a stiffer, colder blast. In July 1939, Assam was informed that the question of future action *vis-à-vis* Tawang was to be decided after the expiry of one year while New Delhi hoped that, in the interval, nothing would be done to incur any commitments in that area.[28]

New Delhi's July 1939 fiat, which, in its essence, amounted to a slowing-down, a soft-pedalling and even a postponement of all vital decisions concerning Tawang taken during the preceding two years, marks a distinct watershed in the story of the eastern frontier. Not long after it was taken, intervened the grim years, and the total mobilisation, of World War II, with Tawang, and much else, consigned to the limbo. No wonder the decree remained, for all practical purposes, operative all through the years now left to British rule in India. For clearer analysis, it may help to pinpoint the factors that led to it.

To start with, it may be recognised that a major role in the drama was played by Basil Gould, then Political Officer in Sikkim. It may be recalled that New Delhi's initial reaction, in 1936, in response to mounting pressure from Assam, and clear advice from Norbu, that 'posa' be discontinued straightaway, was to steer a middle course. In a telegram to Gould, then in Lhasa, on 19 November (1936) a three-pronged policy was spelt out: one, that while 'posa' may not be discontinued for historical reasons, it would be made clear that it was purely a 'compensation for territorial adjustments'; two, Assam officials would be asked to undertake 'annual' tours to Dirang-dzong, but 'biennial' only to Tawang; and three, Assam would be permitted to institute direct revenue collection in the entire area while granting a fixed annual sum to the monastery in Tawang. At the same time, it was to be clearly stipulated that all Tibetan dzongpons would be withdrawn.[29]

Intimation of the new policy was made to the Governor in Shillong on 9 December[30] while, a day previously, Gould, then in Lhasa, was reminded that apart from the March 1914 'notes', Tibet had reaffirmed its acceptance of the McMahon Line in connection with the Kingdon-Ward case. What was more, Gould was asked to obtain a 'written reaffirmation' of the 'Red' Line.[31]

---

ing to their fate those who have been told to regard themselves as dependent upon us '; *two*, ' the permanent occupation of Tawang ', a policy ' which obviously is the most desirable '; *three*, ' a further visit on a small scale this spring' which, 'if it is to be worthwhile, would have to be repeated periodically '. Reid to Linlithgow, 3 January 1939, in *IOR*, L/P&S/12/36/29.

[28]*Reid*, p. 300.
[29]India to Gould, 19 November 1936, in *IOR*, L/P&S/12/36/29.
[30]New Delhi to Assam, 9 December 1936, in Ibid.
[31]India to Gould, 8 December 1936, in Ibid.
New Delhi had, *inter alia*, pointed out that neither at the time of the exchange of notes,

On 12 December Gould despatched a long telegram from Lhasa. The burden of it was a counsel of patient deliberation rather than of precipitate haste. He was clear, ' on close investigation ', that

> it is improbable that the Kashag made any useful admission on the occasion of interview with Battye on the Kingdon-Ward case.

This was to knock the bottom out of New Delhi's, as indeed Whitehall's, entire premise. Nor did Gould favour asking for a written assurance on the lines India had demanded. He 'apprehended' that this would create difficulties. For, he argued, the weary, and time-consuming, process of consulting the Regent, the Prime Minister and above all the National Assembly and the monasteries would generate an ugly situation that China was bound to exploit. He was equally opposed to what he called the ' unambitious programme ' of penetration which was now proposed, for

> while it may raise suspicions and cause irritation and no doubt provoke protest and argument (it) is likely to be insufficiently impressive and decisive.

What did he advocate then? Gould pleaded for ' definite action ' backed by a reiteration of an *oral* explanation (at Lhasa) of ' our indubitable rights ' rather than raising the question of reaffirmation. The latter, he argued, presupposed a better knowledge of the area, and what was involved, besides a more thorough discussion with Assam.[32]

Visibly frustrated, New Delhi withdrew its request for a written reaffirmation and countermanded the measures it had earlier proposed to Assam, pending further discussions with Gould. At the same time, Assam was reassured that the Government of India had decided to exercise its rights in Tawang and had ' merely agreed ', on Gould's advice, to postpone a decision on the exact steps to be taken.

It may be recalled that, on 7 February 1937, India had directed Gould that Tibet be informed ' in general terms ' about ' our intentions ',[33] a view successfully contested by the Political Officer who felt that ' we must know how we intend to act before we talk '.[34] Later, it was as a result of Gould's consultations with Assam[34a] that Captain Lightfoot's ' preliminary and exploratory ' expedi-

24–25 March 1914, nor in the more recent Kingdon-Ward case was there ' any suggestion that Tibetan Government's observance of the McMahon Line was dependent on securing definite Sino-Tibetan boundary '. It concluded, therefore, that the attitude of the Kashag was ' wholly untenable '. Loc. cit.

For Tibet's reaffirmation of the ' Red (McMahon) Line ' see Battye to India, 13 December 1935, *supra*, n. 2.

[32]Gould to India, 12 December 1936, in *IOR*, L/P&S/12/36/29.
[33]India to Gould, 7 February 1937, in Ibid.
[34]Gould to India, 31 January 1937, in Ibid.
[34a]In May 1937, Sir Robert Reid, then Governor of Assam, had expressed the view that

tion to the Tawang area, ' in the spring of next year (1938) ', was decided upon. Pending Lightfoot's report, New Delhi was to hold its hand with regard to any definite opinion ' about administering or occupying ' Tawang.[35]

What Gould viewed to be a ' vindication ' of his policy was the protest lodged by Lhasa *after* Lightfoot had arrived in Tawang. On 4 May 1938, Norbu, then stationed in the Tibetan capital, informed his political superior that he had countered the Tibetan protest by maintaining that the Lightfoot expedition will return ' only *after* touring around ' Tawang.[36] Gould felt satisfied that Lhasa's attitude

> even in the face of overt action on our part indicates that it would have been useless to press them to concede in advance acquiescence in our assumption of our treaty rights in the Tawang area....

Further, the Political Officer was clearly of the view that the fact that Lightfoot had arrived in Tawang ' prior to any protest ', was all to the good and thought it ' desirable ' that his garrison should be maintained at Tawang until the Tibetan Government adopted a compliant attitude.[37]

The harsh reality was otherwise, for Norbu found the Tibetans to be far from ' compliant '. Lhasa, he reported on 25 May 1938, maintained that Tawang was, in fact, ' Tibetan territory ' and, therefore, its collection of taxes there ' normal '. How was it, the Tibetans asked, that the question had not been raised in the life-time of the late Dalai Lama? Norbu's rejoinder was that British rights rested on the Simla Treaty of 1914. To his political masters he suggested that, so far as New Delhi was concerned, the answer lay in proclaiming, 'in the widest possible terms', that taxes levied by the Tibetan authorities were ' illegal ', and that the true domiciled inhabitants of Tawang, being ' now British subjects ', should refuse payment.[38]

Even though a slight difference of emphasis may be noticed here and there, it would be wrong to assume that Gould and Norbu were pursuing separate, if contradictory, courses. As a matter of fact, Norbu enjoyed Gould's complete confidence and, in return, was most loyal. In a Memorandum on 15 May 1938, entitled ' Tibetan Activity in the Abor Hills ', which has been cited earlier in the text, Gould highlighted three points which needed clarifica-

though ' undoubtedly British ', Tawang had been controlled by Tibet; that ' more impressive and permanent action ' was required if it was to be effectively occupied; that ' the time has come ' when the policy advocated in 1914, 'and so long held in abeyance', should be carried out. This was to despatch to Tawang a European Police Officer 'with an escort of at least a platoon to stay there for the summer ' and ' return annually '. The local inhabitants, the owners of private estates and the monks were to be treated with courtesy and tact.

Assam to India, 27 May 1937, in *Reid*, pp. 295–96.
[35] New Delhi to Assam, 1 July 1937, in *IOR*, L/P&S/12/36/29.
[36] Gould to India, 4–5 May 1938, in *IOR*, L/P&S/12/36/23, Part II.
[37] Gould to India, 4–5 May 1938, in Ibid.
[38] Norbu to Gould, 25 May 1938, in Ibid.

tion before a protest was lodged in Lhasa: (1) whether incursions complained of were not 'of old standing'; (2) whether there had been a fresh incursion 'this year'; and (3) whether there was a 'good prospect' of local inhabitants, Abor or Tibetan, resisting these incursions in future.[39]

Meantime as Lightfoot's complaints about Tibetan exactions in Monyul continued to pour in, Norbu persisted in his efforts to make the Tibetans accept the British position. Thus an entry in his Lhasa Diary for June 1938 reads:

> Norbu called on the Regent and discussed the question of Tawang in detail and impressed on him that the treaty rights must be observed by the Tibetan Government. The Regent replied that so far the Kashag has not referred the question to him and that he will see his way to abide by the treaty when the Cabinet Ministers refer to him.[40]

Such tactics were typical of the Lhasa regime, whenever it wanted to stall a decision. Nor, for that matter, was New Delhi ready for one and this, despite the India Office,[41] Lightfoot, and the Assam Governor's relentless proddings, alluded to earlier. It is not unlikely that New Delhi's conclusion, towards the end of December 1938, to stay its hand for another year and to veto Assam's suggestion for a 'second expedition on a smaller scale' was based on Gould's recommendations. For apart from what has been said above, on 3 November 1938, in his observations on the report of Lightfoot's expedition, the Political Officer had made the following pertinent comments:

1. That so downtrodden were the Monbas that they 'themselves are likely to contribute little towards their liberation' from Tibetan influence;
2. That a more thorough 'investigation' of local conditions, emphasised in McMahon's Final Memorandum, was necessary before a firm decision was taken on Tawang's future administration;
3. That any interference with Tibetan officials in the Tawang monastery would invite the 'active intervention' of the 'largest monastery' in the world (Gould revealed that even Bell had, in 1914, given an undertaking that Tibetan Government 'would be consulted' whenever a new head Lama was appointed).

In the upshot, his 'own inclination' would have been

> on the one hand to advocate a more imposing exhibition of strength at the outset, and on the other hand to avoid any present decision, pending further experience on such matters as the levy of a cash tribute, the abolition of

---

[39] Gould to India, 18 May 1938, in *IOR*, L/P&S/12/36/29.
[40] The specific entry is for 20 June 1938, in Ibid.
[41] India Office minute, 15 August 1938, in *supra*, n. 23.

certain forms of taxation and of free labour or the introduction of a panchayat system....

If Government were financially tight, as they persistently complained they were,

> the most convenient course might be to let the whole position simmer until the financial position improves or until the Tibetan Government raises some definite issue in regard to Tawang.[42]

It would thus stand to reason that New Delhi's decision, reached in December 1938 and later formalised in April and July 1939, against 'either the occupation of Tawang or the sending of a second expedition' rested squarely on the twin arguments used by Gould, namely, 'financial stringency' on the one hand and letting 'the whole position simmer' on the other. For Tawang's future and the security of the eastern frontier it was not, as the retrospect shows, either a sensible or a statesmanlike conclusion.

---

[42]Gould to India, 3 November 1938, in *IOR*, L/P&S/12/36/29.

Chapter 37

China's Cartographic Aggression: New Delhi and London

TIBET'S VAGUE admission of the 1914 Red Line, coupled with its actual administration of some pockets to the south of it, was a revelation that dawned upon New Delhi only in 1936. The latter's subsequent efforts to exercise jurisdiction were handicapped by the advice of Basil Gould, its man on the spot, who understandably was opposed to any action unless all its consequences had been fully weighed in advance. While Lhasa in its own characteristic way was mulishly stubborn, contradictory advice from Assam and Gould made New Delhi hesitant. No wonder, despite proddings from Lightfoot and the Governor in Shillong, it prevaricated, played for time and, in the final count, refused to act.

Just about this time New Delhi awakened to another ugly reality—China's cartographic aggressions against large slices of India's tribal territory. This was borne out by the fact that in its maps delineating the boundaries of the province of Sikang it had shown as part of its territory areas which were, without doubt, part of India. To New Delhi's persistent demand that a strong protest be lodged in Nanking, Whitehall took a soft line and this in the face of similar advice from its Ambassador in China. London argued that unless the Chinese took steps to translate their cartographic encroachments into attempts at incorporating these areas as part of their territory, no useful purpose would be served by arousing their ire!

Apart from Caroe's demi-official to Walton at the India Office in April 1936, alluded to in the preceding chapter, India's formal communication to Whitehall on 17 August (1936) revealed a sad neglect in regard to Chinese intrusions into Indian territory. 'Latest Chinese Atlases', Sir Aubrey Metcalfe, then Foreign Secretary, wrote, actually showed

> most of the whole of the tribal area south of the McMahon Line up to the administered boundary of British India in Assam together with a portion of northern Burma as included in China.

It may be noted here that the context in this case was general (and not Tawang alone) covering in its gamut the whole of what is now known as NEFA. As New Delhi viewed it, the position was far from satisfactory:

> Briefly . . . the cartographic activities of the Chinese have set up a claim to

absorb in China a very large stretch of Indian territory while in a portion of India just west of the area claimed by the Chinese as part of Sikang province namely Tawang, the Tibetan Government over whom the Chinese claim suzerainty are collecting revenues and exercising jurisdiction many miles on the Indian side of the international frontier.

The present apart, it was the future that was at stake and with a prophetic vision, rare in bureaucratic memoranda, the dangers that lurked around the corner were succinctly spelt out. China's claim, the note pointed out,

> does not at present actually include Tawang itself, but there can be little doubt that it will be extended to Tawang and even to Bhutan and Sikkim, if no steps are taken to challenge these activities. There is moreover the danger that the exercise of jurisdiction by Tibet in the Tawang area might enable China, or other power in a position to assert authority over Tibet, to claim prescriptive rights over a part of the territory recognised as within India under the 1914 Convention.[1]

Unfortunately for New Delhi 'saner' counsels in Whitehall were not prepared to challenge China and for reasons which, at best, appear to be narrow and sordid. A protest in Nanking, it was argued, would be 'inconsistent' with the decision to be 'unostentatious' regarding the publication of the 1914 documents; what was more, it might arouse Chinese displeasure! Again, the latter may brush aside British protests by pleading: (a) that they (Chinese) were not responsible for private cartographers who had published the offending maps; (b) that atlases such as the *Times* were guilty of much the same offence; and (c) that in any case China did not recognise the 1914 agreement on which the McMahon Line was based.[2]

The British Ambassador in Nanking, although he did not favour the 'strong protest' that New Delhi had initially demanded—on the plea that China was not a party to the 1914 Convention and had taken exception to the boundaries laid down in it—viewed the matter differently. Since he had already told the Chinese Foreign Office that Tibet was an autonomous region of China, he could

> see no objection to pointing out that the maps complained of (were not acceptable).... (Besides they could be informed) that our maps (were) being amended to show the boundary as agreed upon by the British and Tibetan plenipotentiaries at the Simla Conference and also that the boundaries of

---

[1] India to India Office, 17 August 1936, in *IOR*, L/P&S/12/36/23, Part II.

[2] India Office minute by M J Clauson, 22 August 1936, in *IOR*, L/P&S/12/36/29. On 31 August, Clauson noted that India's suggestion about a protest to China was 'of no immediate urgency' and could be 'left over'. Nine days later, Walton minuted that a protest 'against the geographical encroachments of China' could be taken up 'separately' with the Foreign Office. For the texts see Ibid.

Sikang province, insofar as they infringe Indian Territory, are not recognised by HMG.³

It may not be out of place to point out here that the above position, as outlined by Sir Hughe Knatchbull-Hugessen, did not conform to the true facts of the situation. In 1914, or even subsequently, it may be recalled, the Chinese had taken exception to the Sino-Tibetan, *not* the Indo-Tibetan, boundary and the latter was part of the Convention map over which Ivan Chen had slept for weeks and which he had *signed*, not initialled, at three places. While he might have conformed more closely to the facts, and put things in more forceful language, it may be recognised that Sir Hughe took a stand which was in such refreshing contrast to the pusillanimous attitude of the India Office to Chinese claims, both actual and prospective. As it turned out, thanks principally to its own timidity, Whitehall overruled both New Delhi as well as Nanking with the result that the British Ambassador was informed, on 24 November, that the proposed protest to China regarding her 'cartographic aggression' was to be stayed,

> unless the latter should endeavour to assert their territorial claims on the northern border of Assam otherwise than on paper.⁴

From New Delhi's standpoint it was far from being a happy position, the more untenable as it soon became clear that although the *Shen Pao*, which had carried the offending maps, was an unofficial atlas, a Chinese Ordinance had laid down that

> no maps and charts showing the boundaries of China may be published in China without the imprimatur of the Central Government authorities.

It would thus be obvious that even the *Shen Pao* maps had the seal of official Chinese approval. And yet, this approval notwithstanding, London was 'still' against 'any protest' and harped on the 'undesirability' of making representations to the Chinese Government regarding the boundary as shown in the Atlas.⁵

---

³Knatchbull-Hugessen (Ambassador to China) to Orde (Foreign Office), 12 October 1936, in *IOR*, L/P&S/12/36/23, Part II.

⁴Foreign Office to Knatchbull-Hugessen, 24 November 1936, in Ibid.
Earlier Walton had written to Metcalfe to point out that, *inter alia*, the Chinese could 'quote the manner in which the boundary is shown on British maps including the map printed in the present edition of the India Office List.' This, he intimated, was being corrected 'in future editions' while at the same time the India Office agreed to the issue 'as soon as possible' of a revised edition of Volume XIV of Aitchison's *Treaties*.
Walton to India, 15 October 1936, in Ibid.

⁵Revised Ordinance governing the examination of 'Maps and Charts', 8 September 1936, cited in British Embassy (Nanking) to Foreign Office, 15 December 1936, in Ibid.

Nor, for that matter, were the Chinese the sole offenders. The *Times* 'India number: 1937', it seems, perpetrated the same error even as some other, though by no means all, British cartographers had over the years.[6] What was more, official Indian publications persisted in it at a time when New Delhi itself had awakened to the harsh realities.

The only way out, it was argued, was the publication of new maps which would show the correct position. A decision to this effect, as we know, was taken in New Delhi in August 1936[7] and later communicated to London. Despite this, and for a variety of reasons—among them the fact of an undemarcated eastern boundary of Bhutan with Tawang—these maps took a long time in coming.[8] And this in the face of some polite, and not quite polite, reminders from London.[9] As it turned out, the long-awaited map, christened 'Highlands of Tibet and the Surrounding Regions', was not issued until early in January 1939.

In retrospect, what is interesting is that instead of publicising the new map and thereby making the Indian boundary better known, London appears to have been satisfied that not much notice was taken of it. A Reuter message about the 'New Map of India', originating in New Delhi, was carried, it would seem, only by London's *Evening Standard*. The paper underlined the fact that

> for the first time on a map of this scale is a definite boundary between the tribal areas of northern Assam and Tibet (indicated).... The new demarcation shows that the Assam tribal tracts cover a much larger area than was generally imagined....[10]

Not unlike its earlier attitude on the publication of the 1914 Simla Convention, it was typical of London's squeamishness that here too it wanted to avoid 'any unnecessary' publicity. Thus, a minute of 29 August 1938 recorded that the

> correct frontier should be unobtrusively marked ... that we desired nothing should be published on the subject at all....[11]

---

[6]For the *Times*, see Clauson to Caroe, 2 April 1937; for Indian official maps showing the boundaries incorrectly see 'Report on the Administration of Assam for 1935–36' and Menon to Dawson (Assam), 25 March 1937, in Ibid.

'Cassel's New Atlas', 4th edition, 1928, showed the eastern frontier correctly as did the end map in Bell, *Tibet, Past and Present* (Oxford, 1924).

[7]Metcalfe to Walton, 17 August 1936, in *IOR*, L/P&S/12/36/29.

[8]Surveyor General (India) to New Delhi, 23 March 1937, in *IOR*, L/P&S/12/36/23, Part I.

[9]Clauson to Caroe, 2 April 1937: 'Walton (is) already exercised about the making of the international frontier'. And Rumbold (India Office) to Hill (India), 26 May 1937: 'when we may expect the map?' *IOR*, L/P&S/12/36/23, Part II.

[10]*The Evening Standard* (London), 19 January 1939.

[11]India Office minute, 29 August 1938, in *IOR*, L/P&S/12/36/23, Part II.

Whitehall's attitude was the more disturbing in that knowledgeable Indian officials were not unaware of the dangerous implications of China's cartographic aggression. Thus a letter of 4 March (1937) from Olaf Caroe to R A (later Lord) Butler, then Under Secretary at the India Office, underlined the position sufficiently clearly:

> Owing mainly to our failure to publish the 1914 agreement with Tibet relative to the Indo-Tibetan frontier... Chinese cartographers have absorbed in China a slice of India some 500 miles long and 100 miles in depth, and included this slice, together with a larger mass of territory which is really Tibet in an imaginary Chinese south-western province which they call Sikang....

Nor was that all, for they had 'also' created

> an imaginary Chinese province out of what is really North-east Tibet and call it Kokonor or Chinghai.

Even though Kokonor did not touch Indian territory, its creation typified the

> Chinese custom of pretending that a state of affairs exists and so persuading as many people as possible that it does exist.

Caroe drew attention to the omissions of 'our own unofficial' cartographers and thought it to be a

> typical result of British or British Indian apathy in all matters affecting the North-east, as apart from the North-west Frontier, and is an instance of the lack of contact between Whitehall, Delhi and Peking in Far Eastern Affairs.

Furthermore, he cautioned, the impending separation of Burma from India by setting up two British authorities *vis-à-vis* China and Tibet

> must complicate appreciations of future dangers and will make it more than ever necessary to keep awake....[12]

Did New Delhi, or London for that matter,[13] ever heed these words?

---

[12] Caroe (then on leave in England) to Butler, 4 March 1937, in Ibid.
A Chinese scholar refers to the province of Hsi-kang (created in 1938) as an 'ethnological museum' and lists as many as ten different races inhabiting it. *Yao-ting Sung*, pp. 171–72.

[13] The immediate aftermath was a note by Walton wherein he underlined the steps already taken or contemplated:
> We have asked the Government of India to send either direct or through the India Office copies of the new Survey of India maps to the leading firms of cartographers in this country, and draw their attention to the point. The Royal Geographical Society and the War Office will also be informed. The map in the India Office List has already been corrected in this year's edition.

Minute by J C Walton, 13 March 1937, in *IOR*, L/P&S/12/36/23, Part II.

Chapter 38

Tibet and China, 1940–47

IN THE decade that elapses between Lightfoot's Mission to Tawang (1938) and the British withdrawal from India (1947), the broad pattern of events sketched out in the preceding chapters repeats itself, albeit with a pronounced difference in emphasis. For one, Tibetan encroachments south of the 1914 'Red Line' persist, although Indian efforts to counter these are now more consciously pursued. Again, China's cartographic aggression against the McMahon frontier continues unchecked and, unwittingly, gets support from some ignorant British, and Indian, map-makers. A significant development is World War II which, owing to powerful Japanese onslaughts on the mainland, push China's KMT regime, and with it her political centre of gravity, to the country's extreme south-west. Other things apart, this had a powerful impact on Chinese efforts, both direct as well as indirect, to stage a comeback in Tibet. Another result, no doubt, was the latter's growing awareness of its political status which found an increasing degree of expression in persistent enquiries about the scope and content of its ' autonomy ' and of the overlord's claim to ' suzerainty'. British India's own interest in the maintenance of Tibet's integrity (of which the ' Mongolian fringe ' from Nepal to Burma was a part) was further aroused. Evidence of this growing involvement was the fact that the tenure of the temporary Lhasa Mission of 1936, grudgingly extended from year to year, now assumed a semi-permanent character while India's long-neglected fences along the eastern frontier began to be mended at last.

For China, World War II had started two years earlier when, in 1937, Japan launched, without much ceremony, a direct, frontal attack on the country. For a time the League of Nations, and its Western stalwarts, played at the game of compromise and 'containment' of Japanese aggression, meeting China's urgent needs by fitful shipments of arms and ammunition. By 1938, however, this became virtually impossible for the Japanese navy began to dominate the China coast and made all shipping hazardous, if not impossible. To counter this, the British opened the Burma road which, through the backdoor of Yunnan, kept up a trickle of much-needed supplies to the hard-pressed Chinese armies.

By the fall of 1939, the war assumed global proportions, with Britain openly arrayed on China's side as an ally. Lhasa found this somewhat disconcerting, a fact that would partly explain its refusal openly to espouse the 'Allied' cause unreservedly. This was in such sharp contrast to its attitude during

World War I when it had made a generous offer of men to fight on the British side. Understandably, in 1939, Tibet decided to stay scrupulously neutral.

The Burma-Yunnan road, with its small trickle of a tenuous, if uncertain, supply-line, even at the best of times, soon became inoperative as a result of Japan's victories (in Burma). By 1941, with the road-link severed, the Chinese Government suggested an alternate route. Cutting through the north-eastern tip of the Lohit and the Tibetan province of Zayul, it was designed to link up the plains of Assam with south-western Szechuan and all that was left of Kuomintang China. Although the project looked neat enough on paper, and scrupulously skirted Japanese-occupied territory, the lie of the land posed formidable problems which would no doubt have strained known, and available, engineering skills, and equipment, to the utmost. Besides, at its most optimistic, the link would take 2-3 years to build and would thus subserve no immediate needs. Another fact, which understandably found no mention in public debate, may perhaps have been uppermost in New Delhi's thinking—a refusal to expose Assam's oil and other rich natural resources to direct Chinese needs then, or their covetous looks later.

But perhaps the most significant aspect of the proposal, which finally drew a blank, was China's refusal to consult with Tibet. The latter, while broadly sympathetic to the Chinese cause in terms of the unequal struggle in which that country was now engaged, was sternly opposed to allowing its own territory to be used for road-building. Nor was India prepared to steam-roller Tibet into submission. The resultant situation is well summed up by Mr. Richardson:

> The Chinese then bluntly informed the Tibetan Government that they were going ahead with their proposed road. The Tibetan Government, after deliberations by the National Assembly, determined to resist. Both sides were urged by the British Government to come to an agreement, failing which co-operation in India could not be forthcoming; but the Chinese, without further argument, sent a survey party to the Tibetan border. When it tried to enter the country, it was turned back by Tibetan troops. In spite of a visit by a Chinese official from Chinghai, who mixed persuasion and threats, the Tibetans refused to yield.[1]

A Tibetan historian would have us believe that the Chinese 'threatened to wage war' (viz., if Lhasa did not give way) and 'even instigated (its) provincial governors' to initiate hostilities. Tibet too, he assures us, was 'ready to face' the challenge. In the last round, in the first half of 1942, however, the Chinese withdrew their surveyors and the crisis blew over.[2]

[1] Richardson, *History*, p. 159.
[2] *Shakabapa*, p. 286.
On 13 July 1942, U S Ambassador Gauss informed his government that the Chinese had 'abandoned whatever plans they may have had' for constructing a motor road because it would

A corollary to the abortive Western Szechuan-Zayul-Lohit valley road was Lhasa's grudging willingness, under considerable Indian pressure—Rai Bahadur Norbu, we are told, ' strongly requested ' the Tibetan Government and ' even warned ' that ' a continued refusal ' might result in the loss of ' British support '.³—to permit pack animal supplies through its territory to Kham and onwards to Szechuan. At no stage too enthusiastic, Lhasa finally persuaded itself to allow the transport of non-military goods. And that principally because it ' did not wish to embarrass ' the British Indian Government which, we are told, was prepared to threaten it with ' economic sanctions '.⁴

Interestingly enough, the British apart, even the United States exerted a great deal of diplomatic pressure. It was in this context that, in July 1942, Washington despatched two of its officers, Captain Ilia Tolstoy and Lieutenant Brooke Dolan on what was described as a ' most secret ' project of ' strategic importance '.⁵ The objective, in concert with the British and Chinese Governments, was to ' speak plainly ' to Tibet so as to make it ' change its attitude ' in regard to the passage of supplies to China.

When Lhasa did finally give in, China insisted, as Tibet's overlord, on stationing its men and setting up its agencies along the entire route—a demand which Lhasa stoutly, and successfully, resisted. Suspect as Chinese motives had always been, Tibet saw in the injection of this alien personnel an ill-disguised attempt, thinly cloaked, to sabotage its independence. For it would have been evident, even to the most casual observer, that the route could have, at best, a very limited value, reduced further by Tibet's refusal to permit transport of any military hardware.⁶ As the then US Ambassador in China wrote home:

have ' no early value to the war effort '. Ambassador Gauss to Secretary of State in *Foreign Relations of the United States: Diplomatic Papers: 1942: China* (Washington, 1956), p. 627.

The suggestion that the ' Tibetans used the lever of China's desperate need of a land supply route to attempt to pressure the Chinese into entering into a tripartite agreement (China, Tibet and India) about the proposed road '—*Karunakar Gupta*—is not supported by any evidence. Besides it smacks of misplaced emphasis. For it was the Chinese who made use of the War to pressurise the Tibetans; the latter did not want the road anyway while British pressure on Tibet, as may be evident, had its limits. See *infra*, notes 4, 6–8.

³*Shakabapa*, p. 286.

⁴*Inter alia*, Hull (Secretary of State) told Gauss that the British Government were prepared, ' in association with the Chinese ', to ' speak plainly ' to Tibet, to ' exercise joint pressure ' and even to threaten ' economic sanctions ' if, in return, the Chinese Government ' give definite and public undertaking to respect Tibetan autonomy and to refrain from interfering in Tibet's internal administration '. On its own, Washington desired a ' practical solution ' of ' any existing difficulty.'

Secretary of State to Ambassador Gauss, 3 July 1942, in *Foreign Relations*, n. 2, p. 626.

⁵Donovan (Director, Office of Strategic Services) to Secretary of State, 2 July 1942, and Hull to President Roosevelt (enclosing a draft letter for the Dalai Lama), 3 July 1942, Ibid., pp. 624–25. Hull underlined the fact that the letter to the Dalai Lama was addressed to him in his capacity as the religious leader of Tibet ' thus avoiding any possible offence to the Chinese Government ' who included Tibet in the territory of the Republic of China.

⁶In a communication to the Department of State, the British Embassy defined ' non-military '

Transit through Tibet is practicable by pack animal trains making one trip a year but the amount that could be transported (maximum estimates placed it at 3,000 tons annually) renders the project of minor importance as a supply route to China. The round trip requires six months and about half of the year travel is impracticable.[7]

Significantly, by 1943, initial Chinese ardour had cooled off, albeit in the process President Chiang is said to have ordered the governors of Chinghai, Yunnan and Sikang to move troops to Tibet's borders. Lhasa, however, kept its nerve and stood its ground while China, failing ' to make any political capital' out of the scheme, lost all interest in the passage of goods through Tibet.[8]

On another front, however, China's gains were impressive. It may be recalled that since General Huang Mu-sung's mission in 1934, a Chinese presence in Lhasa had been maintained. And here, in the course of less than half a dozen years, Huang's two wireless operators had been transformed into the ' Regional Office of the (Kuomintang's) Committee for Mongolian and Tibetan Affairs', CMTA for short. In 1940, on the occasion of ceremonies connected with the formal installation of the 14th Dalai Lama, the Chinese sent a high-power mission, through India, headed by Wu Ching-hsin, then Chairman of CMTA. According to Chinese accounts, Wu's primary objective was to ' supervise' the oracle's revelation and the lot-drawing procedures

supplies to include petroleum ' but *not* arms, ammunition and explosives'. *Inter alia*, it put forth the view that the Chinese seemed to be ' more anxious' to extend their influence in East Tibet than to obtain supplies; that the ' present' position was that Tibet had ' now agreed *during the current year only*' to the despatch from India of these non-military supplies; that in consequence the Chinese had been asked to agree: (a) to the selection of the Changlam as the main route and of Jyekundo as the delivery point; (b) to dispense with liaison officers or supervisors; (c) to delegation of authority to the British and Chinese representatives at Lhasa to negotiate a contract with Tibetan carriers. Telegram, (British) Foreign Office to Embassy in Washington, 15 August 1942, delivered to the Department of State, 27 August 1942, Ibid., pp. 630–31.

[7]Ambassador Gauss explained that the term ' non-military' was not to be strictly interpreted. Gauss to Secretary of State, 13 July 1942, in *supra*, n. 2.

Also see Vincent (Counsellor of Embassy in China) to Gauss, dated Chungking, 30 July 1942. Vincent noted that the Chinese had conceded that the earlier estimate of 3,000 tons was ' much too high' (Richardson, then attached to the Indian Agent General in Chungking, thought the estimate would not ' exceed' 700 tons) and that the Chinese had suggested that ' to overcome' Tibetan fears a commercial company be organised in which Indian as well as Tibetans and Chinese would take part. *Foreign Relations*, n. 2, pp. 628–29.

[8]Richardson, *History*, pp. 160–62.

Also see Philipps (Personal Representative of President Roosevelt to India) to Secretary of State, 20 January and 8 February 1943, in *Foreign Relations of the United States: Diplomatic Papers: 1943: China* (Washington, 1957), pp. 620–21.

Inter alia, Philipps revealed that the ' practicability' of this route was being ' re-considered' in Chungking and it was ' inferred' that its decision would be ' negative'; that while New Delhi had ' no objection' to use of Tibetan routes, it refused to reopen discussions ' except on basis of joint arrangements with both Chinese and Tibetan governments'. The Chinese,

which go with the selection of a new Dalai Lama.[9] Later, however, these formalities were waived off and instead, 'at a private interview', Wu is said to have 'identified' the boy whom the Tibetans had brought from Amdu and whom they were now to instal as their future ruler. At the installation, on Chinese insistence that the 'precedent set by the Resident of Amban' be followed, Wu 'sat on the same side as the new Dalai Lama', as well as his parents and his tutor. The arrangement was important for from the

> seating of Mr.Wu alone we can see that the Chinese representative asserted the traditional position of China in Tibet and did much more than present a ceremonial scarf.[10]

Apart from Wu, another first-hand eye-witness of the installation ceremonies was Basil Gould, then Political Officer in Sikkim. The fact that his description, and narrative, was later adopted by the Tibetan Government as an 'official' account,[11] lends it greater credibility than the somewhat colourful, if contradictory, version detailed above and doled out by Dr Li. Gould underlines the fact that it was because the Chinese representative ' had been dissatisfied' with the position accorded to him, that he absented himself from the Potala at the time of presentation of gifts from China. This, however, made scant difference to the role he is alleged to have played, for the Chinese furnished in the newspapers

> an account, as detailed as it was inaccurate, of the ceremony as it might no doubt have been conducted if the Chinese representative in Lhasa had been the chief actor in the scene.[12]

Whatever his role at the installation, in another direction, however, Wu did

---

however, he intimated, considered Tibet ' an integral part' of their country, and would 'reject any proposal for tripartite negotiations including Tibetan government.'

[9] Li, *Tibet*, p. 181.
See also ' Observer ' (P L Mehra), ' The Dalai and the Panchen: Tibet's Supreme Incarnate Lamas ', *India Quarterly*, XV, 3, July–September 1959, pp. 262–89.

[10] Li, *Tibet*, p. 181.
According to Dr Sung, the 14th Dalai Lama's installation took place on 22 February 1940 and both Yencheng, the Tibetan Regent, as well as General Wu, the Chinese representative, 'jointly presided' over the ceremony. *Yao-ting Sung*, p. 190.

[11] B J Gould, *The Jewel in the Lotus*, (London, 1957), pp. 209–33.

[12] Gould reveals that a newspaper, ' of which I knew nothing ', had asked him to send it separate reports of the ceremony. This, however, he refused, agreeing nonetheless to send a telegram ' announcing the bare fact that installation had taken place '. Later,

> when a copy of the paper arrived, I found in it a column which began with the statement that I had reported that the installation had taken place on a certain date. It then went on without any indication that the words were not mine...to retail a version which obviously the Chinese had supplied.

Ibid., pp. 234–35.

assert himself, and successfully. And this was his decision to set up in Lhasa 'a permanent office' of the CMTA. His original purpose, we are told, was to establish a High Commission but evidently the Tibetan Regent objected and Chungking did not specifically approve. Hence the permanent office inaugurated on 1 April (1940) to which a Director and a Deputy Director were appointed.[13]

A side purpose of Wu's visit appears to have been to assure the British, as also the Tibetans, that China's aims were peaceful, that it did not contemplate aggression and would not stand in the way of Tibet choosing its own, if need be separate, path. This assurance may have been deemed necessary in view of the fact that, with the Chinese Government located in Chungking, Lhasa would, no doubt, have felt the giant almost breathing down its neck. The latter may also have been afraid lest the KMT regime should seek compensation, at Tibet's expense, for its loss of territory and prestige elsewhere.

It may be recalled that, on 3 July 1942, the American Secretary of State Hull had told his Ambassador in Chungking that Tibet's refusal to cooperate in regard to the proposed road-link through its territory, was 'due to fear of Chinese penetration'. Ten days later the Ambassador wrote back to say that

> Tibetan authorities are being assured that these technicians (to be deployed on the trade route) will not engage in any political activities; that they will be instructed to confine themselves to the matter of supervising transport.

The Ambassador, however, added that even though Chungking considered Tibet to be a part of the Republic of China, it 'had no intention of altering' a situation in which internal administration in Tibet was 'in fact autonomous'.[14]

Apart from Lhasa, the British too had been aroused to unabashed Chinese designs on Tibet and the Indian frontier. It was then widely believed that Chungking was 'more anxious' to extend its influence in Eastern Tibet than to obtain supplies; for, if supplies alone were desired, the proposed supervisors appeared 'unnecessary'.[15] The situation was further complicated by the fact that this distrust of China could not be publicly aired, for the latter was now an 'ally' in a global war.

As Director of CMTA's permanent office in Tibet, Wu had appointed one Dr. Kung Ching-tsung. A couple of years later, Lhasa requested his recall.[16] His replacement, in August 1944, was a highly placed Chinese

---

[13]Li, *Tibet*, pp.185–87.

[14]It may be recalled that Vincent, the American Counsellor in Chungking, had reported that in his talks with Dr Tsiang, Director of the Political Affairs Department of the Executive Yuan, the latter had promised to eschew from the transport project all 'political considerations and factors,' and, among other things, had made mention of Tibet as a 'self-governing dominion'. Vincent to Gauss, 30 July 1942; *supra*, n. 7.

Also see *supra*, notes 2 and 4.

[15]British Embassy to Department of State, 27 August 1942, *supra*, n. 6.

[16]*Shakabapa*, p. 287.

functionary, Sheng Tsung-lien who, being on the personal staff of General Chiang Kai-shek, would appear to represent Chinese policy at its very fount. According to Dr Li, Shen's appointment was made with a view ' to re-adjust ' China's strained relations with the ' unfriendly ' Lhasa authorities. Whether he actually succeeded in this objective, is a matter of debate for while the Chinese believe that he met with ' no success ',[17] the Tibetan version is that ' with his fine diplomacy ' he did succeed in ' improving ' relations between the two countries.[18] According to Mr. Richardson, while failing to obtain any ' sweeping concessions ', Sheng,

> an able, unostentatious, and broad-minded man, well-supported by a capable staff, certainly won a higher degree of Tibetan confidence and regard than any of his predecessors.[19]

By the time Sheng arrived in Lhasa in the latter half of 1944, British policy *vis-à-vis* Tibet had been restated with a certain added emphasis. The provocation, it would seem, was a continuous, and relentless, Chinese pressure, sustained by unqualified US support, about British policy in regard to a country which Chungking viewed to be an integral part of the mainland. Washington, though not always outspoken, had been consistently punctilious about ' avoiding ' giving ' any possible offence' to Chiang Kai-shek and, as early as July 1942, informed its Ambassador in Chungking that the Chinese government had long claimed suzerainty over Tibet, that the constitution had listed the country among the areas comprising the territory of the Republic of China and that it (Washington) had ' at no time raised questions ' regarding either of these claims.[20]

1942 was also to mark the visit to India of General Chiang Kai-shek, then head of the Kuomintang regime in Chungking. During the course of his stay, the General made no secret of his concern over the Indian government's reluctance to forge ahead with the Lohit valley road through Assam and southeast Tibet, or the stationing of Chinese personnel on the existing trade route through Tibet. It has been noticed that New Delhi was not very willing to push Tibet around, even though Norbu had exerted considerable pressure, on China's behalf, at Lhasa. Nor, as events proved, would the latter readily agree.[21]

Tibetan recalcitrance, as well as British inability to coerce it into submission

[17]Li, *Tibet*, p. 190.
[18]*Supra*, n. 16.
[19]Richardson, *History*, pp. 165–66.
[20]Ambassador Gauss had revealed that the Chinese Vice-Minister for Foreign Affairs had made it clear to him (Gauss) that 'there was no occasion for giving assurances regarding " autonomy "' and that Tibet was considered a part of the Republic of China. For details *supra*, notes 2 and 5.
[21]In its communication to the Department of State, *supra*, n. 7, the British Embassy made the point:
> The present position is that the Tibetan Government have now agreed during the current year only, to the despatch from India of non-military supplies, preferably via the

was made a subject of considerable grievance by the Nationalist Chinese Foreign Minister, Dr Soong. This was during his meetings with the then British Foreign Secretary, Mr Eden (now Lord Avon), in Washington, in March 1943. Later, in May that year, at the Pacific Council's meeting, the Chinese returned to the charge. The considered British response took the form of what has come to be known as the Eden Memorandum of August 1943, which made British recognition of Chinese suzerainty *conditional* on the latter's acceptance of Tibet's autonomy. Essentially, the Memorandum stated that HMG

> have always been prepared to recognise Chinese suzerainty over Tibet *but only on the understanding* that Tibet is regarded as autonomous.

Its own interest, which foreswore any ' political ambitions ' in Tibet, was

> the maintenance of friendly relations with, and the preservation of peaceful conditions in an area which is conterminous with the North-east frontier of India.

Nor was the approach entirely negative in character. For Whitehall was prepared to ' offer any help ' and indeed ' welcome '

> any amicable arrangements which the Chinese Government might be disposed to make with Tibet whereby the latter recognised Chinese suzerainty in return for an agreed frontier and an undertaking to recognise Tibetan autonomy....[22]

The fact that Tibet had, since 1911, enjoyed *de facto* independence, that it refused to compromise its neutrality in a global war in which China was directly threatened and that despite Chungking's threats—which for a time, in 1943, assumed serious proportions[23]—it had refused to be intimidated or browbeaten, lent considerable support to this thesis. To an extent perhaps Sheng's appointment at Lhasa in 1944 may be viewed as Chungking's offer of an olive branch

---

Changlam to Jyekundo, avoiding Lhasa, and as they cannot undertake to handle transport themselves they suggest that a contract be made with a Tibetan firm *for this year only*. As regards the appointment of Chinese technicians or experts, no such request has, they state, been received from the Chinese representative at Lhasa and if made will be refused, since in the Tibetan Government's view neither British nor Chinese supervisors should travel up and down the supply route in Tibetan territory.

[22]The citations are from the memorandum ' sent to Dr Soong (in London) by Mr Eden, 5 August 1943, in a personal letter '. Later, the British Embassy (Washington) handed a copy over to the Department of State, 14 September 1943. For the text see *Foreign Relations*, 1943, pp. 637–38.

[23]For alleged Chinese troop movements on Tibet's borders, British anxiety, and persistent US efforts to defuse the situation resulting in Chinese denials see Merrell (*Charge* in India) to Secretary of State, 15 May; Secretary of State to Atcheson (*Charge* in China), 18 May; Atcheson to Secretary of State, 25 May; British Embassy to Department of State, 28 August;

to woo the Tibetans. Another effort in the same direction was a 'solemn' declaration made by Chiang Kai-shek, in August 1945, while addressing a joint session of his country's National Supreme Defence Council and the Central Executive Committee of the KMT, in Chungking. *Inter alia*, he pledged that

> if the Tibetans should at this time express a wish for self-government, our Government would, in conformity with our sincere traditions, accord it a very high degree of autonomy. If in the future they fulfil economic requirements for independence, the nation's government will, as in the case of Outer Mongolia, help them to attain that status.

The sting, however, was in the tail, for

> Tibet must give proof that it can consolidate and protect its continuity so as not to become another Korea.[24]

It is not unlikely that, apart from mollifying uneasy public opinion at home and abroad, Chiang's real objective in making this prouncement was to sound a note of warning that he would not sign Tibet away, even as he had Outer Mongolia. It may be recalled that the Sino-Soviet treaty had just then been concluded. *Inter alia*, it had provided for a plebiscite in Outer Mongolia, a face-saving device which appeared to be so thinly disguised as not to cloak the latter's real sell-away. This apart, there was the additional fact that Chiang's views on the five races were known to go to an extreme and, in fact, were far in advance of the theory, or practice, of Yuan Shih-kai or the Manchus. Thus in *China's Destiny* he bemoaned the fact, that if only the Ch'ing

> had treated the Hans, the Manchus, the Mongols, the Mohammedans and the Tibetans within the state without discrimination; if it had recognised the five classes as integral parts of a single whole and granted equality . .

Secretary of State to Atcheson, 21 September; Berle (Acting Secretary of State) to Gauss (Ambassador to China), 27 September; Gauss to Secretary of State, 28 September; Berle to Gauss, 29 September and Gauss to Secretary of State, 4 and 29 October, all in 1943, in Ibid., pp. 631–43.

Richardson too affirms that,

in April 1943, Chiang Kai-shek directed the governors of Chingai, Yunnan and Sikang to move the troops to the Tibetan border. His intention was probably to overawe the Tibetans....In 1943, when the threat of Chinese aggression against Tibet was brought to their notice, the United States Embassy in Chungking appeared to consider that the danger was exaggerated, but it seems probable that they exerted some pressure on the Chinese government to prevent a blatant misuse of military supplies, for most of which the Chinese had to rely upon their allies.

Richardson, *History*, pp. 161 and 164.

[24]Li, *Tibet*, p. 190.

The *New York Times*, 25 August 1945, gives a slightly different version, so does the *Times* (London), 27 August 1945.

China would have been able to advance together with the contemporary European . . . countries.²⁵

Actually what Chiang now sought to prove was that the races were no better than tribes springing from a single race—the Han!²⁵ᵃ

Another interesting Chinese endeavour, in 1946, was for Sheng in Lhasa to persuade the Tibetans to send an official delegation to China. Ostensibly the aim was to negotiate the boundary and other outstanding questions, even though in reality Sheng wanted them to participate in a meeting of the National Assembly which had then been convened and stood charged with the responsibility of framing a new constitution for Republican China. At Nanking, efforts were made to represent the Tibetan visitors as though they were delegates to the Assembly— and one of them was declared to be a member of its Presidium! Despite their lack of initiation in the ways of higher diplomacy, the Tibetans did not fall into the trap and refused to be a party to any resolutions adopted by the Assembly. It appears that Lhasa had instructed them 'not to sign any sort of document' and, accordingly, they not only declined but 'made a public demonstration' of their refusal.²⁶ Not that they did always conform to Lhasa's wishes for, according to Shakabapa, 'without the permission or orders' of the Tibetan government, the Mission had attended a meeting of the Chinese National Assembly on 5 May 1946. For its part, however, the Mission explained that it had 'gone only to watch the proceedings' and that it neither recognised nor signed the new constitutional law' passed by the Assembly.²⁷

It would seem from the above that over the years, and despite persistent Chinese endeavours, Tibet had refused to be coaxed or cajoled into accepting the former's hegemony. An instance in point was the 1947 non-official Asian Relations Conference in New Delhi to which, among others, the Tibetan government had been invited. The Conference convened early in 1947 and in spite of the Chinese row over the map showing Tibet as a separate entity, which served as an eye-opener and took the late Mr. Nehru completely by surprise, Lhasa's delegates functioned as a distinct group, separate from the Chinese and with their own independent flag.²⁸

---

²⁵Chiang Kai-shek, *China's Destiny, and Chinese Economic Theory* (London, 1947), pp. 47–48.
²⁵ᵃ 'Commentary' by Philip Jaffe, in Ibid., pp. 307–8.
²⁶Richardson, *History*, pp.166–67.
According to Dr Li, the 'delegates' had arrived 'in response' to an invitation and 'yet' took the position that they had 'no power' to discuss the draft constitution, demanding, *inter alia*, deletion of the proposal that 'Tibet's local autonomy shall be decided by law'. A 'compromise solution' however, we are assured, 'was reached'. Li, *Tibet*, p. 191.
²⁷*Shakabapa*, pp. 290–91.
²⁸Richardson, *History*, p. 168.

Chapter 39

End of British Rule: Tibetan and Chinese Encroachments on the Eastern Frontier

AFTER CHINA'S KMT regime had won the War against Japan by proxy as it were, its one great effort was directed towards gathering all the threads firmly in its grip in order, among other things, to fit into the status, and role, of a Great Power. Compulsions, both of its domestic and international situations, however, made this a difficult consummation. At home, Mao's armies swept across the whole of the north-east and made Chiang gradually lose his hold; abroad, Stalin exacted his pound of flesh for an alliance of dubious value. The plebiscite in Mongolia, which formed a part of the overall deal and to which a reference has been made already, was a face-saving formula to formalise an existing reality. In the case of Tibet, however, the story was different. By means fair, and not so fair, the Kuomintang regime tried to establish its claims to supremacy and an acknowledgement that Tibet indeed formed a part of the Motherland. Not that it succeeded, for the Tibetans had learnt a lesson or two and despite their own domestic squabbles kept the Chinese at a safe distance.

In addition to more pressing preoccupations at home and abroad, New Delhi in the early forties was up against the problem of Tibetan as well as Chinese encroachments on its eastern frontier. Thus to Tawang, early in 1943, Lhasa appears to have sent its officials, accompanied by a small body of troops, and entrusted with the task of holding some enquiries. In ostensible discharge of their duties, the Tibetan representatives issued summons to certain individuals in Shergaon, Kalakthang and Rupa, all in the Kameng division, to furnish some evidence. This was tantamount to exercise of authority in a region south of the McMahon Line which did not belong to them. From New Delhi's point of view this was bad enough; what was worse was that Lhasa now asked Bhutanese officials to undertake to return about 400 families of Tibetan extraction who had, over the past several decades, crossed the border and settled in that country. Merits of the case apart, since Bhutan's foreign relations, under the treaty of 1910, could only be conducted by, and through, India, the Tibetan move constituted a clear violation of accepted norms of diplomatic behaviour. No wonder, to both these encroachments, in Kameng and with regard to Bhutan, New Delhi took strong exception and it would appear that, in deference to its protests, Lhasa recalled its officials from Tawang and countermanded the negotiations with Bhutan.

Clearly India's approach towards Tawang was motivated not merely in terms of counteracting Tibetan incursions, irritating as these were, but to forestalling to the extent it possibly could, problems arising from the not unlikely absorption of Tibet by China after the War was over. The fact that the Indo-Tibetan frontier was a part of the Simla Convention, to which the Chinese were not a party, was disturbing enough. But an even more disquieting situation would arise if the Tibetans also evaded implementation of the agreements in question while India itself had no effective control over the territory allegedly in dispute. Unfortunately, pious resolutions to the contrary notwithstanding, New Delhi's control over these areas was far from effectively established at the time of transfer of power in 1947, a fact that was to have disastrous results in the years to come.

An interesting aspect of persistent Tibetan encroachments on Tawang during these years was a certain measure of academic debate, conducted behind the scenes, in regard to an alternate frontier in the Kameng division, just south of the McMahon Line. In March 1939, an Assam official, the then acting Governor, Henry Twynam who argued this thesis, cast some serious doubts on the general validity of the 1914 treaty. Article IX of that solemn compact, he maintained, did not refer to the interchange of letters with Shatra laying down the India-Tibet boundary, but to the small-scale map attached to the Convention. Besides, since 1914, no steps had been taken to make the McMahon frontier effective by an actual exercise of authority. Was it fair, in equity, he asked, to make good the claim now, after this long lapse of years? Besides, he sought to point out, it was not really necessary to include Tawang within the Indian frontier when the same purpose could as well be served by a boundary line along the Sela and the Digien rivers which constituted formidable natural barriers. Insofar as it was dispensable, Tawang, he argued, could in fact be used as a bargaining counter to make Lhasa tacitly accept the rest of the McMahon frontier.[1]

Another argument, a variant on the above theme, was pressed into service to justify a re-drawing of the boundary in this sector. It was maintained that, in 1914, the chief preoccupation of the British Plenipotentiary was to obtain a frontier that would look well on a map, although it was far from being a convenient ethnic and political boundary; that, in fact, Tawang was ' as Tibetan in character ' as the Chumbi valley. To buttress the Sela boun-

---

[1] In a long, and reasoned, letter Twynam put forth his point of view cogently and with considerable skill. *Inter alia*, he argued:

Humanitarian grounds alone would scarcely be sufficient to justify a 'forward' policy as similar grounds could be urged for the occupation of other areas of Tibet.... It is true that last year's expedition may have excited hopes and raised claims, but it is possible that much could be done to fulfil expectations without going so far as to occupy an area which has always been oriented towards Tibet ethnographically, politically and in religion and is even now in Lightfoot's words 'dominated by representatives of the Tibetan Government'.... The crux of the whole question apart from the financial aspect appears to lie in Lhasa's reactions to a forward policy and the extent to which these should be allowed for....

Twynam to Linlithgow, 17 March 1939, in *IOR*, L/P&S/12/36/23, Part I.

dary it was suggested that a trade-route via Tashigong might be developed, which would thereby tend to reduce a demand for free transport in the Dirang-dzong-Kalakthang areas. Besides, the Sela boundary would cost only 'about one-fourth' of what the McMahon alignment, including Tawang, would. And with a regime obsessed with rupees, annas and pies, an argument like this, more than any other, was bound to clinch an issue.[2]

Another interesting line of reasoning employed centred on serious doubts being entertained about the Monbas proving, in effect, to be good and effective 'Wardens of the Marches'. For here, in an exposed position on the frontier, was a 'plug of tribesmen' closely allied by race and language to the principalities in their rear, a fact that would make them increasingly suspect in terms of withstanding pressures from the other side.[3]

It is somewhat amusing to recall in this context that later, during the meeting of the officials of the two governments in 1960, Peking made use of this argument to maintain that even the British held the McMahon Line to be 'invalid' and 'difficult' to cling to; and that, in 1944, they had expressed 'their willingness' to change the boundary in the Monyul area 'south of Tawang', between the McMahon Line and the 'traditional customary line maintained' by China.[4] Actually, the significance of this admittedly defeatist approach which, because of its plausibility, may have proved acceptable at the highest level,[5] lay in two

---

[2] A few weeks later the Acting Assam Governor underscored his earlier arguments emphasising that he could *not*
> but feel that to take over the Tawang area would inevitably alienate those in authority in Tibet *without any particular advantage* to ourselves.

Twynam to Linlithgow, 3 April 1939, in *IOR*, L/P&S/12/36/29.

[3] Gould to India, 9 May 1940, in *IOR*, L/P&S/12/36/23, Part I. Herein Gould was offering his observations on Olaf Caroe's 'The Mongolian Fringe', a paper in which the then Foreign Secretary set out cogently the problems of India's north-eastern frontier and which was widely circulated among officials in Assam and along the eastern frontier.

It may be recalled that, as early as November 1938, Gould had maintained that the Monbas were so downtrodden that they 'themselves were likely to contribute little towards their liberation' from Tibetan nfluence. Gould to India, 3 November 1938, in *IOR*, L/P&S/12/36/29.

[4] The Chinese position regarding the Monyul area is stated in the *Report of the Officials of the Governments of India and the Poeple's Republic of China on the Boundary Question* (New Delhi, 1961), pp. C R (Chinese Report) 104–6, 153, 160 and 172. Subsequently this reference has been cited as *Officials' Report*.

It is interesting to note that in making use of it, *Karunakar Gupta* has been selective and thus, to an extent, unfair to his evidence. After citing the Chinese version that Gould, in December 1944, proposed to the Lhasa authorities a willingness 'to change the boundary...(running) not to the north but to the south of Tawang', he omits to add:
> But since it (British Indian government) still insisted on occupying the southern part of Mon-yul, this aggressive proposal was never approved by the Tibet local government.

His reference to an aide-memoire of the Political Officer which allegedly showed that Gould's offer was 'definitive and formal' is unsubstantiated.

For the Indian reply to the Chinese assertions see *Officials' Report*, pp. I R (Indian Report) 228–29; also Ibid., pp. 115 and 134–36.

[5] On 17 April, the Viceroy told Twynam that even though he had 'no reason to suppose'

factors. One, it was symptomatic of a general, and fairly widespread, reluctance to take any firm action. A preceding chapter makes abundantly clear how in 1938 ' financial considerations ', or a ' need for economy ', were held to justify a stern refusal to implement the measures which Captain Lightfoot recommended and the Assam Government supported to the hilt, which Norbu Dhondhup in Lhasa held to be necessary and which Gould thought desirable.[6] Even Whitehall was not prepared for the sell-away which New Delhi had then advocated and, in fact, helped to stiffen its attitude a little.[7] In retrospect, it seems strangely odd that such considerations as an expenditure of a 100,000 rupees weighed heavily in the balance and were made to cloud a clearer concept of national integrity and of the need to protect the country's borders.[8]

A second factor that emerges is the almost paranoiac obsession both in New Delhi, and in Whitehall, which amounted to a refusal to do anything that would, in the slightest degree, upset the Chinese apple-cart. It was feared, for instance, that if Tawang and other frontier incursions were taken up seriously with Tibet, the resultant hullabaloo in Lhasa, and the discussions in the Tsongdu, would reach Chinese ears and thereby help to upset a delicate balance. Similarly, the fact of making the frontier effective, it was argued, might be used by the Chinese to drum a propaganda offensive to the effect that while a deadly struggle against Japan was still being waged, the British were busy in a game of ' imperialist aggrandisement ' at the expense of their weak and helpless neighbours.[9] Thus, as New Delhi viewed it, it was a harsh choice between

that ' we are on insecure ground with regard to our treaty rights', there was, 'from the practical point of view no advantage and considerable risk' in pressing the matter further with the Tibetan authorities. Later, on 24 August, he told the Secretary of State that

there is much to be said for his (Twynam's) proposal both on general and financial grounds particularly as he thinks that a boundary on the Se La would only cost about one-fourth of the expenditure estimated to be necessary if we were to decide eventually to go right up to the McMahon Line and include Tawang....

Earlier, on 25 July, the Secretary of State had asked the Viceroy for ' some expression of your views ' on Twynam's suggestion.

Viceroy to Twynam, 17 April and Viceroy to Secretary of State, 24 August 1939, also Secretary of State to Viceroy, 25 August (para *included* 25 July) 1939, all in *IOR*, L/P&S/12/36/29.

[6]For details, *supra*, Chapter XXXV.

[7]In according its approval to the Government of India's policy towards Tawang, the India Office made it clear that it did not view the prevailing situation 'with equanimity' and would await the promised review at the end of a year hoping that, when ' time for action' comes, ' clearer information ' would be available. Secretary of State to India, 13 July 1939, in *IOR*, L/P&S/12/36/23, Part I.

[8]An India Office minute by E G Crombie, on 23 June, underlined New Delhi's ' preoccupation with financial stringency ' and ' indifference ' to the plight of (Tawang's) inhabitants—an aspect which had been treated ' somewhat casually '. Another minute by Peel, on 3 July, expressed the view that New Delhi appeared ' so concerned with their financial difficulties'. Later, in according its approval to India's ' do nothing ' fiat for a year, Whitehall expressed the view that it did so in the light of New Delhi's plea for ' financial stringency'.

For the minutes see *IOR*, L/P&S/12/36/29; also *supra*, n. 7.

[9]Typical of the genre was the following:

As HMG understand your intentions, you do not contemplate any immediate forward action, driving out Tibetan encroachments with all the friction that it might entail and acquiescing in an unsatisfactory frontier with a growing awareness that if China absorbed Tibet, at the end of the war the problem would become a hundred times more difficult, intractable.

A necessary, and indeed important, corollary to the Tawang ' concession ', contemplated by the British, may not be overlooked, namely that it was conditional: to be made in return for Lhasa's implicit, and unqualified, acceptance of the rest of the boundary to which it had agreed in 1914. More explicitly, as a later India Office minute recorded,

> there was general agreement in India (in 1940) that *if* it came to discussions with the Tibetans on the question of the boundary, it might be useful to agree, *as a bargaining counter*, to draw the boundary south of the Tawang area.[10]

From the above it should be obvious that the Indian Government's mottoes of ' appeasement ', ' peace at any price ' and ' let sleeping dogs lie ' were by no means different, except perhaps in the time-lag, from Neville Chamberlain and his ilk at Munich. In sum, with a lot of argument and counter-argument in New Delhi and London, added to the exigencies of a difficult situation in Lhasa itself, the resultant policy remained one of soft-pedalling and sweeping under the carpet as it were, all questions of a controversial character. Whatever its temporary gains, it proved in the long run to be a sordid, short-sighted approach for which, later, a heavy price had to be paid.

Apart from Tawang, two other areas in which Tibetan encroachments were pronounced were in the Siang valley and in the Lohit. The McMahon Line, it appears, had cut in half the territory of the ruler of Po and since occupation right up to the frontier had not been immediately effected, not until 1928 at any rate, the semi-independent king of Po continued to exercise a vague authority over areas strictly south of the Line. In the Lohit, too, a few square

> and they would emphasise the importance of avoiding a clash if possible between our forces and Tibetan troops partly because of its effect on our relations with Tibet and partly because it would presumably come to the ears of the Chinese and be used by them to stir up propaganda both in China and in popular press in the United States on the line that we are up to our old Imperialist game. . . .Danger of this propaganda being effective and difficult to counteract is particularly present at the moment.

Secretary of State to Viceroy, 15 April 1943, in *IOR*, L/P&S/12/36/23, Part I.

[10]Minute by Peel, 26 February 1943, in *IOR*, L/P&S/12/36/29.

Also see extract from letter No. 73, from Governor, Assam, dated 5 August 1940, summing up the conclusions of a meeting, on 1 August 1940 at Shillong, of a number of officials including the Governor, Gould, Political Officers of the Sadiya and Balipara Frontier Tracts and Raja Dorji of Bhutan, which read in part:

> The general opinion was that commonsense demands that we should not press our claims on Tawang, but tacitly assume that a more suitable line than the McMahon Line would be one farther south, either at the Se La or farther south in the neighbourhood of Dirang-dzong.

For the text see *IOR*, L/P&S/12/36/23, Part I.

miles of uninhabited territory, south of Rima, which had been included into India, was said to fall within that town's orbit. The harsh reality, however, was that Lhasa's own control over Rima was so tenuous that its further extension of authority could, at best, be very loose in nature. The broad approach in New Delhi was that its claims in these two small pockets should be made effective before disturbing the *status quo* in Tawang, and that, in order of priority, areas should be occupied as from the east to the west. Again, it was felt that places nearest to China—and the Lohit and Siang were much nearer —should be taken first.[11] It was only, if and when manpower and resources were available, after these priority needs had been attended to, that Tawang was to be brought in.

By 1944, British road-making activity in the Lohit, at Sanga Cho-dzong, in the Subansiri and even in Monyul, were such as to arouse Lhasa's interest and curiosity. This would, if partly, explain the latter's blanket claims to territories to which it had no title whatsoever. It may be recalled that a necessary corollary to road-building was the establishment of posts at Walong and in Dirang-dzong and that steps were taken, albeit half-heartedly, to stop Tibetan exactions, monastic or otherwise. A distinction between the latter two imposts was hard to draw for officials of a monastery would often-times exact civil taxes in the guise of monastic dues. In the early forties, when Lhasa is said to have resisted the Assam Government's proposal to despatch vaccine to Tawang on the plea that it was 'unquestionably' Tibetan territory, New Delhi played it decidedly cool. Those who knew the country maintained that any attempt at an abrupt assertion of authority, after nearly thirty years of studied inactivity, would arouse suspicion, and that as the Tibetans believed only in accomplished facts, action to be meaningful must be at once impressive and decisive. At the same time New Delhi appears to have concluded that while it was not necessary to offer Tibet any boundary rectifications north of the Sela as a sop, the fact of extending regular administration into that area could be used as an effective weapon when the time came for serious *pourparlers*.[12]

[11] For a first-hand account of the extension of British administration into these areas see J P Mills, ' Problems of the Assam-Tibet Frontier ', *JRCAS*, XXXVIII, April 1950. Mills, an anthropologist and a senior civil servant, was acting as Advisor to the Assam Governor on tribal matters.

[12] An India Office minute of 16 March 1946 reads:
The Se La Sub-Agency: in which we are prepared to make an adjustment of the boundary. The sooner we can secure Tibetan agreement to what is the frontier the sooner—we hope— these petty annoyances cease.
IOR, L/P&S/12/36/29.

Again, as early as 1943, Lhasa foreswore any claims to some of these areas. This was in reply to New Delhi's protest against Tibetan encroachments. The latter now conceded:
The Red and Blue Lines in the (1914 Convention) map indicate the boundaries of Inner and Outer Tibet as China and Tibet . . . if Rupa, Shergaon and Kalaktang are within the territorial jurisdiction of the British government. . . . The Tibetan government have accordingly issued orders to the officer incharge of the enquiry commission of Tsona area not to call up the villagers or endeavour to levy taxes. [n. contd. overleaf]

Another argument pressed into service was that if the British took away territory which Tibet, rightly or wrongly, held to be its own, it would weaken the latter considerably in dealing with China and in reclaiming areas which it regarded to be indubitably Tibetan.[13]

As it happened, New Delhi's speed in effecting control in areas south of the Sela was painfully slow. This was largely because while the Kashag persisted in issuing written orders to its dzongpons in Talung, Dirang-dzong and Tsona, the British were determined to exhaust every resource of tact and diplomacy which, to all practical purposes, foreswore any use of force. The dzongpons themselves behaved as no better than tax-gatherers and were determined to make the largest pile they could during their brief tenures and were unscrupulous and callous to a degree. Since their own interests were intimately involved, they were more than zealous executants of orders from Lhasa and evaded, by all means possible, such regulations as the British belatedly endeavoured to introduce.[14]

In the early forties, a constitutional knot of considerable complexity, which related to a definition of the precise administrative position which these areas occupied, presented itself. It may be recalled that before the Government of India Act, 1935 was promulgated, what later constituted NEFA was defined as ' Excluded and Partially Excluded Areas ' forming part of the province of Assam. Under the new constitutional dispensation, however, their position remained somewhat anomalous. In the first place, while they were a part of India, technically this was not *British* India; in the second, while their administration was a charge on central revenues, these areas were part of the province of Assam—thereby making the charge, on federal account, irregular. New Delhi's way out of the dilemma was to seek to declare them, through an Act

Foreign Office (New Delhi), telegram, dated 20 March 1943 handed to Foreign Office (Tibetan) 24 March and Foreign Office (Tibetan), letter, to Ludlow (Additional Assistant Political Officer, Sikkim), dated Lhasa, 9 April 1943, both in Ibid.

[13]Thus, on 31 October 1944, the Tibetan Foreign Office had told Gould ' by direction of the Kashag ' that while it ' did not wish in any way to dispute the validity of the McMahon Line as determining the limits of territory in which India and Tibet respectively (subject to such minor adjustments as contemplated then) are entitled to exercise authority ', in view of the ' territorial and political settlement ' with China then pending (and which was ' a matter of overwhelming importance '), ' extension of their (British) regular administration up to the Line be postponed '.

India to Secretary of State, 4 November 1944, in *IOR*, L/P&S/12/36,/23, Part I. Also see *Officials' Report* p. IR 229.

[14]A note by J P Mills, then Advisor to the Governor of Assam on his discussions with the Tsona dzongpons and representatives of Tawang held at Dirang-dzong on 29 May (1945) is instructive:

> They admit that we are in occupation south of Sela....I trust I was successful but it strained my powers of diplomacy to the utmost to put the correct position clearly to the dzongpons without seeming to imply that their government had sent them orders which were not in accordance with the truth....

For the text *IOR*, L/P&S/12/36/29.

of the British Parliament, tribal areas.

The India Office in London, and public opinion in India, however, were deeply aroused by this proposal. It was widely believed to be part of a deep-laid conspiracy to ferret these areas out of the provincial sphere before the whole constitutional set-up went into the melting pot. Besides, their exclusion would lend support to those at the highest levels of government who had argued for keeping frontier defence, and even external relations, out of the hands of a purely Indian Government, then in the offing. Some of the tribal leaders, however, viewed the New Delhi proposals 'with dismay' and saw in it an attempt to create a 'North Eastern British protectorate' which, they presumed, would be 'a non-regulated area' ruled by '(British) political officials'. This was early in 1946.[15] Later, in July that year, a Conference of the leaders of tribal communities in Assam published a Memorandum of their demands in which, *inter alia*, they asked for 'autonomy' for the hill tribes.[16] In October 1946, the late Mr Nehru who, a few weeks earlier, had joined the 'interim' government in New Delhi as Vice-President of the Viceroy's Executive Council, took the opportunity to assure the tribal leaders of 'as much freedom and autonomy' as was consistent with 'the close association' which they had developed with the people of Assam.[17]

By May 1947, the Advisory Committee of the Indian Constituent Assembly on 'Tribal and Excluded Areas' had summed up the position fairly succinctly in a memorandum that it drew up. After pointing out that constitutionally there was a distinction between tribal and excluded areas and that the sole *de jure* tribal area in Assam was the Naga Hills, the Memorandum underlined the fact that

> through an oversight no notification for the northern boundary of the province (had been issued) and thus the whole territory upto the Indo-Tibetan frontier is *de jure* excluded area and so theoretically forms part of the province; this area however (was) never *actually* administered by the province and, in recognition of the *de facto* position, the Central Government has assumed responsibility for those parts of the Balipara, Sadiya and Tirap Frontier tracts which are truly tribal in character ... as well as that part of the Naga Hills which lies beyond the administrative boundary.

The Memorandum further listed the Balipara, Sadiya and the Lakhimpur Frontier Tracts among the seven 'Tribal and Excluded Areas' of Assam.[18]

---

[15] *Memorandum of the people of the Garo Hills, Assam* to the Chairman, British Parliamentary Delegation, 25 February 1946.

[16] *Demands of the Tribal Communities of Assam* (Conference of the Leaders of the Tribal Communities of Assam, Shillong, July 1946).

[17] *Press Information Bureau*, New Delhi, 2 October 1946.

[18] *Memorandum on the Tribal and Excluded Areas of the North-east Frontier* prepared for the Advisory Committee on tribal and excluded areas of the North West Frontier, Baluchistan and the North East Frontier (New Delhi, May 1947).

One may thus deduce that, on the eve of India's independence, New Delhi's proposals about what its detractors had called a ' North-eastern protectorate ', or a ' non-regulated area ', were overtaken by events. In any case, it should have been evident that a constitutional change of such a far-reaching character as to require Parliamentary legislation in London would, in 1946, not only have detracted from the quantum of power with which the constitution-making body in India was to be clothed but would have faced that body with an inconvenient *fait accompli*. Apart from being ill-timed and undesirable, the motives underlying it would have been grossly suspect.

It may be of some interest to note here that, on the eve of transfer of power in August 1947, the Tsongdu in Lhasa, after the fullest deliberation, placed on record its tacit acceptance of the Simla Convention and the Trade Regulations of 1914, albeit it was of the view that these should be revised in due course of time. The Tsongdu's decision is the more important insofar as, about the same time, it lodged a strong protest in Nanking against the manner in which the Tibetan goodwill mission of 1946 to that country, referred to earlier in the narrative, had been treated.

Mention has often been made of Tibet's demand on New Delhi for ' return ' of ' Tibetan territories ' all the way from Ladakh in the west to parts of NEFA in the east. Since, later in 1959, the Chinese Prime Minister made use of this communication as an expression of the Tibetan local authorities' 'dissatisfaction ' with the McMahon Line and of their demand for ' return (of) all the territory of the Tibet region of China south of this illegal line ',[19] a word about it may not be out of place here.

The cable in question was dated 16 October 1947, and was from the Tibetan (Foreign) Bureau in Lhasa. *Inter alia*, it asked for the return of territories

> such as Zayul and Walong, and in the direction of Pemakoe, Lonag, Lopa, Mon, Bhutan, Sikkim, Darjeeling and others on this side of river Ganges and Lowo, Ladakh etc. upto boundary of Yarkhim.

It should be obvious that the demands presented were far from well-defined; more, that the areas listed comprised large chunks of territory to which Tibet could lay no claim whatsoever. Understandably New Delhi's reply was couched in very general terms and took the position that it

> would be glad to have an assurance that it is the intention of the Tibetan Government to continue relations on the existing basis until new agreements are reached on matters that either party may wish to take up. This is the procedure adopted by all other countries with which India has inherited

---

[19]Letter from the Prime Minister of China to the Prime Minister of India, 8 September 1959, *White Paper*, II, pp. 27–33.

treaty relations from His Majesty's Government.[20]

Even a casual perusal of the note would make it clear that there could have been no question of entertaining claims to large areas of Indian territory, that what New Delhi sought was a 'stand still' agreement until an opportunity offered itself for bilateral talks. An eye-witness of the scene, in Lhasa, when these exchanges took place was Mr Richardson who in his person not only represented the continuity of the transformation from the British to the Indian Mission, but had first-hand knowledge of the various goings-on in the Tibetan capital on the eve of the transfer of power in India. According to him the initial Tibetan demand

> was, perhaps, an attempt to test the Indian attitude to border regions where their British predecessors had, by a series of agreements, established the frontiers of India; but it was also an example of the way in which the Tibetans interpreted the political testament of the late Dalai Lama by seeking to balance their actions towards one of their neighbours by similar action towards the other. The request to India was the counterpart of the message conveyed to the Chinese Government by the Goodwill Mission in 1946, in which they asked, in equally wide terms, for the return of all Tibetan territories still in Chinese hands.[21]

Nor, it may be noted, was there any ambiguity about the Indian response to Lhasa's 'demands'. It had been made clear that while existing agreements which India, as a successor state, would inherit from the British Government may continue, discussions about any future modifications thereof could be taken up later. And it was only after what has been called 'further deliberation for several months', that Lhasa accepted the change-over of government in India, *without* any known reservations.[22]

---

[20] Letter from the Prime Minister of India to the Prime Minister of China, 26 September 1959, *White Paper*, II, pp. 34–52.
[21] Richardson, *History*, p. 174.
[22] *Shakabapa*, p. 294.

Epilogue

THE BRITISH quit India in August 1947, handing over power to two newly emergent dominions of India and Pakistan. As it worked out, Tibet and the North-east Frontier, by geographic compulsion, became a charge on the residuary state of India—Pakistan, with no physical contiguity, had precious little to do with either. For all practical purposes, therefore, in the pages that follow New Delhi's responsibilities, as a successor state, towards Tibet and the eastern frontier remain as they were in the earlier part of this study.

Following closely on the emergence of India as an independent state, a revolution of gigantic proportions brought the Communist Party to power in Peking. As a direct corollary, by 1949, the KMT regime of Chiang Kai-shek was driven to Taiwan where it remains to date, the sole repository of all that the 'Republic of China' had stood for. Not long after they took over, an early objective the Communists proclaimed was the 'liberation' of Tibet from the alleged intrigues and machinations of western imperialists, and the manner and mode thereof had the most profound inpact, among others, on relations with India—and on the frontier.

After the British quit in August 1947, New Delhi continued, at an accelerated pace, the left-over legacy of making its authority good and effective right up to the farthest limits of the eastern frontier. Significant as British departure was, an event of no small import that synchronised with it was an attempted *coup d'etat* in Lhasa led by an ex-Regent. The latter had not only sought the intervention of Generalissimo Chiang Kai-shek but claimed the powerful backing of a pro-Chinese faction in the Sera monastery, located a stone's throw from the Tibetan capital. A Tibetan writer views the conspiracy, with its dark shadow of 'mystery, fear and intrigue', as constituting a 'threat' of a 'possible' civil strife. Mr Richardson, an eye-witness, saw in it not so much a proof of 'internal dissensions' as of 'continuing Chinese machinations' at a time when, with an independent India in the offing, Tibet's traditional links with the British were on the point of being severed.[1] Predictably, Dr Li views it as a conspiracy of the 'predominantly pro-British Young Tibet' party.[2] As events in China itself were moving fast towards a Communist take-over, the attempted coup in Lhasa assumed added importance. Meanwhile, New Delhi, shortly after independence, stationed an Indian official at Tawang while a military post at Walong, in the Lohit valley, had been established a little earlier. In

---

[1] For details, *Shakabapa*, pp. 292–94 and Richardson, *History*, pp. 169–72.
[2] Li, *Tibet*, pp. 187–88.

the Subansiri area, thanks to the remarkably patient work of Furer-Haimendorff and Ursula Graham Bower, a great deal more was known about the Apa Tanis and the Miris.[3]

An interesting innovation brought about at this time was the administrative reorganisation of the entire eastern frontier into what has since been known as the North East Frontier Agency, NEFA for short. To man it was established a newly constituted administrative personnel—the Indian Frontier Administrative Service—under the direct control of the Ministry of External Affairs in New Delhi. Nor, as Verrier Elwin later explained in his *A Philosophy for NEFA*, was there any intent to exploit the area or its people to narrow, selfish, ends. In the late Mr Nehru's words, the objective was to help the tribal people to 'grow according to their own genius and traditions', and not to 'impose' anything on them.[4]

Soon after India became independent, there were considerable stresses and strains in its relationship with China owing principally to the latter's approach towards Tibet. Not unlike the Kuomintang before them, the Chinese Communists viewed the country as an integral part of the mainland where all that needed to be done was to 'liberate' it from 'imperialist oppression'.[5] It is not necessary to rehearse here the oft-repeated story of the events that preceded Tibet's 'liberation' in October 1950 but, relevant to the narrative, a few salient points need to be underlined.

At the outset it may be noted that, until 1949, before the Communists completed the establishment of an apparently stable control over mainland China, the Lhasa Government did not regard itself as subordinate to Peking. And yet, before long, it was ready, and indeed prepared, to negotiate with the Communist regime a new treaty arrangement that would be mutually acceptable. Thus a Tibetan delegation had arrived in New Delhi, *en route* to Peking, in August 1950 and conducted some preliminary *pourparlers* with the (Communist) Chinese Ambassador stationed there. When intimated that further talks could take place only in Peking, it left New Delhi for Calcutta, on its

---

[3] Christoph von Furer-Haimendorff, *The Apa Tanis and Their Neighbours* (London, 1962), and Ursula Graham Bower, *The Hidden Land* (New York, 1963).

[4] Verrier Elwin, *A Philosophy for NEFA*, Second Edition (Shillong, 1959).

[5] *Hsinhua* (New China News Agency) release, 24 October 1950.

The release stated, *inter alia*, that before the 'liberation', the 'United States and British Imperialists' had continued to send spies and arms into Tibet.

A Chinese scholar, Dr Yao-ting Sung who was a functionary of the Kuomintang and had served a brief tenure in Hsi-kang, came to the conclusion that two considerations were of 'paramount importance' in solving the Tibetan question. The first was the security of Western China, which is the 'primary concern' of the Chinese and revolves around Tibet; the second, the preservation of Buddhist religion and of 'an independent way of life' which were Lhasa's minimum demands. The lack of an 'adequate adjustment of these conflicting interests' had been responsible for their mutual discord. His own solution, which he terms 'the most feasible arrangement': 'conditional independence'. *Yao-ting Sung*, pp. 210–11.

It may be noted, if in passing, that Dr Sung's study was completed in 1949, before the Chinese Communists ousted the Kuomintang from the mainland.

way to the Chinese capital, on 25 October but before the last leg of its journey could commence, events had completely overtaken it. For on 7 October, the People's Liberation Army had marched into Tibet and, less than a fortnight later, Chamdo had fallen to its advance guards.[6]

Another point that bears emphasis is that, prior to the 'liberation', the Indian government did use its good offices to put the Tibetans into touch with the new masters of Peking. Thus negotiations between the Tibetans and the Chinese in New Delhi, in August–September 1950, were brought about through Indian contacts. Again, it was India that informed Peking in October that the Tibetans were proceeding thither 'immediately'. All this notwithstanding, at no stage is India known to have offered to act as an intermediary. One would suspect that New Delhi had learnt the lessons so powerfully impressed upon the British in the crisis of the early thirties although, as would be noticed presently, even for its new role of a go-between it was not only suspect but earned some stern, if ill-deserved, rebuke.[7]

The maximum, however, that Tibet's 'liberation' produced was a sharp, wordy duel between New Delhi and Peking which, other things apart, underlined a remarkable divergence in their respective outlooks *vis-à-vis* the Tibetan question. New Delhi, for its part, as its Memorandum of 21 October had pointed out, deplored 'military action'; was convinced that by resort to it the Chinese position 'will be weakened'; more, it remained throughout a powerful advocate of 'peaceful negotiations'. As to Tibet's status, its Note of 31 October was fairly eloquent, underlining as it did

> the legitimate Tibetan claim to autonomy within the framework of Chinese suzerainty.... Tibetan autonomy is a fact which ... the Chinese Government were themselves willing to recognise and foster....[8]

As for itself, its repeated suggestion

> was not, as the Chinese Government seem to suggest, unwarranted interference in China's internal affairs, but well-meant advice by a friendly

---

[6] For graphic, first-hand accounts of the Chinese 'liberation' of Tibet, see Robert Ford, *Captured in Tibet* (London, 1957) and Dalai Lama, *My Land and My People* (London, 1962).
Also see Heinrich Harrer, *Seven Years in Tibet* (London, 1953), as well as Richardson, Li, Shakabapa, op.cit., and the International Commission of Jurists, *Tibet and the People's Republic of China* (Geneva, 1960).

[7] For the Indian Memorandum of 21 October 1950 and texts of the subsequent notes exchanged between New Delhi and Peking see Carlyle (Editor), *Documents on International Affairs* (Oxford, 1953).
In its 'note' of 30 October Peking accused the Tibetan delegations of having 'intentionally delayed' its departure for Peking 'under outside instigation'. Later, in the text, New Delhi was directly charged with having been affected 'by foreign influences hostile to China'.

[8] Indian note of 31 October 1950. It is interesting to recall that in reproducing it, the Chinese consistently substituted the word 'sovereignty' wherever the Indian version had used 'suzerainty'. For the Chinese version see *Hsinhua*, Supplement No.59, 21 November 1950

government which has a natural interest in the solution of problems concerning its neighbours by peaceful methods.

To Peking, both the tone and content of India's 'Notes' were unwelcome. Its reply, dated 30 October, stated *inter alia* that

> Tibet is an integral part of the Chinese territory and the problem of Tibet is entirely a domestic problem of China. The Chinese People's Liberation Army must enter Tibet, liberate the Tibetan people, and defend the frontiers of China....

After this, one need hardly waste any breath on Tibet's status, as viewed from Peking. For it is significant that in its own version of the Indian notes, the term 'sovereignty' was substituted wherever 'suzerainty' had been mentioned in the (Indian) text. Again, in its 16 November reply, Peking rubbed in *ad nauseam* China's 'sovereignty' and 'sovereign rights', apart from an emphasis on the 'protection of the integrity' of its territory. Equally it expressed itself as 'greatly surprised' that New Delhi had 'attempted to influence and obstruct' the exercise of China's 'sovereign rights' in Tibet even though it welcomed

> the renewed declaration of the Indian Government that it has no political or territorial ambitions in *China's Tibet* and that it does not seek any new privileged position.

By May 1951, 'negotiations' between Tibetan 'delegates' and Chinese officials in Peking had resulted in a 17-point 'Agreement on Measures for the Peaceful Liberation of Tibet'. *Inter alia*, the agreement assured the 'Tibetan nationality' that

> all nationalities within the boundaries of the Chinese People's Republic are equal and that they shall establish unity and mutual aid and oppose imperialism and their own public enemies, so that the C.P.R. will become a big family of fraternity and co-operation, composed of all its nationalities.[9]

One is struck by the remarkable similarity of this jargon with the 'imperialist lackey' Yuan Shih-kai's Presidential 'mandates' about the equality of the five races, within the fraternity of the Great Motherland!

In April 1954, New Delhi concluded an 'Agreement on Trade and Intercourse between Tibet Region of China and India'. In Notes exchanged on the occasion, which were to constitute 'an agreement' in their own right, New Delhi undertook, among other things, to 'withdraw' its military escorts, 'hand over' the postal, telegraph and public telephone services 'along with their

---

[9] For the text, *Hsinhua*, 23 May 1951.

equipment', as also the twelve rest-houses which it owned en route. After exactly half a century since Younghusband marched to Lhasa in 1904, the wheel appears to have come round full circle.

The April 1954 Agreement constituted an important landmark in the history of Sino-Indian relations, for *inter alia* it enshrined the five principles of ' Panch Shila '. The latter were viewed at the time not only as eloquent of the peace and amity that had characterised Sino-Indian relations in the past but as harbingers of their future concord.[10] The euphoria about ' Hindi-Chini Bhai Bhai ' reached a new pitch with an exchange of visits between the two Prime Ministers, providing occasions for considerable mass hysteria. On the surface, at any rate, Tibet and the frontier dispute seemed a long way off if not indeed forgotten.

The rift in the lute, however, was soon apparent if, for the moment, cleverly hidden from the public gaze. Against the powerful current that seemed to sweep nearly everyone away, a few lone voices could still be heard, though the prevalent din made them almost inaudible. One of these was that of Sir Olaf Caroe. In a letter to the *Times*, in November 1954, he pin-pointed in particular the problem of the North-eastern frontier and underlined the fact that China's

> absorption of Tibet now makes the location of this frontier a matter of direct international dispute between herself (China) and India. In effect she may claim a slice of Indian territory measuring 250 by 100 miles in extent. This is much more than infiltration.

Sir Olaf warned too against Imperial China's expansionist role, ' as opportunity offered and strength allowed ', and underlined its relevance:

> That the tradition holds in Communist China, as in Soviet Russia, is proved by the absorption of Tibet.[11]

As later events were to bear out powerfully, the ink on the 1954 agreement was scarcely dry when reports about Chinese incursions across the frontier began to pour in. The first of these related to Bara Hoti, not far from Nepal's border. As the years rolled by, the ' incidents ' swelled both in number and resultant bitterness. Nor did discussions help: in argument, the Chinese proved unyielding, intractable. The cartographic aggression continued too, and unabated. In contrast to the frontier infiltra-

---

[10] For the text, *White Paper*, I, pp. 98–105. The actual handing over took place at Lhasa on 1 April 1955. *Survey of China Mainland Press*, 2–4 April 1955, pp. 1–2.

For a commentary on the agreement see P L Mehra ' India, China and Tibet, 1950–54 ', *India Quarterly*, XII, 1, January–March 1956, pp. 3–22.

[11] Sir Olaf Caroe, letter to the *Times*, under the heading ' Mr. Nehru and China', 11 October 1954. Extracts from the letter were reproduced in the *Hindu* (Madras), on 6 November 1954.

tions, which New Delhi for years scrupulously enshrouded in secrecy, the published maps could neither be hidden nor wished away.

In fairness to Mr Nehru, it must be said that he was not oblivious of the Chinese threat, even though it took him time to be fully aroused. Thus in October 1954 when the Indian Prime Minister was on a visit to China:

> In the course of our talks I briefly mentioned to you (Chou En-lai) that I had seen some maps recently published in China which gave a wrong borderline between the two countries. I presumed that this was by some error and told you at the time that so far as India was concerned we were not much worried about the matter because our boundaries were quite clear and were not a matter of argument. You were good enough to reply to me that these maps were really reproductions of old pre-liberation maps and that you had had no time to revise them. In view of the many and heavy preoccupations of your Government, I could understand that this revision had not taken place till then. I expressed the hope that the borderline would be corrected before long.

Later, towards the end of 1956, when Chou En-lai paid an extended return visit to India, Nehru again brought up the question of the eastern frontier. The Chinese Prime Minister, who had earlier talked over matters concerning the Sino-Burmese frontier with the Burmese Prime Minister U Nu, referred to the McMahon Line. Nehru recalled that he remembered

> your (Chou) telling me that you did not approve of this border being called the McMahon Line and I replied that I did not like that name either. But for facility of reference you referred to it as such.

> You told me then that you had accepted this McMahon Line border with Burma and, whatever might have happened long ago, in view of the friendly relations which existed between China and India, you proposed to recognise this border with India also. You added that you would like to consult the authorities of the Tibet region of China and you proposed to do so.

Later, the Prime Minister penned a minute to keep a record of this talk, ' for our personal and confidential ' use. The relevant part read:

> Premier Chou referred to the McMahon Line and again said that he had never heard of this before though of course the then Chinese Government had dealt with this matter and not accepted that line. He had gone into this matter in connection with the border dispute with Burma. Although he thought that this line established by British Imperialists was not fair, nevertheless, because it was an accomplished fact and because of the friendly relations which existed between China and the countries concerned, namely

India and Burma, the Chinese Government were of the opinion that they should give recognition to this McMahon Line. They had, however, not consulted the Tibetan authorities about it yet. They proposed to do so.[12]

The subject, Nehru recalled, had been discussed 'at some considerable length' and the Chinese Prime Minister had been 'good enough' to make this point 'quite clear'.

Unfortunately for Nehru, and India, Chou's thinking was completely at variance. He had no doubt discussed the question with Nehru, as with U Nu, but as

> you (Nehru) are aware, the McMahon Line was a product of the British policy of aggression against the Tibet region of China and aroused the great indignation of the Chinese people. Juridically, too, it cannot be considered legal. I have told you that it has never been recognised by the Chinese Central Government. Although related documents were signed by a representative of the local authorities of the Tibet region of China, the Tibet local authorities were in fact dissatisfied with this unilaterally drawn line. And I have told you formally about their dissatisfaction.

Despite all this, however, Chou was prepared to give the matter another thought,

> In view of the various complex factors mentioned ... the Chinese Government on the one hand finds it necessary to take a more or less realistic attitude towards the McMahon Line, on the other hand, cannot but act with prudence and needs time to deal with this matter.[13]

The tyro that Nehru was in foreign affairs, his flair for them notwithstanding, Chou's epistle must have been a great shock, though not perhaps such a surprise. The Chinese Prime Minister had questioned not only the validity of the McMahon Line but, what was worse, the whole basis of the Sino-Indian boundary which, he maintained, had 'never been formally delimited'. More, Chou made it clear that historically 'no treaty or agreement' concerning it 'has ever been concluded' between the Chinese and Indian governments. Nothing could have been more disturbing to New Delhi's *amour-propre*, for China now threw into the maelstrom of the crucible the whole basis of what India had long regarded as a settled fact of life!

Replying to the Chinese Prime Minister on 22 March 1959, Nehru recalled the 1914 Simla Convention:

> The Line was drawn after full discussion and was confirmed subsequently

[12] Nehru to Chou En-lai, 14 December 1958, *White Paper*, I, pp. 48–51.
[13] Chou En-lai to Nehru, 23 January 1959, Ibid., pp. 52–54.

by a formal exchange of letters; and there is nothing to indicate that the Tibetan authorities were in any way dissatisfied with the agreed boundary. Moreover ... there is no mention of any Chinese reservation in respect of the India-Tibet frontier either during the discussions or at the time of their initialling the Convention.[14]

Again, as Nehru was quick to point out, the line had the advantage of running along the crest of the high Himalayan range which, in this sector, formed a 'natural dividing line' between the Tibetan plateau in the north and the submontane region in the south.

Chou's reply to Nehru's letter was despatched on 26 September. He realled that the McMahon Line 'was never discussed' at the Simla Conferencec; that it was determined 'behind the back' of the Chinese representative; that it was 'a product of the British policy of aggression'; that it had 'never been recognised' by China and was 'decidedly illegal'. What was more,

for quite a long time after the exchange of secret notes (March 1914)... Britain dared not make public the related documents, nor change the traditional way of drawing this section of the boundary on maps.

Chou recalled too that 'great indignation' had been aroused in China and that in 1947 Lhasa had asked for the return of all the territory of the Tibet region 'south of this illegal line'.

As for accepting it now:

Mr Prime Minister, how could China agree to accept under coercion such an illegal line which would have it relinquish its rights and disgrace itself by selling out its territory—and such a large piece of territory as that.

The correct position, Chou maintained, was that the

delineation of the Sino-Indian boundary east of Bhutan in all traditional Chinese maps is a true reflection of the actual situation of the customary boundary before the appearance of the so-called McMahon Line.[15]

The Indian Prime Minister tried to put the record straight by pointing to a number of relevant facts which have been noticed at length in the preceding pages. Briefly, negotiations at Simla were tripartite and this with China's fullest knowledge and concurrence; the boundaries of Tibet, both with China and India, were the Conference's major preoccupation; the Chinese representative at Simla was fully aware of the McMahon Line—indeed, he appended his signature, not initials, at three places on the map (attached to the Convention)

[14]Nehru to Chou En-lai, 22 March 1959, Ibid,. pp. 55–57.
[15]Chou En-lai to Nehru, 8 September 1959, *White Paper*, II, pp. 27–33.

over which he (and his government) must have pored for weeks before signing it, as also the Convention, on 27 April. Neither on 25 April, nor on 13 June (1914) when China retailed its objections to the Convention's terms, as also the map, was the question of the Indo-Tibetan boundary even remotely mentioned. Nor, as we have seen, was it brought up five years later when, on 30 May 1919, Peking presented fresh proposals for a 'final' settlement. As to holding up publication for years, the hope was that a settlement with China would be reached both as to Tibet's status as also the boundaries of Outer/Inner Tibet. Later when the treaties were published in Aitchison's 1929 edition, and the maps amended accordingly, 'neither then nor subsequently' was 'any objection' raised by the Chinese authorities.[16]

The wordy duel which took the form of these epistolary exchanges—and with time it grew sharper in tone, and ever more bitter—was bad enough. What was worse was that Peking synchronised it with large-scale deployment of force to give shape and form and put substance into its territorial claims. This was more true of Ladakh in the Western sector where not only a road had been built through the Aksai Chin plateau, but large chunks of territory that lay to the south of it were claimed by the establishment of military posts in what was, at worst, disputed territory.

The pattern of events in the eastern sector was no whit different. Thus in 1957, Chinese survey parties had moved, in force, into the Lohit division while in August 1959, they overpowered the Indian outpost at Longju and took the (Indian) personnel stationed there prisoner.

For once, the cartographic aggression had developed teeth!

II

THE DELHI-PEKING war of words which synchronised with an actual deployment of force by the two sides and some stray 'incidents' that followed in its wake had, by 1959, made the situation along the border extremely explosive.

As the long citations in the preceding section, culled from the exchanges between the heads of government in the two countries, lay bare there was a wide chasm that now separated them with regard to their respective thinking on the McMahon Line. This was no less true of differences in other sectors of the boundary, as indeed in regard to the maps. As a matter of fact, so wide was the gap that by the end of 1959 it was clear, even to the most casual of observers, that there was a complete breakdown in communications. It may perhaps bear mention here that the March 1959 rebellion in Lhasa, which resulted in the flight of the Dalai Lama and a large influx of Tibetan refugees that followed, helped further to muddy the waters between New Delhi and Peking. The latter now openly charged the former with complicity

[16]Nehru to Chou En-lai, 26 September 1959, Ibid., pp. 34-52. An 'annexure' provided 'A Note on the Border Disputes'.

in the Lhasa Rebellion and with shielding armed Tibetan rebels in its frontier areas on the north-east. Even though stoutly denied in New Delhi, these allegations could only serve to worsen the already tense situation that now prevailed in the relations between the two countries.[17]

An aspect of the dispute which comes out clearly and bears mention here was Nehru's apparent anxiety to avoid, 'at almost any cost', a head-on confrontation with China. It is not without significance that despite what had happened in Ladakh, on the Aksai Chin, at Bara Hoti, in Longju, not to mention his long exchanges with the Chinese Prime Minister, Nehru had kept things entirely to himself. To be precise, it was not until 28 August 1959 that he told a shocked parliament, and through it the country, that the Chinese had built a highway through the Aksai Chin. More, another two years were to elapse before he was willing to concede that the border incursions were not isolated instances but part of a general probing of India's defences by the Chinese army, poised for an attack all along the frontier.

Typical of New Delhi's approach at this time was the fact that the first reconnaissance party to the Aksai Chin in Ladakh—preliminary intelligence reports regarding Chinese road-building activity had reached the Indian Government between October 1957 and February 1958—was not sent until the middle of 1959 and then only *after* informing the Chinese Government![18] The latter responded by arresting and detaining Indian patrols for a whole month during which confessions were sought to be extorted from them![19] Nehru's anxiety not to annoy Peking may also be manifest in his steadfast refusal to encourage the Dalai Lama—and this despite a loud public clamour to the contrary—to engage in any political activity on Indian soil.[20] This gave much-needed ammunition to his political adversaries who accused him of leaning over backwards to appease China.

After Nehru's long and unusually detailed letter of 26 September (1959) referred to earlier, there was a marked shift in emphasis in the diplomatic exchanges between the two leaders. Thus in his reply, Chou in place of an elaborate rejoinder, dismissed the entire data marshalled by New Delhi with the solitary remark that it completely 'disregards', in many respects, the 'basic facts' of the boundary. To avert clashes in future—and some serious

---

[17]*Inter alia,* Nehru wrote to Chou:

The charge that India has been shielding armed Tibetan rebels in the frontier areas in the north-east is wholly unfounded and we firmly reject it. On the contrary, our personnel disarmed the Tibetan rebels as soon as they crossed the frontier ... the few who showed disinclination ... were told ... would not get asylum in India and made to leave our territory finally.

Nehru to Chou En-lai, 26 September 1959, *White Paper,* II, pp. 34–52.

[18]Nehru's statement in the Lok Sabha, 28 August 1959, in Jawaharlal Nehru, *India's Foreign Policy* (New Delhi, 1961), p. 328.

[19]For details of the Indian and Chinese versions, *White Paper,* II, pp. 13–24.

[20]Nehru's statement in the Lok Sabha, 28 April 1959, *India's Foreign Policy,* pp. 319–26.

ones had already taken place, albeit not on the north-east frontier—and help improve a fast-deteriorating situation, Chou proposed

> that the armed forces of China and India should each withdraw 20 kilometres at once from the so-called McMahon Line in the east, and from the line upto which each side exercises actual control in the west and that the two sides undertake to refrain from again sending their armed personnel to be stationed in and patrol the zones from which they have evacuated their armed forces....

Peking also put forth the view that, in order to discuss the boundary question further, the two Prime Ministers 'hold talks' in the 'immediate future'.[21]

New Delhi's response was cold and sceptical for in between, in October 1959, had intervened a gruesome clash in the Chang Chenmo valley in Ladakh. Here the Chinese had inflicted heavy casualties on an Indian police patrol and, for a time, held back the prisoners and the dead bodies despite repeated demands for their surrender—a fact which aroused public opinion to a fever pitch. Coupled with the fact that there really were no Indian armed personnel manning the check posts, as New Delhi had pointed out in its reply, this made it difficult for the latter to accept the Chinese proposal for a 20-kilometre withdrawal. *Inter alia*, Nehru had underlined that

> on our North-east frontier, the entire territory up to the border ... has been for long years part of India. Our civil administration has been functioning there.... At no point, except at Longju, are Chinese forces in occupation of any area south of the Indian border. The boundary in this area passes over a terrain, the height of which varies from 14,000 to 20,000 feet above sea level. In this extremely difficult terrain, almost all our border check posts are situated on high hill features.... It would be extremely difficult in practice to establish a new line of outposts in the rear, where they are to be ten or twenty kilometres from the international boundary.

There was another serious difficulty—the two sides were in a complete deadlock as to what each viewed as the real facts of the boundary. It followed that

> an agreement about the observance of the status quo would, therefore, be meaningless as the facts concerning the status quo are themselves disputed.

New Delhi's counter suggestion, therefore, for preventing clashes was that the two sides should strictly enforce a ban on all armed border patrols. What was more to the purpose, in order to lay down a basis for talks between the two

---

[21] Chou En-lai to Nehru, 7 November 1959, *White Paper*, III, pp. 45–46.

Prime Ministers, who might get bogged down 'in a forest' of data, it was 'necessary'

> that some 'preliminary steps' were taken and the foundation for our discussion laid.[22]

Chou's response to Nehru's proposals was argumentative. He reiterated his earlier view that the withdrawal of armed forces by the two sides to a depth of 20 kilometres would 'thoroughly' eliminate the risk of border clashes but was prepared to apply to the whole frontier the Indian proposal (specifically made *vis-à-vis* Longju) about the non-stationing of armed forces in disputed places, as also the ban on armed patrols from the frontier outposts. After furnishing what he called 'eloquent proof' that the Aksai Chin area had always been under Chinese jurisdiction, Chou turned his attention to the eastern frontier and recalled that 'up to now' his government had made no demand in regard to the area south of 'the so-called' McMahon Line, either as a pre-condition or an interim measure. In this context, he emphasised that up to the 1938 edition of the Survey of India maps, the delineation of the eastern section of the boundary 'still corresponded' to what was shown on Chinese maps.

Why 'suddenly in recent years', Chou queried, had the un-delimited boundary been changed into a delimited boundary? He rubbed in what he viewed as a major Chinese 'concession' and stressed that although the McMahon Line

> has never been recognised by past Chinese governments, nor by the Government of the People's Republic of China, yet (the latter) ... has strictly abided by its statement of absolutely not allowing its armed personnel to cross this line in waiting for a friendly settlement of the boundary question.... China ... has not even stepped into the vast area ... which, not long ago, was still under the jurisdiction of the local government of the Tibet region of China.

In contrast, the Chinese Prime Minister emphasised, New Delhi had taken 'an unreasonable attitude' of 'refusing to discuss' the eastern sector of the border while laying territorial claims to an area in the western sector 'which has never been' under its rule.

Polemics apart, Chou proposed a 'speedy' holding of talks between the two Prime Ministers

> so as to reach first some agreement of principles as a guidance to concrete discussions and settlement of the boundary question by the two sides....

[22]Nehru to Chou En-lai, 16 November 1959, Ibid., pp. 47–51.

(Without it) concrete discussions ... may bog down in endless and fruitless debates ....

He even proposed a date—26 December.[23]

Unfortunately for Chou's anxiety for an early meeting, Nehru's rejoinder was a complete damper:

How can we, Mr Prime Minister, reach an agreement on principles when there is such complete disagreement about the facts?[24]

Not in December 1959—as Chou had initially proposed—but towards the close of April 1960, the two Prime Ministers did, however, meet in New Delhi. At the end of six days (April 19–25) of talks, differences on the boundary remained unresolved, although what was euphemistically called 'a better appreciation of the points of view' of the two governments was said to have been achieved. A concrete outcome of the meeting was an agreement

that officials of the two Governments should meet and examine, check and study all historical documents, records, accounts, maps and other material relevant to the boundary question, on which each side relied in support of its stand, and draw up a report for submission to the two Governments. This report would list the points on which there was agreement and the points on which there was disagreement or which should be examined more fully and clarified. This report should prove helpful towards further consideration of these problems by the two Governments.[25]

The officials were to meet between June and September—alternately in the capitals of the two countries—and by the latter date complete their findings.

The 'Officials' Report', as it came to be called, was published in February 1961 and is an extremely useful documentary study of the frontier dispute between India and China.[26] Significantly, the only common ground discovered seems to have been an outer cover which holds the two distinct, and entirely disparate reports together! For apart from a brief, 3-paged, 'joint statement' furnishing the background to their talks and forwarding the 'Report' to their respective governments, each side gives its own version even of the statement leading to the adoption of an 'Agreed Agenda' and, of course, wrote its own report.

[23]Chou En-lai to Nehru, 17 December 1959, Ibid., pp. 52–57.
[24]Nehru to Chou En-lai, 21 December 1959, Ibid., pp. 58–59.
[25] 'Joint Communique issued by the two Prime Ministers' New Delhi, 25 April 1960, cited in *Officials' Report*, infra, n. 10, p.1.
[26]*Report of the Officials of the Government of India and the People's Republic of China on the Boundary Question* (Ministry of External Affairs, New Delhi, February 1961) cited, et seq., as *Officials' Report*.

Epilogue

The 'Agreed Agenda' for the meetings of the officials listed the subject-matter thus:

1. Location and Terrain Features of the Boundary;
2. Treaties and Agreements, Tradition and Custom;
3. Administration and Jurisdiction;
4. Miscellaneous.

Items 1 and 2 were to be dealt with separately for the entire length of the boundary, while items 3 and 4 were to be treated sector-wise.[27]

In the preceding pages, a great deal of ground in regard to the eastern frontier has been covered in the light of all available documentary evidence. The reader would thus have what may be called a reasonably objective assessment of how the McMahon Line came to be drawn both before it was put on the map in 1914 and of what happened to it in the years that have elapsed since. It would therefore help understanding if the Chinese viewpoint, as spelt out by their officials, is now stated and, for the most part, in their own words.

One of the important Chinese contentions has been that Tibet had no *locus standi* to conclude a treaty, for it

> is a part of Chinese territory and China enjoys full sovereignty over Tibet. This premise denies Tibet the right to conclude treaties separately with foreign countries independently of the Chinese Central Government. Unless authorised and consented to by the Chinese Central Government, the Tibet local authorities have no right to conclude treaties with foreign countries....[28]

To the argument that, before the Conference, China had accepted Tibet's status as an equal, represented by its own Plenipotentiary, and that this fact was not challenged during the Conference, Peking's rejoinder was that this did

> not tally with the facts. It was only because Britain insisted on the Tibet representative attending the Conference on an equal footing ... that the Chinese Government stated that 'the Chinese representative would go to India in any circumstances'. This was a statement of reserving its opinion as there was no other way out. It absolutely cannot be considered as an indication of accepting the British demand.

Again, in the course of the Conference

> the Chinese representative still raised objections repeatedly. For example, in the proposal of the Chinese representative put forward on 30 October

[27] Ibid., p. I R (Indian Report), 12.
[28] Ibid., p. C R (Chinese Report) 25.

1913, apart from stating that 'Tibet forms an integral part of the territory of the Republic of China', it was particularly pointed out that 'Tibet undertakes to be guided by China in her foreign and military affairs and not to enter into negotiation with any foreign power except through the intermediary of the Chinese Government'. Another example: on 15 April 1914, in his talks with Rose... the Chinese representative first of all raised an objection to the equal standing given to Tibet *vis-à-vis* China and Britain in the preamble of the draft Simla Convention.

China recognised that the representative of the Tibet region 'signed' the Simla agreement,

> but they have always clearly pointed out at the same time that this is illegal, and that Tibet has no right to conclude treaties separately.[29]

The question of the Sino-Indian (actually Indo-Tibetan) boundary and how it evolved out of the bilateral discussions between the British delegate and Lonchen Shatra was raised too:

> True, at that time the Chinese representative and the British representative did conduct bilateral discussions. But the question is: why was it that the results of discussions between the Chinese and British representatives could not constitute an agreement, but must be referred to the plenary session, while only the so-called McMahon Line required a secret exchange of notes and did not need to be referred to the plenary session? It was precisely because the question of the Sino-Indian boundary was never put forward at the Simla Conference, that the Chinese representative did not and could not raise any objection.... It can be seen from the counter-proposals of the Chinese representative made at the Conference on 30 October 1913, ... (which) unequivocally demanded that Britain must not annex Tibet or any portion of it.[30]

The Chinese started with the premise that not only was the McMahon Line 'illegal' and 'null and void' and could not constitute 'a legal basis for the boundary', but also that

> the Simla Convention is even more unrelated to the question of the Sino-Indian boundary. Since the Indian side insisted... the Chinese could not but go further into this question.[31]

Its illegality sprang out of the British

[29]Ibid., p. C R 26.
[30]Ibid., pp. C R 23–24.
[31]Ibid., p. C R 19.

unilaterally changing the traditional customary line in the eastern sector of the boundary, and a line which Britain tried to impose on China.[32]

The aim of the British imperialists at Simla was

> to push, in collusion with the Tibet local Government, the dividing line between Tibet and the other parts of China eastwards and north-eastwards into the administrative districts of the various provinces in north-west and south-west China.[33]

The Indian argument that the McMahon Line did not delimit a fresh boundary but confirmed an existing one, that in a mountainous terrain the international boundary must, of necessity, be consistent with the boundary following the watershed, was dismissed with scant grace, for such

> an assertion . . . in total disregard of the various complicated factors involved in forming a traditional customary line is obviously erroneous. . . . Geographical features have a certain bearing . . . but they are by no means the only or decisive factor. . . . It is thus evident that the argument . . . that the Sino-Indian boundary must consistently run along the main watershed is untenable.[34]

Peking also pressed into service another line of reasoning, namely that no Chinese regime had accepted the McMahon Line. Even the Chiang Kai-shek 'clique', it pointed out, had in July, September and November 1946 and again in January as well as February 1947 sent notes 'protesting against the British gradual invasion into the Chinese area in the eastern sector' north of the traditional customary line. Again, Peking maintained, as late as 1949 the KMT Ambassador in India

> sent a note to the Indian Ministry of External Affairs, repudiating the Simla Convention which the Indian Government held to be valid.[35]

Tibet too, New Delhi was reminded, had made protests—in 1944, 1945 and 1951—and expressed the hope 'that the original status of the boundary in the Monyul area will be maintained', as before. *Inter alia*, Lhasa had accused the Indian Government of

> seizing as its own what did not belong to it. This we (Tibet) deeply regret and absolutely cannot accept. . . . Please tell the Indian Government at

[32]Ibid., p. C R 24.
[33]Ibid., p. C R 173.
[34]Ibid., p. C R 177.
[35]Ibid., pp. C R 24–25.

once.... to withdraw immediately the officers and soldiers who have arrived in Tawang.[36]

Another argument was that as a result of 'repeated representations' made by Tibet,

the British Government was compelled in 1944 to express willingness to change the so-called McMahon Line by marking the boundary in the Mon-yul area south of Tawang between the so-called McMahon Line and the traditional customary line maintained by China.... It shows that even the British felt the so-called McMahon Line invalid and difficult to cling to....[37]

What was more,

in the course of negotiations between the Tibet local Government and the British Government, the latter more than once offered to return to Tibet that tract of territory north of Sela.[38]

Since the scope of this study is limited to the first half of this century, it has not been deemed necessary to dig up the bones of the 5th Dalai Lama and of his disciple Mera Lama, who brought 'politico-religious rule' to Mon-yul in the 17th century. For much the same reason 'the pledges, avowals etc.' of 'contemporary officials and people' in Tibet, affirming their determination 'not (to) allow the sovereignty of the frontiers' of the Motherland to be threatened, have been kept out.[39] Only one observation is called for and it is to the effect that there was a broad consensus of opinion, both in India and the world outside, that as between the two, New Delhi's case on the frontier, while by no means fool-proof, was sounder, rested on a reasonably solid sub-stratum of factual data and was indeed more convincingly put forth.

Between the presentation of the Officials' Report in December 1960[40] and the large-scale offensive mounted by the Chinese in October–November 1962, two developments of some significance intervene. The first relates to the conclusion, on 1 October 1960, of the Sino-Burmese boundary treaty which affected the eastern sector directly. It would be evident that the western

---

[36] Ibid., p. C R 153.
[37] Ibid., p. C R 172.
Earlier the Chinese had maintained that
in the course of negotiations between the Tibet local Government and the British Government, the latter more than once offered to return to Tibet that tract of territory north of Sela.
[38] *Supra*, n. 20.
[39] Ibid., pp. C R 44–46.
[40] The *Officials' Report* was signed in Rangoon on 12 December 1960 and published later in February 1961. *Supra*, n. 10.

extremity of the Burma-China boundary, now settled, touched the easternmost point of the India-China boundary. New Delhi was, therefore, quick to point out that the tri-junction of India, Burma and China was five miles to the north of the Dipu L'ka pass, and *not* at the pass itself. While it is true, India contended, that the text of the treaty had left the exact location of this point unspecified, the fact was that the attached map had shown it in an 'erroneous manner'.[41] The Chinese response was that the question of the tri-junction could be taken up only when a 'reasonable settlement' of the boundary question with India itself came up.[42]

Another issue, though not directly related to the eastern boundary, was the holding of Sino-Pakistani border talks. New Delhi protested that the Chinese were 'seeking to exploit' the troubled situation in Kashmir and 'India's differences with Pakistan' to their own advantage.[43] Peking's rejoinder was a homily on 'friendship among Asian countries and peace in Asia' and its counter-charge that New Delhi was making use of Sino-Pakistani negotiations 'to whip up anti-Chinese sentiments'. The sting, however, was in the tail:

> Would it not be better (for India) to make some earnest effort towards a peaceful settlement of the Sino-Indian boundary question, rather than wasting its strength in such fruitless quarrel?[44]

Name-calling could not have gone further. Already the euphoria of Hindi-Chini Bhai Bhai days seemed an ancient tale!

III

THE MARCH 1959 Rebellion in Lhasa, the Sino-Pakistani honeymoon with its somewhat hazy, if uncertain, beginnings in March 1961 and Peking's conclusion of a border agreement with Burma in October 1960—followed later by similar compacts with Nepal, Pakistan, Afghanistan and Outer Mongolia—mark a phase of growing acrimony in relations between New Delhi and Peking. Already, by the middle of 1962, the language of their 'Notes' was getting increasingly bitter with slander, calumny and mutual name-calling a bye-word for so-called diplomatic exchanges. Wordy duels were bad enough; what was worse was the growing frequency of armed clashes—ambushing of patrols, exchange of fire, establishment of posts in each other's rear in what both sides claimed to be their territory. Mercifully most of this activity, until August 1962, was confined to one part of the frontier—the western or the Ladakh sector—and it was its extension to the eastern half which set in train

[41] India to China, 30 December 1960, *White Paper*, V, p. 20.
[42] China to India, 21 February 1960, Ibid., pp. 21–22.
[43] India to China, 10 May 1962, *White Paper*, VI, pp. 96–97.
[44] China to India, 31 May 1962, Ibid., pp. 99–102.

events leading to the large-scale fighting of October–November 1962.

It is neither necessary nor perhaps pertinent to this study to retail at length either the course of events that brought matters to a head, much less attempt a close scrutiny of the various phases through which the month-long fighting passed. Two factors alone need emphasis: the crossing by the Chinese, on 8 September, of the Thag La ridge in the western extremity of the Kameng division, and developments that followed it in fairly quick succession.

A word about the Chinese crossing of the Thag La ridge and the fighting at Dhola or Che Dong. It may be conceded, without qualification, that in terms of the co-ordinates on the McMahon boundary maps of 1914, both the places lie to the north of the Line and, therefore, strictly speaking, India was occupying what was technically Tibetan-Chinese territory. And yet to say all this is to ignore a most important aspect of the question.

The 1914 maps, attached to the Convention, were small-scale—1″=8 miles—sketch maps designed more to be illustrative than definitive. Since a knowledge of the area was far from accurate, and detailed surveys lacking, the parallels and the meridians were shown only approximately. All that they were designed to make clear was that the boundary ran along the main watershed ridge of the area—and the main watershed ridge is Thag La, and Dhola lies to the south of it.

A footnote about the co-ordinates may not be out of place either. If those shown in the 1914 map were to be strictly followed, the Chinese should yield to India both Migyitun and Tulung La, in which case Indian territory would advance a further 7 miles and take in nearly 70 square miles. To Chinese propaganda it is more germane, indeed extremely handy, to ignore this aspect of the question and to concentrate on the inaccurate co-ordinates given in the maps where these are favourable to their claims. In other words, Peking would accept the highest watershed as a boundary in parts of the Eastern Sector where it suits, albeit the watershed there may not conform to the co-ordinates given in the 1914 maps. And yet it would quote the co-ordinates in the maps which go in its favour in other parts of the Sector to make demands for territorial concessions from India.[45]

To get back to Thag La. Prior to the Chinese crossing it on 8 September, most of the fighting, all through 1962 and earlier, had been in Ladakh: an exception though was January (1962) when the Chinese crossed the eastern frontier near Longju, and proceeded to the village of Roi, half a mile within India. With the Thag La crossed, a small detachment of the para-military Assam Rifles, stationed near the frontier, was completely swamped, both out-numbered and out-manoeuvred. On 20 September, there was heavy fighting between the Indian and Chinese troops at Dhola, referred to as Che Dong by Peking. Skirmishes continued and on 10 October there was another round

---

[45]Annexure in Nehru to Chou En-lai, 14 November 1962, *White Paper*, VIII, pp. 15–17.

of bitter fighting claiming many Indian casualties. On 16 October there was another heavy attack on Dhola.[46]

In between, two developments intervened. *One*, early in October the Chinese proposed holding of talks—and even named a date and place: 15 October, in Peking—on the basis of the Officials' Report, and with no pre-conditions.[47] The Indian reaction was: no talks under duress and, as a pre-condition, the Chinese must pull out of NEFA to their pre-8 September positions.[48] *Two*, on 12 October Prime Minister Nehru told the press in New Delhi while on his way to Colombo: ' Our instructions (to the Army) are to free our territory in NEFA from the Chinese'. These remarks, torn out of their context, and blown out of all proportion to their true import, were widely publicised as: ' I have ordered the Army to throw the Chinese out '.[49]

On 20 October the Chinese launched a massive assault all along the frontier and, since Peking had loudly proclaimed that the Indians were the first aggressors, called it ' a counter-attack in self-defence '. It ranged all over, from the westernmost extremity in Ladakh to Kibitoo and Walong in the Lohit division. Far from fully prepared, and in NEFA with logistics heavily weighed against it, the Indian Army reeled back, and in considerable disarray.[50] In the month-long fighting—on 21 November, Peking was to announce a unilateral cease-fire—two principal offensives may be clearly discerned. The first, 20–24 October, claimed Dhola and Khinzemane, while the Chinese mounted a two-pronged attack on Tawang; in the Lohit division, Kibitoo was abandoned and as for Ladakh nearly all the forward posts fell. The second major thrust was from 16–19 November, when Sela and Bomdila in the Kameng division fell— Tawang had fallen on 9 November—as did Walong in the Lohit. Ten days after the unilateral cease-fire of 21 November, the withdrawal of the ' frontier guards' commenced, as from 1 December. By the end of the year, Indian

---

[46] S H Ahmed, ' Chronology of Sino–India Border Dispute,' *International Studies* (New Delhi), V, 1–2, July–October 1963, pp. 212–20.

[47] Note by the Ministry of Foreign Affairs Peking, to the Embassy of India in China, 3 October 1962, *White Paper*, VII, pp. 96–98.

There is an obvious error in G Narayan Rao, *The India China Border* (Bombay, 1968), p. 103 when he suggests that it was India which proposed to China ' a definite date (15 October 1962) for holding negotiations '. Actually, it was the other way round.

[48] Note given by the Ministry of External Affairs, New Delhi, to the Embassy of China in India, 6 October 1962, *White Paper*, VII, pp. 100–102.

[49] The *Hindu* (Madras), 13 October 1962.

Also see P L Mehra, ' The Institutions at work during the 1962 conflict ', in *Foreign Policy Making in India and China* (University of Brussels, 1968), pp. 1–26.

[50] The best, first-hand, account of fighting in the NEFA, particularly the Thag La ridge-Dhola area, is in Brigadier J P Dalvi, *Himalayan Blunder* (Bombay, 1969). General B M Kaul, *The Untold Story* (Bombay, 1967) is informative but must be accepted with considerable reserve. For other secondary sources see General K S Thimaya, ' Chinese Aggression and After ', *International Studies* (New Delhi), V, 1-2, pp. 50–53, John Rowland, *A History of Sino-Indian Relations* (Princeton, 1966), pp. 166–73, V B Karnik (Editor) *China Invades India* (Bombay, 1963), pp. 222–90 and J N Nanporia, *The Sino-Indian Dispute* (Bombay, 1963), pp. 9–24.

personnel had begun slowly to move back into areas evacuated by the Chinese.[51]

Important though it was, it is not necessary here to follow the blue-print presented by the six Colombo powers to bring about a workable cease-fire and thereby generate an atmosphere

> in which the problems created by the border dispute would be discussed amicably in a spirit of friendship between China and India.[52]

The harsh truth was that the much hoped for 'spirit of friendship' proved to be a vain dream. Actually the reverse was the case, with the Colombo proposals themselves becoming a subject of discord and distrust and each side accusing the other of lack of sincerity. How wide was the gap is made clear by the exchanges between the two Prime Ministers which took place early in 1963. Thus writing to Nehru on 3 March 1963, Chou En-lai urged an early meeting, deprecating

> any more reason to delay the holding of talks between Chinese and Indian officials. As for the fact that there is a difference between the two sides in the way they interpret the Colombo proposals, it can well be discussed and resolved in the talks and should not constitute an obstacle to the opening of the talks. China reserves its two points of interpretation of the Colombo proposals, but does not make their acceptance a pre-condition for the opening of the talks.[53]

Nehru's rejoinder was more to the point: India had accepted the Colombo proposals unreservedly, China had not. What was more, the latter

> insists on unilateral implementation of the Chinese Government's statement of 21 November 1962. This is the only obstacle to the next step of talks and discussions to implement the Colombo Conference proposals with a view to the creation of the appropriate climate....[54]

On 20 April 1963, Chou retorted:

> Indeed, is it not because the Indian Government, by exploiting the ambig-

---

[51]For some facets of the Sino-Indian conflict see Augustin Palat, 'Tibet as a Mirror in Policy-making in the field of Sino-Indian Relations', Miloslav Krasa, 'Some Aspects in the Background of India-China Border Conflict', and P L Mehra, 'The Institutions at Work during the 1962 conflict', in *Foreign Policy Making in India and China*, op. cit. n. 5, pp. 27–43, 104–21 and 1–26 respectively.

[52]Mrs Bandaranaike (Prime Minister of Ceylon) at a banquet given in her honour by Mr Chou En-lai in Peking, on 1 January 1963. The *Hindu* (Madras), 2 January 1963.

[53]Chou En-lai to Nehru, 3 March 1963, *White Paper*, IX, p. 4.

[54]Nehru to Chou En-lai, 5 March 1963, Ibid., p. 6.

uities of the Colombo proposals, had interpreted the proposals as conforming with the Indian stand that it ostensibly proclaimed its unreserved acceptance of the Colombo proposals?

And, by asking China to

> accept in toto the Colombo proposals and the so-called clarifications ... as a pre-condition to negotiations, you are actually serving an ultimatum for China to accept the Indian Government's interpretation.... This absolutely will not do....[55]

The reply from New Delhi was no better:

> No amount of casuistry, Mr Prime Minister, can conceal the fact that the Government of China while claiming to accept the proposals in principle, has been constantly opposing these proposals by maintaining its so-called reservations.

And later:

> It seems to be a strange kind of logic for you to reject the Colombo Conference proposals just because the Government of India has accepted them.... The obvious reason for the Government of China's attitude in this matter is its desire to retain at least partially the gains of its latest aggression and no amount of camouflage can hide this particular design.[56]

Given the background, is it any wonder that, despite India's acceptance ' in toto ' and China's much-advertised ' positive response ', the Colombo proposals failed to come off the ground? While no one could gainsay their contribution in defusing an explosive situation, it was a pity that, in more ways than one, they proved still-born. Besides, and this could never be over-emphasised, the proposals provided at best a framework of reference, a means to an end—and the end was a direct confrontation, across the table, between the principal antagonists. And here, unfortunately, the gap was widened by mounting distrust, bedevilled by grim memories of a sudden avalanche, confounded by humiliating military reverses.

If the language of their diplomatic exchanges alone was to be a yardstick of the growing deterioration in the relations between the two countries, the situation had worsened precipitately. The following passages, picked up at random from the large mass that the White Papers contain, are designed to be more representative than exhaustive.

---

[55]Chou En-lai to Nehru, 20 April 1963, Ibid., pp. 11–13.
[56]Nehru to Chou En-lai, 1 May 1963, Ibid., p.17.

China to India, 9 October 1963:

Apart from reporting ... the hackneyed slander about Chinese aggression against India ... the Indian Government pretentiously suggested five so-called constructive steps.... Well, then, the Chinese Government, might as well use some ink and paper and analyse the substance of these so-called constructive suggestions made by India and see what stuff they are really made of....[57]

And later an exhortation:

(Indian Government) should discard all useless pretexts and subterfuges and accept the Chinese Government proposal for both sides to accept the Colombo proposals in principle as a basis for the immediate holding of direct negotiations....[58]

A fortnight later, and referring to the Chinese proposal for a renewal of the 1954 Trade Agreement relating to Tibet, Peking had this to say:

India's extraordinarily rigid attitude and totally unreasonable position on this question.... (It) tried to take the opportunity to blackmail and swindle China on this question. It deliberately linked the question together with the Sino-Indian boundary question in a far-fetched way and absolutely insisted on China's unconditional acceptance of India's unilateral claims on the boundary question as a precondition to the negotiation of the proposed agreement....[59]

Two years later, things were no better. In its note of 17 May 1965 Peking sought

to advise the Indian Government if it wants to deliver itself from isolation, it should change its stand of serving imperialism and undermining Afro-Asian solidarity, abandon its policy of great power chauvinism and expansionism and handle India's relations ... in accordance with the Five Principles of Peaceful Co-existence and the Ten Principles of the Bandung Conference.[60]

Nor had the Indian language much to commend itself. In its note of 19 June (1965) it referred to Peking's 'propagandist arguments and slander', to the 'legally invalid and politically mischievous' Sino-Pakistan boundary agreement, suggesting that

[57] *White Paper*, X, p. 8.
[58] Ibid., p. 11.
[59] Ibid., p. 53.
[60] China to India, 17 May 1965, *White Paper*, XII, p. 4.

Pakistan is a neighbour of China only by virtue of aggression and what the so-called Sino-Pakistan boundary agreement has done is to share between them the fruits of aggression at the expense of India.

There was name-calling too:

Great-power chauvinism and expansionism is a cap which fits the People's Republic of China more than any other Government in Asia and Africa, and indeed in the whole world today....[61]

With such diplomatic (!) exchanges to go by, it was no surprise that in the Indo-Pakistani war of September–October 1965 Peking took a markedly pro-Pakistani stance. It accused New Delhi of 'an act of naked aggression' against Pakistan and called its ruling circles 'the greatest hypocrites' of whom the Chinese have had 'a deep experience'. It will be recalled that at the height of the conflict, the Chinese served a three-day 'ultimatum' on India (later extended to five) calling upon it to withdraw its 'military works for aggression' on the 'Chinese side of the China-Sikkim boundary', or else 'grave consequences' would ensue.[62]

Exactly a year later, in September 1966, India was accused of hiring itself to 'US imperialism', allying with the Soviet Union, bullying 'its neighbours', practising 'expansionism', and carrying out 'ruthless national oppression'. New Delhi was reminded that its 'iniquitous conduct' ran 'diametrically counter' to the interests of the Indian people who 'wanted to make revolution'.[63]

By 1967 things had reached a stage where even such formal courtesies as mark the beginning and end of diplomatic notes—viz., of a Government presenting 'its compliments' or having 'the honour' to reply or renewing 'assurances of its highest consideration', etc.—ceased.[64] They had lost all meaning anyway but the harsh crudeness of the language now employed jarred on sensitive ears— if there was indeed any sensitivity left in them.

A new development of some significance was Peking's overt intervention in the domestic affairs of India and its unabashed encouragement to the Marxist (Naxalbari) revolt in West Bengal. The latter was hailed as the 'front pew' of the 'revolutionary armed struggle' launched by the Indian people 'under the guidance' of Mao Tse-tung's thought. Further the

emergence of this struggle in India, a big country which is colonial and

[61] India to China, 19 June 1965, Ibid., pp. 4–5.
[62] For the texts of the notes, China to India, 16 September and China to India, 19 September 1965, *White Paper*, XII, pp. 42–44 and 46–48.
[63] China to India, 15 September 1966, *White Paper*, XIII, pp. 51–52.
[64] The first note containing the new phraseology: 'The Ministry of Foreign Affairs ... addresses the present note ...' is from Peking dated 16 January 1967. New Delhi lost no time in adopting it. For the texts see *White Paper*, XIV, pp. 1–2 et. seq.

semi-feudal ... with an unbalanced political and economic development, signifies a new stage in the Indian people's surging struggle against reactionary rule.[65]

It is not necessary to detail here the insulting treatment meted out to Indian diplomats in Peking in the summer of 1967 when the Cultural Revolution was at its height.[66] For one, the Indians were not an exception, as there was hardly a mission that escaped the Red Guards' close scrutiny. It may also perhaps be pointed out that the Great Proletarian Cultural Revolution has, if China watchers are to be believed, just about spent itself and one would hope Peking may soon return to accepted norms of international intercourse.

The Cultural Revolution, however, lies outside the scope of these pages and albeit there is nothing of any great moment that happens on the frontier in the years after the 1962 conflict, and the stalemate that ensued, a brief recapitulation may help to place things in sharper focus.

The impact of the 1962 fighting on the North-Eastern Frontier was profound, and in more respects than one. However valid, and convincing, Indian explanations of a lack of preparedness, of the difficulties of terrain and logistics, of the incompetence of some of the commanders at the top,[67] of a complete failure of the political leadership then at the helm of affairs,[68] Chinese successes had a most powerful influence on the people in the frontier areas. In Kameng, and in the Lohit, their arms had the most resounding of successes and, for effect, nothing could have been more impressive than their proud, disdainful, gesture of a 'unilateral' withdrawal, after having carried all before them. The Monbas and the Mishmis who were in the front line, no less than the Akas, the Daflas and the Miris who were not, must have been deeply impressed by Peking's armed prowess and no doubt disconcerted by India's inability to protect them against onslaughts from without.

In the years that have elapsed since the ' cease-fire ', and the ' witdrawals ' of the closing months of 1962, a few changes on the eastern frontier may be

---

[65] Peking broadcast, 26 June 1967, in India to China, 5 July 1967, in Ibid., p. 95.

[66] For details, Ibid., pp. 98–124.

[67] For excerpts from the Henderson-Brooke report on the NEFA debacle, presented to the Lok Sabha on 2 September 1963, by Mr. Y B Chavan, then Minister for Defence, see *Asian Recorder*, New Delhi, 1963, p. 5418.

[68] Apart from J P Dalvi's *Himalayan Blunder* and B M Kaul's *The Untold Story*, both in *supra*, n. 6, see Kuldip Nayar, *Between the Lines* (Bombay, 1968) and his more recent, *India: the Critical Years* (Revised Edition, New Delhi, 1971), as also D R Mankekar, *The Guilty Men of 1962* (Bombay, 1968). S S Khera, *India's Defence Problems* (Bombay, 1968), G Narayan Rao, *supra*, n. 3, and P C Chakarvarty, *Evolution of India's Northern Border* (Bombay, 1971) though peripheral, are of interest in providing useful insights. A well-presented, if highly controversial, study is Neville Maxwell, *India's China War* (Bombay, 1970) and that remarkably self-complimentary if also extremely informative, B N Mullik, *My Years with Nehru: The Chinese Betrayal* (Bombay, 1971). Also see P L Mehra, ' India's China War ', *India Quarterly*, XXVI, 4 October–December 1970, pp. 410–16.

readily discerned. At the outset is the criss-crossing of a network of roads and air-strips which, it would seem, now reach the farthest check-posts near the frontier, with its deep impact on the morale, both among the soldiers and the civilians, in and around the frontier areas. Here too, one would imagine, the lessons of 1962, in terms both of men and munitions, have not been lost and the necessary leeway been made up.

Over the years since 1962, which in the story of the frontier marks a watershed and a landmark, some significant developments on the international plane have altered the picture almost beyond recognition. One of these, and perhaps of the greatest moment, is the growing bitterness in the Moscow-Peking wrangle over their frontier disputes.

Wordy duels, name-calling and mass-hysteria apart, the armed clashes of a few years ago on the frozen waters of the Heilungkiang and across the Ili, in the Sinkiang-Uighur-Kazakhistan areas, added to China's unqualified denunciation of the 'unequal' treaties (and its principal beneficiaries, the social-Imperialist masters of the Kremlin) serves to lend the Sino-Indian boundary conflict a newer, if entirely different perspective. To an extent, it does help to answer those who, perhaps unwittingly, have accused New Delhi of 'intransigence' and thrown in its face China's 'magnanimous' gestures, in terms of territorial compromises, towards Burma, Nepal, Pakistan, Afghanistan and the Mongolian People's Republic.

Another event of the utmost importance has been the development by Peking, since 1964, of a nuclear capability. While the precise details and assessment of this capability, in terms of the threats it poses to peace on the periphery, must remain a matter of debate, the fact of China becoming a nuclear power of some significance completely alters the picture—and not in Asia only. This is the more significant in terms of the revelations, now eagerly awaited, of the shadow-boxing going on in the top echelon of the People's Republic where the disappearance of Lin Piao (Mao's hand-picked heir-apparent), and a host of top-brass in the armed forces, has yet to be satisfactorily explained while, to all outward appearances, the pennants of the Cultural Revolution remain firmly nailed to the flag-masts, aflutter in winds that proclaim that the 'East is Red'. There have been feelers and talk too, at both ends, of a gradual normalisation in the relations between New Delhi and Peking—the former committed, to-date, to a refusal to go nuclear; the latter, to be a party to the (Nuclear) Nonproliferation treaty. To maintain that in this extremely complicated situation, the frontier in general, and the McMahon Line in particular, is reduced to its proper proportions in the fuller, larger scheme of things is neither to minimise its importance, nor yet to gainsay its relevance.

Bibliography

I. MANUSCRIPT SOURCES
(a) *Archival*
The basic source-material made use of in this work are the records of the Government of India preserved in the National Archives in New Delhi. It would be tedious, and perhaps far from rewarding to the reader, to list the individual records — mostly files — which add up to a sizeable number. Those used here, for most part, are the *Foreign and Political Department Proceedings*, marked Secret-External, External A and, in very few cases, External B. Sometimes it is possible to find the same proceedings at more than one place but, up to 1921, conveniently for the researcher, they are indexed together under various subject-heads (viz., 'Affairs of Tibet'). Among the most interesting and revealing are those containing — apart from the official proceedings — the notes, marginal comments, and (official) annotations. In 1921, when the new filing system was introduced in the Foreign and Political Department, the pattern underwent a sea-change with the result that in the post-1921 period there is a vast plethora of files, each containing a relatively small number of proceedings. The task of piecing together bits of information for these years becomes more complex, requiring a great deal of patient and careful handling.

The Whitehall end of the picture comes mostly through the records in the India Office Library in London. The principal collection used here are the *Political and Secret Department Subject Files*. These are mostly distinguished by the year (indicated by a stroke at the end) in which the compilation was done. Lately, however, a new system of cataloguing designated as L/P&S/10/- has taken their place. Apart from the subject files, there are the *Political and Secret (Department) Memoranda* listed as L/P&S/18/- and the very useful *External Collections*, under L/P&S/12/-, most of them in facsimile.

In the Public Record Office, which serves as the archives for the Foreign Office, there is a lot that supplements the records in the India Office. Of great use among these, and perhaps the easiest to reach, are the *Foreign Office Confidential Print Series*, 'Affairs of Tibet' and 'Affairs of Tibet and Mongolia' listed as FO 535 and the much more ponderous, if fulsome, series for China marked as FO 371.

Among the collections of private papers the *Jordan-Langley* correspondence in the Public Record Office, the *Morley Collection* (MSS. Eur. D. 573) in the India Office Library and the *Hardinge Papers*, on microfilm, in the Nehru Memorial Museum and Library, New Delhi, have been drawn upon. Sir Henry McMahon's 'papers' in the India Office Library (MSS. Eur. F. 101/I-) are singularly unsatisfactory for their principal content comprises a 'Note', dated 30 September 1907, relating to the attitude of the (North-west Frontier) tribes 'in the event of an attempted invasion of India by Russia'.

For maps, the library of the Royal Geographical Society and the Map Rooms of the India Office and the Foreign Office Libraries have proved most rewarding.

(b) *Unpublished Theses*
Osborn, George Knox III, 'Sino-Indian Border Conflicts: historical background and recent developments', unpublished thesis, (University of Stanford, 1963).
Sung Yao-ting, 'Chinese-Tibetan Relations, 1890–1947', unpublished thesis, (University of Minnesota, 1949).

II. PRIMARY SOURCES
Demands of the Tribal Communities of Assam (Shillong, 1946).

Foreign Relations of the United States: Diplomatic Papers: 1942/1943/1944: China (Washington 1956, 1957, 1958).
Memorandum of the People of the Garo Hills, Assam (Gauhati, 1946).
Memorandum on the Tribal and Excluded Areas of the North-east Frontier (New Delhi, May 1947).
Notes, Memoranda and Letters Exchanged Between the Governments of India and China (Ministry of External Affairs, 1958 –), I-XIV.
Report of the Officials of the Governments of India and the People's Republic of China on the Boundary Question (New Delhi, 1961).

III. RESEARCH ARTICLES

Bailey, F M, 'Journey through a portion of South-east Tibet and the Mishmi hills', *The Geographical Magazine* (London), 39, 1912.
Bell, Charles Alfred, 'The North-east Frontier of India', *JRCAS* (London), 17, 1930.
Caroe, Sir Olaf, 'The Geography and Ethnics of India's Northern Frontiers', *The Geographical Journal* (London), 126, 1960.
Cheng, Y C, 'The Organisation of the Wai-chiao-pu', *Chinese Social and Political Science Review* (Shanghai), I, 1916.
Choudhury, Deba Prosad, 'The North-east Frontier of India', *Modern Asian Studies* (Cambridge), 4, 1970.
Gupta, Karunakar, 'The McMahon Line, 1911–45: the British Legacy', *China Quarterly* (London), 47, 1971.
────── 'India's China Relations', *Seminar* (New Delhi), 50, October 1963.
Kingdon-Ward, F W, 'The Assam Himalaya: Travels in Balipara', *JRCAS* (London), 25, 1938; and 27, 1940.
Mehra, P L, 'India's China War', a Review Article in *India Quarterly* (New Delhi) 26, 1970.
────── 'The Institutions at Work during the 1962 Conflict', in *Foreign Policy Making in India and China* (University of Brussels, 1968).
'Observer' (P L Mehra), 'The Dalai and the Panchen: Tibet's Supreme Incarnate Lamas', *India Quarterly* (New Delhi), 15, 1959.
Rose, Archibald, 'Chinese Frontiers of India', *The Geographical Journal* (London), 39, March 1912.
Shao Hsung-cheng, (review of) 'Tibet in Modern World Politics', *Chinese Social and Political Science Review* (Shanghai) 16, 1932–33.
Sigel, Louis T, 'C'hing Tibetan Policy, 1906–10', *Papers on China*, Vol. 20 (East Asian Research Centre, Harvard University, Cambridge, Mass.), December 1966.
Twynam, Sir Henry and Sir Olaf Caroe, exchanges, *The Times* (London), 2, 4, 10, September 1959.
Yang, S C, 'The Revolution in Szechuan, 1911–12', *Journal of the West China Border Society*, (Chengtu), 6, 1933–34.

IV. SECONDARY SOURCES

Bacot, J, *Le Thibet Revolte* (Paris, 1910).
Bailey, F M, *China–Tibet–Assam, A Journey, 1911* (London, 1955).
────── *No Passport to Tibet* (London, 1957).
Banerji, Anil Chander, *The Eastern Frontier of India*, 1st Edition (Calcutta, 1943).
Bell, Charles Alfred, *Tibet, Past And Present* (Oxford, 1924).
────── *Portrait of the Dalai Lama* (London, 1946).
Bower, Ursula Graham, *The Hidden Land* (New York, 1953).
Chen, Jerome, *Yuan Shih-kai, 1859–1916* (London, 1961).
Chiang Kai-shek, *China's Destiny and Chinese Economic Theory* (London, 1947).
Dalvi, J P, *Himalayan Blunder* (Bombay, 1969).
Eekelen, W F van, *India's Frontier Policy and the Border Dispute with China*, 2nd Edition (The Hague, 1968).

Elwin, Verrier, *A Philosophy for NEFA*, 2nd Edition (Shillong, 1959).
Ford, Robert W, *Captured in Tibet* (London, 1953).
Furer-Haimendorff, Christoph von, *The Apa Tanis and Their Neighbours* (London, 1962).
―――― *Ethnographic Notes on the Tribes of the Subansiri Region* (Shillong, 1947).
―――― *Himalayan Barbary* (London, 1955).
Gilbert, Martin, *Servant of India* (London, 1966).
Gould, Sir Basil, *The Jewel in the Lotus* (London, 1957).
Hedin, Sven, *Trans Himalaya: Discoveries and Adventures in Tibet*, 3 vols, (London, 1910).
Ho Kan-chih, *A History of the Modern Chinese Revolution* (Peking, 1959).
Hu Sheng, *Imperialism and Chinese Politics* (Peking, 1955).
Kaul, B M, *The Untold Story* (Bombay, 1967).
Lamb, Alastair, *The McMahon Line*, 2 vols (London, 1967).
Lattimore, Owen, *Inner Asian Frontiers of China*, 2nd Edition (New York, 1951).
Li Chein-mung, Ssu-yu Teng and Jeremy Ingalls, *The Political History of China, 1840–1928* (New York, 1956).
Li, Tieh-tseng, *The Historical Status of Tibet* (New York, 1956).
McNair, H F, *Modern Chinese History: Selected Readings* (London, 1927).
Maxwell, Neville, *India's China War* (Bombay, 1971).
Mayers, William Fredrick, *The Chinese Government*, 2nd Edition (London, 1886).
Mehra, Parshotam, *The Younghusband Expedition: An Interpretation* (Bombay, 1968).
Monger, G W, *The End of Isolation* (London, 1963).
Mullick, B N, *My Years with Nehru: The Chinese Betrayal* (Bombay, 1971).
Nayar, Kuldip, *Between the Lines* (Bombay, 1958).
―――― *India: the Critical Years* (New Delhi, 1971).
O'Connor, Fredrick W, *Things Mortal* (London, 1940).
Pavlovsky, Michel M, *Chinese–Russian Relations* (New York, 1959).
Phillimore, Colonel R H, *Historical Records of the Survey of India*, 4 vols, (Dehra Dun, 1945–58).
Pu Yi, *From Emperor to Citizen*, 2 vols, (Peking, 1964).
Rao, G Narayan, *India–China Border: a Reappraisal* (Bombay, 1968).
Rose, Leo E & Fisher, Margaret W, *The NEFA of India* (Institute of International Studies, Berkeley, 1967).
Reid, Sir Robert, *History of the Frontier Areas Bordering on Assam, 1883–1941* (Shillong, 1942).
Rockhill, W W, *The Dalai Lamas of Lhasa and Their Relations with the Manchu Emperors of China* (Leiden, 1910).
Shakabapa, *Political History of Tibet* (Princeton, 1967).
Tang, Peter S H, *Russian and Soviet Policy in Manchuria and Outer Mongolia, 1911–31* (Durham, 1959).
Teichman, Eric, *Travels of a Consular Officer in Eastern Tibet* (Cambridge, 1922).
Tung, L, *China and Some Phases of International Law* (London, 1940).

Index

Afghanistan: and Tibet, 203;
'defining' northern Afghanistan, 257, 259-60;
and Russia, 416 n
Aitchison's *Treaties*: and publication of Simla Convention, 418, 418 n., 419, 423-24
Alston, Sir Beilby: negotiations with China for tripartite talks, 166, 167;
changed policy towards Tibet, 353;
support to Bell's Lhasa visit, 360-62;
on conditions in China (1921), 372
Assam, 3, 4, 8, 9, 16, 421-22, 426-27, 429, 431-33, 437, 443, 448, 458-59

Bailey, Lt Col F M: journey from Peking (1911–12), 70 n., 71 n., 88, 93;
exploration on the Kameng frontier (with Morshead), 232 n.;
visit to Lhasa (1924), 376, 377;
reports on neglect of Tibetan forces/polity, 384, 385
Batang, 9, 68, 69, 72, 76, 76 n., 188, 190, 209, 303
Bell, Sir Charles Alfred: 1; administration in Chumbi valley, 36, 37-38;
and Panchen Lama, 37;
and Chang Ying-tang, 39;
negotiations on India-Tibet boundary, 227-28;
and Inner/Outer Tibet, 342 n., 343;
changed policy towards Tibet, 350, 355;
mission to Lhasa (1920–21), 356, 357, 370;
instructions, 358-59;
communication to Tibetan government, 361-62;
assessment of Tibetan polity, 364-67;
settlement of Tibetan question, 394
Bhutan, 8

Caroe, Sir Olaf: 'rediscovers' the McMahon Line, 413, 422 n., 423;
regarding China's cartographic aggression, 441;
and 'The Mongolian Fringe', 454 n.;
warns of Red China's aggressive intent, 466

Chang Ying-tang: 37;
and Tibetan administration, 38, 38 n., 39 n.;
and Sven Hedin, 39, 52, 53;
and Tibetan Trade Regulations, 58-60;
proposed as Chinese delegate to tripartite talks in India, 153
Chao Erh-feng: 67-69;
conquest of Eastern Tibet, 70-71;
expedition to Lhasa, 72-78;
Viceroyalty of Szechuan, 76;
and collapse of Chinese rule, 79, 155
Chen, Ivan: appointment as delegate to the tripartite talks, 162, 165-66;
status and powers, 164-65, 167;
departure for India, 168;
life-sketch, 174;
'coerced' into signing the Convention, 261-62;
acceptance of Simla Convention, 276, 287
China: and 'Adhesion' Agreement (1906), 25-26, 249;
and October (1911) Revolution, 103;
accepts bipartite basis for talks, 150-51;
requirements for a settlement, 179-80;
'demands' at Simla, 184;
rejection of McMahon's boundary proposals, 213, 215;
'five-point' proposal, 216, 220;
boundary between Inner/Outer Tibet, 223;
repudiates Ivan Chen's initialling of the first Convention, 242-43;
proposes continuation of negotiations in London/Peking, 263-64;
territorial claims and 'concessions', 265-68, 271-72;
initiative for reopening negotiations (1915), 301;
and civil war (1916–18), 307-9;
and fighting in East Tibet, 310;
refusal to negotiate, 321;
May 1919 proposals, 330, 333;
and Bell's mission to Lhasa, 363, 368-69;
and Washington Conference (1921–22), 371-72;
anti-British campaign (1922), 385;

repudiates tripartite basis for negotiations (1931–32), 388-91;
overtures to Dalai Lama (1930), 397;
proposes direct talks with Tibet (1931–32), 403;
cartographic aggression, 437-38;
and HMG's refusal to protest, 438, 438 n.;
and 'Shen Pao' Atlas maps, 439, 439 n.;
and Olaf Caroe, 441;
and Tibet during World War II, 442-43;
and US pressure on Tibet, 443 n., 444, 444 n., 445, 445 n., 447-48, 448 n.;
and Wu's mission (1940) to Lhasa, 445, 447;
and Sheng's appointment as representative at Lhasa, 448;
and McMahon Line, 454, 454 n.;
and Tibetan 'autonomy', 464;
and Tibet's 'liberation', 464, 464 n.;
17-point Agreement with Tibet, 465;
and boundary settlements, 479
Chung Ying, General: appointed commander of Chao's expedition to Lhasa, 73;
march to Lhasa, 107;
and revolt in Lhasa, 108-9;
appointed Amban, 124;
leaves Lhasa, 125;
crosses into India, 126, 140
Curzon, Lord: 1; on North-East Frontier, 7, 11;
on China's 'Adhesion' (1906) Agreement, 23, 30, 35

Dalai Lama (13th): gets new title in Peking, 28-29, 29 n.;
and Dorjieff, 43; enters Lhasa (1913); 123;
refuses compliance with Yuan Shi-kai's directive, 134;
and 'negotiations' in East Tibet, 157-61;
for a rapprochement with Russia (1915), 301;
quarrels with Panchen Lama, 375;
strikes at the 'Progressive Party', 377-78;
cools off in relations with Britain, 379;
and Chinese overtures (1932), 392-93, 398;
and appeals to the British (1932), 400;
exchanges with Chiang Kai-shek, 401-3;
and Williamson's visit to Lhasa (1933), 407, 409;
death (December 1933), 413-14
Dalai Lama (14th): selection and installation (1940), 446, 446 n.;
and his flight (1959), 470
Dane, Sir Louis: and negotiations with China (1905–6), 58-61

Dorjieff, Aguan: and Russian intrigue, 16 n., 42-43;
meets Dalai Lama (in Tibet), 127-28

Eekelen, W F van, 22, 22 n
Elwin, Verrier, 11, 12 n

Feng Chuan, 68, 69
Fu Sung-mu: and the new province of Hsi-kang, 155, 157, 157 n

Gould, Sir Basil: and meeting with Chung Ying (1912), 125, 125 n., 126;
and Tawang, 427-28;
'differences' with Norbu Dhondhup, 429-30;
recommendations (1936), 432-34;
reactions to Lightfoot's report (1938), 435-36
Gregorson, Dr: his murder, 93

Hardinge, Lord: policy on the N-E Frontier, 94-96;
and Abor Expedition, 97;
and Dalai Lama (13th), 112, 123
Hedin, Dr Sven, 31, 31 n., 45
Hsiang Cheng: (Tibetan, Changtreng), siege and fall, 69;
mutiny in, 75 n., 78
Huang Mu-sung, General: visit to Lhasa (1934), 414, 414 n.
Hu Ching-yi: and new Chinese province of Hsi-kang, 155-57, 157 n.
Huthukthu, Bogdo: and Dalai Lama (13th), 26-27;
exchanges with Yuan Shih-kai, 103-5;
proclaims independence of Mongolia, 127-28

India: boundary with China, 463-64, 464 n.;
Chinese incursions, 466-67;
'Officials Report', 474-75;
and Chinese crossing of boundary, 480-81, 481 n., 482;
and Colombo proposals (1962), 482, 482 n.;
and bad language of 'Notes', 483-87

Japan: sabotage of May 1919 proposals, 339, 339 n., 340;
influence in Chinese politics, 373
Jordan, Sir John: advises *status quo* by China in Tibet, 138;
presents (to China) August (1912) Memorandum, 140-43;

Index

discussions with Chinese Foreign Office, 144-45;
favours tripartite negotiations, 148-150;
negotiates for talks in India, 152-53, 162-63;
reaction to the first draft for a settlement, 147;
'sell-out' on Kokonor, 214;
territorial settlement with China, 267-69;
'volte face', 269-71;
and final round of talks at Simla, 278, 280-81, 283;
talks with Yuan Shih-kai, 302-3;
and Yuan Shih-kai's death, 303 n.;
and Teichman's Memorandum (1917), 306;
territorial settlement in East Tibet, 320-21;
differences with Teichman, 326-29;
assessment of situation in China, 332;
May 1919 proposals, 334-39, 347-48, 350;
and Japanese sabotage, 339-40;
anti-Dalai Lama bias, 353

Kalon Lama: and Teichman, 318-19, 324-25, 327
Kingdon-Ward, W F: visit to Mon-yul, 420-21, 421 n.

Laden La: mediation in Tibet-Nepal dispute, 385
Lampson, Sir Miles: and Tibetan question, 408-9
Lien Yu (Amban): appointed Assistant Amban (1906), 55, 55 n.;
opposes Chao Erh-feng's appointment as Additional Amban, 72 n.;
deposed and besieged, 104, 108;
his charges against Chung Ying, 126
Lightfoot, Captain: visit to Tawang (1938), 428-29;
his brief and report, 430-31, 431 n.;
New Delhi's reluctance to accept his recommendations, 432
Line, Inner: (on the N-E Frontier), definition, 5-6, 6 n., 90
Line, Outer: (on the N-E Frontier), definition, 6, 90, 94
Liu, General: and Teichman (1918), 317-18 321, 323, 326, 329
Liu Man-ching (Miss): visit to Lhasa (1930), 395-96, 396 n.
Lu Hsing-chi: 132-33, 133 n.;
and Panchen Lama, 135;
and Dalai Lama (13th), 136, 154;
as Amban-designate, 164;

and settlement at Simla, 212, 273-74
Macdonald, David, 315
McMahon, Sir Arthur Henry: brief sketch, 173, 173 n., 174;
strategy at Simla, 181;
his draft for a tripartite settlement, 198-200;
and Arthur Hirtzel's draft, 204, 206, 249;
'verbal statement' regarding Chinese position, 210-12;
and India-Tibet boundary, 231-32;
and negotiations with Ivan Chen, 241;
explains Chinese repudiation of the first Simla Convention, 243-44;
'strategy' for negotiating with Russia, 254;
obtaining Chinese signatures, 274-75, 277, 280-81, 282, 283-85;
summoning final meeting of the Conference, 286-92;
appointed High Commissioner in Egypt, 415-16
McMahon Line: Tibet's reaffirmation, 421-22, 425;
and Kingdon-Ward case, 426, 426 n.;
and Tibet, 428;
correctly shown, 440, 440 n.;
modifications suggested, 453;
Tibetan encroachments, 433, 456, 457-58, 458 n.;
proposed British protectorate, 459, 459 n., 460;
Tibetan claims to areas to its south, 460-61;
China's repudiation, 468-70;
Chinese proposal for withdrawal, 472-73;
Chinese version, 476-78
Minto, Lord: 23-24; and Chinese 'Adhesion' 30;
and Sven Hedin, 31, 31 n., 32 n.
Mongolia: 15; and Russia, 35; and China, 35, 127;
Russo-Mongolian agreement, 140, 148, 151, 177, 204;
and Sino-Soviet Agreement, 450
Morley, John: as Secretary of State for India, 31, 54, 54 n

Needham, Jack Francis: 1, 11;
assessment of his work, 91
Nicolson, Arthur: negotiations with Russia (1905–6), 42-48
Norbu Dhondhup: visit to Lhasa (1925), 378, 379;

'differences' with Gould, 429-30;
policy towards Tibet (regarding McMahon Line), 434-35

O'Callaghan, T P M: and post at Menilkrai, 82, 83, 83 n., 84;
and the Walong 'promenade', 98
O'Connor, W F T : 8, 8 n., 9;
dealings with Chang Ying-tang, 39, 39 n., 40, 40 n.;
and Panchen Lama, 40

Panchen Lama, (9th): and British policy, 40;
and Lu Hsing-chi, 135;
relations with the Dalai Lama, 375;
his flight from Shigatse (1923), 375, 375-76 n.;
his plans to return to Tibet (1934), 414, 414 n.
Peng Jih-sheng, General: and fighting in East Tibet, 310-17;
Teichman's opinion of, 318

Reid, Sir Robert, 1 n.
Richardson, H E: on Chung Ying's entry into Lhasa, 74;
and Tibetan claims to Indian territory, 461, 461 n.;
and *coup d'etat* in Lhasa (1947), 462
Rockhill, W W: 16 n.; and Dalai Lama (13th) 27 n., 28 n
Rose, Archibald: brief sketch, 176;
discussions with Ivan Chen (1914), 234-36
Russia: and war with Japan, 41;
and Tibet, 44, 46-48;
and Convention with England (1907), 49-51;
modifying the (1907) Convention, 151, 247-49, 253;
Convention no longer valid, 417, 417 n.;
concurrent negotiations (by the British) with (Russia and) China, 1914, 205;
and Indo-Tibetan boundary, 222;
and Mongolia, 250-55;
and validity of 1914 Simla Convention, 417

Sadiya, 1 n., 11, 14
Sazonov: exchanges with Buchanan, 252-60;
as negotiator, 261;
and final (1914) Russian position on the Simla Convention, 279
Shatra, Lonchen: brief sketch, 174-75;

negotiations with Bell on India-Tibet boundary, 227-30;
exchange of letters with McMahon, 230-31;
as negotiator, 233;
and the Second Simla Convention, 285;
McMahon's opinion of him, 295-300;
his political eclipse, 299
Simla: Conference at, 171;
date of meeting, 172-73;
different sessions at Simla and Delhi, 175;
first draft of Convention, 176-77;
second draft, 177;
British representation at Lhasa, 198-202, 203-4, 206-7;
first Convention, 237-40;
second Convention, 289-92

Tang Shao-yi: and negotiations with the British (1905), 18, 19, 19 n.;
and 'Adhesion' Agreement, 20-21, 24, 52
Tawang: 8, 225, 232 n.;
Captain Nevill's visit (1928), 421;
and Gould (1936), 427, 427 n., 428, 428 n., 429;
as bargaining counter, 456
Teichman, Sir Eric: 67 n., 295;
'Memorandum' on Tibet (1917), 303-6, 315;
and boundary agreements between China and Tibet (1918), 317-19, 321-22;
and Chamdo Agreement, 322-24, 325;
and Rongbatsa truce (1918), 327;
differences with Jordan, 327-29;
assessment of situation in East Tibet, 331;
changed policy towards Tibet, 353-54
Tibet: and Trade Regulations (1908), 56-57, 148;
agreement with Mongolia (1913), 140, 151, 193;
desiderata for a settlement, 178-79;
'claims' at Simla, 182-83;
its (physical) 'limits', 185-90, 194-95;
boundary with India, 221, 223-25;
anxiety for a settlement with China, 310, 319-20;
request for arms, 332-33;
and Chinese proposals of May 1919, 341-42;
and Kansu Mission, 347-48, 349, 394;
question of arms supply, 350, 350 n., 351-53, 367;
'modernisation', 374-75;
fighting with China (1932), 387, 390, 399;

negotiations for a 'local' settlement, 410 n.;
Mission to China (1946), 451, 451 n.;
and Asian Relations Conference (1947), 451;
and March (1959) Rebellion, 470-71, 471n.
Tibet, Inner/Outer: McMahon proposes, 191-92;
HMG accepts in principle, 193;
boundaries of, 195-97;
political difficulty of, 208-9;
and Ivan Chen, 209-11;
and China, 218;
British insistence on principle, 219;
acceptance by China, 220;
abolition of, 342, 342 n.
Tuan Chi-Jui, 347
Twynam, Sir Henry: proposals for modifying McMahon Line, 453, 453 n., 454, 454 n., 455 n.

Weir, Lt Col: visit to Lhasa (1930), 385, 397, 398 n.;
and Tibet's anxiety about Chinese advance in East Tibet, 388;
not invited (to Lhasa, 1929), 395
Wellington Koo: 266; as Chinese delegate to the Pacific Conference (1921-22), 371;
as Chinese Foreign Minister, 383
White, John Claude, 11
Williamson, F W: on unpopularity of Lhasa police, 377, 377 n.;
opposed to direct Sino-Tibetan talks, 404-5;
change of stance, 406-7;
and Dalai Lama (13th), 408;
visit to Lhasa (1934), 415
Williamson, Noel: as successor of Needham, 12-13;
tours and exploration, 91-93;
his murder, 93, 95, 96

Yang Feng, 132, 140
Yin Chang-heng: appointed Commander of 'Chinese Western Expeditionary Forces', 131;
reaches Tachienlu, 139, 154;
adventure in East Tibet, 312-13
Younghusband, Francis Edward: 16, 17, 17 n.; and Lhasa Convention, 19, 26
Yu T'ai, 17, 33 n., 68
Yuan Shih-kai: proclaimed President, 103;
and Bogdo Huthukthu, 104-5;
and Tibet, 110-11, 113, 124;
decrees for Tibet and Mongolia, 129-30;
restores Dalai Lama's titles, 130, 137;
expedition into Tibet, 139, 155, 162;
talks with Jordan, 302-3;
his death, 303 n.
Yuggon Dzasa: negotiations with Dalai Lama (13th), 396-97;
negotiations with China, 402